Leadership and Administration of

OUTDOOR PURSUITS

Second Edition

Leadership and Administration of

OUTDOOR PURSUITS

Second Edition

by

PHYLLIS FORD

and

JIM BLANCHARD

designed and illustrated by

ANNE BLANCHARD

Copyright © 1993
Venture Publishing, Inc.

No part of the material protected by this copyright notice may be reproduced or utilized in any form by any means, electronic or mechanical, including photocopying, recording, or by any information storage and retrieval system, without written permission from the copyright owner.

Printed in the United States of America

Production: Bonnie Godbey
Printing and Binding: BookCrafters, Inc.
Manuscript Editing: Michele L. Barbin

Library of Congress Catalogue Card Number 92-63339
ISBN 0-910251-60-6

10 9 8 7 6 5 4 3 2 1

This book is dedicated to our parents, Wendell and Mary Ford, and Bob and Jane Blanchard, who taught us to enjoy and respect the out-of-doors and to want to share it with others, and to Ian Blanchard who is already following in his parents' footsteps.

table of contents

✱part three   Leadership and Administration

part four   Planning and Field Leadership

Phyllis Ford

Phyllis Ford retired as Chair of the Department of Recreation and Park Resources at Michigan State University and now is the director of Green Bough Programs, an outdoor recreation/education consulting business. She earned a B.S. degree in Recreation from the University of Massachusetts, an M.A. in Education from Arizona State University, and a doctorate in Recreation from Indiana University, where she also received the Garrett Eppley Alumni Award and the W.W. Patty Distinguished Award. She is the author of *Principles and Practice of Outdoor/Environmental Education,* and *Take a New Bearing,* as well as co-author of *Camp Administration and Leadership in Recreation and Leisure Services.* She has written many articles and papers and has held program, leadership, supervisory, and administrative positions in youth agencies, resident and day camps, public schools, and universities.

Dr. Ford was in the Department of Recreation and Park Management at the University of Oregon from 1961 to 1969, then served as Chair of the Recreation Education Program at the University of Iowa until 1971. She returned to Oregon as Department Head from 1971-1975, served as Graduate Student Coordinator from 1975-1981, and again as Department Head from 1981-1985, when she accepted the position as Chair of the Department of Physical Education, Sport, and Leisure Studies at Washington State University. She moved to Michigan State in 1987, but returned to Oregon to retire from academia.

Phyl started camping at age four, and participated in her first backpack trip at age nine. She has hiked and camped in the New England States, the Midwest, the Northwest, and Canada. She has backpacked most of the Pacific Crest Scenic Trail in Oregon and climbed most of that state's mountains, including several ascents of the ten highest peaks. Her outdoor leadership experiences include Girl Scouts, climbing clubs, and high school and college courses. She is an avid naturalist and has taught environmental interpretation, outdoor education, and recreation and natural resources on the university level.

With her major interests in outdoor education/recreation, Dr. Ford has served as an officer for the American Camping Association both nationally and regionally. A life member of the ACA, she received that organization's Hedley Dimock Award for contribution to the advancement of youth camping in 1971. She also received the Julian Smith Award for outdoor education from the American Alliance for Health, Physical Education, and Recreation, and the Taft Campus Award from Northern Illinois University. She has served on one Bureau of Land Management and two U.S. Forest Service Advisory Committees, and has done volunteer work for the U.S. Forest Service.

James Blanchard

James Blanchard holds a B.S. degree in General Science and an M.S. degree in Recreation and Park Management from the University of Oregon, where he has been a member of the faculty of Physical Education since 1979. He developed and coordinates the University of Oregon Outdoor Pursuits Program, which provides approximately 1,300 student credit hours of instruction per year in an integrated array of land-based and water-based skills and outdoor leadership training opportunities including approximately 40 courses and 30 outings annually.

As owner and director of Best of the Alps Trekking, he spends summers leading hiking and climbing adventure tours in eastern and western Europe and in Japan. He also owns and operates Outdoor Safety Consultants, specializing in risk assessment and leadership training for private and public providers of outdoor pursuits.

Jim has extensive experience in backpacking, mountaineering, and skiing, and has pursued these interests across the U.S., Canada, Mexico, and 36 countries in Europe and Asia. He has taught these activities for elementary and secondary schools, colleges and universities, park districts, and other public and private institutions in the United States and Europe, including several seasons with Outward Bound.

Blanchard is an expert in mountain rescue techniques, avalanche safety, and backcountry first aid, and he has taught courses in these skills since 1967. In 1965, he was President of the Mountain Rescue and Safety Council of Oregon, and he remains active as a team member, rescue coordinator, and member of the Board of Directors of Eugene Mountain Rescue.

Through most of the 70s, Blanchard worked seasonally for the U.S. Forest Service as a Wilderness Ranger, where he developed a biocentric philosophy and a sensitivity to the complex interactions of man and the natural environment. He has applied his knowledge of environmental issues in training backcountry personnel for the U.S. Forest Service, in a ten-part wilderness series for public television, and in numerous college courses and lectures.

Anne Blanchard

Anne Blanchard holds an A.A. degree in Graphic Design from Lane Community College and a B.A. degree in Telecommunications and Film from the University of Oregon. She is a freelance graphic designer and an accomplished mountaineer, ski instructor, and guide with outdoor leadership experience in the United States, Europe, and Asia.

introduction

This second edition of *Leadership and Administration of Outdoor Pursuits*, like the first edition, was written primarily as a textbook for college and university students studying outdoor recreation. Much of the material may be applied to the National Recreation and Park Association curriculum standards for accreditation. A second purpose of the book is to help administrators of existing or potential outdoor pursuit programs to understand the intricacies of administering an outdoor recreation program. Of course, a third purpose is to help current and future outdoor leaders to use the best and most current practices employed by reasonable and prudent professionals.

This second edition has been completely rewritten and greatly enhanced. The order of the chapters has been rearranged into four sections: Background, Skills and Knowledge Specific to the Outdoor Leader, Leadership and Administration, and Planning and Leading. There are new chapters dedicated to Marketing the Outdoor Program, Transportation, and a very comprehensive chapter on Strategic and Tactical Planning. The materials on Preparation for Survival, First Aid in Outdoor Emergencies, Search and Rescue, and Land Navigation have been completely updated and are more inclusive than in the first edition.

Because the current topographical maps use the metric system and because of the number of readers from the countries that have adopted that system as the official unit of measurement, most of the references to distance and weight have been listed two ways. It is intended to help American students, as most of the rest of the world now uses the metric system.

The authors want to acknowledge the contributions of others who have made the book possible. Michael Strong, co-coordinator of the Outdoor Pursuits Program, provided a great deal of information, advice, and support throughout the rewriting process. John Pitetti, Volunteer Search and Rescue Coordinator for the Lane County Sheriff's Office assisted with technical details in Chapter Eight "Search and Rescue." Special thanks are owed to the student leaders in the Outdoor Pursuits Program, whose insightful critiques and suggestions have been invaluable in rewriting this text.

We also want to acknowledge Joann Brady, the only typist we know who can make order out of chaotic penmanship, inserted comments, and lightly penciled additions. Without her typing the first copies of the revision, the final copies would never have materialized.

part one

BACKGROUND

OUTDOOR PURSUITS AND OUTDOOR PARTICIPANTS

Introduction

When the first settlers came to North America, their primary task was to develop homes and farms and, later, towns and cities. They cut and plowed the vast forests and prairies to build their cities, farms, and factories. The areas they thought of as wilderness were to be conquered, controlled, or eradicated. For the most part, the only settlers who roamed the woods, mountains, and rivers were explorers, trappers, and hunters. Like the native Americans, they followed game trails or just struck off into the forests without trails.

For the early hunters, trappers, and explorers, camping equipment was simple. They had no special clothes unless they made them from the skins of the game they had killed. Their shelters were often openings in rock formations and hollow trees, or beneath boughs, branches and animal hides. Their protection from the elements was often no more than a piece of hide, a deerskin, and perhaps a raccoon skin hat made so that the rain dripped off the end of the tail. Their camping equipment was made up of the few things they owned—clothes, a blanket, rifle, powder, bullets, a piece of flint for lighting a fire, stiff leather or hide shoes, probably no socks, a boiling pot, a knife, and a sack for carrying everything that was not hung onto the belt or carried in the hand.

Food was often some meat shot during the day or dried from an earlier trip—rabbit, squirrel, deer, elk, bear, fish, or whatever was available. If they were fortunate in finding any salad plants they recognized, a few sprigs of miner's lettuce, spring beauty, watercress or something similar could be nibbled for fresh greens. Their mainstay was some sort of cornmeal biscuit or johnny (journey) cake. These early campers packaged their food in rags, brown paper, or skins. They reused the wrappings until they were tattered, completely soaked with fat, and highly flammable. Then they burned them as tinder for their fires. They may have cut boughs for their beds in areas where fir trees were plentiful, and they probably dug "hip and shoulder holes" in which to sink their weary bones as they slept. They used the woods for their toilet, and leaves, cones, or other natural plant materials for toilet paper. If women or children accompanied them, sanitary materials and babies' diapers were fashioned from mosses, particularly the absorbent sphagnum moss. As recently as World War I (1917-1918), sphagnum moss was sanitized and used as dressings for wounds. In those days, there were no gauze bandages.

The land was vast, and the explorers and trapper/hunters were few. In spite of cutting trees for beds, building fires for warmth and cooking, and digging a few hip holes, there was little noticeable damage done to the environment. Any damage done was rarely permanent, and the slight scars were few and far between. The early users of natural areas used natural materials over and over until they fell apart or were used for fuel. They had no plastics, foil, or sleeping bags, and seldom traveled in large groups. They camped right next to the source of water but had no worry about drinking from any stream. While they rarely washed with soap or swam, their sanitary practices contributed to pollution of the water. Only the scarce number of early settlers kept water-borne diseases from becoming wide-spread epidemics. Most of the water-borne diseases brought to the rivers and streams by man or beast were limited to the water supplies of the towns and villages.

Because their lives depended upon it, they learned to "read" the environment for signs of animals, other people, or previous campsites. They "knew" where they were. They recognized edible, poisonous, and medicinal plants. They were curious to know what each plant and animal meant to the area. They studied the "signs" of the area much like we study the signs in a strange city today. Many times, they traveled alone knowing there was probably no help for miles around. If they became injured or ill, they had to take care of the problem themselves—or die alone. When they traveled in groups, they depended upon their comrades for help, although medical practices were primitive by modern standards. In times of illness, most people had only folklore, guesses and self-taught remedies to call on.

As European populations expanded and the native populations were decimated by warfare and disease, proportionately fewer people lived in direct contact with the wilderness. Outdoor survival skills and knowledge seemed relatively less important than mastery of the specialized trades necessary for success in an increasingly complex urban society. About 1890, families living comfortably on the East Coast began to seek the outdoors for recreation including nature study, hiking, camping and sightseeing. By the early 1900s, youth groups such as Boy Scouts, Girl Scouts, Camp Fire, YMCA, YWCA, and private organizations had developed summer camps where the participants were taught outdoor living skills such as fire building, use of axe and saw, cooking,

tenting, nature crafts, and nature study. These activities were taught to youth for several purposes: to understand the ways of the Native Americans, to learn how to be "scouts," to become self-sufficient, and to perform everyday living tasks such as planning and preparing meals and getting along with others at a time when the required public school curriculum was focused upon reading, writing, and arithmetic, and none of what progressive educators considered "practical" education.

Interest in the outdoors for recreation caught on and grew by leaps and bounds, interrupted only briefly by World Wars I and II, until, in the 1950s, literally hundreds of thousands of Americans went camping each summer. But by 1945, thousands of acres of forests and prairies had been cut and plowed to make way for towns and farms. The abundance of potential outdoor recreational land had decreased to less than a fourth of what it had been in Colonial days.

Today, almost everyone from the United States and Canada and thousands from countries all over the world spend some time each year out of doors eating, cooking, sleeping, traveling or playing. Many trails are overcrowded. Unlike early explorers, most people don't go off the trails for fear of getting lost (probably wisely), and the trails get wider and muddier every year. Instead of seeking new areas, finding game or exploring, people today flock to the sites known for recreational activities, spectacular views, temperate climates, excellent fishing, and beautiful scenery, often lured to heavily used sites by influential marketing techniques such as advertisements, guide books, documentary videos, and magazine articles.

The practices of modern campers, hikers, backpackers, paddlers or backyard cooks differ from those of the earlier hunters, trappers, and explorers in many ways. Most equipment is now made of non-biodegradable materials and may be tossed away after one use or when worn out. Synthetics, such as nylon and plastic, are used to make clothing and equipment. Food wrappings consist of foil, plastic, and treated paper—sometimes all on one package— and these materials do not burn or decay. Heavy shoes protect the feet but tramp down or erode the land. Wood used for cooking has become more and more scarce. In some areas, it has been cut and burned far faster than it can be regrown. With so many people using the outdoors, human waste has created a problem. Toilet paper takes several years to disintegrate and return to the soil. Fecal material can be sighted along almost any trail, and diseases from humans and animals have made it necessary to purify every stream before drinking the water.

The modern camper may be confused or frightened even by plants and animals that have been studied for many decades and shown to be harmless. Lack of understanding too often leads to fear, and fear blocks vision, clouds judgment, and delays development of a constructive relationship between the person and the environment.

Most people today do not cope well with emergencies, accidents or unforeseen survival situations. They seem to think that whenever something goes wrong, someone will soon come to help. Where there are trail signs, people assume they will not get lost, or if they do, a ranger will swoop from nowhere to rescue them. Unfortunately, many such overconfident and underskilled people stray from the trails and become hopelessly confused and lost. Evidence of the inability to cope with survival emergencies is found in the numbers of people who get into trouble each year. They were snowbound on highways with no survival equipment in their cars. Or they were ill-prepared to weather out periods of darkness, loss of water and/or power, and lack of normal food supplies and cooking facilities following tornadoes, hurricanes, earthquakes and other natural phenomena.

The ways of outdoor enthusiasts today are so different from the ways of the early explorers that new methods and regulations must be enforced. Nothing seems to stop the growth of interest in outdoor activities; yet if people continue to participate in these activities as they have up to the present, the potential quality of all outdoor experiences will diminish as the available land becomes overrun with litter, debris, waste, water pollution, barren sites, and crowds of people.

Since the end of World War II in 1945, the quantity of all outdoor activities has increased astonishingly. In a veritable explosion of numbers, millions are backpacking, cross-country skiing, rafting, canoeing, bicycling, hiking, climbing or caving. In short, millions are moving across land and water seeking enjoyment through physical activity in primitive settings. Accompanying this rise in outdoor recreation have been predictable increases in environmentally-related accidents, injuries, and deaths, with a concomitant increase in environmental degradation.

Most of the participants in outdoor pursuits have had no formal or informal education which addresses either care of the natural environment or care of themselves in that natural environment. It is now recognized that the user needs to be educated in care of self and in stewardship of land and water resources. Those who are charged with educating users must, in turn, have been educated to teach them.

Organized outdoor pursuit activities are inherently complex. On the one hand, there is the human element—people who desire experiences based on utilization of natural resources. On the other hand, there is the nonhuman element—the natural resources that can contribute to either successful or disastrous experiences and which may be affected adversely by excessive or improper use. The connecting elements are the activity sponsors, the resource management agency, money, transportation, and equipment; all must be coordinated by a leader who, it is assumed, has the knowledge and ability to integrate these elements in such a way as to yield safe and environmentally responsible outdoor experiences that result in attainment of proper objectives.

One answer to the dilemma is expert leadership, and the preparation of expert leaders begins with the proper education. This book is designed to meet the needs of both outdoor leaders and administrators. While specifically addressed to leaders and instructors, the contents should be understood by administrators of outdoor programs as well. The managers of these educational and recreational programs are, with increasing frequency and urgency, being pressed to extend the scope of their programs to include outdoor pursuits. Unfortunately, many administrators do not know enough about such activities to be able to select qualified leaders and to monitor and evaluate the development and implementation of the activities adequately. A better understanding by administrators of the specific demands of outdoor leadership should improve the process by which they select and supervise leaders. Thus, program quality improves while exposure to liability is reduced.

Through the use of the material in this text, readers should become aware of the accepted standards, policies, controversies, principles, methods, and skills of leadership of outdoor activities. Readers should be able to plan, organize, and carry out safe and responsible programs for land-based or water-based activities in natural settings. Further, they should understand the roles and functions of both leaders and administrators of outdoor pursuit activities.

Outdoor Recreation Defined

This book is focused primarily on activities perceived as outdoor recreation. The words "outdoor recreation" connote a wide variety of meanings. In its broadest sense, the terms were used by the U.S. Department of the Interior in its report, *The Recreation Imperative*, to the U.S. Senate in 1974. As a result of the 1962 Public Law 85-470, the Outdoor Recreation Resources Review Commission (ORRRC) was organized and mandated to review the outdoor recreation wants and needs of the American people in 1962 with projections for the years 1976 and 2000, and to inventory the available resources and recommend policies and programs to insure that the needs of the people would be met. In carrying out the charge, the commission defined outdoor recreation as follows:

"…those activities that occur outdoors in an urban and man-made environment as well as those activities traditionally associated with the natural environment. With the advent of indoor-outdoor facilities, such as convertible skating rinks and swimming

pools, an additional dimension has been added to the complex of areas and facilities encompassed in the term outdoor recreation" (Outdoor Recreation Resources Review Commission, 1962).

As a result of this broad definition, and by surveying thousands of Americans, the following list of the twenty-six most popular activities was generated:

Picnicking
Driving for Pleasure
Swimming
Sightseeing
Pleasure Walking
Attending Sporting Events
Playing Outdoor Games and Sports
Fishing
General Boating
Bicycling
Sledding
Attending Concerts and Plays
Nature Walking
Camping
Day Hiking
Hunting
Ice Skating
Hiking with Pack (Backpacking)
Water Skiing
Bird Watching
Canoeing/Kayaking
Downhill Skiing
Cross-Country Skiing
Sailing
Photography (Primarily mammals and birds)
Mountain Climbing

In 1984, a research report from the University of Maryland reported that the rank order of the activity popularity was the same as in 1962, but that the numbers of participants had grown astonishingly.

This broad definition of outdoor recreation, encompassing urban and rural participants, includes more than most single books on outdoor activities are able to cover. Other definitions may be equally broad. The following definition, adapted from Reynold Carlson, is more limiting:

Outdoor recreation is an enjoyable leisure-time activity pursued outdoors or indoors involving knowledge, use, or appreciation of natural resources (Carlson, 1960).

The essence of Carlson's definition is the emphasis on "natural resources," thus eliminating outdoor facilities which are developed and maintained according to carefully planned specifications (e.g., golf courses and tennis courts). Carlson's definition, however, because of its inclusion of indoor activities (e.g., looking at slides of natural resources and reading guidebooks), even though they involve use, knowledge, or appreciation of natural resources, is broader than many outdoor enthusiasts are willing to accept.

A third definition of outdoor recreation is proposed by Clawson and Knetsch in their book, *Economics of Outdoor Recreation*. In spite of the fact that this book was written in 1966, no natural resource economist since then has challenged or altered the definition or the premise upon which it is based. This definition is based on the premise that outdoor recreation occurs on large tracts of land and/or water located at considerable distances from the homes of the recreationists and, consequently, includes several phases. This multiphased concept of outdoor recreation entails the activities, attitudes and economic values of anticipation (planning the event, which includes purchasing equipment, determining the route, and organizing the schedule), travel to the site, activities at the site (hiking, climbing, rafting), travel from the site, and recollection or reflection. While most outdoor leaders and their respective followers seem to be mainly concerned with activities at the site, it is clear that pre-trip planning and transportation, and post-trip evaluation are also integral parts of the leader's responsibility; thus the multiphased concept of outdoor recreation has logical application for this book.

These three definitions may serve to confuse, or even annoy, some outdoor enthusiasts who consider their personal outdoor recreational interest to be far removed from, and even antithetical to, the interests of others. The authors of this book recognize, accordingly, that the

terms used here will not be generally accepted by all outdoor leaders. For the sake of clarifying the contents of this book, the following discussion will serve to define outdoor pursuits as we see them. It is important to understand that, while the principles for activities pursued by *individuals* are basically the same as those for activities carried out by *groups*, this book focuses upon administration and leadership functions that are carried out with and for *groups* of people. Further, it must be understood that the outdoor pursuits referred to here are usually those undertaken voluntarily for the sake of the activities themselves and with no gain in mind other than the intrinsic value of the activity. This, then, is a book on the administration and leadership of activities usually considered to be recreational.

In the twentieth century, there have been many studies and attempts to define the terms recreation and leisure. For the sake of simplicity, most recreational professionals agree that *recreation* consists of activities chosen voluntarily during leisure time for the sake of the activities themselves. *Leisure* is defined as freedom from duties or responsibilities or time remaining after the necessities of life (sleep, nourishment, and day-to-day responsibilities such as work, school, and chores) are accomplished. Leisure is correlated with discretionary time (time to choose.)

There are many recognized definitions of recreation, but a statement from Jensen (1970) summarizes them most appropriately:

(Today, of course, the statement would be written in nonsexist language; however, in 1970 the male gender was understood to include both sexes.)

Upon analysis of definitions it seems that many of them, even though stated differently, say essentially the same thing. The following elements are common to the several definitions:

1. Recreation directly involves the individual.
2. It is entered into voluntarily.
3. It occurs during leisure time.

4. The motivating force is enjoyment and satisfaction, as opposed to material gain.
5. Recreation is wholesome to the individual and his society.

These common points distinguish recreation from work and other necessary activities; however, they do not give the term the strength it deserves. They do not *clearly distinguish* recreation from amusement, time-filling, or low-quality participation. They do not add a strong characteristic of *quality* to this meaning.

The term "recreation" implies that the participant is recreated in some aspect— physically, psychologically, spiritually, or mentally; that he becomes refreshed and enriched; that he becomes revitalized and more ready to cope with his trials. In order to qualify as recreation, an activity must do something desirable to the participant. It must enrich him and add joy and satisfaction to an otherwise routine day (*Outdoor Recreation in America*, 1970).

Many outdoor scientific expeditions (i.e., studying glaciers and testing new equipment on Mt. Everest, exploring the Mojave Desert, or charting the Colorado River) entail the same skills and often identical leadership principles as recreational activities. However, the goals are specific to the accomplishment of the task, and the process often requires strict discipline, arduous functions, forced effort to succeed and even drudgery, hardship and deprivation—always with the accomplishment of the task in mind.

Recreational experiences may involve the same discipline, ardor, effort, drudgery, hardship, and discomfort. However, the end product is not the accomplishment of a required task; it is the accomplishment of an internal feeling of success, safe return, and joy of accomplishing something of personal value. While the goal of a funded expedition may be to reach the destination and to return with a "product" in the form of information, the goal of recreation is personal satisfaction and, a safe return with a chance to try again, if desired.

It is a moot point to try to determine when an enjoyable outdoor recreation activity becomes an unpleasant bit of drudgery or a life-endangering crisis. Hopefully, leaders and administrators will apply the principles of group guidance and avoid turning recreation into a goal-oriented torturous experience. The major purpose of this book is to discuss the role and function of professional leaders who are paid employees or volunteers leading members of the general public in voluntarily chosen activities with positive, enjoyable expectations.

The term "outdoor pursuits" is widely applied to those activities which entail moving across natural land and/or water resources by nonmechanized means of travel. In this context, this book limits the scope of outdoor pursuits to nonmechanical and nonanimal means of travel. Included in this perception of outdoor pursuits are such activities as hiking, backpacking, climbing (rock and snow), cross-country skiing, primitive camping (summer and winter), canoeing, rafting, caving, and snowshoeing. Specifically included are group activities based on land, snow, or water resources. Excluded are downhill skiing, car camping, motor boating, horseback riding, dog sledding, etc. While the book is focused on nonmechanical group activities involving human judgment in areas remote from modern convenience, much of the material is applicable to the excluded activities. All of the activities are based upon the interrelationship of humans with the natural environment, particularly where that environment may present discomfort, danger, and unique situations.

The terms "outdoor adventure" or "adventure activity" are similar to but slightly different from "outdoor pursuits." Adventure activities are those outdoor pursuits that, in addition to being based upon the interrelationship of the human with the natural environment, apply stress to or challenge the participants *purposefully*. Advanced skills, tenacity, stamina, and courage are elements added to usual outdoor pursuits that cause them to be termed "adventure activities." The point at which an outdoor pursuit becomes an "adventure activity" is often moot and may be determined by the participant who finds the skills, tenacity, and stamina required by the program are greater than had been anticipated. The novice participant in river rafting may *perceive* the experience as an outdoor adventure, but if the instructor does not apply stress purposefully, the activity, from the instructor's point of view, is an outdoor recreational pursuit.

It must be recognized that many activities necessitating leadership in the outdoors are not perceived as recreation by the sponsors, leaders and/or participants. Classes required by various educational institutions, military training, referral programs for potential or adjudicated delinquents, and any program whose purpose is to develop self-concept, character, stamina, or other personal attribute cannot be labelled "recreation." Such programs should, nevertheless, follow the same leadership standards and principles as recreational programs. The purposes of each are different; however, the means of achieving those purposes differ little. Philosophically, it is believed that the attitude and technique of the leader can turn an otherwise unpleasant situation into an enjoyable one so that the purpose of the outing can be achieved more willingly, even with enthusiasm. Regardless of the ultimate goal, leadership should never result in an antipathy toward the resources upon which the activities are based, nor in anything other than an attitude of care for those resources.

It must further be understood that there is a fine line between voluntary and required activities. There are times when participants in required activities find themselves enjoying the experience and desiring to participate again. By the same token, there are times when the outdoor recreation enthusiast wishes only to get home and away from the activity. Picture two friends who have climbed a glacier-covered peak in the sunshine and then descended into a cold rain. As they subsequently try to warm themselves over a miserable sputtering fire of wet subalpine fir twigs, one turns to the other and asks, "Is this recreation?"

Thus, regardless of the diversity of outdoor recreation definitions and the vast potential for definitions of outdoor pursuits, this book focuses mainly upon the administration and leadership of voluntarily chosen nonmechanized outdoor activities undertaken in natural environments, remote from the city, for the purpose of enjoyment, self-realization and the intrinsic value of the experience itself.

The Leisure Experience

In recent years, attempts have been made to define the "leisure experience." It is important that the outdoor leader understand this definition because, while some outdoor pursuits are conducted for the purposes of education or character development, the vast majority of outdoor pursuits are conducted for the purpose of recreation or leisure. Even the activities conducted for the purpose of education may eventually become recreation; thus the understanding of what composes a leisure experience becomes important to the leader.

Defining the "leisure experience" is an attempt to explain the personal nature of an individual's activities as opposed to just having free time. There seems to be agreement that the leisure experience is really a continuum of experiences that vary in intensity from those that are barely perceptible to the individual to those which may go beyond ecstacy into what Maslow (1968) terms the "peak experience" (complete immersion into the experience and a state of oblivion to other forces). Individuals differ in the range and intensity of their leisure experiences. Thoughts, images, feelings, and sensations differ in intensity so, while some individuals feel only slightly exhilarated, others feel at the peak of stimulation. These individual differences, when recognized by the insightful leader, will influence the method of leading.

Further, it has long been recognized that the feeling of the leisure experience changes and is transitory. For example, one may find pleasant emotions in planning an outdoor activity and start out with high expectations of joy. However, after several hours of trudging uphill under a heavy pack, the leisure experience may well resemble drudgery. Upon reaching a level spot and a view of cascading waterfalls, the experience of leisure may well reoccur. Certainly those who start out with trepidation in an outdoor venture because of extrinsic motivation such as parental or peer coercion and return having found the experience to have been personally satisfying and thrilling have moved from one range of the leisure experience continuum to the other.

It is believed that four conditions must be present for a person to experience leisure: perceived freedom of choice, intrinsic motivation, facilitative arousal, and commitment. Understanding each of these conditions can help a leader appreciate why one individual may hate the outdoor experience while another may love it. Even if the outdoor program is *not* basically recreational in purpose or nature, the leader may be more successful if the conditions for leisure experience are understood.

1. *Perceived freedom of choice.* If the participant perceives that he/she has the freedom to choose the activity (and to choose to end it at any time) a leisure experience may be present. If, on the other hand, the participant feels that there is no choice in participating and does so only as an assignment, a punishment, a required learning experience, or because of peer pressure, then the experience is not one of leisure.

2. *Intrinsic motivation.* If the participant is paid, bribed or enticed into outdoor pursuits, or if participation is for any reason other than personal desire, he/she is not motivated intrinsically. Intrinsic means for the value within something. For example, the intrinsic value of a one hundred dollar bill is no more than that of a one dollar bill. Its intrinsic value is that of a piece of special paper with special printing. The intrinsic value of an outdoor pursuit is purely for the feelings of joy or satisfaction or inner contentment—for the value of the activity itself. The psychological needs of the individual play a big part in determining intrinsic motivation.

3. *Facilitative arousal.* Facilitative arousal in the vernacular refers to "what turns you on." It may be curiosity, variety, novelty, challenge or countless other stimuli or motivations. This level of stimulus also differs from person to person or from event to event. A novice might find

rapelling from a 50 foot cliff to be too frightening. A person who has rapelled that same cliff many times over a period of ten years might find it boring. But one who is trying it for the first time, after many successful attempts at a lower cliff, might find that experience facilitatively arousing. (He/she is "turned on" by the experience.)

4. *Commitment.* If the participants aren't personally committed to the activity it is not going to be a leisure experience. All other conditions might be met but, because of minimal interest, psychological burnout, or other priorities, a personal commitment is lacking, and the true leisure experience is lacking. Some people may want to repeat a trip many times and find it exhilarating each time so are committed to continuing it in high spirits. Others may be bored and want to quit because they are no longer committed to the experience. For them, a new route may rekindle the commitment. Those who aren't committed to the activity in the first place will be a challenge to the leader.

Ideally, the leader wants participants who: (1) choose the activity voluntarily, (2) are there for no motivation other than to participate in the activities themselves, (3) are stimulated by that level of activity, and (4) are committed to the program. If all these conditions are met, the individual will participate in what is known as a "leisure experience." The intensity of the experience will vary from individual to individual.

(Philosophically, if the outdoor program is purely punitive, or forced upon the individual for some purpose other than contact with the natural environment, the leaders might consider using a different site. Using natural resources with their finite ability to withstand the impact of humans for any purpose other than enjoyable use, understanding or appreciation of natural resources may no longer be acceptable conduct. Certainly one of the purposes of any outdoor program should be the eventual enjoyment, understanding and appreciation of the outdoors in the true context of leisure.)

Participants

Many outdoor leaders perceive their followers to be similar to themselves, but such is rarely the case. Leaders would do well to consider some or all of the following as potential clients:

- Five-year-old youngsters with grandparents in their 80s;
- Families with parents in their late 30s or early 40s with children aged 14, 11 and 8;
- Participants who are hearing impaired, partly or totally blind, physically disabled, mentally disturbed, or learning impaired;
- Minorities (African-American, Oriental, Chicano, and others);
- Students from elementary schools, high schools, or colleges;
- Young men and women who find the outdoors their main source of personal challenge and gratifying recreation;
- Inner-city youth who find the outdoors frightening, alien, and even punitive.

It is especially challenging and not uncommon to find several of the above in one outing group. Leaders of outdoor pursuits must expect a wide range of participant ages, abilities, and backgrounds, many times in combination. While some activities should be limited to the very fit, most groups include a wide range of abilities, interests, and attitudes. The leader must be willing and able to lead the slow, tired, frightened, or recalcitrant follower. Leaders and administrators of outdoor programs often seem to assume that leadership is being offered to segments of the population whose interests and skills in the out-of-doors are the primary reasons for being there. This is more often *not* the case.

Usually participants are grouped with some common denominator as a tie. Regardless of ability, intelligence, income, or even equal liking for the activity, youth groups are tied together by their membership in a nationally sponsored organization with specified goals and behavior patterns. Boy Scouts, Girl Scouts, Camp Fire, YMCA, YWCA, and other similar groups are usually involved in outdoor

programs as a sponsored group or troop. Each participant may have different reasons for being there. Social interaction, peer pressures, desire to excel, parental hopes, desire to earn an award, or other motivations may be stronger than a desire for any of the purposes of outdoor pursuits recognized by the leader.

Family groups may participate in outdoor programs for reasons primarily related to family cohesiveness. The main purpose may be to have a chance to interact on a recreational level in a new setting. Here, as in the youth groups, the outdoor experience may be secondary to the family interaction. Leaders of two or three diverse families in a group may even find conflicting objectives from one family to another and may need to make changes in the program objectives and the leading/teaching methods planned for the occasion.

Mixed groups may attend outdoor pursuit programs sponsored by municipal recreation departments, schools, or clubs. Usually participants in such programs are there because of personal goals. Unlike the youth agency groups, they may have no common denominator for belonging to the group and may not even be interested in being part of it. People who join city-sponsored programs, clubs, and college classes may be doing so because the desire to participate in the activity is primary and the temporary group association interest is only secondary or perhaps nonexistent.

The physically or mentally disabled, the adjudicated delinquent, and the social misfit or miscreant are increasingly being programmed into outdoor pursuits for the purpose of developing self-confidence, experiencing success, learning to adjust to new situations, and experiencing group work. The physically disabled, including those with orthopedic, congenital, and neuro-muscular disabling conditions, can usually adjust to the environment and are usually in the program voluntarily with attitudes and skills as attainable (within the limitations of the disability) as any nondisabled person.

The mentally disabled, on the other hand, may not know or understand why they are present or what they should do. Coping with problems caused by snow, danger, cold, rain, heavy loads, toileting, lack of comprehension, and length of time needed to perform tasks means a different approach to leadership.

The elderly may range in age from 55 to 90 or more. Some may be in better shape mentally and physically than some people much younger. Some may need a slower pace, warmer clothes, more frequent rest, or other considerations. A totally mixed group could contain physical disabilities, mental impairment, the teenager, the retiree, young adults, the middle-aged, and the elderly. In short, the outdoor-pursuit leader can anticipate responsibility for every category of person imaginable and will profit by learning as much about human diversity as he/she can.

The Nonexistent "Typical" Participant

It is unwise to focus all our attention on the "average" or "typical" person involved in outdoor recreation because such an individual is not to be found. The "average" is a composite of many pieces of information—not the description of a verifiable individual. Because of different locales, motivation, and personal attributes, outdoor enthusiasts are as different as are the members of the general public. For example, in 1990 it was found that of the enthusiasts visiting the Inyo National Forest in California, 91 percent were white, 60 percent were males, and 53 percent were college educated. Only five percent were Asian, three percent were Hispanic, and less than one percent were African-American. We cannot generalize that the outdoor recreationist is an educated white male. In *this* case, we can state that the typical participant was white, male, and college educated. In contrast, however, 64 percent of the visitors to the San Gabriel Canyon of the Angeles National Forest were Hispanic and only 22 percent were Caucasian. In this second case, the typical outdoor recreationist was *not* Caucasian. While the reason for the differences is not known, it is surmised that they may have been due to distance factors, socioeconomic differences, motivation and knowledge of opportunities.

In another study of the Angeles National Forest, four major cultural groups made up the sample: U.S.-born Anglos (6 percent), U.S.-born Hispanics (26 percent), Mexican-born Mexicans and Hispanics (45 percent), and Central/South American-born Hispanics (23 percent). The motivations of the respondents varied in respect to place of birth. The respond-ents born outside the United States had stronger motivational responses for all fifteen reasons (listed on a questionnaire) for going to the forest than those born in the United States. Strongest were the motivations to get away from noise, be with the family, learn about nature, experience new things, and enjoy peace and calm. The fact remains, while we may expect to find most of the participants to be white males, we can also expect to find many participants who are neither white nor male. And we can expect to find participants with many motivations for being in the outdoors. We should not generalize about any population.

Sponsoring Agencies

Participants in outdoor pursuits are of two types: common adventurers or proprietary groups. As common adventurers, they, in essence, sponsor themselves, all taking equal responsibility for cost, equipment, leadership, and success or failure of the event. Common adventure, also known as joint venture, assumes an undertaking wherein all participants have an equal voice in directing the conduct of the enterprise. In other words, common adventurers have no legally designated leader. They are a self-sponsored group with shared leadership responsibilities. They may be members of a college outdoor program, a private climbing club, a group of acquaintances, or a family.

While the principles of outdoor leadership may be applied sagaciously by groups of common adventurers, this book is specifically addressed to those proprietary groups operating under sponsored programs with designated volunteer or employed leaders. Proprietary groups may be discussed under the following six categories. Within each category, leaders may be part- or full-time volunteers, or part- or full-time paid professionals.

1. *Tax-supported Outdoor Programs*
   Municipal recreation departments and districts offer many outdoor activity programs.
2. *Youth-agency Outdoor Programs*
   (Includes Scouts, Camp Fire, YMCA, YWCA, YMHA, etc.)
   These organizations sponsor resident and day camps as well as an extensive array of outdoor trips.
3. *School-sponsored Outdoor Programs*
   Elementary and middle schools offer outdoor education programs, often for five days away from home. Colleges and universities often offer elective outdoor skill classes. Recreation and physical education departments provide a variety of outdoor-related courses for their majors and minors. And many natural science departments (e.g., geology, botany, and zoology) require field trips to natural areas.
4. *Church-sponsored Outdoor Programs*
5. *Membership Programs*
   These programs include hiking, climbing, and boating clubs, native plant societies, and bird watchers' organizations.
6. *Private Businesses*
   These include many types of "for-profit" programs some of which are educational development programs, wilderness use education courses, guided nature tours, tours to other countries, and guide businesses sponsoring water and land trips.

The Values of Outdoor Recreation

One might ask the question, "What good is outdoor recreation that we should spend so much time and money on it?" Or, "What are the values of outdoor pursuits?" One could spend much time relating the *economic* values of outdoor recreation in terms of money spent on equipment, transportation, guide service, and such amenities as photographic equipment,

lightweight food, and how-to books. This book, however, is about people and the benefits of outdoor pursuits to the human being.

In spite of the lack of quantitative data supporting the value of outdoor pursuits, there are *perceived* values that are undeniable. Human beings may be viewed holistically as a combination of mind, body, and spirit. Another way of looking at the holistic individual is as a complex organism whose nonbiological essence is composed of knowledge, skills, and attitudes or emotions. The values of outdoor recreation may relate to each of those domains separately and in combination.

Physical Values

The physical values of outdoor recreation include the benefits of exercise, development of endurance, and increase in cardio-muscular function. With the increase in strength and endurance comes energy, an increase in muscle tone, an increase in the flow of oxygen to the brain, and a general feeling of well-being. Other physical benefits may well be fitness, skills, strength, coordination, exercise, and balance.

Mental Values

The knowledge gained from good-quality outdoor pursuits includes knowledge of self and self-concept, knowledge of safety measures and the need to follow them, and knowledge of skills that relate to the physical values. The knowledge of outdoor skills should be accompanied by the knowledge of the environment in which the activity takes place. Weather, flora, fauna, rock and soil formations, water quality, and changing ecosystems provide the individual with understandings of the world that can last throughout life and make other experiences more interesting.

Emotional Values

The emotions or attitudes one develops through outdoor pursuits may relate to the self, to others, to society, and to the environment. One can gain a sense of achievement, overcome stress, find relaxation, increase self-concept, or just simply enjoy the experience. One may develop new attitudes toward the members of the group because of the closeness of the individuals in accomplishing difficult tasks. From appreciation for the natural environment and a commitment to save it from destruction may emerge a real concern for the survival of the planet after witnessing the results from acid rain, mining, blasting, burning, logging, or herbicides when they are seen face to face in the seemingly untouched wild lands.

Psychological-Sociological Values

The values of outdoor activities may be greatest in terms of the contribution to the individual and to the group. Research has shown that changes in self-esteem as a result of outdoor experiences are both positive and quantitative. Ewert (1987) has identified the potential psychological benefits of outdoor adventure recreation as being: Self-concept, Confidence, Self-efficacy, Sensation-seeking, Actualization, Well-Being, and Personal Testing. He lists potential sociological benefits as: Compassion, Group Cooperation, Respect for Others, Communication, Behavior Feedback, Friendship, and Belonging.

There is research to document the theory that a primary human motivation is to establish control over one's environment. Certainly if participants perceive they have control of the outdoor situation, their behavior is markedly different from behaviors of those who feel they do not have control. Both physical and social space introduces perceptions of control and different reactions. Successful coping with stress leads to enhanced feelings of control. In the outdoor environment, individuals who learn to perceive that they are in control of themselves and the situation are believed to have greater psychological and physiological well-being than those who feel a lack of control. It is important that the leader understands this, for not only will the individual benefit by positive perceptions of the natural environment, those perceptions may be induced by positive leadership.

In addition to a desire to feel "in" control, outdoor participants seem to desire a freedom "from" control. They feel that they do not have control of their recreational choices if someone or something dictates where and how they must travel. They often resent being controlled by an agency after they have chosen where to go for their recreational pursuits. This results in problems of management, particularly management of wilderness areas. (See Chapter Two for more on this.)

Overall Values

While the following passage was written during a 1954 workshop on recreation, it is interesting to note that the words are still valid today. If the six objectives listed are met, that in itself may be the greatest value of outdoor pursuits.

The first principle of recreation is that the experience must give satisfaction to the participant. This does not mean, however, that certain other values might not be derived. Neither does it mean that the leader and the organization or agency responsible for the activity should not have specific objectives. Objectives are generally stated in terms of values to the individual. Most of them, however, also have social significance, and programs are planned to meet social needs. The fostering of love of the land and pride in country, the understanding and practice of democracy, the strengthening of social institutions, and the development of conservation attitudes—these are values that might come from the participation in desirable outdoor recreation activities. Contributions of recreation to the health and happiness of people are themselves important social values.

The principal purpose of outdoor recreation is to provide for enjoyment, appreciation, and use of the natural environment. Certain more specific objectives are the following:

1. To develop a sense of responsibility for the preservation, care, and wise use of the natural environment;
2. To develop an awareness and understanding of the inter-relatedness of all nature, including man;
3. To develop an understanding and appreciation of man's heritage of outdoor living, skills, and pursuits;
4. To develop good outdoor citizenship;
5. To make a contribution to physical and mental health;
6. To develop resourcefulness, self-reliance, and adaptability (*Athletic Institute*, 1954).

Summary

The principles of outdoor leadership are based on the need to assist those desiring outdoor experiences in making logical and safe transitions from the routine of every day life to a positive interaction with the natural world. This book is designed for outdoor leaders and administrators of both land-based and water-based outdoor activities. While mainly concerned with recreational (voluntary) pursuits, the book also addresses nonrecreational outdoor programs. While the content is focused upon nonmechanical and nonanimal means of travel, much of the material is applicable to other outdoor activities.

There are countless locations for outdoor pursuits, a wide variety of participants, and many benefits to outdoor experiences. Physical, mental, emotional, social, and psychological values have been identified for outdoor pursuits as well as values for the entire outdoor-recreation experience. Regardless of differences among participants, professional quality leadership techniques are needed in every activity.

References

Athletic Institute. (1954). *The recreation program*. Chicago, IL: The Athletic Institute.

Brown, C. N. (1982). New handshake: Management partners along the Appalachian Trail, *Parks and Recreation*. National Recreation and Parks Association, June, pp. 36-42, 62.

Carlson, R.E. (1960). Lecture. Bloomington, IN: Indiana University.

Clawson, M., & Knetsch, J. L. (1966). *Economics of outdoor recreation*. Baltimore, MD: The Johns Hopkins Press.

Ewert, A. (1987). Research in outdoor adventure: Overview and analysis. *The Bradford Papers*. Volume II. Bloomington, IN: Indiana University.

Jensen, C. (1970). *Outdoor recreation in America*. Minneapolis, MN: Burgess Publishing Co.

Knudson, D. M. (1984). *Outdoor recreation*. Revised edition. New York, NY: Macmillan Publishing Company.

Maslow, A.H. (1968). *Toward a psychology of being*. New York, NY: D. Van Norstrand Co.

Nash, R. (1967). *Wilderness and the American mind*. New Haven, CT: Yale University Press.

Outdoor Recreation Resources Review Commission (ORRRC). (1962). *Outdoor recreation for America*. Washington, DC: U.S. Department of the Interior.

Tinsley, H. E., & Tinsley, D. J. (1986). A theory of the attributes, benefits, and causes of leisure experiences. *Leisure Sciences*, 8:1, pp. 27-49.

USDA Forest Service. (June 1990) *Recreation*
    Research Report. 2:2. Riverside, CA:
    Pacific Southwest Research Station.

RESOURCES FOR OUTDOOR PURSUITS

Locations for Outdoor Pursuits

The sites for outdoor pursuits are many and include natural outdoor areas, indoor facilities, and swimming pools. Indoors, the innovative leader may use walls for climbing, bleachers for practicing belaying techniques, and beams for practicing ascending techniques. In swimming pools, one can teach rescue techniques, entering and leaving watercraft safely, basic use of paddles and oars, fundamental kayak rolls, and rescue techniques. Use of indoor sites can facilitate learning by reducing transportation time as well as eliminating distractions such as wind, rain, and cold. Participants can thus enter the land or water resources at a higher skill level, resulting in higher safety margins for the individual and lower risk to the environment.

The natural resources for outdoor pursuits are made up of the land, water, plants, animals, air, and climate of many areas. Potential sites include millions of acres of land and lakes, miles of rivers, and countless caves. Forests, jungles, deserts, prairies, rocks, snow, ponds, streams, and beaches with their accompanying challenges of weather, steepness, currents, cliffs, plants, and animals abound throughout the world. These resources are administered by various government agencies, youth-serving organizations, private businesses, timber companies, individuals, schools, and churches.

Life zones occur within definable geographic areas, usually determined by either elevation or latitude. Life zones are areas in which, because of identifiable climate, specific forms of plant and animal life exist. Major life zones are the Tropical, Lower Sonoran, Upper Sonoran, Moist Temperate, Dry Temperate, Canadian, Hudsonian, and Arctic-Alpine. The existence of life zones and their associated plant and animal species makes the outdoor pursuit activity more challenging, interesting, and varied. Since life zones change as one moves either south or north and also as one climbs or descends in elevation, it is important that outdoor leaders learn about all life zones into which the group will travel. The change in life zones as one ascends and descends is of importance to the hiker, backpacker, and climber and, at times, to the river rafter who moves from one life zone to another when descending long distances.

Since species of plants and animals are different in different life zones, it stands to reason that the human being must make climatic allowances and adapt accordingly. Geographic areas of the world are so diverse that knowledge of flora, fauna, geology, and weather are of vital importance to the outdoor adventurer. The American who tries backpacking, climbing, or river activities in New Zealand, Australia, the Orient, or Europe must be able to learn new things very rapidly. Drinking-water sources, obnoxious or even dangerous plants and animals, useful plants, emergency fuel sources, and changes in weather patterns are all important to the safety and well-being of the participant. By the same token, the New Englander who has spent years in the northern Appalachians is not automatically equipped to lead a group in Florida, New Mexico, the Washington rain forest, the glaciers of any state, or the high plains and prairies. Nor is any outdoor leader who is an expert in his/her own geographic area equipped to lead groups in any other area in the world without some preliminary examination of the weather, geography, geology, plants, and animals of the new area.

Resource Classification for Recreation

Before looking at the agencies that manage outdoor areas, it might be helpful to look at the methods by which recreational lands are classified.

Recreational Land Classification

It is possible to classify land by many methods. Commonly used systems include those based upon forest types, life zones, hunting zones, water districts, agricultural soils, minerals, climate zones, topographic areas, and recreational uses. In 1962, however, the Outdoor Recreation Resources Review Commission (ORRRC), in its study of resources available for outdoor recreation, recommended a land classification system based upon recreational uses. This system has now been adopted worldwide and has become the single land classification system of value in understanding the *recreational uses* of large areas that often serve other purposes. Figure 2.1 indicates the six classifications (always identified by Roman numerals), examples of each, and available activities.

The greatest amount of outdoor pursuit activity takes place on Class III lands, partly because this category includes the largest number of acres and partly because it includes thousands

of miles of trails and rivers for hiking and boating. Class II and Class V lands are also frequented by large numbers of outdoor enthusiasts. Class II lands contain many fine campsites and many miles of trails or rivers; however, these lands are usually parts of parks with fairly well-developed facilities, telephones, and close emergency aid. This land classification makes them suitable for beginners or novices. Class V lands are usually utilized by those who expect no amenities other than trails and maybe not even those. Included in Class V are legally designated wilderness areas, roadless areas, and other areas that have no legal designation but are remote, primitive, and lacking any development. Class IV and VI lands are limited to activities involving sightseeing and nature and historical study only. It is important that leaders recognize the types of recreational activities that are appropriate to the lands under consideration for use. The outdoor pursuits discussed in this book should not be conducted on Class I, IV or VI lands nor on many portions of the Class II lands. It is also important that outdoor-pursuit leaders realize that much natural land is used for activities other than recreation.

Outdoor recreation land managers and users also designate many land areas by legally accepted terms. In addition to the ORRRC classification system that defines recreational limits and gives guidelines for appropriate management, certain lands are designated by law for specific uses. Wild, Scenic, and Recreational Rivers; Scenic Trails; and Wilderness Areas are all titles of land or water resources specifically managed similarly no matter which agency owns and administers the lands on which they exist. The following definitions clarify these differences.

Wild, Scenic, and Recreational Rivers

Wild rivers are truly primitive on at least four counts. They are unpolluted, inaccessible except by trail, free of impoundments, and have primitive shorelines or watersheds. River management focuses on preservation and enhancement

---

FIGURE 2.1   ORRRC Land Classification

CLASS	EXAMPLES	ACTIVITIES
1. High-density Recreation Areas	Coulter Bay in Grand Teton National Park Yosemite Valley Huntington Beach, CA Jones Beach, NY	sports, games, sightseeing; use of many man-made facilities, marinas, etc.
2. General Outdoor Recreation Areas	state parks county parks large city parks	picnicking, camping, hiking, biking, skiing, water sports, fishing, ball playing, many man-made facilities

3. Natural Environment Areas	parts of:
	  National Forests
	  National Parks
	  large land holdings
		hiking, camping, boating, fishing, hunting, almost exclusively; many trails, some picnic facilities, some pit privies

4. Unique Natural Areas	Old Faithful Yosemite Falls Bristle Cone Natural Area (in the Inyo National Forest)	sightseeing, nature study

5. Primitive Areas	legally designated wilderness areas
	  (Boundary Waters Canoe Area,
	    Lostine Wilderness)
	roadless areas
	primitive areas
		canoeing, hiking, climbing; some trails, no other man-made amenities

6. Historic or Cultural Sites	Valley Forge Casa Grande Ruins Mesa Verde	sightseeing, history or cultural study

---

of primitive qualities as the dominant priority, and no facilities for recreation, except trails, are provided.

Scenic rivers (or river sections) are free of impoundments and have largely primitive watersheds and undeveloped shorelines, but are accessible by road in places. Management emphasizes maintenance of a natural, though somewhat modified, environment, and a modest range of facilities for recreation is allowed.

Recreational rivers may have been much more affected by man but are still essentially free-flowing. Some past impoundment or diversion is permissible, but usually such activities are precluded in the future. Limited shoreline development and pollution may be present, but roads and railroads are nearby, providing easy accessibility.

Management of recreational rivers is strongly oriented toward providing for the visitor but maintaining an aesthetically pleasing environment. Recreational river areas usually provide a wide range of readily accessible recreational opportunities, more elaborate and numerous than in the other classifications. The environment may reflect substantial evidence of man's activity. Different classifications may be applied to segments of streams. For example, one part of a designated segment may be labeled "wild," another segment "recreational," and a third segment "scenic," or any combination of these. Few rivers or streams in the system are of one classification only, and any single segment must be at least 25 miles long to be categorized.

National Scenic Trails

National scenic trails are major cross-country trails administered by the Secretary of the Department of Agriculture, or the Department of the Interior. They provide opportunities for extended trips on foot or horseback. These trails may cross through lands administered by the U.S. Forest Service, National Park Service, Bureau of Land Management, Bureau of Indian Affairs, and other federal agencies, as well as lands owned by states, counties, and private individuals and corporations. None of the trails is entirely complete, and all users should inquire about and procure all necessary permits before attempting to travel on them. The Pacific Crest National Scenic Trail is administered by the U.S. Forest Service, while the Appalachian Trail is administered by the National Park Service. Figure 2.2 lists the national scenic trails.

Wilderness

The term "wilderness" holds different meanings for different people. Psychologically, wilderness connotes a primitive, pristine, often remote and adventurous area. To some, the woods on the edge of a large city, the forested areas of a state park, or any area with a hiking trail can be perceived as a wilderness. On the other extreme, some people regard wilderness as only those areas that have no obvious mark of humanity—no trails, no signs, no fire rings, not even any vestiges of earlier human occupation or travel. This is often referred to as the *sociological* or the *psychological* definition.

Legally designated wilderness, however, is land set aside by Congress and defined in the Wilderness Act of 1964:

> A wilderness, in contrast with those areas where man and his own works dominate the landscape, is hereby recognized as an area where the earth and its community of life are untrammeled by man, where man himself is a visitor who does not remain. An area of wilderness is further defined to mean in this Act an area of undeveloped Federal land retaining its primeval character and influence, without permanent improvements

FIGURE 2.2	National Scenic Trails		
NATIONAL SCENIC TRAILS	**LENGTH (km)**	**(mi.)**	**ADMIN.**
Appalachian	3,300	2,050	NPS
Pacific Crest	3,700	2,300	USFS
Continental Divide	4,990	3,100	USFS
North Country	5,200	3,200	NPS
Ice Age	1,600	1,000	Wi. DNR
Potomac Heritage	1,126	704	NPS
Natchez Trace	1,110	694	NPS
Florida	2,080	1,300	USFS

or human habitation, which is protected and managed so as to preserve its natural conditions and which: (1) generally appears to have been affected primarily by the forces of nature, with the imprint of man's work substantially unnoticeable; (2) has outstanding opportunities for solitude or a primitive and unconfined type of recreation; (3) has at least five thousand acres of land or is of sufficient size as to make practicable its preservation and use in an unimpaired condition; and (4) may also contain ecological, geological, or other features of scientific, educational, scenic, or historical value.

The word "untrammeled" is defined as untouched, unaltered, or unhampered.

This Act, then, provided special areas managed for preservation and available for recreation by those seeking natural settings. As with many resources, the preservation of this environment is dependent upon the behavior of the visitor. While most visitors are concerned about environmental quality, sensitive to ecological factors, and appreciative of the psychological benefits of primitive areas, preservation ultimately requires aggressive management. Each wilderness area is administered by the federal management agency responsible for the land in which the designated wilderness area lies.

Classification by Difficulty

Mountains and rivers have been classified according to the difficulty of navigation. The following is a description of the difficulty levels of rivers and climbs.

International Scale of River Difficulty

Class I: Moving water with a few riffles and small waves. Few or no obstructions.

Class II: Easy rapids with waves up to three feet and wide, clear channels. Most are obvious without scouting. Some maneuvering is required.

Class III: Rapids with high irregular waves often capable of swamping an open canoe. Narrow passages most often require complex maneuvering. Many require scouting.

Class IV: Long difficult rapids with constricted passages most often requiring precise maneuvering in very turbulent waters. Scouting often necessary and conditions make rescue difficult. Generally not possible for open canoes.

Class V: Extremely difficult long and very violent rapids with highly congested routes which nearly always must be scouted. Rescue conditions difficult and significant hazard to life in event of mishap.

Class VI: Difficulties are carried to extreme of navigability. Nearly impossible and very dangerous. For experts only, after close study and all precautions taken.

NOTE: If the water is below 50°F (10°C) or if the trip is extended in wilderness areas, the rapids on the river should be considered one class more difficult than usual.

Climbing Classifications

There are many different systems used to rate climbs. Currently, the most often used are the Yosemite Decimal System (YDS), the National Climbing Classification System (NCCS), the Union Internationale des Associations d'Alpinisme (UIAA), the Australian and British systems, and the Alpine systems. The following scheme is widely used and forms the basis of the current YDS and NCCS systems. It is sometimes referred to as the Sierra Club System, but is actually based upon the German Welzenbach System of the 1920s.

Class 1: Hiking cross-country without use of hands.

Class 2: Using hands in "scrambling" style. Rope usually not needed.

Class 3: Easy climbing using hands. Rope may be used by the inexperienced.

Class 4: Roped climbing with belaying, usually short pitches.

Class 5: Roped climbing in which the leader places protection. This class was originally divided into levels from 5.0 to 5.9. Later, as routes more difficult than 5.9 were climbed, 5.10 was added. Recent advances in free climbing have pushed the upper limits to 5.14, and higher levels seem inevitable.

Class 6: Roped climbing with artificial assistance such as pitons and etriers. In the YDS system, Class 6 is designated with an "A" and divided into levels from A.0 (fixed lines) to A.5 (30 feet or 10 meters or more of very weak placements).

In addition to classification of climbs by the difficulty of individual pitches, as in the above system, most current schemes also provide an overall grade for the route. The YDS and NCCS systems use Roman numerals as follows:

I = Several hours
II = Half a day
III = Most of a day
IV = Long hard day usually averaging around Level 5.7
V = 1 1/2 to 2 1/2 days usually averaging around Level 5.8
VI = Greater than 2 1/2 days

Wilderness Permits

As the numbers of wilderness users increase, the environmental value and quality of the resource may be diminished, creating a need to control the numbers of users. Before 1940, wilderness travel was rare; therefore, natural resources remained in a relatively natural state. Little information was needed about the backcountry traveler. In some areas, registration cards were designed merely to "count heads," but these were rarely filled out by wilderness enthusiasts. With the increase in backcountry and wilderness travel, preservation of these areas has become a problem, and the wilderness permit has become an important management tool—particularly in those areas mentioned above where the impact of visitor use is endangering natural and wildlife resources.

According to the U.S. Forest Service, census and control are the main reasons for issuing wilderness permits. As census tools, permits provide a source of information on the numbers of visitors, visitor characteristics, and distribution of use. These raw data are keypunched and processed, and computer programs compile and translate the permit data for management planning and administrative decisions. This gives the Forest Service information on how many wilderness seekers are traveling into which popular areas for what length of time. Analysis of data helps managers design regulations and helps to maintain a high quality wilderness resource and to protect the aesthetics of the wilderness experience. The wilderness management plan considers all appropriate and compatible methods to distribute use (theoretically) within the capacity of the area.

The second reason for issuing wilderness permits, therefore, is to assist the Forest Service with visitor distribution. Methods of visitor distribution may include:

1. Limiting the number of users;

2. Restricting specific areas for certain forms of visitor travel;

3. Informing visitors about less congested areas and distributing information to encourage visits to lightly used or relatively unknown areas;

4. Limiting the number of people in parties or the number permitted to stay overnight at specific locations;

5. Regulating the use of saddle horses and pack stock;

6. Stressing the experience and value to be found outside the peak-use period.

A third reason for wilderness permits is to maintain the spiritual aspects of a quality wilderness experience. According to ecologist Raymond Dasmann (1968), man needs this. Without the wild country, there will be no space left for that last wild thing—the free human spirit. Clinical evidence shows the spiritual benefits of wilderness to man's mental health. Sociologists agree that camping under primitive conditions provides people with a rare opportunity to release their hidden qualities and establish their identities. U.S. Forest Service wilderness policies are designed to minimize the noise, crowding, and deterioration that are typical of modern day high-speed living—and from which the wilderness visitor seeks to escape.

The fourth reason for issuing permits is to improve behavior through educational contact between the user and the Forest Ranger. User awareness of the proper "Rules of Behavior" helps to protect fragile features, and this personal contact may be an important educational link between wilderness conservation practice and visitor habits.

The wilderness permit offers many benefits to our wilderness resources and to the outdoor recreationist. It also assists the USFS in terms of administrative decisions, regulation of high-use wilderness areas, educational contacts, and the preservation of natural resources. Unfortunately, it also creates many problems, both administrative and philosophical. One current administrative problem is that of uniformity in permit distribution. Issuance methods are inconsistent among and even within, the managment agencies. People are confused about which areas supply self-issuing permits and which require personal contact with the Ranger by obtaining the permit at the Ranger Station. Furthermore, some wilderness areas may not even require a permit.

While plans are being implemented to unify wilderness permit distribution methods within wilderness areas and among management units, one can expect significant differences to remain between agencies and between units within each agency.

Advanced reservations are available in some very popular regions, such as the Mt. Rainier and Olympic Wilderness Areas and Yosemite National Park. Advanced reservations, however, pose certain problems. For instance, the number of users within Yosemite's travel zones is closely regulated. Wilderness permits for fifty percent of the carrying capacity may be obtained through "advanced reservations," while the remaining permits are issued on a "first-come-first-served" basis. However, individuals and groups may reserve three or four areas in advance, then make a choice as to which "reserved" wilderness area and permit they will use depending upon weather, travel distance, etc. As a result, the quota in some zones is not filled, but there is no way to predict the number of "no shows" to balance the quota with "first-come-first-served" permits.

Another administrative problem involves regulation of high-use areas. Data obtained from permits indicate that visitor use of most wilderness areas will eventually have to be regulated. This means that many wilderness enthusiasts will not be allowed into the area they want to visit because the requested areas or travel zones will be full.

With such regulations and restrictions being imposed upon visitors, philosophical problems arise. Many people do not like the idea of wilderness regulation. Merely filling out the regimented form produces resentment; the wilderness permit imposes implied restrictions contrary to wilderness philosophy. The regulations interfere with the participants' perception of "freedom from control" discussed in Chapter One. The participants view these regulations as an outside "control" of their activities. They chose those activities voluntarily because they had the "freedom to choose"; yet, they were denied "freedom from control" within their choice. As enforcement becomes a necessity, the quality of the wilderness experience is altered by the presence of enforcement personnel—a further imposition to the perception of "wilderness." Resource managers must consider the quality of the experience a visitor receives if he/she encounters a policing agent while in the backcountry.

Philosophical problems tend to create ill feelings, and Roderick Nash expresses them very well in *Wilderness and the American Mind*:

> ...the idea of the intense control that quota systems entail is difficult to square with the meaning of wilderness. Essentially a man-managed wilderness is a contradiction because wilderness necessitates an "absence" of civilization's ordering influence. The quality of freedom so frequently associated with wilderness is diminished, if not destroyed, by regulation. Campgrounds become sleeping-bag motels with defined capacities and check-out times (p. 273).

Philosophical controversies and administrative problems are numerous regarding wilderness regulations and enforcement methods. Management agencies are caught in the middle—working for the preservation of natural resources while aiding in the advancement of public outdoor recreation—damned by angry wilderness users if they regulate high-use areas and condemned by others if they don't. Management agencies are in a no-win situation, if winning is defined as pleasing all of one's constituents. Problems will continue to exist because no "compromise" can fully satisfy all of the demands. Figure 2.3 (pages 23-24) delineates the impact of alternative rationing systems as seen by the Forest Service.

In summary, it can be said that the wilderness permit acts as a management tool on which to base moral decisions in order to serve the public and protect the wilderness.

Permits and the Outdoor Leader

There are two main types of permits with which the leader should be familiar. Both are in common use by all of the major federal and state land management agencies.

Single-Use Permits: The "single-use" or "single-visit" permits are, as the name implies, designed to apply to single visits by individuals or groups. In some cases, they are obtainable in unlimited numbers at trail heads. Increasingly, however, it is necessary to obtain them at Ranger Stations or National Park Offices, and there may be limits placed upon the number of permits issued, group size, or length of stay.

Routes and campsites may also be specified in the permit. The availability of such permits and the associated rules and regulations varies widely both by place and by season. Group leaders need to be especially careful to contact the management agency well in advance, preferably in the earliest stages of planning an outing to determine whether a permit will be available and what rules and regulations will apply.

Special-Use Permits: The second type of permit is usually referred to as a "special-use" permit. These permits are generally required for any use of federal or state lands other than for purely casual, non-commercial use. Under current policies, essentially all use by schools, municipal recreation departments, park and recreation districts, and even use by some outing clubs must be authorized by special-use permit. Unlike single-use permits, these permits cannot normally be obtained quickly. The typical special-use permit application is rather lengthy, requiring substantial detail about the nature of the organization or institution that wishes to use

the resource, the nature of the proposed activities, the routes and campsites to be used, the dates of proposed use, and the number of participants and staff expected on each outing.

Special-use permits almost always include insurance provisions, wherein the permittee must carry specified types and amounts of liability insurance and conform to agency policies with regard to the wording of certain key elements of the policies. Many special-use permits include user fees and other fee structures, which sometimes involves a percentage of profits arrangement.

Basic information for permits includes the name of the permittee(s), the exact location of the program, the itinerary, the program activities, and the dates of the program. Standard provisions usually found on all program permits include policies related to: the fee structure, fire control, damage to the environment, transferring and subletting, nondiscrimination, disposal of waste and refuse, insurance, advertisements, qualifications of leaders, safety plans, natural hazards, and protection of historical and cultural resources.

In many locales, all camping groups are required to obtain and obey state permits for campfires and individual state licenses for fishing and hunting as well as the federal permits for traveling. Those hiking National Scenic Trails that cross Forest Service, Park Service, and other boundaries as well as wilderness areas *may* be able to procure permits to cover wilderness and fire use for the entire trip.

Obtaining special-use permits for use of the National Parks for backcountry pursuits can be a bit more involved because there is usually a very substantial application fee, along with the above mentioned fees and the park admission fees. In other nations, there is currently less paperwork and expense. Most developed nations and a growing number of third world nations do, however, have effective controls and regulations in place. It must be realized that the National Parks of the United States are "living museums," and the management policies to date preclude much "use" (or abuse) of the resources. The U.S. Forest Service and other land management agencies have adopted permit systems

FIGURE 2.3a   Summary of Impacts and Consequences of Alternative Rationing Systems

USER EVALUATION CRITERIA

Rationing System	Clientele Group Benefited by System	Clientele Group Adversely Affected by System	Experience to Date With Use of System in Wilderness	Acceptability of System to Wilderness Users[1]
Request (reservation)	Those able and/or willing to plan ahead; i.e., persons with structured lifestyles.	Those unable or unwilling to plan ahead; i.e., persons with occupations that do not permit long-range planning, including many professionals.	Main type of rationing system used in both National Forest and National Park wilderness.	Generally high. Good acceptance in areas where used. Seen as best way to ration by users in areas not currently rationed.
Lottery (chance)	No one identifiable group benefited. Those who examine probabilities of success at different areas have better chance.	No one identifiable group discriminated against. Can discriminate against the unsuccessful applicant to whom wilderness is very important.	None. However, this is a common method for allocating big-game hunting permits.	Low.
Queuing (first-come, first-served)	Those with low opportunity cost for their time (e.g., unemployed). Also favors users who live nearby.	Those persons with high opportunity cost for time. Also those persons who live some distance from areas. The cost of time is not recovered by anyone.	Used in conjunction with reservation system in San Jacinto Wilderness. Also used in some National Park Wilderness.	Low to moderate.
Pricing (fee)	Those able or willing to pay entry costs.	Those unwilling or unable to pay entry costs.	None.	Low to moderate.
Merit (skill and knowledge)	Those able or willing to invest time and effort to meet requirements.	Those unable or unwilling to invest time and effort to meet requirements.	None. Merit is used to allocate use for some related activities such as technical mountain climbing and river running.	Not clearly known. Could vary considerably depending upon level of training required to attain neccessary proficiency and knowledge level.

[1] Based upon actual field experience as well as upon evidence reported in visitor studies (Stankey, 1973).
[2] This criterion is designed to measure how the different rationing systems would directly affect the behavior of wilderness users (e.g., where they go, when they go, how they behave, etc.).
(Source: USDA *Wilderness Management*, p. 329)

FIGURE 2.3b

ADMINISTRATIVE EVALUATION CRITERIA

Rationing System	Difficulty for Administrators	Efficiency–Extent to Which System can Minimize Problems of Suboptimization	Principal Way in Which Use Impact is Controlled	How System Affects User Behavior [2]
Request (reservation)	Moderately difficult. Requires extra staffing, expanded hours. Record-keeping can be substantial.	Low to moderate. Under utilization can occur because of no shows, thus denying entry to others. Allocation of permits to applicants has little relationship to value of the experience as judged by the applicant.	Reducing visitor numbers. Controlling distribution of use in space and time by varying number of permits available at different trailheads or at different times.	Affects both spatial and temporal behavior.
Lottery (chance)	Difficult to moderately difficult. Allocating permits over an entire use season could be very cumbersome.	Low. Because permits are assigned randomly, persons who place little value on wilderness stand equal chance of gaining entry with those who place high value on the opportunity.	Reducing visitor numbers. Controlling distribution of use in space and time by number of permits available at different places or times.	Affects both spatial and temporal behavior.
Queuing (first-come, first-served)	Difficulty low to moderate. Could require development of facilities to support visitors waiting in line.	Moderate. Because system rations primarily through a cost of time, it requires some measures of worth by participants.	Reducing visitor numbers. Controlling distribution of use in space and time by number of persons permitted to enter at different places or times.	Affects both spatial and temporal behavior. User must consider cost of time and of waiting in line.
Pricing (fee)	Moderate difficulty. Possibly some legal questions about imposing a fee for wilderness entry.	Moderate to high. Imposing a fee requires user to judge value of experience against cost. Uncertain as to how well use could be fine tuned with price.	Reducing visitor numbers. Controlling distribution of use in space and time by using differential prices.	Affects both temporal and spatial behavior. User most consider cost in dollars.
Merit (skill and knowledge)	Difficult to moderately difficult. Initial investments to establish licensing program could be substantial.	Moderate to high. Requires users to make expenditures of time and effort (maybe dollars) to gain entry.	Some reduction in numbers as well as shifts in time and space. Major reduction in per capita impact.	Affects style of camping behavior.

which may be used to regulate visitors *as the need arises.* The permit systems also help the agencies obtain important data about visitors which can be used to improve wilderness management.

Federal agencies in the United States are responsible for assuring use of government land on an equal basis to all citizens regardless of race, religious faith, creed, or national origin. Furthermore, the government has developed a set of regulations designed to ensure that paid leaders charge fees that are fair to all, carry adequate insurance, conduct specifically approved activities, and care for natural resources appropriately. The various federal agencies administer leader permits differently, and the policies are subject to periodic change. Leaders, therefore, are advised to check with the proper authorities before taking a group onto federal property.

Federal Land Managers

In the United States, land and water utilized for outdoor pursuits consists of large holdings by the federal government, states, counties, and cities, as well as land owned and managed privately. Privately owned land useful for outdoor activities includes timber areas, farms, ranches, and natural preserves.

Most of the federal acreage is in states west of the Mississippi River, but every one of the fifty states contains at least some federal land. Most outdoor recreation in the United States occurs on U.S. Forest Service lands. To learn more about who manages the federal lands, it may help to study Figure 2.4 which delineates the major federal organizations that hold the land used for outdoor pursuits. It can be seen that three federal departments administer most of these lands.

The Department of Agriculture

In the United States, the greatest amount of outdoor recreation takes place on land managed by the U.S. Forest Service, a division of the Department of Agriculture. Forest Service lands are considered agricultural lands because of the timber crop that is planted, managed, and harvested there. The Forest Service, unlike the single-purpose National Park Service, performs a variety of functions. These are, simply, to manage:

Timber—The greatest amount of American lumber is harvested on National Forest lands;

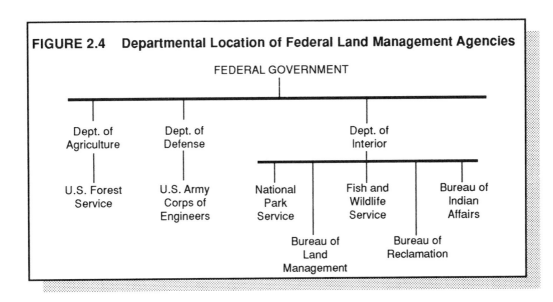

FIGURE 2.4   Departmental Location of Federal Land Management Agencies

Forage—Grazing for domestic and native animals, such as cattle, deer, antelope, and moose, is controlled by the USFS.

Wildlife—Most wild animals of all kinds, but particularly large species, reside within National Forest boundaries;

Water—Much city water for the western half of the USA comes from water stored in water tables deep under the carpeted floors of the national forests. It falls as snow or rain and eventually trickles through the soil to rivers, streams, and reservoirs;

Recreation—In the United States, most hunting, fishing, boating, hiking, camping, skiing, climbing, etc. occurs on U.S. Forest Service land.

For the most part, outdoor activities are held on Class III and V lands. Forest Service facilities for these include:

1. Over 100,000 miles of trails for hiking, skiing, and snowmobiling;
2. Nearly 300 winter-sports sites, including ski lifts;
3. Most of the National Wilderness Preservation System outside Alaska;
4. Over 120,000 miles of fishing streams;
5. Two million acres of lakes;
6. One third of the big-game animals in the nation;
7. Approximately 5,000 campgrounds with a capacity to handle more than 500,000 persons at one time;
8. Approximately 2,000 picnic grounds;
9. Nearly 200 interpretive sites, 52 of which are major interpretive centers;
10. Recreational special-use residential areas;
11. Seven National Recreation Areas;
12. Three National Monuments.

The Department of the Interior

America's Department of the Interior has often been nicknamed the Department of Natural Resources, for it manages national parks, wildlife refuges, flood plains, mining, oil, gas, and several other resources. Within the Department of the Interior, the four agencies discussed below manage large amounts of acreage used for outdoor pursuits. The purpose of each component of the Department of Interior is different, as are their policies for recreation. The user is advised to be familiar with the differences in the following four agencies, the National Park Service, the Bureau of Land Management, the Bureau of Reclamation and the Bureau of Indian Affairs, and their policies before considering their land for recreation.

The National Park Service

The National Parks of America may be referred to as living museums of natural and cultural resources. Included in the over 79 million acres administered by the National Park Service are the National Parks, most of the National Monuments, national historic sites, battlefields, cemeteries, memorials, parkways, and the White House and National Visitor Center. Only the National Parks and some of the National Monuments are available for outdoor pursuits. Nearly 55 million acres of national park land exist in the State of Alaska, and over 24 million acres are in the contiguous 48 states and Hawaii.

It has been said that the National Park idea is one of the few cultural ideas given to the rest of the world by the USA. The idea was actually conceived by George Catlin, an artist who painted Native Americans, and implemented by Congress with the establishment of Yellowstone National Park in 1872. Today, there are parks worldwide, including Canada, Russia, Germany, Australia, Kenya, Zaire, Zambia, Tanzania, and Switzerland.

The U.S. National Park Service, formed in 1916, was charged with the administration of national parks and national monuments:

The service thus established shall promote and regulate the use of the Federal areas known as national parks, monuments, and reservations hereinafter specified by such means and measures as to conform to the fundamental purpose of said parks, monuments, and reservations, which purpose is to conserve the scenery and the natural and historic objects and the wildlife therein and to provide for the enjoyment of the same in such manner and by such means as will leave them unimpaired for the enjoyment of future generations. (Tolson, 1933.)

An analysis of the purpose of the parks shows that their management must be a balance between preservation and use. This may appear paradoxical to many until they learn that national parks are not playgrounds and that any recreation taking place there must be appropriate to the setting. National parks are basically single-purpose lands—lands to preserve unique national resources. All other management agencies recognize a multiple-use or a conservation-use philosophy as opposed to the Park Service policy of preservation. This preservationist policy (to save—not to use) coupled with the provision of "enjoyment" causes trouble for the Park Service as they attempt to accommodate all the demands of the users and, at the same time, to preserve the natural resources for which each park is unique.

The backcountry of most national parks offers excellent opportunities for outdoor pursuits, if carried out according to park regulations. Because national parks are to be treated as biological entities, hunting, fishing, and campfires are often prohibited, and areas for boating, hiking, climbing, etc., are carefully monitored. In some parks, such activities are allowed only with a permit, qualified guides, or approved equipment. Anyone pursuing backcountry recreation in a National Park should learn about the uniqueness of the area and should practice camping and traveling skills compatible with management policies.

The Bureau of Land Management

The Bureau of Land Management (BLM) manages approximately 20 percent of the land in the USA, most of it west of the Mississippi River. The agency is not well understood by most people, and Knudson describes it succinctly as follows:

The Bureau of Land Management has a longer history and broader jurisdiction than almost any other federal government land agency. One of the agency's predecessors was formed in 1792, five years after the Constitution was signed. The General Land Office was the official holder, recorder, and dispenser of public lands in the expanding United States. This is the group that administered the Homestead Act. It gave lands to the railroads to open the West. It took title to Alaska, Oregon, and most other western states. It handles drilling on the outer continental shelf and federal lands today.

These functions were inherited by the Bureau of Land Management, formed in 1946 by a merger of the General Land Office and the Grazing Service, which had been established in 1934 by the Taylor Grazing Act. The BLM combined the duties of custodian and manager for grasslands, forests, deserts, and tundra that had not been claimed by the Forest Service, National Park Service, school grants, railroad grants, homesteaders, ranchers, speculators, miners, or states and their subdivisions.

The Bureau of Land Management is responsible for the residue of America's rich land bounty. Most of the BLM property looks like the residue with some spectacularly notable exceptions. These exceptions include the highly productive timber lands of the reverted Oregon and California Railroad Grant, as well as beautiful mountain, desert, and arctic scenery.

This agency is not well known among the general public, especially east of the Mississippi. Until recently, its major constituents have been ranchers who graze their cattle on public lands for nominal fees, miners who prospect and stake claims there, and a dwindling supply of homesteaders and settlers (Knudson, *Outdoor Recreation*, 1984, p. 256).

In recent years, recreationists have discovered the beauty of BLM lands as well as many other attributes conducive to outdoor pursuits. The 150 recreational areas administered by this federal agency make up five percent of the land under its management. In 1989, the BLM identified special resources for recreational purposes, including:

1. 544 developed recreation sites, including 5,552 overnight units in 14 states;
2. The California Desert, King Range, and Steese National Conservation Areas;
3. 15 designated Wild and Scenic Rivers;
4. 20 designated National Recreation, Historic, and Scenic Trails, totaling over 1,600 miles;
5. 56,509 acres of designated wilderness in eight states.

In 1989, land-, water-, snow- and ice-based recreational activities on BLM land accounted for 61 million visits and 493 million visitor hours.

The Bureau of Reclamation

The Bureau of Reclamation, like other federal agencies, was not created to provide recreation. It was formed in response to public demand for development of water supplies for irrigation and for low-cost electrical power. The Reclamation Act of 1902 empowered the Bureau of Reclamation to build dams for irrigation and hydroelectric power in seventeen western states, though many of the rivers dammed by the Bureau of Reclamation are now used for rafting, floating, kayaking, etc. This agency usually contracts with the U.S. Forest Service, the National Park Service, the Fish and Wildlife Service, or state and local agencies to develop and manage camping sites and sanitary stations along the routes.

The Bureau of Indian Affairs

Within the Department of the Interior is the Bureau of Indian Affairs. Unfortunately, many people assume that tribal holdings comprise part of the United States' "public" lands because the National Park Service, Bureau of Land Management, and Fish and Wildlife Service are "public" lands. It must be made clear that the approximately 51,000,000 acres of land granted to various Native American tribes by government treaty are *private* lands administered by tribal councils with assistance from the Bureau of Indian Affairs.

For all recreational activities conducted on tribal lands, permission must be granted by the tribal councils of the various reservations. Many National Forests and National Parks have boundaries contiguous to reservations, and often trails and rivers pass through Native American land. Part of the Pacific Crest National Scenic Trail in the southern half of California is a good example, as is part of the Mount Jefferson Wilderness Area in Oregon.

Routes of hikers and boaters may cross Native American land. It is the responsibility of the leader to recognize boundaries designated on maps and to respect the tribal lands as being private. Any time a trip includes camping on tribal lands, permission should be gained in advance—just as on any other private land.

The United States Fish and Wildlife Service

Another Department of the Interior agency that manages large amounts of land with limited facilities for outdoor pursuits is the U.S. Fish and Wildlife Service. Of the almost 89 million acres administered by this service, about 718 thousand acres have been designated as wilderness. This may be misleading to anyone who perceives wilderness as a legally-designated area for camping. In fact, Fish and Wildlife Service wilderness areas are set aside as portions of the National Wildlife Refuge System for the main purpose of protecting rare, endangered, and/or migratory animals. Recreation on refuges, therefore, consists primarily of wildlife observation, photography, sightseeing, and nature walks. Less than five percent of the visits to Wildlife Service lands are devoted to camping, and those are by special arrangement, usually in connection with government-approved research.

Participants in the outdoor pursuits discussed in this book should not plan to use wildlife refuges for overnight trips or climbing. In some areas, day trips for hiking, cross-country skiing, and boating practice are allowed with permission. Boat trips for those wishing to experience the solitude of the Okefenokie National Wildlife Refuge are conducted by licensed guides who have been granted permission to enter the wildlife refuge for a short distance. These guides are associated with a private non-profit organization that has leased adjacent land from the State of Georgia to carry out this activity—a rare use of wildlife refuges.

The Department of Defense

The Federal Government regulates commerce in the United States; consequently, it has the power to keep navigable streams and rivers open and free and to authorize and control dams. The Secretary of the Army has the primary responsibility for regulating navigable streams and also for studying and controlling floods. As a result, the U.S. Army Corps of Engineers manages the largest water-resource recreation program in the country—nearly 8,000,000 acres of land and 3,000,000 acres of water.

For the most part, the Corps shares the management of lands adjacent to its water resources with other federal agencies, or with state or county agencies. Furthermore, most of the visitors to Corps of Engineers' water resources are day or weekend guests who use facilities developed for camping, picnicking, boating, or swimming. Nevertheless, because of increasing demand for hiking trails, the Corps and its co-managers have started to encourage more nonfacility-based recreation.

While not usually considered the ideal location for outdoor pursuits away from the amenities of civilization, Corps of Engineers' waterways do make excellent training areas for water skills needed in primitive settings.

The same may be said for the thousands of lakes managed by the Tennessee Valley Authority, created in the 1930s, and the Land Between the Lakes area, created in western Tennessee and eastern Kentucky in 1964. Outdoor activities popular on these lands and waters include boating, fishing, and camping in developed campgrounds. These experiences provide opportunities for developing skills to use on less developed lands and waters.

Privately Owned Lands

In much of the USA, particularly east of the Mississippi River, much privately owned land is available for the outdoor enthusiast. Generally, private land conducive to outdoor recreation may be categorized as that belonging to timber companies, ranchers, or farmers. Since 65 percent of the marketable timber in America grows on privately owned land, there is much potential for outdoor pursuits here. Much of the privately owned land, however, is heavily roaded and, in timber areas, extensively logged. Permission *may* be obtained from individual landowners to cross private land and to camp there. Usually, the landowner will be cooperative if some assurance can be given for minimum impact on soil, plants, and animals and if respect for property boundaries, fences, and gates is guaranteed.

Summary

The purpose of this chapter is not to educate leaders in the details of government and private lands and their management. It is to help the leader understand the responsibilities inherent in using public and private lands for outdoor pursuits. Thus, the leader has several responsibilities when planning any trip on land or water. These include:

1. Determining who has jurisdiction over the land or water to be traveled;

2. Ascertaining a list of policies or regulations for using the land or water;

3. Obtaining necessary permits or permission to use the land or water for recreation;

4. Following the regulatory policies precisely.

References

Brockman, C. F., & Meriam, L. C. (1979). *Recreational use of wild lands.* New York, NY: McGraw-Hill Publishing Company.

Dasmann, R. F. (1968). *An environment fit for people.* Public Affairs Pamphlet No. 421. New York, NY: Public Affairs Pamphlets.

Hart, J. (1977). *Walking softly in the wilderness.* San Francisco, CA: Sierra Club Books.

Hendee, J. C., Stankey, G. H., & Lucas, R. C. (1990). *Wilderness management (2nd ed.),* Golden, CO: Fulcrum Publishing Co.

Jensen, C. R. (1985). *Outdoor recreation in America (4th ed.)* Minneapolis, MN: Burgess Publishing Co.

Knudson, D. (1984). *Outdoor recreation (rev. ed.)* New York, NY: Macmillan Publishing Co.

Nash, R. (1967). *Wilderness and the American mind.* New Haven, CT: Yale University Press.

Personal interviews. (March 11, 1992). USFS, Willamette National Forest. Eugene, OR.

Stankey, G. H., & Baden, J. (1977). *Rationing wilderness use: Methods, problems and guidelines.* Washington, DC: USDA Forest Service Research Paper, INT-192, July.

Stone, G. P., & Taves, M. J. (1956). Research into the human element in wilderness use. *Proceedings of the Society of American Foresters.*

Tolson, H. (1933). *Laws relating to the national park service, the national parks and monuments.* Washington, DC: U.S. Government Printing Office.

U.S. Department of Agriculture. (1983). *Land uses of the National Forest systems as of September 30, 1983.* Washington, DC: USDA.

U.S. Department of the Army, Correspondence, April 2, 1984.

U.S. Department of the Interior. (1984). *Annual report of lands under control of the U.S. Fish and Wildlife Service as of September 30, 1984,* Washington, DC: USDI.

U.S. Department of the Interior, Correspondence, April 1, 1984.

U.S. Department of the Interior. (1984). *Summary Statistics—Water, land, and related data, Bureau of Reclamation,* Washington, DC: USDI.

U.S. Department of the Interior. (1989). *Public land statistics.* Washington, DC: Bureau of Land Management.

THE NATURAL ENVIRONMENT

To many people, the natural environment is an undifferentiated mass of plants, animals, dirt, and things that go bump (or worse) in the night. To others, it is a super-abundance of fresh air and water, fish, trees, flowers, and open space. To still more, it represents a challenge that must be overcome or conquered, or a vehicle to be utilized for self-aggrandizement. The average person in today's society does not feel at home or secure in an outdoor setting, and this feeling of discomfort manifests itself in fear, shyness, bravado, indifference, boisterousness, silliness, and other expressions of emotion. People who are not ready to learn will learn ineffectively or not at all. Those who are ill at ease with any topic cannot concentrate, for their attention focuses only on ways to become more comfortable. People who are not comfortable in the outdoor setting are not ready to learn in the outdoors.

One of the responsibilities inherent in outdoor leadership is to help outing participants understand and feel comfortable in the natural environment, regardless where it may be. We are talking about psychological at-homeness, not physical comfort. The leader has a triple responsibility: to nurture natural curiosity, to revive lost or stifled curiosity, and to whet the appetite for more knowledge.

What is "out there" is basically the same no matter what part of the world one is in. The natural environment is comprised of nonliving (abiotic) and living (biotic) components. Nonliving components are the air, soil, and water, and the living components are the animals and plants. The initials of these items spell "a swap"—easy to remember when we realize that, when we exchange our urban life for life in the outdoors, we experience "a swap"—an exchange of things with which we are familiar for things with which we are not. Air, soil, water, animals, and plants. What should participants know about each in order to feel at home? There is more to be known about each than any one person could ever learn. Fortunately, there are some universal concepts that can be applied throughout the world. Knowing these basic concepts can help one become more environmentally literate, understand potential dangers, and feel more comfortable in the outdoors.

Understanding the Natural Environment

As in any other subject, outdoor teaching has various levels of difficulty, starting with programs for the beginner and leading to advanced activities. Many people, adults as well as children, are not ready to learn about the natural world because the out-of-doors does not interest them, because they are ill at ease, or because they are overwhelmed by the endless complexity of nature. A child in a new school needs to know about new friends, the cafeteria, recess, the playground, the gymnasium, teachers, rest rooms, new books, and seating arrangements before becoming involved in the daily lesson. So it is with outdoor teaching. Learners need to be comfortable in what may be a very strange environment before they can learn effectively.

A simple two-level approach to understanding the environment (environmental comfort and ecological knowledge) will help participants feel more "at-home" and will give them a basic understanding of what is going on in the natural world. By introducing the participants to these two levels of outdoor awareness, leaders can stimulate at-homeness, interest, and initial confidence in both the knowledge and understanding of the natural environment.

Level One: Environmental Comfort

Environmental comfort is brought about by having participants relate to the confusion of outdoor objects in terms of what is already known or familiar. Scientific facts are not used at this point; the objective is to arouse interest, develop observational skills, and to make people feel at ease. This level is made up of three simple awareness steps: *art, analogies,* and *sensory involvement,* that are basic to familiarity with the out-of-doors and the feeling of comfort and understanding. These three steps are of importance to all, regardless of the age or ability of the learner. It is axiomatic that one must learn standing before walking and walking before running. So it is with teaching in the out-of-doors. Everyone learns through the same progression regardless of age or mental acuity. Those who are more mature, sophisticated, and intelligent will progress at greater speed, in greater depth, and through much more complicated processes than those at more elementary stages.

Each of the three basic comfort steps of outdoor teaching must be undertaken for optimal value. As in any field, advanced concepts can be completely comprehended only if the basic fundamentals are well-learned. The mentally disabled must spend much time working with art, analogies, and sensory awareness, and some

will not progress beyond an elementary knowledge. Hours and days may be spent in repetitious activities based upon these three steps. Children and adults of average or above average intelligence may learn faster, and they may review the concepts in greater depth and with greater mental stimulation throughout life. Attaining knowledge of ecology (the second level) best occurs after the learner feels at home in the outdoor setting and has developed a curiosity toward it.

Step One: Art Forms

It is difficult to make a clean break between the three steps of the comfort level; however, they can be clearly described. The *art form* step of outdoor learning is designed to develop a degree of appreciation, sensitivity, awareness, and discrimination toward the visual environment. It draws on the learner's ability to recognize basic art forms found in the urban setting and to seek visual evidence of similar forms in the natural world. Seven art forms can be identified in the natural setting by visual perception. Recognizing and identifying these forms is the initial step in feeling at home in nature.

Lines: Figure 3.1 illustrates the types of lines one can find in art, the urban setting and the outdoor setting. One can experiment further with combinations like half circles, wavy lines, and a line collage. The mature participant may find the existence of spirals in plant life to be fascinating. For example, following the seed arrangement of a sunflower will show that the arrangement is a spiral—not concentric circles as many assume. Following the pattern of scale arrangement on a pine cone reveals a spiral. Examination of a tree trunk of a tree where the bark has been removed by lightning, insects, old age, or other natural processes reveals that the tree grew in a spiral—slowly but evenly and always in the same direction. In the Northern Hemisphere, this growth is to the right as one's eyes follow the spiral from bottom to top.

Shape and Form: Shape is two-dimensional, while form is three-dimensional. Mature participants should be able to differentiate between

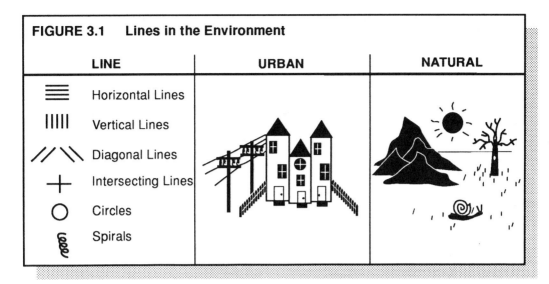

FIGURE 3.1   Lines in the Environment

LINE	URBAN	NATURAL
Horizontal Lines		
Vertical Lines		
Diagonal Lines		
Intersecting Lines		
Circles		
Spirals		

the two; however, during night hikes, objects can only be viewed two-dimensionally, so basic two-dimensional shapes should be learned by all. See Figure 3.2.

Color: Intensity (the brightness or dullness of a color), value (the lightness or darkness of a color), and hue (the name of the color) are all observable in the natural world; however, persons who are color blind will have less success identifying these values than those with normal vision. The most common form of color-blindness is a chromosome anomaly found only in males.

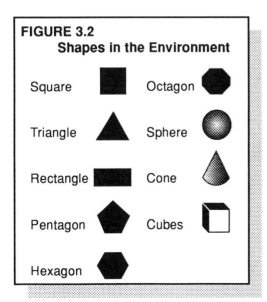

FIGURE 3.2
Shapes in the Environment

Square		Octagon	
Triangle		Sphere	
Rectangle		Cone	
Pentagon		Cubes	
Hexagon			

For such individuals, colors that are seen as red and green to those with normal vision are seen as brown by those who are color-blind. This causes a minor problem with recognition of colors in the natural setting, and leaders are cautioned to be alert for signs that some males in a group may not be able to spot the brown cone hidden among the green needles or the red bird flitting among the green leaves.

People who are bored driving across long expanses of desert or forest often find the trip more pleasing after they have learned to analyze the various hues as well as the intensity of each one. The person who feels the woods are "all green" soon learns that there is a great variety of color to be seen. A search for color may reveal a great preponderance of intensities, values, and hues. Many are surprised to learn that "true blue" is rare in nature—the sky, however is a notable exception. Crater Lake is "true blue" as it represents the blue of the color spectrum refracted back to the eye after the water has absorbed all the other colors. According to artists, the "blues" of flowers, birds, etc., are combinations of blue with purple, red, and other colors.

Texture: Texture is the tactile quality of an object and is best understood in the natural world through activities involving sensory awareness. Until the beginner is convinced that touching things in nature has value, his/her understanding of the natural world must be through the visual sense and the imagination. Such tactile descriptors as rough, smooth, fuzzy, prickly, soft, hard, etc. can be comprehended by the viewer, even though texture cannot be verified without experience.

Balance: In both art and nature, balance refers to symmetry. In formal (symmetrical) balance, there are identical forms on each side of an imaginary line. Informal (asymmetrical) objects have different sized or shaped forms on either side of an imaginary line. Examples of formal balance in nature are:

The opposite branching patterns of maples, ashes, and dogwoods;
The sepals of dogwood blossoms;
The arrangement of petals on a daisy;
The placement of fins on most fish.

Examples of asymmetry in nature would be:

A rock worn smooth by water on one side but not on the other;
The arrangement of petals on many flowers;
The mitten-shaped sassafras leaf;
The different sized and shaped main claws of the fiddler crab.

Contrast: Contrast refers to light and dark areas. In nature, dark areas are often caused by shadows that change visual perception of the environment. Understanding shadows and thus contrast helps those who are insecure in the depths of an unknown forest. Furthermore, an ability to adjust to the changes from light to dark at twilight aids participants in making the psychological transition from day to night.

Patterns, Repetitions: Once one has identified lines, forms, colors, textures, balance, and contrast, it is time to notice any continuity in design created by a pattern or a series of repeated lines or objects. Seeing the repeated zigzag on conifers against the skyline or the repetition of the half circle created by the tops of deciduous trees helps people perceive nature as something other than a "mass of sticks and weeds." Seeing

the patterns on caterpillars, beetles, frogs, snakes, and other creatures help to defray some of what seems to be an inherent fear of small animals.

Step Two: Analogies

One way to help people feel at home in a natural setting is to have them relate to nature in terms of items which are familiar to them. An analogy is a resemblance between the attributes, circumstances, or effects of two things. Through mental analogies, people can find that the unfamiliar reminds them of the familiar. Participants must be cautioned, however, that an analogy does not make the item *identical* to its partner.

To introduce people to a natural community (i.e., pond, woods, meadow, stream), discuss and identify the analogous components of the community from which the group comes. Generally, through brainstorming, participants can list inhabitants, factories, jobs, residences, transportation systems, water supply systems, garbage collectors, alarm systems, stores, schools, etc. Further discussion will show that they can expect to find a resemblance in some particulars between communities that may otherwise appear to be dissimilar: those in the Southwest and those in the Northwest; urban and rural communities; a community of Chinese and a community of Norwegians; and so forth.

Following a discussion of the components of the human (man-made) community, one can ask the group to observe a natural community to locate similar components. For each of the components in the previous list, there are analogous items to be located in a natural setting. Green plants are the "food factories," the voice of a raucous blue jay serves as an alarm system, the underground tunnels of ants or other small animals are "subways," and the trails of the larger animals serve as "transportation systems." One can even watch a squirrel ride a branch to the ground and jump off, leaving the "elevator" to return to the "top floor" for another passenger. Imagination goes a long way to help the urban dweller realize that what goes on in a forest environment is analogous to what occurs in the city.

A second way to utilize analogies in learning about the natural environment is by describing new things in familiar terms to which everyone can relate. Utilizing analogies helps people form pictures in their minds, and these mental images are more easily retained than plain descriptions. Nearly all outdoor leaders use a few.

Commonly used American analogies include:

The top of the hemlock tree looks like a tired boy's farewell, or a debutante's farewell, or a buggy whip;

The five main veins of the maple leaf are like the five fingers of a hand;

The red tips on the sepals of the dogwood are like drops of blood on the crucifix;

The needles of the Douglas fir are like the bristles of a bottle brush;

The shape of an elm is a vase (or a feather duster);

Cirro-cumulus clouds look like mackerel scales or buttermilk;

A jellyfish may look like swimming jelly but is neither a fish nor jelly;

Porcupines look like pincushions;

Flowers are named shooting star, Dutchman's breeches;

Rock formations are named "Old Man of the Mountain," "Monkey Face," or the "Needle."

Step Three: Sensory Awareness

In order to understand the natural world, people must have a readiness to learn, and this comes about through successful first-hand experiences that whet intellectual appetites for information. Most individuals seem to approach inspection of the out-of-doors in the same position as they would approach the inspection of a new home— i.e., erect. But, in inspecting the new home, they might change their position from upright to one more conducive to analyzing a house. They might kneel down and feel the carpet, stretch up and feel the top bookshelves, sniff the air, and notice the odor of newness. In short, looking over a new home could involve using several senses at various heights.

Investigation of a forest or meadow should entail similar behavior, yet, because of insecurity, self-consciousness, or indifference, people seem to look at a forest or field from a standing position, hands in pockets, head down, and chin on chest. Everything is viewed through eyes held five to six feet above the ground without utilizing all senses effectively. Ideally, one should view the natural world from many positions, several distances and through several senses. The more ways in which one can examine natural objects, the greater the appreciation and subsequent enjoyment.

In a pamphlet entitled *Forest lands in management,* the U.S. Forest Service states that, in terms of the total use of the five senses, 87 percent is sight, 7 percent is hearing, 3.5 percent is smell, 1.5 percent is touch, and 1.0 percent is taste. Even with these percentages, though, far less is actually perceived correctly. We look but do not really see. A person examining the seed of an elm tree might notice an oval but probably fails to see that it has a clear indentation in one end. And how many people looking at trees realize that branch placement is opposite in some species, but alternating in others? People can see aspen leaves quiver and quake; however, few look closely or touch to discern the reason for the action. Outdoor recreation participants can learn to see colors, shapes, and patterns in the world around them. Use of the senses makes up the third step of becoming environmentally comfortable.

Sight: When learning to see, the first imperative is to look at various levels. Some things are best observed while the viewer kneels or lies down. Certain plants are even referred to as "belly" plants because of the prone position that must be assumed by the viewer. Some items are best viewed by climbing, others by looking at an opposite side. (Whenever the viewer needs to move an object for better study, it is mandatory that it be replaced exactly as it was found. Rocks harbor larva homes, and disturbing them is tantamount to destroying them.)

Hearing: Even people with good hearing need instruction in listening. We tend to block out superfluous sounds in our everyday lives, for we find traffic, air conditioning, elevators, footfalls, and other noises distracting. Some people use radios constantly, either to provide or to block out background sounds. Such sound tends to destroy the ability to discriminate various other sounds because it is meant to be a sound *masker*. Thus, people in the out-of-doors must be taught to listen discriminately to background noise or they will not hear it because of their conscious effort in the past to shut it out.

When listening in the outdoors, we may successfully hear sounds of the wind or rain. But if we have been concentrating on a low tone, such as the buzzing of bees, we may not be able to hear a high one, such as a cricket. People must train themselves to "listen high" or "listen low" and to focus their attention on background noises. Bird watchers have been known to pick out songs of migrating birds above traffic noise or the music of an orchestra. The true knack of listening also enables a person to carry on a conversation intently as both a listener and a speaker at the same time, and being able to interrupt and call attention to a bird singing in the nearby shrub or to the footfall of an approaching animal.

Smell: Seeing and hearing are simple and safe activities, and, for the most part, so is the sense of smell. There are times when one may find a good strong inhalation results in gagging and nausea, just as ammonia is tolerable if sniffed gently, but obnoxious if inhaled strongly. It is a good idea to smell everything as if it *might* be unpleasant, sniffing gently at first, then more strongly until the odor is clear.

Smelling objects enhances appreciation. Roses are known for their fragrance as well as their form; honeysuckle is appreciated for its aroma as much as for its greenery. Most people develop an increased appreciation for the Ponderosa pine when they realize that, in the heat of the summer, the pines living in their native habitat give off a distinct vanilla odor from crevices in the bark. This smell is absent in the winter or in rain. The millipede's protective device consists of an ability to curl its hard body into a circle while releasing folic acid, a chemical odor resembling that of peach or cherry pits (prussic acid). In the winter, the millipede's odor often resembles the odor from a miner's or climber's

lamp (carbolic acid). Picking up the insect and smelling the exuding chemical odor thus helps one to understand the protective device better than just hearing about it.

Incidentally, poison ivy and poison oak flowers are extremely fragrant, and, where they grow profusely, they may be detected at a ten-foot distance without harm! Things are also sniffed more easily in the mist than in dry or cold air. (Foxes and coyotes lick their noses to enhance the ability to smell.)

Touch: The sense of touch is easily used; however, people seem to be conditioned not to touch and are reluctant to take their hands from their pockets to learn about things through feeling them. Of course, touch can have more serious consequences than smelling if burns, cuts, rashes, etc., result. But one can learn to touch gently at first with the pads of the fingertips, then with more pressure. Large areas such as sand, moss, bark, or rocks may be touched with the palm. Patting is an acceptable way to feel some natural objects. "Patting prevents picking," is a saying used by educators who are teaching observational skills simultaneously with ethical conservation.

The forms of some objects will even be more evident through feeling than through sight; the diamond shape of spruce needles, for example, are best understood through the sense of touch. Attempting to roll one between the thumb and index finger results in the discovery that it is impossible to "roll" a spruce needle. Through the first hand experience of feeling the waxy slanted top of spruce needles, one can understand how rain slides off and why, consequently, spruces can thrive in heavy rains that would devastate the more flexible, grooved needles of other evergreen types. Feeling pine needles makes one realize that the tips are soft and pointed—letting ice and snow slide off easily. Some pines have soft flexible needles that would be easily ripped apart by heavy winds, while other pines have short stubby needles that can withstand harsher climates. Feeling the needles helps make this clear to the beginner who may be uncomfortable among evergreens that have sharp points and stiff branches.

For understanding the extreme smoothness of some items, parts of the face are used. Only through touching it to the cheek, for instance, can one fully appreciate the texture of a rose.

Taste: Perhaps the reason that taste is the least used of all our senses is because unpleasant tastes and poisonous items come to mind. Certainly this sense must be developed with great care. Leaders should probably attempt to teach taste recognition only to normally intelligent persons over six years of age. Everyone must be aware of plants which should not be sampled because of deleterious effects, i.e., poison ivy, poison sumac, etc. Tasting is best done under careful supervision of a leader who knows plants thoroughly, or one who discriminates against plants that are *not* known.

Techniques for tasting involve several steps and the knowledge that it is done with the *tongue.* Certain things are savored on the tip of the tongue while a few at the back. At no time should tasting necessitate swallowing. The steps are:

1. Touch the tip of the tongue against the object.

2. If no flavor is evident, bite the object gently with the incisor teeth, then touch the tip of the tongue to it.

3. If you still can't taste anything chew some of the material and spit it out.

4. If no taste is evident after this, go no further.

There are only four tastes: sweet, sour, bitter, and salty. Certain items of interest for taste experiments are: any of the sour grasses or wood sorrel; peppermints and spearmints; inner bark of wild cherry and sassafras in the spring; and ripe wild grape, blackberries, blueberries, and strawberries.

Some words of caution for tasters. Plan on leaving all white berries alone. They tend to be poisonous and, if swallowed, could mean trouble. Some red, black, or blue berries may be safe; however, there are enough exceptions to warrant caution. Some edible plants share locales with very similar looking but highly toxic plants. Confusion of safe and toxic species has caused numerous fatalities. Leaders might well decide *not* to investigate the sense of taste because of the potential of liability should a participant select the wrong plant or swallow something that should not be ingested. Leaders should recognize that saying something like, "Never, taste the _____ because it is extremely hot and peppery," will cause the more curious participant to taste the object anyway. Immature participants may make wrong decisions. *The value of teaching participants to taste natural objects is debatable and should probably be left for the advanced participant who is already very knowledgeable concerning plant identification.*

Acquiring comfort with the outdoors through "art forms," analogies, and sensory awareness are logical first steps toward developing environmental understanding. Such comfort, however, does not help one to understand what is being observed. Nor does it do anything for developing an environmental consciousness. It only provides a sense of familiarity with the natural environment that is the first level to learning basic ecological concepts.

Level Two: Ecological Knowledge

After the participants are comfortable in the natural world through viewing things in terms of those with which they are familiar, they should be ready for the second level—learning about how everything fits together. They should be ready to learn basic ecological concepts. The word "ecology" comes from two Greek words meaning the study of the home. The home which, in this case, is the place where we live—the biosphere or life-support part of the earth. It consists of a thin layer of soil, water, and air beyond which no life can exist. The invention of the word "ecology" is credited to a German zoologist who coined it in 1866; however, it wasn't widely accepted until the early 1900s. When ecology became a household word in the 1960s and 1970s, its meaning became lost in the excitement over the cause known as the "ecology movement."

Simply put, ecology is the study of the interrelationships of all living and nonliving components of the biosphere. In the study of ecology, reference is made to ecosystems which are major identifiable segments of the biosphere. The components of the ecosystem are similar to the building blocks of a human dwelling or a human body.

At its lowest level, protoplasm is combined into cells. Groups of cells become tissues, and similar tissues make up organs (heart, kidney, lungs). Organs are combined into organ systems (e.g., cardiovascular, urino-genitary), and these systems make up organisms or individuals. Individuals of like kind make up populations; a group of populations becomes a community, and several communities become an ecosystem.

In any ecosystem, there will be many different kinds of individuals. All the individuals of any one species become a population of that species. All the dogs in a city are the dog population; all the mice make up the mouse population; and all the people make up the human population. These combined populations are a community. In an urban setting, the community may be primarily human, but there are also cat, dog, mouse, canary, goldfish, and other populations. In a forest community, there are virtually hundreds of populations: oak, hickory, red bud, maidenhair fern, hepatica, lady's slipper, red-headed woodpecker, scarlet tanager, cardinal, mouse, squirrel, mosquito, snake, beetle, ant, mushroom, grass, and on and on. Recognition is also given to those who pass into and out of the area, but do not reside there (birds flying through, deer crossing rocky areas, migrating monarch butterflies.) We identify forest communities, meadow communities, grassland communities, marshlands communities, and others. When reference is made to an ecosystem, it means a community and its nonliving elements (all the plants and animals plus air, water, soil, and minerals). Another name for ecosystem is biome (home for life). Commonly studied ecosystems include oceans, salt-water estuaries, sea shores, streams, rivers, lakes, ponds, marshes, deserts, tundra, grasslands, and forests.

Components of an Ecosystem

People involved in outdoor activities work, play, and learn in one or more ecosystems and are vitally involved with all its components. They can develop a basic understanding of what is going on around them by learning and remembering a few basic facts and concepts about ecosystems. There are four components of any ecosystem, each with specific and different functions.

Abiotic Substances: The basic nonliving parts of an ecosystem consist of elements and their compounds. Abiotic substances include water, air, and the mineral and chemical components of soil. The quality and quantity of each are vital to life, and their make-up, along with certain ecological forces, determine the components of various ecosystems.

Producers: In any ecosystem, there must be producers that are capable of manufacturing food; in a natural ecosystem, these are largely the green plants. A prime characteristic of green plants is that they are autotrophic; that is, they are self-nourishing. Green plants can fix light energy and manufacture food from simple inorganic substances. This function is made possible by chlorophyll which acts as a catalyst to aid in the process of photosynthesis (synthesizing light into energy).

Plant life derives the raw materials for building its own substance from air, water, and soil. Within the green leaves of plants, the elements so procured are combined into carbohydrates, from which all food matter is derived. From the air, oxygen and its compound, carbon dioxide; are derived while from the soil, the roots draw up water and small quantities of nitrogen, phosphorus, potassium, calcium, magnesium, and trace amounts of other elements. Sunlight furnishes the energy to bring about the combining of the raw materials. The process, known as photosynthesis, is the basis of all food production.

All other organisms are dependent upon plants for their source of food; thus, the green plants are considered *dominants.*

Consumers: Consumers are organisms that depend upon the plants for their energy. They are heterotrophic (other-nourishing) and utilize, rearrange, and decompose the complex materials synthesized by the autotrophs.

Consumers are categorized into several levels. The *plant eaters* (herbivores) are made up of very small to very large animals. While most people think of the cow eating grass as a prime example of an herbivore, the largest amount of plant consumption is done by the plant-sucking and chewing insects. Insects and rodents, which are considered of minor interest (or great bother) to many outdoor people, are, nevertheless, "key-industry" animals since they support the predators that depend upon them for food.

After the herbivores are the *first-level carnivores (meat eaters).* They feed on the key-industry animals and, like the herbivores, they range in size from very small to very large. Lady-bird beetles eating aphids, birds eating insects or worms, snakes eating mice, and coyotes feeding on cottontails are all examples of first-level carnivores (animals that eat animals that have eaten plants).

Second-level carnivores are those animals that prey on and eat the first-level carnivores. They tend to be larger, more fierce, and fewer in number (within each species) than the first-level carnivores. If the snake that ate the mouse is, in turn, eaten by a hawk, the hawk is the second-level carnivore. Similarly, the coyote that ate the cottontail might be eaten by a mountain lion.

Two other types of consumers complete the list. *Parasites* live off, but do not kill, their hosts (though their hosts may die eventually from weakness), and *scavengers* eat dead, decaying animals. Combinations such as the omnivores (eaters of both plant and animal matter) and third- and fourth-level carnivores are also present, but the basic consumers are the five explained above.

Decomposers: Decomposers are scavengers and decay organisms such as many types of bacteria which break down dead plant and animal material into chemical (abiotic) elements. These chemical elements subsequently become the ingredients for the food manufactured by the green plants. Other decomposers are made up of the plants that have no chlorophyll, such as mushrooms (fungi) which live on decaying material.

The Food Chain

A linking of the "eating-eaten" relationship is known as a food chain. Generally, there are three-link chains of organisms; however, many-linked food chains also exist as shown in Figure 3.3 (see page 40).

Each chain is a part of the "energy cycle" revolving through the producers, consumers, decomposers, and abiotic elements and powered by the energy-giving sun. (See Figure 3.4, page 40)

The food chain, if left alone, usually produces enough for the consumers; although, most organisms are eaten before they reach the adult stage. Each link in the food chain consists of larger species than the one before it and usually supports fewer numbers. An animal gains only 10 percent of the energy of the plant it eats. Ninety percent is lost to heat. That animal must be larger than the ones it eats (or its prey would eat it) and must eat great numbers of its prey to gain enough energy to live. That animal is eaten by another (usually larger) animal which gains only 10 percent of the energy of its prey as ninety percent is again lost to heat.

It is often said that it takes 100 cottontails to feed ten coyotes to feed one eagle. This is confusing because the number of animals eaten is irrelevant. It takes 100 *energy units* of cottontails to make 10 *energy units* of coyotes to make one *energy unit* of eagle. This energy-loss-to-heat is called the food pyramid. It is best illustrated in correct dimensions but this is rarely done because the width of each unit would have to be at least nine inches wider than the level below it.

Limiting Factors

The four items upon which each organism depends for life are light (from the sun), air, water, and soil. These are known as "limiting factors" and can be easily remembered by using the initials, LAWS. It is the multitude of varying combinations of these four items that creates

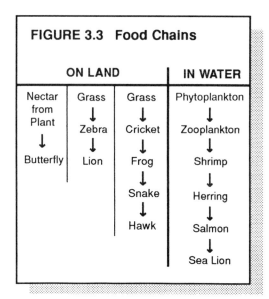

FIGURE 3.3   Food Chains

ON LAND			IN WATER
Nectar from Plant ↓ Butterfly	Grass ↓ Zebra ↓ Lion	Grass ↓ Cricket ↓ Frog ↓ Snake ↓ Hawk	Phytoplankton ↓ Zooplankton ↓ Shrimp ↓ Herring ↓ Salmon ↓ Sea Lion

different ecosystems and helps us understand the distribution of vegetation and animal life all over the world. Less water creates a desert; more water creates a marsh; less sunlight results in different species of trees and shrubs; poor soil supports only certain plants; richer soil produces greater growth; pure air helps growth; polluted air retards or stops it. What lives in any ecosystem depends upon the quality and quantity of the limiting factors—Light, Air, Water, and Soil (LAWS).

Ecological Forces

In addition to the limiting factors, what lives in various ecosystems (or how it lives) is dependent upon ecological "forces" such as wind, temperature, humidity, fire, gravity (landslides, avalanches), earthquakes, volcanism, and even the basic topography of the land. Given equal amounts and qualities of light, air, water, and soil, two areas in the same life zone may differ in their plant and animal species because of the effect of one or more of the natural forces. Youth can usually remember that "LAWS and forces control the lives in the ecosystem."

In summary, an ecosystem is made up of abiotic substances, producers, consumers, and decomposers. These interact in a continuous energy cycle. Ecosystems and life zones differ because of varying amounts and qualities of sunlight, air, water, and soil and because of the

effect of natural forces. People involved in outdoor activities can better understand and appreciate the different ecosystems through which they travel if these basic concepts are understood. The answer to the question, "Why is this area unlike another?" is found in knowledge, understanding, and application of these concepts.

Ecological Concepts

Knowing the basic components of an ecosystem leads to learning about basic ecological concepts. There are virtually hundreds of ecological concepts, and different authors and science curricula recommend different lists. The following seven basic concepts are taken from several sources, but appear to be the essence of most of the current beginning outdoor education programs that teach ecological principles.

In many youth camps, outdoor education programs, schools, youth groups, church programs, and community centers participants in environmental education programs can be heard going around chanting, "E-C, D-C, I-C, A"; "E-C, D-C, I-C, A"; "E-C, D-C, I-C, A." (Van Matre, 1979). What on earth are they saying? What are all these letters, and what do they mean? They stand for the first letters in seven easily understood ecological principles that can help people understand the world around them.

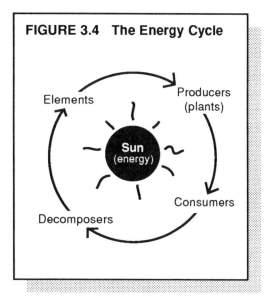

FIGURE 3.4   The Energy Cycle

Elements

Producers (plants)

Sun (energy)

Consumers

Decomposers

By using this little chant, one can remember the first letters of these principles. The principles are revisions of those explained in *The Closing Circle* by Barry Commoner, a popular book in the 1970s. Commoner has been called, "the Paul Revere of ecology," and is credited with putting ecological principles into common phrases. While he described four "laws" of ecology, those have since been expanded and incorporated into the seven explained here.

"E-C, D-C, I-C, A" stand for Energy, Cycles, Diversity, Community, Interrelationships, Change, and Adaptation. Chanting the letters over and over can help one to remember the words. What do they mean? It really is quite easy.

Energy: One way of looking at energy is to remember, "The sun is the source of all energy." We can see examples of this in many places. Green plants cannot grow in the dark. If one puts a house plant in a dark closet for several months, it will die—even if the door is opened occasionally to give it a drink of water. Without sunlight, green plants cannot produce energy. If the food chain is understood, then one can understand why sunlight affects (directly and indirectly) the health of animals, too.

Since green plants get their energy from the sun, animals that eat green plants get their energy from the plants that get their energy from the sun. Animals that eat the animals that eat the plants get their energy from the animals that got their energy from the plants that got their energy from the sun.

Energy is essential for ecosystems to survive since it is required by all living components. When an animal eats a plant or another animal, energy passes from the eaten to the eater. Energy is also responsible for wind, tides, the water cycle, and other vital ecological cycles.

Cycles: In simple ecological terms, cycles mean, "Everything is going somewhere and coming back." The sun comes up in the east every morning, goes down in the west at night, and comes up again in the east the next morning. Day and night are cycles. So are the seasons, bird migration, and the bloom and fruitation of the trees.

Maybe the most important cycle in the natural environment is the cycle created as we use the air over and over again. Oxygen is inhaled and carbon dioxide is exhaled. Plants take in carbon dioxide and transpire oxygen. The cycle goes on and on.

When rains fall, the water goes to the soil and into the streams and rivers and lakes and oceans. From there, it evaporates and becomes part of the clouds. From the clouds, it becomes rain and falls back to earth. This water cycle maintains moisture in the ground, water in the wells, and water for rivers and oceans. Understanding the water cycle is important to any outdoor living activity because of its effect on the weather.

Soil gives plants nutrients they need for growing. When the plants die, bacteria break down the waste matter and return it to the soil as nutrients for new plants. Leaves falling in the autumn and decaying into organic nutrients for future plants is a very observable example of this concept of cycles.

It can be very reassuring to those whose lives are chaotic and disjointed to realize that there is consistency in nature. Understanding the cyclic nature of our reality is reassuring; we bear the harshness of winter, knowing that spring will soon follow.

Diversity: Life, as it is known, depends upon diversity. Diversity means differences. All people are all different in genetic background, with resulting diversity in size, shape, color, race, intelligence, athletic ability, and so forth. Diverse cultural backgrounds add further to individual differences making the human species extremely diverse. Plants and animals differ, also. There are many kinds of trees, and there are many kinds of species within trees. There are many different types of needle-bearing trees such as pines, spruces, hemlocks, cedars, firs, junipers, etc., and there may be a hundred different kinds of pine trees. Each kind of pine tree has thousands of needles, all of which are similar yet different. These things are true about every species of plant or animal.

Through the existence of diverse species, it is possible for plants and animals to live in all the various life zones and ecosystems created by the multiple factors of Light, Air, Water, and Soil. Also, diversity greatly enhances the chances of survival of a species. Genetic differences within populations make it possible for one species to collectively possess more traits than any single member of the population could possibly possess. Accommodation of the species to long-term changes in the ecosystem is made possible by this diversity. Differences in genetic makeup between individuals make it unlikely that any single disease will be able to override the defenses of 100 percent of the population of any species. The survival of a species is also critical to the health, and sometimes survival, of ecosystems.

Furthermore, there is a great diversity of species within every ecosystem. The old growth forest on the Pacific Northwest may appear to be a single species (Douglas fir) forest; however, the diversity is manifested by the thousands of smaller plants, insects, bacteria, birds, microbes, etc., that make up the total ecosystem. For one to become environmentally literate, it must be understood that there is a great value in this diversity. In many ecosystems, stability depends upon diversity. If one species becomes diseased or is devoured by insects, there should be another species to maintain the life in the area. While complex ecosystems (those with relatively large numbers of species) tend to be inherently more stable than simple ecosystems, the loss of even one species can have profound consequences. Complex ecosystems tend to be more stable because more species may occupy any one niche; yet, even in a complex system, the loss of a single species may add to destabilization, "tumble down" serial effects, and irreversible decay. Because of the critical importance of diversity, much concern is now focused on the extremely rapid and accelerating rate of human caused extinctions of plant and animal populations worldwide.

Community: Plants and animals live where the conditions (LAWS and forces) are suited for them. Each plant and animal has a "niche," or role, in that area. Roles may be: holding soil in place, breaking down rocks into smaller pieces, storing water, providing shade, pruning leaves and branches, feeding birds, etc. Another way of saying this is, "Things must fit how and where they live." We know that certain animals depend upon certain plants for their food and that those animals and plants live only where the environment is suitable for them. We also know that there are many different communities or ecosystems. We travel through prairies, mountainous areas, along glaciers, and alpine meadows. We canoe or raft down streams and rivers; we explore the tidal pools, beaches, and estuaries. Each community consists of plants and animals that "fit" there and each of which has a "niche" or role.

Interrelationships: It must seem obvious by now that each of these ecological concepts is connected to every other one. And all are connected to the LAWS of Light, Air, Water and Soil. Interrelationships is the concept that recognizes this connectedness. Animals depend upon several different kinds of plants for their food. Plants also depend upon each other. Some plants shade others so they can grow out of the scorching sun. Some plants (vines) use others for climbing supports. People depend on each other—on parents, friends, teachers, the police, shopkeepers, farmers, manufacturers, and on and on. Everything on earth is somehow connected.

For years, people have asked the question, "What good is it?" "What good is poison ivy?" "What good are mosquitoes?" "What good are dandelions?" These questions imply that we mean, "What good is it to *me*?" If it were understood that all things are interrelated, the question might be, "What part does this thing play in the scheme of things?" What is its niche, or role, in the *world*? Mosquito larva sometimes help purify the water in high mountain lakes, and they certainly feed the birds. Poison ivy makes shade for other plants, holds soil in place, and provides food for some birds. Dandelion leaves are used for food by many people, and young rabbits like the new leaves. Everything is related to something else. All are interdependent.

This is what John Muir meant when he wrote: "When we try to pick out anything by itself, we find it hitched to everything else in the universe." Barry Commoner's first ecological principle is: "Everything is connected to everything else." And the final lines of a lengthy poem, "Vision of the Lady of the Misty Isle," are: "Thou canst not touching of a flower/ Without the troubling of a star." (Sir Francis Thompson). These well known quotations are examples of the concept of interrelationship.

Change: It is a known fact that things change. The energy from a plant becomes an animal's energy. Live leaves become dead leaves. Seeds become plants. Little trees become big trees. Everything is changing. Companions change, as do families, homes, classes, interests, and knowledge. Mountains become smaller with erosion. Rocks are worn down and become soil. Soil is leached, utilized, moved, and compacted to become other forms of rock. Plants come to life, bloom, bear seeds, die, decompose and are utilized for nutrients for other plants. Understanding this concept helps people understand that a forest, a pond, or a meadow cannot be preserved. Meadows, if left alone, generally become forests; ponds become marshes; and rivers change their courses. Nothing in nature is static. "Everything is becoming something else."

Adaptation: Adaptation is the ability of a plant or animal to change in order to fit the environment. Examples of what is called "situational" adaptation can be seen frequently. A tree that has lost its top in a windstorm may have adapted through one of its branches reaching toward the sun to become a new top, or "leader." An evergreen tree that has had its trunk bent and broken by a heavy snowstorm may have adapted by straightening up and reaching for the sun even though the trunk remains crooked. We see a lot of these trees in forests where there are heavy snow falls. They are called "pistol butt" trunks because they resembled the grip of the old-fashioned gun to the early settlers (another example of how we use analogies to give names to things when we don't know what else to call them).

If you hike along a trail or along a country road that has been dug a little below the level of the forest floor, you will see that the trees on either side look as if they had started to grow sideways and then turned and grew up straight. When the road was built, the force of gravity caused the trees alongside of the cut to slump toward the lower level. Their roots held them from falling down and their ability to adapt caused them to straighten up and point their tops toward the sun. These three examples demonstrate that trees are "phototropic," or "sun loving," and can adapt to various negative environmental situations to reach toward the sun.

The long-range and permanent adaptation of specific species is evolution. The members that possess favorable traits of a species are more likely, in the long run, to pass their genetic material to the next generation, thus they adapt permanently to the environment. The kangaroo rat of the American Southwest has adapted to its need to utilize every precious drop of water it ingests and has no liquid urine—only a hard pebble of solid waste. Carnivorous plants have developed leaf structures to trap insects that are subsequently ingested to augment an inadequate supply of nitrogen in the soil.

We know that different bird bills have changed over the centuries and adapted for feeding on certain nutrients. A hummingbird bill, used for penetrating into the calyxes of flowers, would not do for a hawk that needs a bill suitable for tearing meat. A duck's flat bill would not do for a seed eater.

Much of the diversity we see among plants and animals is because of the ability to adapt. In times of adverse conditions, plants and animals die, adapt, or move (the biologists' DAM Law). Many animals and plants have adapted permanently to changing conditions. Here, we see the interrelationship of three ecological principles (diversity, change, and adaptation) and again we understand that everything is connected to everything else.

Biological Concepts and Identification

As stated earlier, it is impossible for anyone to know everything about the natural environment. The outdoor leader should have certain basic knowledge, however. A good course in physical science will help one understand the basics of soil, water, and air, as well as the influences of natural forces upon them. Basic geology and meteorology are fundamental to understanding the ecosystems through which one will be traveling. A course in basic biology with emphasis on plants and animals is also a necessity.

Identification by itself is useless to most participants unless they possess the ability to sort, file, and retain such information in their brains as files for future reference. Many learners do not assimilate such data and find identification to be a dead end exercise. While knowing the name of a plant does not help anyone understand it, labels allow us to catalogue, sort out, and remember things, and the very process of pointing out objects causes people to notice what they may otherwise have missed. Photography can similarly enhance perceptions as people aggressively seek out new, interesting subjects. Interesting bits of information about what is being observed can help focus attention while moving the observers toward a better understanding of the interrelationships of all the components of the system.

It is recommended that every outdoor leader develop one area in which he/she is well-versed. It may be trees, flowers, birds, rocks, or another aspect of physical or biological science. This will help the leader explain some things in depth and enable him/her to move into other areas of natural history more readily.

It is not the purpose of this book to teach physical science of biology. Some facts, however, may help the neophyte to become more observant while learning about the natural world. A list of what a leader should know is moot; however, some leadership ideas follow. Each leader will have a special set of needs for information depending upon his/her responsibilities and locale.

Plants

Leaders might make it a goal to know a specific number of flowering and nonflowering plants (trees, flowers, ferns, mosses, and fungi) depending upon where the program is located and the preponderance of species. Knowing the differences among plant families helps in identification.

The difference between mosses, fungi, ferns, and flowering plants relates to the differences in the reproductive processes. In the flowering plants, there are gymnosperms (naked seeds) and the angiosperms (seeds in containers). Most cone-bearing trees are gymnosperms, while the fruit trees are angiosperms. This is easy to see in the apple which is a fruit that covers the seeds.

Once one is familiar with several major plant families, many individual species may be looked up fairly easily. Many species require hand lenses and detailed dissection; thus, the leader may want to stick to generalities such as, "This is one of the many species of buttercup." When one becomes familiar with several plant families, more can be added to the list until one develops an accumulation of data useful in identifying literally hundreds of plants.

When identifying a flower, one should know how to look at it. Describe the stem, leaves, and flower arrangement. Look at the flower and notice the sepals, petals, and corolla. Examine the stamens and pistil, if possible. And, of course, observe where the plant is growing, e.g., marsh, dry area, rocky outcrop, or shady conifer forest.

The difference between trees and shrubs is not precise—even to botanists. *Usually* shrubs are woody plants, smaller than trees, with several stems growing together in one clump. Often, however, there are trees (such as the vine maple of the Northwest and the goose foot maple of the Northeast) that are under 20 feet tall and have several stems growing together. The differences are so difficult that the amateur naturalist admits that most people should not try to be too pedantic here. It is easier to distinguish among the deciduous trees, the broad-leaved evergreens, and the conifers.

Deciduous trees lose all of their leaves every autumn, while evergreens lose some leaves throughout the year. Individual leaves or needles are retained for two or more years so the tree always has greenery. There are exceptions such as the larch which is a deciduous needle bearer (but not a conifer). Most trees, however, fall into one of the three major categories. Leaders should learn to recognize the major species of trees in the areas in which they are traveling.

Animals

The major animals in an area are usually easily learned and, while they may seldom been seen, are easily recognizable if viewed.

Outdoor leaders should know the differences among vertebrates which include the mammals, fish, amphibians, reptiles, and birds. It is expected that these will cause few problems among most leaders; however, a good review of the major classes of vertebrates might be a good idea!

There are literally millions of species of invertebrates in nature, and every outdoor leader should know something about several of the over one million species of arthropods—those animals with external skeletons making up about 80 percent of all known animals. Because many arthropods can cause problems, e.g., itching, poisoning, and pain, the following should be understood:

Arachnids: Animals with eight legs and no antennae.
- Spiders have a two-region body of head-thorax and abdomen.
- Ticks have a one region body and are parasites on land mammals.
- Mites are minute to pea-sized and parasites on land and aquatic mammals.
- Scorpions have large pincers, elongated tails with stingers, and are terrestrial.

Diplopoda: Millipedes with two pairs of legs per body segment. They are slow moving, their bites are not poisonous. They emit a protective odor and curl up when disturbed.

Chilopoda: Centipedes with one pair of legs per body segment. They are fast moving, and their bites are often poisonous.

Insects: Arthropods with one pair of antennae, a body divided into three segments (head, thorax, and abdomen), and six legs. There are about 1,000,000 species. Outdoor leaders should be familiar with several of the 29 orders of insects.

There are literally hundreds of books, booklets, and pamphlets available today to help people identify plants and animals in their natural habitats. Every outdoor leader should have a constantly growing library of such books. Take notes on the unknown while on trips and attempt to look them up upon return. Many times, there will be participants who are quite knowledgeable about some plants or animals, and the group should be encouraged to learn from those people. The amount of information shared by the participants and leaders will create good morale as well as lead to more rewarding experiences.

Basic Physical Science Concepts

Before attempting to teach participants about the environment, the leader should have a basic understanding of physical science including mathematics, physics, and chemistry. The extent of the leader's understanding of basic science will determine the extent to which the concepts and theories of physical science can be understood and taught.

Astronomy and Cosmology

Leaders should acquaint themselves with current theories on the evolution of the universe, and basic astronomy, including the structure of the galaxy and solar system and the linear and temporal dimensions of the universe. The leader should also be familiar with at least the primary constellations and brightest stars, as well as some of the most interesting features of the night sky. Such knowledge is required to capture the interest and attention of participants. Pointing out a few key stars, constellations, or patterns can inspire curiosity and receptivity and lead to discussion of cosmological or astronomical concepts. Leaders in the southern hemisphere have need for knowledge of the southern constellations.

Geology

The leader should be familiar with basic geological concepts including the general structure of the earth, plate tectonics theory, the various processes by which the rocks and minerals of the earth's crust are formed, eroded, and transformed, and the geologic time scales. A knowledge of the most abundant rocks and minerals in the region and their relationship to the area's geologic history should be considered necessary. Furthermore, the leader should be prepared to supply a basic explanation of the area (Why is this hill here?; Why is there a valley over there?; From a geological point of view, when and how did it form?).

The capable outdoor leader conducting groups in rugged canyons or mountainous terrain must be able to distinguish between types and qualities of rocks. Different rock types often require different equipment and techniques. Variations in rock types may determine the acceptable routes as well as the necessary safety precautions. It is assumed that the leader knows the rock thoroughly, and it is his/her responsibility to convey this knowledge to participants. Learning to climb on a rock with no knowledge of the rock itself is analogous to learning to canoe with no knowledge of water conditions. Skills must be adjusted to known environmental conditions.

Basic knowledge of rock types is vital and can be summarized as follows:

Igneous rocks are those formed when molten rock, called magma, cools and hardens. These rocks are called intrusive when they cool underground and extrusive when they solidify after spilling onto the surface (as occurs from

volcanoes). Slow cooling results in larger crystals, while more rapid cooling leads to finer grains—even to glass-like structures.

Sedimentary rocks are, as the name implies, formed by deposition of materials. This may occur on land or underwater, and the individual particles may be microscopic to immense in size. Sedimentary rocks are usually classified as detrital, or chemical and organic or inorganic, depending upon the type and mechanism of deposition.

Metamorphic rocks are metamorphosed, or changed, rocks. They are typically hard and dense, having been subjected to great heat and pressure over long periods of time.

A good review of basic geology will help the leader become familiar with the common rocks in each category.

Weather

For both safety and comfort, outdoor leaders and their participants should understand basic concepts about weather. Weather is the atmospheric condition (interaction of wind, sun, precipitation, humidity, and air pressure) over a short period of time. Climate refers to weather over a long period of time.

Next to daylight and darkness, weather has the most significant effect on the outdoor experience. When asked to predict the weather, most people are completely reliant upon their recall of the latest radio or television forecast. Many outdoor people are only slightly more sophisticated. While they generally pay a bit more attention to the forecasts, they are often painfully unaware of the differences between valley, mountain, or desert weather and lack any ability to forecast weather for themselves.

Nothing can replace the careful review of a good meteorology text, and local guidebooks and other resources should always be tapped for insights into specific weather hazards and conditions in your area. There are, however, several general principles to keep in mind. Like the sun that drives it, weather follows patterns. While never so precisely predictable as sun movements, weather *can* be forecast with some degree of accuracy. Government and private broadcasts over the news media usually attempt twenty-four hour and longer estimates based upon computer models and a wealth of information from hundreds of stations. Still, we all know minor errors are frequent and major errors not uncommon.

Believe it or not, you can probably do just as well, or even better, yourself given the basic ideas listed below—if you change the rules a bit. First, don't try to pin things down too closely. If you predict an eighty percent chance of rain by 10:00 a.m., you will likely err. "It will probably rain by lunch" is a safer statement. Keep in mind that all you really want to be able to do is to decide whether or not to modify your trip plans; you know you can't possibly reach one hundred percent assurance, so you travel prepared for anything anyway. Your predictions *can* help you decide when and where to camp, whether or not tomorrow will be a good day for picture taking, for climbing, or for lounging in the tent all day. Keeping one eye *always* on the weather is characteristic of all experienced outdoor people since surprises can be unpleasant or even deadly. Second, do not try to predict too far into the future. Take it four to six hours at a time. You can usually forecast tomorrow morning's weather, but if you try before late evening, don't bet your last cookie on it.

The major concern of the outdoor leader is *bad* or *foul* weather—storms, winds, rain, and snow. Such conditions are usually associated with low-pressure areas, generated at the interfaces of major air masses, and moving from west to east like giant pinwheels. These lows rotate counterclockwise in the Northern Hemisphere and actually consist of a set of fronts. Fronts are boundaries between elements of the air masses that originally rubbed together to form the low. Figure 3.5 (page 48) shows cross sections indicating the cloud and weather sequences typical of cold and warm fronts, respectively.

Note that the vertical scales in the sketches are very much exaggerated. The entire low pressure system is thinner in proportion than a pancake. Note also that what might be experienced at a given point on the ground depends upon many factors, including where the storm is relative to the group, how fast the storm is moving,

and wind velocities, temperatures, and humidities within each air mass. You can, however, make some fairly accurate guesses. Some useful considerations are listed below:

1. Storms (lows) generally move from west to east. You should check locally to find out what is normal for each season in your area. In most areas, the storm will approach from somewhere between the southwest and the northwest. Along the southern and southeastern coast, however, hurricanes can be a significant exception. Know where your weather comes from, and pay attention.

2. Cirrus clouds, with their distinctive "mare's tales" of tiny hexagonal snow crystals, usually precede warm fronts by about twelve hours. If you see these clouds, watch to see what happens next. If the warm air behind the front is unstable, you are likely to see cirrocumulus (or "mackerel" clouds), followed by turbulent buildup of cumulus clouds and, quite possibly, lightning. If the warm air is stable, you should see a thickening and lowering of the clouds, with altostratus changing to stratocumulus, nimbostratus, and stratus—i.e., drizzle and steady rain, or snow. Cirrus clouds in the late afternoon? You had better stake out your tent fly, even though the evening will likely be dry.

3. Storms (lows) move at varying speeds, usually from twenty to thirty miles an hour. They speed up and slow down, but generally progress at about twenty-five miles per hour. Look to the west or southwest, northwest, or from wherever *your* weather comes to make long-term (three-and-a-half hour) forecasts. If you see the characteristic low grey line of an approaching storm coming over the horizon, estimate how long it will be before it gets to you.

In rolling low hills, you may be able to see only fifty or sixty miles, or about two or three hours into the future.

In the desert, or if you are in the mountains with a good view into the west, you may be able to see well for a hundred and twenty miles, or as much as five hours into the future.

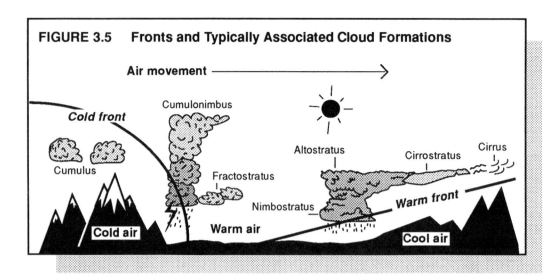

FIGURE 3.5   Fronts and Typically Associated Cloud Formations

When one is facing an oncoming low, with its counterclockwise circulation, the winds will actually be coming from as much as 90 degrees or more to the left. To make a shorter range forecast, perhaps up to an hour or two, look directly into the wind.

For example, in the Pacific Northwest, experienced backcountry travelers frequently scan the horizon, starting in the south/southeast to be sure to catch the short-term forecast, then sweeping around to the northwest to see what might happen several hours later.

4. Some of the nastiest weather is not always related to fronts. Thunderstorms are a particular problem, and while many backpacking and mountaineering texts give advice on what to do if you are caught in one, few mention techniques for prediction. Those thunderstorms that buildup unrelated frontal disturbances usually do so in reasonably predictable fashion—unstable air is uplifted due to strong heating of the ground or sharp differences in ground temperature. The points to remember are: (1) it is common for huge, active storms to develop within an hour from clear sky (thirty minutes is not unusual), and (2) cumulonimbus clouds tend to form in certain predictable areas and usually drift in directions characteristic of the region. There is no excuse during hot, humid, and unstable weather, when thunderstorms are a possibility, for not keeping a careful eye in the direction of likely buildup. Thunderstorms are serious business.

5. Consider the effects of elevation. In clear air, expect temperatures to drop by about 5.5°F for every 1,000 feet elevation gain (approximately 1°C per 100 m). If condensation (cloudiness) is occurring, the rate of cooling drops to about 2.5°F per 1,000 feet (approximately 0.5°C per 100 m). A figure often used for estimates, when conditions can't be predicted, is about 3.5°F per 1,000 feet (approximately 0.6°C per 100 m). Thus, a good guess would be that the mountain campsite at 8,000 feet (2,438 m) is at least 28°F (–2.2°C) cooler than a sea-level hometown. This means that freezing temperatures are not at all uncommon even in midsummer in most of the mountainous regions. A cool 60°F (15.6°C) summer evening at sea level could mean freezing temperatures at just over 5,000 feet (1,524 m).

6. When the sun rises, the mountains begin to heat up and do so faster than the sea. As a result, once the sun has begun to "cook" the land, morning winds tend to blow inland and upstream. The reverse happens at night. These winds can be a frustration for river runners unless paddling plans are adjusted accordingly.

On or near the high mountains, the effects can be very severe on otherwise cool, clear nights. Radiant cooling of the surface of exposed high-elevation rock and snow can send torrents of very cold air flowing down gullies and streams. Usually the primary effects are poolings of subfreezing air in lake and meadow basins, and gentle but frosty breezes icing the sleeping bags of those careless enough to sleep near creeks. Occasionally, these winds blow in a strange pulsing rhythm that stops almost completely for a few minutes, then rushes down slope with tent-shredding force.

7. Be aware of the effects of mountain ranges on weather, especially precipitation. When moisture-laden air is forced upward by mountains, it is cooled, and cool air cannot hold as much moisture as warmer air. Condensation often results, forming clouds and perhaps precipitation. Notice that since the general motion of storms is from west to east, the west side of mountain ranges usually receives much more moisture than equivalent elevations on the downwind, or eastern, side of the range. See Figures 3.6 and 3.7 (page 50) to help understand clouds and winds.

Water

Most people seem to take water for granted, giving it little thought as long as it is clear and cool; yet, water is as important as sunlight, air, and soil. It is necessary for life, and all forms of life are dependent upon it. Additionally, humans use water for consumption, industry, irrigation, fish hatcheries, and recreation. Water helps leach nutrients down into the soil so plant roots can use them. Some of the water that plants use is lost through the leaves by a process called transpiration, which is analogous to perspiration in people. Water in the soil is additionally used by plants to manufacture food, and wildlife needs it in order to live.

The water on our planet moves through what is commonly known as the "water cycle." The elements that make up the weather (heat, pressure, wind, and moisture) cause precipitation, evaporation, and condensation in an endless cycle. Because of heat, water in lakes and

FIGURE 3.6   Clouds

HIGH CLOUDS
are composed of tiny ice crystals and found at elevations of 20,000 to 40,000 feet.

Cirrus
Thin, wispy, and feathery; sometimes called "Mares' Tails". Often seen in advance of warm fronts.

Cirrostratus
Thin and patchy; rarely seen.

Cirrocumulus
Small, white flakes, or a ripple pattern.

MIDDLE CLOUDS
occur at elevations of 6,000 to 20,000 feet.

Altostratus
Layers, or sheets, of gray or blue. They look slightly striped. The sun looks as if it is being seen through frosted glass.

Altocumulus
Patches, or layers, of puffy or roll-like clouds; whitish gray.

LOW CLOUDS
occur from near the earth up to 6,500 feet.

Stratus
Low and fog like. Only light drizzle can fall from these clouds.

Nimbostratus
True rain clouds. They have a wet look, and often there are streaks of rain extending to the ground.

Stratocumulus
Odd-shaped masses spreading out in a rolling or puffy layer; gray with darker shadings.

TOWERING CLOUDS
may reach from low elevations to over 40,000 feet.

Cumulonimbus
These are thunderheads; with puffy (water cloud) bases and flat (ice cloud) tops.

Cumulus
Puffy and cauliflower-like. The shapes constantly change.

FIGURE 3.7   Beaufort Scale of Wind Force

Beaufort Number Symbol	Specifications For Use on Land	Miles Per Hour	U.S. Weather Bureau Forecast Terms
0	Calm; smoke rises vertically.	less than 1	light
1	Direction of wind shown by smoke drift but not by wind vanes.	1-3	light
2	Wind felt on face; leaves rustle; ordinary vane moved by wind.	4-7	light
3	Leaves and small twigs in constant motion; wind extends light flag.	8-12	gentle
4	Raises dust and loose paper; small branches are moved.	13-18	moderate
5	Small trees in leaf begin to sway; wavelets form on inland waters.	19-24	fresh
6	Large branches in motion; whistling heard in telegraph wires; umbrellas used with difficulty.	25-31	strong
7	Whole trees in motion; inconvenience felt in walking against wind.	32-38	strong
8	Breaks twigs off trees; generally impedes progress.	39-46	gale
9	Slight structural damage occurs.	47-54	gale
10	Seldom experienced inland; trees uprooted; considerable structural damage occurs.	55-63	whole gale
11	Very rarely experienced; accompanied by much damage.	64-75	whole gale
12	Heavy damage.	above 75	hurricane

oceans evaporates and rises into the atmosphere. Here, it cools and condenses, forming clouds which are blown by the wind. When the clouds get too full of moisture, it starts to rain. As the rain falls to the ground, some of it soaks into the ground and is stored in underground streams, caverns, or air spaces between soil particles. Underground streams form springs (a welcome sight to the hiker) when they reach the surface of the earth. Water that does not soak into the ground runs off into streams, lakes, and oceans, where some of it evaporates and returns to the air to form clouds again. Thus, the cycle repeats itself. Understanding the "water cycle" helps one to predict the weather and to appreciate the plants and animals that depend upon water.

Interpretation

Interpreting the environment is an art that should accompany instruction in outdoor skills. Interpreting is not the same as telling, nor is it identification. The major principles of interpretation explained by this century's foremost interpreter, Freeman Tilden, are as follows:

1. Interpretation must relate to the personality or experience of the participant. Here, the leader must be careful not to allude to scientific principles or facts that are not within the current knowledge or understanding of the participant. Nor should the material address the participants as if they were younger, older, or more or less experienced than they are. Referring to the odor of the hay-scented fern as, "Just like that of the haymow back home," is meaningless to the participant who has never smelled hay or even seen a haymow! Stating that "Everyone recognizes the state tree of Indiana" is untrue and is derogatory to those who have no idea what the tree is, let alone know what it looks like. Interpreters cannot assume that everyone ever recognizes or knows something. To state that something is "obvious" may make those who don't find it at all obvious to feel inferior or at least slightly ill at ease. Better words would be "If you recognize _____," or "Those who have lived in the country may remember the odor of _____." It all depends on how it is said.

Furthermore, the interpretation should focus on what is actually present. Mentioning that something occurs in another land or country or that you remember seeing something like it elsewhere confuses the participant who wants to know about the item that is present. *After* discussing the feature that is present, it may be useful to discuss where else the feature is known to occur, or ask if participants have seen something similar elsewhere, as a prelude to investigating why the feature occurs at this spot.

2. Interpretation contains information but is not solely information. Interpretation reveals *meanings* of objects based upon information or facts. Just handing out information is meaningless and a dead end bit of trivia. Explaining that a certain tree is "shade intolerant" or that a

merganser has a "serrated bill" means nothing until the learner finds out the importance of shade intolerance or serrated bills. In other words, if it is important to point out something, it is even more important to explain the overall meaning, such as how the concept relates to the total environment, why the difference in something is important, and what happens if something changes.

3. Interpretation is an art made up of several arts. It is a skill that requires creative communication, humor, dramatics, lucid use of analogies, questions, audience participation, and knowing when to stop lest the learner becomes supersaturated with knowledge and meanings. A good interpreter knows when to stop. Maybe a half-dozen interpretive facts a day is enough!

4. The chief aim of interpretation is to provoke curiosity and interest. It is not to have the learner go away with a list of unrelated facts, but to have the participant go away with the desire to know more. Outdoor leaders can whet interest in learning about the outdoors that can last long after the muscles and joints have stiffened and ceased to carry the participant over rough terrain.

5. Interpretive facts should present a whole idea. This may be difficult when trying to explain the ecological components of one type of forest; however, one should be alert to trying to give both sides of an issue. "What happens if? When this happens, then _____. Because this is so, then _____ is so." If the tree is shade intolerant, it means that the young tree must have bright sunlight, or it cannot grow to maturity and may die after only one year. The interpreter should go on from there to explain what happens in a forest that consists of only shade intolerant species. One can talk about the need to maintain a minimum impact environment in a popular campsite but that is incomplete information unless one also explains the whole thing, i.e., what happens if the campsite is overused?

6. Interpretation to those who are 12 and under should be done in a separate program. Interpretation for children takes a different

approach. Adults may feel as if someone is "talking down to them" if they are given a child's program, and most children will find the adult program to be rather boring. Children usually react more favorably to more analogies, dramatics, and creative imagination.

As one sets out to interpret the environment, it is well to remember that the opportunities for environmental education in outdoor-pursuit activities are the result of direct contact with the natural world. This contact also results in real or potential damage to the environment and major challenges for the outdoor leaders. Any activity, anywhere at any time, has consequences. The hike or canoe trip that is invaluable in sensitizing participants to the environment and its problems also leaves its mark, wearing hard on what may be especially fragile or overused lands.

Summary

Understanding the natural environment seems to be a very complex task to most people. With knowledge of a few basic facts and skills, however, the leader can enhance the possibility of every participant enjoying the natural surroundings and feeling comfortable in every ecosystem. Most important for leaders, perhaps, is a good basic understanding of the physical and biological characteristics of the area to be visited. Leaders should at the very least know enough about the area to identify major geologic and geographic features and the more common plants and animals. Ideally, leaders should know a lot more than just the names of features, plants, or animals; yet, names alone are often valuable in helping participants gain an appreciation of the environment. This points to the value of leaders having a good comprehension of basic physical and natural science. The leader who understands basic physical, geological, meteorological, and biological principles and processes can take his/her participants much farther along the path toward enlightened action. If this leader is also excited by, and about, environmental issues and is an effective and personable teacher, he/she can induce (even on a short excursion) major and long-lasting changes in participant attitudes and behaviors.

Recommended Resource Books

Brown, V. (1987). *The amateur naturalist's handbook.* Englewood Cliffs, NJ: Prentice-Hall.

Brown, V. (1982). *Reading the outdoors at night.* Englewood Cliffs, NJ: Prentice-Hall.

Brown, V. (1983). *Investigating nature through outdoor projects.* Harrisburg, PA: Stackpole Books.

Gale, L. (1984). *A field guide to the familiar.* Englewood Cliffs, NJ: Prentice-Hall.

Peterson, T. C. (1986). *Heaven and earth: A fieldbook of foolproof nature identification.* New York, NY: Dell Press.

Finders Series. Berkeley, CA: Nature Study Guild.
   Finders for east of the Rocky Mountains:
       Flower finder
       Tree finder
       Winter tree finder
       Track finder
       Berry finder
       Life on the intertidal rocks
   Pacific coast tree finder
   "   "   *bird finder*
   "   "   *berry finder*
   "   "   *fern finder*
   Redwood region finder
   Sierra flower finder
   Pacific intertidal life finder
   Pacific mammal finder
   Desert tree finder
   Rocky mountain tree finder

Golden guides, edited by H. S. Zim. New York, NY: Golden Press.
   Golden nature guides to:
       Trees
       Birds
       Weeds
       Flowers
       Insects

Pond life
Cacti
Spiders
Reptiles and amphibians
Stars
Mammals
Seashores
Fishes
Rocks and minerals
Butterflies and moths
Nonflowering plants
Ecology

Golden field guides to:
Birds of North America
Seashells of North America
Trees of North America
Rocky mountains
Everglades
Northwest

Peterson field guides, edited by R. T. Peterson. Boston, MA: Houghton Mifflin Co.
Eastern birds
Western birds
Butterflies
Mammals
Rocks and minerals
Animal tracks
Ferns and their related families of north Eastern and central north america
Trees and shrubs
Reptiles and amphibians
Rocky mountain wild flowers
Stars and planets
Western reptiles and amphibians
Wild flowers of northeastern and central North America
Pacific states wild flowers
Beetles
Moths
Southwestern and Texas wild flowers
Birds of Texas

The Stokes nature guide series, edited by D. Stokes and L. Stokes. Boston, MA: Little, Brown and Company.
A guide to nature in winter
A guide to enjoying wild flowers
A guide to observing insect lives

References

Buchsbaum, R., & Buchsbaum, M. (1957). *Basic ecology.* Pittsburgh, PA: The Boxwood Press.

Commoner, B. (1971). *The closing circle.* New York, NY: Alfred A. Knoph.

Calder, N. (1974). *The weather machine.* New York, NY: Viking Press.

Ford, P. (1980). *Principles and practices of outdoor/environmental education.* New York, NY: Macmillan Publishing Company.

Ford, P. (1991). *Take a new bearing.* Martinsville, IN: American Camping Association.

Muir, J. (1967). *My first summer in the Sierra.* In The Sierra Club (Ed.), *Gentle wilderness.* New York, NY: Ballantine Books.

Odum, E. P. (1959). *Fundamentals of ecology.* Philadelphia, PA: W. B. Saunders, Co.

Rey, H. A. (1975). *The stars.* Boston, MA: Houghton Mifflin Co.

Tilden, F. (1977). *Interpreting our hertiage, 3rd ed.* Chapel Hill, NC: The University of North Carolina Press.

U.S. Forest Service. (no date). *Forest lands in management.* Washington, DC: Department of Agriculture.

Van Matre, S. (1979). *Sunship earth.* Martinsville, IN: American Camping Association.

(Also miscellaneous handouts from the Audubon Camp of the West, 1970. National Audubon Society.)

chapter
four

CARE OF THE ENVIRONMENT

For tens of thousands of years, man was a minor, or even trivial, component of the delicate web of life on earth. Human connections to the system were clear, at least pragmatically. Survival itself depended upon relative stability in the environment. Primitive tools were inefficient, and populations were small and mobile, so if one pristine site was temporarily overtaxed, another could be found nearby. The limits of resources were approached only rarely.

Now, of course, the situation has changed. We have vast populations and an ever-expanding tool kit giving us almost unlimited power to affect our environment. Unfortunately, our innate drives haven't changed much over the centuries. We still seek to gather unto ourselves as much as we can from the world around us and do so with the aid of ever more efficient tools and techniques. More, more, more. The more we know, the faster we learn. The more we learn, the faster we manufacture. The more we manufacture, the more we buy. The more we buy, the more we want. The cycle is hypnotic and captivating, playing upon our most basic urges.

Few people appreciate, or even think about, the ecosystem upon which their lives depend. The environment filters through to us by media channels. Only when the wheels of the car spin in the snow or the precious electric power is cut by an ice storm do we momentarily acknowledge our relationship to the natural world.

The problem is that we are, on a global scale, no less dependent upon the ecosystem than we were in the beginning; yet, we continue to abuse the system in ever more profound ways. The environment to which we and our societies are so finely tuned is only the current equilibrium state in an ongoing process of adjustment and readjustment, and shifts in this equilibrium can threaten every aspect of not only the human experience but the survival of all life on earth.

Wearing blinders of ignorance, dogma, or faith in technology, we forge ahead in pursuit of our personal goals. Meanwhile, populations, already overly large, continue to grow as the earth's natural resources are gobbled up at accelerating rates by the industrialized nations. Clearly, the current path can lead only to disaster for the ecosystem, of which we are a part. It is hard to be optimistic! Nevertheless, there is no point in giving up. Outdoor leaders and administrators are in an exceptionally favorable position to help.

What can we do to significantly alter the seemingly inexorable course of events? Plenty! Outdoor pursuits can provide participants with an initial sensitivity toward the environment, the first and essential step on the path toward increased understanding of environmental processes, increased understanding of our place in, and dependence upon, the ecosystem, and finally to action on behalf of the environment. The environmentally conscious outdoor administrator can recognize sensitization as a major program goal and encourage appropriate outings and leadership techniques. Outdoor leaders can accelerate the development of the environmentally responsible participant in several ways.

Since it is obvious that the human alters the state of the environment with every sortie, what can be done to make sure the impact is kept to a minimum? Land managers recommend "no-trace camping," "minimum-impact camping," or "low-impact camping." Each means camping, hiking, boating, or engaging in any outdoor pursuit in a manner that leaves little or no trace of human evidence on either the land or water. One can camp without leaving a visible trace of presence and still pollute the water. One can bury cans, papers, garbage, and old socks and appear to leave no trace; yet, the negative effects may remain years later. Furthermore, even "low-impact" camping may still have unacceptable effects on the land, water, plants, and animals. The effect of human presence may not be low enough to retain the quality of the environment; it may also not be the lowest one can afford to make. Thus, the term, "minimum-impact" is the most realistic one.

The opportunities for environmental education in outdoor pursuit activities are the result of direct contact with the natural world. This contact also results in real or potential damage to the environment and major challenges for outdoor leaders. Any activity, anywhere, at any time, has consequences. The hike or canoe trip that is invaluable in sensitizing participants to the environment and its problems also leaves its mark, wearing hard on what may be especially fragile or overused lands.

The river is a special environment. Travel may be on the water via rafts or boats, or it may take place on the riparian zone close to the water. Eating and sleeping often take place within this fragile zone. Whether one is enjoying the peaceful solitude of a lazy day on the river or accepting the challenge of a new section of white water, river running is a very satisfying outdoor experience. As more and more folks of all ages turn to rafting, kayaking, canoeing, and drifting, environmental damage in and along the river increases, including: lost equipment, fire damage to soil and vegetation, human waste, water waste, and litter.

Minimizing environmental impact on river trips begins during the planning stage. A good place to start is with the literature available in libraries, the Forest Service, and the Bureau of Land Management Offices, or the Outdoor Program room at colleges and universities. Each river has a different management plan. Check the information on the river you plan to run. *The Whitewater Source Book* is a good source of information for specific river regulations and includes addresses and phone numbers of the management agencies if additional information is needed. Most river regulations center around campfire use, human waste, waste water, and garbage disposal.

Clearly, one essential characteristic of a leader, if he/she is to accomplish anything environmentally substantive, is personal behavior consistent with that desired among participants. If the leader shows excitement, interest, and appreciation vis-à-vis the environment, so will most of the participants. If the leader modifies his/her behavior as needed to minimize impacts on the environment, so will others. If the leader stops to pick up litter in the parking lot before setting out on the trail or stream, most of the group will notice, a few will actually help, and even the most thoughtless and inconsiderate individuals are likely to think twice before littering, at least on this outing.

The following material contains a number of suggestions for minimizing ecological and social impacts on natural areas—both land and water. Many of the suggested techniques require some additional time or energy from participants who may not understand enough to appreciate what is being asked of them. Discussing the issues in a broader perspective can help participants appreciate the need for what might otherwise seem to be fanatical behavior. If time is limited, it is sometimes useful to throw out some interesting ideas or facts to ponder such as: In the contiguous 48 states, there is more land under asphalt and concrete (about 1.5 percent) than in wilderness (less than 1 percent).

Carrying Capacity

Recreational carrying capacity—the ability of the land to carry the impact of human use without perceptibly decreasing in quality—is a concept in education and recreation land use literature that became popular in the 1960s. The notion of recreational carrying capacity is a carry-over from the use of the term for rangeland and livestock. The number of acres needed to feed certain kinds of stock at certain rates of growth is known, as are the rates of rejuvenation of the land after so many animals have grazed on it for a specified period of time. Carrying capacity is the number of grazing animals the land can "carry" without destroying its ability to return to its natural state.

The original definition of "carrying capacity" is adequate for lands managed for grazing; however, that definition is inadequate for the education and recreation fields. Managers of grazing animals need to know what, perhaps irreversible, ecological damage is done to the land by foraging, trampling, and littering. Humans, on the other hand, have *opinions* about how they want their natural land to look and what their outdoor experiences should be like. The original meaning does not provide for the feelings and attitudes of human beings. People have definite expectations and anticipations when they embark on an outdoor experience, and this complicates things greatly, especially where carrying capacity is concerned. Recreational carrying capacity is no longer measurable in terms of biological-ecosystem rejuvenation only, but comprises other factors dealing with the subjective concept of how much is too much. In most of the literature, carrying capacity is used in relation to wilderness; however, that is only because the majority of the literature on the topic is in response to the question of wilderness management. Carrying capacity, as defined today, refers to *any* land used for human purposes.

Roderick Nash (1967) defines wilderness carrying capacity simply as "the ability of an environment to absorb human influences and still retain its wildness" (p. 255). Lime and Stankey (1971) state it more abstractly: "The recreational carrying capacity is the character

of use that can be supported over a specified time by an area developed at a certain level without causing excessive damage to either the physical environment or the experience for the visitor" (p. 175). In determining carrying capacity, both the ecological resources of an area and the attitudes of the users must be weighed, along with management objectives. Nash divides the components into biological, physical, and psychological, whereas Stankey (1973) calls these "ecological and sociological components of carrying capacity." Some people refer to ecological impact as physical impact. In each case, the conclusions are the same, even though the nomenclature differs. This book refers to ecological and sociological impact, because those are the terms used currently by most management agencies.

Ecological Impact

Ecological carrying capacity deals with the physical/biological changes brought about by natural processes and human or recreational impacts on these processes. It is the ability of a biotic community to survive under use. Any use creates some change, so unless we disallow it, we must be able to accept change. Most studies on carrying capacity have dealt with the ecological aspect and have included such things as present vegetation, importing hardier ground cover, soil compaction, erosion, wildlife census and behavior patterns, coliform count in streams, watershed runoff patterns, air quality, fire history in an area, and climate. Perhaps most of the focus has been on the effects of ecological carrying capacity rather than on the complex, nebulous area of the social consequences of increasing use pressures because ecological carrying capacity can be more easily measured and because the rates and types of change must be known before management can implement its objectives.

Ecological carrying capacity here refers to the capacity of the land to accommodate people without destruction to, or diminished quality of, the physical features such as rocks, soil, water, air, and topographic features, as well as to the ability of the flora and fauna to withstand constant contact with the humans who visit the area. Where there are too many roads, trails, drainage fields, and the like, the physical features of the land are needlessly destroyed or changed. Soil compaction, either from humans or mechanical equipment, is the cause of much ecological disturbance. Water quality issues are both biological and social in effect, and may be discussed as both ecological and social impact.

Soil Abrasion and Compaction

Certain soils, especially where very wet or very dry, are subject to disturbance and erosion when walked on, especially by lug-soled boots. Some soils, even those soils which at other times might be easily abraded, are compressed and hardened when stepped on. This process is one of the most common ways in which people have an impact on the ecosystem and is most difficult to reverse. Compaction prevents normal permeation of water into the soil, resulting in the death of many kinds of plants. Compaction also promotes erosion when, unable to sink in and no longer slowed by plant life, water on a slope runs along the surface and gains energy until some noncompacted normal soil is reached. The high-speed, high-energy water then washes away the weaker and more vulnerable normal soil. Compaction damage is a quiet, slow, cumulative process that is almost impossible to reverse.

Suggestions

Several things can be done to lessen the impact of human-caused abrasion and compaction.

When traveling:

1. When possible, use existing trails and footwear that are no more abusive to the soil than necessary. Lug-sole boots are often the worst possible choice. The deeper the lugs and stiffer the sole, the greater the damage to certain types of soil. Leaders can suggest that participants use heavy lug soles only when they are necessary to protect the feet from rocks, snow, and ice. For simple trail use, lighter weight soles are more comfortable and easier on the environment.

2. Avoid widening the trail. This means not stepping on the shoulder of the trail but walking right in the middle of it. Don't form multiple trails by walking alongside a water- or weed-filled path. If you must stay out of the water or away from dew-covered plants, stay well off the trail and have the group fan out to avoid creating a second parallel path.

3. Don't cut corners or switchbacks! Follow the trail around the corner even if less considerate hikers have worn a shorter path. If you can spare the time, take a minute or two to place barriers, such as branches and rocks, across or in the second trail to reduce further damage! Getting participants involved in trail repair focuses their attention on the problem and makes it less likely that they will cause similar problems elsewhere.

4. When you come to a damaged section of trail, or if rocks, trees, or limbs block the trail, try to repair the damage or at least to clear a path through the debris. Making a path around the obstacle causes unnecessary damage, magnified by hikers and game that follow. Most trail-maintenance programs are poorly funded, and even the best can't get to every problem site in time. Doing minor maintenance is one way in which organized groups can, in a sense, compensate for the great impact of their numbers.

5. When traveling off-trail, don't create new paths! Every attempt should be made to avoid leaving any sign of passing. The most sensitive areas are hillsides and meadows. In either case, single-file travel by a group should be avoided. Fanning out reduces the impact at any one point. On hillsides, individuals should fan out and walk in a zigzag pattern to prevent starting stream courses down the hill. This is especially important in soft soil.

In most cases, leaders have to be strongly assertive until participants get used to the idea of finding their own separate paths. No one wants to put out any extra energy, especially on hillsides. The easiest path, or that taken by the leader, is usually the route everyone wants to take. It helps to stop before such sensitive areas, explain the problem and course of action, and then start people from separate points. Even so, frequent reminders may be necessary along the way to prevent people from converging onto common paths.

6. When traveling off-trail, use snow or rock when possible. Here again, minimizing impact may require people to put out a little bit of extra energy, and the leader may need to provide both control and encouragement while setting a good example.

7. When traveling off the marked trail, don't mark your route with flagging or rock piles (known in English-speaking parts of the world as cairns, ducks, or birds) unless there is a need to follow the exact route again, in which case all markings should be removed on the last passage over the route. Old unneeded plastic flagging left by less considerate pathfinders should be removed as well. Marked routes encourage concentrated use, and plenty of marked routes exist already. It should go without saying that in no case should trees be blazed (notches cut in the bark) to mark a route.

When camping:

1. Select campsites carefully! Good choices for durability include river or shore sands, glaciated rock surfaces, areas of deep fir or pine-needle duff, and previously hardened campsites. When using a site that is already beaten down to a hard and nearly vegetation-free surface, be sure to limit activity to well within the existing limits of the site. Don't expand the site by allowing too many people to camp in it, or by allowing tent placements or activities that produce wear on the surrounding ground cover. Never camp on the fragile grasses of meadows or near bodies of water, except on maintained or developed campsites. These sites are usually extremely sensitive to abrasion and compaction, as well as being colder and having far greater social impact than hidden sites away from the shoreline.

2. Control the foot-traffic patterns in the camp area so that new trails aren't formed between camps or to viewpoints, latrines, or water sources. This is important even when the campsite will only be used for a day or two.

3. Encourage the use of camp shoes with soft or smooth soles.

4. Never cut trenches or otherwise modify a site. Modern tents have floors, thus eliminating the need to dig drainage trenches around them. Help the participants to select safe, comfortable, and environmentally stable sites and show them how to avoid disturbing the soil.

5. If sticks and stones must be moved to make a bed or tent site, relocate them before you leave! Try to leave the site in a condition that is as close to the natural state as possible.

6. Police each campsite carefully for all litter, including the little pieces of foil, "twisties," and other small but tell-tale evidence of human presence. Groups should remove all "clues" to their presence before they leave a site.

When building fires: Compaction and abrasion are by no means the only ways in which hikers directly affect vegetation in the backcountry. Several very significant types of damage relate to the use of campfires. The most obvious is wildfire damage caused by escaping fires. Wildfires can be prevented by digging a trench down to mineral soil around the fire site and, after use, putting the fire out completely.

Most people make some effort to extinguish their fires; yet, most fail to do so completely. The usual reason for failure is that most of the applied water runs off, or sinks into, the soil, and what is left is baked out of the ashes by residual heat in the ashes and soil. If a fire ring of stones has been used, the heat in the stones finishes the job so that, in a few hours, the fuels are totally dry. All it takes is one tiny spark to restart the fire, and many embers usually remain protected under the stones of the fire ring. Another common reason for fires continuing to burn after attempts to extinguish them is that roots and other underground vegetable matter in the duff layer may smoulder far away from the confines of the fire ring if the trench was not dug down to mineral soil. The fire can spread a long way, not uncommonly springing up on the surface fifty feet or more away from the original fire site. Wilderness rangers tell tales of amazingly long escapes, up to 100 yards or so, and of extensive areas of underground smoldering fires lasting through entire winter seasons under the snowpack. These fires can be extremely hard to control, requiring tedious hands-and-knees digging and a lot of damage to the soil surface. There are records of these fires requiring several seasons of hard work to extinguish. It is far easier to spend a few extra minutes to select and prepare the site properly.

When selecting the fire site: Leaders need to supervise the selection of campfire sites to be sure that the sites are free of nearby or over-hanging combustibles, that there are no oppor-tunities for wind-driven sparks to set fires else-where, and that the duff layer (the top layer of soil containing organic material) is not too thick. If rocks are to be used, leaders should suggest the use of only one or two stones rather than a whole ring—just enough to support a pot and provide some wind protection. This will help make it easier to put out the fire later. Large existing fire rings should always be dismantled down to a minimal number of rocks, and the unneeded rocks should be carried back to their original locations. This approach can help re-duce the risk of future human-caused wildfires by making participants aware of fire control when they are on their own in future trips.

Participants should be shown how to prepare a fire site by digging a trench around the out-side of the fire ring and down to mineral soil. If the group consists of adults, the leader can usually expect them to put the fire out properly; that is, to stir in lots of water with a stick, roll the rocks back, and feel the site with bare hands for hot spots. If the group consists of children, then this chore usually falls on the leader; how-ever, the children should certainly be involved, with due caution observed to avoid burns. In either case, regardless of the ages of the partici-pants, the leader needs to check each fire site by hand, feeling carefully throughout the fire bed, rock sites, and trench for any signs of re-maining or escaping fire.

Campfires produce a lot of heat focused on a small area. The result is sterilization of the soil at the site combined with an increase in certain

minerals left over from combustion of the wood. Sterilization of the soil produces long lasting scars. These scars range from charcoal debris in sand and carbon stains on rock to unsightly and essentially permanent blackened spots on mead-ows. Leaders can help by pointing out such scars to participants and by guiding the site se-lection process if fires will be used. Concrete or metal fire sites should always be used if possible. If not, try to find a site where the least damage will be caused. This may be an existing site, but should in no case be a meadow. A once popular but ineffective technique is that of cutting out a complete disk of grass and topsoil and replacing it after having used the site. The replaced ring may initially appear to look natural when set in with care, but within a few days it begins to die. At best, the result is a circle of sickly grasses, occasionally fringed or spiked with invading plant species seeking the fire-concentrated min-erals beneath. See Figure 4.1.

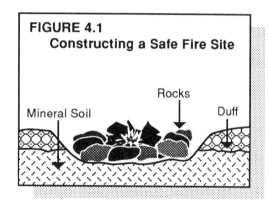

FIGURE 4.1
Constructing a Safe Fire Site

Rocks

Mineral Soil   Duff

When using wood for fuel: Perhaps the most significant impact of campfires is overcon-sumption of natural fuels. Problems resulting from overuse have severely damaged wilderness and backcountry resources around the world. Popular misconceptions and outdated habits abound among users of our wilderness lands and waters, adding to the difficulty of resolving the problem. The delicate balance of nature is easily upset, especially at higher elevations.

The potential for harm depends upon how much burnable dead woody material is produced by the site, how much of it must remain in place for the health of the ecosystem, the amount of fuel consumed, and the method of gathering the fuel. Generally speaking, high-elevation sites produce less fuel than low-elevation sites. For example, a forest in the Pacific Northwest of the United States might produce nearly a hundred times more fuel per acre of contiguous forest at 3,000 feet (900 meters) than in the zone of meadow and grove vegetation at 6,500 feet (2,000 meters). Unfortunately, consumption often exceeds production even in the low-elevation sites. Outdoor pursuits are typically concentrated along rivers and trails. Sad as it may seem, the environmental consciousness-raising campaigns of the last decades haven't significantly diminished the appeal of the campfire. The result is thousands of seriously over-taxed sites nestled within forests otherwise well-endowed with burnable woody debris.

In many wilderness and backcountry areas, the problem is compounded by the tendency of hikers to favor the high-elevation trails and campsites. Anyone who has wandered through the alpine areas of the United States or Canada over the last fifteen or twenty years can testify to the recent ravages of fuel-hungry campers who have laid waste to countless trees, including the spectacular silver-gray gnarled snags that once were so common. In many areas, almost all of the accumulated fuels and many living trees have been consumed. In some popular areas, where fuel production is low, management agencies now prohibit campfires altogether. In most areas, however, the option of whether or not to have a fire is still left to the individual, who unfortunately may lack either understanding of, or sincere concern for, the environment, or both. Sites where options exist provide valuable opportunities for leaders. Given an option, the leader can help the participants decide whether or not to have a fire. Working the participants through the decision process will make them aware of the immediate site-specific concerns related to fire safety and broader environmental issues and should provide a basis for future decisions about campfires.

Concerns that might be addressed before deciding to use a campfire include, but are not limited to:

1. What is the normal concentration of fuel materials in the area? Careful observation of vegetation and ground cover in areas well away from the site should provide an indication of the normal amount and distribution of fuels in the area. Often the most accurate sense of a normal state comes from observations made along the trail during the day's hike because disruption of normal fuel supplies may extend a half mile out from campsites in popular areas. Unless fire suppression or other artificial means have altered natural patterns, the amount of potential fuel material on the ground far from campsites should approximate the normal and healthy balance for that area.

2. Is the amount of fuel, at and near the site, close to normal? Has the site been partly stripped of "dead and down" wood? Have trees or branches been cut for fuel? A common pattern in popular areas shows no fuel left on the ground within 50 feet (15 meters) or so of the fire ring. Signs of minor damage to trees extend even farther. In a heavily abused area, broken-off limbs and axe and saw scars near the fire site usually indicate a lack of dead and down wood nearby. Most people gather these fuels out to a radius of 100 feet (30 meters) or more before hacking into standing wood. If the site appears to have nearly a normal fuel distribution close at hand, then a fire may be a reasonable option if fuels are gathered over a wide area and not lazily scavenged from the closest possible site.

3. Can the fire be safely contained and extinguished?

4. Will the site be scarred by the fire?

5. Is there sufficient air movement to carry the smoke away? Many lake basins have serious pollution problems caused by campfire smoke.

6. Can fuels be gathered over a wide area without using axes or saws? These tools leave permanent unsightly scars and are totally unnecessary in almost all cases.

7. Will the fire disturb animals or other people in the area? A campfire makes a group's presence obvious to any wildlife or other campers within a wide area due to noise (wood gathering, chopping, or breaking), visual impact (smoke during the day and firelight at night), and smell (often noticeable miles downwind). The result is greater disturbance to the lives of local animals as well as less privacy and possible disruption of the experiences of other campers who may be seeking some sense of solitude.

8. Will it be possible to keep ashes and smoke away from shelters? Is there likely to be damage to gear, such as burn holes in tents, and will the smoke blow into anyone's camp, creating a permanent odor of wood smoke on clothing, or away from the camp?

9. Will the fire interfere with awareness of the environment? Fires tend to mask the sights and sounds and smells of the night, as campers sit transfixed by the flames.

10. What about campfires along river banks? Many rafters (as well as land travelers) find stoves to be the fastest, easiest, and cleanest method of cooking. In fact, some resource managers *require* the use of stoves. Fire pans are the next best option for minimizing fire damage. They are required on some rivers, recommended on some, and even provided on a few. Fire pans can be garbage can lids or the bottom parts of charcoal stoves. Necessary equipment includes fire pan, grill, small shovel, and water container for fire control. To use the fire pan:

a. Locate it below the high-water mark so that any coals that may spill out will be washed away.
b. Douse the area and set the fire pan on rocks to prevent scorching the substrata and destroying soil microorganisms.
c. Small sticks burn hot and break down into small ashes. Large logs burn slowly and sometimes never burn completely.
d. Keep a bail bucket or other container of water nearby for fire control.

e. Once you've enjoyed the meal, moisten the ashes until they are cool and shovel them into an ammo can. (These may be purchased from surplus or outdoor stores.)
f. When finished, it is a good idea to douse the area again to prevent burned feet.
g. At the next camp, empty the ashes into the fire to break them down to a finer ash as the trip progresses.

All of this is by no means intended as a blanket condemnation of backwoods campfires. The intent has been to point out some concerns that might not be obvious and to offset what, especially in America, amounts almost to campfire-mania. Leaders concerned about the effects of fires should study the matter carefully to gain an understanding of the role of fires in the ecosystem and to understand the difference between natural fires burning fuels in place and campfires fueled by collected materials.

It is also important to recognize that, in many parts of the world, forest fuel accumulations are far higher than normal because of fire suppression by land managers. This is in many regards just as hard on the system as excessive building of campfires, since it precludes natural processes necessary to the maintenance of open lands. Open lands, like fire-caused meadows, are vital to a host of plant and animal species. In areas of excessive fuel buildup, it should be remembered that the potential for wildfire may be extremely high and that more campfires aren't the solution. The only way to return such areas to normal is to let nature take its course.

If a decision is made to make a fire for cooking food or boiling water, one option is a stick fire consisting of two or three small rocks and pencil-sized fuel. Such a fire is quickly made, easy to cook with, uses little fuel, and produces little smoke. Usually the site can be returned to a near-normal state in a couple of minutes. See Figure 4.2.

FIGURE 4.2   Low Impact Fire

Use 2 to 3 rocks and pencil-sized twigs

Water Quality

Washing dishes, bodies, or clothes in otherwise natural lakes, rivers, and streams alters both the purity and visual quality of the water. Soap and food residues are unpleasant to view and unpleasant to ingest (even when invisible). When tested in midsummer, after hordes of hikers have used the area for swimming, bathing, and cooking, the bacterial count of high-altitude lakes may be higher than that permitted by municipal sanitarians. Of course, this diminished quality of the water can have extreme results in the quality of the outdoor experience.

Suggestions

Food, soaps, and detergents in amazingly small quantities can add enough nutrients to lakes and streams to cause major shifts in both plant and animal populations. Consider not taking any soap or detergent at all! Many experienced backpackers make do very well with moss, sand, or fir cones for scrubbing, followed by a hot-water rinse. Swimmers should be careful to rinse off repellents and lotions well away from lakes and streams, especially in subalpine or alpine regions. Even dyes and soap residues

can harm these fragile waters, so clothing, if it must be worn in the water, should be carefully rinsed as well. The idea here is to distribute the toxic residues on the more resistant land-based life forms which spares the more sensitive ecological balance of the waters.

For meals with numerous plates, cups, silverware, and pots, the best procedure for washing dishes is the three-bucket wash method:

1. In the first bucket, add very hot water and some biodegradable dishwashing soap.

2. Use the second bucket for rinsing.

3. In the third bucket, add a cupful of chlorine bleach to disinfect the dishes.

To dispose of the waste water, dig a hole above the high-water mark and at least 100 feet away from a river or stream. Remove the sod carefully. Use a colander or cheesecloth to strain off food particles which should be disposed in the garbage. Waste from brushing teeth can also be disposed in the waste-water hole. Unfortunately, even this system is not ideal, as coyotes, bears, and other animals often dig out such pits in search of the source of the interesting odors.

When you leave the site, carefully replace the sod and stamp it down. If you must shower with soap, use it sparingly. Have a friend rinse you off well away from the river. Never put soap in side streams or in the river.

Disturbance of Plant Life

How many pairs of trampling feet can a meadow tolerate in March? May? July? November? In sun, rain, snow, or drought? How many people crossing through grazing land will it take to drive the deer away permanently? These things are unknown, yet when the ecological carrying capacity is surpassed, the quality of the environment diminishes as does the opportunity for optimal enjoyment.

Plant life is especially vulnerable to human impact. Abrasion and compaction combine to destroy countless plants each season, from tiny micro-species to giant forest trees. Some plants will die if stepped on only once. Most will die if stepped on repeatedly. At low elevations and mid-latitudes, the growing season is relatively long, many species flourish, and the ecosystem is quite resilient. As elevation increases, the growing conditions become less favorable. As a result, higher elevations reveal both fewer species and fewer members of each species and an ecosystem that is much more easily disturbed. After being walked on by a group of hikers, a low-elevation field might, if left undisturbed, return to normal within a few weeks, while a high alpine meadow often shows visible signs for many years and may be impaired in less obvious ways for decades.

Many subalpine and alpine plants give the impression of being tough and able to withstand the fiercest storm or abuse when, in reality, quite the opposite is often true. These plants may be, in fact, just barely hanging on, just barely able to maintain themselves under the harsh conditions and extremely sensitive to damage by abrasions or compaction. Heather, for instance, a widespread and hardy-looking subalpine plant, gives the impression of great durability yet has been shown to succumb to only a few passages by people in lug-sole boots. As another example, hundreds of backcountry and wilderness trees are lost each year in campsites. When soil profiles are lowered by abrasion and compaction, tree roots become exposed and abraded, inviting disease and impairing their functions.

Often and even more critical, the amount of water reaching the deeper roots is reduced because the hardened top layer of soil sheds the water rather than allowing it to permeate downwards.

Suggestions

Minimizing impact on plant life starts with following the steps for lessening physical impact. In addition, add the obvious considerations like: Do not to pick wild flowers, no matter how plentiful, and do not cut down or scar living shrubs or trees. Those who like to identify species will be much more successful if they take small field guides with them to the outdoor site than if they try to preserve bits and pieces of picked flowers to identify upon their return home. The botanical knowledge of the leader can play a major role in helping participants identify plants.

Disturbance of Animal Life

People affect animal life in many ways; yet, a group of hikers may see no obvious signs of disturbance. There is no good equivalent in the animal kingdom to the axe-scarred abused old tree that stands for years as testament to its mistreatment. Animals respond to disturbance by changing in their numbers and/or their habitat. Individual animals rarely exhibit obvious signs of abuse. Whatever our hikers can see will likely be taken as "normal" for the area, unless they are informed otherwise. Actually, of course, there are few places on earth where animal populations haven't been profoundly disturbed by man. "Normal" is an elusive concept in this case. Hunting, fishing, and game-management policies have altered the populations and distributions of virtually every large animal on earth. Many animals, which are not affected by these processes, have been affected, if not eliminated altogether, by agricultural or industrial pressures.

Even in formally designated wilderness areas that are supposedly intended to serve as "biologic baselines," the animal population continues to be profoundly disturbed. How natural and undisturbed can one expect the animal population to be in the typical wilderness area? Often encroached along all sides by logging and farming, the land abounds with deer and other game enjoying the good eating typical of farm and clear-cut forest. Since control programs have all but destroyed the old balance provided by predators, these unchecked populations, often exceed their normal populations and outgrow their natural food supply. Inside the wilderness area, the balance is typically shifted in the other direction, except where the abnormally high adjacent populations temporarily intrude. Fire suppression over the last fifty years or so has greatly reduced the rate at which new meadows are cleared by fire, causing meadows to grow dense with trees and choke out the vital food plants that grow only in full sun.

Another major disruption is centered on wilderness and backcountry lakes. Thousands of these lakes, including virtually every lake that doesn't freeze to the bottom in every wilderness area, are stocked each year for the benefit of fishermen. This has usually been done with the good intent of dispersing activity from overly crowded natural fishing streams and lakes of lower altitudes. Almost all of the stocked lakes were once naturally devoid of fish, so adding them totally changes the water's ecosystem and has major effects on a wide range of animals including a variety of predators outside of the lake. Just as permanent or popular campsites lure and provide sustenance for increased populations of rodents, birds, and predators of rodents and birds, so stocked lakes become focal points for new or expanded populations. This is completely inconsistent with the notion of wilderness as a "biological entity" or "biological baseline." We might ask the question, "Where, if not within these areas which comprise only about one percent of the United States, are natural processes to dominate?" And, "How many artificially introduced attributes are necessary for a successful and enjoyable outdoor experience?"

Suggestions

What can leaders do to reduce group impact on animal life? Here are some suggestions:

1. Check with the resource management agency and/or local wildlife manager to find out what particular problems or concerns may exist in the area of your proposed route. Adjust your route and activities accordingly. Remember that many animals need large areas of undisturbed territory.

2. Travel quietly, camp away, and preferably downwind, from meadows and feeding areas, and keep children and dogs under control at all times.

3. Leave a clean camp. Food wastes should be either carried out or burned. It takes only a little debris from each camping party to begin attracting rodents and other scavengers into

camp, along with the snakes and predators for which they themselves are food. Feeding wild animals changes their diets and feeding habits, so all feeding is to be avoided.

4. Keep all foods, shampoos, other soaps, detergents, toothpaste, insect repellents, and sunscreen products out of the water supply!

Sociological Impact

The concept of sociological carrying capacity deals primarily with the attitude of the user towards the wilderness and backcountry experience. Many factors makeup and influence this attitude, and the user may not be aware of all of them. They are subjective and changeable opinions and are difficult to measure in terms of acceptable limits of change. The student of sociological impact also asks whether there are accepted norms that govern outdoor behavior and to what extent violations of these norms affect others. The three primary influences are: (1) recreational-use influences, (2) environmentally-related influences, and (3) management-related influences, all leading to a loss of quality experience.

1. Recreational-use influences. Stankey (1972) gives four categories under this heading.

   a. Intensity of use—when the user's perception of solitude is exceeded by too many encounters.

   b. Character of the encounter—conflict between types of use, such as meeting large groups or those going under their own steam (hikers, canoeists, snowshoers, skiers), versus those being carried by horsepower (on horseback, in motorboats, snowmobiles, or recreational vehicles).

   c. Spatial aspects—the location of the encounter, whether at the trailhead, on the trail, or at the campsite.

   d. Destructive visitor behavior—evidence of littering, vandalism, and campsite overuse.

2. Environmentally-related influences. One example is the visitor's *perception* of the resource quality, including opinions on the ecological components of carrying capacity.

3. Management-related influences. This includes Nash's physical component of carrying capacity. It is in part the resource's capacity to " 'absorb' constructed trails, bridges, roads, signs, and other man-made features" (Nash, 1967, p. 267).

The tolerance level of these factors in combination with others, such as mental attitude, belief systems, physical condition of the area, and especially expectations, determines for one individual at a given moment what a quality experience will be. One way to determine quality experience, and therefore sociological carrying capacity, is to find out what value the user puts on each of these factors and what the user is willing to give up to attain and enjoy them. By studying the economics of recreation, i.e., supply and demand, one may determine what kind of recreational experience the visitor will have. Supply and demand of scarce resources should be balanced in the most fair and beneficial of ways. How much a user is willing to give up for a quality recreation experience may be stated in nondollar terms, and, according to David Greist (1975), there are three nondollar costs to the user:

1. Decreased chances of entry if use limits are imposed;

2. For solitude seekers, decreased satisfaction due to high-use levels;

3. For those who seek undisturbed natural environments, decreased satisfaction due to environmental change associated with high-use levels.

The carrying capacity could also be stated as the use level demanded by users after they consider costs. Frissell and Stankey (1972) and Marion, Cole, and Reynolds (1985) refer to this as the "limits of acceptable change," which focuses most of the attention on the users' perception of this change.

In relation to outdoor recreation, the aesthetic (or psychological) carrying capacity affects the amount of space a person needs for privacy and an absence of a feeling of crowdedness. At the same time, it also affects the need for human proximity to dispel loneliness, fear, and isolation. This feeling of space is different for different people at different times.

Other aesthetic features of land include noise, wind, vistas (both long and short), diversity in plant life, topography, color, shadow, openness, and so on. Some people like open forests, some like dense stands of trees; most find the sound of running water soothing, yet some find it tiring. No known formula has been devised for calculating the aesthetic quality of land. At times, however, it seems obvious that because of noise, confusion, or the sight of one logged area after another, the aesthetic quality of the land has been diminished. Littering, personal sanitation, and other habits all have an impact on sociological carrying capacity.

Littering

All of the foregoing impacts have both ecological and social significance; however, the social effects are relatively less important. In the case of littering, the ecological impact is relatively small compared to the social. Litter is unsightly and highly disturbing to all but the most insensitive observers; yet, it is the only impact discussed so far that is easily reversed in most instances. Except for the growing problem of small bits of wind- and animal-dispersed litter, most can simply be picked up and removed. In comparison to the difficulties of reversing the effects of compaction or other abuses of the ecosystem, littering is a minor issue.

Fortunately, most outdoor enthusiasts are conscientious about not leaving debris behind. Unfortunately, litter continues to accumulate wherever people go. Some of the debris is accidentally dropped—bits of gum wrapper or foil intended for the pocket. Most is left by people who are insensitive, inconsiderate, un-caring, and/or sloppy. The behavior of most of these people can be changed, while the behavior of certain others can be modified only by coercion, e.g., the intimidating power of regulations and the threat of fines. Inevitably, much debris will have to be picked up by more considerate and caring users. Leaders have an opportunity here to help the environment and raise consciousness of the issue among participants, as few resource managers have budgets sufficient to fund enough rangers and garbage men to clean things up.

Suggestions

1. With the help of participants, take a few minutes at the trailhead or put-in point to pick up the litter in the area. The site will look better, you and the participants will feel good, and the amount of litter left by participants will be reduced. A person who has spent some time cleaning up litter isn't likely to remain part of the problem. Have smokers pick up all the cigarette butts! Maybe they can be convinced that stepping on them doesn't make them vanish!

2. Set a good example by picking up any and all litter found along the trail. Some leaders of children like to use an incentive program with prizes for those who find the most litter. This may work for some groups; however, praise and a sense of pride may be better than material rewards.

3. Providing litter bags for each person helps to overcome reluctance based on fears of getting their pockets or gear dirty.

4. Never bury trash. Set a good example and carry it out. Trash pits result in unnecessary damage to the soil and are usually uncovered by foraging bears and other animals who then scatter the debris. Even if burial is successful, the trash is still there and will take an extremely long time to decompose if it contains plastic, aluminum, or glass. Teach the slogan, "Never bury it. Carry it!"

5. Before heading out, consider repackaging foods and other supplies to minimize or eliminate unnecessary packaging.

6. If a fire is used, don't try to burn plastics or metal—especially aluminum cans or foil. It is far easier to put empty plastic, aluminum, and foil wrappers and containers into a trash bag and carry them out. If foil-lined wrappers are burned, the foil remains in the fire. Initially blackened, it is hard to see and messy to retrieve and carry out. After one or two rainstorms, scorched foil is washed clean and shiny, then blown by winds out into the surrounding area to accumulate as part of a permanent legacy of debris.

7. Consider stopping by the office of the land-management agency on the way back from the outing to present the trash your group has collected. If this isn't convenient, you might send in a few photographs of the group and the bags of litter you've collected. Organized groups are often criticized by individuals and small private parties because of real or imagined overuse of certain resources, so this action is a public relations gesture designed to better the image of organized groups in the eyes of managers and the public.

Sanitation

The disposal of human wastes is primarily a social concern. The ecological impacts of human waste disposal are rarely significant, except in certain exceptionally fragile or overused sites where water supplies may be sensitive to excessive input of nutrients. Social problems relate to both health and aesthetics; many diseases are carried by feces, contaminated insects, or water supplies, and aesthetic concerns range from odors and unpleasant sights to the delights of finding oneself walking through a "mine field" near a camp.

The extent of the potential problems is determined mainly by the degree of use and the elevation of the site. At high elevation sites, biodegradation typically proceeds at a much slower pace than at lower elevations. From sea level to elevations as high as 3,000 feet (900 meters), in temperate climates at middle latitudes, biodegradation of organic matter, such as fecal wastes, is relatively rapid. At high elevations this is not the case. In middle altitudes of 6,000 feet (1,800 meters), for example, organic material may take six times longer to decompose than at sea level. Above 6,000 feet, the rate of biodegradation declines rapidly.

Unfortunately, many of our wilderness areas are at relatively high elevations. High rates of use and a slow rate of biodegradation of wastes often result in buildups that all too often reach water supplies. Deserts present a different problem. Because there is little organic matter in the soil, microorganisms that are needed to break down fecal material are few or absent. Fecal waste dissipates very slowly and often filters through the ground following natural drainage systems.

Outhouses and chemical toilets are rarely adequate solutions, since most outhouses eventually drain into water supplies and because such facilities usually end up being filled more with garbage than with sewage. In addition, such facilities are only used by a few people, unless they are very close at hand, and/or when there are so many people they become essential for privacy. When camping out in the backcountry, how far will the typical camper go out of his/her way to use an outhouse? How far if it is dark and no one is around? Most people prefer the bushes to an outhouse full of creepy crawling things and an unpleasant odor.

Suggestions

Several steps can be taken to minimize health risks and aesthetic problems related to sanitation.

1. When possible, minimize the amount of fecal waste and urine deposited in the wilderness. This doesn't mean teaching techniques of self-control—what we have in mind is using the facilities at home or at trail heads, considering day hikes or shorter visits to sensitive areas, and keeping food intake moderate on longer outings.

2. Reduce impact on sensitive sites by taking appropriate steps outside of the sensitive areas and at lower or higher sites.

3. Carefully assess the possibility of contamination of water supplies, and issue clear directions to participants. Remember that, in many areas, especially at high elevations or in glacially scoured areas, the bedrock may be near the surface. Rain or spring-snow melt can easily wash water into the water supplies, so note drainage patterns!

4. Select campsites that are near desirable toilet sites and well away from bodies of water. Some land managers specify 200 feet (60 meters) or more. This is because it is well known that, in the middle of the night, most campers are not going to stumble 200 feet off into the bushes unless required to. If tent partners are tolerant, they are more likely to take about two giant steps away from the tent. It is necessary, therefore, to place the camp itself in a carefully selected place vis-à-vis sanitation.

5. Discuss procedures clearly and openly with all participants. If a latrine is used, explain how to find it and how to use it. Usually, however, latrines are not a good idea unless the site is at low elevation, has a very thick (2-3 foot) duff layer, and does not drain into any water supplies. Cat holes are generally superior and are almost always the best solution at high elevations. Like a cat, scratch a shallow depression, no more than a few inches, into the duff. This insures that the fecal matter will be within the upper level where biologic activity can begin the process of biodegradation. Afterwards cover the spot with the scratched-out material. Small logs or rocks can also be temporarily moved and the space beneath used. This is a considerate thing to do in places where others may walk later.

In a desert environment, surface disposal is often the best solution, *ecologically*; however, the desiccated human feces will remain in view to other visitors for a long time. Humans do not find viewing the feces of their own kind with the same interest that they view those of the wild animals that are native to the region. The optimal solution is use of shallow cat holes where the high temperatures can destroy pathogens fairly quickly.

6. Toilet paper, if brought along, should be used sparingly, then ignited. The unused portions will burn, and the rest will be disposed of by insects and other decomposers. *Be sure that the duff isn't ignited too.* In many areas, there is so much organic matter (leaves and small roots) that burning toilet paper creates the beginnings of underground smoldering fires! Consider disposing of toilet paper in double plastic bags and disposing of the contents when you get back home. In all cases, sanitary pads and tampons should be disposed of that way. Also, consider using natural toilet paper, including soft leaves, fallen bark, pine cones, moss, and snow. They aren't as uncomfortable as they may sound.

Figure 4.3 illustrates methods of handling human waste.

Food and Water Wastes

Disposal of waste water has more ecological than sociological implications. In addition to impact on the ecological balance of the land and water resources, however, the sight of soap suds and scum on the surfaces of small lakes is aesthetically unpleasant.

Suggestions

Large plastic bags are good for garbage. Burn the burnable if you are using a fire pan. Do not burn plastic, Styrofoam™, or aluminum foil. The rest of the garbage may be segregated into recyclable and nonrecyclable, placed in double or reinforced bags to prevent puncture and loss, then carried in the pack or watercraft.

Noise and Visual Disturbance

Many users of natural areas do not understand that noises can carry for long distances. Radios, dogs, and clanking pots and pans can sometimes be heard for more than a mile, and some users

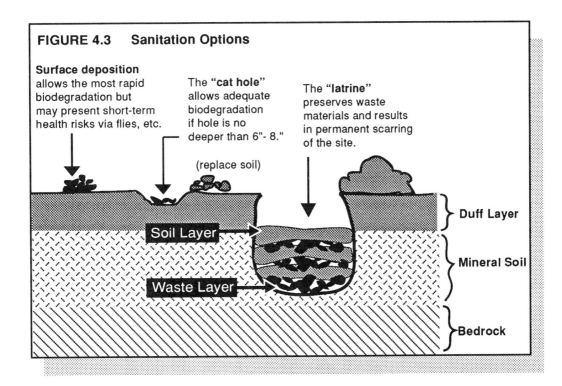

FIGURE 4.3   Sanitation Options

don't seem to understand that most backcountry users do not want to be disturbed by the sounds of other users. Even a loud conversation can disturb people in nearby campsites.

In a primitive natural setting used for backpacking, bright, obtrusive shades are disturbing to those who want to "get away from it all." To many people, bright colors are reminiscent of the neon-lit urban environment left behind and are antithetical to the greens and blues and browns of the natural world. Other visual impacts include campfire rings, litter, broken branches, and any evidence of disregard for the natural environment that impairs the visual harmony of the outdoors.

Suggestions

When possible, campers today should buy and use tents and tarps in earth tones so as not to disturb others with incongruent colors. Leaders might well hold discussions on the merit of brightly colored tents that can be seen from higher elevations. Is there value in seeing the campsite from a distance, or can the group rely on their own navigational skills to return to camp without the aid of colors that are incongruent with the natural surroundings?

Pets and Beasts of Burden

There are a number of serious ecological and sociological impacts related to the presence of dogs, horses, mules, burros, llamas, and other pets and beasts of burden in natural areas. Dogs can harass wildlife, pollute water supplies, and disturb human users by barking and, in some cases, through their very presence, as some people do not like dogs. Dogs can also be a nuisance and a hazard on ski trails. Horses and other beasts of burden can cause extensive damage to trails, campsites, and meadows. Wet trails can be rendered almost impassable to foot traffic, and campgrounds can be turned into horse-fly and manure-ridden wastelands. Hoofed animals tied to trees paw nervously, exposing and abrading the soil and the roots, and inviting plant infections. Like humans, grazing animals tend to eat all of their favorite foods first. If animals are hobbled, or if tether

posts are not moved frequently, the animals will consume all of their favorite vegetation first, often decimating fragile plant populations.

Suggestions

Dogs may or may not be allowed by the policies of the agency managing the area in question, e.g., National Park backcountry and wilderness areas and most groomed cross-country ski trails. If they are allowed, there are several things one can do to minimize adverse impacts. First and foremost, dogs should be considered for wilderness and backcountry travel if, and only if, they will remain in control at all times. This means that the dog needs to be very well-trained so that firm control is maintained verbally or by hand signals or that the dog is restrained by a leash. Dogs are free-roaming and inquisitive by nature, and their carnivorous nature and resemblance to coyotes and wolves does not endear them to local wildlife populations. Dog owners also need to be sensitive to the effects of barking or howling. Such sounds carry for long distances and can be highly disturbing to wildlife as well as to human users. Puppies and dogs prone to barking should be left at home and, under no circumstances, should dogs be tied in camp while the owners are away on a hike or climb. Even dogs who don't bark at home usually bark when left in a strange camp. They seem to feel completely abandoned.

No dog should be taken to an area where grizzly bears may be found, as grizzlies have been known to chase dogs. Serious injuries have resulted when dogs being chased by grizzlies have sought refuge behind the legs of their owners.

Bears aren't the only thing a dog may bring back to the campsite. Since the dog runs randomly through plant life, many a dog owner, who has carefully avoided all the poison ivy or poison oak in the area will develop a serious case of the dermatitis after stroking the apparently clean pet. Anyone who has accompanied a dog near water knows that dogs can hardly resist the odor of dead fish. After rolling in a week-old dead trout, the dog returns to the campsite bearing a long-lasting and foul odor that is almost impossible to get rid of. Other serious problems include the chance meeting with a skunk or the terrible encounter with a porcupine that may inflict hundreds of quills into the dog's mouth, body, and feet. Taking a dog home to the vet instead of finishing the trip is no one's idea of a successful outing.

Now that *Giardia lamblia* has become a widely distributed menace, there is a new concern about dogs. The domestic dog and its wild relatives are among the animals known to carry Giardia. It is, therefore, important to keep dog's fecal matter away from lakes and streams, just as it is necessary with human fecal matter. Many dogs also carry Parvovirus which can be picked up by other animals. There is evidence that the sharp decline of the wolf population on Isle Royale National Park was caused by domestic dogs carrying this virus. In spite of the fact that dogs are prohibited on the island, it is known that unthinking people who visit by yacht or cruiser, frequently go ashore and take their dogs with them in order to give the pets a respite from the cramped quarters of the boat. It is believed that one or more dogs carried the Parvovirus ashore and it was picked up by the wolves, almost wiping out the entire colony before they developed their own immunity.

Again, this relates back to control. If one is unwilling to follow the policies of the agency and/or does not have or is unwilling to exert sufficient control over the behavior of the dog, then the animal should not be allowed on the outing. From a social perspective and simply as a common courtesy, one should also consult the other members of the party to ensure that no one objects to the presence of the animal.

Finally, and of equally importance, is the issue of whether or not the dog can enjoy the trip. Many dogs are simply not up to the rigors of hiking or backpacking. The dog should be over two-years-old, in fit condition, and able to withstand the weather. Many a hiker's dog has succumbed to heat or cold. Short-haired dogs and even many long-haired varieties are not able to withstand either prolonged heat or periods of cold rain. Many dogs have become dehydrated and died on the trail. If one must take a dog on a trip, extra water must be carried because dogs require more water than humans to sustain their needs.

The domestic dog is not as hardy as its wild counterpart. In addition to the weather, dogs are also vulnerable to a variety of discomforts and injuries for which city dwellers many be poorly prepared. Most dogs have relatively tender feet. Rocky trails or spring and early summer snowfields may abrade the dog's footpads over a surprisingly short distance. It is not unusual to see bloody footprints of dogs out for their first hike of the year. Long-haired dogs are especially vulnerable to burrs and grass seeds. The dog will naturally try to bite these and pull them from the fur, which is painful in itself and can be lethal if seeds, like those of certain grasses, become lodged in the throat. In any case, the tedious process of deburring a dog is not pleasant for either party. Pet owners might consider procuring a dog first-aid kit from the veterinarian before taking animals for prolonged trips.

Summary

One (perhaps the most important) outcome of outdoor recreation is the development of a sense of stewardship, a sense of caring for the land, and a commitment to protecting the land from damage. Because no one knows how to determine the fine line between land of good quality and land of poor quality, the outdoor leader must be careful that the impact of the group does not to approach the peak of carrying capacity. Evidence of change in quality and return to a state of quality is difficult if not impossible to measure.

It is the responsibility of the outdoor-pursuit leader to practice a strong environmental ethic and to teach participants to do likewise. Caring for the natural environment includes understanding the concept of carrying capacity from both the ecological and sociological points of view and practicing minimum-impact camping techniques. Developing an attitude of stewardship for the land is one of the major goals of outdoor leaders. Participants need to understand how to prevent soil compaction and abrasion and how to avoid altering the quality of water, plant, and animal resources. Furthermore, they must understand the social problems of litter, sanitation, waste water and food, noise and

visual disturbances, and pets and beasts of burden. They must learn how to leave the natural
environment as nearly natural as possible. Most
participants will begin to appreciate the issues
if they are clearly explained.

The recommendations are many; yet, if followed, become an ingrained environmental
ethic and, to some, an irrepressible way of life.
Following these recommendations will make a
difference in the quality of both the environment
and the outdoor experiences both now and for
years to come.

References

Cockrell, D. (Ed.). (1991). *The wilderness
educator: The Wilderness Education Association curriculum guide.* Merrillville, IN:
ICS Books, Inc.

Cole, D. N. (1990). Some principles to guide
wilderness campsite management. In D. W.
Lime (Ed.) *Managing America's enduring
wilderness resource: Proceedings of the
Conference.* (September 1989). Minneapolis, MN.

Ford, P. (1991). *Take a new bearing.*
Martinsville, IN: American Camping
Association.

Frissell, S., & Stankey, G. H. (October 1972).
*Wilderness environmental quality: Search
for social and ecological harmony.* Paper
presented at the annual meeting, Society of
American Foresters, Hot Springs, AR.

Greist, D. A. (1975). Risk zoning: A recreation management system and method of
measuring carrying capacity. *Journal of
Forestry, 73*(11), 711-714.

Greist, D. A. (1976). The carrying capacity of
public wild land recreation areas: Evaluation of alternative measures. *Journal of
Leisure Research. 8*(2), 123-128.

Hendee, J. C., Stankey, G. H., & Lucas, R. C.
(1990). *Wilderness management. (2nd
ed.).* Golden, CO: Fulcrum Publishing Co.

Hampton, B., & Cole, D. (1988). *Soft paths:
How to enjoy the wilderness without harm-
ing it.* Harrisburg, PA: Stackpole Books.

Hart, J. (1977). *Walking softly in the wilderness.* San Francisco, CA: Sierra Club
Books.

Leopold, A. (1966). *Sand County almanac
and sketches from here and there.* London,
England: Oxford University Press.

Lime, D. W., & Stankey, G. H. (1971). Carrying capacity: Maintaining outdoor recreation quality. *Forest Recreation Proceedings.* Upper Darby, PA: USFS, Northeast
Range and Experiment Station.

Lucas, R. C. (1973). Wilderness: A management framework. *Journal of Soil and
Water Conservation, 28*(4), 150-154.

Manning, H. (1972). *Backpacking: One step
at a time.* Seattle, WA: Recreational Equipment, Inc. Press.

Marion, J., Cole, D., & Reynolds, D. (1985).
Limits of acceptable change: A framework
for assessing carrying capacity. *Park
Science, 6*(1): 9-11.

Meyer, K. (1989). *How to s—t in the woods.*
Berkeley, CA: Ten Speed Press.

Nash, R. (1967). *Wilderness and the American
mind.* New Haven, CT: Yale University
Press.

Penny, R. (1989). *The whitewater source
book.* Birmingham, AL: Menasha Press.

Royte, E. (April 1992). She knows if you've
been bad or good. *Outside,* pp. 70-86, ff.

Stankey, G. H. (1971). Wilderness: Carrying capacity and quality. *Naturalist, 22*(3), pp. 7-13.

Stankey, G. H. (1972). A strategy for the definition and management of wilderness quality. In J. V. Krutilla (Ed.) *Natural Environment: Studies in theoretical and applied analysis.* Baltimore, MD: Johns Hopkins University Press.

Stankey, G. H. (November 1973). *Visitor perception of wilderness recreation carrying capacity.* USDA Forest Service Research Paper, INT-142. Washington, DC: Department of Agriculture.

Stankey, G. H., & Baden, J. (July 1977). *Rationing wilderness use: Methods, problems and guidelines.* USDA Forest Service Research Paper, INT-192. Washington, DC: Department of Agriculture.

VanDerWege, D. (Summer 1989). Low-impact camping: Loving nature softly. *Outdoor Ethics, 8*(3), pp. 1, 7.

part two

SKILLS & KNOWLEDGE SPECIFIC TO THE OUTDOOR LEADER

UNDERSTANDING HUMAN NEEDS

Leading people in outdoor pursuits entails knowledge and skill in two very diverse aspects of responsibility. Outdoor pursuits and their inherent skills may appear to be the major focal point of the program; however, a more important consideration is the second aspect of the responsibility: *leading human beings* in an adverse, and often fragile, environment. The needs of the environment as related to use by humans were discussed in Chapter Four, "Care of the Environment"; this chapter deals with the needs of humans. In many ways, the activity, be it skiing, hiking, rafting, or any other, is a means to an end—end being human growth and development, enjoyment, and participation in the leisure experience. It is thus apparent that the leader of outdoor pursuits is really a leader of *participants* in outdoor pursuits and, as such, should be aware of the physiological and psychological needs of human beings.

The novice leader may be so over zealous about the outdoors and the activities in which the followers will participate that the needs of the followers may become secondary. The result can be frustration for the leader and reduction in the quality of the experience for the participant, leading to frustration on one end of a continuum and fatality on the other end.

The primary concern of all leaders—regardless of program—must be to meet, at least, the basic needs of each participant. Leader-determined goals and objectives are vital in some situations, but must be secondary to individual requirements. If the needs of all individuals are met, at least partly, the chances of the group goals being reached become a reality. If the needs of one individual are not met, at least minimally, the progress of the entire group could be deterred. There are, of course, times when meeting all the demands of one individual could create problems for the entire group, and compromises must be made to insure that the goals of *everyone* are met minimally but not optimally. People's needs can be categorized in several ways, but for the application of the material in this text, the writers believe physiological and psychological groupings may be the most easily understood and applied.

One of the most widely quoted views on human needs is that of Abraham Maslow, who developed a hierarchy of needs, each based upon the fulfillment of the previous one. At the base of Maslow's hierarchy is the need for life-sustaining elements. This is a physiological demand—a demand for the things upon which life depends. In the human, life continuation depends upon adequate oxygen, maintenance of body warmth, adequate sleep, liquid, and food. (These will be discussed in greater depth later in this chapter.) After the physiological, Maslow identifies the psychological need for security and safety which, in his analysis, is basically the freedom from harassment. The third requirement is that of belonging and acceptance which is manifested in the gregarious and caring nature of people. Following the need to belong is the need for self-respect and respect from others. The fifth and final human need is the one for self-actualization, which Maslow feels is not possible to define sharply but is an "ongoing actualization of potentials, capacities and talents, as fulfillment of mission (or call, fate, destiny, or vocation), as a fuller knowledge of, and acceptance of, the person's own intrinsic nature, as an unceasing trend toward unity, integrity or synergy within the person." (Maslow, A., *Toward a Psychology of Being,* 1980, p. 25.)

Analysis of the foregoing descriptors reveals that self-actualization is closely related to the recognized goals of the leisure experience discussed in Chapter One. It may be that it is through participation in leisure activities that self-actualization has its greatest potential. With Maslow's hierarchy in mind, analysis of physiological and psychological needs can take place as they apply to outdoor pursuits.

Physiological Needs

Physiological needs are discussed first because, if these are not fulfilled, the individual could become so disabled and weak that death could result. In many cases, physiological deprivation may not be reversed, while deprivation of psychological needs may be reversed. Physiological needs may be ordered according to the possibility of death caused by total deprivation. Beginning with shortness of survival time, these needs include an adequate air supply, adequate shelter, sufficient drinking water, adequate rest and sleep, an adequate quantity of appropriate food and, in some cases, exercise of body organs and systems. All of the foregoing are essential to the production of metabolic energy and/or to the maintenance of a viable body temperature. These priorities are important to remember when preparing survival kits, as will be discussed in Chapter Six, "Preparation for Survival."

People need air, water, certain nutrients, and an environment that allows maintenance of body temperatures within narrow limits. In our normal, everyday lives, we seldom consider these needs except momentarily when hunger or thirst compels us to seek food or drink. Setting out into the wilderness means leaving behind the warm and secure home, the supermarkets, and the city water system, and asking our bodies to perform with great efficiency, sometimes in harsh weather at high altitude, sustained by whatever food and shelter can be carried in a pack, and by natural ground-water sources. On one day excursions at modest altitudes in the summer, this is rarely a major problem. Most outdoor enthusiasts, however, want the option of trips of weekend length or longer, sometimes at relatively high elevations or in extremely arid deserts. Comfort and, in the long run, safety depend upon an understanding of basic physical needs and how to obtain them in backcountry settings.

Air

Most people take air for granted and live at or near sea level. As one ascends in elevation, an adequate supply of oxygen cannot be assumed. The efficiency with which the body takes up oxygen has much to do with the pressure of the air we breathe. At 5,000 feet (1,500 meters), a common elevation for ski areas and trailheads, the percentage of oxygen in the air is essentially the same as at sea level, but the air pressure is significantly less (as may be noticed in a bulging water bottle). Most people experience the first signs of hypoxia, an inadequate supply of oxygen, at about this altitude. For most, fortunately, adverse symptoms are barely noticeable, except for shortness of breath upon heavy exertion. The most likely sensation is, in fact, one of exhilaration—that delightful mountain high that, like other "highs," is actually a function of mental impairment, in this case, caused by an inadequate oxygen supply to the brain. As elevations increase, the effects of hypoxia increase and are compounded by other physiological responses to lowered air pressure. Above an elevation of 5,000 feet (1,500 meters), acute mountain sickness (AMS) may begin to appear, and, at higher elevations high altitude pulmonary edema (HAPE) and cerebral edema (CE) can be life threatening. Altitude-related ailments are discussed in greater detail in Chapter Seven, "First Aid in Outdoor Emergencies."

Body Temperatures

The human body has little tolerance for temperature variation. The normal internal body core temperature is maintained at a constant 98.6°F (37°C) plus or minus a few degrees. Should the body core rise above 105°F (40°C) or descend to lower than 85°F (29°C), serious physiological problems, including death, can occur.

Body temperature, hyperthermia, hypothermia, equipment for protection from the elements of weather and some related materials on water and food are discussed in depth in Chapter Six, "Preparation for Survival," and Chapter Seven, "First Aid in Outdoor Emergencies."

Shelter

The need for shelter is related to the need to maintain a normal body core temperature. Wind, precipitation, and intense sun all can take their toll on the temperature of the body. Wind promotes convective heat loss and accelerates evaporation. Precipitation cools without evaporation and greatly reduces the efficiency of the insulating materials commonly used in clothing and bedding. Sun desiccates and can raise body temperature. Excessive solar radiation can contribute to hyperthermic conditions and, especially at higher elevations, can cause minor short-term and major long-term damage to skin and eyes. Shelter from the elements is, then, a basic human requirement. Shelter is discussed in greater length in Chapter Six, "Preparation for Survival."

Water

Problems related to the consumption of water probably cause more distress than the sum total of all other concerns discussed in this chapter. People think little about water in everyday life! It is readily available, fresh from the kitchen tap, filtered and otherwise purified by the city. Furthermore, many people don't drink very much plain water because their foods tend to be high in water content. There is also a great tendency to consume many other types of liquid such as soda, tea, coffee, juice, beer, wine, and a lot of other modified forms of water. In the United States, the consumption of soft drinks far surpasses that of plain water!

Since, during an average day of light work in town, the average person loses about two liters of water through urination, perspiration, and respiration, that amount must be replaced. The average diet contains about three cups (750 ml) of water taken in liquid water form, and we gain another cup (250 ml) through the metabolism of foods, a process in which water is one of the end products. That leaves about one quart (about one liter) to replace each day. That is only about four cups, not much when you add all the sips from the drinking fountain, colas, and other sources on a typical day.

What happens when people head for the hills? First, the increase in elevation (and resulting lowered air pressure) results in a more rapid water loss. Several other factors can also increase loss of water. Low humidity, high temperature, and wind all contribute. Increasing the level of exertion dramatically increases the losses. Overall, one is probably going to lose at *least* three quarts (three liters) of water per day during moderate outdoor activity. This means that even if the diet provides a full liter of water in and from solid food, it will be necessary to consume at least *two* liters of fluids per day or double the amount needed on a normal day in town. It is common in hot, dry, or strenuous circumstances to lose four or more liters per day, and one of the authors once had to abandon a climb in Mexico when two gallons (almost eight liters) per day proved insufficient. While the rate of water loss can be moderated by avoiding excessive perspiration, avoiding daytime travel in hot deserts, or by the use of vapor barriers, the daily losses in typical outdoor activities are inevitably greater than in normal city life.

In the short run, a small amount of unreplaced water is not of much concern. In a day of ski touring, if only a liter of water is replaced, the only symptoms may be less energy and greater sensitivity to cold. Chances are that thirst will inspire replacement of part of that deficit before turning in for the night, and a few glasses of water in the morning will complete the job.

But what if one is out for several days? Here is where the trouble begins. On most outings, water is lost at a much higher rate than usual, the food one carries tends to contain less free water, and water sources may be hard to find. In the winter or in cold conditions, the situation is further complicated by a lack of interest in drinking (in part due to a true lack of thirst caused by mild hypothermia), the freezing of water bottles, or frozen water sources that require slow and fuel-consumptive steps to melt ice. A common result is dehydration, and a surprising number of hikers, climbers, skiers, and river runners suffer from this condition. One widespread myth is that thirst is an accurate indicator of one's need for water. The thirst mechanism works quite well for small deficiencies, but unfortunately it tends to sound an alarm only intermittently and is easily silenced by a small amount of water. The occasional sip of water, every half hour or so, usually eliminates almost all sensation of thirst. Thus, one can gradually become more and more seriously dehydrated without feeling constantly thirsty.

What happens when one becomes dehydrated? Aside from weighing less (the one result that some people seem to enjoy), one is likely to feel weak and sometimes nauseated. Wilderness rangers and others who deal with large numbers of backcountry travelers report that the overwhelming majority of complaints of illness among these travelers involves feelings of weakness and slight nausea, and that almost all of these people respond almost miraculously to a substantial dose of water and a little rest. Acute Mountain Sickness may also be involved at high elevations, but the role and frequency of dehydration seem clear.

Beyond simple discomfort, dehydration can have some very serious consequences. In dehydration, blood volume is decreased, blood chemistry is altered, and the oxygen-carrying capacity of the blood is impaired. Perhaps the most important consequence is a reduction of

metabolic efficiency. This results in weakness and limits the body's ability to produce heat. In a winter environment, this is an especially serious effect since efficient metabolic heat production is essential. Other effects include a predisposition to thrombophlebitis as a result of the thickening of the blood. Thrombophlebitis is blood clotting, usually in the leg, which can result in a coronary, pulmonary, or cerebral embolism if a clot breaks loose and travels to the heart, lungs, or brain. Dehydration also upsets the body's electrolyte balance and hinders elimination of wastes. Women should be especially careful to maintain good hygiene and a substantial urine volume since they are especially susceptible to bladder infections—a common and frustrating condition predisposed to by dehydration.

How can dehydration be recognized? Among the best known signs are sunken eyes and dark circles. Another sign is changes in urine color. If the urine noticeably decreases in volume, becomes darker or more intense in color, or begins to cause a burning sensation, one should suspect dehydration.

Prevention of dehydration is not as easy as it might seem. This is due partly to lack of awareness of how much water is needed to maintain hydration, partly to the inefficiency of the thirst response, and partly to the difficulty of obtaining adequate supplies of safe water in some backcountry settings. It is essential to acknowledge the importance of maintaining hydration, to understand the quantity of water needed to replace losses, and to willfully override the temptation to rely solely upon thirst as an indicator of need. A good rule of thumb is to drink frequently during periods of activity and to double the amount that seems to satisfy thirst. That is, drink what seems to be enough, then down another equal quantity. This practice should result in reasonably frequent, "clear and copious" urination. When the water isn't very palatable due to purification processes, or for those who simply don't care for straight water, there are many commercially available flavorings. Some contain various electrolytes and other compounds that may (or may not) provide some additional, if marginal, value.

Sources of Water

Even if one is aware of the danger of dehydration, obtaining the necessary water can be difficult. In dry areas, water may be hard to find, and, in the winter, the price of water may be high in terms of fuel consumption and time. Under either of these conditions, the problem can be partially avoided on short trips by carrying water from town. On longer trips, the weight of the needed water usually makes it impractical to carry enough water from town. A good plan on longer trips is to drink as much as possible when in camp (when one presumably has access to water and time to purify it properly) and to carry at least a full liter of safe water from camp each day. In this way, one is assured of an adequate safe supply and, less tempted by marginal, or unsafe, water sources encountered along the way.

When relying on natural local ground-water supplies, it is always advisable to study maps, and consult guidebooks and knowledgeable users of the area before departure. Keep in mind that maps are only approximations based upon interpretations of aerial photographs and that water supplies vary widely with the seasons; that lake on the map may be a meadow in the dry season. The creek that the local guide has been drinking from for twenty years may be heavily polluted. Water pollution is variable and is very hard to predict, and the local guide may be immune or asymptomatic to local pollutants, or just very lucky. In backcountry water supplies, there are many potential pollutants ranging from soaps and detergents to an array of organisms including viruses, bacteria, and organisms like *Giardia lamblia* and *Entamoeba histolytica*.

How can backcountry travelers avoid water pollution? The answer, for all practical purposes, is that avoidance of all dangerous pollutants is virtually impossible almost everywhere that one is likely to lead an outing. Well into the sixties, it was still possible to find many safe ground water sources, at least throughout the western states and provinces of the United States and Canada. Unfortunately, this has changed dramatically over the last few decades. The current and cumulative effects of increased

human usage on shrinking backcountry areas have resulted in widespread pollution of ground water supplies. Although by no means the only culprit, *Giardia lamblia* is perhaps the best known. Until about 30 years ago, this flagellate was rare in the United States and Canada, even though it was common in many other parts of the world. It was probably introduced by tourists and has rapidly spread throughout North America. It is spread through fecal contamination by humans, dogs, and such ubiquitous indigenous species as the beaver. Adolescent beavers carry the organism as they seek new streams to colonize.

Whatever purification system is used, it is best to start with the purest possible water. What are the best sources of water in the backcountry? Perhaps the most obvious choice is fresh rain or snow. Normally, these provide a very safe supply, if common sense is applied. The authors have seen snow that is: (1) grey from pollutants in eastern Europe; (2) too sour with natural acids to drink, downwind from an active Japanese volcano; and (3) too radioactive to handle safely on Mt. Hood in Oregon after the Chernobyl accident thousands of miles away.

Old snow can be safe but must be used with caution. By late spring, most snowfields contain an abundance of plant and animal life. Throughout the midlatitudes of both hemispheres, one of the most common problems is "watermelon snow." This red algae typically blooms at elevations just above timberline and can result in streaks and splotches of intense watermelon-pink coloration by early summer. The pink color is due to the presence of phenolphthalein, a powerful laxative used in some commercial preparations. Boiling is quite useless unless one prefers *hot* laxatives. Small amounts of the algae infiltrate streams and lakes fed by alpine snowfields, and this probably contributes to the frequency of mild diarrhea so commonly experienced by summer hikers in the high country. More than one youngster has munched a bright pink snowball with predictable, and prompt, results.

When ground water is considered, the choices (in the order listed) are usually springs, ponds, lakes, and streams. A deep spring is usually the best choice, as such a source generally has the smallest chance of being contaminated. Care must be taken, however, to assess the terrain uphill of the spring to be sure that no likely sources of pollution exist. The second best choice is likely to be a small pond with no evident human use or sources of pollution nearby, and no surface stream entry.

To understand *why* one must realize that, as a human, one is trying to avoid human diseases. These diseases are, with a few exceptions, transmitted via the fecal tract of humans or of domestic or wild animals. The organisms, mainly bacteria and viruses, thrive in the dark and special environment of the fecal tract. The pond is often a good water supply choice because: (1) with no incoming stream, fecal contamination is unlikely; (2) what contamination does reach the pond will be subjected to intense insolation (irradiation by sunlight) and will likely be killed; (3) the pond is shallow and oxygen can permeate the waters and kill many types of pathogens; (4) surviving pathogens encounter competition in the pond and will likely be consumed in the active food chain there; and (5) since the pond is relatively warm, the few surviving "bad guys" will grow (that is, move through their life cycles) faster than in colder waters. This is good, since while they "age" faster, reproduction is inhibited in this strange environment, so "die-off" occurs more quickly. The overall process is called the "reservoir effect," which has been known and used for centuries as a means of purifying water. Certainly there are parts of the world where nasty organisms may infest any pond, and, even at middle latitudes, one must be sure that people or dogs haven't been in or near the pond.

Purification, as stated before, is always the safest course. If you can't purify the water, though, such a pond is a fairly safe bet. You may have to suck the water through your teeth to hold back the frog eggs, but then a little extra protein shouldn't hurt.

The next best choice is a large lake. Here, one may be lucky to find water that has been in the lake long enough for the reservoir effect to have reduced the level of contamination. On the other hand, lake hydraulics are complex. The water of a highly polluted incoming stream may circulate near the surface, or currents may yield seepage fresh from a lakeside campsite. Since lakes are colder and deeper than ponds, the effects of sunlight and oxidation are reduced, and die-off is slower.

The last choice, which should always be highly suspect, is the surface stream. One of the most prevalent outdoor myths is that a mile of rapidly flowing stream purifies the water. A number of studies have shown that only slight improvement results from the effects of even miles of rapids and falls, especially when the water is very cold. In cold water, the "bad guys" live a long time, and, if the stream is fast, they may travel a *long* way. The dilution factor may be in one's favor, but it is a big gamble to drink from any surface stream.

In many popular outdoor areas, there are fast, clear, cold streams that are badly polluted as a result of the accumulation of human fecal matter in popular valleys. Even in areas not often frequented by people, there is always the possibility that a surface stream contains *Giardia*, an animal carcass, or some other contaminant worthy of a purification tablet or two.

One last thought. When hiking in an area where streams or spring sources could include agricultural or timber harvesting areas, be very careful. A wide array of deadly sprays is used in these areas and contamination of water supplies is inevitable. The danger continues all year long. High water and rains flood more contaminants into the waterways, while low flow may result in less dilution.

Water Purification

Unless you are melting clean fresh snow, the only way to be *sure* of the water supply is to purify. There are several methods in common use among backpackers; yet, all seem to be rather poorly understood or, at least, inadequately utilized. Boiling can provide safe drinking water, assuming the pollutants are living organisms. As can be seen in Figure 5.1, boiling is effective against all major types of pathogens likely to be found in ground water. This figure also shows the effect of common treatments on microorganisms.

FIGURE 5.1   The Effectiveness of Heat, Halogens, and Filters Against Various Pathogens

	BACTERIA	VIRUSES	PROTOZOAN CYSTS	PARASITE EGGS & LARVAE
BOILING	yes[1]	yes[1]	yes	yes
FILTRATION	yes[2]	no	yes	yes
HALOGENATION	yes	yes[3]	yes[3]	no

no = Not effective for field purification
yes = Very effective
yes [1] = Effective but requires longer boiling
yes [2] = Must have pore size less than 0.2 micrometers to catch enteric bacteria
yes [3] = Effective, if proper dosage, pH, and treatment times are used

The usual mistake made in boiling the water is failure to boil it for an adequate length of time. Too often, people seem to think that boiling the water (as a purification process) simply means bringing the water to a boil. At sea level, one may be justified in feeling confident after one or two minutes; however sterile water cannot be assured unless it is boiled for five minutes. At higher elevations, one needs to boil the water somewhat longer to achieve the same effect, as the boiling point of water is reduced by approximately 1.8°F (1°C) for every 1,000 feet (300 m) of elevation increase. A common mistake is failure to decontaminate all containers. Some people empty their water bottles into a big pot, boil it for awhile, and then pour it back into the same bottles without boiling the bottles. It depends upon how much risk one is willing to take. It is instructive to watch how a past victim of *Giardiasis* treats his/her water supply. *Very carefully!*

Many people prefer to use halogens, iodine crystals, or a bromine or chlorine compound such as Halazone or common bleach. These compounds work well against bacteria. Viruses and protozoan cysts, including *Giardia*, are more resistant, especially to chlorine; however, any of the halogens can be effective *if* they are used properly. The labels on the bottles of most

commercial products may be misleading as treatment recommendations assume clear water at 70°F (21°C). Water containing silt or visible organic material may require additional treatment time, and/or additional quantities of the chemical, or both. Water temperature also affects treatment time and/or dosage. For example, for most halogen water purification compounds, it is necessary either to double the amount of chemical or double the treatment time for clear water at 40°F (4.4°C). Halogen cannot be relied upon to kill parasite eggs or larvae such as may be found in surface water in undeveloped countries and in many warmer climates.

A third and increasingly popular method is filtration. Here again, the method is often misunderstood and misused. Most of the filters that have recently appeared on the market employ a combination of filtration and chemical (usually iodine) treatment. Many claim to deliver perfectly safe water. Caution is advised since some of the filters in these devices are not small enough to catch Giardia cysts. Some units do have filters fine enough, but those units are sometimes painfully slow. One of the best is the Katadyne pump. It has been around for a long time and is very reliable, though it is a bit slow, rather heavy, and quite costly. Filters alone cannot be expected to capture viruses so it is essential to use them in combination with secondary halogen treatment, especially in undeveloped countries. Figure 5.2 gives suggestions for field treatment of drinking water.

Adequate Rest/Sleep

The human being can go more hours without sleep than many think; however, a lack of sleep is accompanied by reduced muscle energy and reduced mental agility. A participant in outdoor pursuits needs to be alert and in top physical and mental condition to minimize risks. In several cases of death or near disaster by hypothermia, there has been evidence that the victims were fatigued before the trip, a condition which may have been a contributing factor in subsequent unwise and life-threatening decisions and which clearly predisposes one to hypothermia.

It is recommended that all participants have extra sleep before a strenuous trip and that the leader insist on extra rest for himself/herself. At least eight hours of sleep per 24-hour period is recommended for each adult, preferably for one to two weeks in advance of a trip lasting five or more days. On the trip itself, occasional long rests or even midday or midafternoon naps will help the body recover from fatiguing

exercise and prepare it for more. A careful leader recognizes that a tired participant is a normal one at the end of a difficult stretch of terrain or water; however, a fatigued individual whose physiological need for sleep has not been met at the *beginning* of a trip—or even well into the trip—is an individual who may be a hazard to himself/herself as well as to the rest of the group. While most leaders have no control over pre- and post-trip behaviors, part of pre-trip training should stress the responsibility of the individual to self and group for meeting personal physiological needs.

Food

The quality and quantity of the foods people eat determine the limits of their physical well-being and can affect their psychological states. Leaders must understand nutritional needs and be sensitive to the psychological implications of diet. While there is some truth in the old adage that one can live only three minutes without air, three days without water, and three weeks (at least) without food, there are very few situations wherein such desperate extremes need to be considered. That is, we are seldom concerned with the limits of survival. In most cases, air, water, and food are sufficiently abundant to allow us to focus on optimal

---

FIGURE 5.2   Suggestions For Field Treatment of Drinking Water

North American wilderness areas and most developed countries:	Tropical or subtropical areas and most "developing" countries:
CLEAR SURFACE WATER: (there are 3 options) 1. boiling 2. halogenation 3. filtration	**URBAN TAP WATER (clear or cloudy):** (there are 2 options) 1. boiling 2. halogenation
CLOUDY SURFACE WATER: (there are 2 options) 1. boiling 2. sedimentation followed by either halogenation *or* filtration	**ALL SURFACE WATER:** (there are 2 options) 1. boiling 2. filtration followed by halogenation

* See the text for cautions regarding the use of boiling, halogenation, and filtration techniques.

FIGURE 5.3   Approximate Energy Expenditure During an Hour of Activity by a 150 Pound Person With No Pack

ACTIVITY	CALORIES
Sunbathing	80
Walking on smooth level pavement at 2 mph	115
3 mph	160
4 mph	230
Hiking on level but rough trail at 2 mph	175
Cross-country skiing on level track at 2 mph	600
Bicycling on level road at 6 mph	240
Canoeing on still water at 2 mph	180

achievement of program goals which, in turn, equates to providing the sustenance necessary for optional physical and mental performance by all participants and staff.

Food provides substance and energy. The elements and compounds are needed to build and replace body tissues and fuel metabolic furnaces. In the short term, the body is capable of energy output and self-restoration without nutritional input. The food stored normally within the body allows up to several hours of very heavy exertion before replacement becomes essential. The period over which activity can be maintained without consumption of food is largely determined by the level of exercise and the time can be extended to a day or more if energy output is limited to light activity. Thus, as a general rule, the importance of providing a well-balanced diet varies according to the length of the trip. The implications of this will be discussed later in this chapter.

Nutritional Needs

What are the basic nutritional needs? There is no simple answer, as evidenced by the immense volume of scientific and popular writing on the topic. Individual caloric requirements and nutritional needs vary by gender, weight, and a host of other criteria. Caloric needs are measured in calories. For dietary purposes, the "large" calorie is used as the standard energy unit. The "large" calorie is equal to 1000 "small" calories, which are in turn the amount of energy needed to raise one gram (approximately one cubic centimeter) of liquid water one degree Celsius. Figure 5.3 gives the approximate caloric energy expended in one hour of various activities by a 150 pound person with no pack.

The estimates in Figure 5.3 include basal metabolism, which is approximately 1,100 calories per 100 pounds (45 kg) of body weight per day, or 68.75 calories per hour for a 150 pound (68 kg) person. The figures in the table are averages drawn from many sources, some of which disagree by a considerable margin. In practice, such estimates are of little value as they do not reflect the influence of factors such as surface type, equipment design, the fitness and skill level of the individual, environmental conditions, or changes in elevation. For example, carrying 100 pounds (45 kg) of weight (includes body weight and any carried weight) 1,000 feet (305 m) requires about 110 calories, which is equivalent to 198 calories for a 150 pound (68 kg) person carrying a 30 pound pack. Thus, the energy needed for an hour of hiking, at two miles (3.2 km) per hour, could be doubled if 1,000 feet (305 m) are gained, and the energy could be increased by an additional 25 percent or more by an adverse combination of poor footing, lack of skill, or other factors that reduce efficiency.

Estimates of daily caloric needs are somewhat more reliable and useful. They are arrived at by adding basal metabolism, additional energy required for activity, and the specific dynamic action (SDA). The SDA is a measure of the energy released as heat and, therefore, not available to the body for performing work. Assuming an SDA of about 7 percent (it varies from 5 to 12 percent of the caloric value of food), then the total calorie need of a 150 pound (68 kg) person ranges from about 2,800 calories for a typical day of office work to around 4,500 calories per day for strenuous work. Mountain climbing or other particularly demanding activities may consume 5,000 or more calories per day, though this level of activity is unlikely to be maintained over a period of many days.

Fats, Proteins, and Carbohydrates

Other nutritional needs are even more difficult to identify precisely. Fats, proteins, and carbohydrates provide needed nutrients, vitamins, minerals, and fiber. Fats contain the most caloric energy per pound (4,100 calories) as well as fat soluble vitamins. There is much dispute about the amount of total fat that should be included in one's diet and about the effects of saturated, unsaturated and polyunsaturated fats.

Proteins provide the amino acids necessary to the production of body tissues. Various amino acids are needed in rather precise ratios in order to be used by the body to form the new tissue proteins. Some foods, including most animal proteins, are referred to as "complete," while most vegetable proteins are referred to as "incomplete" and so must be combined with certain other vegetable proteins to provide acceptable amino acid ratios. Proteins provide approximately 1,800 calories per pound (816 per kilogram), and about 70 grams (2 ounces or so) are needed every day regardless of the level of exercise.

Carbohydrates include starches, sugars, and cellulose. As a group, carbohydrates are primarily useful as sources of easily, and quickly, available energy, except for cellulose, most of which is indigestible but serves as bulk fiber. Starches digest more rapidly than proteins but not as rapidly as simple sugars. Carbohydrates, like proteins, provide about 1,800 calories per pound.

Food Planning

When planning food requirements, there are several things to consider. The length of the trip is obviously important. Regardless of the intended trip length, it is always wise to include a substantial supply of emergency food as well. This extra supply, at least equal to a large extra lunch, should be stored deep in the pack and, under normal conditions, not touched until safely back at the trailhead. Trip length alone isn't enough to determine the needed quantity of food accurately. It is also necessary to predict the activity levels throughout the period, the average weight of the participants, and the approximate temperatures to be encountered. As a general guideline, plan on providing 15 calories per pound of body weight per day for relatively sedentary activity, 20 calories for moderate activity such as hiking, and 25 calories for strenuous activities such as climbing. Add at least 5 percent for cold weather activities to compensate for the energy needed to makeup for increased heat losses. For example, a 150 pound (68 kg) person engaged in moderately strenuous trail backpacking probably needs about 3,000 calories of energy supply per day in temperate conditions and about 3,150 calories per day in cold weather. A 175 pound (79 kg) mountain climber might need 4,375 calories per day in warm conditions and about 4,600 calories per day in cold conditions.

There are various formulas for calculating the optimal percentages of fats, proteins, and carbohydrates in the diet. Many have been published in reputable outdoor magazines and texts in recent years, and each proposes a different balance. In the dozen examples reviewed by the authors, recommended percentages by weight of fats vary from 11 to 35 percent. Recommendations for proteins varied from 10 to 30 percent, and recommendations for carbohydrates varied from 40 to 61 percent. The broad range, especially for fats and proteins, reflects differences in opinion as to the dietary importance of each type of food, different assumptions of trip duration, exercise level, altitude and temperature, and the extent to which long-term health interests are compromised. For example, at 4,100 calories per pound (1,860 per kilogram), fats are an efficient way to meet caloric needs when weight must be kept to a minimum. On the other hand, fats are harder to digest, especially at higher elevations, and high fat intake over long periods is associated with a host of chronic ailments. It is probably best, at least for trips of short or moderate duration, to plan a diet that closely approximates the normal diet of the participants.

Fats are contained in many foods, including meats, cheese, and nuts, as well as in the more obvious oils, butter, margarine, and lard. They are typically hard to handle, being messy and prone to spoilage in hot weather, and hard to clean from utensils. While desirable on longer and colder trips due to their high caloric density, they become less digestible at higher elevations.

"Complete" proteins are contained in meats, eggs, and dairy products, and "incomplete" proteins are found in grains, legumes (such as beans and peas), and nuts. The utility of incomplete proteins can be substantially increased by combining grains, legumes, and seeds or nuts to provide balanced and complete sets of amino acids. For example, soybeans and rice, beans and corn, and peas and wheat are combinations that yield "complete" arrays of essential amino acids. It is usually easier to pack and store grains, legumes, and nuts than meat, eggs or dairy products; however, dried milk is an easily obtained exception. Bread, pastas, crackers, and cereals all contain both protein and carbohydrates and are excellent sources of each if care is taken to select products that are high in whole grain content and low in fat and sugar.

One should take care not to provide, or to consume, excessive amounts of simple sugars. Many backcountry enthusiasts carry large quantities of high fat/high sugar mixtures commonly known as GORP (for "good old raisins and peanuts") containing the aforementioned items and/or chocolate, dried dates, and a variety of other sweets shunned in everyday life as being too costly or unhealthy. The mixture is usually rationalized as "energy food" (for which

purpose it may be well-suited); however, it is too often consumed by the fistful at each rest stop, "just in case." The resulting stomach upset isn't surprising. The simple sugars, that are so abundant in GORP, can produce a phenomena known as "glycemic swing." By entering the bloodstream very rapidly, they inspire an increase in insulin which, in turn, may cause a rapid reduction in blood sugar to, or below, levels prior to eating the sugar. GORP-like mixtures should contain only modest amounts of sugar and should be eaten in small quantities along with bread and crackers, to forestall hunger pangs and maintain a constant level of energy supply.

The leader needs to consider the ways in which food and meal planning affect the course of events during an outing. It is best to know something about the intended diet before attempting to create a detailed time management plan. If the diet includes foods that need to be cooked, sufficient time must be allocated for cooking. If the diet is high in carbohydrates and relatively low in fats, it will be necessary to eat, or at least to snack, at least every two hours since carbohydrates are digested in about two hours. Groups bent upon accomplishment of a goal that requires optimal output may choose to minimize cooking and rely upon frequent breaks throughout the day. Leaders often find that there is a great advantage to carrying only foods that don't require cooking. The time demands of supervising participant cooking efforts and attending staff meetings may mean that the time needed for cooking chores must be taken from needed sleep or relaxation time.

Whatever the diet and whatever the plan for mealtimes, it is very important that the participants know what to expect. Ideally, they should be part of the process, and, at a minimum, they must be consulted to ensure that any special dietary needs are met. If the participants are expected to provide part or all of their food, it is best to provide clear guidance. This is especially important when beginners are involved or when preparation time, or facilities, are limited.

As mentioned earlier, there are important psychological effects associated with the preparation and consumption of food. For most

people, the enjoyment of food is a central pleasure in life, and mealtimes are important opportunities for social interactions. Given all of the
practical concerns to be dealt with in planning
meals, it is easy to overlook the importance of
palatability. Ideally, the meals need to provide
every participant with sufficient food that is
enjoyable to eat. This is a formidable task for
two people sharing meals on a weekend backpack trip, and palatability can be next to impossible for the leader who must plan meals for a
large group. In general, the more the participants
are involved in planning, providing, and preparing the meals, the happier everyone will be.
When the institution provides the meals, the
cost per meal per participant is usually higher
than when participants provide and prepare their
own meals. Savings on bulk quantities of foods
and other economies of scale are offset by the
costs of labor needed to acquire, store, package,
transport, and prepare the food. Even when
participants carry the food and regular staff
double as chefs, communal meals aren't likely
to save money.

On the other hand, there are many situations,
such as Outward Bound or the National Outdoor
Leadership School extended backcountry programs, where the institution has no choice but
to provide the food. In such cases, the participants generally carry and prepare the food according to institutional guidelines. Youth camps
and most commercial raft guides and horse packers provide and prepare full-meal service for
their clientele. Youth camps do so as a matter
of efficiency, having little or no recourse, while
guides and packers do so because it has become
an integral part of the expectations of those who
patronize such services. While direct involvement in the provision of meals can be costly,
labor intensive, and oftentimes frustrating (it is
impossible to please everyone), it is also potentially profitable and constitutes, for some guides
and packers, a major aspect of the services they
provide.

Other Necessities

Vitamins, which provide the enzymes to help
break down the food into usable or stored energy, are found naturally in most foods, and a
well-balanced menu should preclude a need for
supplementary vitamins. On *long* trips (of several weeks), evidence has been found that vita-
min deficiency can cause irritability, mental
depression, or night blindness. For this reason,
leaders of long trips might consider recommending supplementary vitamins or carrying a
complementary supply. Minerals are water
soluble and found in adequate amounts in meats,
vegetables, and fruits. Like vitamins, however,
it may be wise to carry a supplementary supply
on trips lasting several weeks.

Because of the taste factor and need for enjoyable eating experiences, condiments are considered necessary additions to the menu. Individuals preparing their own meals or groups
cooking together can decide on garlic, paprika,
oregano, lemon pepper, dried green pepper,
dried onions, onion salt, bullion, or a myriad
others spices; each enhances flavor but each is
not equally appreciated by all people. The in-
discriminate use of curry in a casserole may
create a range of emotions from anger and dis-
gust to pure ecstasy. While condiments are
important, wise selection and use is of greater
importance.

The frequency and size of meals is something the leader may choose to plan, advise,
implement, and control for the benefit of the
group. Two rules of thumb may help:

1. Recommend eating small portions of
carbohydrates frequently (several times a day).
They supply immediate energy. Carbohydrates
usually are digested in about two hours. One
should eat twice as many energy units of carbohydrates as all other foods combined.

2. Advise eating proteins and fats at night.
They break down slowly. Fats take up to six
hours to leave the stomach, providing a fuel
source through most of the night.

Menu planning, food selection, packaging,
preparation, and preservation are topics covered
in many outdoor activity books. The recommendations vary relative to geographic location, type of group, availability of food stuffs,
and tastes of the participants. The following
guidelines for menu planning can be followed

nearly anywhere, and the planner can complete the details from reading material relative to the particular locale, season, and group being served.

1. Breakfast: cereal and quick snacks for early energy

2. Snacks: carbohydrates for immediate energy between meals

3. Lunch: carbohydrates for immediate energy and light protein for later energy

4. Dinner: the *big* meal; protein for slow break down and fuel storage during rest and sleep

Good Health

A final physiological need directly related to success in outdoor pursuits is good health, which is defined simplistically as absence from disease or illness. Neither participant nor leader should embark on a strenuous or lengthy trip (in distance or duration) with any sign of illness that might significantly impair physical or mental well-being. Colds and flu are especially common and debilitating; yet, they are often shrugged off as "minor." The reduction in participant or leader stamina caused by a cold could be just enough to endanger a trip. When there is a need to move rapidly or continuously, a problem is created by having to wait for one whose normal energy has already been sapped before the trip started. More important, an ill individual may be less able to cope with an emergency, and would undoubtedly be less able to contribute to the group, and/or would require special attention in an emergency.

Safe, enjoyable, and worthwhile trips can be run for any level of fitness. It is important for the leader to ascertain the fitness levels of all participants prior to an outing so that the program and route are designed accordingly. Mixed levels can create dissatisfaction among participants and create a substantial challenge to the creativity and patience of the leader. Fitness provides an important margin of safety in backcountry travel, and an entire group can be compromised by one unfit participant. In order to eliminate or reduce problems in the field, leaders often administer fitness tests to determine a poor condition or a wide disparity of fitness levels within the group.

Exercise

It goes without saying that under ordinary circumstances, leaders need not concern themselves with the human physiological need for exercise, for every outdoor pursuit requires the use of many muscle groups, including the heart. In the case of a group stranded in a storm and holed up in a tent, snow cave, or crevasse, and in the case of energy and the long wait to be rescued, the human body will suffer from lack of exercise. Muscular activity increases circulatory and respiratory rates and develops and maintains strength. A leader should not expect participants of any age to "sit still" very long. In cramped quarters, there must be opportunity for exercise. Isotonic exercises (muscle stretching and tensing) can be done while the participant is lying in a sleeping bag, but they may be boring and thus are not desirable over prolonged periods of time. It is incumbent upon the leader to understand the need for exercise and to develop a series of activities to maintain muscle tone as well as cardiovascular efficiency.

Without exercise, muscles atrophy quickly, and lose their elasticity and strength. Persons who are weak after a long illness are often weak because of a lack of muscle use, not from the illness itself. Campers waiting out a long storm in a small tent must exercise their muscles, or they too can weaken.

A prolonged period of inactivity compounded by dehydration can be extremely dangerous since such circumstances predispose people to the formation of blood clots as mentioned earlier in this chapter.

Summary

It is thus the leader's responsibility to assure that the participants' physiological or life-sustaining needs are met. Adequate fresh air, a body temperature controlled near 98.6°F (37°C), shelter from inclement weather, adequate drinking water, adequate rest and sleep, adequate and proper nourishment, and adequate and proper exercise are all on the first or bottom level of human needs. If these requirements are not minimally met, one will probably not be able to meet the next step of Maslow's hierarchy on human needs.

In outdoor pursuits, people need strength, endurance, and mental agility for success in what may be, or become, harsh environments. Only the human resources of mind and body can overcome these difficulties as survival may depend upon the mental and physical capabilities of the participants. Leaders, therefore, should be first and foremost dedicated to assuring that basic human physiological needs are met before and during the trip.

Psychological Needs

If we utilize Maslow's hierarchy as a base and recognize that the first level consists of physiological needs, it will be seen that level two—the need for security and safety—is the first *psychological* need an outdoor leader must address.

Security

While Maslow initially referred to security as freedom from harassment (meaning freedom from having to look over one's shoulder to spot oppressors), security also means a feeling that no one in the group to which one wishes to belong will harass or ridicule. Individuals first need to feel secure and safe with themselves and then with the members of the group.

Insecurity is characteristic of many participants in new ventures, particularly those ventures containing elements of risk, adventure, suspense, and development of technical skills. People may feel insecure within themselves (lack a positive self-concept) because they are unsure of their skills, their stamina, their ability to perform adequately, the appropriateness and adequacy of their equipment, or their ability to get along in the group. People who are insecure may perceive the rest of the group to be opposed to them on every move. It may be difficult to visualize harassment actually occurring in a recreational or educational event, but it does

occur among those of all ages. The imagined (or real) harassment takes the form of teasing, ridicule, avoidance, or jokes. An insecure person may react to innocent teasing as if it were total harassment. Being alone in a group, being unskilled, or being teased all lead to feelings of insecurity and potentially to elements of fear.

It is important for leaders to understand that meeting the need for security within the self includes dispelling imagined (or real) harassment. Vindictive teasing, ridicule, or harassing behavior can take place in an outdoor situation if the group has a wide variety of skills and knowledge. However, this behavior can be prevented if the leader makes an effort to be sure that all feel secure and capable of succeeding. The leader must be confident that all participants will be able to execute the skills necessary for the activity. This means that he/she has some pre-trip responsibilities to the individuals. They must learn, practice, and become adept at skills needed for the trip. They must have physical conditioning to develop strength and stamina. They must develop a feeling of personal security *prior* to embarking on the journey. People who are confident in their own ability tend to act secure; thus, tend not to harass others or to perceive harassment coming at them.

In addition to feeling insecure because of inferior ability, some participants may feel insecure because they see themselves as solitary individuals in a group of strangers. When meeting a group for the first time a leader should first warmly welcome them. Second, not only should the leader learn everyone's name but he/she should expedite the process by asking everyone to learn everyone else's name. Learning something positive about everyone helps subsequent conversations. Learning people's names and being able to carry on conversations with each other not only helps each participant feel secure, but it helps the leader develop a closeness with each individual in the group and to understand their interests and experiences.

Related to the need for security, fear is one of the most common psychological problems. Symptoms of fear include:

1. Increase in the pulse rate;
2. Muscular tension—even inability to move in extreme cases;
3. Perspiration of palms and soles of the feet;
4. Dryness in the mouth;
5. Feelings of "butterflies" in the stomach.

Fear of the unknown, fear of discomfort, and fear of the result of personal weakness all seem to be apparent in outdoor recreational situations. *Fear of the unknown* is that experience of anxiety found among people in job interviews, students prior to examinations, and any outdoor participant about to tackle a new challenge. In the outdoors, fear of the unknown is seen in the fear of being alone (no companions, no voices, no help), fear of darkness (inability to see), and fear of animals (imagined attacks). It is also the fear of "what lies ahead" (unknown terrain, weather, hardships, route, and environment). It tends to be more severe in some people than in others and in some circumstances rather than others. People display fear in different ways. Some are obviously frightened and show it in open-eyed, open-mouthed, white-faced staring, while others internalize the fear or even disguise it with bravado. A leader should assume a degree of fear of the unknown is present in every member and should take steps to lessen it unless it is in the form of controlled stress applied purposefully in an "adventure recreation" setting. Even then, the leader must be extremely careful that the fear doesn't reach the extreme of panic.

The *fear of discomfort*, or of suffering, includes fear of no relief from cold, heat, thirst, or hunger as well as fear of anticipated or real pain. Fear of discomfort can usually be controlled through proper equipment. The fear of cold or dampness may be alleviated by the feeling of security given by carrying sweaters and rain gear, proper shelter, sleeping bags, and ground cover. The fear of hunger and thirst may be alleviated by feeling secure that adequate and proper nourishment and water are available. It is the responsibility of the leader to realize that such fear of discomfort may not develop until the participant is a long way from home and the environmental conditions have deteriorated to

a point of potential hardship. If the participant has not brought adequate food, liquid, source of heat, clothing, shelter, and rain gear, there is little the leader can do to prevent this fear. This situation underscores a need for adequate clothing and equipment.

In the case where, in spite of every precaution, the leader realizes one or more people fear discomfort, there is a need to assess whether the potential discomfort is imagined or real. If it is imagined, the positive attitude of other group members may be effective in changing the person's mind. If it is a real possibility, the leader's responsibility is to take precautions to prevent it by improvising or borrowing clothing or equipment, or by changing plans.

Fear of personal weakness includes a fear of death and its imminent inconvenience to family and loved ones as well as the natural fear of the unknown. It also includes a fear of society through loss of face, ridicule, admitting failure, guilt, and reprisal.

Fear of one's own weakness is a reality usually brought about by little or no adequate practice or conditioning prior to the trip, or as a result of a debilitating injury. "I can't make it" generally means "I don't think I have the strength or stamina" (a fear of weakness). If the participants have been in a long-term conditioning course, they will realize they have developed strength and stamina. Activities, such as running, jogging, bicycling, weight lifting, jazzercise and many others, develop strength and stamina if performed continuously and regularly. Those who have not exercised recently may need professional advice on type of activity and duration. Many people start with a brisk walk of 30 minutes daily. Adequate rest and nutrition, of course, must accompany the programs. No one should start a trip without adequate rest, nourishment, or conditioning exercise.

Belonging

The third need recognized by Maslow is the need to belong and to be accepted. Fulfillment of this need is a particularly important aspect of the outdoor pursuit leader's responsibility, for outdoor recreation leadership implies leadership of social groups involved in outdoor skills. Even the most highly-skilled, well-equipped, and well-conditioned member of the group needs to feel accepted by others and must have any psychological barriers to acceptance broken down.

Some excellent activities for developing group security and group trust are described in the *New Games* series edited by Andrew Fluegelman and *Cowstails and Cobras* and *Silver Bullets* by Karl Rohnke of Project Adventure. These activities, initiative tasks, and cooperative games are designed to bring about group continuity, a sense of group cohesiveness, and the indoctrination of attitudes which recognize the need for a total group effort to accomplish difficult tasks. Through pre-trip participation in initiative tasks, each person can start to understand how members of the group need each other, can help each other, and can work together for the success of the unit regardless of size, age, sex, or any other variable. The sense of belonging may follow the completion of group-building skills, for the participants may gain it through participating in the activities. That feeling must persist throughout the activity.

One way to help participants feel that they belong is also to make them feel needed or important. In some sponsored outings, it is the practice for leaders to cook, clean up, and pack up. Some clients pay high prices for trips wherein all cooking, clean up and camp chores are performed for them. Many times participants who share in these tasks gain a feeling of cohesiveness to the group and a sense of being needed—hence belonging.

Respect for Self and Respect from Others

The need to feel respected follows the need to belong and may certainly appear as a concurrent need. Belonging to a group in which one feels secure from harassment is basic to belonging to a group in which one feels an element of respect. People want to feel good about themselves and want others to respect them. The two are probably never mutually exclusive, for self-respect seems to grow with the increase of group respect. The outdoor leader is in a position conducive to encouraging and guiding interactions among group members. Group members can respect each other for knowledge of plants, accurate weather predictions, ability to tell jokes, strength, humor, or any other human skill, knowledge, or attitude if the leader facilitates the process by demonstrating respect first. The leader can facilitate the process by demonstrating respect for every group member, and by purposefully facilitating the development of mutual respect among group members.

Self-Actualization

Self-actualization is an ongoing process through which individuals grow toward their own unique capabilities, potentials, or talents. It is the process in which, because all other needs have been met, one is free to develop one's talents and capabilities to their fullest. The need for self-actualization may be the same in each person; however, because each person is a unique individual, no two people will move toward it identically. Since self-actualization is a process, it has no ending; consequently, it is never attained.

The challenge to the leader here is to understand the uniqueness of each participant with accompanying differences in goals, skills, capabilities, motivations, perceived and real barriers, and a host of other factors that contribute to individual differences. Individuals have been influenced by their own physical and mental ability, by their own body structures and their physical and intellectual fitness levels, by race, family, economic or geographic factors, as a result of local customs and mores, because of educational factors, and many less obvious forces.

For some, climbing a 4,000-foot mountain or canoeing through a series of short riffles is a big step in the self-actualization process. Others may need a glacier climb or a 12,000 footer, a trek across 150 miles of desert or a 200-mile raft trip on a roaring river. For some, the self-actualizing process reaches the point where they are helpers, teachers, and sharers. Maslow describes healthy people as those with the following 13 clinically observable traits (Maslow, p. 26):

1. Superior perception of reality;
2. Increased acceptance of self, of others, and of nature;
3. Increased spontaneity;
4. Increase in problem-centering;
5. Increased detachment and desire for privacy;
6. Increased autonomy and resistance to enculturation;
7. Greater freshness of appreciation and richness of emotional reaction;
8. Higher frequency of peak experiences;
9. Increased identification with the human species (i.e., greater empathy with others);
10. Changed (the clinician would say, improved) interpersonal relations;
11. More democratic character structure;
12. Greatly increased creativeness;
13. Certain changes in the value system.

Mood Differences

It is an accepted fact that participants have many moods or emotional reactions to various situations. We can assume that the moods of one participant will not be the same as those of others in the group. The moods of a person who is generally optimistic will differ from those of a typically pessimistic person. The leader should understand that the moods of every individual may be so different that a group mood cannot be described accurately.

It is not generally understood that both individual and group moods change at different phases of the activity; thus it is difficult to lead with the same group emotions in mind throughout the activity. Even the moods of the leader may change from elation to fatigue to peaceful to powerful depending upon the stage of the trip.

Two studies on mood changes in outdoor education experiences may be of interest here. In each case, eleven mood factors were analyzed at each of the five phases of the outdoor recreation experience identified by Clawson and Knetsch: (a) planning, (b) travel to the site, (c) participation on the site, (d) travel from the site, and (e) recollection. The first study took place on a three-day winter camping experience on Mt. Hood in Oregon by a class training to be outdoor leaders; and the second study took place with sixth graders attending a one-week residential outdoor school near the Pacific Ocean in the northwest in May. Each group was different in age, size, location, and purpose of trip. The weather was mixed rain and snow on Mt. Hood, and three days of rain and two days of sunshine in the outdoor school.

It was not expected that the moods or mood changes would be the same from group to group. The eleven moods studied were: social affection, fatigue, concentration, elation, surgency (playfulness), anxiety, aggression, vigor, skepticism, sadness, and egotism.

Each mood was measured during each of the five phases of the experience, and the means and standard deviations were computed and analyzed for significant differences. Analysis of the two groups (college class winter camping and sixth grade outdoor education), showed that, as the experience progressed for the college group, statistically significant mood changes occurred in nine of the eleven categories: social affection, fatigue, concentration, anxiety, aggression, vigor, skepticism, and sadness. The sixth graders, however, showed significant mood changes in only four categories: elation, aggression, sadness, and egotism. Overall, the sixth graders appeared to be more friendly (social affection) and elated throughout. In the case of the college students, the mood changes might have been caused by the miserable weather they encountered, causing wet tents and sleeping bags, and presumably a decrease in enthusiasm for the experience. It is also interesting to note that the sixth graders started their outdoor experience feeling much more elation than the college students.

For the prospective leader, these two studies demonstrate the fact that different people's needs, emotions, and attitudes differ at various phases during a trip and differ among groups. It may be conjectured that similar differences might be demonstrated for every possible group in every possible situation. This means the leaders cannot have set expectations for the emotional makeup of any group at any time and must be prepared for and expect changes in the individual and group attitudes from time to time. It becomes obvious that meeting the psychological needs of people is a complex matter which cannot be oversimplified by being aware only of Maslow's hierarchy.

Individual Differences

The outdoor pursuit leader cannot afford to be just a leader of outdoor pursuits. He/she is always a leader of people, all of whom are different. Beyond the basic physiological and psychological needs are specific needs that may have an impact on the basic needs. The inexperienced person whose glasses are broken has a different fear and security problem than does the experienced person who carries an extra pair (and who, incidentally, may not remember the frightening experience that caused him/her to pack an extra pair regardless of the situation). The hypoglycemic (low blood sugar) person has different dietary needs from others and needs more frequent snacks of protein and fats than others. The person over 65 years of age may have a slower pace than a 25-year-old but may also have a higher tolerance for periods of sustained exercise. Older people usually have more endurance while younger people have more speed. Most 45-year-old adults cannot imitate all the actions of a 10-year-old in the same manner and at the same speed. The 10-year-old requires more rest and has shorter bursts of pep at high-energy activities; yet, he/she may be taking a two-hour nap while the adult can go at his/her own slow pace tirelessly for eight hours or more.

Individual differences have such an impact that no two people can be said to have the same "amounts" of any needs. Each person's needs are similar but in dissimilar proportions. The competent leader understands this phenomenon. In actuality, the term "leader of outdoor pursuits" is really a misnomer. To be a leader implies one has followers. An activity or pursuit cannot follow anyone. The title of this book notwithstanding, we are referring to leaders of outdoor-pursuit *participants* here.

Summary

The leader of outdoor pursuits needs to understand the physiological and psychological needs of participants. Physiological needs include adequate air for breathing, a body temperature near to or at 98.6°F, shelter from harsh elements, drinking water, rest, food, exercises, and good health. Psychological needs, based upon the hierarchy proposed by Abraham Maslow, include security, belonging, respect for self and others, and self-actualization.

Leaders should be cognizant of both kinds of needs and methods to help participants attain them. Since each person differs in each differing situation, the meeting of individual needs in a group experience in the out-of-doors becomes a complex and challenging responsibility.

References

Backer, H., MD. (1991). Presentation. Wilderness Medicine Conference. Boulder, CO.

Buell, L. (1980). *Leader's guide to the 24-hour experience.* Greenfield, MA: Environmental Awareness Publications.

Clawson, M., & Knetsch, J. L. (1966). *Economics of outdoor recreation.* Baltimore, MD: Johns Hopkins Press.

Dickman, S. R. (1988). *Pathway to wellness.* Champaign, IL: Life Enhancement Publications.

Fear, E. (No date). *Outdoor living: Problems, solutions, guidelines.* Tacoma, WA: Mountain Rescue Council.

Flugelman, A. (Ed.). (1976). *The new games book.* New York, NY: Dolphin Books/Doubleday & Co.

Ford, P., & Cloninger, K. (Winter 1982-83). Multiphasic mood changes in a five-day residential outdoor education experience. *The Journal of Environmental Education, 14*(2).

Maslow, A. (1980). *Toward a psychology of being (2nd ed.).* New York, NY: D. Van Nostrand Co.

McArdel, W. D., Katch, F. I., & Katch, V. L. (1981). *Exercise physiology.* Philadelphia, PA: Lea and Febiger.

Prentice, W., & Brucher, C. A. (1988). *Fitness for college and life. (2nd ed.)* St. Louis, MO: Times Mirror/Mosby Publishing.

Rohnke, K. (1984). *Silver bullets.* Hamilton, MA: Project Adventure.

Rohnke, K. (1989). *Cowstails and cobras II.* Hamilton, MA: Project Adventure.

Winterburn, D. (1979). *Participation mood during each of Clawson's multi-phase theory of outdoor recreation.* Unpublished master's thesis. University of Oregon.

PREPARATION FOR SURVIVAL

To some people, it may seem unnecessary to discuss survival in a leadership book because it is usually assumed that an outdoor leader would be very knowledgeable in the art of surviving in the out-of-doors. Most outdoor leaders understand and practice the skills of living in the outdoors but have never been in a situation that calls for survival in an actual *emergency* situation. Fortunately, most leaders never have to prove their ability to survive or to guide a group under emergency survival conditions. Unfortunately, when the rare survival situation occurs, some participants, some leaders, and some groups fail the ultimate test.

The term "survival" has many connotations. For some, it brings to mind physically and psychologically harrowing near-death scenarios, such as being stranded in a raft at sea, lost for months in the Arctic wilds after a plane crash, or being forced to dig a snow cave to survive a week-long bitter storm. While such circumstances have occurred, and will occur again, the typical outdoor enthusiast or leader is far more likely to encounter situations that are much less dramatic and of considerably shorter duration. In today's world, the importance of long-term survival skills is minimal even for most outdoor leaders. Given modern technology and the dwindling undeveloped and roadless areas remaining worldwide, there is little need to be familiar with edible foods or the improvisation of snowshoes. This is not to say that there is *no*

value in these skills; it is simply a reality that one can usually survive with no food whatever for more than a week and that virtually every individual or party lost in the wilds is found within a few days if they stay put. Fatalities occur often, but they are almost always due to failure to survive short-term (one or two day) scenarios. It seems best, therefore, to focus on those topics and skills that are most likely to be needed and most essential to the central definition of survival, which is a safe return home by all involved.

Possible Emergency Situations

The unexpected emergency situation is usually a situation that is a distinct possibility, but of low probability. The situation may be related to the *participants* themselves or to environmental factors. Most potential emergency situations can be identified and plans can be made to prevent them or to protect the participants if they do occur. The conscientious leader will consider and prepare for every reasonable contingency.

Emergency survival conditions involving individuals or a group are usually classified as being *personal* or *situational*. *Personal* conditions that necessitate survival techniques include those where one or more of the group members become ill, fatigued, or injured. *Situational* conditions are those related to one or more people getting lost or stranded. Being stranded is often the result of environmental factors; however, it may be the result of poor judgment, accident, or (*very* rarely) equipment. Rather than "equipment failure," such stranding is usually the result of inadequate equipment, or through improper *use* or *application* of the gear. In other words, it is often the result of poor judgment in the planning stage or of inadequate instruction in the use of the equipment.

The following list includes some of the more common environmental hazards that may result in situational emergencies:

1. *Weather conditions*
   Rapid changes in weather, lightning, whiteouts, hail, very high winds.

2. *Temperature-related trauma*
   Hypothermia, frostbite and other cold injuries, heat exhaustion, heatstroke.

3. *Sun-related trauma*
   Sunburn, sun blindness, allergic reactions to sunlight.

4. *Snow and ice hazards*
   Deep snow, avalanches, cornices, snow bridges, crevasses, snow and ice falling from trees, thin ice on lakes and streams.

5. *Dangerous terrain*
   Steep slopes, rockfall, falling limbs and snags, brush and vegetation.

6. *Water hazards*
   Floods, high tides, swollen streams, cold water.

7. *Altitude*
   Acute mountain sickness, cerebral edema, high altitude pulmonary edema.

8. *Nightfall*
   Unexpected darkness, inability to negotiate terrain, navigational difficulties.

9. *Wildlife*
   Large predators, toxic or allergic reactions to bites by rodents and birds, poisonous snakes, spiders, scorpions, and insects.

10. *Poisonous plants*
    Contact irritants and ingestion of poisonous plants.

Every potential environmental hazard should be considered and planned for. The ten environmental hazards listed previously must be addressed. The leader must plan for each of these hazards as an individual and must be sure the participants have addressed them, too. If a participant says, "I can't plan for this," or, "I don't know what I would do," or "My equipment isn't adequate," the leader should not allow that participant to go on the outing until the individual is adequately prepared in knowledge and equipment. Such firmness is essential to the well-being of the individual and to the welfare of the entire group.

Planning for Survival

In all cases, leaders need to understand the survival needs of people, the survival equipment needed, and techniques for survival. It is assumed that aspiring leaders have basic camping knowledge and experience including fire building, knots, water procurement and purification, cooking, climbing, and other applicable outdoor skills. Survival requires basic skills plus the ability to make correct decisions under exceptionally stressful circumstances. In this chapter, we are not concerned with the usual day-to-day living in the out-of-doors. We are concerned with preparation for surviving the unexpected emergency. Furthermore, we are concerned with the responsibilities and actions of the leader to ensure that the participants are prepared to survive the emergency.

Outdoor pursuit leaders have no greater responsibility than that of ensuring the safe return of all participants and staff. Those who sign up for an outing have the right to assume that the leader is capable of handling any and all reasonably foreseeable contingencies, including "personal" emergencies (being lost or stranded due to environmental factors, accidents, equipment failure, navigational error, or poor judgment). All are real possibilities for which the leader must be fully prepared and for which the leader must equip and prepare the group. *There is no excuse for any leader conducting a group into a situation wherein either the whole group or any individual separated from the group cannot survive for at least one or two unplanned nights out.*

It is the leader's responsibility to know the area and the possible weather conditions for the period in question, and to know what knowledge, skill, and equipment each person must have to assure survival under a reasonably likely worst case scenario. What is a "reasonably likely" worst case scenario? It isn't "reasonably likely" that a comet will strike the campsite, but it is *always* possible for one person to wander off and lose track of the group. The worst reasonably likely case usually lies somewhere in between and is often, for land-based backcountry activities, considered to be a lost individual in foul weather. In any case, the determination is critical and is a measure of the experience and judgment of the leader.

Generally speaking, leaders are skilled practitioners of the activity they are conducting or of the skills they are teaching. Clearly, the quality of service or teaching is largely determined by the experience of the leader. In a survival situation, the stakes are far higher. The leader's actions may determine whether individuals live or die; yet, in the great majority of cases, the leader has no real survival experience. He/she may have read about survival skills and may know a great deal about the topic but have no experiential basis upon which to act. The result is lack of self-confidence on the part of the leader, potential lack of confidence in the leader by the participants, and certainly lack of preparedness for maximally efficient action in an emergency.

The following guidelines and suggestions are necessarily of a general nature. It is impossible to define precisely the particular set of knowledge and skills needed under all possible circumstances. Leaders are encouraged to commit themselves to the task of identifying their own needs and the needs of those for whom they will be responsible and then to the task of practicing the necessary skills.

Survival experiences can be simulated on survival practice outings. Under supervision, one or more leaders or leaders-in-training can spend the night out doors using only the items taken in their day packs. Camped within a safe distance of the "survival" site, supervisors should monitor the health and welfare of the "survivors." A great deal can be learned in as short a period as one night or a weekend. Certainly, there is far less psychological stress associated with such a contrived situation. Nevertheless, the real and potential benefits are great. At the very least, self-confidence is enhanced and, more importantly, the first *real* need for survival skills will not be the leader's first experience in the art of survival. As with anything in life, the first time is awkward and inefficient, but the second time is much more successful. Furthermore, this type of experience reinforces the leader's understanding of what constitutes adequate survival equipment and tends to reinforce his/her conviction that such equipment must be carried at all times—even on day hikes!

If the leader is to respond effectively, practice for survival is essential by selecting the best techniques from a large mental "tool box" and by efficiently implementing the chosen strategies. Survival techniques can easily be incorporated into virtually every outing. On a wild flower hike or at a lunch break, discuss what one might do if lost overnight in the area. During a ski lesson, point out possible locations for making a kick hole in a sheltered tree well, and spend some time orienting students to the general area to reduce the chance of becoming lost. *Practice* solo and group survival with backpacking and mountaineering classes. An hour or so of mock survival experience may be all it takes to open the eyes of naive beginners and inspire greater attention to preparation for their personal survival or future outings.

When outdoor activities result in injury or death, the cause can usually be traced back to the living room, dining table, or desk at which the outing was planned. In virtually every case, the incident, or its negative consequences, could have been prevented, or at the very least

*moderated, by better planning and more con-
scientious attention to preparations for the outing.* The best way to improve one's chances
for survival is to reduce the likelihood of encountering serious problems in the first place.
This in turn requires knowledge of the area and
enough experience to know what activities are
safe and appropriate under the particular circumstances. As will be discussed at length later
in this book, careful planning by a mature and
experienced leader can result in optimal excitement, challenge, and adventure with a minimal
chance of having to test one's powers of survival.

The first line of defense is preparation for
emergencies. Participants who are experienced
in outdoor pursuits know that when people interact with the natural world, it is only prudent to
"expect the unexpected." Preparation for emergencies entails:

1. *Recognizing the existence of potential
hazards and dangerous circumstances.* All too
often leaders fail at this early stage. Leaders
must develop an exceptional ability to detect and
analyze potential dangers. We say "exceptional"
because it seems clear that most people do not
demonstrate proficiency in this area. If this
sounds harsh, observe any freeway in the country for ten minutes. In outdoor pursuits, the
dangers are far less obvious than those facing
high-speed drivers.

2. *Accurately estimating the risks associated
with hazards and the likelihood of adverse circumstances, and acknowledging the need to take
corrective actions.*

3. *Taking the necessary actions.* Too often
the danger is acknowledged but nothing substantive is done. The leader, due to lack of experience, laziness, or overconfidence, does not
act on the available information to ensure that
every participant and staff member enters the
field with the knowledge, skill, and equipment
necessary for survival. The leader must also
take such essential basic precautions as filing a
"trip plan" which include detailed routes and
emergency instructions, with a responsible party

in town. See Chapters Five and Nine for material on human needs and navigation skills, respectively, and refer to Chapter Seventeen for
lists of recommended minimum equipment for
various activities.

The second line of defense is the exercise of
good judgment in the field. Many individuals
and even whole groups have died because the
leader did not elect to abort the outing in the face
of inclement circumstances. Most outings are
goal-oriented, whether the goal is to reach a
summit, run a river segment, or meet an educational objective. Too often, leaders (and participants) are too reluctant to modify plans, or simply go home. Healthy, well-rested, nourished,
fully-hydrated, warm people with reserve dry
clothes and reserve supplies of water and food
have a margin of safety. If *any* one of these factors is compromised for *any* one individual in the
group, the leader must resolve the deficiency,
or alter or abort the agenda. If this sounds a bit
extreme, ask any experienced leader; most can
relate many examples of having to make major
changes in plans to stay within safe margins of
group and individual well-being.

The last line of defense is action taken in
response to an existing emergency. The range
of available options will, in most circumstances,
depends upon the extent of group preparation,
as survival usually depends upon rational behavior and access to knowledge, skills, and key
items of clothing and equipment. Accident and
injury response is covered in Chapters Seven,
"First Aid in Outdoor Emergencies" and Chapter
Eight, "Search and Rescue." In this chapter,
emphasis will be placed on the lost or stranded
individual or group.

From the well-equipped group of experienced adults stranded by a blocked trail at a low
elevation site in mild weather to the marginally
equipped youngster separated from the group
in unexpected foul weather during a late fall
field trip in the mountains the range of possible
scenarios is vast. Fortunately, it is possible to
define certain actions or behaviors that can significantly increase the odds for survival under
almost any circumstance.

The Lost Individual

The most likely scenario is that of an individual who is separated from the group, so to be of any use, the following guidelines *must* be conveyed to *every* member of the group *prior* to the outing.

(1) *Stop* as soon as it is apparent that you are separated from your group, lost, or in trouble. Further attempts at travel usually reduce chances of survival. Those who stay put within a short distance of the last seen point are almost invariably found alive, while those who try to find their way back to civilization suffer a higher risk of death. This is because traveling, even a relatively short distance, greatly reduces the probability of being found by searchers. A circle with a one-mile (1.6 km) radius has an area of about 3.14 square miles (8.4 km). At a radius of two miles (3.2 km), the area increases to 12.56 square miles (32.53 sq km), and so on. It is true that most people (about 80 percent, depending upon whose figures one uses) do find their own way out. However, among the 20 percent who do not succeed in finding their own way out, fewer than half are found alive by searchers. In most cases, the odds are far better if one stays put—if someone will know exactly where to begin looking and will implement a search in a timely manner. The solo hiker who did not file a "trip plan" or failed to stick to the expressed route may have no option but to travel.

(2) *Sit down.* Survival depends upon rational behavior and the will to survive. The natural, and almost universal, response to being lost is anxiety verging on panic, sometimes accompanied by some of the symptoms of psychogenic shock. Fears (of the unknown, of wild animals, of the impending discomfort, and of death) come early, and later are often exceeded by loneliness, boredom, and despair. Sitting down really helps. It is harder to panic when you are sitting! Anxiety is the greatest danger, as it impairs logical reasoning, and, because it interferes with the efficient production of metabolic heat, it predisposes the anxious individual to hypothermia. Simple relaxation techniques (rhythmic breathing, counting, or hard tensing of the body followed by relaxation) can help.

(3) *Think carefully.* What just happened? How did you arrive here? From where? What time is it?

(4) *Assess all of your gear and clothing carefully.* In a remarkable number of tragic cases, victims have been found with, or near, supplies that could have saved their lives had they had the presence of mind to make use of them.

(5) *Make noise* and make it easy for people to see you. If weather conditions and the immediate environment allow, move to the most visible or open area in the very close vicinity while not losing track of your original site. Three of anything, such as three mirror flashes, yells, or whistle blasts constitute the equivalent of "SOS" in the U.S. (Hunters fire three shots.) In Europe, the equivalent distress signal is six of anything. Know what is locally recognized. Early signalling can help the group relocate its missing member before a full-scale search is required.

(6) *Explore* the immediate area. Try to follow your tracks back, but be careful not to lose track of where you were. From the point where you sat down, carefully try going out and back in each of four directions, and each at right angles. In forested areas, it may be possible to blaze or mark trees by extending the legs of the "X" carefully for a considerable distance and by lining up marked trees; always be sure that the way back to the center is not lost. In desert or open country, it may be possible to do the same thing using cairns (rock piles) as guide posts, to build, in essence, a "picket fence" in each of four directions. This may allow discovery of a trail or other aid to location, and, if the markers are obvious, would make it much easier for the searchers to find you.

(7) *Prepare shelter.* Long before dark, locate the most sheltered site nearby and begin building a shelter, gathering insulation, and collecting fuel. Allow at *least* three hours to do this! Do it while you have time, energy, and daylight in your favor. Mark the area well so

that searchers will not miss it in the dark. *Know how* to build emergency shelters in the areas you frequent. Each area lends itself to different possibilities, from leaf and vine structures in the tropics to pole and bark structures or bough piles in the Pacific Northwest to a host of snow shelters (quinzees, caves, trenches, and igloos), each suited to certain conditions.

Do not rely totally upon being able to construct a shelter of native materials. The "personal shelter" in the list of suggested survival kit contents is an invaluable aid in an actual survival situation.

(8) Stay put. For the reasons discussed above, not to mention the need to conserve energy, it is generally best to stay where you are. If circumstances dictate a need to travel, move only in daylight and only if you are sure of your goal. One exception to daylight travel may occur in some deserts during very hot weather, wherein it may be necessary to hole up during the day, to avoid the desiccating effects of extreme heat and low humidity, and to travel only at night. If you find a trail, it may not be the one from which you strayed. Beware of taking the wrong trail or taking a trail in the wrong direction! *A cardinal rule for lost persons is never, ever leave a trail or road except to follow a larger or more heavily used trail or road!*

A program for lost children, called "Hug-A-Tree," might be taught to adults as well as children. The program was initiated after the death of a child who had become lost, and not knowing how to respond, had succumbed to the cold and dampness. While the program is recommended for children, it makes good sense for adults also. Hug-A-Tree has six basic steps to remember. Three are "things to do," and three are ideas to help prevent panic.

1. *ALWAYS CARRY A TRASH BAG AND WHISTLE ON A PICNIC, HIKE, OR CAMPING TRIP.*
   By making a hole in the bag for the face (without this hole, there is a danger of suffocation) and putting it on over the head, it will keep you dry and warm. The whistle will carry farther than the voice, and takes less energy to use.

2. *HUG A TREE ONCE YOU KNOW YOU ARE LOST.*
   One of the greatest fears a person of any age can have is of being alone. Hugging a tree, and even talking to it, calms one down and prevents panic. By staying in one place, the person is found far more easily.

3. *MAKE YOURSELF BIG.*
   From helicopters, people are hard to see when they are standing up, when they are in a group of trees, or when they are wearing dark and drab clothing. Find your tree to hug near a small clearing if possible. A brightly colored garment, tarp, or other large surface is very helpful to searchers. Lie down when the helicopter flies over. Make crosses or "SOS" in broken shrubbery or rocks, or by dragging your foot in the dirt or the snow.

4. *NO ONE WILL BE ANGRY AT YOU.*
   Time and again, people (especially children and the mentally disabled or learning impaired) have avoided searchers because they were ashamed of getting lost and afraid of punishment. Anyone can get lost, adult or child. If they had known that a happy reunion filled with love was awaiting, they would have been less frightened and proned to panic, and they would have worked harder at being found.

5. *THE ANIMALS OUT THERE WILL NOT HURT YOU.*
   This may not be an absolute truth; however, the risk of injury by wild animals is always small, even in "grizzly country." If you hear a noise at night, yell at it. If it is an animal, it will run away. If it is a searcher, you will be found. Fear of the dark and of "lions and tigers and bears" are a big factor in panicking children and others into running. They need strong reassurance to stay put and be safe.

6. *YOU WILL HAVE HUNDREDS OF PEOPLE LOOKING FOR YOU. SOMEONE WILL FIND YOU!* Many children and adults who are lost don't realize that if they sit down and stay put, one of a few hundred people will find them. Some are afraid of strangers or men in uniform so they, don't respond to yells and have actually hidden from searchers they knew were looking for them. Children especially need to learn that this is one time that it is permissible and wise to talk to strangers.

Group Survival

What if a group, rather than a single individual, is lost or stranded? In almost all circumstances, there are advantages to having more than one person in a survival scenario. More people mean more brainpower, more collective knowledge and skills, companionship, more combined strength, and usually more resources of clothing and equipment. On the other hand, the complexity of group dynamics increases with each additional survivor; travel is limited to the pace of the slowest member; and, if resources are finite, each additional person reduces the quantity of resources available to each individual. Survival situations are potentially the ultimate test of a leader's ability to induce positive behaviors in a group. When anxieties are high and resources are limited, survival chances are optimized when the group acts cohesively and efficiently, taking full advantage of the collective potential of each and every member. Under such circumstances, however, every member of the group will be impaired by the effects of stress, fatigue, and concern for his/her personal welfare. As conditions deteriorate, some people maintain a clear focus on collective needs and the well-being of the group, while others may become increasingly self-centered unless someone intervenes.

Generally speaking, negative behaviors stem from personal anxieties and lack of rest. Measures aimed at alleviating or at least moderating the anxiety, and/or providing rest, may be far more effective than attempts to stop specific behaviors. In a survival situation, survivors are

likely to feel an acute loss of control unless they are, or believe they are, fully engaged in resolving the crisis. Participants in any group may feel anxiety due to loss of control if they do not understand and appreciate what the group is doing, or about to do. In a survival situation, group and individual morale is benefitted by clear, frequent, and detailed briefings by the leader, frequent opportunities for communication to the leader, and a well-defined plan that allocates meaningful responsibilities in proportion to each individual's abilities and needs.

In truly life-threatening situations, democracy is an unaffordable luxury. The leader must have the ability and will to take the helm, seek and accept all available advice, make decisions, and see to it that the group acts in a way that maximizes survival potential in the collective sense. Anyone who may consider accepting a role as a leader of a backcountry or wilderness adventure would do well to read some of the many excellent firsthand accounts written by survivors of shipwrecks, air crashes, and other disasters that led to epic group ordeals. Such accounts provide valuable insights, facilitate mental rehearsal, and, if nothing else, inspire an extra measure of caution in planning and preparation for outings.

There are many good survival books available in most large bookstores, and specific survival skills are discussed in numerous articles in popular magazines and in backpacking, snow camping, and mountaineering texts. While much of the information is useful, many "survival books" tend to focus on unlikely scenarios requiring long-term survival, and most books and articles focus on solo survival. The leader should be well-versed (and, ideally, practiced) in solo survival skills and must be prepared to deal with group survival.

There are many possible reasons for a group being forced to spend an extra day or more away from civilization. Groups on remote rivers may be unable to proceed due to changes in water levels or equipment failure, or land-based expeditions may be unable to proceed due to extreme weather. One of the most frequent causes of the delay of a group is injury, illness to a group member, or a missing group member. If the weather is summer-like with warm nights, an unexpected night out should present no great hardship for a group, even if they are not prepared for camping. A group equipped for camping should be able to handle several extra nights outdoors, even in cool weather, if adequate water supplies are available. A hiking group, properly equipped for a summer day, should carry ample supplies to assure overnight group survival even in cool, wet weather. If each person is required to carry basic, common sense survival items such as extra insulation and a personal shelter, these resources can be shared and heat conserved by huddling together.

Basic Survival Needs

In Chapter Five, the basic needs of individuals were discussed in terms of physiological and psychological needs. Survival needs are identical to the basic needs of all humans; however, the order and intensity of the needs may change. The most important element for survival is a psychological state that is even more basic than those described in Chapter Five. It is the *will to live*—the challenge to stay alive. During World War II, among sailors tossed into the cold North Sea waters after their ships had been torpedoed, a greater proportion of old and middle-aged men survived than the young who were thought, by some, to have given up more easily. This theory is said to have been one of the reasons Kurt Hahn founded the Outward Bound Schools, which attempt to build self-confidence by helping people persist through hardships. Thus, survival priorities and the length of possible survival are often listed as:

1. Will to live (depends upon the individual).

2. Oxygen or air (about three minutes).

3. Shelter from temperature extremes (four minutes to several hours).

4. Water (up to three days). See Chapter Five, "Understanding Human Needs."

5. Food (up to three weeks or more). See Chapter Five, "Understanding Human Needs."

The chance of survival without any one of the above may be decreased by the state of mental health, injuries, lowered (or raised) body temperature, and diseases that affect the body's defense mechanisms. Chances of survival may be increased through knowledge, equipment, planning, and mental and physical health.

The Will To Live

There is no way we can predict how strong a person's will to live is, but we know that death comes hard to those who struggle against it. There are cases where people have survived emergencies for which they were unprepared—just by determination. In an outdoor excursion, however, it is the leader who needs to provide the example of tenacity. It is the leader who must instill hope into the minds of the participants. If they are prepared and know it, there is a better hope for survival than if there is inadequate or insufficient equipment or knowledge. The leader has a two-fold responsibility: maintain a personal will to live, and foster the will to live among the participants. It is easier to have the will to live if there is a sound rational basis for hope. The leader must, by word and deed, instill hope in the mind of each group member, for belief in the possibility of success is the essential precursor to a "will to live." Hope sustains the will to struggle. In an actual emergency situation, preparation in terms of fitness and equipment is the best foundation on which to build hope.

Shelter, Clothing, and Equipment

It is certainly possible to conceive of a situation in which an individual participant in the program is lost and seriously injured during a period of foul weather. Though the likelihood is low, especially if the leader modifies the program in the event of foul weather, such a situation could develop. Most experienced leaders, however, require clothing and equipment adequate for:

1. Reasonable individual comfort in all temperatures and weather likely to be encountered,

2. Group survival for several days in the case of highly unlikely but possible situations such as extremes of weather or the group becoming lost or stranded,

3. Individual survival in the event of separation from the group for one or two nights,

4. Treatment of serious injuries or minor illnesses in a group setting, including overnight care, and,

5. Evacuation of an incapacitated individual if there is any uncertainty regarding the ability of rescue services to perform a rapid evacuation regardless of weather conditions.

In the case of a one-day trip, Item 1 is usually satisfied rather easily. Some pessimism is called for, since weather is hard to predict, and the list should be issued well in advance of the outing. A little extra gear isn't nearly as inconvenient as having to change plans due to lack of equipment. Because leaders are typically skilled, fit, and may be used to needing relatively little insulation, they need to be especially sensitive to the considerably greater needs of participants. The pace of the group outing is usually slower than that of small, private outings; thus, even the leaders may need more warm clothing. Participants are typically less efficient, less fit, less skilled, and more anxious than leaders, and for each of these reasons may need more protective gear and clothing than the leader(s).

Item number 2, group survival, requires some form of group shelter and some provision for obtaining an adequate water supply. In most cases, this consists of at least a large tarp, means of starting a fire, and a cooking pot for boiling water (supplemented by a stove and fuel for where fires would not be feasible). Food is always useful here, though rarely absolutely essential.

Item 3, individual survival, assumes that a single individual loses track of the group and must survive independently for two or more days before being found or finding his/her way to assistance. Since the weather can change considerably in a period of several days, the gear list has to address the worst and provide adequate insulation and weatherproofing. Minimum requirements generally include a personal shelter, water, matches, and sufficient insulation to protect against the wettest or coldest nights the individual would be likely to encounter. These items complement the group-survival items suggested above but must be carried by each individual at all times to be useful.

Item 4, injuries or illnesses, implies the need for first-aid equipment and for adequate shelter and insulation to protect the injured person. The group tarp provides the shelter; the additional insulation is usually an insulating pad and a sleeping bag. In snow-covered terrains, especially above the timberline, more insulating pads may be necessary.

Item 5, a means of evacuation, could consist of a climbing rope or several pack frames—provided, of course, that someone in the group knows how to construct effective litters from these items.

Suggested items of equipment are listed in Chapter Seventeen starting with "Hiking". Notice that the lists for participants are briefly annotated to help insure that appropriate items are brought to the outing. Also note that the required items are simply described, while the optimal items are, in some cases discussed at greater length because of participants have a choice to make on *optimal* items. The extent to which annotation is useful depends upon the experience level of the participants and upon the extent to which the clothing and equipment requirements have been explained to them. If at least one substantive pre-trip meeting is held well in advance of the outing, the list may not need extensive annotation. Substantial annotation is usually worthwhile, though, given the limitations of verbal communication and the potentially serious consequences of inadequate gear. While requiring too much gear may eliminate potential participants due to cost barriers, may perpetuate dependence upon material goods, and otherwise may degrade the experience, requiring too little may have far more serious consequences.

Participants rightfully expect to return home healthy, well, and happy. The leader must anticipate and require sufficient gear to insure not only survival, but reasonable comfort as well. This isn't easy to do since the environment is unpredictable, and each individual has physical and psychological tolerances that vary in response to myriad variables. Those who contest the leader's responsibility to require adequate gear often cite the personal responsibility of individuals and the advantage of learning by experience. The argument with regard to individual responsibility, while generally valid, assumes that each individual involved is fully knowledgeable about equipment and clothing demands of the particular outing and activity, is fully aware of the implications of taking or not taking each item, and is willing and able to come prepared in a manner consistent with the goals and philosophy of the group. These are assumptions that can rarely be made even on professional expeditions!

No one is likely to contest the advantages of learning by experience. Many of us who now manage outdoor schools and programs learned in this way, through many years of alternative success and failure. Unguided experiential learning is a fine way to learn, if one survives the process and if the resource base can withstand the abuse of the learners. Guidance may alter the learning/teaching process adversely, but it can also reduce the risk of injury to the participants and to the resources during and following the experience. Comfortable participants are more observant and receptive learners and are far more likely to be considerate of natural resources.

How does a leader determine what clothing and equipment to take? What should be required and what should be simply suggested? What gear does the leader take? What items should the group carry in addition to the personal gear carried by each individual?

The following material is a proposed system for arriving at a concise list for any outing. Keep in mind that the leader is ultimately responsible for seeing that adequate clothing and equipment are taken on the outing. In a positive light, conscientious effort at this point in the planning process can greatly facilitate the attainment of the trip. In a "worst-case" scenario, where an injury or accident occurs, the leader may be in more than just a moral dilemma if his/her requirements weren't adequate. In a legal action, the leader may be asked to explain and justify any variance between his/her gear requirements and those endorsed by other professionals conducting similar activities. It might be nice to be positive about all this, but a touch of paranoia may be healthy here.

Gear planning is largely a matter of prediction, and the accuracy of the prediction depends upon the leader's understanding of the environment in which the activity will take place, the demands of the activity itself, and the needs and expectations of the participants. Conscientious gear planning should also include a consideration of "common practices in the trade" when considering whether to require an otherwise marginal or questionably necessary item. The quality of the final list depends upon the leader's ability to predict needs combined with good judgment in balancing the costs and benefits of each item. Uncertainty is inevitable. Therefore, once a list is determined, it may be compared to that of established and respected operators of similar programs. No two lists are likely to be identical; however, this comparison can provide insights, ideas, and an opportunity to alter the list.

Consider what causes a rise or fall in body temperature. If you understand what causes these temperature fluctuations, you may understand the need for so many clothes. To maintain the heat of the body, the effect of five elements must be considered and appropriate measures taken to provide shelter against them. Rain is a serious concern because it can occur suddenly at virtually any place on earth. Many people seem to be optimistic and assume that, if it isn't raining when they leave home, it won't rain before they return. As a result, rain gear is left behind. *Rain* can rob clothing of 90 percent of its insulation value. Even wool (advertised as "warm when wet"), polypropylene (advertised as "warmer than wool"), and 60/40 cloth (advertised as *"water repellent"*—not waterproof) are of minimal value if worn in the rain for very long without a protective outer layer of rainwear.

Wind can blow heat away from the body faster than the body can replace it. Coupled with rain, winds of speeds even as little as five miles per hour (8 kph) can drive away heat and cause hypothermia in temperatures as warm as 45°F (7°C). *Still cold air* can cause body-heat loss through radiation. *Immersion in water* (falling in a river or stream) causes rapid cooling of the body with an accompanying need for rapid drying and warming. The *sun* causes the reverse problem: an increase in body temperature with the accompanying need for rapid cooling and addition of moisture.

Gear Lists

There are several reasons for generating gear lists. The leader needs a list as a tool for organizing and comparing options, and as a reminder during the packing process. Participants need lists in order to know what to bring. From a pessimistic perspective, the list itself, if effectively enforced, provides a means of establishing the quality of the pre-outing planning if one should be subjected to legal litigation.

Examine the process of assembling a comprehensive clothing and equipment list for a specific outing or event. Assume that the site, the program, and the participants have been determined in advance. A method of listing that works well is to construct three lists: one for participants, one for leaders and staff, and one for group gear. The "staff" and "group" lists usually need only be single listings of items, since the purpose of these lists is to serve as reminders. The "participant" list needs to be more detailed and is often annotated, since the users of the list presumably have less experience in the activity. Look at the sample lists in Chapter Seventeen. Clothing and equipment are listed separately, and the required and optional portions of the lists are clearly defined.

The actual listing process can be confusing and inefficient if no logical order is applied. People might develop a complete and appropriate gear list starting with sunglasses, then the cooking pot, then the sweater, etc. The simplest way we know to list clothing is to start at the ground and work up: boots first, then socks, underwear, pants, rain pants, and so on, to the hood over the hat. A partial equipment list can also be started this way, beginning with the ground and working through waxes, skis, or whatever meets the ground, and ending with helmet, head lamp, or whatever is likely to be on top. The equipment list can be completed by following a chronological sequence through the entire program. For example, think through the camping process (setting up tent, sleeping pad, sleeping bag, cooking pots, stove, fuel, etc.) to generate a list of items in the order in which they might be used.

Once a basic list has been established by the above process, it is time to review the list in terms of safety. Be a pessimist! Consider everything that might go wrong, and how the clothing and equipment requirements might affect the outcome of the situation. Experience and good judgment are essential here. The leader's obligation is to consider any and all reasonably foreseeable problems. Changes in the weather, injuries or illness, and the possibility of an individual or the group becoming lost are all "reasonably foreseeable" in virtually all outdoor pursuits; however, the relative importance of each will vary with each outing.

Building Shelters

Leaders who have experienced or practiced in foul weather insist upon carrying a large group tarp in addition to requiring individual survival gear. A large tarp can make a marginal situation quite comfortable and could make a critical difference in extreme weather. A 15' x 15' coated nylon tarp, preferably with tie points as shown in Figure 6.1 (page 108), can shelter at least a dozen people in severe weather.

In extreme cold, between periods of warming exercise, such a tarp can be used to cover the group, then snow or leaves can be piled on top as insulation. If there is enough snow to pile on the tarp, there may also be enough to make a quinzee. Figure 6.2 shows the quinzee and other types of snow shelters.

If the snow is relatively warm, so that sintering (bonding) occurs rapidly, the process of constructing a quinzee can be accelerated, and most group members kept out of the weather, by asking them to huddle, covering them with a tarp, and then burying them. If, and only if, the group is perfectly still for about ten minutes following burial, the snow shell will harden enough so that a hole can be dug in the side, allowing some people to exit. After another ten minutes, the walls will be strong enough to pull out the tarp and to do some finishing work while others begin a second structure if needed.

If the snow is deep, try digging a large pit, then using the same technique to form a dome, a sort of "quigloo" hybrid of quinzee and igloo. The smaller the dome, the faster and easier it will be to make, and the stronger it will be.

All are capable of sheltering large groups but, as with quinzees or quigloos, they require practice. No amount of study can replace real practice in making snow shelters, and first attempts are invariably pitiful. There are several serious hazards to be considered when constructing and using snow shelters, especially when large structures must be constructed. First, snow shelters take considerable time to construct. From one to three hours may be required to develop enough snow volume in which to house a dozen people. During this time, inactive group members may be vulnerable to hypothermia, while those engaged in making the shelter risk becoming soaked, especially when making caves or hollowing quinzees. Care must be taken to shelter inactive group members and to protect active members against overheating or saturation of clothing.

Large roof structures must be avoided unless well-domed. A nearly flat roof more than a meter wide will usually sag and may collapse. Inner surfaces must be smooth, and there *must* be good ventilation, to ensure that the temperature stays just below the freezing point, despite the temptation to allow the temperature to rise. Insulation is rendered ineffective by saturation in water vapor, an inevitable result without good ventilation, because a group puts out a great deal of heat (about 100 watts per person!). It is also important to allow any drips that may occur to fall into snow on the floor and not to puddle on tarps or on a hardened, icy layer. An air

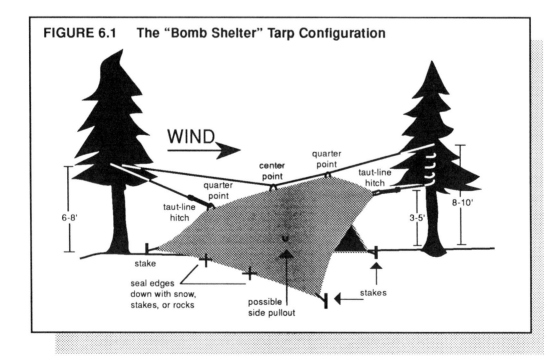

FIGURE 6.1   The "Bomb Shelter" Tarp Configuration

WIND

quarter point
center point
quarter point
taut-line hitch
taut-line hitch
8-10'
taut-line hitch
6-8'
3-5'
stake
seal edges down with snow, stakes, or rocks
possible side pullout
stakes

FIGURE 6.2   Snow Shelters

QUINZEE
(snow pile shelter)
Transparent View

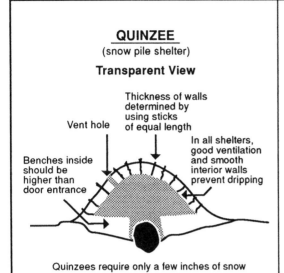

Vent hole

Thickness of walls determined by using sticks of equal length

In all shelters, good ventilation and smooth interior walls prevent dripping

Benches inside should be higher than door entrance

Quinzees require only a few inches of snow

SNOW CAVE
Transparent View

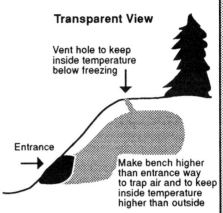

Vent hole to keep inside temperature below freezing

Entrance

Make bench higher than entrance way to trap air and to keep inside temperature higher than outside

Snow caves require deep snow or drifts

SNOW TRENCH

To prepare snow for block making, stomp with skis or snowshoes, then wait 30 minutes

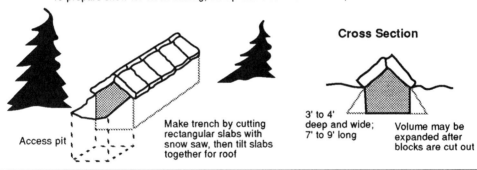

Cross Section

Access pit

Make trench by cutting rectangular slabs with snow saw, then tilt slabs together for roof

3' to 4' deep and wide; 7' to 9' long

Volume may be expanded after blocks are cut out

IGLOO

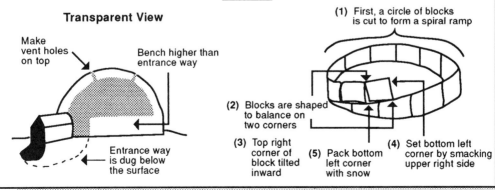

Transparent View

Make vent holes on top

Bench higher than entrance way

Entrance way is dug below the surface

(1) First, a circle of blocks is cut to form a spiral ramp

(2) Blocks are shaped to balance on two corners

(3) Top right corner of block tilted inward

(5) Pack bottom left corner with snow

(4) Set bottom left corner by smacking upper right side

temperature of 30°F (-1.1°C) is tolerable in dry insulation. At 40°F (4.4°C), fog soaks clothing and reduces insulation value, and thus, much more insulation is required than for survival in dry clothing at 30°F.

If a tepee or other large fabric shelter can be devised, then it is possible to raise the temperature to well above freezing, since one doesn't have to contend with melting walls and a limitless supply of moisture. Still, ventilation is critical, especially if the fabric is either waterproof, wet, or both. Each day, each person passes a liter or more of water into the atmosphere. This moisture has to escape in cold weather or else it will raise humidity and cause dripping from the walls, or it will freeze on inner surfaces of the shelter. In dire cases of water shortage, this water could be collected for use, but, in most cases, it is a serious liability. Stones heated outside in a campfire can be used to heat a shelter, and body heat alone can raise temperatures to a comfortable level, even though insulation of the shelter walls may be necessary. Two tarps can be used to create an effective leaf or bough "sandwich." Another good heat source is a buried bed of coals. Make a large fire in a pit; let it burn long enough (an hour or more at least) to heat up the surrounding soil and stones; then cover the pit with a six-to-eight inch layer of mineral soil (soil with *no* vegetable matter in it). Place the shelter directly over the buried coals for effective floor heating for many hours. Use a ground sheet or provide good ventilation to avoid build-up of toxic gases.

Other concerns

Sometimes it is necessary to travel with the group in order to find a suitable survival site, and sometimes it is best to move a group "out of the woods" rather than accept the risks associated with bivouacking under emergency conditions. Such decisions demand experience and good judgment, because a decision to keep moving, if it does not result in getting the group to a safe environment, could lead to disaster. Leaders should practice techniques for close control of groups in adverse weather and darkness. There are some highly effective techniques, including roping up (end persons tied

in and others clipped to sliding runners) and close-order hand-on-shoulder trail walking at night. In both cases, batteries can be conserved by using only one light held by the lead person.

Water

The human body is approximately 80 percent liquid. Intake and output of liquids are necessary for life processes and the normal functions of the vital organs. When water loss exceeds intake, dehydration takes place. Dehydration of 6 percent to 8 percent of the body weight will result in decreased body efficiency; if uncorrected, it will end in a complete body collapse. Water is, therefore, a necessary ingredient to survival. While it is possible to live for up to three days without water in moderate climates, the victim will become weaker and weaker and be more subject to other body ailments. Even those "holed up" in snow shelters should replenish the water in their systems while waiting rescue.

Humans lose water three ways: perspiration, breathing, and urination. Excess body heat must be dissipated by evaporation of perspiration on the skin. Sweating uses salt; salt deficiency causes disruption of body chemistry (muscle cramps, headaches, nausea). Adequate salt intake will also help retain moisture in the system. When hiking, it is wise to drink 3 to 4 quarts of water or juice per day to prevent dehydration.

For a person whose water supply is limited, the problem is to ration water loss rather than intake of water. Conserve the water in the body by reducing the body's basic needs for water. Drink available water until your thirst is satisfied, instead of attempting to stretch the supply. A fuller discussion of the need for water was covered in Chapter Five, "Understanding Human Needs."

Survival Kits

Many are the lists of equipment necessary for survival, and many are the people who purchase such kits and take them on every trip with little or no knowledge of why some items are included or even know how to use them. Fishing hooks, nylon lines, and waterproof matches are of no use to the lost camper in the desert or in the snowy mountains. They are also of little use to the nonfisherman next to a trout stream in July. The service an outdoor leader can perform related to survival kits is to be certain the participants know what should be taken on *every* trip and how to use each item.

There are many lists of the "10 Essentials" necessary for survival, yet there is no universal agreement as to what the *ten* "essential" items are. Often the lists recommend an 11th item or become a list of 10 plus 2. Rather than look at a list that might not cover every contingency, the leader should look at situations and prepare to meet them. The items in a "survival kit" should consist of:

1. Items needed for immediate survival.

Short-term survival items aid in the retention of an existing viable body temperature. Whether the weather is warm, cold, dry, or moist, the individual members of the group must have equipment to wear that will maintain their body temperature at or near normal while they prepare for long-term survival. Such items as rain gear and *extra* insulation (sweaters, jackets, warm head coverings, gloves) are necessary for cold or temperate climates. Sun screen, sunglasses, brimmed hats, long-sleeved light-colored cotton shirts, and long pants are all essential for desert or hot areas of the world. These items must be included in the initial gear of every group member.

Along with clothing come items to protect the eyes. Sunglasses or goggles for snow, sand, sun, or higher elevations are just as essential as the extra clothing.

2. Long-term survival items to (a) preserve or maintain the body temperature and (b) produce metabolic heat.

Items to help maintain body temperature over a period of several hours or days include a shelter (tent, tarp, large poncho, "space blanket," or any large weatherproof cover to provide personal or group shelter), plus the tools to erect the shelter (cord or rope of sufficient length and strength, and a knife to cut the cord into useful lengths).

To produce metabolic heat, a means of heating liquids and food is needed. Where there is adequate firewood, it might be possible to make a small fire. In most cases, it is better to carry a small stove, as firewood is often sparse, wet, or too large to break into small sticks. Prerequisites for the fire or stove are waterproof matches and fire starters. Beware of matches soaked in paraffin as they soak up moisture during storage. Better matches are those completely covered with nail polish or carried in a completely waterproof and sealed container to be opened only for emergency purposes. Many people carry disposable butane lighters—but only bring relatively new and unused ones. They are much more foolproof than matches. Fire starters (fire ribbon, candles, balls of paraffin soaked in wax, etc.) are carried to help light a fire in damp and stormy weather.

Along with the means to heat liquids and food, survival kits must include a supply of water (preferably that which has been purified in advance and carried in case of need), a metal cup or pan in which to melt snow and heat the water, and extra food in the form of high energy carbohydrates such as instant soups, broths, nuts, crackers, and cheese, as well as a small amount of sweets for morale boosters. Many outdoor enthusiasts carry a special packet of such food and plan never to use it except in emergencies. They carry the same packet on trip after trip and replace it about once or twice a year. The extra food should be at least the equivalent of an extra-large lunch, especially in cool weather. In any case, one should plan on enough food for an unplanned night outdoors.

3. Items for travel.

There are times when traveling to a different location can improve the odds of survival. Moving to a lower elevation, a more stable site, or into the shelter of trees may be the wisest action for survival of the group or an individual. If and when it is necessary to travel, survival items include a flashlight with extra batteries and bulbs. Small types using "AA" cells may be adequate in the late spring and early summer; however, larger "D" cells are recommended for the darker months. To prevent battery drain should the switch be activated accidentally, flashlight batteries are carried with one in a reversed position or with paper inserted between them. Extra bulbs are recommended because, unlike the battery that fades slowly, bulbs burn out without warning. A small second flashlight, the butane lighter, or matches should give enough light to replace the main bulb. Not only is a light a means of finding the route, it is a means of signaling at night and provides a great psychological boost. Most people are extremely uncomfortable in a "survival situation," and the advent of darkness adds more anxiety to the scene.

Current maps of the area and a navigational compass are necessary for travel. Unfortunately, many novices think that just carrying such items prevents getting lost. Maps and compasses are of no use unless the participants are capable of using them competently.

4. Signaling items.

Signaling items include fire, the flashlight mentioned above, mirrors, and, *of great importance*, a whistle. Many search and rescue organizations recommend that everyone carry a referee's whistle for signaling. Such items are small, lightweight and can always be a part of the survival kit. Blowing the whistle three times every few minutes will help rescuers locate the lost or stranded individual(s). A word of caution: youngsters may be tempted to blow the whistle for fun, or even to try to fool people into thinking they are lost. Placing the whistle in a sealed plastic bag, explaining that the bag is to be opened only in case of emergency, and requiring the youths return the whistle and bag upon return from a trip, may help preclude any youngster from "crying wolf" by playing with the whistle.

5. Other items.

Many people think that a watch is a good item for a survival kit. A watch may help a person calculate how much daylight is likely to remain, can be an aid in keeping track of distance covered when traveling and can aid in orientation and navigation. Furthermore, a watch is often of psychological value as most people cannot keep track of time, and many feel that hours have elapsed while only a few minutes have passed.

A first aid kit is a given in the list of any experienced outdoor person. Its utility depends upon its contents, and the skill and knowledge of its users. The contents will vary somewhat with the geographic locale and season. Snake bites are not likely on glaciers or cross-country ski trips, but sunburn could occur almost anywhere!

Regardless of anything else, *the most important elements in any survival kit are shelter from the elements and drinking water.* Conscientious advanced planning reduces the chances of needing survival skills, while increasing the likelihood that survivors will be adequately skilled and equipped. Even in emergencies of relatively short duration, survival may depend upon the participant's *will to live* as well as the proper gear.

Teaching for Survival

It is incumbent upon the leader to prepare the participants to plan for their own survival. As was said earlier, part of this is planning for survival in advance. The leader should make the advanced plans and teach them to the participants so that they, in turn, will follow the same patterns of behavior when they are on their own. The advanced plans may be as follows:

1. Know where you are going. Gather as much information about the area as possible. Seek information on trail or water conditions from management agencies and people who have been there recently. Check on all conditions en route to the site and at it: roads, snow, water levels, etc.

2. Make a list of equipment. Follow the list and check it before leaving. Many experienced outdoor people keep standard checklists of gear and equipment for a variety of trips (day, backpacking, cross-country skiing, climbing, and water travel) and post them where they store their equipment. No trip is ever taken without checking the appropriate list. Old-timers who seem to pack their gear by second nature have been known to forget such vital gear as sleeping bags or extra jackets because they packed automatically rather than by plan.

3. Tell someone (friend, family, supervisor) where you are going, what time you are leaving, and when you plan to return. Be sure to call them when you do return. If you are not back by a designated time, they will look for your vehicle first and then for you at where you said you'd be. This means the next point is important.

4. Stick to your plans. (Or inform people where an alternate route might be.) If you plan to run Silver Creek or climb Haystack Peak and tell people, that is where they'll look for you. If you change your mind and go down White River or up Old Baldy, no one will think of looking for you there! Do not alter your plans.

5. In case someone in the group becomes separated from the others and is lost, that person should know what to do. If everything discussed so far has been followed, there is really only one thing to do. **STAY PUT.** Given the fact that the lost member has adequate gear, there is no need to move. The search party will be able to locate a lost person easily if the person doesn't roam further astray and become "loster."

Summary

Surviving outdoor emergencies starts with being prepared for survival and making plans for the worst case scenario likely to exist for the regions and time of year of the activity. If advance plans have been made for shelter, equipment, and water, and if the times and routes have been communicated, a group in an emergency situation should be able to wait until help comes or to send for help. (See Chapter Eight, "Search and Rescue"). In advance of every outing, individuals and groups should plan to carry emergency gear and should be well-educated in steps to follow if lost or stranded.

Even if the group or individual must wait several days for help to survive, survival should be a definite possibility. A well-skilled leader enhances survival chances by being able to get more water and build shelters and fires. While it is hoped that the leaders have such skills, they will go to waste if the initial survival shelter and water are not available or if no one knows where to start looking for a missing group.

References

Boswell, J. (Ed.). (1980). *The U.S. Airforce survival manual.* New York, NY: Times Books.

Darst, P. W., & Armstrong, G. P. (1980). *Outdoor adventure activities for school and recreation programs.* Minneapolis, MN: Burgess Publishing Co.

Fear, D. (1971). *Surviving the unexpected.* Tacoma, WA: See-Hear Communications.

Fear, E., Simac, J., & Lasher, E. (Eds.). (no date). *Guidelines for outdoor living.* Tacoma, WA: Mountain Rescue Council.

Fear, G. (1972). *Surviving the unexpected wilderness emergency.* Tacoma, WA: Survival Educational Association.

Heet, J. (1984). *Hug-a-tree and survive.* 6465 Lance Way, San Diego, CA.

Merrill, B. (1974). *The survival book.* New York, NY: Arco Publishing Co., Inc.

Merrill, W. K. (1965). *Getting out of outdoor trouble.* Harrisburg, PA: Stackpole Books.

Province of British Columbia. (1979). *Outdoor safety and survival.* British Columbia Forest Service Information Branch.

Risk, P. (1983). *Outdoor safety and survival.* New York, NY: John Wiley and Sons.

Stoffel, R., & LaValla, P. (1980). *Survival sense for pilots.* Tacoma, WA: Survival Education Association.

Wiseman, J. (1987). *The SAS survival book.* London, England: Collins Harvill.

BACKCOUNTRY FIRST AID

Most outdoor leaders acknowledge the need for specialized training in first aid. Someone might be injured and need care, and the treatment of an injury in a backcountry setting may require more advanced "second aid" skills. This is certainly true; yet for some this is not sufficient motivation for extra training. Each leader has a different perception of the level of risk inherent in outdoor pursuits, and this perception varies widely with the particular activity, time, and place. Some leaders don't see the risk of injuries in outdoor activities as sufficient enough to justify a substantial investment of time and money in first aid training. Their rationale is often based on having experienced little need for more than basic first aid skills. In that sense, they may have a point.

Outdoor pursuits, taken as a whole, are *not* particularly risky. For example, outdoor-pursuit activities in the mountains claim 400 to 600 lives per year in Japan, a similar number in the combined Alps of France, Switzerland, Germany, Austria, and Italy, and about sixty in the United States. These figures, especially those for Japan and Europe, seem extremely high; yet, when viewed in the context of the great number of participant days, the death rate (and presumably the injury rate) per hour of activity turns out to be not far above the average rates for the recreational activities of the general population. Hour for hour, climbing may not be much more hazardous than driving, and backpacking is no doubt

safer than everyday living in many urban areas! Some people simply don't see this level of risk as warranting a special effort. Nevertheless, leaders do need first-aid training for reasons that transcend their perceptions of, and attitudes toward, risk.

Leaders are responsible for the well-being of others. As explained earlier, the leader is both morally and legally bound to provide certain basic forms of care, and adequate response to injuries is perhaps the most basic of all. While it is certainly true that all adult participants in an outing *should* know first aid, the leader can never count on this assumption. He/she is expected to provide all necessary care, which in all likelihood will exceed the capabilities of any member of the group unless the injury is very minor. Furthermore, the provision of such care requires skills and knowledge beyond that taught in "urban" first-aid courses. Our legal system tends to support the expectations of participants, and competence in first aid is widely acknowledged as a basic requirement of outdoor leadership, professional or otherwise. It isn't "reasonably prudent behavior" to go beyond the rapid availability of professional medical care and facilities without sufficient means to take care of yourself and your party members.

Those leaders working with youth, organized camps, church groups, etc., must follow the first-aid guidelines of their respective agencies.

Usually, no activity or trip is undertaken without first procuring standing orders from a doctor. Such standing orders should include the types and strength of any medications and antibiotics the leader may administer. In some cases, even administration of aspirin may be considered an unreasonable and imprudent act, whether the recipients are allergic to aspirin or not. In all cases, participants should be required to complete health forms and relevant information (i.e., allergies, daily medication, and chronic health conditions), and these forms should accompany the leader on each trip. Some programs require each participant under the legal age to give all medication to the leader who will administered it during the trip. This is standard practice for all youth camps in the United States and is included in the standards to be followed for youth camp accreditation by the American Camping Association. *While the following material is advised for all outdoor leaders, each is strongly cautioned to look into the recommendations of the medical officer employed by the sponsoring agency.*

In this chapter, the intent is not to reiterate the contents of a basic first aid course. Rather, it is to highlight aspects of basic first aid that are especially important in outdoor situations, to provide supplemental information on topics not adequately covered in standard courses, and to provide a list of resources for further study. It is assumed throughout this chapter that the reader is thoroughly familiar with current practices in basic first aid, at least with those equivalent to the American Red Cross Advanced First Aid Course. Much of this chapter relates to those outdoor pursuits conducted in areas remote from help and which require advanced skill and leadership.

Outdoor leaders need first aid skills and knowledge *beyond* the scope of most Red Cross, St. John's, or other courses designed for urban dwellers. Standard EMT (Emergency Medical Technician) courses generally provide little information on improvisation and long-term care since there is little need for these skills in proximity to sophisticated medical treatment. The material provided here is intended only as a supplement to Red Cross, EMT,

or other standard training, however, and cannot replace hands-on experience in a comprehensive outdoor-oriented course.

Anyone planning to lead outings in wilderness or backcountry areas should invest in advanced courses and also pursue good supplementary study in backcountry first aid. Outdoor-oriented Red Cross first aid courses are available in some major cities, as are a growing number of Wilderness First Responder and Wilderness Emergency Medical Technician (WEMT) courses. To locate courses in your area, try contacting the local Red Cross office, parks and recreation department, school district, community college, or university. Many times, Wilderness First Responder, WEMT, and similar courses are advertised in backpacking and mountaineering magazines.

Initial Responses to Emergencies

Most first aid books give advice for the "critical response" period, the critical interval between first awareness of an accident or injury and direct "hands-on" contact with the victim. This period is especially important in outdoor situations. In town, a would-be rescuer or first aider can make repeated mistakes or even become a victim; however, the situation is usually remedied quickly by others. Assistance and expertise are never far away in or near cities in the United States and in most developed countries. Out of town, the situation is very different, and mistakes can be far more costly. Sophisticated support systems are generally not immediately available, and the prognosis for the injured patient can be affected seriously by the quality of care given by the first aider. Too often, an urgent but noncritical situation is turned into a nightmare by errors in the initial response!

Imagine a possible situation. Since the transportation phase of any outing is where a major accident is most likely to occur, imagine driving down the highway with a van full of clients, en route to the trailhead for a day of hiking. You're a couple of hours out of town and a half-hour past the last telephone. There is not much traffic. As you round a corner, you see a pickup truck on its side in the ditch on the outside of the next curve, its wheels still spinning. No other cars have stopped yet. What do you do? You may not be legally obligated to provide first aid; yet, morally, you feel obliged to be of help. You are tempted to pull up close to the pickup, leap out, and run over to check on the occupants, with the knowledge that saving lives may depend upon speed if by chance there are breathing or other time-critical problems. Before you slam on the brakes, hesitate for a second! Think very carefully and clearly at this point. Don't panic, and, most importantly, don't fix your attention too quickly on that vehicle in the ditch.

There are many factors to consider here, and your action will affect you, your passengers, and other motorists, as well as the occupants of the pickup. Take in the *whole* scene and the *whole context* of the accident. Your actions should reflect concern for the welfare of *all* of the people potentially involved. Usually, this means that you have to spend precious time finding a safe place to park and making sure that no further accidents occur. In many situations, the placement of flaggers, flares, or other warning systems can be more valuable to the victims than anything else you can do since secondary accidents are all too common.

Assume you have stopped your van in a safe place and that traffic is adequately warned. Now what? Your options rely on the capabilities of your passengers. Let us assume you have a mixture of children and adults and can leave the youngsters confined to the van under the supervision of an adult while you and the others go to the wreck with whatever blankets and first-aid supplies are available. A word of caution here— take extreme care with regards to traffic, as drivers will be distracted by the accident.

As you approach the vehicle, keep looking around. Don't fix your attention on one thing to the exclusion of the rest of the scene! Are the flares slowing traffic safely? Was another car involved? Look around! Was anybody thrown out? What about across the road? Once at the pickup, announce your arrival but don't risk a costly mistake by diving into the cab too quickly. Is the vehicle stable? What about gasoline? **Look around!** This may be especially difficult at this point, since your pumping

adrenalin is now surely accelerated by the sight and sound of the victim(s). Keep calm and *give clear directions to your helpers.* Make sure that you, your assistants, and the victims aren't endangered by movement of the vehicle, by fire, or by a possible gasoline explosion. Turn off the ignition key if you can. Then, finally, it is possible to approach the victim(s) and begin treatment. A safe approach may cost seconds or even minutes, and there is no alternative.

People should have something constructive to do or stay well away from the scene. At the site of an accident, unnecessary people are distracting, get in the way, and often dilute the efforts of the rescuer by becoming victims themselves. It is common for onlookers to faint, especially if blood is visible. Be firm in your control of onlookers. You can explain your actions later.

At this point, you may encounter ambulatory and concerned companions of the injured parties. This is usually the case, since most people travel with friends or relatives. Just as with your own party, you have to take care not to compound the situation by allowing well-meaning but nonproductive people on the scene. Usually, these companions want to help and can assist in meaningful ways, and they may have a right to stay at the scene. Nevertheless, it is sometimes necessary to remove individuals if their behavior compromises treatment of the victims.

The next stage will be discussed in the next section. Meanwhile, think through some other scenarios, this time in the backcountry. As on the highway, the same careful, eyes-wide-open approach is just as essential in a hiking, climbing, skiing, or water accident. Don't fail to protect yourself, the healthy members of your party, and the victims from environmental hazards. Rockfalls, avalanches, and lightning *do* strike twice in the same place! Both authors of this book can attest to that through personal experiences. Remember that the best final resolution of the situation will depend upon how well you are able to control all of the variables in this critical interval. You want to employ all of your resources to assist the victims, not compound the problem by adding more victims.

Direct Care of the Victim

Approaching the Victim

Once it is possible to deal directly with the patient, make your approach as quickly as possible but with care not to cause further injury. It is a good idea to talk to the victim as soon as voice contact is possible, and the very first communication should be a request for the victim to "Stay still," or the order "Don't move." Do whatever is necessary to keep the person from moving until it is possible to assess the nature of his/her injuries. Reassure the person that help is coming, but be sure not to cause the person to move. On approach, be careful not to slip or trip, causing yourself or some object to slide into, move onto, or otherwise injure the victim. On a hill, try to approach from the side or from below. It is also a good idea, when possible, to approach from a direction that won't elicit undesirable movement by the victim. The victim will naturally try to turn toward the rescuer, which could cause major complications in the event of spinal injury or a precarious position. Coming in from the front of the patient may help prevent spontaneous turning, as there is a tendency for victims to turn to greet the rescuer.

Surveying the Injuries

At this point, it is important to scan the victim quickly for those injuries or conditions that can be immediately life-threatening. *Avoid fixation on any one injury.* Check quickly for adequate respiration, cardiac function, major bleeding, and any sign of spinal injury. These concerns, along with a very few others (certain poisons, diabetic conditions, etc.), can cause death or serious long-term disability if not treated promptly and correctly. Once the major injuries are dealt with, the time element becomes far less critical. Shock, fractures, and other injuries must be promptly attended to, but in a time frame of minutes, not seconds. It is most important to remain calm and *assess the victim from head to toe with great care.* Major injuries are easily hidden by clothing, and victims often are unaware of, or

even strongly deny, serious injuries. Outdoor clothing can be especially concealing; too often, major injuries are not discovered because they are hidden underneath costly ski pants or rain wear. Consider the cost of one day in the hospital! If it is necessary to examine or treat the patient, cut away any clothing that cannot be removed intact safely. In cold situations, extra effort may be warranted to keep protective clothing as useful as can be.

Psychological Support

Remember that the psychological well-being of the patient can greatly affect the final outcome greatly. This is an even greater concern in wilderness and backcountry situations due to added stress and prolonged treatment. Put yourself in the victim's place. How did you feel the last time you were hurt in an accident? Chances are, you were responsible for what happened, knew you were pushing your luck a bit, and afterwards felt rather embarrassed. You may also have felt foolish, guilty, and concerned about the future. Victims begin to worry about the consequences even in the midst of the accident. "What are the injuries?" "How long will they take to heal?" "How much will treatment cost?" "What about loss of employment?" "What will so-and-so think?" The physical outcome for the patient is significantly affected by his/her mental state, and outdoor situations provide a lot of time for worrying and sometimes a lot to worry about. When you were last injured, what sort of help did *you* want? Most likely, if your injuries were major, you wanted someone who *looked* and *sounded* competent. One of the best ways to improve your ability to help others is to spend a few minutes thinking of first aid from the victim's point of view and working through some scenarios.

In the backcountry or on a country road, no ambulance is going to whisk away the victim within minutes. Establish a rapport with him/her as quickly as possible, and stay *in communication* throughout the incident. Establishing a trusting and comfortable rapport can be difficult, and it requires maturity and a degree of self-control on the part of the first aider. Try to keep your voice calm, and try using the victim's name in conversation. Even if that is not your usual style, give it a try. A person who is seriously injured will appreciate being called by name. Be careful when using humor; what may work for a small child with a cut finger may not be appropriate for the injured adult. Honesty goes a long way toward establishing credibility. In virtually all circumstances, it is best to keep the victim well-informed of what is happening and of what is about to happen. The most difficult situations are those involving deaths of family or friends. Since you are not a medical examiner, it is usually best to assure the victim that you really don't know. There may be no life-threatening reason to stop you from telling the truth; however, you cannot predict the result of psychogenic shock on a severely injured victim.

Record Keeping

Another important aspect of victim care is record keeping. Circumstances may not allow note taking during the first few minutes, especially if you are alone; but some time should be allocated for this chore at the earliest possible moment. At the very least, note your time of arrival on the scene and the times of critical events. Better yet, assign someone to this task. The final outcome for the patient may depend in large part upon accurate diagnoses upon arrival at the hospital, and accurate records can provide clues to the nature and extent of injuries or illness. Good notes should include clear and detailed commentary on the patient's medical history, condition, and current treatment. The acronyms in Figure 7.1 can be used to facilitate thorough assessment and record keeping. Changes or events should be noted even when they don't seem important at the moment. Seriously injured patients should be monitored *continually*, with vital signs and the patient's condition noted at least every half-hour.

First Aid in Outdoor Emergencies

Conventional urban-oriented first aid courses assume quick access to professional care and facilities. While the initial treatments proposed in conventional courses are generally appropriate in backcountry situations, some conditions

FIGURE 7.1

Helpful Acronyms for Patient Assessment and Recordkeeping

AMPLE
(Medical history)

Allergies
Medications
Past medical history
Last meal *(When, what)*
Events leading to incident

AVPU
(Level of consciousness)

Alert *to person, place, and time*
Verbal *stimulus response*
Painful *stimulus response*
Unresponsive *to sound or pain*

SOAP
(Standard assessment format)

Subjective
Information obtained by questioning, including AMPLE history
Objective
Observations during exam, including AVPU level
Assessment
Estimation of medical status and likely changes
Plan
How is patient to be cared for

The SOAP format is widely used in the medical profession. Its use can facilitate thorough assessment of the patient, effective on-site planning, and efficient communication with medical and SAR personnel.

and injuries need special attention if access to a hospital or another specialized care facility will be delayed.

The following advice is intended only as a supplement to a thorough understanding of Red Cross, St. John's, EMT, or other standard procedures, and is by no means fully comprehensive. Leaders are urged to seek appropriate training in advanced first aid, extended care, and improvisation, using equipment common to the activities to be led. They must also understand and abide by the relevant policies regarding emergency care that have been established by the sponsoring agency and its medical advisor.

Altitude-Related Problems

As elevation increases, air pressure decreases. The body, finely tuned to near sea-level air pressure, responds poorly to decreased air pressure. Several effects combine to create problems for mountain travelers and pilots. First, adequate hydration becomes more difficult to maintain because water evaporates from the body more rapidly under lowered pressure, and because air at high elevations tends to have a lower relative humidity. In addition, prolonged exposure to lowered air pressure leads to shifts in fluid distribution in the body. Lowered air pressure usually causes hypoxia, which reduces heat production efficiency.

Hypoxia occurs because oxygen is not picked up by the body at low pressure as efficiently as it is at normal pressure. This oxygen deficit can be felt at elevations as low as 5,000 feet (1,500 meters), even by perfectly healthy, fit people. The brain is one of the first organs affected by an oxygen deficit, which is why many people feel a bit exhilarated, giddy, or "high" when moving quickly to such elevations. While most healthy people will experience no worse than a little shortness of breath when exercising at 6,000 feet (1,800 meters), some people may begin to experience symptoms of Acute Mountain Sickness (AMS). These symptoms range from mild to severe headache, insomnia, loss of appetite, nausea, vomiting, periodic breathing, lassitude, and ataxia (loss of coordination) to very serious life-threatening complications such as pulmonary and cerebral edema. At higher elevations, AMS symptoms are more likely to occur and are generally more severe.

For practical purposes, the AMS complex can be divided into three categories: mild, moderate, and severe. In mild AMS, the symptoms are limited to a slight headache, perhaps some insomnia and loss of appetite, and shortness of breath when exercising. While these conditions

alone usually aren't terribly uncomfortable or limiting, they should be taken as an indication of a need to rest and perhaps take an extra day to acclimatize before going up to a higher elevation. Moderate AMS is indicated by such symptoms as a bad or severe headache, lassitude, nausea, and ataxia. Not all of the symptoms need be present to warrant concern because this level of AMS is very serious and clearly indicates a need to descend. Simply stopping the ascent is usually not sufficient therapy. A descent of 2,000 feet (600 meters) is usually necessary to achieve a substantial therapeutic effect.

Ataxia is easy to check for, and its presence is an ominous warning. Common "sobriety" tests work well; ask the suspected AMS victim to walk heel to toe in tiny steps on a 10 or 15 foot-long line scratched in the soil or snow. Any abnormal difficulty should be considered a sign of ataxia and cause for concern. The Romberg test is also useful. Have the patient stand as if at attention. Place your arms on each side of the person and assure the person that you won't let him/her fall. Then ask the person to close his/her eyes. Most people can stand quite still with almost no swaying, while an ataxic person will, within ten to fifteen seconds, sway back and forth and even fall into your arms. Failure of either test should be taken as an indication of possible moderate AMS.

It must be remembered that the various degrees of AMS are only convenient subdivisions of a progressive condition; a person with moderate symptoms is likely to develop severe symptoms soon, if therapy is ignored. Severe AMS is associated with a number of life-threatening conditions such as high altitude pulmonary edema (HAPE) and cerebral edema (CE). Even if these don't develop, the mild ataxia detected in the above tests can progress to complete inability to stand up in a few hours or less. Anyone planning to travel at elevations above 8,000 feet (2,400 meters) should study a good treatise on the topic of altitude-related problems. Peter Hackett's *Mountain Sickness* is a small, concise, and easily read resource that is highly recommended for this purpose.

Respiratory Problems

Asthma

Many of the factors that may contribute to asthmatic symptoms are common in outdoor settings. Cold or dry air, exercise, and a wide range of allergies can bring on an attack. The initial attack can often be controlled through medication if appropriate drugs are available. Often the chronic asthmatic individual will be carrying an inhaler or antihistamine, or these may be included in the first aid kit. As with all drugs— prescription *or* over-the-counter types—take care in prescribing their use. Unless you feel the situation is truly desperate, it is always best to allow the individual to make the decision to use the drugs and to avoid putting yourself out on a legal limb by stating or implying that the drug is safe and will help the person. In any case, read the label carefully and see that directions are followed explicitly.

Again, we offer the caveat to obtain standing orders from the medical profession, and to follow standing orders for youth members who have brought their own antihistamines. No youngster with any known allergy should be permitted on the trip without approval of the family/agency physician.

Another helpful technique for asthmatics is to provide warm moist air. This can be done by guiding steam towards the person's face with a piece of cloth. Be careful, however, not to construct a device that is too efficient, since hot steam and the gases given off by stoves can seriously complicate the problem. A backpacking stove or a fire can be used to boil water, and the steam guided by the sleeve of a coat or shirt. A hot steaming towel can often provide enough relief by resoaking often in very hot water. Once the initial attack has ended, give the individual plenty of time to rest, and avoid further exposure to the conditions that brought on the initial attack. As with most respiratory problems, it is a good idea to go down in elevation.

Bronchitis

Bronchitis is an infection of the trachea and the major air passages of the lungs. Although it may be caused by a virus, most typically it occurs during or after a viral cold and is caused by a bacterial infection. The symptoms usually include a frequent cough that, after a day or two, begins to produce thick greenish or yellowish sputum. The person usually doesn't appear to be very ill otherwise and may or may not have a slight fever. The treatment consists of moderate rest, avoiding prolonged or hard exertion, general "TLC," and antibiotics.

Antibiotic therapy is something rarely attempted on outings since success depends upon having a sufficient quantity of the proper drug to attack the infection, and the drug must be one to which the patient has no adverse reaction. Antibiotics need to be given in specific doses in a pattern designed to raise the initial level of the drug in the body very rapidly, and to maintain it at a constant level throughout the course of treatment. Failure to maintain a high enough drug level can allow the resistant bacteria to multiply. For these reasons, in most cases carrying "just a few" of one or two kinds of antibiotics is probably a waste of time. If the outing is so lengthy or remote as to preclude escape to medical care in a day or two, then a substantial quantity of antibiotics might be brought along, with types and quantities worked out in consultation with a physician.

Pneumonia

Pneumonia is an infection of one or both lungs. The disease varies considerably according to the nature and extent of the infection. Viral pneumonias tend to be less severe than bacterial pneumonias; yet, either type can be extremely disabling, and even fatal, if not properly treated. The symptoms include coughing, a fever of 102°F (39°C) or higher, weakness and a general appearance of being quite ill. If the infection is bacterial, chills and a very high fever may be present.

Even though coughing can sometimes be extremely painful in these cases, the patient must be encouraged to cough deeply at least several times a day to minimize fluid buildup in the lungs. Antibiotics and rest are also very important. The fever and infection increase the body's demand for oxygen while fluid buildup reduces the oxygen-transfer capabilities of the lungs.

This situation alone can be life threatening. High elevations can tip the balance, so get the patient down to a much lower elevation as quickly as possible.

Dehydration

Even in the absence of general systemic dehydration, the lungs can become dry and irritated due to dry air. Low pressure, as at high altitudes, contributes by increasing the evaporation rate. The result may be a hacking dry cough which is usually alleviated by a night of rest, especially if humidity in the tent can be raised by periodically boiling a pot of water outside and letting it cool off in the tent. This problem is most common among ski-tourers and climbers in cold, dry conditions, and usually isn't particularly serious unless the irritated and vulnerable lungs become infected.

Hyperventilation

Hyperventilation is a fairly common occurrence in outdoor activities. An often cited example is accidental hyperventilation that occurs in swimmers attempting to load up on oxygen before a dive. Another common cause is anxiety. The ski run or the next pitch of the climb may not produce anxiety in the leader, but may well terrify a beginner. Watch participants before particularly challenging events, and you may well see forced or rapid breathing. Yet another common cause is improper breathing while hiking or climbing. Too often hikers or climbers are told to breathe and step in a certain pattern— a once popular but highly counterproductive method of breathing control, that all too often overloads the system with oxygen. It is far better to let people find a comfortable need-determined breathing rate. Usually, the adverse symptoms can be easily resolved by breathing into a stuff sack or paper bag. Ten minutes of this method followed by a half hour of rest and relaxation will usually restore a normal carbon-dioxide reflex and reduce the anxiety level. A much reduced pace for an hour or so can help avoid relapses which are common.

Respiratory Arrhythmia

While uncommon below 6,000 feet (1,800 meters), respiratory arrhythmia (Cheyne-Stokes breathing) is fairly common above 10,000 feet (3,000 meters). It is unnerving to experience since the pattern consists of a minute or two of very heavy breathing followed by up to several minutes of no breathing at all. Waking up in the nonbreathing phase is quite an experience, usually resulting in a quick review of your day for any reason why you might now be dead! Both breathing and the desire for breath are absent, a state to which we are unaccustomed. This can be equally distressing if one's tent partner is affected. Normally, the person attracts your attention by breathing heavily, then declines to no breathing at all. Fortunately, this odd pattern does provide adequate oxygenation, even if it causes loss of sleep. Sometimes getting up and moving around a bit, or even taking a short walk and having a bite to eat, can help; otherwise, the problem usually resolves itself in a few hours. Going down in elevation by a few thousand feet (1,000 meters or so) usually ends the problem.

Respiratory Arrest

Whatever the cause of breathing cessation, care must be taken to observe the victim constantly once breathing is restored because relapses are likely. Traumatic events, such as blows to the chest, may result in fluid accumulation or swelling of the lungs over time. Drowning in salt water has a similar effect. The fluid from the body enters the lungs to dilute the salt water since the concentration of salts is higher than that in bodily fluids. Victims can then drown in their own fluids long after being initially resuscitated. Fresh-water near-drowning victims must also be watched carefully, since fresh water is absorbed by the lungs and can cause dangerous shifts in blood chemistry. A survivor of respiratory arrest should be immediately evacuated by the most expedient means, despite evident initial recovery. These cases usually warrant a helicopter evacuation if it can be arranged.

A question that is often heard is "How long should mouth-to-mouth resuscitation be continued?" Certainly, if the victim's heart is still beating, mouth-to-mouth resuscitation should be continued until professionals can take over. It is possible to imagine a situation where one must choose between giving mouth-to-mouth and going for help. There is no good answer to that dilemma; it simply reinforces the argument for leaving detailed plans with responsible people at home, and especially for traveling in groups of three or more people. Leaders should consider this when planning an outing. Even on a day outing, a group should have an assistant leader and enough clothing and equipment to allow simultaneous long-term care of the patient and evacuation of the remainder of the group.

Cardiac Problems

Arrhythmias

Most arrhythmias are not especially dangerous. Extra systoles are common and, while alarming to the patient, should not be a source of great concern if the condition is sporadic and short-term and if extra beats don't occur more often than five times per minute. These "extra beats" are sometimes associated with heavy consumption of caffeine, though many other causes are possible. Paroxysmal tachycardia, a very rapid but regular heartbeat that may last up to an hour or more, is very distressing but usually not life threatening. Forced breathing against a closed glottis or painful pressure on closed eyes can sometimes provide the electrical stimulus necessary to reverse the condition. The patient should be evacuated unless the episode is brief and easy to control, as this form of tachycardia is likely to recur. Atrial fibrillation, a rapid *irregular* heartbeat, usually responds to complete rest for a few hours; otherwise, evacuation is called for. Bradycardia, or a reduced heart rate, may be more serious and related to the use of certain drugs or to cardiac disease. Any prolonged duration of arrhythmias, or any arrhythmia associated with pain, warrants cessation or reduction of exercise, if possible, and prompt evacuation for medical care.

Angina

Angina is symptomatic of heart disease or impending heart attack. The symptoms include a dull, heavy, constricting pain in the center of the chest that characteristically appears when one is active and fades when the activity stops. The pain may spread to the throat, jaw, back, and arms. It may be accompanied by sweating, nausea, and dizziness.

The best treatment for sufferers of angina is usually complete rest coupled with the use of nitroglycerine tablets. These tiny white pills, usually carried by adults who have suffered the condition before, are taken under the tongue where the nitroglycerine is readily taken up. The result is dilation of the coronary arteries and rather rapid relief. Unfortunately, cerebral vessels are also affected, and rather severe headaches can accompany use of this drug. Patients may be able to walk out under their own power, though not without risk. Ideally, the patient should be flown or carried out; yet, this may not, in all cases, be possible without prolonged delay. Chances are the attack is not the first, and the person, usually a middle-aged or older male, will know how much rest is needed before proceeding. Certainly in no way should these patients be subjected to stresses anywhere near as great as those that overtaxed the coronary blood supply. The best plan is usually to head for the car at a leisurely pace after an extended period of rest.

Heart Attack and Heart Failure

Patients surviving the initial episodes of either a heart attack (myocardial infarction) or heart failure need to be handled with great care. As with respiratory arrest, helicopter evacuation is warranted if it can be arranged. If not, these patients need complete rest. In any case, psychological support is crucial as such situations can be terrifying for the victim, and for friends and relatives on the site. Rough or primitive evacuation should be put off for at least 6-8 hours unless a smooth, gentle evacuation can be assured. The patient will want to sit or lean up slightly to minimize respiratory difficulty, which makes carrying still more difficult. Thus, rest may be better than a traumatic and lengthy evacuation. After several days, the person may be able to walk very slowly out or down a trail, with no pack load and plenty of rest stops. This alternative isn't ideal, but, in a party of two or three, it may be necessary, especially if food or water supplies or foul weather make waiting for help impractical, and carrying is impossible.

Anaphylactic Shock

Anaphylactic shock can be caused by exposure to allergens such as pollens, insect bites or stings, medications, or even foods. In urban settings, rapid access to professional care is advisable. In backcountry settings the patient's life may depend upon proper administration of adrenalin (epinephrine) within minutes, or in extreme cases seconds, of the attack. Leaders should be prepared to administer treatment using an inhaler, Anakit, or EpiPin. The Anakit is preferred to the EpiPin for field use, as it contains two injections of epinephrine. It is best for the leader to carry the Anakit separately from the group first aid kit in cold weather to protect it from freezing. Yellow jackets linger after the first frosts, and stings are not the only possible cause of anaphylaxis. A frozen kit wouldn't be very useful. Participants and staff known to be sensitive to bee stings or severely allergic to other substances should be identified prior to the trip. They should have completed health forms, and the leaders should be informed of all participants who suffer from allergies. These people should have their own physician's prescribed medications with them. After an anaphylactic reaction has been controlled, the patient must be monitored for at least 24 hours. Several organizations automatically evacuate victims of anaphylaxis, and there have been a number of incidents wherein a patient has seemingly recovered, only to suffer a fatal, or near fatal, delayed second reaction.

Snake Bite

While there are many types of poisonous snakes, only four major kinds are found in the United States: rattlesnakes, copperheads, cottonmouths, and coral snakes. We reinforce the need for leaders to be familiar with, and to be able to recognize, the major types of snakes found in the areas in which the trip takes place. As might be expected, many people are bitten each year. Fortunately, in many cases, envenomation does not occur or is very slight. Even when envenomation is successful (from the snake's perspective), most victims survive. There is, however, considerable danger for small children, and even adults can suffer major damage to limbs due to the extreme swelling that can follow a bite.

In a backcountry setting the initial response to the bite is especially important, since there will almost inevitably be a long delay before receipt of professional care and the possibility of anti-venom administration. Unless the snake can be immediately ruled nonvenomous, have the patient try to relax and sit quietly. If the snake was a pit viper (such as a rattlesnake), the patient may experience a tingling sensation in the mouth along with a metallic or rubbery taste, well before any other symptoms or signs appear other than burning pain at the bite site. The limb should be held level with the heart or elevated slightly, and wrapped firmly with an elastic bandage between the bite and the body, leaving the wound exposed. Monitor pulse and sensation at the end of the extremity to ensure that the wrap is not *too* tight.

An "Extractor" should be carried at all times in snake country, as it is far superior to conventional suction devices. Use it immediately and do not make incisions as they actually reduce the effectiveness of the device. If an "Extractor" is *not* available, use incisions and suction following conventional techniques described in Red Cross texts. It is important to begin suction or use of the Extractor immediately, as the opportunity for removal of venom virtually disappears within a half hour. *Do not* apply cold, as this increases damage. The full effects of the bite may not be evident for many hours, and long-term damage can be severe if swelling is not controlled by pressure and elevation. Care must be taken, of course, to be sure that the pressure is not so great as to restrict blood flow to parts distal to the injury.

If the victim was bitten by a coral snake, the above procedures should be followed; however, incisions will usually not help. Coral snake toxin is a neurotoxin and quite serious. Keep the victim immobilized, and seek medical help at once.

Head Injuries

Conventional first aid texts say little about head injuries other than to suggest rest, treatment of symptoms as they appear, and careful observation of the patient. One of the major concerns in head injuries is the development of sub- and extra-dural hematomas over time. Another concern is the development of a hematoma from secondary bleeding, that is, bleeding not from the original wound but caused by stress on weakened or damaged vessels. These concerns reinforce the importance of observing the patient and limiting activities for several days following any serious blow to the head.

A good rule of thumb might be that if the blow raises an "egg" or causes any unconsciousness, rest for an hour or so and then head for civilization if it can be reached in a few hours over safe and easy ground at a gentle pace. Otherwise, a few days of *complete* bed rest are in order, followed by very slow and easy travel. The danger is compounded by the fact that, while blood clots form early, they might not adhere fully for a few days. Clots that break loose can travel through the vascular system and lodge elsewhere, causing blockage of arteries in the heart, lungs, brain, or other vital organs.

Another general rule of thumb is that blows causing unconsciousness for less than thirty minutes *usually* don't result in long-term consequences. Blows causing longer periods of unconsciousness probably will have more serious results. This rule may offer encouragement in cases where a person is unconscious for only a short time, but should not be used to avoid treatment. It is better to be conservative.

Fractures and Dislocations

There are two major differences between town and backcountry treatment of fractures. First, in backcountry settings, there is a greater likelihood of having to move or manipulate the injured part. Second, splinting is usually complicated by the lack of conventional materials and devices; yet, the splint must usually be far more secure, with better support and padding than in town. The patient will probably either walk out or be carried out, and, in either case, the limb will have to withstand far more than the amount of abuse typically given an in-town injury. The basic principles of splinting still apply—immobilization of the joints above and below the fracture site and ample padding.

While these skills seem quite straightforward, we have yet to see an adequate splint applied on the first try by a first aid class student. Probably the only way to fully appreciate the amount of padding and the proper method of securing a splint for a backcountry evacuation is to participate in a rescue practice, preferably as the victim. Failure to splint adequately can result in loss of limb function, bedsores (death of tissue due to pressure on the hard parts of a splint), or, at the very least, distress for the patient when splints are readjusted.

There are plenty of excellent splinting materials available in a typical backpacker's kit. Foam pads make excellent padding, and the stiffer foams when rolled up, can add rigidity to splints. Stuff sacks can be filled with various substances to provide padding. Tent poles and pack-frame parts are good stiffeners, as are walking sticks, ice axes, ski poles, and skis. When looking for splints, pads, and ties, keep in mind what it now costs to stay in a hospital! Don't hesitate to "modify" some gear to suit the purpose; in economic terms, it is a bargain, not to mention the value of reducing further pain and injury. Traction splints, which are almost always essential for femur fractures, can be constructed from ski poles, skis, ice axes, or pack frames. See Figure 7.2 (page 126) for an illustration of several improvised traction splints. Evacuation devices (litters, sleds, etc.) will be discussed in Chapter Eight, "Search and Rescue." It cannot be overemphasized that hands-on practice is absolutely essential. The first real need to treat a fracture is *not* the time to learn.

If the part of the limb distal to the injury shows signs of lack of circulation or of compromised nervous function, and if several hours will pass before the victim can be seen by a doctor, there is a good chance that permanent loss of function might occur. Careful manipulation of the part may help. Keep in mind that a nerve or a vessel is probably already being compressed, or may have been cut by the broken ends of the bone. Movement may relieve the pressure, or it may cause irreparable damage. The danger of further injury is reduced somewhat if the movement is made soon (within thirty minutes at least), gently, and with respect for the victim's sense of pain.

Gentle traction can help relieve pressure between bone ends. The directions of motion should be toward the position of function, that is, toward the position the limb would normally assume when relaxed. Another reason for moving a limb may be to allow for transportation. A person with a broken arm sticking straight out to the side will make a very awkward passenger on a litter, and will probably develop a bad attitude toward the brush and trees along the trail. During transportation of the patient, check periodically to be sure that the parts distal to the fracture continue to have adequate circulation and nervous function.

Dislocations are all too common in outdoor activities. Leaders should be aware of previous injuries to participants as dislocations often recur. Ski instructors should be particularly attentive to teaching techniques that reduce the likelihood of shoulder, hip, knee, and ankle dislocations. Leaders who have carefully studied the anatomy of body parts particularly vulnerable to dislocations will be better prepared to conduct emergency field reduction of these injuries. While it is never ideal to attempt to reduce a dislocation in the field, it is often reasonable to attempt reduction of fingers (not *thumbs*) and shoulder dislocations in backcountry situations. The specific methods for reducing these dislocations in the field are beyond the scope of this book, but are well covered in available books and guidelines such as those listed at the end of the chapter.

Spinal Injuries

In order to reduce the risk of extremely serious long-term complications, patients with spinal injuries must be fully immobilized. Because of

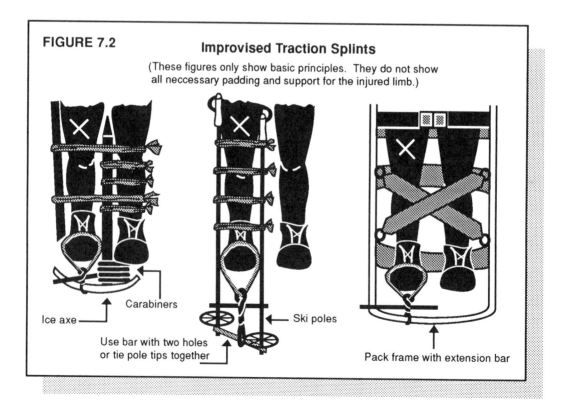

FIGURE 7.2　　　　**Improvised Traction Splints**

(These figures only show basic principles. They do not show all neccessary padding and support for the injured limb.)

Carabiners

Ice axe

Use bar with two holes or tie pole tips together

Ski poles

Pack frame with extension bar

the potentially devastating and irreversible consequences that can result from improper handling of the spinal injury patient, conventional protocols call for complete spinal immobilization and rapid transportation to a medical facility whenever the mechanism of injury could have produced spinal damage. While such first-aid care is ideal, it is extraordinarily difficult to achieve in many outdoor settings. A well-trained first aider can usually improvise a means of keeping the patient fully immobilized at the site of the accident, but it is virtually impossible to immobilize a patient well enough to allow transport by improvised means. Safe transportation of the spinal injury patient requires a well-equipped rescue team, and, ideally, helicopter evacuation. Thus, a diagnosis of possible spinal injury almost invariably requires a time consuming, costly, and potentially dangerous rescue operation. It is therefore advantageous to be able to perform a thorough assessment of the patient, to assure adequate care and to avoid the risks and costs of an unnecessary rescue.

The procedure suggested in Figure 7.3 (see page 128) is designed to help the first aider assess the likelihood of spinal injury. It is not a perfect system. Due to the severity of the potential consequences of inadequate treatment, *if in doubt one should take full precautions whenever the mechanism of injury is such that spinal injury is possible.*

The procedures suggested in Figure 7.3 are recommended for use only in situations when full spinal immobilization would be difficult or impossible to improvise before the patient must be moved, or in situations where transportation of the patient would be dangerously complicated or delayed by spinal immobilization. In these cases, the risk of further injury must be compared to the risks associated with a delayed or dangerous evacuation.

Foot Care

In most outdoor activities, no part of the body takes more abuse than the foot. Injuries to the feet are common, often painful, and potentially dangerous. Most foot injuries are caused by failure to use adequate footwear or by footwear that does not fit properly. Going barefoot increases the risk of cuts, abrasions, and stings or bites. Footwear that is too light for the activity, e.g, light canvas, aerobic, or tennis shoes used for backpacking or rugged off-trail hiking, may result in sprained ankles or deep bruises to the soles of the feet. Shoes or boots that are too short may produce painful blisters on the toes if the person walks downhill for very long, and oversized shoes or boots may result in slippage of the foot with resultant blisters.

Leaders should be highly attentive to participant footwear, and they should provide specific guidance well in advance of the outing as well as during the activity. The frequency and severity of blisters can be reduced by making sure that the feet are kept as dry as possible and by encouraging preventive taping of incipient blisters, preferably while the only symptom is mild irritation. The use of skin toughening treatments is not sufficient to overcome the effects of footwear that does not fit properly. To treat a blister in the field, first assess the damage. If the blister top is torn, it is usually best to remove the loose skin. If the top is intact, the blister may be drained by running a sterilized needle under some "good" skin near the blister edge, to form a drain hole. In either case, the use of antiseptic soap is important as infection is always a danger. The blister or sore area should be covered by a small piece of nonstick material or, ideally, a piece of hydrous gel, and then "donuts" of adhesive-backed felt or adhesive-backed foam can be applied. The idea is to transfer the pressure to the area around the wound. Several donuts of adhesive felt may be needed to equal one layer of adhesive foam. Be sure to round the edges of the donuts to reduce "rolling," and then cover the donuts with adhesive tape. Keep the foot dry, change to clean socks as often as possible, and watch for any signs of infection. In difficult cases, straps or donuts cut from foam pads can serve as insoles or as extra thick "donuts."

Toenails that protrude past the end of the toes can produce major problems as the hiker constantly pushes the nail against the end of the boot. This causes the nail to be forced back into the toe, resulting in a black and blue and entirely loosened nail. Young or beginning hikers may not realize the need for carefully trimmed and shortened nails.

FIGURE 7.3   Exceptions to Spinal Immobilization

Remember:

Whenever the mechanism of injury is such that spinal injury is possible, complete spinal immobilization is the rule. *Exceptions should be made **only** if:*

A. **All** of the following conditions are met. That is, all of the following must be true statements with respect to the patient, **and**

B. Spinal immobilization would result in real and unavoidable danger to the patient and/or rescuers. That is, **there needs to be a good reason for not following the normal procedures.**

  1. The patient is alert and oriented to person, place, and time.
  2. The patient is not under the influence of alcohol or drugs and appears capable of rational communication.
  3. The patient does not complain of neck or shoulder pain.
  4. The patient has no other signs or symptoms of neck, head, or brain injury.
  5. A head to toe exam does not indicate any numbness.
  6. The patient has full finger movement, a good grip in both hands, can extend and flex each arm and leg, and can move both ankles and both feet fully.
  7. The patient can extend and flex each arm and each leg against moderate resistance, and can push and pull with the toes against moderate resistance.
  8. An exam of the neck area finds no spasm, guarding, or tenderness. **If these symptoms are present, do not proceed to #9.**
  9. While the patient's head is being supported, the patient can gently flex the neck, with no pain. **Proceed to item #10 only if there is no pain or other indication of spinal injury.**
  10. The patient exhibits no neck pain, stiffness, numbness, or pain when allowed to move his/her head without support.

Note:

The protocol suggested above is attributable to no single source. It is a conservatively biased composite based on articles in U.S., German, Austrian, and Japanese publications, discussions with physicians and SAR personnel, and personal experience.

Gastrointestinal Ailments

Diseases of the gastrointestinal tract are often accompanied by nausea, vomiting, diarrhea, constipation, jaundice, or pain. There are many possible causes of gastrointestinal distress ranging from relatively benign "indigestion" to life-threatening ailments. Participants in outdoor activities, and travelers in general, are somewhat more likely to contract certain "g.i." ailments, particularly those that are carried by the water supply. In addition, some problems, such as appendicitis, can be difficult or impossible to treat effectively without access to medical facilities. Prevention is always best. The leader should instruct the group in the proper disposal of human wastes and necessary supervision the cleaning of food, purification of water, and washing of dishes and utensils. With care, the group can be somewhat isolated from organisms in the local food and water supply, and the spread of ailments within the group can be minimized.

It is often difficult or impossible to identify specific maladies in the field. The first task of the leader or first aider is generally to differentiate between those conditions that warrant immediate evacuation of the patient and those that may be resolved on-site. Because appendicitis is a relatively frequent occurrence, leaders should be particularly well-versed in its symptoms and field care. Other conditions that warrant immediate evacuation include a perforated peptic ulcer, intestinal obstruction or incarcerated hernia, acute pancreatitis or gall bladder diseases, kidney stones, and peritonitis.

Diarrhea is a particularly common complaint that may have many causes. Mild diarrhea that comes on rather rapidly (and usually lasts only a few hours to a few days) may be caused by staphylococci (*Staphylococcal enteritis*), food allergies, various viruses (viral enteritis), or by offending strains of *E. coli*, the bacteria normally found in one's bowel tract. Certain strains of *E. coli* produce toxins thought to cause the all too common "traveler's diarrhea" which has various nicknames. Chronic mild diarrhea may have many causes such as emotional colitis (spastic colon), changes in food or surroundings (always suspect in outdoor activities), and various underlying diseases.

Severe diarrhea, which may include "explosive" episodes and may be accompanied by vomiting, may be particularly nasty cases of any of the above causes of diarrhea, or may be caused by more serious diseases such as cholera, typhoid fever, or bacillary dysentery (Shigellosis). *Entamoeba histolytica* and the flagellate *Giardia lamblia* are now widespread and can cause particularly obnoxious symptoms.

Whatever the cause of the diarrhea, the concerns are similar. The patient must be kept well-hydrated, and reasonable precautions should be taken to avoid spread of the disease-causing organism. Paregoric, codeine, antibiotics, and other drugs are often prescribed for specific types of diarrhea; however, the use of any of these compounds can be very dangerous. Stopping the flow of stools can have dire consequences if the infecting organism multiplies in the intestinal tract. Antibiotics are useful only when the correct drug is used. Generally, it is better to provide only fluids, and evacuate the patient to a physician's care if the symptoms are not significantly improved within a few days.

Solar Radiation Injuries

Because outdoor activities tend to involve periods of many hours outdoors, participants often are exposed to far more sunlight than in their everyday lives. When activities take place on water, snow, or any surface with high reflectivity, the effects of the sun may be multiplied several fold. At higher elevations, the level of ultraviolet radiation increases markedly. At 5,000 feet (1,500 meters), it only takes about 20 minutes to receive as much UV as in an hour at the seashore. Especially as the ozone layer thins, there is increased awareness of the need for protection, and an ever increasing number of protective compounds have been available to the consumer. All participants should be encouraged to use effective sun screen products, which are now available at SPF ratings of 30 or more, and appropriate headgear and clothing. Leaders who aspire to long careers in the outdoors are advised to consider the *long-term* effects of maintaining a "healthy" looking tan.

Snow blindness is not even mentioned in some first aid texts, as it is a condition now almost solely in the domain of skiers and climbers. The surface of the eye can be sunburned when exposed to very bright sunlight, especially at higher elevations where the UV concentration is higher. Leaders should be very cautious in fog or clouds, at moderate snow elevations, and at high elevations. The visible portion of the spectrum is greatly reduced under foggy or cloudy conditions, while the UV portion of the spectrum, which causes most of the damage, is affected very little. As a result, one may be tempted not to wear sunglasses or not to require participants to wear them. The consequences can be extremely painful and debilitating. Many leaders have made this error once, but it is doubtful that any leader would make it twice.

The treatment for snow blindness consists of cool towels, painkillers if needed, and ophthalmic analgesic ointments if available, in response to the acute pain often described as "ground glass" or "hot nails" in the eyes. Invest in good quality, UV-rated sunglasses with attachable side shields; carry them always; and use them if there is any doubt!

Heat Stress

In the human body, the ability to get rid of excessive heat is limited by such factors as water and salt intake, intensity and duration of exertion, cardiovascular fitness, and prior acclimatization to the heat. A rise in body temperature (*hyper*thermia) of only 6°F (3.3°C) from normal (98.6°F or 37°C) renders the person incapable of providing for his/her immediate needs of water, shade, salt, and rest. A prolonged body core temperature of 106°F (41°C) usually results in death. It is interesting to note that, in a *hypo*thermic condition (exposure to cold and lowering of the core temperature), death occurs at a core temperature of about 78°F (25.5°C)—that is 20°F (11°C) below normal. Therefore, excessive heat gain may be a *greater* danger than an equal amount of body heat loss. Ironically, a winter skiing or snowshoeing trip on a clear, sunny day can create heat stress problems through sunlight reflected off the snow, and through heat gain caused by prolonged hard exercise and compounded by extreme dehydration and sunburn.

An understanding of how the body gains heat can be important in preventing and dealing with heat-stress problems. Essentially, the body gains heat through *absorption* (heat gain from warm air, radiated and/or reflected sunlight, and direct contact with warm objects), and through *internal generation* (heat produced by working muscles and normal body metabolism). Both require attention and preventive measures.

It normally takes the human body two or three days to adjust to the additional cooling and metabolic requirements of a hot climate. The following are suggested as ways of helping the body adjust:

1. Drink plenty of water whenever thirsty. Thirst is the body's earliest warning of impending dehydration. In hot weather, an adult will need a *minimum* of 2-3 quarts of water per day to maintain normal body functions, even with no significant exercise. Adequate hydration is necessary for the body to cool itself by evaporation of perspiration.

2. Add a small amount of extra salt to food, water, or drinks if perspiring heavily but remember that sweat contains more than just table salt, so other replacements may be needed. *Normal diets contain more than enough salt to replace losses in normal temperature at normal activity levels.* Too many people use too many salt tablets, causing negative side effects, one of which is nausea. Extra salt is *rarely* needed!

3. Realize that salt tables are *not* substitutes for proper acclimatization.

4. Minimize perspiration. Remember: *Ration sweat, not water.*

5. Stay out of the direct sunlight as much as possible.

6. Keep your clothes on. Sunburn is not only uncomfortable, sunlight is a heat source which will raise the body core temperature. Also, exposed skin loses water faster than covered skin and results in less cooling.

7. Wear a hat that will shade the head, neck, and face.

8. Slow down activities to minimize the body's heat production. Pace yourself carefully.

9. Eat only as much as necessary for the activity. Eating increases the body's heat production through the digestive process.

10. Frequently rest the cooling system, as well as arm and leg muscles. If cramps develop in the extremities, it is probably from water depletion and lactic acid build-up in overworked muscles. Sit in the shade and drink water. About one-half teaspoon of salt per quart (liter) of water may help, if sweating has been profuse or if the diet has been deficient in salt.

11. Realize that water lost through perspiration, breathing, and urination must be replaced or the body's mental *and* physical efficiency will suffer. When the body's cooling system is over-exerted, mental and physical side effects appear. If the cooling system runs out of water and can't cool the body, the core temperature will begin to rise, and the person's ability to deal with the impending emergency will decrease. Leaders should be prepared to recognize and treat *heat exhaustion* and *heatstroke* under field conditions. The *American Red Cross Advanced First Aid Manual* is a good source of basic information on the symptoms, care, and treatment of heat-related problems.

Hypothermia

Hypothermia has become a well-known word in the last decade, even though the news media occasionally uses the old catchall phrase "exposure." In most first aid books, hypothermia is discussed too briefly to meet the needs of outdoor leaders. Leaders are strongly encouraged to study *Hypothermia* by Pozos and Born, and *Hypothermia, frostbite, and cold injuries* by Wilkerson, Bangs, and Hayward.

Types of Hypothermia

Hypothermia is a condition in which the core (or internal) body temperature is reduced. The body can withstand only a very slight reduction in core temperature without significant impairment of function. When it declines over a period of hours, as might occur in mountain or back-country situations, the condition is known as "chronic exposure" hypothermia. In cold water, the rate of heat loss is so great that severe suppression of body temperature can occur in minutes. Since such rapid cooling almost invariably requires immersion in water, this condition is known as "immersion" hypothermia.

Signs and Symptoms of Hypothermia

Stick your finger in an icy cold stream for a few seconds, then pull it out. Chances are that it will turn red; your system is doing its best to keep the finger warm by adding circulation. Put your finger in the water again for about thirty seconds, and the result will be an ashen, almost numb extremity. What is happening, of course, is that your system is protecting itself from excessive heat loss through the finger.

The body is capable of great variation in blood flow to the surface and can change blood flow volume quite rapidly. In this case, the extremity was, in a sense, sacrificed to save vital core organs. In hypothermia, the body surface and all of the major extremities may be compromised in order to maintain the highest possible temperature of the vital organs.

In either chronic or immersion hypothermia, the blood flow to the skin and other tissues near the surface decreases as the core temperature of the body declines. There may be attempts by the body to generate warmth by shivering, but if this fails to maintain the body's heat balance, circulation will be slowed to the extremities and to the head and brain. Figure 7.4 (page 132) includes the most common signs and symptoms of hypothermia and the temperatures in which they are likely to occur.

In some cases, some symptoms never occur, and, at any given temperature different, individuals may exhibit markedly different signs or symptoms. Therefore, a sign or symptom indicated as occurring in a certain temperature range may appear at higher or lower temperatures. Hypothermia may be thought of as two rather different conditions. The treatment for "mild hypothermia"—hypothermia wherein the patient's core temperature is above 90°F (32.2°C)—varies greatly from the care required in treating victims of "profound hypothermia"—in which core temperatures are *at or below* 90°F.

Perhaps the most frustrating, and certainly one of the most dangerous, effects of hypothermia is the decline of reasoning power that occurs very early in the process of cooling. Unfortunately, loss of mental acuity is an early result of the body's response to cold stress. Ironically, the victim quickly becomes unable to manage his/her own treatment!

Impairment of judgment due to early hypothermia has been implicated in several tragic cases wherein leaders made very poor decisions

FIGURE 7.4   Signs and Symptoms of Hypothermia

BODY TEMPERATURE	COMMON SIGNS AND SYMPTOMS (Expect considerable differences between individuals)
99-97° F 37.2-36.1° C	Mild controllable shivering
97-94° F 36.1-34.4° C	Reduction of ability to do complex mental tasks Moderate to severe shivering Loss of fine motor control (can't do detailed tasks with hands) Increased desire to urinate
94-90° F 34.4-32.2° C	Routine decline of mental status Patient may be withdrawn, depressed, or unconcerned with survival Amnesia may begin Uncontrollable shivering Some loss of thirst and appetite Speech slurred as facial muscles become impaired Larger muscles become sluggish Ataxia (lack of balance; victim may be unable to walk a straight line)
90-86° F 32.2-30.0° C	Patient may appear oriented, but interrogation may reveal incoherence Possible irrational behavior Paradoxical disrobing (victim may feel too warm or restricted by clothing) Stumbling Shivering stops Skin pale or puffy
86-82° F 30.0-27.8° C	Patient may be stuporous Acetone breath may be detectable Slow movements and increased muscular rigidity Uncontrolled urination Slow pulse and respiration Pupils may dilate
82-78° F 27.8-25.6° C	Unconsciousness Pulse not easily detected Erratic respiration and heart rhythm
78-74° F 25.6-23.3° C	Pulmonary edema or cardiac arrhythmias may cause death

that they would almost certainly not have made under normal circumstances. All too often, the group participants in a group do not know how to recognize and treat hypothermia or are unwilling to take control of the situation from the impaired leader. Pre-trip preparation of participants should, therefore, stress the importance of early recognition of symptoms and aggressive treatment of *whomever* may be affected.

Mechanisms of Heat Loss

The body maintains constant internal temperature if heat gain and heat losses are in balance. Heat is lost from the body through radiation, conduction, convection, evaporation, and respiration. The rate of heat loss depends upon environmental conditions, clothing, shelter, and the effectiveness of the body's defense mechanisms. For example, the body can regulate surface temperature, and thus it affects radiant, conductive and convective heat loss rates. This capability relies on the fact that the rate of heat transfer is proportional to the difference in temperature between two objects or substances. For example, at a constant air temperature, heat is lost more readily at a skin temperature of 90°F (32.2°C) than at a skin temperature of 80°F (26.7°C). By controlling blood flow to the surface, the body partially moderates the amount of heat lost to the environment. On a 50°F (10°C) day, a person at rest with light clothing would need to conserve heat. Skin temperature might drop to 70°F (21.1°C) in light clothing, while the core would exhibit almost no shift in temperature. On the same day, while the participant exercises hard, the skin may be maintained at a toasty 90°F (32.2°C) to help radiate unneeded excess heat.

Evaporative cooling can be accelerated or slowed by increasing or decreasing perspiration rates. In severe or prolonged cold stress, the body's defenses serve to reduce the rate of heat losses, even if normal body temperatures cannot be maintained. Figure 7.5 illustrates the common mechanisms of heat loss.

Conduction is direct transfer of heat to any colder body. The rate of transfer is related to relative temperatures and to the conductivity and thermal capacity of the object. Thus, a 50°F (10°C) metal engine block will feel colder than a 50°F (10°C) stone. Heat is lost through long wave *radiation* to any colder body or area. Thus, heat can be lost at a nearby cold object, a cold cloud, or the open sky. In fact, it is only our atmosphere that moderates potentially extreme radiation losses to the near absolute zero cold of interstellar space.

Convection is the term for losses caused by moving air or water across the body. In the absence of air or water movement, a thin layer next to the skin would be warmed, so that the air or water next to the body would be warmer than the ambient environmental temperature. One can step out of a dry sauna and stand naked in very cold air with little distress *if* the air is still. Should a breeze come up, the person will likely leap back to the sauna. Convection is a very effective cooling mechanism. As can be

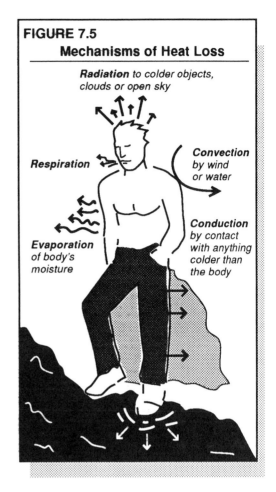

FIGURE 7.5
Mechanisms of Heat Loss

Radiation to colder objects, clouds or open sky

Respiration

Convection by wind or water

Evaporation of body's moisture

Conduction by contact with anything colder than the body

seen in Figure 7.6 (page 134), the effect of each additional increment of air speed is greater at lower speeds and less at higher speeds, because it doesn't take much wind or water current to efficiently displace the air or water "buffer" that has been warmed next to the body.

Wind chill charts, such as the one in the Figure 7.6, attempt to relate ambient air temperature, wind speed, or current, to the temperature or "wind chill factor" (the temperature at which the same cooling rate would occur in still air). There are many wind chill charts in use, each based upon certain assumptions vis-à-vis the humidity of the air, air pressure, and clothing, all of which affect the resultant "wind chill." Convective heat loss in water is much more rapid than in air. Water has 240 times the thermal capacity of air and can strip heat away from

FIGURE 7.6   Wind Chill

EQUIVALENT STILL AIR TEMPERATURE

WIND SPEED (MPH)														
40	1	-4	-15	-22	-29	-36	-45	-54	-62	-69	-76	-87	-94
35	3	-4	-13	-20	-27	-35	-43	-52	-60	-67	-72	-83	-90
30	5	-3	-11	-18	-26	-33	-41	-49	-56	-63	-70	-78	-87
25	7	0	-7	-15	-22	-29	-37	-45	-52	-58	-67	-75	-83
20	12	3	-4	-9	-17	-24	-32	-40	-46	-52	-60	-68	-76
15	16	11	1	-6	-11	-18	-25	-33	-40	-45	-51	-60	-65
10	21	16	9	2	-2	-9	-15	-22	-27	-31	-38	-45	-52
	35	30	25	20	15	10	5	0	-5	-10	-15	-20	-25

AIR TEMPERATURE (°F)

A wind speed of 20 mph combined with an air temperature of 30°F produces approximately the same effect on human skin as still air at 3°F.

the body approximately 30 times faster than air at the same temperature. The body can usually withstand convective losses in an air environment for several hours. However, for a lightly clad person immersed in fast moving 40°F (4.4°C) fresh water for 15 minutes or less, survival chances drop to less than 10 percent. In 30°F (-1.1° C) sea water (which is just above the salt water freezing point), survival times may be less than two minutes.

Evaporation is an effective cooling process, especially when the air is relatively dry. The change in state from liquid to gas requires energy, which comes largely from the body surface. *Respiration* is listed as a separate mechanism for convenience, though it is actually a composite effect. Air at the ambient environmental temperature is inhaled, warmed mostly by convection and conduction, then exhaled.

Heat Gains

Heat gains include heat produced as a product of the metabolic process, as well as heat gained from external sources such as the sun, fire, and hot food or drink. In actual field settings external sources rarely provide more than a small percentage of the caloric energy necessary to maintain viable core temperatures. Heat gain is almost totally from metabolic heat production.

The easiest way to review the major concerns vis-à-vis heat production is to consider those factors that inhibit metabolic processes. Metabolic heat production is inhibited by hypoxia (inadequate oxygen uptake), dehydration, inadequate diet (too little, improper, or poorly timed food intake), fatigue, most illnesses, anxiety, and, unfortunately, by hypothermia itself.

Hypoxia. Metabolism requires oxygen, and it is harder for the body to obtain adequate oxygen at higher elevations. While rarely a significant factor below 5,000 feet (1,500 meters), hypoxia can be a major factor on high-altitude climbs. Even at 5,000 feet, more insulation may be required to stay warm than at the same temperature at sea level.

Dehydration. This is a common and significant factor. Metabolic efficiency depends upon adequate hydration. Even moderate activities can greatly increase the need for water, and if lost water is not replaced promptly, dehydration will occur. The result is a reduced ability to produce heat. Unfortunately dehydration is very common and most problematical in cold weather situations when water is difficult to obtain and may be unappealing.

To compound the situation, hypothermia itself causes increased elimination of fluid and reduction of the feeling of thirst. The best remedy is careful attention to fluid intake and output. Maintain a "clear and copious" outflow by consuming about three liters per day when exercising moderately. This is often most conveniently done by consuming one liter in the morning, one liter in the evening, and at least one liter during the day.

Inadequate Food Intake. While the human digestive system is amazingly tolerant of variations in diet, individuals subject to a cold and hostile environment cannot afford to compromise the body's ability to produce heat. Leaders should consider the caloric requirements of an outing, being especially careful on trips of more than two or three days. Consider, also, what these needs would be in the event of an unexpected extra day or so due to injury or other mishap. Food consumption should be monitored during the outing. While there are several possible reasons why someone may not feel hungry on an outing, lack of hunger may be a symptom of the initial stages of hypothermia. This is one of the several ways in which hypothermia tends to accelerate itself.

Other causes of inadequate food intake may include dieting (some people see outings as an opportunity to lose weight), illness, unappetizing foods, or not enough time to eat. Leaders should provide ample time for food preparation and eating; an experienced person might arrive at camp at 8:00 p.m. and retire at 9:00 p.m., fully fed, while the beginner may still be struggling with the tent! This problem can be minimized by careful attention to the camping process, so that all participants are ready to begin cooking and eating as soon as possible. If care is taken to provide many short snack breaks during the day, the evening meal can be small and simple.

On an outing where the environment is cold but not extremely hostile, an argument can be made for meal planning based on no cooking at all, except for the occasional hot drink or soup. This can save both time and fuel. At high elevations (above about 12,000 feet or 3,700 meters), adequate palatable food becomes both more critical and more difficult. Hypoxia and stress reduce appetite, making it important to provide appetizing food, and yet cooking is extremely time consuming, even with a pressure cooker.

Fatigue. Fatigue reduces the amount of heat generated by the body, and this factor alone can tip the critical balance to a net heat loss. When it is well-rested, the body can withstand at least a few hours a remarkable amount of cold stress. (The exception to this, of course, is immersion hypothermia.) When it is fatigued, the body is highly vulnerable to hypothermia. As most experienced leaders know all too well, the difference between a mild degree of tiredness and complete, stumbling exhaustion can be amazingly small whether measured in meters or in minutes. Again, planning and careful monitoring of the status of each participant can all but eliminate the problem.

Illness. Most illnesses drain the body's energy reserves. While the specific mechanisms vary, any current or recent disease should be a matter of concern for the leader. A participant may not want to miss an outing despite an apparently minor illness, or may participate shortly after recovery from some ailment. On easy outings in fair weather, this may not represent any significant liability, except for the risk of party members who might contract the disease. On longer, more stressful outings where cold may be significant, such individuals should be strongly urged to reconsider or not be allowed to participate.

Anxiety. Studies of real-life survival situations have shown that anxiety significantly reduces an individual's survival time in a cold environment. In two well-documented cases, involving several individuals with nearly identical clothing and equipment, the body temperatures of the survivors corresponded perfectly with their experience levels (which were measured objectively). Interviews with the survivors revealed that anxiety levels during the survival situation were inversely proportional to experience levels; that is, the least experienced were the most anxious, and the most experienced were the least anxious. In other words, those who were most anxious suffered the greatest temperature declines. The effects of anxiety on heat production are also recognized by the military; consequently, the cockpit heating systems of some fighter aircraft are designed to provide extra heat for the pilot during combat situations. While the mechanisms at work here are not well understood, at least part of the negative effects of anxiety are probably due to earlier onset of fatigue, caused by extra mental activity, less efficient muscular activity, and loss of sleep.

Leaders need to pay careful attention to the emotional state of participants, and keep in mind the effects of anxiety on the level of fatigue and on resistance to cold. Remember that, for many people, just being away from the road and out in the woods can be highly stressful! This is not to imply that mental stress is to be avoided at all costs; it is, in fact, an inherent and valuable component of all outdoor activities. Nevertheless, anxiety alone can be a significant suppressor of heat production, and it can compound existing heat-balance deficits. Leaders in programs such

as Outward Bound, wherein mental stress is intentionally induced, need to be especially aware of this possibility, and maintain ample compensating reserves of energy, clothing, and equipment. Leaders should also bear in mind that *they* are not immune to the same effects!

Hypothermia. No doubt the most dangerous factor contributing to hypothermia is hypothermia itself. Lowered body temperature reduces metabolic efficiency and heat production. Figure 7.7 shows thin lines representing constant rates of cooling—as would be expected with constant rates of heat production—and heat loss.

The thick lines illustrate the actual case, wherein the rates of decline for core temperature increase as core temperatures decline. The cooler the body, the less heat is produced. As a result, the condition of a hypothermia patient

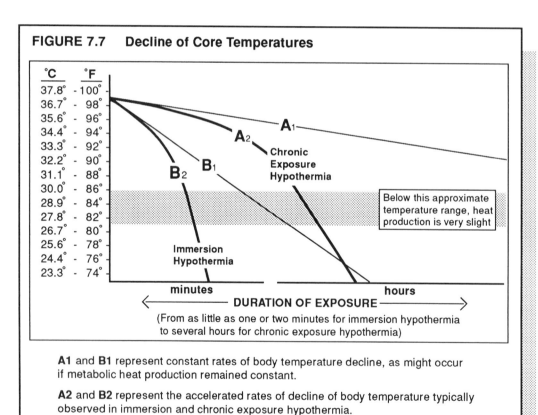

FIGURE 7.7   Decline of Core Temperatures

A1 and **B1** represent constant rates of body temperature decline, as might occur if metabolic heat production remained constant.

A2 and **B2** represent the accelerated rates of decline of body temperature typically observed in immersion and chronic exposure hypothermia.

The rate of decline increases as body temperature decreases. Once the body temperature reaches approximately 86°F (30°C), there is almost no heat production, so the rate of decline is constant.

worsens at an accelerated rate until the core temperature reaches about 86°F (30°C), below which point metabolic heat production is so slight that it is almost insignificant. From this point, the body cools at approximately the same rate as an equivalent mass of steak or hamburger (depending upon one's self-image). Hypothermia also has a prolonged aftereffect, leaving an individual predisposed to the condition for many months. Some studies indicate decreased resistance to cold stress for a year or more.

Prevention of Hypothermia

Hypothermia is a major cause of death in outdoor pursuits, second only to drowning. As will be obvious in the discussion of field treatment, this is a condition that is almost invariably the result of poor planning and inadequate preparation. Most of the fatalities involve poor judgment with regard to clothing and equipment. Fall and spring are the worst seasons in terms of mortality, probably because the seasonal weather may seem temperate in the valleys, while in the mountains it can quickly turn wet, cold, and windy. During winter, the weather is sufficiently intimidating to inspire caution by most users of the outdoors. In summer, experienced mountain hikers and climbers generally understand the danger and equip themselves appropriately. In higher country, less experienced people sometimes succumb to hypothermia even in midsummer. A mid-August snowstorm at 6,000 feet (1,800 meters) is no surprise to an experienced person, but the novice may be completely unprepared, both mentally and in terms of gear, for such an event.

Leaders can no longer plead ignorance of hypothermia or of its prevention or treatment. The majority of beginners in outdoor pursuits know little or nothing about this condition. Given this fact, the leader has to assume responsibility for assessment of the environment, the route, and the intended activities; for the determination and enforcement of minimum clothing and equipment standards; and for the education of the participants. The treatments given below are by no means 100 percent effective in saving lives, and even these sometimes inadequate

measures depend upon specific resources of clothing, shelter, cooking equipment, and food. These resources are not necessarily expensive or hard to obtain, and they are not an unreasonable burden if distributed among the leaders and participants.

Successful treatment of a hypothermia patient in the field requires knowledge, skill, luck, and the foresight to have certain gear on-site. In maritime mountains, the absolute minimum group gear, *in addition* to personal survival gear, for day hiking or climbing includes a tarp shelter, a sleeping bag or half bag, fire-making tools or a stove with fuel, a pot for heating water, and extra food. Above timberline, a stove becomes essential. Many leaders consider a stove mandatory in *all* terrain since the conditions that may cause hypothermia also make fire building difficult, and speed is essential. Insulating pads are also considered necessary by many leaders, especially in winter. There is no perfect, universal set of gear and no single plan that can be applied to all possible circumstances.

It is up to the leader to determine what the basic elements of the outing will be—who, when, where, and what; and, furthermore, the leader must see to it that adequate margins of safety are maintained at all times. By margin of safety, in this case we mean those factors that act to limit the possibility of, or consequences of, hypothermia.

The most important of these factors are:

1. Participant awareness: Every participant should be aware of the risk of hypothermia and should become familiar with significant signs, symptoms, treatments, and preventive measures.

2. Health and fitness: The leader needs to be aware of the state of health, the fitness level, and the energy reserves of each group member. Adequate rest, food, and water, must be continually monitored. No activity should be of such difficulty or duration that less than several hours of reserves remain in each person. Leaders with extensive experience in leading intentionally stressful outdoor activities can sometimes cut this margin to perhaps two hours, but the difficulty of estimating these limits is so great that even experts sometimes miscalculate. Be conservative!

3. *Alternative plans:* In the initial planning of the outing, the leader must consider the possible consequences of changes in the weather, unexpected variances in the rate of travel, accidents, injuries, or health patterns. Alternative plans must be continually updated and reviewed throughout the outing.

4. *Equipment and clothing:* The leader must let only adequately equipped individuals take part in an activity. It is the leader's responsibility to specify this gear and to accept or reject items brought by participants. *The minimum allowable gear must be sufficient to allow survival in the event that the individual is lost alone in the worst weather reasonably foreseeable. The leader must also see to it that the group has sufficient gear to treat hypothermia (as well as any other reasonably foreseeable injury or illness) in the field.*

Leaders should always consider the possibility of having to explain every action, or lack thereof, in court, and a lack of adequate prevention measures (or insufficient means of treating hypothermia in the field) would be extremely hard to defend. In such cases, the court would probably base its decision on the opinions of experienced outdoor leaders who have worked under similar conditions. No two outings are the same, and no one set of rules or lists of equipment can adequately cover all of the possibilities. *It is vitally important that the leader understand the standards of practice among established outdoor leaders in the area and maintain standards at an equivalent level or be prepared to justify variances.* This is not to say that the way something has always been done is necessarily the best or safest way. Clearly this is not always the case. Nevertheless, the leader is expected to understand accepted practices and be able to show cause for any variance.

Treatment of Hypothermia

There are several possible treatments for hypothermia, though the options available in the field are usually limited, and unfortunately, often inadequate. Ideal treatment in a hospital setting may involve the use of sophisticated support systems and techniques such as peritoneal dialysis or the use of a modified kidney dialysis machine. These have a high success rate provided that the victim's condition is not too dire. Unfortunately, such treatments are unavailable to most hypothermia victims within a reasonable time span.

More commonly, and in any case where the patient's condition is not critical, hospital treatment consists of immersion in a warm-water bath. Initial water temperature is usually about 70°F (20°C), raised as rapidly as the patient can safely tolerate to about 110°F (42°C). Care must be taken throughout this process to avoid too-rapid mixing of core and shell blood. The blood in the extremities is cold and has undergone chemical shifts so premature mixing may be dangerous. Mixing can be caused by rough handling, by chemical stimulants, or by tricking the body into dropping its defense and allowing more normal circulation. Care must be taken, for example, to avoid warming the wrists or the back of the neck. Warmth in these sites can trick the body into thinking that the environment is no longer hostile, resulting in reduction of the shunting mechanism that protects the core areas.

In the field, options may be extremely limited if the leader's planning was inadequate. At best, the field treatment of anything beyond the early stages of hypothermia carries a very high risk of mortality.

There are two basic options available. The first assumes the patient's condition is diagnosed very early, before the core temperature has dropped to not lower than 91°F (33°C), and certainly *before* any late-stage signs or symptoms have appeared. The patient must be in what is clinically known as "mild" hypothermia and *not* in profound hypothermia. From the perspective of treatment, it doesn't matter whether the hypothermia is acute (immersion) or chronic.

This option also assumes that the patient has significant reserves of energy and that dry clothing, food, and water are available.

The key to success in this option is to act quickly and aggressively. It is vital to remember that the patient will almost undoubtedly be suffering from some loss of reasoning power. Denial of need and resistance to care are normal, and must be overridden by the first aider. In the course of at most five minutes, get dry clothing on the patient and provide as much readily digestible food as possible, ideally as a mixture of sugars and complex carbohydrates. Give the patient lots of water, then walk the patient at a rapid pace, preferably toward the trailhead, for at least 45 minutes, or until the patient has been perspiring lightly for at least one-half hour and appears fully normal.

If travel toward the trailhead is not practical, consider heading toward a sheltered campsite or perhaps walking in a circle around the camp, or in whatever direction provides heavy exercise and an option of shelter. A good plan, if time, distance, and other considerations preclude leaving the area, is to have the group set up a good camp and prewarm a sleeping bag for the patient while assistants walk the patient on a closed route. If it isn't practical to exercise the patient, use huddling, a large campfire, hot water bottles, or any available heat source to provide warmth, taking care not to injure tissues rendered numb by cooling.

If the patient exhibits more than just early signs of hypothermia, or has a temperature of 91°F (33°C) or less, profound hypothermia must be assumed. Set up a tent or substantial tarp to provide complete wind and rain protection while others huddle tightly around the patient, giving sugary foods if the patient is sufficiently conscious. Be extremely careful about handling the patient. Patients in profound hypothermia can be killed by rough handling, and should be treated as gently as someone with a spinal injury!

As soon as the tent or tarp is in place, add or improvise a couple of sleeping pads and a sleeping bag, and while the shelter is being finished get a healthy person, naked, into the bag. If a choice is available, choose a big bag or one that is part of a zip-together pair since this will make things more comfortable and even allow a third person to enter the bag. While this is being done, someone should set up a stove and warm a large pot of water. As soon as the sleeping bag is warm (aggressive isometrics help), the patient should also be gently stripped naked and slipped into the bag with the valiant bag warmer. Most people have had to put up with sharing their bed with someone with cold feet or hands, and most experienced outdoor folks have on occasion warmed a friend's numb feet on their bellies. Few, however, have experienced the delights of being completely squashed up against someone with a *very* cold body. Expect the bag warmer's eyes to cross and teeth to rattle! A thin dry layer of clothing may be added once the victim has rewarmed well above 91°F (33°C).

Many novices do not understand why skin-to-skin contact is useful or necessary. A sleeping bag does not warm a person, it simply insulates. In the case of hypothermia, there is not enough warmth being generated and just being inside a sleeping bag is not sufficient therapy. However, the warmth from the body of another person will pass to the cold body of the victim at least compensating for inevitable heat losses. In damp conditions, where down may get wet and soggy, a sleeping bag lined with synthetic material works best.

Resist the temptation to rub the patient's arms and legs. Remember the danger of premature mixing of the shell and core blood. At this point, it is probably best to just be still, to let the patient recover from the inevitable stresses of being moved into the shelter and bag. If the patient can be moved to a medical facility within one and one-half hours or so, it is best *not* to try to add warmth beyond that which can be transferred by skin-to-skin contact. Attempts at aggressive warming through the use of external heat sources can easily lead to catastrophic events, such as ventricular fibrillation, if not done gently and correctly.

If medical facilities are more than an hour and a half away, or if the patient's temperature cannot be stabilized, extra heat can be added, using hot water bottles or warmed stones in the groin and armpits taking great care to protect the skin by wrapping the bottles or stones in light clothing. If the patient is fully conscious, feed warm sugary drinks to him/her, keeping in mind that caffeine and alcohol should be avoided, and that the sugars, other nutrients, and water are more important than the heat in the drink. As long as the drink is not much below body temperature, it should do no harm, and will provide needed fuel and hydration. Hot drinks are psychologically beneficial, but sugary fluids should not be delayed if a source of heat is not readily available to warm them up.

A common and unfortunate effect of hypothermia is an enhanced desire to urinate, which is voluntary in the early stages but involuntary later. Field treatment in a sleeping bag is often complicated by urination, which can make things miserable for all concerned; however, there are several ways of dealing with this problem. A wide-neck bottle (for males) or a pan (for females) can be held in place, again taking care to avoid excess moisture. A funnel can be made from a plastic water bottle cut diagonally, to assist in directing urine flow from women. In the absence of such containers, sleeping bags (especially ones with full zippers) can be opened to allow the patient to urinate through an appropriately placed hole in the tent floor (which can be easily patched, by the way, if made at a seam). If those solutions are not possible, the patient must be gently moved to another prewarmed bag. Accidental urination is so common that it is best to be prepared. If the incident occurs on a day hike or climb, then extra care must be taken to prevent soaking of the sleeping bag since only one is usually carried as group gear. The patient should be kept in the bag until he/she appears fully normal and has a normal oral temperature. Given the best and most aggressive field treatment, this may take many hours and may commit the party to an extra night out.

Would-be rescuers must be prepared for the possibility of failure when treating profound hypothermia. If the patient's temperature was very low when treatment in the field was started, the odds are stacked dramatically against survival. Patients with profound hypothermia often die despite competent and aggressive field treatment, and, in fact, they have a good chance

of dying even when hospital water-bath therapy is available. The lesson, of course, is to *prevent* profound hypothermia by planning well and by being proactive in diagnosis and treatment of mild hypothermia.

Frostbite and Trench Foot

Frostbite and trench foot (or immersion foot as some prefer) are injuries often, but not necessarily, related to hypothermia. While either could occur in the absence of hypothermia, hypothermia strongly predisposes an individual to these conditions by reducing blood flow to extremities. Almost all of the damage in trench foot and most of the damage in frostbite is related to circulation loss. In frostbite, tissues freeze, but the overall damage in trench foot may be as severe as in frostbite. Leaders should carefully study texts such as *Hypothermia, frostbite and cold injuries* by Wilkerson, Bangs, and Hayward, if outings in cool weather are to be among the leader's responsibilities. Both frostbite and trench foot are serious conditions that can lead to permanent disability and/or loss of limb. Leaders should know how to prevent, diagnose, and treat each condition, in the field if necessary.

Some individuals are more prone than others to cold injury, and, in most groups the leader can expect to have some people who have a predisposition to injury. Anyone who tends to have cold hands or feet when in a cool environment (which numbers about 10 percent of the population) needs to be especially careful. In cold environments, participants may need information and warnings relative to foot and hand protection, and, in very cold weather, face protection. Remind participants of the need to maintain *dry, loose* insulation on hands and feet, which may mean *reducing* the number of socks and/or frequent changes to assure dryness. Plastic boots are becoming increasingly popular, but they can be dangerous because they cannot expand. This is especially problematical in plastic boots with felt liners, since the liners expand when dampened by perspiration. In any case, it is important to move (flex) fingers and toes often, to maintain awareness of these conditions, and to use a "buddy system" to monitor the noses, cheeks, and ears of every member of the party—including the leader—in very cold conditions.

First-Aid Kits

There is no perfect first-aid kit. There are probably as many "standard first-aid kit" content lists as there are outdoor leaders. Every circumstance is different, and the content of the kit must be adjusted to meet the needs of the leader and/or organization. First-aid kits should contain enough materials to allow whatever level of care might be necessary, for those injuries or medical conditions that might have to be cared for in the field. A youth camp operating near a major urban center may need only basic supplies to allow on-site, moderate term stabilization, while an expedition to the Karakoram might need a fully equipped medical kit in addition to a more complete set of trauma care supplies. Provisions for administration of oxygen, IVs, and drugs are appropriate only when there are personnel on-site who are trained to use these techniques safely and effectively.

Many first-aid kits are hopelessly inadequate, outdated, or contaminated by careless handling or storage. Kits should be checked thoroughly, after every use. After a year of occasional use and being carried on many trips, most kits need a complete assessment, upgrade, and repackaging, even without having been used. There are many possible ways of packing and carrying first-aid kits. Among the best for regular institutional use are large nylon belt ("fanny") packs, plastic food containers, and various watertight boxes, ranging from army surplus ammo cans to high tech plastic supplies designed for rafters. Each has certain advantages. For land-based outings, a fanny pack is very convenient and can be carried below a day pack or strapped to a backpack. It isn't rigid or watertight, however, so despite plastic bags, linings, and requests for gentle handling, the expensive contents may rapidly degrade. Plastic food boxes, if sturdy and sealed with tape, work very well and usually survive abusive handling and even total immersion. Ammo cans and heavy cases are ideal for water-based or residential settings, but are too heavy for backcountry use. It is also helpful to have several smaller kits on hand, for situations that do not warrant use of the full kit.

Figure 7.8 (page 142) illustrates the contents of a first-aid kit recommended for land-based and water-based outings. These supplies have proven adequate for frequent use on single and multi-day outings in remote backcountry areas. They are designed for basic trauma stabilization and care and are carried by leaders only, all of whom are certified at or above the level of the American Red Cross Advanced First Aid course. Note that the rubber gloves and CPR shields are recent additions unfortunately now considered essential due to growing concerns vis-à-vis HIV infection.

References

American Academy of Orthopedic Surgeons. (1977). *Emergency care and transportation of the sick and injured.* Menasha, WI: American Academy of Orthopedic Surgeons.

American National Red Cross. (1990). *Standard first aid and personal safety, and advanced first aid and emergency care.* New York, NY: Doubleday & Co.

American National Red Cross. (1990). *Advanced first aid and emergency care.* New York, NY: Doubleday & Co.

Auerbach, P., MD (1991). *Medicine for the outdoors.* Boston, MA: Little, Brown and Co.

Auerbach, P., MD, & Geehr, E., MD (Eds.). (1983). *Management of wilderness and environmental emergencies.* New York, NY: Macmillan Publishing Co.

Breyfogle, N. (1981). *The common sense medical guide and outdoor reference.* New York, NY: McGraw-Hill.

Clem, B. (1990). The head bone's connected to the... *Rescue Forum 3*(1).

FIGURE 7.8 Suggested Group First-Aid Kit For Backcountry Activities	
	QUANTITY
CONTAINERS	
Belt bag, plastic box or ammo cans	1
Self-sealing plastic bags (sm.)	8
Self-sealing plastic bags (lg.)	6
TOOLS	
Airway (tubular)	1
Scissors (bandage)	1
Plastic wrap	2 sq. ft.
Tweezers	1
Razor	1
Safety pins	6
Needle	1
Thermometer (low range oral)	1
Snake-bite kit	1
Venom extractor	1
Anakit	1
Wire splint	2
Flagging (surveyor's tape)	1
Lighter	1
Notebook and pencil	1
Accident report form	1
Ear syringe	1
Rubber gloves	4 pr.
CPR shields	1
DRESSINGS AND BANDAGES	
Adhesive bandages (1")	12
Adhesive bandages (lg.)	6
Hydrous gel dressing	1 pkg.
Butterfly closures	10
Surgipads (5"x9")	2
Gauze pads (4"x4")	12
Nonstick pads (3"x4")	6
Gauze compresses (lg.)	2
Conforming roller bandage	4
Adhesive tape (2" roll)	1
Adhesive tape (1" roll)	1
Triangular bandages (40")	3
Elastic bandages (4" w/ clips)	2
Adhesive felt (36 sq.")	1
Adhesive foam (36 sq.")	1
Cotton swabs	6
Tampons	4
Antiseptic soap solution (4 oz.)	1

Committee on Injuries of the Academy of Orthopedic Surgeons. (1970). *Emergency care and transportation of the sick and injured.* Menasha, WI: George Banta Co.

Forgey, W. W., MD (1985). *Hypothermia—Death by exposure.* Merrillville, IN: ICS Books.

Forgey, W. W., MD (1987). *Wilderness medicine (5th ed.).* Merrillville, IN: ICS Books.

Ganci, D. (1991). *The basic essentials of desert survival.* Merrillville, IN: ICS Books, Inc.

Hackett, P. H., MD (1980). *Mountain sickness.* New York, NY: The American Alpine Club.

Harkonen, W. S., MD (1984). *Traveling well.* New York, NY: Dodd, Mead & Co..

Houston, C. (1983). *Going higher: The story of man and altitude.* Burlington, VT: Queen City Printers.

Isaac, J., & Goth, P. (1991). *The Outward Bound wilderness first aid handbook.* New York, NY: Lyons and Burford.

Kodet, E. R., MD, & Angier, B. (1986). *Being your own wilderness doctor.* Harrisburg, PA: Stackpole Books.

Pozos, R. S., & Born, D. O. (1982). *Hypothermia: Causes, effects, prevention.* Piscataway, NJ: New Century Publishers.

Prentice, W., & Brucher, C. A. (1988). *Fitness for college and life. (2nd ed.).* St. Louis, MO: Times Mirror/Mosby Publishing.

Setnicka, T. (1980). *Wilderness search and rescue.* Boston, MA: Appalachian Mountain Club.

Tilton, B. (July-Aug 1991). Sweat, hydration, fatigue and the need to drink. *Wilderness Medicine Newsletter* 2(4).

Tilton, B. (July-Aug 1991). Heat and the need to eat. *Wilderness Medicine Newsletter 2*(4).

Wilkerson, J. (Ed.). (1985). *Medicine for Mountaineering.* Seattle, WA: The Mountaineers.

Wilkerson, J. A., Bangs, C. C., & Hayward, J. S. (1986). *Hypothermia, frostbite and other cold injuries.* Seattle, WA: The Mountaineers.

SEARCH
AND RESCUE

Much of the excitement and value of outdoor pursuits stems from the uncertainty inherent in performing an activity in an uncontrolled natural environment; yet, along with this uncertainty comes a real risk to the well-being of both participants and leaders. Every year, some people die while engaged in outdoor recreation, and many more are injured. People get themselves into all sorts of trouble. They fall into crevasses or get stuck on rock faces; they wrap their watercraft around midstream boulders; and, most of all, they get lost. The possibilities and permutations are endless. While first aid was covered in the previous chapter, this chapter focuses upon situations involving lost persons and on problems of access, extrication, and transport.

When emergencies occur in a group with a designated leader, that leader is almost always expected to save the day. While a host of legal, ethical and other factors may modify the formal responsibility of a leader in a given situation, the leader is expected to know what to do. Unless clear and specific agreements to the contrary have been reached with the participants, the leader(s) of an outing should expect to bear full accountability for the resolution of emergencies.

Planning and Preparation

Leaders should understand that good planning and effective field leadership are essential to the conduct of a reasonably safe outing and that both depend upon awareness and conscientious action. Prevention is always best, and good planning can reduce the chance of major mismatches of terrain, weather, activities, and people. Qualified leaders, using state-of-the-art techniques and maintaining high standards in terms of equipment and clothing, can reduce the risks to an extremely low level. Nevertheless, mishaps will occur, and this possibility must be considered in the planning process.

Planners need to consider all reasonably foreseeable problems. Unexpected changes of weather or mobility might necessitate a change en route or a need for escape to civilization. Any number of events might cause a group to be significantly delayed, which might require extra food or water. Injuries or accidents might require technical apparatus or skills in order to gain access to, extricate, and transport the victim. Thus, planners need to be sure that:

1. Reasonable exit routes, known as "escape routes," exist and are known to the field leaders of any land- or water-based outing away from civilization;

2. Enough supplies of water, food, gear, and clothing are carried by the group to meet any reasonably foreseeable need;

3. The group has sufficient expertise in first aid and search and rescue (SAR) techniques appropriate to the activity and site;

4. The location and capabilities of search and rescue resources are known, and the group has sufficient on-site resources to compensate for any deficiencies in the level of service expected from outside resources.

Field leaders shouldn't expect, or be expected, to avoid all problems, but they must maintain the skills and equipment necessary to resolve any reasonably foreseeable emergency situation. This includes up-to-date training in applicable specialty areas such as mountain rescue techniques, water rescue, or avalanche rescue. *Lack of foresight or unsupported optimism is no excuse, morally or ethically, for allowing an outing to proceed without adequate preparation for emergencies.*

Even though on the bottom line the leader may have to orchestrate group response to an emergency, participants should expect to bear some responsibility. Every effort should be made by the leader to explain clearly the risks and specific hazards of the activity as well as what is being done to control risks or provide options in the event of an accident. Participants deserve to know what they are getting into; they need this information to be able to respond appropriately when, at other times, they are not accompanied by a leader; and, they should be expected to maintain a significant portion of the responsibility for their own well-being. *There is no better defense against unforeseen happenings than an alert, informed group.*

Search and Rescue (SAR) Resources

In urban areas, a phone call brings a quick response to virtually any emergency, thanks to nearly instantaneous communication and high-speed transportation systems. Out of town,

response time elongates rapidly. Any emergency that occurs more than about a half-mile away from a road is usually considered to be beyond the reach of conventional emergency service personnel. Their footwear, clothing, equipment, and, sometimes, fitness aren't compatible with backcountry travel. Snow, steep terrain, wild water, or severe weather can further limit the range of effectiveness of conventional fire departments, police, and ambulance services.

Coverage of areas beyond the roadheads is typically the responsibility of a government agency. In the United States, the legal burden for search and rescue (SAR) operations generally falls to the sheriff of the county in which the incident occurs. It is important that leaders know exactly what agency is responsible and how to initiate a search and rescue operation.

There is a wide range in the quality of SAR assistance one can expect. It depends primarily upon the location. One might anticipate differences in services between two separate countries, and yet one might be surprised by differences across county, state, provincial, or other divisional lines within one country. Striking contrasts exist. Counties with big populations, relatively high incomes, and a lot of outdoor recreation activity can and must maintain substantial SAR capabilities. Counties with smaller populations and budgets are in no position to maintain equivalent resources. Mutual-aid agreements help, but the service still suffers in some areas. Similar disparities exist throughout the world. In many places, SAR services are all but nonexistent.

Just about the only thing one *can* count on is that a call for help will eventually bring one or more people to the scene. Quality SAR response is very, very costly. Quality response means prompt response by enough qualified and properly equipped personnel to maximize the chance of finding, assessing, extricating, treating, and transporting the victim to safety. A topnotch SAR team supported by aircraft and a sophisticated communication system is a luxury available in very few places on earth. One such example is Switzerland, where a dozen teams on 24-hour standby can rightfully claim a fifteen-minute response time to any point in the country if the weather cooperates. This sort of assistance doesn't exist anywhere else outside of the Alps, except in the movies. The only places that come close to the Swiss model are a few popular regions in the United Kingdom, parts of Western Europe, the United States, Australia, New Zealand, and Japan.

In some cases, the individual may be held liable for all of the cost of a SAR mission, while, in other cases the charges may be minimal or there is no charge at all. There is a good deal of difference between the various countries of the world in terms of cost of SAR. SAR liability insurance is available in Europe and elsewhere.

Leaders should ascertain just what sort of outside assistance is available in the event of need, and do so early in the planning phase. The quality of SAR services is an important factor in determining routes and activities. Any group has to be capable of at least stabilizing an accident scene, and both groups and individuals should always be prepared to survive for an unplanned night or two, even when quality SAR services are available. It usually takes a long time to get to a telephone or radio; delays may be caused by weather or other factors; and considerable time is usually required for searches, rescues, and transportation of victims. If efficient SAR services are not available, then the group itself will have to assume a greater portion of the responsibility.

Backcountry Rescue

In the event of any emergency, the leader should fight to maintain internal calm and keep an objective perspective on the situation, resisting the urge to respond emotionally or irrationally. Stabilization of the accident scene and concern for the welfare of uninvolved people are both essential. In backcountry settings, it is vital to avoid additional victims or missing people. Help is always in short supply in these cases, and the last thing needed is one less helper and one more victim. The most important thing a leader can do in any emergency is maintain control of the group so that the actions of the group do not further aggravate the situation.

Often the very first task of the leader has to be directed toward the unaffected part of the group. Whether hiking or running a river, the

order to stop or return to the scene of the incident must be conveyed quickly and effectively unless previously established plans will automatically return the other party members to the scene in time to help. In most emergency situations, urgent priorities usually include: (1) getting someone safely to the victim to provide first aid and stabilization, and (2) getting the group assembled, organized, and protected.

Leaders may have to contend with any number of situations requiring skills in search, extrication, or transportation. Each type of outdoor activity has its own special set of potential problems and solutions. Leaders have an obligation to themselves and their clients or students to know and to be able to employ effective SAR methods. There are many excellent books available giving detailed information about these methods for virtually every activity in the realm of outdoor pursuits. These texts provide a valuable foundation of knowledge and reference; however, they cannot be substituted for practice. There is no reasonable alternative to hands-on experience in rescue techniques and search tactics.

While an ability to carry out self-rescue is essential, leaders also need to understand the specific capabilities of the agencies upon which they may have to call, and leaders must know how to contact these agencies. Should a real need arise, it helps a great deal to know and be known by those who might come to your aid. This isn't always practical or possible, but put yourself in the shoes of the rescuer or searcher and the value becomes clear. The organization and execution of an effective SAR operation depend, in large part, upon the information the organizers have about the emergency situation. This information is almost never complete and is always subject to question and interpretation. The more the organizers know about the people at the scene, the better they can interpret and predict from the information on hand.

In the United States and Canada, most outdoor activities take place in semi-remote locales. Typically, the accident or missing person scenario unfolds many miles from the trailhead, and the leader must decide whether to seek outside help, attempt resolution using the resources available on-site, or both. This is often a difficult but critical decision. In the following examples, our purpose is to illustrate advantages and disadvantages of each course of action. Examine how a typical minor climbing accident scenario might be resolved using outside help. Then, for comparison, imagine how it might be resolved using only self-help techniques.

Assume that the accident occurs in a mountainous backcountry area at an elevation of 7,500 feet (2,300 m), a mile (1.6 km) above a major trail, and that the terrain between the accident site and the trail is moderately steep, partly snow covered, and doesn't require any special skills to traverse. Furthermore, assume that it is five miles (8.0 km) to the trailhead on an easy downhill grade, an hour's drive to a telephone, and another hour's drive to town and hospital. The victim's two climbing partners are with the victim. The climbers were smart enough to carry a foam pad, sleeping bag, tarp, stove, and extra food and water with them, so they are capable of surviving for at least one night. The weather appears to be fairly stable.

Note that this scenario isn't extreme. It is not uncommon for hikers, hunters, fishermen, skiers, or climbers to spend a substantial portion of their outing time at least this far from the road. Assume optimism as to the times required at each stage, but do not assume the help of helicopters. Helicopters are remarkable machines, and, although an effort is usually made to use them, they cannot be taken for granted. All too often they cannot be used, as will be explained later.

Assume that the injury occurs at about 2:00 p.m. The victim takes a short but fast slide down a small snow patch and hits a rock which results in a fractured tibia. The process of assessing and treating (splinting) the injury, then getting the victim into a sheltered and reasonably comfortable place will take at least half-hour. It will usually take at least another few minutes to decide on the best course of action; we will assume, in this case, that one person will stay with the victim, and one will go for help. This course of action isn't ideal; it would be much better to have two people stay with the victim to insure continual observation and to assist in nursing and camp chores. For safety, it would be better for

two to go for help. Nevertheless, if it is decided that help is needed, little recourse is available. Signaling might be effective, but it would probably result only in catching the attention of others elsewhere on the mountain, and waiting for more manpower might delay the call for help for hours. (The use of radios is discussed later in this chapter.)

The person who goes for help should carry a written note, to be sure that all important details are communicated to the rescue group. The note should include all the information that the rescue group will need to perform an efficient job. Think about what the rescuers need to know if called upon to conduct a rescue operation. Essential data includes a description of the victim (name, age, sex, approximate height and weight, address, and names of physicians and relatives or contact persons). Police agencies usually request a driver's license number through which they can access more information on the individual. They are ultimately in charge, and it is their normal procedure to procure a driver's license number. If it isn't available at the initial contact, it may be requested later. A large percentage of SAR incidents are not related to outdoor pursuits and involve "other issues;" police agencies use the same procedure for all cases.

Describe the nature of the injuries carefully, including the signs and symptoms as well as your diagnosis. In addition to the specific patient-related information described in the last chapter, be sure to note others on the scene (names, affiliations and qualifications in relevant areas such as first aid and SAR), available gear and equipment (Can the party survive the night?), and a very specific and detailed account of the location (the *exact* location by reference to the map and local features, ground cover, and terrain), and the weather (exactly what's happening and what you predict). It is also important to note any plan to move the patient. In addition, if there is any chance of using a helicopter, possible landing sites should be carefully described.

Taking a few extra minutes to be sure the details suggested above are noted accurately can save hours in the long run. Leaders are strongly encouraged to carry a Search and Rescue Information Form as an aid to recall the necessary categories of information. See Figure 8.1 (pages 150-151). By now, it will be at least 3:00 p.m., The person going for help will need at least two-and-a-half-hours to get to the trailhead, especially since time must be taken to mark out the cross-country portion of the route. Care and caution are essential here; this is not the time to run madly down the trail!

By about 5:30 p.m. the messenger should be at the trailhead, having, we hope, remembered to bring along the car keys. An hour of driving is required to get to the phone, so, at about 6:30 p.m., the SAR agency (usually the county sheriff, or park headquarters in some national parks) is finally contacted. If the person taking the call is efficient, the messenger will be thoroughly interrogated. Usually, the messenger will also be asked to stay at the phone or at an agreed-upon contact point until a deputy or ranger can meet him/her. What happens next depends upon the structure and resources of the agency and upon the availability of personnel. Typically, it will take at least an hour to organize a quick response team. This will consist of either volunteers or professional rescue workers equipped with basic first-aid equipment and radios. The party is usually small, and its purpose is to get to the accident scene as quickly as possible, to locate and stabilize the victim, and to provide by radio any information needed to fine tune the effort of the larger team to follow.

If all goes well, the quick-response people should be heading out of town by 7:30 p.m. or so. By about 9:30, they should be at the trailhead, and by 10:00 p.m., in the company of the very tired messenger, they should be ready to head back up the hill. Six miles (9.6 km) of uphill travel under heavy loads, at a time when the body is ready to retire for the day, is not easy. The mile (1.6 km) of off-trail travel may be tedious or nearly impossible in the dark, depending upon how well the route was marked and upon the recall of the messenger. Five hours may seem like a long time for a six-mile (9.6 km) trip, but experience has shown the need to allow at least that much time. This means that it will be 3:00 a.m. or later when the victim and companions are reached.

Meanwhile, back in town, a large party may have been organized quickly enough to arrive at the trailhead perhaps two hours behind the quick-response team. We'll be optimistic and assume this time frame, although in common practice this large party is sometimes withheld until first light in the morning. This group may consist of members of search-and-support groups, technical rescue teams, or both, depending upon the anticipated mission needs. This large back-up and transportation group will usually bring with them an array of equipment ranging from medical supplies to litters and technical hardware to facilitate care and transportation of the victim. By about 5:00 a.m., all of the help has arrived at the accident site, and by perhaps 6:00 a.m., the tired rescuers might begin the six mile (9.6 km) carry out. For a trail of this length, the carry-out time should take about seven hours. It can vary considerably, depending upon the type of stretcher, the trail characteristics, amount of snow, and the number of rescuers. By about 1:00 p.m., the victim should be at the trailhead, and in another two hours, at 3:00 p.m., in the hospital.

Twenty-five hours is a long time, long enough to affect the prognosis in some injuries quite seriously. What if the group hadn't had the basic equipment needed to survive a night out? What if the weather had been worse? It is also worth considering the costs of the rescue, not just in terms of who pays the bill (you *may* have to pay, and costs of $10,000 or more aren't uncommon) but also in terms of costs to society and to the rescuers themselves. If the victim doesn't pay the bill, taxpayers have to. Some rescuers are professionals; it is part of their job. Most mountain search and rescue personnel are volunteers, and for them a mission can cost heavily in terms of time lost from work and wear and tear on personal equipment.

Perhaps the risk factor is most important here. Rescues can be hazardous. It is not possible to move large parties of people into backcountry areas in a hurry, often at night or in foul weather, without risk. Every year, some rescuers die in attempts to locate or rescue people in the outdoors. A call for SAR assistance is a very serious matter. Nevertheless, it is important not

FIGURE 8.1a   Search and Rescue Information Form

Please fill out both sides of this form *clearly* and *completely*, and give the form to the authorities responsible for search and rescue. (This is usually the County Sheriff.) If more than one person is lost or injured, attach a separate sheet with all subject data. **BE SPECIFIC.**

SUMMARY

Person Reporting: _____ Date: _____

Address & Phone Of Above: _____

Time Of Incident (AM/PM): _____ Time Of Report (AM/PM): _____

If Organized Group, Give Name Of Organization: _____

City, State Of Above: _____

Name Of Leader(s): _____

Trip Or Course Title: _____

Agency Contact Person (name): _____ Phone Of Above: _____

GENERAL INFORMATION

What Happened? _____
(Describe incident in detail. Victim data section follows.)

What Assistance Do You Need? _____
(Personnel, equipment)

What Are Your Plans? _____
(What *exactly* are your plans?)

What Personnel Are On Site? _____
(Names, experience, associations. Attach separate list if necessary.)

What Equipment Is On Site? _____
(Shelter, sleeping bags, lights, food and water, stoves, fuel, etc., with *quantities*)

If A Helicopter Might Be Used, Give Best Landing Sites _____
(Detail locations, dimensions and obstructions, distance to victim).

LOCATION

A precise location is extremely important. Describe location of all significant points by as many methods as possible.

Location Of Trailhead _____
(Name and/or number of trail, road name and number, etc.)

Location Of Victim Or Party_____
(Use legal description *and* relationship to major features.)

Where And When Will You Meet Search-And-Rescue Team?_____
(How long will you wait, and what will you do?)

To Find You, What Should Searchers Look For? _____
(Colors, markings, signals at meeting point)

FIGURE 8.1b   Search and Rescue Information Form

WEATHER

Current Temperature:_____   Visibility: _____
(Estimate °F.)   (Specify feet or miles)

Wind Direction:_____ Windspeed: _____ Steady Or Gusty: _____

Clouds, Fog: _____ Precipitation: _____ Describe Snow Cover:_____
(Describe)   (Amount, type)   (If any)

Weather Summary, Past Day: _____
(Include max./min. temp.)

Weather You Predict, Next Day:_____

INJURED OR LOST PERSON DATA

Name: _____ Age:_____Sex:_____

Height: _____ Weight: _____ Hair: _____ Eyes: _____

Address: _____ Phone(s): _____
                  (# street   city   state   zip code)
Driver's License Number:_____ State: _____

Person To Contact: _____ Relationship: _____

Address: _____ Phone(s): _____
                  (# street   city   state   zip code)
Alternate Person To Contact: _____ Relationship: _____

Address: _____ Phone(s): _____
                  (# street   city   state   zip code)

IF LOST, GIVE INFORMATION

Footwear Type: _____
(Describe shoes, boots, skis, snowshoes etc., including size and tread pattern)

Coats & Rainwear: _____ Pants:_____ Hats: _____
(Color, size, type, brand)   (As above)   (As above)

All Other Gear: _____
(As above for all equipment, shelter, clothing; be complete and include colors)

Is Person Alone Or In A Group? _____ Place Last Seen: _____
(Explain)   (Exactly)

Time Last Seen: _____ Day And Date: _____ Direction Of Travel: _____
(am/pm)   (Trail, road, etc.)

Person's Plans At Last Contact: _____

Physical Condition Of Person: _____

IF INJURED, GIVE INFORMATION

Time Of Injury (AM/PM): _____ Time Of Report (AM/PM): _____

Can Victim Walk Safely?_____ Ride Sitting Up? _____

Nature Of Injuries (Give full details of *all* signs and symptoms): _____

Treatment Given (What, when, and caregiver's qualifications): _____

to delay if help is truly needed because delay might only make things worse in the long run. SAR teams are there to help, but users of their services have an obligation to do everything possible to avoid unnecessary costs and risks.

Now try to resolve the same incident without calling upon the assistance of a rescue group. Remember, there are three people, one of whom is the victim. Again, assume an injury at 2:00 p.m. If party members know enough about first aid to assess injuries accurately, to stabilize them effectively, to construct or devise a means of transporting the victim, and to predict the effect of improvised transportation, then movement without outside aid might be possible. Any improvised transportation system is probably going to be a lot harder on the victim than that provided by professional rescue teams. In addition, there will be only two carriers unless other nearby campers or climbers can be recruited. Consider, too, that going only partway and running out of energy could be disastrous.

Nevertheless, the advantages of a self-contained, self-help rescue may outweigh the disadvantages. Improvising an effective splint and constructing a strong, durable, comfortable, sturdy litter may take two hours or more. In some cases, a rope-seat "piggy-back" can be used, or a two-person carry can be devised using ice axes or poles. Under these conditions, carrying out the victim will probably take 12 hours or more, and even that figure might be low unless help is obtained from others in the area. However, if all goes well, the victim will probably be at the trailhead at 4:00 a.m. and to the hospital at 6:00 a.m. This is nine hours ahead of the outside-help alternative. There are several other advantages, including: (1) the group stays together and can pool resources and skills; (2) the group gets off the mountain quickly, a possible life-saving benefit if the group isn't prepared to survive the night; (3) group members probably learn more than if outside help were called, and they can feel good about having taken care of themselves; (4) substantial costs may be avoided; and (5) rescue teams are not exposed to unnecessary risks.

Leaders of organized groups are in a different position than members or leaders of private parties, mainly because of fear of liability. If the group is well-prepared for survival, and if the is no special need for haste in getting the victim to a hospital, the very safest course may be to call for outside assistance. In real life, the number of possibilities and variables is enormous, and the decision will always be a judgment call. The more SAR and first aid experience the leader has, the better that decision is likely to be.

Most of the time the leader will have to assume ground-based assistance only, and will have to make strategy choices on that basis. Intermediate solutions, such as sending out for help while having the group begin the transportation or search process, may be possible and desirable. This is a common practice; although, it has also caused a number of frustrating situations where rescuers and the distressed party have passed each other in the night, each laboring for many needless extra hours due to poor communication.

Searches

When someone is missing, the leader has to decide how long to wait before responding. In some cases, response must be immediate. For example, if a small child is missing in harsh weather or hazardous terrain, quick action is called for. On the other hand, one or two overdue adult backpackers, who are well-equipped for the weather conditions and terrain, would usually be given considerable time in which to find their own way out unless there were reasons to suspect urgent need for assistance. Generally speaking, initial cursory search procedures require few searchers and may be accomplished by a small party of adults, while any more thorough searching requires large numbers of personnel. The leader must decide whether to commit all of his/her resources to the initial search attempt, or send one or two people out for help. In a small group, one or two people may constitute a major portion of the potential search party. The initial search may result in locating the missing person; however, every hour of delay in sending someone for help may delay assistance. In most cases, an uneasy compromise is reached, wherein a limited search is conducted by the group before anyone is sent out to instigate a full-scale response. A good decision is critical and requires careful analysis and sound judgment.

As in any emergency, the leader must maintain objectivity and perspective. Group control is essential but may be more difficult if the group members are anxious or distracted by events. This is the time to pull the group together, physically and psychologically, so that all of the human and material resources of the group can be effectively focused on the task at hand. The most effective strategy in a search depends on many variables, including the likely behavior of the missing person, the urgency based on the victim's projected survivability, the terrain, and the number of searchers available.

In any search, even in those involving highly trained teams, lack of information and problems in communication are the greatest sources of inefficiency and frustration. Take as much time as is necessary to ensure that accurate information about the lost person(s) is obtained, provided to all who need it, and clearly recorded. Collect every available item of information about the victim, including not less than the information requested under "Lost Subject Information" on the Search and Rescue Information Form in Figure 8.1 (page 150-151).

Typically, a search starts at the "last seen point," which must be specifically identified, preferably on-site, by whoever last saw the victim. The "last seen point" should be carefully marked. Great care must be taken if trackers or tracking dogs may be called in. Well-meaning searchers may destroy tracks or evidence and confuse the scent trail.

The leader who tries to organize a search for a missing participant has to be extremely careful, since sending searchers out involves loss of contact, unless the group is carrying radios. No one should be dispatched unless the leader is absolutely sure that the individuals know their routes and instructions and are fully capable of safe conduct. In every case, it is essential that the leader establish cutoff times for returns to some fixed and well-known assembly point.

Too often, searchers are allowed to leave with no fixed time of return, so that it becomes impossible to control the operation effectively.

Personnel should be assigned to man the last seen point, any obvious nearby destinations, and key trail or route junctions. If there are not enough available personnel, these points must be very clearly marked, and a note must be left with concise instructions (usually, "Stay here, we will be here at _____ o'clock a.m./p.m."). A piece of bright plastic survey tape on a branch by the trail is *not* enough. Tie the survey tape across the trail with the note tied in the center. It must be so obvious that a disoriented, anxious, possibly hypothermic person will notice it even at night! Check it as often as possible, in case the missing person may be waiting, and also make sure that animals, wind, or snowfall haven't damaged or obscured the marker.

The leader must decide when to call in the searchers and when to either make camp or leave the area. Sometimes enough resources and experienced people are available to allow a "skeleton crew" to stay on-site, while the rest of the group is taken out of the area. Those who remain on-site may be able to alternate duties of tending a bright fire and patrolling key sites until relieved by other searchers the next day. The welfare of the lost individual must be weighed against the welfare of the individuals in the group. Certainly, it is not in the best interests of the lost person to have the energy of a search team diverted to the care of others.

If and when search teams are called upon to assist, the leader must be prepared to provide a detailed, accurate account of all data and an account of all search efforts, so that the search coordinator will have every possible advantage when developing a strategy.

When an organized search is conducted, the leader should be prepared to serve as a resource person for those officially responsible for the search. In some cases, this may be the leader of the search and rescue team, while, in other cases, it may be a sheriff's office deputy, a park ranger, or a representative of the land management agency. On larger searches, when many agencies are involved, the Incident Command System (I.C.S.) is often employed, in which case the leader may be asked to report to the search manager (often called the Incident Commander) or to someone else in the hierarchy. See Figure 8.2 for an overview of the I.C.S. structure.

No two searches are alike, and each country and region has its own terminology and procedures. Nevertheless, there are some common patterns. These have evolved from experience and from extensive study of lost person behavior. Information on effective strategies and tactics has been conveyed worldwide by such international organizations as the Mountain Rescue Association (MRA), by national organizations such as the National Association for Search and Rescue (NASAR), and through the personal travels and communications of search and rescue personnel worldwide.

The first stages of a search usually consist of patrolling every reasonable travel route, and inspecting every likely destination in the area. When possible, an attempt is made to monitor the boundaries of the area—roads, trails, streams, or ridges—in an attempt to limit the possible search area and, ideally, confine the subject. It is relatively easy to search linear features. Once this possibility has been exhausted, the areas between travel routes must be searched. This is a far more time consuming stage!

While one mile (1.6 km) of trail can be walked in half an hour or less, a square mile (2.6 sq. km) of woods or rough country may require 200 hours, or 20 searchers working in efficient lines, spaced 50 feet apart, making at least 5 passes at a pace of about 1/2 mile (0.8 km) per hour for ten hours. If a lost person travels one mile (1.6 km) from the last seen point in an unknown direction, the area of possibility is over 3 square miles (8 sq. km). If the person moves swiftly for an hour and consequently travels three miles (4.8 km), the possible area is over 28 square miles (73 sq. km), which would take a team of 20 dedicated searchers at least a full month to search. For every patch of open country that allows wider spacing of searchers there's a patch that requires closer spacing, so these estimates aren't too far off. Any leader who finds little enthusiasm for keeping careful track of his/her group should participate in this type of search! Finding a person in a square mile of forest can be harder than finding the fabled needle in the haystack; to face the chilling reality is a sure way to turn any leader into a confirmed "mother hen."

Helicopters

It was mentioned earlier that helicopters, while potentially valuable, often can't be used. This is contrary to popular notions about SAR operations, which probably stem from film or television productions in which helicopters invariably play a major role. When they can be employed, helicopters are a tremendous aid, saving rescuers or searchers a lot of work and making the evacuation faster and more pleasant for the victim. The following list points out some of the limitations of helicopters:

1. A helicopter capable of doing the work safely must be available. Not all of them, in fact relatively few, can carry significant loads at higher elevations and still fly safely in the mountains. At lower elevations and in less rugged terrain, more options exist.

2. Qualified pilots who are willing to undertake the risk are not easy to find. Helicopter rescue work can be extremely hazardous and requires exceptional skill.

3. Fuel supplies and maintenance for the helicopter must be obtained if the mission is prolonged, or if the site is remote. Most helicopters require frequent refueling.

4. Flying conditions must be safe. Visibility, amount and type of precipitation, air temperature, air pressure, and wind velocity all have to be within the limits of the aircraft.

5. A safe landing site near the scene, or winch capability, is usually required unless the helicopter is being used only for observation or communication.

6. In many areas, permission has to be obtained from government agencies before using or landing aircraft. Policies vary widely, but,

FIGURE 8.2   Incident Command System

Incident Command Systems have been used for many years in various military and fire-fighting applications and have been adopted for use by many search and rescue organizations. These systems are modular and designed to be expanded as needed. In a very small operation, all functions may be carried out by one person. On larger operations, individuals may be assigned responsibility for one or more of the areas indicated by boxes in the following diagram. Ideally, no individual should be responsible for supervising more than five people.

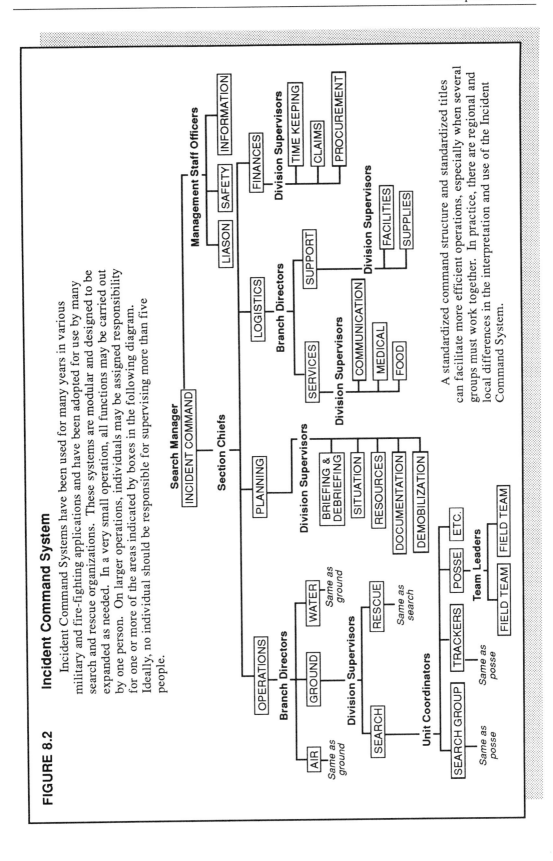

A standardized command structure and standardized titles can facilitate more efficient operations, especially when several groups must work together. In practice, there are regional and local differences in the interpretation and use of the Incident Command System.

in many cases, air support is disallowed. In the United States, for example, there are strict policies regarding the use of helicopters in wilderness areas, where they are usually prohibited unless the emergency is truly life-threatening.

7. Someone has to pay for use of the helicopter and the services of the pilot and crew. This cost is sometimes absorbed by military units or government-funded emergency services, so the burden is spread out among taxpayers. In other cases, individuals may have to pay for the rescue helicopter and pilot, which can be very costly. Typical rates range from $300 to $1,500 or more per hour for the kinds of helicopters commonly used in rescue work.

All told, helicopter assistance is often unavailable. In most cases, SAR agencies begin and maintain a ground-based operation, regardless of whether or not a helicopter may be employed, with the knowledge that air support could be delayed or cancelled for any of the reasons listed above. In addition, there is always the possibility of an accident or mechanical failure. Nevertheless, leaders should be prepared to work with helicopters, which means learning basic rules for approaching and exiting and understanding the general specifications of landing sites. Figure 8.3 illustrates a helicopter landing zone, danger areas, and approach and exit routes.

Radios and Beacons

Radios can, at least in theory, provide instantaneous communication between field groups and between field parties and "civilization." They are used extensively in field applications by the U.S. Forest Service and the National Park Service, the military, search and rescue groups, ski patrols, and a growing number of providers of recreational outdoor activities, including youth camps. With each passing year, there seem to be more capabilities packed into smaller and less expensive units. It seems likely that radios will eventually become standard items of group gear for most kinds of outdoor outings.

This prediction is based only partially on the actual utility of radios in the field. As will be explained shortly, real utility is severely limited

in most nongovernmental applications. For many organizations, a more compelling rationale is found in the need to conform to "current practices in the trade." When major providers of any activity adopt safety related behaviors as standard policy, others who provide similar services may not want to explain why *they* haven't adopted the new policy or technology, even when adoption would produce little real change in risk levels.

Potential users of field portable radios should be aware of the following limitations:

1. All radios are not created equal. There is a wide variety of radios on the market. Very durable units designed for field use may cost twice as much as models designed for urban use, yet have fewer features.

2. Field portable radios usually have low power and virtually require line-of-sight situations in order to function adequately. In dense woods or brush, radio range is severely limited, and even small hills can block radio waves. Thus "repeaters" or "relays" are placed on the crests of strategically located hills and ridges to facilitate effective communication in the area.

This is not to say that radios have no utility in such circumstances. It may be possible to communicate between field units and/or distant stations when line-of-site or near line-of-sight can be achieved.

3. Most repeaters and relays are limited for use by authorized employees of certain government agencies, and most FM frequency bands are assigned by the Federal Communication Commission (FCC) to specific user groups, for which licenses are required. In many areas, commercial licenses are difficult to obtain as frequency bands become increasingly crowded. In some areas, there are amateur radio repeaters in appropriate locations; however, access to these frequencies is limited to those holding certain types of "ham" licenses, and, in many cases, licensed users must also belong to the club or organization that operates the repeater and must know the access code. Another drawback to the use of amateur radio is that *every* user must be licensed, whereas any authorized

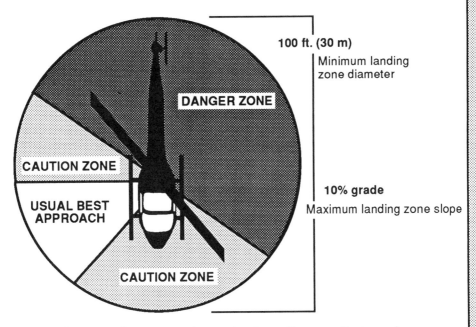

FIGURE 8.3   Helicopter Landing Zone Safety

100 ft. (30 m)
Minimum landing
zone diameter

DANGER ZONE

CAUTION ZONE

USUAL BEST
APPROACH

10% grade
Maximum landing zone slope

CAUTION ZONE

Minimum landing zone diameter may be greater depending upon the type of helicopter, the load it is carrying, the elevation and air pressure, wind velocity and visibility, and the height of the trees or other objects surrounding the zone.

WARNING:
1. Tail rotors are deadly and are often hard to see due to rapid rotation.
2. Main rotors "flap," so approach in a low posture even if clearance seems adequate.
3. Secure all loose objects as wind blasts can be substantial.
4. Approach only when directed by pilot or crew member. Safest approach may vary depending upon the helicopter type and the slope and contour of the landing zone.

employee may use the frequency assigned to a commercial licensee. Access to citizens bands is essentially unlimited, but most channels are extremely overcrowded.

4. Effective field use of a radio is simple under ideal line-of-sight conditions, but can be problematical in more typical circumstances in the field. Antenna positions and many other factors influence the effectiveness of attempted transmission.

5. Batteries are a continual expense and concern. Rechargeable battery packs must be recharged after a day or less of use. Alkaline

batteries last longer and are usually somewhat lighter. Most batteries are less efficient in cold conditions. Most commonly available units are capable of "listening" for several days on a single set of alkaline cells. However, they can receive for a much shorter period of time, and total transmission time may be counted in minutes. Under typical operating conditions, a second spare set of batteries must be carried, even for one or two day outings.

6. *The presence of radios on an outing can instill false confidence.* Leaders may be tempted to make plans on the assumption that radios will provide reliable communication in normal

operations and/or in emergencies. Too often, leaders equipped with radios tend to rely excessively on the technology. When planning to meet at Lake A, two leaders may, as a "backup plan," agree to check in on the radio if one or the other fails to arrive at the lake by a designated time. This may be a reasonable first recourse, but too often such a plan is used to the exclusion of a "bomb-proof" nontechnological backup. What if the radios don't work, as is so often the case? Participants are also inclined to be less cautious when radios are available.

7. *The presence of radios inevitably alters the outdoor experience.* As anyone who has carried a radio can confirm, a backcountry experience with a radio transceiver in one's pack is different. It is more difficult to feel a sense of immersion in the natural world when one carries an instantaneous voice link with civilization. In some programs, radios are carried by leaders but not revealed to participants except in emergencies.

If radios are used, there are a few "tricks of the trade" that can enhance their effectiveness in field use.

1. Use alkaline cells and always carry fresh spares.

2. Set up a schedule for monitoring or check-ins, to limit drain on batteries.

3. Keep batteries warm to maintain efficiency.

4. Think carefully before transmitting. Is the call necessary? What is the briefest and clearest possible way of saying this? (Instead of "Base Camp, this is Fred, do you read me?," try "Base, Fred.") Short transmissions save precious battery power.

5. Find a good location (one likely to produce a successful contact) *before* transmitting. Hold the antenna vertically. Seek a point that is as close to line of sight as possible. In forested areas, try going to the center of a meadow. In lake basin areas, if all else fails, wade chest deep into a lake, to provide an effective ground plane.

Public and Press Relations in Emergencies

The public relations aspect of a serious accident is in many ways like day-to-day contact with the public. The reader might want to read the end of Chapter Thirteen, "Marketing," for a more complete discussion of public relations. The public relations following a serious accident requires some special consideration. The "image" projected can be no better than the job that is being accomplished. One must be honest, accurate, and reasonable. Due to the possibility of litigation, one must also be prudent in all communications. If negligence has contributed to the accident, whoever is responsible (usually the leader) will be in an extremely difficult situation, personally and professionally. If there was no negligence, however, and the leader responded swiftly and efficiently, the supervisor should be able to maintain public confidence by explaining the circumstances and the leader's response to the situation. Litigation is sometimes necessary to determine whether negligence was involved, and this possibility makes prudence essential.

Regardless of whether a situation involved negligence, there are several things to keep in mind that could simplify the ramifications. The items listed below represent the public-relations point of view; however, the staff should be well-aware that public relations cannot be the only consideration at this point.

1. The welfare of the injured party comes first. This may seem like a simplistic statement; but it is an important part of how the public will evaluate what has happened. Included in the protection of the injured party is keeping bystanders and/or witnesses calm and in control from the outset. Someone needs to assume authority to minimize unwelcome help or interference.

2. After the injured person has been provided the necessary first aid or other emergency medical attention, be sure that the family is notified immediately with as clear an evaluation of the status of the injury as is possible. The family certainly has the right to know the situation before any information is released to the news media and before the information can reach them in a distorted form through secondhand sources.

Common sense dictates that it is important to communicate the actual seriousness of the situation, but be sure to present the information calmly and without dramatic interpretations of a "great rescue effort." At least in the initial announcement, the family does not need and probably does not want to know the shocking or graphic details of the injury, or any unfounded rumors or speculation in the event of a search. Rather, you should tell them the important facts, giving only useful information about the injury, illness, or search.

3. Be sure that your supervisors or other parties likely to be contacted about the accident are immediately and thoroughly informed about the incident.

4. If possible, anticipate inquiries from the media. Prepare a written statement for them if time permits, or at least be prepared to give the pertinent information as you know it, but do not release it without talking to the information coordinator or your supervisor.

5. Cooperation with the press and public in providing the best information possible is important at this point. Try to accentuate the positive whenever you can. For example: "Although the girl fell backward off the diving platform, *the doctor indicated* she has probably suffered only a minor concussion. She was able to move all her limbs and to speak clearly before she was transported to the hospital."

Unless you have a medical source to quote regarding the condition of the injured, be very careful about evaluation. Clearly refer them to a hospital or a doctor for confirmation and clarification of the condition.

6. Despite the need and desire to inform the media and the public about the actual occurrence, be careful about giving out information which might jeopardize the rights of either the agency or the individual should a legal suit result from the accident. No statements regarding fault or liability should be made. If possible, the supervisor should handle all media inquiries. That person should be very well-informed and, if possible, be the most knowledgeable about the incident.

A word of caution—if litigation seems possible or probable, be wary of people who call and "just ask questions" or who identify themselves by name only and not by agency. People have been known to ask leading questions in order to establish a legal case. There is no need to be rude, but it is completely appropriate to ask why they need the information. A reasonable answer to that question can help you provide more useful information for legitimate inquiries, protect the privacy of the injured party, and sort out those who really should have information from those who should not.

This is a very touchy area. *If there is any question, it is better to defer public comment until contact has been made, by your supervisor, with an attorney for your agency. The more serious the accident, and/or the more likelihood of responsibility by the agency, the more important this aspect becomes.*

When approached in this kind of situation, give some sort of "bare bones" statement if possible. For example, you might say that the patient has been taken to the hospital and a report on the incident is being prepared which will be available at a later time. It would also be appropriate to suggest what person to contact and an approximate time to do so. In some cases, it is better to give no statement. These types of situations should be discussed beforehand by all supervisors and staff members.

7. The most important thing you can do is also the most difficult; *stay calm!* This is especially important if your actions and statements might affect the welfare of the victims. Your ability to make prudent decisions and statements

under stress is vitally important. Anxiety, over-excitement, or loss of firm control of your behavior can very seriously alter both the actual and the publicly perceived outcomes of the incident. Work through scenarios in your head and with your supervisor before you encounter a real emergency. Talk to people who work in emergency services and/or in public relations, and develop your skills and confidence by reviewing past incidents.

8. Follow through after the emergency. Let the family know that you are concerned for the outcome of the patient. Visits to patient and family are expressions of caring and are good for public relations. Follow through if you can provide additional information about the incident. Let your staff and supervisors know anything you find out so they, too, can answer questions which are likely to be asked by the public.

9. Make sure that a complete accident report is on file, and record all related contacts and actions taken. See Figure 8.4.

Summary

While search and rescue (SAR) operations are not needed in the vast majority of outdoor activities, emergencies can and do occur, and the leader is expected to know what to do to procure help from the outside. Careful planning and effective leadership usually precludes the need for such help; however, unforeseen happenings, such as accidents and lost participants, often necessitates the need for search and rescue. Leaders must understand that there is a wide difference in SAR services throughout the world and even within individual countries.

When outside help is needed, the decision must be made whether to transport a victim to the help or to send for the help to come to the victim. Either decision requires careful understanding of the advantages and disadvantages of each action. Regardless of the decision, procuring help from the outside takes a very long time, usually a minimum of 24 hours.

In order to be effective, a search for lost or missing participants requires a specific plan of operation that must be followed assiduously.

Among other problems, searches require much time and many people. Helicopters and radios are sometimes employed and are extremely valuable assets in SAR operations; however, they are often unavailable or cannot be fully-utilized due to adverse weather, rugged terrain, technical limitations, or other factors. Because search and rescue generates much interest by the news media, public relations following a serious accident or a lost participant must be handled very carefully and should usually follow steps discussed beforehand with the organization's administrator and other staff in the program.

References

Emergency Response Institute Network. (no date). *Search in an emergency.* Olympia, WA: Emergency Response Institute, Inc.

Mariner, W. (1963). *Mountain rescue techniques.* Seattle, WA: The Mountaineers.

May, W. G. (1973). *Mountain search and rescue techniques.* Boulder, CO: Rocky Mountain Rescue Group.

McInnes, H. (1972). *International mountain rescue handbook.* New York, NY: Charles Scribner's, Sons.

Oklahoma State University. (1988). *Field operations guide for incident command systems.* Stillwater, OK: Fire Protection Publications.

Person interviews. (1992). John Pitetti. Lane County, OR: Sheriff's Patrol, Search and Rescue Team.

Risk, P. (1983). *Outdoor safety and survival.* New York, NY: John Wiley & Sons.

Setnicka, T. (1980). *Wilderness search and rescue.* Boston, MA: Appalachian Mountain Club.

FIGURE 8.4   Accident Report Form

Name _____ Date Of Birth _____ Sex _____
               (last   first   middle)

Address _____ City _____ State _____ Zip Code _____
          (number   street)

Telephone   (home) _____   (work) _____

Person Notified _____ Telephone _____
(parent or legal guardian)

Address _____ City _____ State _____ Zip Code _____
(if different)   (number   street)

How Notified _____ When Notified _____

Date Of Injury _____ Time (AM/PM) _____ Weather Conditions _____

Place Of Injury And Circumstances _____
(include equipment involved)

Describe Injury _____

First Aid Given _____

_____ By _____ When _____

Disposition Of Patient _____
(continued activity, went home, taken to hospital, etc.)

WITNESSES

Name _____ Address _____ Phone _____

Name _____ Address _____ Phone _____

Name _____ Address _____ Phone _____

On back, explain relevant details, what went wrong,
and how accident might have been prevented.

Follow-Up Actions (date, action, by)   _____

Submitted By _____   **Date** _____

LAND
NAVIGATION

People are navigators from birth. Motivated by their needs, they learn quickly how to move through their environments efficiently. For most purposes, a mental route map is enough. (To get to the refrigerator, turn left at the kitchen table.) Later in life, a somewhat longer series of turns take one reliably to the supermarket, and the reverse series brings one home. Another sequence of cues and turns takes folks to the bank and back.

Simple "route mapping" is a very basic survival skill, and it is, for most people, all that is needed for survival. Most people, though not all, are able to master a far more sophisticated skill. They can go from home to the supermarket and then, even if they have never done it before, they can find the bank without going home first! To do this, they have created in their minds a reasonably accurate two-dimensional mental image, or map, of the area. Then they can estimate the relative positions of the supermarket and bank. Most people get around quite efficiently by employing a combination of route and cue memorization, mental mapping, marginal ability to read a simple road map, and occasional advice from a friendly service station attendant.

The Need for Navigation Skills

Aren't these skills sufficient for outdoor activities? Perhaps they are for those who participate in some activities. For example, the alpine skier who always stays within the boundaries of the area is guided by simple maps and abundant signs. The sport climber may follow a hundred yard long trail to the popular rock quarry near town, and follow a route meticulously described in word and photo in the local guidebook. The cross-country skier at a resort may follow the red signs on a two kilometer loop. In the central European Alps, a mountaineer may join a line of fellow climbers on a well-worn path to the summit, seldom losing sight of the village in the valley below. Do these people need to be able to navigate? Maybe not, unless they venture, intentionally or inadvertently, beyond the safety of well-marked and well-signed routes.

Who *does* need to be able to read maps, use compasses, and practice navigational skills, and what do these people need to know? There are some activities and some types of terrain wherein participants need more than "urban" navigational skills. Whenever people enter areas devoid of conventional orientation cues, navigation skills become important. Map reading skills may be valuable even when orientation is not an issue. For example, in the steep and rugged

Alps of Europe or Japan, trail signing is excellent, and trails are well-marked for "urban" users. However, the significance of taking a given route cannot be fully appreciated unless the shape of the land is understood, a skill that requires an ability to interpret contour lines. In most backcountry areas, self-reliant trail travel depends upon the ability to read a map.

Off-trail travel requires ability in both map reading *and* compass use especially if the terrain is wooded or if major landmarks are obscured by foul weather. Thus, competence in the use of maps, compasses, and navigational techniques is more important in parts of the western and northern United States, in Canada, and in most of Scandinavia than in some southwestern U.S. desert regions or the central Alps of Europe. Mountaineers, off-trail backpackers, ski-tourers and snowcampers (who are active when trails, and usually trail signs, are buried), and open water or wilderness canoeists need to be adept at navigation, as do orienteerers, whose sport is based upon navigational competency. Anyone traveling on backcountry trails where winter snow often remains in place obliterating trails until late August, or all summer, must also be competent with map and compass. Many times they will lose the trail and suddenly be dependent upon navigation skills, perhaps for their own survival!

While it is clear that the definition of adequate competence in navigation varies between activities and regions, leaders should recognize that *their* needs may exceed those of the typical participant. There are at least three reasons for this. First, competence in map reading is an extremely valuable, if not essential, prerequisite to effective planning. Second, orientation and navigation skills are central to safety. Leaders must know where they are and what their options are at all times. Third, most participants in outdoor pursuits need at least basic instruction in navigational skills. The leader should be well-ahead of the participants in knowledge, skill and experience to enable effective teaching.

Any leader intending to conduct outings in wilderness or backcountry areas, whether off-trail travel is intended or not, should be well-versed in all of the techniques addressed in this chapter. The purpose of this chapter is *not*,

however, to teach map and compass skills. Rather, it is to suggest what types of information might be most useful to participants and suggest ways of teaching map and compass skills.

The leader or instructor who attempts to convey the basic knowledge and skills outlined in this chapter will find that the task requires considerable time and endless patience. The ideas to be conveyed are not particularly complex, and there are only a few essential skills to be taught. Many people, however, are poorly prepared to grasp even the most basic geometrical and mathematical concepts, and others may have great difficulty reading maps due to deficiencies in their ability to conceptualize spatial relationships. In virtually all cases, however, these difficulties can be overcome by creativity, patience, and persistence.

Teaching Map and Compass Skills

Teaching the use of maps and compasses is not difficult, but it can be frustrating. The most common pitfalls for the instructor are:

1. Lack of personal skill, knowledge, or experience in navigation. It is hard to teach what is not known, and hard to be convincing if there is a lack of reinforcing experience;

2. Trying to teach to an unmotivated audience. Do the participants believe they *need* the information?;

3. Trying to teach, even to the most eager audience, in the face of significant environmental or other distractions. The tired beginning backpacker facing another two miles to camp, the climber anxious about the next pitch, or the cross-country skier pondering survival on the next hill will be distracted by other, more pressing concerns; and

4. Falsely assuming that participants understand basic concepts of mapping and/or the measurement of angles. Trying to teach too much, too fast is a common error in any teaching endeavor.

Look at these concerns more closely. What constitutes adequate competence for an instructor? The answer clearly depends upon the nature of the activity, the terrain to be covered, and the program itself. At the very least, the leader should be able to:

1. Interpret a topographic map accurately; includes an ability to envision three-dimensional land forms as expressed by contour lines, and an ability to determine elevations and elevation differences using a topographic map;

2. Use a compass to measure bearings on the map, to measure bearings in the field, to plot bearings on the map, and to follow bearings in the field;

3. Determine location in the field by resection and triangulation; and

4. Compute and employ trail gradients.

In addition, the leader should understand at least the basics of orientation by the sun and stars.

The second concern deals with motivation. It is worth considering whether the participants really *need* map and compass skills. Usually the answer is yes, if they will be backpacking mountaineering, ski touring, or otherwise engaging in backcountry activities. There are exceptions, however. Many people employ the service of guides or leaders on *all* of their outings, not uncommonly for the specific purpose of avoiding the need to know how to navigate. While it is always tempting to force self-sufficiency on such people, success is likely to be limited. Besides, as long as they continue to use guides, and never stray from the guide's direct supervision, they may not need to know much about navigation.

Also, participants may not need map and compass skills because their activities may take place in a part of the world where such skills are not essential. For example, hikers in the Kita Alps of Japan or the Berner Oberland in Switzerland will find clearly marked trails on sharply defined ridges between populated valleys, with huts at half-day intervals. This is not to say that maps are not useful to these people—far from it! Yet, in these areas all that is needed is a *very* basic ability to read maps.

Compasses are rarely ever used by hikers in such areas, and only climbers and others venturing well off maintained routes need to be proficient with maps and compasses. On the other hand, travelers may be surprised to learn that in certain areas of Scandinavia, children learn to navigate by compass in the first grade so they can find their ways to and from home in blizzards. The leader should attempt to understand how and where the participants may employ navigational skills, and use this information to motivate their interest in learning.

The third concern has to do with the setting in which learning takes place and the receptivity of the prospective students. Experience has proven that many people find maps and compasses puzzling. The average beginning backpacker needs to focus just about all of his/her wits on the wobbling compass needle and the squiggly contour lines. The instructor, on the other hand, can stride along briskly watching the scenery with one eye while rattling on about the fine points of correcting declination in areas of local magnetic disturbance. The poor beginner, limping from blisters and out of breath from the pace, may be more concerned with avoiding the next mud hole. Short rest breaks may be poor teaching settings, if most of that time is needed for rest, treating sore feet, putting on and taking off clothes, snacking, and dashing into the bushes to relieve the kidneys.

If they are unhurried and participants remain warm and comfortable, rest stops can provide opportunities for viewing the terrain and comparing it to the map. Have participants review the last part of the hike carefully, relating each detail to the map, then predict the hike to the next rest stop. If possible, find a place with a good view of the area. Nothing beats sitting on top of a hill or ridge, looking out on terrain depicted on the map. Features can be related to the map, and bearings measured, sighted, and plotted. Triangulation can also be practiced.

Too often the instructors, needing little time for maintenance, try to teach when the class is not receptive. A common frustration is trying to teach navigation while ski touring. It is a fine and even enjoyable thing to do during a long lunch stop on a warm spring day, but it is doomed to failure while skiing or in wind, snow, or rain unless the participants are exceptionally motivated. Teaching navigation while moving is usually impossible except at a leisurely pace with capable skiers. Remember that a pace that is leisurely for the leader may be exhilarating or even scary for the participant, who may be more concerned about missing the trees than about keeping track of location or direction.

Who cares about compass use when the next piece of ski trail looks like the north face of the Eiger! If the student has to spend significant physical or psychological energy just surviving, little or no attention can be focused on "extraneous" learning. So don't set expectations too high unless the terrain, weather, and activity are well within the fitness and skill limits of the participants. Be patient, and expect some difficulties in transferring concepts from the classroom or the in-town practice course to the field. Simply being in a backcountry area is unsettling for many people.

A closely related concern is the "sheep syndrome," the tendency of people to stop orienting themselves when following another person. This tendency, coupled with tiredness, discomfort, or anxiety, results in little or no capacity for learning or refining navigation skills. Thus, small groups that frequently rotate with the lead person are essential to any attempt at teaching navigation in the field.

One of the best ways to avoid the sheep syndrome is to assign a participant to the navigator's position at the head of the line, and to rotate the position at regular intervals. People tend to pay attention best if they believe they are responsible for their own welfare. As far as can be done safely, the staff should allow the practice navigators to make errors. Under such circumstances, the other participants will often be sufficiently anxious to maintain a healthy level of attention to navigation.

The key is to appreciate the physical and mental stresses on the group, and to modify instructional patterns accordingly. Try to teach in pleasant, nonthreatening settings at times when the participants are comfortable, relaxed, well-fed, and well-watered. These concerns

bring to mind a rather obvious alternative, that of classroom or at least in-town teaching. Classroom settings can be very efficient since a variety of media can be used, and participants are usually comfortable and receptive.

Last, but not least, is the mistake of trying to teach too quickly or to convey too much information. The instructor may overwhelm even the most eager, receptive, and intelligent student if this happens. In any group situation, some individuals will have special needs, and maps and compasses present problems for a surprisingly large number of people.

One common difficulty has to do with understanding a map as a view of the land's surface. For most of us, it is easy to understand the concept of a vertical view; the explanation that most maps are bird's-eye views (actually the simultaneous views of an infinite number of birds) is usually sufficient. Others, however, have difficulty in shifting perceptive. Look at a child's "map" of a city street—all of the building *fronts* are visible though tilted back and distorted. Some people never do become comfortable with conventional mapping systems, and they will require considerable extra instructional effort. The use of compasses, for instance, requires a basic understanding of angles; many people have little idea of what an angle is, much less a bearing, and need assistance in the form of definition and simple examples and analogies.

Since it is difficult to assess the particular needs of everyone in the class quickly, and, since basic concepts of geometry and perspective are so crucial to the entire realm of navigation, it is usually a good idea to begin lessons with a review of these topics. Remember that many people also have a longstanding anxiety about anything that sounds "mathematical." This alone can be extremely limiting, and, if the difficulties are compounded by specific learning problems or by any of the concerns discussed earlier, both the instructor and the student may be in for a frustrating experience unless it is possible to commit the necessary time to those with special needs.

Assume that basic navigation skills are included in the program objectives, and that the leader is fortunate enough to have an eager and receptive audience with appropriate resources and good weather. What should be taught? First, it is necessary to assess the needs of the students carefully and to weigh these against the limits set by constraints of time. Planning is important here, so that limited resources and time may be used effectively. The following progression includes most of the basic navigational concepts and skills useful for hiking, backpacking, and mountaineering. While the relative importance of these concepts and skills will vary for each group (and perhaps for each individual), care should be taken not to skip steps upon which later steps depend.

For most participants in outdoor activities, the fear of becoming lost is the prime motivation for learning navigation skills. The leader responsible for teaching navigation may find it useful to begin with an illustration, preferably recent and from the local area, of a situation wherein such skills helped prevent losing the way, or where problems resulted from lack of navigational competency. It is encouraging to point out that anyone can learn to navigate, and that mastery of only a few simple skills can provide a large measure of security. People need both an incentive to learn and a belief in their ability to learn.

The following topics are suggested as possible contents of a basic introductory course in navigation. At the University of Oregon, this material is taught in three hours of lecture and a six-hour field session, followed by a work sheet and stringent examination, as part of a 40-hour course that is a prerequisite to participation in any backcountry outing course.

Basic Orientation Techniques

It is often best to begin with a brief review of the cardinal directions. Children, even when facing north, are often not sure which way is east and a surprising number of adults are unsure as well. The following points should be made:

1. *Navigation is based upon orientation,* which should be maintained continually throughout a trip.

2. *Orientation requires continual attention to direction and distance.* When we drive a car, lead a group, or travel solo, we pay attention; but too often when we travel as passengers or as followers in a group, we do not. Lack of attention leads to loss of orientation, which in turn leads to dependency on others or the need to employ more advanced navigational skills.

3. *Developing an ability to remain oriented and learning navigation skills is possible only if and when the individual takes responsibility for his/her education.* If the experienced, knowledgeable, or aggressive people in a group are allowed to take the lead every time, the less experienced or more timid people will not become competent and self-sufficient. Learning situations need to be structured to allow everyone, especially those who need it most, the opportunity to be responsible for orientation and navigation. Keep in mind the fact that the ultimate goal is improvement of post-class behavior.

4. *Before beginning a hike, river trip, or any outdoor adventure, study a large-scale map, such as a highway map,* to understand the "big picture" and to form an oriented mental map of the general site and the surrounding features.

5. *Before leaving the vehicles, study the detailed map of the area.* Using the map, predict what the route will be like, then, while traveling, *observe* carefully and *compare* the observations to the predictions. If observations and predictions do not agree, *stop and figure out why.* If the prediction-confirmation interval is limited to a distance of a half-mile (0.8 km) or to a travel time of 15 minutes, then the individual or group should never be more than a half-mile or 15 minutes travel time from a confirmed location. If this one simple concept were applied universally, few people would ever become lost, since under most circumstances it is easy to retrace one's steps for a half-mile.

Solar Clues

A large percentage of the population is remarkably unaware of natural patterns. A brief review of planetary mechanics can help establish the regularity of apparent solar motions and explain seasonal variance in the sun's elevation in the sky. Important concepts include: (1) The sun moves from east to west at about 15 degrees per hour (360 degrees divided by 24 hours), and (2) At noon, Standard Time (if one is near the center of the time zone), the sun is at its highest point (shadows are shortest), and the shadows point north for observers north of the Tropic of Cancer and south for those south of the Tropic of Capricorn. This gives students at least one

way of roughly approximating direction by the sun if they know what time it is and which way the shadows point. See Figure 9.1

A useful related fact is the near symmetry of the day around the noon hour. If, for example, it gets light five-and-a-half-hours before noon, it will get dark five-and-a-half-hours after noon—*Standard* Time, of course. They should also be reminded of the effect of "Daylight Savings Time" or summer time. Noon Standard Time becomes 1:00 on Daylight Time. Thus, on

FIGURE 9.1   Using Shadows to Determine Direction or Time in the Northern Hemisphere

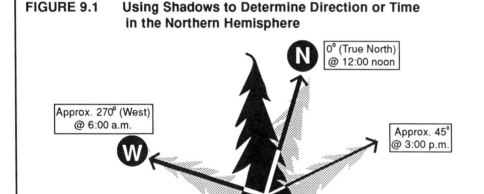

0° (True North) @ 12:00 noon

Approx. 270° (West) @ 6:00 a.m.

Approx. 45° @ 3:00 p.m.

Approx. 90° (East) @ 6:00 p.m.

NOTE:
1. If you are in the northern hemisphere, north of the Tropic of Cancer, and near the center of your time zone, shadows point approximately True North at noon, Standard Time (1:00 p.m. Daylight Savings Time). In the southern hemisphere, south of the Tropic of Capricorn, and near the center of your time zone, shadows point approximately True South at the same times.
2. Shadows are shortest at noon, Standard Time.
3. Shadows move approximately 15° per hour.
4. If you can measure the direction of shadows (i.e. have a compass), it is possible to estimate the time.
5. If you know the time (i.e. have a watch), you can estimate direction.
6. Without a compass or watch, True North (and noon) can be estimated by determining the direction and time of the shortest shadows.

Daylight Time if it gets light at 5:00 a.m. (eight hours before 1 p.m.), it will get dark at about 9:00 p.m. Participants may be able to remember that Daylight Time is always one hour ahead of Standard Time.

Stellar Clues

When using stars for navigational aids, it is best to focus on very basic concepts. The most useful references are the Big Dipper and Polaris (or directions to the more illusive sigma octans for Southern Hemisphere residents). See Figure 9.2. Many other stars have value in navigation; however, these are best left for an evening of stargazing.

Maps

What is a map? A bird's-eye view analogy is useful. Models, globes, and sketches can help explain perspective. A good exercise with children (and sometimes with adults) is to have them draw maps of small areas. For example, have children draw a picture of the top of their own desk and explain that it is a map. Then have them draw a picture of all the desks in the room as seen by someone peering through a hole in the ceiling. Then have them draw the playground, the neighborhood, and their route to school. This progression will help children as young as age six understand the meaning of maps. In youth camps, youngsters may "map" their tent or cabin floors, then the location of a group of tents/cabins, followed by birds' eye views of other facilities in the camp.

Map types. Show planimetric and topographic maps using highway, United States Geological Survey (USGS), or other topographic expressions of the same area. Overheads or slides of these are handy in the classroom. The simplicity and low cost of planimetric maps can be contrasted to the greater amount of information but commensurate increases in cost and complexity of topographic images.

Map making. Explain aerial photographs and the use of overlapping photos to allow interpretation of topography. Explanations of mapping theory and techniques may be interesting to a few people, but it is most important to note that the process involves a combination

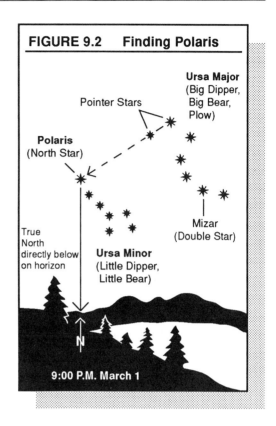

FIGURE 9.2   Finding Polaris

of human and machine work, and that the map is thus just an approximation of reality. Common errors, such as out-of-date or incorrectly placed roads and trails and inaccuracies in designation of ground cover and bodies of water, should be mentioned. These points are best illustrated on maps of the local area.

Map Reading

Symbols, colors, and conventions. On most maps, true north is toward the top of the map; so left or right map edges and any vertical line on the map are approximately true north-south lines. Every country has its own conventions and symbols. Most use green to designate contiguous vegetation, and it is sometimes of interest to explain the standards used. In the U.S., for instance, areas are colored green on USGS topographic quadrangles if the map maker estimates that an acre of such vegetation would be adequate to hide a squad of Marines! Aerial photos, especially low-elevation oblique photos of the terrain shown on practice maps, are valuable aids here.

It is always important to show how water is indicated, and, depending upon the region, how glaciers, lava flows, swamps, or other features are shown. In some areas, it is useful to include the concept of townships, ranges, and sections, even in a beginning class. "Legal descriptions" of location are essential components of more advanced courses and courses for employees of land management agencies or members of search groups.

Scale. Explain the idea of ratios and proportions, and show examples of maps on different scales, ideally of the same area. Derive some easily understood equivalents for common map scales such as 1.0 cm = 0.5 km on a 1:50,000 map; 1 inch = about 1 mile for 1:62,500 maps (62,500 is close to 63,360, the number of inches in a mile); or 0.5 inch = 1,000 feet for 1:24,000 maps. Have the students work through a series of examples of translation from map to reality and from reality to the map. Basic competence includes an ability to predict the real size of a feature shown on a map, and the size on the map of an observed feature accurately.

Contour lines. Classroom presentation of sketches, overheads, and other visual aids is especially useful here. See Figure 9.3.

Suggest that participants imagine the successive shorelines created by placing a little "mountain" of clay in a bathtub, then raising the water level one inch at a time. This idea can be extended to explain the behavior of contour lines on gentle and steep slopes, ridges, and valleys. Other effective techniques include the use of topographic mockups made by layering sheets of cardboard cut on "contour lines," of chalkboard illustrations showing how ridges and valleys might be expressed, and of slides depicting the actual terrain on topographic maps in the hands of students. The use of such slides can be very effective. A set of slides taken from a high point shown on the students' maps can be used to approximate the effect of actually sitting on the point with the class identifying and relating the real view with the topographic map expression.

A valuable exercise at this point is to "take a hike" on the students' maps; 1:62,500 or 1:50,000 scale maps are good choices since they are in common use and are intermediate in scale.

Select a route that includes uphill and downhill portions and a range of landforms and features. Follow the route, describing the trail, terrain, vegetation, and other features one would encounter if actually walking along the route.

Beginners should learn to identify uphill and downhill portions of a route and to determine elevations of selected points. Intermediate groups should learn to estimate vertical gains and losses accurately, and to compute trail gradients.

Approximate trail gradients are easy to calculate. They are simply the vertical gain or loss divided by the horizontal distance traveled. Yet, an amazing number of people have trouble even with primitive mathematical calculations. A diagram or "cross-section" of the trail helps clarify the process. The phrase "rise over run" may help. Thus, a trail that climbs 800 feet in a mile will have a gradient of 800/5,280 or about 15 percent. In practice, since most people can't accurately picture 100 feet or meters, it is usually best to scale down to 10 feet or meters. For example, a 15 percent slope (15 units of vertical change per 100 units of horizontal change) is the same as 1.5 units of vertical change per 10 units of horizontal change. Knowing that the trail climbs 1.5 feet for every 10 horizontal feet of trail allows one to visualize the actual trail slope. Gradients are a simple way of understanding how steep a trail will be. It is easy to misread the steepness of trails, especially if one is relatively new at map reading or must use maps of many different vertical and horizontal scales.

Compasses

There are many types of compasses, each best suited for a particular use. The orienteering compass is by far the most useful for recreational navigation in the backcountry. There are many sizes and shapes available, and some have mirrors attached by a hinge to the end nearest the capsule containing the needle. In general, the longer the base, the greater the potential accuracy, and the mirror feature, if used correctly, can further reduce errors by about half. Figure 9.4 (page 172) shows a typical orienteering compass.

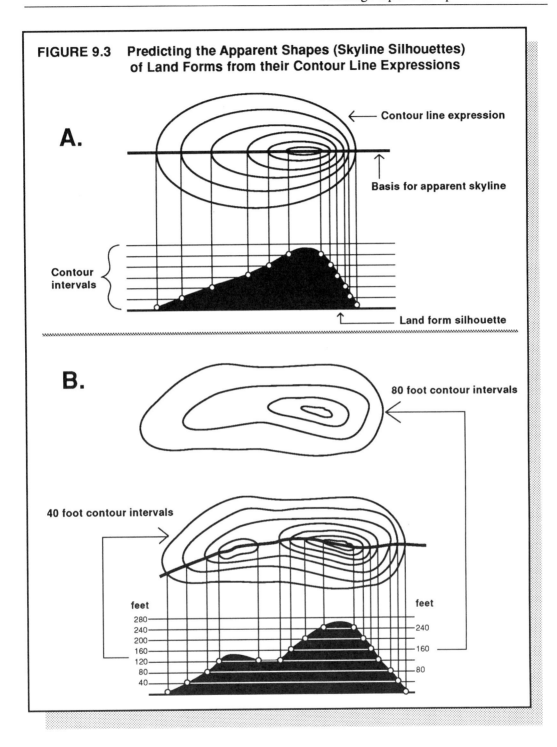

FIGURE 9.3   Predicting the Apparent Shapes (Skyline Silhouettes) of Land Forms from their Contour Line Expressions

A.

Contour line expression

Basis for apparent skyline

Contour intervals

Land form silhouette

B.

80 foot contour intervals

40 foot contour intervals

feet

280
240
200
160
120
80
40

feet

240

160

80

Ideally, each student should have an orienteering compass. It is, however, sometimes necessary to share a limited supply or even fabricate paper or plastic replicas, which can serve well in the classroom. Some people have military models not designed to be used on a map. If the owners of these compasses want to use them, it will be necessary to use a protractor to measure angles on the map. This is quite easy, but more time consuming and less convenient than using an orienteering compass.

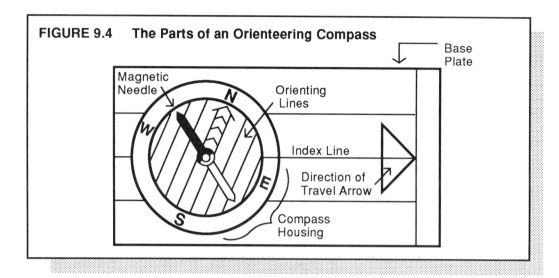

FIGURE 9.4   The Parts of an Orienteering Compass

Now and then, someone from the southern hemisphere brings a compass to the northern hemisphere, or vice versa. Since magnetic lines of force are tilted toward the poles, the south end of northern hemisphere (and the north end of southern hemisphere) compasses have to be weighted so that the needle sits horizontally. Even compasses balanced for use near the equator will not work well if taken too far north or south. Ship compasses, by the way, have moveable weights to allow adjustments as needed.

Measuring and Plotting Bearings on a Map

Angles. Too often we leap into discussions without defining basic concepts. Unfortunately, many adults are no better off than young children in terms of understanding basic geometric concepts. Since we are teaching map and compass use, it is helpful to teach geometry concepts that are consistent with the immediate needs. Angles should be measured in clockwise directions from the vertical line, which should be identified as the "reference line." Any discussion of angles should include the idea of a reference line and of the use of a 360 degree circle.

Directions. Figure 9.5 illustrates cardinal directions and bearings. Students must understand that the degree figures define the various lines one could draw from the center of the circle to points on the circle or "scale," and that these lines represent directions. "Bearings" can then

be defined as equivalent to these lines of direction and designated by reference to the scale number, which is the angle, measured in a clockwise direction, between the reference line and the line of travel. Once this is understood, have the students imagine themselves standing in the center of the circle. "Following a bearing" can then be explained as walking from the center straight out toward the appropriate point on the scale. Bearings from one place to another on the map can be shown by extension of the idea; have students imagine the starting place to be at

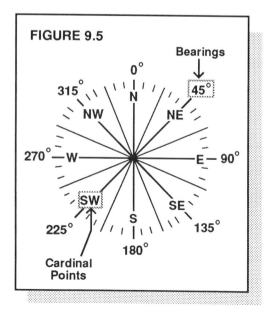

FIGURE 9.5

the center of the circle. At this point, it is worth-while to note that the reference line is due north. The differences between true and magnetic north will be discussed later.

Orienting the scale. The compass is best introduced as a device for measuring angles. Identify the parts of the compass but have the students ignore the needle for now. The scale can be equated to the circle used to illustrate the concept of direction. It probably speeds the learning process to have the students see the scale as fixed and the rectangular base as mov-able to continue the comparison to the circle of directions.

Perhaps the most important idea to be intro-duced here is orientation of the scale using the "orienting lines" visible within the compass housing. The concept of orienting the scale should be discussed in detail because it is crucial to effective use of the compass. Remind stu-dents that a compass is simply a tool for measur-ing angles, and that angles are always measured from a reference line. To be consistent with map conventions, this reference line is the true-north direction line. Orienting the scale to true north on a map means lining up the orienting lines in the housing with any real or imaginary "vertical" (up-and-down) line on the map. For now, it is sufficient to define "true north" as the direction to the North Pole.

Some people have difficulty estimating a ver-tical line on a map. There is a tendency to trust section lines or other lines scribed onto the map, which may not be true north-south lines. Sug-gest folding the right or left edge of the map inward and lining up the top and bottom edges, so that the map edge forms a perfect vertical reference.

Orienting the map. The one basic skill not yet discussed is orienting the map. Sometimes it is useful to orient the map to the terrain, to facilitate visual location or identification of features on the map. The easiest way to accom-plish this is to orient the orienting lines of the compass on the map, then while holding the compass firmly to the roughly horizontal map, rotate the map until the north end of the needle points to the declination figure. Some people prefer to set the compass to zero degrees first; though, it really isn't necessary. If the map is

perfectly oriented, it is possible to line up objects quite precisely. In actual practice, however, it is seldom possible to find a large, flat, magneti-cally neutral surface on which to spread the map.

Measuring bearings on maps. Measuring bearings is most easily taught as a three step process of (1) aligning the compass base plate, (2) orienting the scale, and (3) reading the bear-ing. Aligning the base plate means setting the edge of the compass on a line between the two points, with the "direction of travel" arrow point-ing in the correct direction. (If they have this arrow reversed, they may still reach their desti-nation, but the route will be about 24,000 miles longer!) When the points are small and close together, greater accuracy can be obtained by using the lines scribed onto the base plate, par-allel to the edges. Orienting the scale is done while holding the base plate in place.

The most common errors at this stage are reversal of the orienting lines, putting the south end of the lines at the top, and inaccurate align-ment. Students may need to be reminded that they are only measuring angles on the map, and the compass needle should be ignored. Reading the bearing may or may not be easy, depending upon the compass being used. In many models, the scale is graduated in two degree units, and in others, parallax error results if the eye is not directly above the point where the bearing line crosses the scale. In many cases, such as when plotting bearings or following a bearing, it is not necessary to read the exact bearing unless it must be recorded or compared to another bearing.

Accuracy is important, since a one degree error equates to 92 feet at one mile (5,280 feet), or 17.45 meters at one kilometer, and any errors in measurement on the map may be compounded by errors in following the bearing in the field. At this point, practice is needed. After a series of simple point to point bearing measurements, it is helpful to have students also measure dis-tances, to determine elevations of the end points, and to interpret the shape of the land between the two points as a step toward integration of the skills learned thus far.

Plotting bearings on maps. The next step, plotting bearings on the map, is most easily taught as a four step process as follows: (1) set the bearing on the compass, (2) place the tip of a pencil at the point where the plot is to begin, (3) place the compass edge against the pencil tip and rotate the base plate until the orienting lines are correctly oriented on the map, and (4) draw a line in the direction of the "direction of travel" arrow when plotting a bearing *to* a target or feature, or in the opposite direction when plotting a bearing from a feature (as in triangulation). It is usually easiest to begin practice with exercises requiring students to find features. For example, "What feature lies at a bearing of 246 degrees at a distance of 2 1/4 miles from Scout Lake?"

Most beginning students need to learn nothing more than how to measure bearings on the map, while more advanced students will find resection and triangulation interesting and useful. Resection is best illustrated by using a simple example wherein students imagine themselves walking along a ridge, creek, road, trail, or other linear feature. The first imaginary situation should be simple, for instance, a walk along a nearly straight east-west ridge from which a finite point or feature, such as a peak, appears to be due north of the observer.

Later, scenarios can be as interesting as class ability, interest, and time allowance, and should include examples of how the technique can be applied to realistic situations. Once this "point-line" method is in hand, two point fixations (triangulation) can be illustrated and practiced, again starting with a simple case, such as, "If you can see Spire Peak at a bearing of 60 degrees and Red Bluffs at a bearing of 150 degrees, where must you be?" As with all compass use, lots of practice is essential.

True North, Magnetic North, and Declination

There are several "norths," including "true" north, "magnetic" north, "grid" north, and others. For most recreational purposes, it is sufficient to know that lines of latitude and longitude to which most maps are oriented are centered on the geographic North Pole, and that the direction to the North Pole is called "true north." See Figure 9.6.

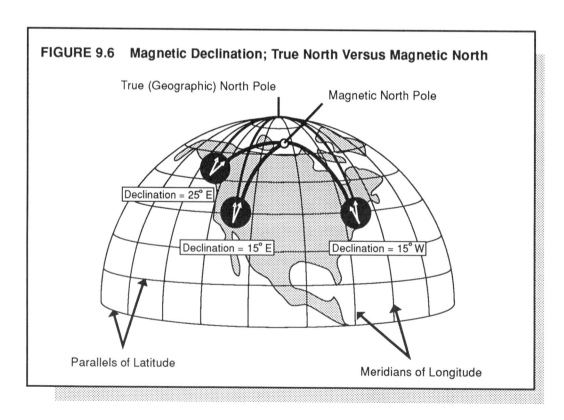

FIGURE 9.6   Magnetic Declination; True North Versus Magnetic North

True (Geographic) North Pole

Magnetic North Pole

Declination = 25° E

Declination = 15° E

Declination = 15° W

Parallels of Latitude

Meridians of Longitude

It is generally sufficient just to know that the magnetic pole is not in the same place as the geographic North Pole, and that "magnetic north" is the direction to the magnetic pole. An illustration, such as Figure 9.6, can help explain the concept of declination, which is the difference between true north and magnetic north. While it is helpful to identify the local declination and its direction, it is also important to show how and where the declination is indicated on maps.

Map and Compass Use in the Field

There are many well-established systems for using maps and compasses in the field. The system suggested here requires no addition or subtraction and is very easily retained. In this system, true bearings are measured on the map as described above, and followed in the field by simply allowing the north end of the needle to point to the declination figure on the scale. The declination figure is the point on the scale that corresponds to the local declination. This eliminates the errors that can occur in other systems due to confusion of whether to add or subtract when going from map to field or vice versa, and eliminates the possibility of error in the addition or subtraction process. Some compasses have special adjustable "declination arrows" that can be set to facilitate correct positioning of the magnetic needle. Compasses used exclusively in one area can be marked to make it easier to see the desired point on the scale.

The steps in following a bearing in the field are: (1) set the compass for the correct bearing, (2) hold the compass about chest high, pointing directly away from the body, (3) turn your entire body around until the north end of the needle points to the declination figure, (4) sight carefully on a target, (5) walk to the target, and sight on the next target, and so on until the destination is reached. This is a simple process in theory; yet, considerable practice is required before one can be considered capable of self-sufficiency in the field. There are, of course, many possible sources of error and frustration in actual backcountry travel.

Students should be advised of the following concerns and tips prior to field practice:

1. *It isn't easy to sight accurately.* Strange as it may seem, the first thing to teach beginners—and even some who claim to be experts—is how to hold the compass. Many people hold the compass flat on one palm and face the direction in which they are headed. They may not realize that the hand holding the compass is not pointing in the same direction as the body but at an angle, either right or left of where they are headed.

The best way for beginners to hold a compass is with both elbows tucked in tight against the body (as if to hold the pants up) and the hands held palm upwards, one on top of the other. The compass should rest on the top hand with the base plate parallel to the waist and the direction of the travel arrow pointing directly forward.

Eye level positioning can also be effective, and it is helpful to compare the advantages and disadvantages of holding the compass at eye level versus the waist-level position. In particular, point out the problem of rotating the compass between orientation of the needle and sighting in the eye-level position, and rotating the eyes or head instead of looking straight out in the waist-level position.

2. *Targets must be chosen carefully.* While it is best to select relatively distant targets, care must be taken to avoid losing site of the target while en route. Young children may have to be reminded that targets like "that post with the bird on it," or "that big black cow" may present difficulties. Point out the possibility of having a person go and stand as a temporary target when no good natural targets are available.

3. Use back-sighting to confirm position when necessary. To take a "back-bearing," place the south end of the compass needle on the declination figure. If all is well, the back-sight should line up perfectly with the starting point. If it does not, move to the correct position.

4. Even when the bearing is followed accurately, *a small feature may be missed unless distance is carefully estimated.* It is worthwhile to review scale issues and to discuss, demonstrate, and practice pacing. A measured, slightly

sloping course will point out the effects on pace length of uphill or downhill walking. A marked distance of 100 meters, yards, or feet can be viewed from each end and from different angles to develop a visual sense of distance. A visual reference is much more useful than counting paces for any purpose other than measuring progress on roads, smooth gentle trails, or other relatively level surfaces allowing for regular, normal strides.

5. *People tend to gain or lose elevation when traversing a sidehill.* Some of this results from a tendency to sight on trees, which may have a considerable vertical extent. There is also a tendency to creep uphill on very steep slopes, or to creep downhill when tired.

6. *It is often impossible to travel directly from point to point.* What's important is to keep track of where the bearing line is. It is not usually necessary to thrash through dense berry patches or build a raft to cross a lake! Explain simple ways of dodging obstacles. Figure 9.7 illustrates simple ways of avoiding obstacles.

7. *It is possible to do everything correctly, but head in the wrong direction!* The reason lies in variations in the magnetic field caused by magnetic rocks or by magnetic fields created by the human being.

Local deviations in the magnetic field are very common and can be frustrating. Iron-ore deposits are often magnetic, as are many fine-grained, dark-colored intrusive volcanic rocks. Dark color usually means high iron mineral content; fine-grained means rapid cooling and a greater likelihood of some noncrystalline (glassy) components; and intrusive means that the molten rock sat in place as it cooled. In such rocks, some of the iron-bearing minerals, which tended in their molten state to orient with the magnetic field of the earth, are fixed in place so that the entire rock mass now acts as a giant magnet. In coarse, crystalline rock, the process of crystallization effectively randomizes the orientation of the magnetic minerals, and, in lava flows, continual motion through the solidification process has a similar effect in greatly reducing the magnetic influence of the rock mass.

Students should be reminded of the need for caution in areas of known iron deposits and on or near rocky outcrops that look suspicious (i.e., meet the above criteria). Intrusive volcanic masses are often exposed at the tops of hills and ridges since this type of rock tends to be highly durable.

Suggest ways in which the students might be able to detect such problems. In many cases the effect can be dramatically illustrated by moving the compass near the rock, causing movement or even reversals of the needle. Show how to test for local effects by sighting on a very distant feature, moving, and sighting again. (If the feature is very distant, no change should occur; a change means something is amiss.) This test is based on the usually valid assumption that such distances vary widely in short distances. Show how to measure and correct for such disturbances by comparing the bearing of a feature measured on the map to the bearing measured by direct field observation.

There are two common sources of "manmade" magnetic anomalies. Any alloy of iron, nickel, or chromium may be magnetic, so students need to be warned about pocket knives, belt buckles (which may appear to be brass but are often brass-plated iron), or even pens or mechanical pencils. On the other hand, there is no need to worry about a solid brass buckle, or an aluminum pack frame since there is no appreciable magnetic field around these metals unless a current is passing through them. This brings us to the other common manmade disturbance, power lines. It is unwise to trust any bearings sighted, or taken, when near high voltage lines. There is often a five degrees or greater distortion a hundred feet or more from a point directly beneath a major cross-country transmission line, so it is best to take a long sight past the lines and/or rely upon back-sighting from distant points.

Navigation Training on Field Outings

Map-and-compass teaching in the field can be highly rewarding or incredibly frustrating. As mentioned earlier, the primary issue is the willingness and ability of the students to pay

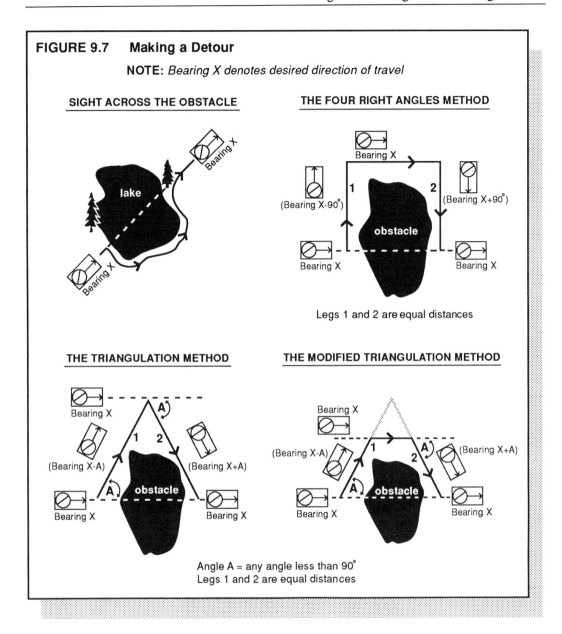

FIGURE 9.7   Making a Detour

NOTE: *Bearing X denotes desired direction of travel*

SIGHT ACROSS THE OBSTACLE

THE FOUR RIGHT ANGLES METHOD

Legs 1 and 2 are equal distances

THE TRIANGULATION METHOD

THE MODIFIED TRIANGULATION METHOD

Angle A = any angle less than 90°
Legs 1 and 2 are equal distances

attention to the subject at hand. This will not occur if the student is cold, tired, or under stress. Extreme care must be taken when letting individuals or small groups travel alone (without staff) to practice reaching destinations.

This is a most valuable teaching method if safety issues are dealt with adequately. Usually, a staff person should "tail" each independent group or individual. If this is not done, then the route must: (1) be surrounded by safe and unmistakable terrain barriers, (2) traverse terrain that is well within the skill limits and fitness of the participants, and (3) be free of significant hazards. In addition, each participant must have adequate equipment and clothing, and be given clear and concise directions as to what to do and how to survive a night should they become disabled or lost.

Developed Practice Courses

Once the basic concepts and skills are mastered in the classroom, it is time to get outside and practice. Sometimes, it is not practical (or even possible) to go directly from the classroom to a backcountry setting. Even when backcountry areas are readily accessible, it is often best to do some beginning practice in an adjacent field or nearby park before taking on the challenge (and risks) of "real" navigation. Have students take bearings on distant features and compare them to the bearings obtained by others. Compare map and field bearings. Call out a bearing and ask students to identify what feature is at that point. Follow preset courses; good ones can be set up quickly even in small areas such as a field or school campus.

First, mark a series of points by walking around the area. For children, the schoolyard or playing field may be large enough. Courses for more advanced participants may cover several square miles of wooded, hilly terrain. Bearings can then be directly measured on a second round through the course so the students can find the points when given premeasured bearings. Better yet, carefully mark the points on a map, so the students must measure and then follow the bearings. If marking the points on, for instance, a park map would make it too easy to find the points, delete all park features from the map so the bearing and distance are the only clues! If the area is larger, maps or aerial photos can be used to locate precise point locations; then points can be placed on-site and confirmed by walking several key legs between points.

If the points are obvious enough that they won't be missed by a person walking on the proper bearing, a flat area can be used to practice by finding points using bearings only. If bearings are the only clue, be sure to establish clear boundaries for the course, so individuals or groups know when to stop if they miss a point! Otherwise, people may wander all over the countryside looking for an illusive point.

Most urban or suburban sites or parks are a mile or less in each dimension. An area of a square mile (two or three square kilometers) is large enough to allow challenging and rewarding practice, but small enough to control if adequate barriers define the site. Clear definition of the site is especially important when the site is bordered by confusing or hazardous terrain or if it will be used by beginners.

Consider what might happen if an individual or group should miss a point on the practice course. What may seem an obvious corrective action to the leader or individual familiar with the area may not be so obvious to the confused beginner. The nature and extent of barriers (limiting features) necessary for safety depend upon the likelihood of error (someone becoming lost and confused) and upon the consequences. Young beginners need more protection than well-prepared groups of college students; sites surrounded by undeveloped land are usually more hazardous than parks surrounded by populated areas, though this may not be the case in urban areas plagued by traffic and crime.

If any significant hazards exist, clear instructions—both verbal and on the map—should be provided. Even in small relatively safe areas, it is common practice to allow only small-group travel. Two or three heads are (usually) better than one, and a small group is easier to keep track of.

Careful fail-safe check-in and check-out procedures are called for on any such course. Adequate clothing requirements and safety instructions play a significant role in reducing risk. Waiver forms should be utilized as on any outing, unless the course is very small and highly controlled.

All manner of games and systems for verification have been devised. These can add interest and excitement for certain groups. The most popular game involves riddles or codes solved by clues found at each point. Verification systems may require the participant to record a code number, to take a coded tag, or even to photograph the point. This level of complexity can be avoided if participants are sufficiently motivated to find points and to improve their skills.

In actual backcountry travel, destinations are seldom found solely by following a bearing line. Land forms, roads, trails, signs, elevation differences, and distance all provide valuable additional information. On a simple short course, bearing and distance clues are often given to participants at the start or by posting at points along the route. Since participants need to learn how to read and measure bearings and distances on maps, the best way to provide the information is in the form of a map. If the purpose of learning to use a map and compass is to facilitate backcountry travel, practice should, if possible, be on terrain that resembles or is as challenging as the intended area of use.

Altimeters and Navigational Aids

While virtually all backcountry navigational problems can be solved with the aid of a compass and a good map, there are other instruments that can be useful (or even essential) under certain circumstances. The most important, and perhaps least obvious, is a reliable, accurate watch. A watch allows one to keep track of elapsed time while traveling, which can be an important means of reckoning distance covered. Knowing the time also allows maximal utilization of available daylight, and it allows navigation by the sun and stars. In fact, the development of clocks played a critical role in early exploration of the globe, for navigational accuracy was limited primarily by the ability to keep precise track of time.

The sextant and alidade are often thought of only as archaic tools of ancient mariners. Used in combination with an accurate clock and tables of sun and star positions, these devices allow remarkably accurate calculation of latitude and longitude, and they have been used by many twentieth century explorers of featureless land areas, as well as seas. Modern high tech versions aren't as aesthetically appealing as the classic old brass versions, but they are easier to use, even more accurate, and do all of the calculations from data stored on computer chips.

In recent years, technological advances have made it possible to compress remarkable navigational aids into small, field portable units. Loran, for example, is a system of long range (thus the name) navigation wherein pulsed signals from two or more stations are used to determine location. Loran has been in service for at least four decades, but until recently, the mobile units were heavy and bulky. Now it is possible to obtain hand-held Loran receivers for about $600.00, capable of operating up to 1,000 miles from Loran transmitters with an accuracy of 60 to 100 feet. The "Global Positioning System" (GPS) is another technological wonder. Using an array of satellites, a GPS hand-held unit calculates position, elevation, direction of travel, and the bearing and distance to any desired point. Current models cost about $1,000.00; however, the sizes and costs of Loran and GPS systems are shrinking each year. It is likely that affordable systems will be available in the not too distant future. They may soon even incorporate other new technologies that allow locations to be displayed as a flashing spot on a video map of the area!

Altimeters are barometers with scales reading in feet or meters of elevation instead of units of pressure. They are always interesting to consult, seldom truly essential, generally costly, and seldom reliable to within less than 50-100 feet of elevation, unless frequently reset. On the positive side, an altimeter can provide useful information when attempting to determine location, and can be very useful when climbing peaks with expansive glaciers or snowfields in foul weather. An altimeter can also be helpful in dense forests or in any circumstance where poor visibility precludes the use of re-section or triangulation. Sometimes the two techniques may be combined, by determining elevation, locating the closest contour line on the map, then plotting an intersecting bearing.

Since altimeters are simple barometers, an increase in air pressure will cause the same effect as a lowering of elevation, while decreasing air pressure, as before a storm, increases elevation readings. Thus, an altimeter sitting on one's desk will often read, over a period of several hours, as if it is rising or falling. Sometimes dramatic changes in air pressure occur, so the altimeter cannot be completely trusted even for short periods. In practice, they need to be reset to the elevation of each known point along the route. When arriving at camp, it is a good idea to note the reading unless the actual elevation of the site is known. By morning, the pressure is likely to have changed, so the altimeter will have to be reset to the setting of the previous evening, which is the best estimate of the elevation of the camp. Temperature and humidity variations also affect altimeter accuracy. Even with their disadvantages, when used with care and a healthy dose of skepticism, altimeters can be potential useful adjuncts to conventional compass navigation.

Summary

In order to plan and conduct outings, all leaders should be able to interpret topographic maps accurately. In addition, leaders should be well-versed in map and compass navigation techniques if they intend to lead any backpacking, mountaineering, cross-country skiing, or other backcountry activity.

It is important to assess the abilities of participants in light of the fact that what should be known depends upon the activity, locale, and participants themselves. Classroom instruction and practice courses that simulate the environment of the actual outing can help prepare participants for backcountry learning experiences. In "real life" backcountry settings, the rate at which an individual gains skill usually depends upon the extent to which he/she is given personal responsibility for navigation.

References

Bengtsson, H., & Atkinson, G. (1977). *Orienteering for sport and pleasure.* Brattleboro, VT: The Stephen Greene Press.

Berglund, B. (1979). *The complete guide to orienteering in North America.* Toronto, Ontario: Paguian Press Limited.

Brower, D. (Ed.). (1971). *The Sierra Club wilderness handbook.* New York, NY: Ballantine Books.

Department of the Army. (1987). *Map reading and land navigation.* Washington, DC: Department of the Army Field Manual 21-28.

Disley, J. (1973). *Orienteering.* Harrisburg, PA: Stackpole Books.

Hart, J. (1977). *Walking softly in the wilderness.* San Francisco, CA: Sierra Club Books.

Kals, W. S. (1983). *Land navigation handbook.* San Francisco, CA: Sierra Club Books.

Kjellstrom, B. (1976). *Be expert with map and compass (4th ed.).* New York, NY: Charles Scribner's Sons.

Outward Bound. (1989). *The Outward Bound map and compass handbook.* New York, NY: Lyons and Burford.

The Mountaineers. (1960). *Mountaineering: The freedom of the hills.* Seattle, WA: The Mountaineers.

Owendoff, R. (1964). *Better ways of pathfinding.* Harrisburg, PA: Stackpole Books.

Riley, M., & Cremer, R. (1979). *Basic Orienteering.* Chicago, IL: Contemporary Books.

part three

LEADERSHIP
&
ADMINISTRATION

OUTDOOR PURSUITS LEADERSHIP

Throughout this book, emphasis has been placed on safety and care of the natural environment, and on those who use it for recreational or educational experiences. Understanding the natural environment and the needs of those who use it, coupled with skills and knowledge specific to the outdoor leader, leads to the topic of actual leadership in outdoor pursuits. It is extremely important that those aspiring to become leaders of participants in outdoor activities know and understand the material in Part I, "Background" and Part II, "Skills and Knowledge Specific to the Outdoor Leader" of this book. Only after that should one attempt to implement the material in the final two sections.

What is a leader? How does one become a leader? What makes some people leaders in title only, while others become leaders without officially sanctioned authority? This topic has filled many books and given rise to many theories, models, and studies. In this chapter, the relevance of modern leadership theory to outdoor pursuits will be discussed. "Leader" is defined here as one who influences the behavior of others and helps them reach their common goals and objectives. The leader may direct or guide people into action with a resulting change or improvement in knowledge, skill, or attitude.

Being a Follower

One of the first exercises in becoming a leader is to serve as a follower and analyze the components of leadership from that standpoint. In a theoretical sense, one can do that by participating in the following exercise.

Imagine yourself signing up for an outdoor-pursuit exercise. It does not matter what the activity is or where it will take place as long as you envision an experience that will hold the potential for a degree of enjoyment, excitement, challenge, and/or adventure. Since the idea is to put yourself in the place of the typical participant or student, you may want to think about some activity with which you are not familiar or that tends to be intimidating to you. If your forte is not fast-water canoeing, imagine you have just signed up for a three-day river trip. If you are an ice climber, imagine a trip to the desert or vice versa. If you are really set on imagining your own favorite pastime, imagine signing up for a very advanced lesson or clinic.

Now try to imagine what expectations you would have for the imaginary leader of your program. If you have been a leader or teacher for many years, it may be difficult to imagine a role reversal. If you are unable to put yourself into the position (imaginary or real) of being a follower (particularly one of your own followers), you may not have what it takes to be a good leader.

What would you expect of your leader? Of the total experience? Can you generate a list of your expectations? First, you probably expect the individual to be friendly, reasonably easy to get along with, and interested in, even excited about, the program. Of no less importance is the maturity and evident good sense of the person. These qualities are often considered the primary criteria for leadership of any sort; however, they are extremely difficult to assess. What else do you have a right to expect? You should expect the person to have a good basic understanding of the terrain, the weather, and the potential hazards of the locale chosen for the activity. You should also expect the leader to be sufficiently concerned about, and aware of, environmental issues and accepted practices to minimize your group's impact on the land and water. Certainly, you expect your leader to understand basic human physical and psychological needs, and to know how to meet these needs in the environment and context of your activity.

You also should expect high levels of knowledge, skill, and experience in the activity, plus familiarity with *backcountry first aid* and *search and rescue* or other appropriate skills so that he/she can handle any reasonably foreseen emergency. You should expect competence in the ability to apply a knowledge of the six other topics covered thus far in this book (i.e., *resources for outdoor pursuits, the natural environment, care of the natural environment, human needs, survival, and navigation*). You may expect to retain much personal responsibility for what happens to you on the trip. Or you may expect that the leader will take full responsibility for all aspects of the trip, including navigating, preparing meals, putting up the tent, preparing the latrine, and anything else that can be done for you. In either case, you want the leader to be a competent and up-to-date professional of the activity.

You have a right to certain expectations in at least two other areas. The leader should be willing and able to *control* and *lead (or teach)* the group adequately. This expectation cannot be assured by the satisfaction of any or all of the foregoing qualities.

Does the foregoing list mean that you, as a leader, need to anticipate and to meet all of these expectations? The general answer is, of course, yes. Generally, the expectations you imagined above are probably the same as the expectations of both adults and parents whose children you may lead. To some extent, the leader is controlled by the hopes of people served. If the expectations of the followers are not met, there may be dissatisfaction and accompanying participant dropout, or, in serious cases, substantial liability and risk of litigation. The imagined situation is a good one for understanding how you might feel as a participant.

Following— The Participant

Obviously, in all leadership situations, there must be followers. Thus, before analyzing leadership and the outdoor leader's characteristics, it is best to understand the people who seek the organized outdoor pursuit experience. Initially, the leader should recognize the fact that outdoor participants are *groups* of people bound by the constraints of time (pre-trip, trip, and post-trip) and by space (the location of the event).

The group will develop an identification as "members," a sense of purpose, a pattern of interaction, and some commonly agreed-upon system of order. Members of outdoor-pursuit groups are members of *social* groups and interact accordingly. They call each other by their first names, and they derive much of their satisfaction from group interaction, including talking, eating, and sharing the exigencies of the outdoor environment. They are aware of being group members and identify with the group by cohesiveness in working together, a sense of shared purpose, and a need for, and acceptance of, others in the group.

An outdoor group may be a *primary* group such as a family, but it is probably more often a *secondary* group. A *primary* group is a lasting group that shares personalities and emotional character, while a *secondary* group is usually one that meets for a short time only and allows one to achieve, to gain recognition, to meet basic social needs, and to polish one's behavior as it relates to the activity. An outdoor pursuit activity may consist of several primary groups (i.e., several families meeting as a secondary group), or it may consist of just a secondary group made up of students or members of a community who did not know each other prior to the outdoor experience. Behaviors in primary groups, where people know each other and live or work together over a long period of time, differ from behaviors in secondary groups, where people meet for only a few days or weeks.

Properties of Groups

Sessoms and Stevenson (1981) have identified nine properties of groups that may be explained in terms of outdoor pursuits as follows:

Purpose

The main purpose of the outdoor pursuit group is usually the same as that of the sponsoring agency. All members of the group are there to accomplish the same end. Common purposes may be: to climb Baldtop Mountain, to learn to cross-country ski, to travel 100 miles by canoe, or to explore Limestone Cave. Such goals are self-evident. There are also, however, three tacit goals for all outdoor pursuit groups. They may not be verbalized; however, they are of greater importance, in the long run, than destination goals. Theoretically, for all outdoor experiences, these should be the main goals of the group *and* the leader. They are: to return unharmed, to maintain the environment in its natural condition, and to have an enjoyable, or at least personally rewarding, experience.

Tone or Social Atmosphere

The group as a whole will have an identifiable social atmosphere. It may be up to the leader to set the tone so that the group is optimistic, careful, friendly, and supportive of each other. A hostile, careless, disgruntled, or frightened member can "set the tone" for the entire group. In such cases, the leader may need to intervene to create a positive atmosphere.

Cohesion

The tone of the group may well be influenced by group cohesion. If the group is divided on what route to follow, what action to take, whether to

go on or to turn back, or even which menu to follow, cohesion may be lacking and this can lead to a breakdown in the social atmosphere. The leader must have the ability to maintain a cohesive group.

Organizational Structure

Some groups are organized on a formal basis, as in a classroom, while others are informally organized, as in a discussion group. The organizational structure of an outdoor-pursuit group may vary within one event or may be entirely formal or informal. The group needs to know who is in charge, what is the positional hierarchy, and when formal or informal procedures will occur. Formal organization is needed when a lot of beginners participate in an overnight cross-country skiing trip, but the organization will be less formal during the evening meal and maybe on the trip home. Lessons, activities performed in high-risk situations, and events involving young children are usually formally organized.

Patterns of Communication

Every group develops a system for receiving and sending messages consisting of specialized vocabulary, body language, and facial expressions. Outdoor pursuit groups have their own unique communication systems. Such terms as "high-tech gear," "skid lid," "60/40," "polypro," "Class III," "on belay," and many others are included. Hikers and river runners alike can understand body and hand language that indicates cold, heat, rain, sleep, fatigue, etc. The participant who is new to the experience actually has a language barrier until the special communication patterns of outdoor pursuit enthusiasts is mastered.

Patterns of Interaction

Watch any group and interaction patterns will become evident. Who speaks to whom? Who speaks the most? How are responses made? Who seems to have seniority? Who never speaks? These are patterns of interaction. A good leader should not monopolize the discussion, and should try to involve everyone (but not to force those who are by nature and/or preference reticent). A functional social group usually has a fairly evenly distributed level of interaction.

Procedures

Groups have definite ways of getting things done. How is the raft packed each day? What goes in first? Last? Who packs what? How is the site of the fire returned to its natural state? Who leads on the trail? For how long? Such patterns are identifiable characteristics of all outdoor groups.

Internal Commitment

All members of the group may not be equally committed to the goal of the event. Some individuals may not really care if the summit is reached, and some may be terribly disappointed and get angry at a leader who turns back in deference to group safety. The leader has the unenviable responsibility of trying to unify commitment even if it means changing the goals. In some cases, the group itself may be involved in setting or modifying these, and commitment may be more unified than if the leader makes an arbitrary, automatic suggestion.

Group History

Each group may be made up of some individuals with a history of similar experiences together, some with similar experiences as members of several different groups, and some with no similar background. Individuals who have traveled together before may exhibit certain behavior and patterns of interaction that preclude socialization with others new to the group. The group made up of participants who have no group history may be the easiest to lead once procedures are defined. The group with a long history together may be the next easiest to lead (although not always), and the mixed group may challenge the leader to achieve a new goal—bringing old and new members into a cohesive unit.

These nine properties give each group its own special identity. No two groups exhibit identical characteristics, and understanding these properties helps the leader to mold his/her style to meet the needs of the followers.

Reasons for Following

Why do some people never want to be leaders while others never sign up with a group with a designated leader, preferring to join a group of common adventurers where the leadership may be shared or everyone may be an autonomous individual? Why do some participants enroll in outdoor pursuit activities with the desire to develop skills that will ultimately lead to leadership positions? And why are some groups made up of individuals who are paying for a leader who will assume all the responsibilities of the trip so they will not have to be leaders? Sessoms and Stevenson (1981) have proposed three answers to these questions: *efficiency, satisfaction,* and *experience.*

Efficiency means that individuals want leaders when they are involved in situations where they are unwilling to undertake certain responsibilities themselves and find it easier to be followers. Many individuals discover that the most efficient and effective way of achieving their goals is through delegating responsibility for that achievement to someone else—the leader. In the outdoors, this reason for being a follower is particularly relevant. If one wishes to climb a mountain or run a river for the first time, it is much easier to achieve that goal by following a leader who knows the route than to chart all potential routes and head forth without firsthand knowledge of what lies ahead. Many people would find the achievement of outdoor goals so difficult without a leader that the activities would never get started in the first place.

Satisfaction refers to the fact that if people are already followers and are satisfied with the way things are going, they tend to continue to follow the current leader. In many outdoor situations where participants could take minor leadership roles (i.e., preparation of meals, teaching others how to pitch a tent, demonstrating simple skills), they prefer to continue to be followers because they are completely at ease and satisfied with the leader's style and accomplishments. In some cases, participants are leaders of significance in their own vocations or homes and are seeking a change where someone else can assume the leadership in their lives. They find it very satisfying for someone else to be the leader while they relax as vacationing followers.

Experience means that many people have not had the experience of being a leader; thus, they remain as followers. Many people are comfortable and secure in the familiar role of follower. The idea of becoming a first-time leader brings a fear of the unknown which is overcome easily by reverting to this familiar role.

Thus, many people are followers because it is efficient, satisfying, and/or comfortable. That is not to say, however, that everyone wants to be a follower. You, the readers of this book, probably aspire to become leaders, and the preceding list of reasons for following should give you a basis for understanding your function as leaders.

Beyond the reasons why individuals follow rather than lead, participants have many reasons for being part of the outdoor pursuit program. Consider the following as a partial list of why they are drawn to the activity:

1. Exploration
2. Self-discovery and self-determination
3. Interest in nature and the environment
4. Relaxation
5. Social relationships
6. Intellectual growth
7. Physical fitness
8. Pleasure
9. Independence
10. Family unity
11. Desire for new skills
12. To reach the destination

Forces Affecting Participants

Inasmuch as the outdoor-pursuit leader is leading people, it is important to understand as much about the participants as possible. While behaviors, reactions, attitudes, or understandings cannot be predicted, it is possible to understand the wide range of forces that have an impact on individuals and groups. Forces that influence people may be obvious, visible, and recognizable *external* forces, or they may be subtle, unspoken, invisible *internal* forces. Sessoms and

Stevenson (1981) have discussed the influences of external and internal forces on participants in typical societal settings such as committees, planning sessions, and municipal recreation activities. Their list has been adapted here to demonstrate how external and internal forces affect the outdoor-pursuit participant.

External Forces

Each of the following forces is the same for everyone in the group; however, individual reactions to each may differ considerably. Some possible reactions are listed beside each external force.

1. Time
    a. When will we get there?
    b. What time do we eat?
    c. Why must we get up so early?
    d. I wish today would never end.
2. Space
    a. This tent is too crowded.
    b. You can see forever.
    c. It must be 2,000 feet straight down!
    d. How come they are camping on our lake?
3. Lighting
    a. It's dark out!
    b. What fascinating shadows.
    c. I should have brought my darker sunglasses.
    d. Thank heaven the sun is coming up.
4. Acoustics
    a. Speak up, I can't hear you above the waterfall.
    b. That darn stream won't shut up and let me sleep.
    c. It is so still here I feel peaceful.
    d. It is so still here I feel lonesome.
5. Isolation
    a. I miss my family.
    b. Boy, is it good to be away.
    c. How close is emergency help?
    d. There's nothing out there!
6. Extended time from home
    a. I wonder if they're all right.
    b. Bet my desk is piled high when I return.

6. Extended time from home (cont'd)
   c. What if Henry called and couldn't reach me?
   d. Did I turn off the stove?
7. Food
   a. This is so easy to prepare.
   b. I really don't care for beef stew.
   c. I don't think we've brought enough.
   d. I'm hungry.
8. Primitive toilet facilities
   a. How inconvenient.
   b. What do you do when you are all roped up on a steep glacier?
   c. What do you do on the river?
   d. Is this really private?

The reader can imagine reactions to other external forces. People respond differently to temperature; height; personal privacy (sleeping, dressing); speed; environmental factors such as vast deserts, deep forests, swamps, or snowdrifts; and many other factors. When the myriad external forces that have an impact on all participants and the accompanying potential reactions are analyzed, it can be seen that outdoor leadership entails a great capacity for understanding people.

Internal Forces

Internal forces are factors that represent ideas, biases, feelings, or perceptions held by individuals within the group. Internal forces can affect the dynamics of the group and individual members within it.

1. Group size
   a. Eight is just right.
   b. We need one more strong person.
   c. There are too many people here.
2. Dress
   a. Everyone else has Goretex.
   b. I wish I had boots like those.
   c. I didn't know I'd need a hat.
3. Sex
   a. Too many women…
   b. I wonder if he's married.
   c. There's no privacy.
4. Age
   a. Look at that old guy go!
   b. Kids have no sense.
   c. I'm too old for this group.
5. Skills
   a. I've run this river fifteen times.
   b. I think I can; I think I can.
   c. I never learned to tie a bowline.
6. Physical characteristics
   a. What does he mean, step on those rocks? He's 6'4", and I'm only 5'2"!
   b. Hope my "trick knee" holds out.
   c. I'm small but tough.

The above list of forces exists within every group, and the possible reactions are only a sample. Other, less obvious, internal forces include:

1. *Motivation*—What makes different people participate?
2. *Perceived status*—How does each person view his/her status in the group?
3. *Group norms*—Certain behaviors are "expected" among outdoor participants (for example, minimum-impact camping).
4. *Homogeneity/heterogeneity*—Is the group made up of similar or dissimilar people in regard to age, experience, backgrounds, education, etc.?
5. *Group atmosphere*—A pessimistic atmosphere imparts pessimism to individuals. This group force must be controlled by the leader.
6. *Personal feelings and attitudes*—Some people bring with them openness or prejudice, courage or cowardice, an innate love for the outdoors or a trepidation about insects, reptiles, and even many mammals.

Responsibilities of Group Members

In spite of the fact that all group participants expect guidance and safety from the leader, they are not without responsibilities to themselves and each other. These responsibilities include judging their own personal skills, abilities, and fitness.

Personal Responsibilities

Fitness. The individual who signs up for a trip without the appropriate and/or required physical conditioning and/or skills may be as much at fault for going as the agency or leader is for permitting him/her to go. The person who slows down because of inadequate personal preparation may endanger the entire group and, thus, may contribute to the discomfort, accident, or injury of others.

Knowledge of the Trip, Location, Schedule, Required Skills, and Equipment. The participant who shows up without mandatory equipment should not be permitted to accompany the group. The person who doesn't attend required training meetings should not go either. Failure to bring a correct map or proper footwear; arriving at the departure point late or requesting to leave the group early; bringing a guest or a pet; or carrying firearms, alcoholic beverages, fireworks, hallucinogens, and other prohibited items are all irresponsible acts.

Knowledge of the Leader's Qualifications. It is the participant's responsibility to verify the leader's qualifications, certifications, references, abilities, and reputation. A participant signing up for a wilderness or river trip with someone whose brochure guarantees an exciting trip through fabulous country may get more excitement than he/she desires. Anyone who fails to know more than that about a leader's qualifications may be a contributing factor to his/her own accident or injury if the leader turns out to be unqualified, irresponsible, or incompetent.

Responsibilities to Others in the Group

Leaders should recognize the responsibility of *each individual to the entire group.* Everyone is expected to be on time and not delay the group, to be organized about their own gear, to be neat, and to dress and act "appropriately." Furthermore, each individual is expected not to offend the group through offensive personal habits, bragging, or complaining. It must be recognized, however, that many longtime personal behaviors cannot be changed.

Participant behavior varies depending upon settings. The *individual alone* may exhibit behavior indicative of his/her true personality, but rarely does a leader see a participant as a lone individual. There are several settings in which the individual must react with one other person; the *experience of two* in a mountain tent or a canoe calls for different behavior. The two must tolerate and understand each other's needs, and each should be reasonably neat and organized with their personal possessions and equipment.

Responsibilities of the Group to the Individual

On the other hand, the *group is obligated to the individual.* Even if the majority rules, the needs of each person should be met. Leaders who side with the majority to the detriment of the minority are not acting responsibly. When seven in a group of eight want to press on and one is in pain or exhausted or close to hypothermia, the group should be made to understand why they must change their goal and respect the needs of this individual.

Group-to-Group Responsibilities

Trail and river courtesy dictates privacy, quiet, and overt contact. Slow groups should let faster ones pass, and groups arriving second at camping sites should move away from those who arrived first—regardless of the attributes of a neighboring site. As mentioned in previous chapters, groups have responsibilities for following agency policies and for following minimum-impact camping skills.

Knowing the foregoing material and anticipating a variety of interactive behavior will help the leader relate to each member of the group emphatically and humanistically.

Leader-Follower Relationships

Like communication, leading and following is a two-way street. Without positive relations and interaction from one to another, the leader-follower relationship may break down and dissolve entirely. Edginton and Ford (1985) have identified a set of eight desirable relationships between leaders and followers. The following examples show how these relate to outdoor pursuits.

Shared Expectations

Some participants may come to the pre-trip meeting expecting the trip to be a guided tour with much of the everyday routine of cooking and cleaning up done by the leader and "assistants." Another may perceive the trip to be completely "roughing it" with a diet of native nuts and berries. The leader's hopes may fall somewhere between these two extremes; but, until the expectations of all are congruent, the chance of a successful trip for anyone is diminished. Expectations must be shared and a consensus reached before any progress can be made in positive relationships.

Trust

In order to produce a satisfying experience, a level of trust must exist between leader and participant. The follower must trust the leader's judgment, and the leader must trust the follower to act according to plan.

Effective Communication

Each leader and follower must develop both speaking and listening skills with opportunity for input and feedback.

Shared Decision Making

In spite of the fact that, on many occasions, the leader must make autocratic decisions for the welfare of the group, sometimes followers can share in the decision-making process during outdoor activities. When to eat, a choice of routes where practical, a choice of activities, and even a determination to turn back or go on can be made by sharing the facts and the risks.

Cooperation

There must be a willingness on the part of the follower to cooperate with the direction given by the leader. By the same token, the leader must be willing to cooperate with the follower so that his/her needs may be met.

Sense of Risk and Spontaneity

Participants appreciate spontaneity because it creates an illusion of freedom and, to some extent, a sense of unpredictability. The leader must, however, share with the group an awareness of true (or existing) and perceived risks. As discussed in Chapter Twelve, risk does not necessarily imply danger. A spontaneous decision on the part of a troop of Girl Scouts, all of whom are strong swimmers, to go skinny-dipping in a mountain lake is "risky" in terms of propriety, but not dangerous if waterfront safety practices are followed. The shared sense of risk and the spontaneity of the situation may bring leader and followers closer together.

Positive Reinforcement

Leaders must encourage followers and usually do so by giving positive reinforcement as the followers progress. Participants, in turn, can reinforce the leader. One says, "You certainly are catching on fast." The other says, "Thanks, I've wanted to learn to do this since I was a little kid."

Social and Emotional Bond

The leader must show interest in each participant in terms of warmth, humor, and understanding. The follower will, in turn, show respect and admiration. Usually, this relationship is initiated by the leader, with the result that participants respond positively and develop a social bond in return.

It is obvious that outdoor leadership and "followership" is strongest when both groups interrelate positively. One cannot expect followers to understand the aforementioned eight interactive relations. Leaders, however, must not only understand them but take steps to initiate them.

The Leader

Having discussed some reasons why people want leaders and what they expect of them, we can now turn to the topic of leadership itself.

How Are Leaders Selected?

Those who become leaders of outdoor pursuits do not all reach their position in the same manner. According to Shivers (1980), there are four possible ways in which leaders attain their positions. These may be related to outdoor situations as follows:

Appointment

Leaders are appointed by a person in a superior position. In recreational and educational settings, they are hired by those with administrative responsibility and assigned specific duties and responsibilities. In volunteer work, they may be selected by a chairperson or council president.

Election

Teams or countries may elect leaders. Outdoor clubs may elect officers, trip chairpersons, climbing coordinators, or river guides. These leaders may be elected because of ability, popularity, or a number of other factors.

Emergence

An emergent leader is one who, while not initially chosen, emerges from the group to assume leadership roles when the "right" (often unpredicted) situation occurs. The quiet follower who takes charge of leading part of the group from a burning forest, the salesperson who directs first aid care before the appointed leader can get to the victim of a landslide, or the teenager who can comfort a peer rapeling for the first time are all leaders who emerge from unusual situations. This type of leader usually assumes that role because he/she possesses and can use special skills, knowledge, or abilities that complement those of the appointed leader in unusual situations.

Charisma

Charisma is an indefinable power to draw others to oneself. Highly attractive, intangible, and often enigmatic qualities combine to create charisma. Because of personal demeanor, the charismatic leader may have a devoted following. In fact, it is because of their charisma that some people are able to become leaders.

None of the above guarantees the selection of the "best" leader or even the most competent. This list merely explains how people become leaders.

Leadership and Power

Many people believe leadership is synonymous with power. In this case, power usually refers to such terms as influence, control, authority, and strength. The outdoor leader actually does exert this force, and a brief discussion of the types of authority he/she may possess is in order. French and Raven (1959) have identified five sources from which power emanates.

Legitimate power is that coming from the assignment of the leadership role to a specific person as well as that derived from laws, regulations, and rules that the leader follows.

Reward power comes from the leader's ability to reward specific behavior. A shoulder patch awarded for the ascent of designated peaks, a first aid certificate, and a scout badge are examples of tangible rewards, while recognition in the form of praise, testimonies, a pat on the back, a thumbs-up signal, or applause are examples of intangible rewards. It is within the leader's authority to offer these rewards.

Coercive power derives its source from the leader's ability to withhold or withdraw a privilege. This type may seem negative, even threatening, and yet it may well be used when safety is the greater issue. "No one will be permitted on this trip without every one of the items of required equipment," or "No raft will proceed until every person aboard is wearing a properly secured life jacket" are examples of acceptable and appropriate use of coercive power, particularly when used along with a proper explanation of the reasons why these things are being required.

Referent power is simply derived from the leader's ability to attract. Charisma is a nebulous, yet forceful, trait that draws people to a certain individual. Some leaders are influential (powerful) by virtue of the "halo" effect and can do no wrong in the eyes of their followers. The wise leader does not let adulation go to his/her head, but tempers it with humbleness and discretion.

Expert power is derived from the fact that the leader was hired due to his/her skill in the particular outdoor pursuit being offered.

The prudent leader understands that these five types of power are tools to be used carefully and responsibly in helping the participant meet his/her own needs. They are not to be used for the self-aggrandizement of the leader.

Role of the Leader

The role of the leader is to guide, to influence, and to direct the participant toward what should be mutually agreed-upon goals compatible with the philosophy and goals of the sponsoring agency. As mentioned several times in this book, the three fundamental goals of outdoor pursuits are: a safe return, care of the natural environment, and an emotionally rewarding experience. Beyond the challenge of helping followers to meet their goals, outdoor leaders may perform the following functions:

1. Help to build group cohesiveness;
2. Help participants to identify and work for goals common to all;
3. Plan the procedures by which group goals can be met;
4. Organize the participants according to their abilities so that the planned procedures can be carried out;
5. Motivate the participants to carry out the plans, energize them, encourage them, and demonstrate behavior conducive to goal attainment;
6. Evaluate the attainment of the goals and the reasons for nonattainment;
7. Serve as spokesperson for the group, represent the group and the sponsoring agency (especially in times of accident or injury), act as contact with government officials, and compose any official communication;
8. Help participants to learn, grow, and improve in knowledge, skills, and attitudes and encouraging self-development;
9. Serve as the catalyst for establishing group climate or atmosphere.

There may be many more roles for outdoor leaders to play; however, these are role expectations common to all leaders.

Leadership Traits

Many studies done since the early 1900s have postulated that successful leaders have identifiable traits or characteristics, and countless lists of leader traits have been generated. Describing these has some merit in terms of helping prospective leaders understand what followers feel are desirable characteristics. Participation in the exercise at the beginning of this chapter was one way of looking at leadership characteristics. You probably generated your own list in addition to the one recommended.

As a result of a research study in 1978, Buell developed two lists (i.e., personal qualities and leadership qualities) that he felt were necessary for all outdoor leaders. Some of these qualities were:

Personal: poise, cooperation, self-discipline, tolerance, patience, concern for others, neat appearance, fit, dependable, pleasing voice, effective speech, integrity, prompt, self-confidence and enthusiasm.

Leadership: realizes objectives, understands participants, gets along with others, shows resourcefulness, gains confidence, can analyze problems, shows initiative, is well-organized, can adapt, can inspire, observes rules and regulations, cares for equipment, and uses time advantageously.

In 1990, Priest identified seven skills (technical, safety, organizational, environmental, instructional, group management, and problem solving/decision making) and seven attributes (motivational philosophy and interest, physical fitness, healthy self-concept and ego, awareness and empathy for others, personable traits and behavior, flexible leadership style, and judgment based on experience) that he claimed must be combined to produce an effective leader. In between these two studies are many more that list variations of the traits necessary to being an effective or competent outdoor leader.

You might add many other traits to each list, but having these or others in any combination and quantity does not guarantee a good leader. Unless a person can act holistically, using his/her own unique characteristics appropriately in a wide variety of situations, the possession of any number of traits is of no value. You can always study lists of recommended traits, try to strengthen those you already think you possess and develop those you do not, but always with the realization that it is how the traits and qualities are combined and utilized that defines the leadership ability.

Actually, the leader should acquire a combination of skills, knowledge, and attitudes that can be interfaced with personal characteristics. Figure 10.1 shows how leadership qualifications can be organized into three interrelated components. Each of the components can then contain lists of relevant traits.

Recommended Competencies for Leaders

With the foregoing material in mind, one might well ask the question, "What competencies *should* outdoor leaders possess?" or "What abilities do outdoor leaders need to develop?" The knowledge, skills, and attitudes needed for success as an outdoor leader are not universally agreed upon. In fact, there is no way to substantiate without doubt just what makes up the qualities and qualifications of the adequate leader. They might be described as "best guess."

When the options of professional leaders are collected and analyzed, the average of the high scores of these potential actions becomes the recommended standard. Yet, no one can prove that these highly agreed upon opinions are actually the most accurate answers. They

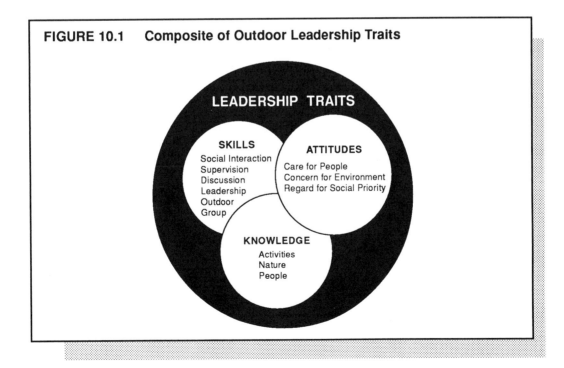

FIGURE 10.1   Composite of Outdoor Leadership Traits

LEADERSHIP TRAITS

SKILLS
Social Interaction
Supervision
Discussion
Leadership
Outdoor
Group

ATTITUDES
Care for People
Concern for Environment
Regard for Social Priority

KNOWLEDGE
Activities
Nature
People

are purely opinions which become the (best guess) recommended standard. These standards remain in effect until overtaken by new ideas. It is assumed that opinions are gained through experience, objective analysis, or real situation and a reasonably consistent degree of knowledge, skill, and attitude.

Two studies on the competencies needed by outdoor leaders are of particular interest here. By competency, we refer to measurable proficiencies of skill, knowledge, experience, and attitudes in outdoor pursuits. They are all deemed necessary for being qualified as a capable outdoor leader, instructor, supervisor, and/or administrator.

Cousineau, in a 1977 study of outdoor pursuit leaders in Ontario, Canada, found that his 113 respondents agreed that, *in order to be certified* as competent outdoor leaders, each should be examined in the following areas of competence:

1. Recognized level of achievement in specific outdoor skills such as canoe tripping, rock climbing, sailing, orienteering, caving, winter camping, cross-country skiing, whitewater canoeing, and kayaking;
2. Successful completion of courses and workshops in outdoor skills;
3. Experience as a participant and leader in outdoor pursuits;
4. Desirable personality traits for outdoor leadership;
5. Establishment of a minimum age;
6. Physical fitness and health (judged essential);
7. Skill in wilderness first aid, lifesaving, and rescue techniques;
8. Skill in aquatic lifesaving.

In 1981, Swiderski conducted a survey of outdoor leaders in five western regions of the United States Forest Service to determine opinions on the importance of fifty land-based outdoor leadership skills. Analysis of the data from his 148 respondents indicated that there were six competencies which appeared among the top ten in all five of the western regions. These six competencies were:

1. Exercise good judgment and common sense while performing duties as a leader under stress and pressure.
2. Handle situations which pose potential safety problems.
3. Foresee and be prepared for situations in which problems and accidents might occur.
4. Prevent illness or injury, but, if either occurs, recognize and apply proper procedures and controls to stabilize or improve the ill or injured person's condition.
5. Teach causes, prevention, symptoms, and physiological effects of environmentally related injuries and illness which may include, but not be limited to, hypothermia, frostbite, heat exhaustion, heatstroke, high altitude, and fluid intake.
6. Follow a personal ethic, which displays sensitivity and concern for the wilderness, reflected in everyday practices and consistent with accepted and sound environmental values.

What Cousineau's and Swiderski's studies tell us is that outdoor leaders can agree upon the competencies they see as necessary in all outdoor leaders. Their opinions should be heeded, for who can assess the needed qualifications for outdoor leadership better than outdoor leaders themselves? Swiderski's study, though, tells us that, while there may be an identifiable core of competencies that should be mandatory for all, leaders in different areas of western portions of the United States do not agree on all competencies. It may be concluded from Swiderski's study that, beyond the fact that some competencies can be agreed upon by the majority, some competencies are so regionally specific because of terrain, weather, climate, resource base, or other reasons that there are significant differences in how the competencies are evaluated from region to region.

This gives the outdoor leader a challenge. What are the *minimum* competencies for his/her region and what *additional* competencies are recommended? It behooves the leader in each part of the world to develop competencies beyond those suggested here.

Leadership Styles

Two logical questions at this point are: "How does leadership work?" and "What works in one situation and not in another?" More relevant, perhaps, is the question: "What works in outdoor pursuits?" Basically styles of leading may be listed as laissez-faire (letting others do it), democratic (sharing), and autocratic (assuming all responsibility). When should each style be used? The following discussion addresses several leadership models which, in turn, explain the changing styles of the leader.

The literature on leadership contains at least eleven explanations of the role and function of leadership (Edginton and Ford, 1985), ranging from the very simple to the complex combination of several simple functions. The authors of this book believe that the tri-dimensional model developed by Hersey and Blanchard (1988) relates best to the styles of leadership needed in outdoor pursuits. The "tri-dimensional leadership effectiveness model" is based upon two previously recommended ones. The Ohio State study defines leadership as a continuum between processes that are concerned with human relations in the accomplishment of a task. The Reddin model suggests that certain styles are effective at times and ineffective at other times. Hersey and Blanchard tell us that, in the continuum between human relationships and the accomplishment of tasks, one's leadership style will vary according to two variables: the *level of maturity* of the group of followers and the *demands of the situation*. They propose that *the leader should determine his/her style of leadership after diagnosing the maturity of the group and the demands of the situation*. This leadership model is particularly relevant to the leader of outdoor pursuits, as will be explained.

Maturity, according to Hersey and Blanchard, occurs on a continuum that is not necessarily related to age. A mature group member in an outdoor pursuit has considerable experience and education relative to the tasks to be performed, is capable of setting high but attainable goals, and possesses the willingness and ability to take responsibility. Immature group members lack *all* of those characteristics, while those on

the continuum between the extremes lack some characteristics. Figure 10.2 shows this maturity continuum expressed vertically.

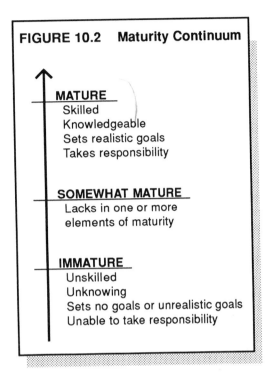

FIGURE 10.2   Maturity Continuum

A group of well-trained, experienced Eagle Scouts may be more mature as outdoor-pursuit followers than a group of parents who are novices—even though the parents may be assumed to be mature in other areas. The parents, because of lack of skill and knowledge, may not set attainable goals, and may lack the ability to be responsible for their own welfare. A group of very young beginners would probably lack skills, realistic goal-setting abilities, and a degree of personal responsibility. They may "feel" they can raft for eight hours on an unknown river; however, in actuality, if they do, they probably will experience the need to call for help. They cannot take responsibility for their choices and actions.

The demands of the situation relate to the task to be accomplished. In outdoor pursuits, the situation may range from formal to informal, tense to relaxed, dangerous to safe. It may demand a great amount of leader control or little or no control. Figure 10.3 (page 196) explains this.

FIGURE 10.3   Demands of the Situation

SITUATION	LEADER CONTROL NEEDED
Child dabbling feet in small creek	No leader control
Child crossing slow creek at waist height	Some leader control
Child crossing roaring, steep mountain stream	Complete leader control

In crossing the roaring mountain stream, the leader may need to be very pedantic—even autocratic and not on an equal basis with the participants. In the case of dabbling feet in a small creek, resting, eating, talking, etc., the situation is such that the leader may, indeed, appear as one of the group.

Combining the maturity of the group with the demands of the situation, we find the tridimensional leadership model proposed by Hersey and Blanchard wherein they propose that styles of leadership change accordingly. Telling, selling, participating, and delegating are the styles of leadership they define as the two continua of maturity and situation overlap. Figure 10.4 portrays this model.

In the case of the leader teaching "beginning rock climbing," the style would be pedantic, direct, and even autocratic (*telling*). In a situation where the participants are somewhat or very well-skilled and the leader tries to convince them of the necessity for carrying the correct type and amount of food, we find the technique is *selling*. If the leader wants a close relationship with participants and the task to be performed requires little direction (i.e., cooking dinner with skilled adult participants), this component is *participating*. Or the task to be accomplished is minimal, as is the need for leader intervention (gathering kindling, group singing, picking berries, or dabbling feet in the creek), and the technique to use is *delegating*.

With a mature group, picking berries can be delegated entirely; however, with youth, who may get disoriented and become lost, some leadership is necessary. Whether it be telling, selling, or participating will depend upon the group maturity and the environmental situation. Thus, we see that the style of leadership depends upon the maturity of the group and the demands of the situation, as is explained below.

High Task Orientation, Low Relationship (with Followers). When teaching complex skills, such as rappeling or raft guiding, to beginners, the leader must explain the necessity of wearing helmets or completely fastened life jackets. Here, the leader's style is one of organizing, directing, telling, evaluating, initiating, and finalizing. The situation is demanding; the maturity level is low; and the leader has a very impersonal relationship with the group.

High Task Orientation, High Relationship. The leader here is concerned with a very important task to be accomplished, such as planning nutritious meals, but, because of the skill, knowledge and responsibility of the group, the leader works *with* them, not *for* them. The leader may participate, interact, motivate, suggest, or integrate, and consequently serve as an enabler with this advanced group.

High Relationship, Low Task. In this case, the leader *participates* in the preparation of the evening meal with an experienced group through techniques involving trust, listening, acceptance, advice, and encouragement. He/she relates to everyone as an equal in a situation when no one really cares if the soup boils over.

Low Relationship, Low Task. In this case, neither the accomplishment of the task, nor the strength of the leader's influence is important.

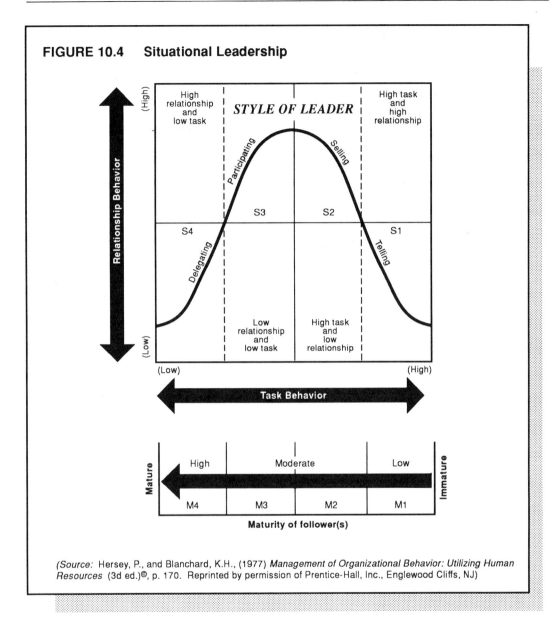

FIGURE 10.4   Situational Leadership

(Source: Hersey, P., and Blanchard, K.H., (1977) *Management of Organizational Behavior: Utilizing Human Resources* (3d ed.)©, p. 170. Reprinted by permission of Prentice-Hall, Inc., Englewood Cliffs, NJ)

When picking berries recreationally, the leader may just set out some time and area limitations, then sit back and wait for the task to be accomplished.

Superimposing situational demands over the continuum of maturity tells us that the leader's *style* will change depending upon the *task/relationship* orientation as well as *group maturity.*

To further illustrate the four dimensions above, assume a group of adults is starting their first whitewater rafting class or winter mountaineering excursion. As a whole, the group's

knowledge, skills, and ability to take responsibility for themselves is very limited or lacking (immature), and safety is a prime concern of the leader who would use a directive task-oriented approach with little interaction with the learners. The leadership style would change to the point where it might even be participative as the learners become as adept as their leader.

Implementation of the Hersey-Blanchard Model

Understanding the foregoing model of leadership style can help a leader understand when and why different styles of leadership will and should change. The model is based upon the premise that the group itself is one that expects strong leadership throughout the program. Phipps (1991) has developed a scheme useful for leadership education (the leader is training others to be leaders). In this model, the designated leader purposefully changes leadership style throughout the course so that more and more of the decisions are made by the followers (leader-trainees). For example, by the end of a course, the leader may take no responsible for the high task activities. Those activities that need organization, direction, and instruction have become the responsibilities of the leaders-in-training. Through group dynamics, the trainees discuss and share responsibilities with the designated leader who takes less and less responsibility. This style of leadership has been recommended throughout parts of this text. For example, in the section on survival in Chapter Six, it was recommended that leaders-to-be participate in a survival situation using only what they brought with them on a day trip. In this case, the course leader "stood aside" and let the participants work out their situation using the equipment they had brought with them. The leader's style was "not to lead."

Phipps' model is recommended for situations where the purpose is to train leaders. Strict adherence to the Hersey-Blanchard model is recommended for the situation where the participants expect to follow the leader and thus enroll in the program with that in mind. For situations in between these two extremes, the leader's style should change according to the group expectations and the importance of the task to be accomplished.

By incorporating Fiedler's contingency model into it, Priest (1989) added the element of conditions to the task orientation-relationship model explained above. According to Priest, factors that determine the favorability of conditions include: environmental dangers, individual competence, group unity, leader proficiency, and decision consequences. His spectrum of conditional favorability is shown on Figure 10.5. Summarizing Priest's model, the style of the leader is based upon the combinations of task importance, the relationships with the participants, and the conditions of favorability. In other words, his model is based upon the Hersey-Blanchard model with the Fiedler's conditions superimposed.

At first glance the choice of leadership style involves analysis of too many factors to be efficient. In fact, if the leader understands that leadership styles will change according to the task, the leader's desired relationships with the participants, and the conditions of the situation, then the leader can plan for a change of style. A knowledgeable leader can justify why he/she changes from a firm, rather autocratic style to a cooperative, sharing style.

In summarizing the above, it can be said that the *styles* of leadership used in outdoor pursuits can change according to the: *importance of the task* to be accomplished, the *relationship* desired between the participants and the leader, and *an analysis of a series of conditions* which will determine the decision-making process.

Teaching vs. Leading

The differences between teaching and leading are not always clear, and there are many times when the outdoor leader teaches and the teacher leads. Perhaps it is simplest to define teaching as learning from an instructor and leading as facilitating self-taught learning. Much of this depends upon the experience or maturity of the group and the tasks to be accomplished.

While theories of leadership may be applied broadly to many situations, the *techniques* of leadership usually relate to specific activities in which one person—the leader—organizes, directs, influences, instructs, or otherwise affects the behavior of others—the followers. The techniques utilized by leaders of outdoor pursuits may often be automatic and unacceptable for other types of human effort. Inherent in outdoor pursuits, however, is an element of risk, danger, and even death. Accordingly, an outdoor leader may use firmness, nondemocratic methods, and

FIGURE 10.5   A Spectrum of Conditional Favorability

FACTORS DETERMINING THE FAVORABILITY OF CONDITIONS	LOW FAVORABILITY	HIGH FAVORABILITY
Environmental Dangers	• Bad weather • Many perils and hazards • Mostly subjective risks not easily controlled	• Good weather • Few perils and hazards • Mostly objective risks under human control
Group	• Disintegrated and divided • Distrustful and competitive • Immature and irresponsible	• Cohesive and unified • Trusting and cooperative • Mature and responsible
Individuals	• Novice members • Incompetent, unskilled, unable • Unsure, inexperienced, unknowledgeable	• Expert members • Competent, skilled, able • Confident, experienced, knowledgeable
Leader	• Deficient and incapable • Lacks power base for credibility • Poor judgment, stressed out, fatigued	• Proficient and capable • Holds strong power base for credibility • Sound judgment, in control, fit
Consequences of the Decision	• Problem cloudy and uncertain • Insufficient time and resources • Challenge high with unacceptable outcomes	• Problem clear and defined • Sufficient time and recources • Challenge low with acceptable outcomes

unilateral decisions. It is difficult to know at what point to be firm and autocratic, particularly since most leadership training programs emphasize group dynamics and leadership by consensus. Before discussing how the leader arrives at decisions, then, it may be wise to examine the inherently different expectations that mature and immature people have for the leaders of their programs.

Teacher-Directed vs. Self-Directed Programs

Many, if not most outdoor pursuit programs consist of adult participants, and it is known that adults learn differently from children. Adult may be defined as a "mature, *self-directing individual.*" This means that adults do not always need the teacher-directed programs of youth. Remembering that leadership style varies with

the *maturity* of the group, it seems that there must be a difference in the way immature and mature participants learn. These differences are summed up in the following four points adapted from Edginton and Ford's *Leadership of Recreation and Leisure Service Organizations:*

1. The immature are dependent learners. As individuals grow, they move from dependency to self-direction. People who have reached maturity need to be recognized as self-directing and given the opportunity to choose their own methods of learning.

2. The immature lack experience or cannot generalize based upon previous situations. Mature learners benefit more from learning conditions in which they can tie in some of their previous experiences.

3. Both immature and mature learners have teachable moments (unpredictable times when they are particularly receptive to learning). For many, these coincide with a stage the individual faces in a specific role. Thus the timing of learning experiences becomes as important as knowing at what stage a group or individual may be.

4. The immature beginner has many basics with which to become familiar while the mature, or advanced, person is interested in a problem-centered approach to learning. The receptivity of the mature learner peaks when the issue being studied is of immediate concern and not just an abstract theory.

Figure 10.6 delineates the differences between an understanding of immature and mature behavior in five different areas. It should be understood that this dichotomy is really based not upon an either-or situation, but upon a continuum. In groups, individuals may be at various points on the continuum and one should not categorically assume that immature and mature

behavior is entirely separated. The dotted line on the table means that there is not a clear demarcation between these two; on the whole, the immature are more likely to be to the left and the mature to the right. (The beginning climber is not very self-directed compared to the veteran of 200 climbs.) The less mature the individual, the more pedagogical (leader-oriented) the approach should be. Learners with intermediate skills may exhibit both immature and mature behaviors, so it is possible to say that they would likely fall within a wide area in the middle of the continuum.

Because of their lack of maturity, limited experiences, interest in the present, and lack of ability to be self-directing, most children are assumed to be immature while most adults are assumed to be mature. Some adults, however, may select leader-directed leisure experiences similar to those for children because of an interest in a specific topic or activity, a desire for an extrinsic reward, a lack of earlier experience, or situational immaturity.

FIGURE 10.6   Continuum of Immature and Mature Learners

ASSUMPTIONS ABOUT	IMMATURE (Beginner)	MATURE (Advanced)
Perception of the Participant	Dependent upon others	Self-motivated individual
Status of the Participants' Experience	Built on progression of earlier experiences leading to selected outcomes	Based on own past experiences with chances to grow
Readiness for New Experiences and New Learning	Varies with maturity	Based on life problems and life tasks
Orientation to Learning-time Perspective	Topic, or activity, centered for future use	Task, or problem-oriented; solutions based upon current need; focus on *now*
Motivation	Extrinsic award (ribbons, badges, trophies) and intrinsic rewards (praise, winning, peer acceptance)	Intrinsic incentives (personal growth, self-actualization, self-esteem, belonging, fulfilling curiosity)

In terms of our *perception of the participant*, leaders should generally view the immature as being dependent upon others and the mature as being self-motivated. In a leader-directed (immature) situation, the participant is viewed as being dependent upon the leader, while, in a self-directed (mature) experience, the participant is self-motivated and self-directed.

In terms of *experience*, leaders should develop progressive programs to meet the needs of the immature based upon earlier programs for beginners, who also need *leader-selected* outcomes. The mature participant is generally viewed as being able to participate in activities that draw from past experience and knowledge with a chance to grow through individually selected goals. With beginners, there is usually one-way communication since the leader is the primary resource for the learning. With the mature, leaders and participants engage in transactional communication where everyone's experience is valued as a resource for learning.

In terms of *readiness*, it is assumed that the readiness of participants in leader-directed programs varies with the level of their maturity whereas self-directed participants are all assumed to have reached a similar level of maturity. For example, children are grouped according to ages, classes, skills, and experiences. The mature learners are group according to interests and experiences. On the whole, the more mature will identify their own program needs. The less mature adults (in terms of their abilities) will select leader-directed programs as they seek new skills and new adventure.

Orientation to learning-time perspectives refers to the topics or activities learned and the time frame within which they will be used. For the less mature, leader-directed participants, the behaviors are usually topic oriented, for example tying knots, basic belaying techniques, or getting up after falling down on skis. From the leader's perspective, the activities are being learned for future application. For the self-directed participant, the level of maturity in the performance of basic skills already exists and the focus is problem centered, i.e., how to scale the rock face using the skills learned in the past. Mature learners may have different objectives such as socialization, skill perfection, or the addition of another

climb to a list of many. Immature learners usually all have the same objective, such as learning the skill.

Motivational behavior refers to the fact that the immature learner often is motivated by intrinsic incentives that have no tangible aspects.

The processes and techniques of leadership will differ for the immature and the mature participant and may need to be adjusted very carefully when the skill maturity of the participants ranges from beginning level to expert level.

Leader-directed (pedagogical) techniques may be utilized in situations involving children, adults, and groups of all ages—whenever people are beginners or immature in experience. In leader-directed programs (for beginners), the setting is formal, organized with predetermined locations for participants, equipment, and so on. The leader and often the sponsoring organization establish the format for the setting, as can be seen with many youth agency badge programs. There is little interpersonal communication.

Self-directed (andragogical) leadership is generally practiced in settings with adults or experienced participants. In self-directed programs the setting is informal. Participants and leader share an equal status wherein the leader is a facilitator rather than a director. Time is devoted to getting acquainted, sharing ideas, and socializing. The site is usually decided by consensus rather than by the leader.

The process of *organization and planning* under leader-directed settings is almost always implemented by the leader, who plans and organizes what activities will be undertaken. In self-directed programs, program organization occurs with participant involvement in the decision-making process. Examples of leader-directed outdoor programs would be a canoeing lesson, a climbing lesson, or a backpacking trip sponsored by a municipality, where the leader structures the format. In a self-directed program, planning is done mutually with the leader involved as a facilitator. Examples would be club programs, common adventurer outings, and advanced trips sponsored by a municipality.

Assessing interests, needs, and values of a leader-directed program is a primary function of the leader. An overnight hike for ten-year-olds, for instance, is usually planned according to his/her perception of participant interests and needs, and his/her own values. If this were not the case, ten-year-olds might plan to hike too long a distance, to bring a mixture of indigestible food, and perhaps even to engage in dangerous activities or those which would annoy other campers. Self-directed programs involve the participants in assessing their own interests, needs, and values in agreement with the group.

In leader-directed settings, *goals and outcomes* are primarily established by the leader, while in self-directed programs, they are created by group negotiations with consensus. The leader-directed program might have a goal of hiking 12 miles, while in a self-directed program, participants might discuss various hike lengths and reach an agreement based upon a consensus from the group members.

In planning the *sequence of events and activities*, the leader of a leader-directed experience will plan purposefully, in a logical sequence, the order in which events are to occur. An example of this is a leading plan where the event may be divided into specific units, each of which contributes to the integral whole. For example, hiking, cooking, map and compass, and survival and environmental ethics are often taught separately before the trip. This sequence of events is planned so that each one builds purposefully on previously learned skills, knowledge, and attitudes.

In self-directed programs, events and activities are conducted according to the desires of the group, assuming everyone already has a foundation of basic skills on which to build and can undertake projects at any stage needed to reach the goal. As a matter of fact, because of the wide variety of individual readiness levels in self-directed programs, different events and activities may be conducted by part of the group rather than having everyone perform every step. In a self-directed canoe trip, for example, the group may start out, travel for a while, then go ashore and analyze how to do things more efficiently.

Implementing activities requires two different processes. In leader-directed activities, techniques, rules, and format are transmitted to the participants by the leader, who may assign practice drills or designate specific steps and projects to be followed for earning badges or awards. In self-directed activities, the program is often conducted independently of the leader's goals and wishes. Instead everyone doing the same thing, the group may plan a variety of activities for independent participation by different people. Instead, the program might be implemented through discussion, sharing, and experimental involvement, with the leader being a facilitator rather than a director.

Evaluation of leader-directed programs is conducted primarily by the leader. It may be in terms of "You did well," "You have made a lot of improvements," or "You have earned your badge." In a self-directed program, evaluation occurs through mutual group consent, with members stating, "We did well," or "We succeeded." They also gather data that support group evaluation of individual portions of the project, parts of which may be assessed as being better than others. Here the final result or product isn't evaluated as much as the *process* the group went through to complete the project. No person loses or fails because of a leader or any other one individual making that decision, and any individual or project deemed successful merits this praise on the basis of group consensus. Success in the self-directed process is measured in terms of group or individual expectations, not those of the leader. In this andragogical process, evaluation is not a dead end, but a move toward assessing more or different needs and finding ways to meet them. Rather than a single-minded orientation toward judgment and comparison with past events or scores, it focuses on changing the situation to bring about success in the future. In the andragogical process, each individual is measured in terms of his/her own ability, not against others in the group. As long as this person contributes to group goals with his/her own unique abilities, his/her achievement can be assessed highly. Through this process, each individual makes the enterprise successful.

Because of situation, circumstance, type of program, age, or ability of the participants, one can never assume that every program will be either entirely leader-directed or self-directed. A leader-directed (formal) setting may be used in a self-directed activity with the group helping to plan, assess, and create goals. On the other hand, the self-directed group may, through consensus or agreement, plan a very logical and purposeful sequence of events and implement precise techniques, rules, and assignments for completing them. The point here is that much advanced adult outdoor leadership occurs in self-directed groups; the prudent leader should understand that he/she may need to make some modifications in the leadership process to meet the goals of the self-directed group. Even in what may appear to be a leader-directed program with an identifiable progression, some participants may require less leadership to meet their self-directed recreational needs.

In conclusion, leaders must be able to adjust their methods of working with groups to adapt to the continuum of the beginner who is both chronologically and experientially immature and the beginner who is chronologically mature but immature in experience. A review of the literature on adult education tells one that adults:

1. Are capable of change at any age;
2. Seek fulfillment or happiness; (Learning experiences can be an avenue for achieving self-fulfillment.)
3. Are extremely capable and become frustrated unless they are given the opportunity for self-direction;
4. Have developed "mind sets" based upon past experiences that have much to do with how they react to a particular learning situation;
5. Are capable of learning from personal experience but need help in determining a logical process for analyzing those past experiences;
6. May be quite mature in relation to one set of standards and quite immature in another; (In cases where the learners are still immature, more guidance may be required from the instructor.)
7. Have periods in their life which make them more receptive to learning certain subjects and give them blocks against other subjects until that problem is solved or that phase is past;

8. Are uniquely different based upon aims, values, social habits, and experience; therefore, each learner should be treated with respect for his/her individuality.

The following guidelines are offered for leaders who work with adults:

1. Adults expect to be treated with dignity and respect. They want to feel valued as individuals and have their opinions respected and given credence.
2. Leaders should recognize the value of the uniqueness of each individual. It is important to remember that each adult in the group will bring unique skills, experience, and knowledge to the group environment.
3. The leader should attempt to determine both individual and group goals since individual goals within adult groups can vary tremendously. Some attempt should be made to identify and respond to individual desires and expectations expressed by group members.
4. Leaders should work to create a supportive social climate. This is important to build a relationship of trust and openness that facilitates positive communication.
5. Adults find leisure experiences more personally meaningful if they are actively involved in the decision-making process.
6. Adults respond to personally relevant leisure experiences; in other words, outings that draw upon the participants' meaningful past experiences are often more successful than those that deal in abstractions.
7. Adults respond to leaders who are genuinely concerned about their welfare, needs, interests, and desires.
8. In developing relationships in groups of adults, the leader should work to create trust between group members and between himself/herself and the group.
9. The leader should attempt to interact with participants in a parallel fashion rather than in a superior/subordinate way. Respect for the leader should be based upon knowledge and skills rather than solely on his/her position within the organization.

10. The leader should be able to adjust the goals of the activity or program, where appropriate, to meet the needs of group members. It is not unusual for the goals of the group to be different from those of the leader, and some modification may be necessary.

Outdoor Pursuit Leadership Training

In virtually all of the economically advanced nations of the world, large numbers of people regularly participate in outdoor recreation. As outdoor activities become more popular, there has been a growing awareness of the need for qualified instructors and leaders at all levels of expertise in each activity. Guide services and schools are often the first to recognize and respond to this need, having a vested interest in the availability of competent staff. Therefore, the first (and sometimes the only) training programs in a given area begin as in-service programs for staff. These staff training programs are often opened to prospective staff, and, in some cases, expanded to offer leadership training to the general public.

In some countries, public funds have been made available to facilitate development of larger, more accessible leadership training programs. The rationale for such expenditures is usually economic, based upon the value of tourism and a desire to reap some of the long-term benefits that can accrue from having more productive local enterprises. In France, for example, a multitude of small, private programs are complemented by the large and prestigious École de Ski et Alpinisme in Chamonix. The school is partly tax-supported, sets national standards, certifies ski instructors and guides, and offers a variety of programs including multi-year in-residence courses of study leading to full guide status.

Of the many leadership training programs available worldwide, those in the English speaking nations are probably the most easily accessible to readers of this text. The following brief survey of outdoor leadership training in the United Kingdom, Australia, New Zealand, Canada, and the United States illustrates the diversity of programs that are available.

United Kingdom

The United Kingdom was the first nation to institute a formal training program for outdoor leaders. In 1969, the Scottish Mountain Leadership Board, on behalf of the three outdoor-leadership training agencies in the United Kingdom, published *Mountain Leadership* by Eric Langmuir. Revised in 1973 and reprinted in 1976, this book provides much of the groundwork for candidates attempting to obtain leadership training and receive a Mountain Leadership Certificate.

Within the United Kingdom, a Mountain Leadership Certificate is accepted as proof of having achieved a minimum standard of proficiency in skills important to teachers and other leaders in charge of children participating in high-risk outdoor activities.

Leadership certificates are awarded to candidates who meet the necessary prerequisites, who fulfill the requirements set forth by the Mountain Leadership Training Board, and who pass the assessment procedures that take place at an approved outdoor-pursuit center.

Applicants who are accepted in the Mountain Leadership Certificate scheme undergo a residency of at least one week or a nonresidential course of four full-weekend outings. A period of at least one year of practical training follows, where the candidate puts into practice the technical skills learned during the basic training period.

The assessment takes place during a one-week residency held at an approved mountain or other outdoor-pursuit center. A written report and recommendations are made on the basis of examined knowledge, and observed performance is evaluated by a field assessor who accompanies the candidate on a scheduled expedition. The report and recommendations are forwarded to the Mountain Leadership Training Board for final approval before a certificate is granted.

Australia

Three of Australia's seven states are actively involved in the training of outdoor leaders. Victoria, South Australia, and Tasmania all offer certification programs in "Mountain and

Bushwalking Leadership." The Victoria program was the first of the three, created in response to the concern that heavy use of outdoor teaching environments might lead to accidents and fatalities. The South Australian program is very similar to Victoria's, but concentrates primarily on training school teachers to care for children involved in outdoor-adventure activities. The Tasmanian program takes the Victoria system one step further by incorporating a unique experimental component aimed more at commercial operators than at school teachers.

Historically, the Australian outdoor-leadership movement began with the first Victorian course offered in May 1969. The program format at that time was heavily modeled on the British Mountain Leadership Certificate scheme with the content adapted to suit local bush settings. Over the years that followed, many alterations were made including the application of advisor and assessor panels and the introduction of preliminary appraisal sessions.

Today, a typical program for leadership applicants begins with an initial week-long residential course during which the technical and safety skills of each applicant are appraised, and recommendations are made on their potential for leadership.

Once they have been recommended for leadership, candidates are assigned established, experienced leaders as advisors for one or two years. During this training period, they experience a wide variety of leadership roles with many different groups in a range of settings. These intensive and extensive experiences are recorded in a log book, then the candidates meet with their advisor to discuss the log. Once the candidates have collectively put in a minimum number of days as experienced apprentice leaders, they are once again appraised and recommended for advancement to the assessment stage.

The assessment stage begins with individual four-day trips in which each candidate takes full leadership responsibility. An advisor attends as backup leader, and members of an assessment panel go along to critique each candidate's leadership performance. If satisfactory performance is demonstrated on this trip, the candidates are advanced to a final, week-long residential assessment course. During this time, a panel of advisors and judges observe and evaluate the leadership performance of several candidates under a wide selection of actual and simulated situations. At the conclusion of the assessment period, candidates who meet the criteria for advancement are recommended for a leadership certificate. At any time during this process, a candidate who fails to meet a criterion has the option of withdrawing from the program or returning to repeat that stage of training.

With a few differences, both the South Australian and Tasmanian programs follow this scheme. The South Australian program is oriented toward outdoor-education for teachers and thus focuses upon teaching strategies, instructional aids, and lesson planning.

In Tasmania, more emphasis is placed on safety skills such as accident response, route finding, weather interpretation, and search-and-rescue. The Tasmanian program also has more stringent application prerequisites than the other two programs. Applicants must be highly experienced in bush and mountain travel before they will ever be considered as candidates. The result is a leadership-trainee group at an advanced technical-skill level that can concentrate on the more critical aspects of leadership development such as group dynamics, decision making, and problem solving.

All three states make use of the manual, Bushwalking and Mountaincraft Leadership, published in 1978 by the Victoria Bushwalking and Mountaincraft Advisory Board. The manual details six areas of concern for the leadership candidate: the leader, trip planning, the walk, food, the elements, and emergencies.

New Zealand

In 1977, the provisional Outdoor Training Advisory Board (OTAB) was formed to examine a national outdoor-leadership training system for New Zealand. The "Hunt Report" had recently been published in the U.K., and it advocated sweeping alterations to the British Mountain Leadership Certificate Scheme. OTAB's recommendations for outdoor-leadership development at home were based heavily upon the changes occurring overseas.

OTAB implemented outdoor-leadership training programs from a new and fresh perspective. They agreed to adopt an open-ended development scheme that did not present a certificate, which thus implied that a candidate should continue to seek lifelong learning opportunities in outdoor-leadership training. A modular approach was also used that allowed the system to be flexible enough to meet an individual's unique needs, to be applicable to many levels of skill or experience, and to be available to potential leaders from many outdoor-pursuit areas and organizations. To encourage leaders to take responsibility for their own training and development, rather than evaluation by a panel of board members, OTAB decided upon self-assessment.

OTAB is designed to be an advisory agency. At present they assist other associations with outdoor-leader training programs at a "grass roots" level rather than dictating a mandatory series of courses for all leaders in general. They also operate a resource-and-information clearinghouse based in the capital city of Wellington, and have two major publications of note: a self-assessment Logbook and an Outdoor Training Guide.

Canada

Canada is relatively new at the work of developing outdoor leaders. No recognized program exists nationally, but, at the provincial level, a few currently operate, and others are under consideration.

The Nova Scotia Outdoor Leadership Development Program serves three functions: a clearinghouse for information on outdoor leadership, a service program providing outdoor-leadership resources and class instructors, and the sponsor of a basic course in leadership training. Applicants attend an introductory leadership school to obtain groundwork in some of the more important leadership skills. As candidates, they apprentice in an experiential leadership role and then attend a leadership assessment school. Once they complete this program a certificate is not granted; instead, graduates are encouraged to continue their training, self-assessment, and development as outdoor leaders.

The stream of leadership training follows a modular pattern which deals with teaching methods, problem solving, group dynamics, trip planning, and expedition behavior. On their own, candidates must obtain the specialized technical skills in the adventure activities where they expect to lead parties and the necessary core skills of navigation, survival, campcraft, environmental ethics, and emergency procedures.

United States

In contrast to the five countries mentioned above, there is no widely accepted broadsided certification program for outdoor leaders in the United States. There are, however, several well-established and nationally recognized training and certification programs for instructors in specific activities. For example, one may become certified as an instructor in skiing, scuba diving, canoeing, or as a guide in several states. In addition, there are dozens of small organizations offering instructor certification in virtually every outdoor pursuit from hiking to hanggliding, and from rafting to rock climbing. With few exceptions these organizations are highly specialized, are recognized only within the local area or region, and are not recognized by any governmental agency. Generalized outdoor pursuits leadership training, designed to address the complex array of skills necessary to the safe leadership of activities such as backpacking or mountaineering, is available through a small number of private organizations and public institutions.

Outward Bound began in the United Kingdom and has since become the largest and most widespread adventure-based educational institution with 32 schools and centers worldwide. There are five schools in the United States. While the Outward Bound schools are best known for an emphasis on building participant self-confidence and self-reliance in experiences ranging from sailing to canoeing and from backpacking to mountaineering, the schools also provide excellent leadership training. The Kurt Hahn Leadership Center, located at the North Carolina Outward Bound School, offers leadership courses to the general public. Most of the training programs devoted specifically to leadership skills are limited to staff and prospective staff; however, Outward Bound does occasionally offer leadership seminars and leadership development programs for the general public, and most of their regular programs include material of value to prospective leaders.

The National Outdoor Leadership School operates an outdoor center which administers a wide variety of outdoor-skills courses, including specialized courses for outdoor leaders and instructors. The Wilderness Education Association offers a number of leadership certification programs within many higher-education degree programs in physical education and recreation.

At the National Outdoor Leadership School (NOLS), the emphasis in leadership training is placed upon teaching capability and technical skills. Certificates at three levels are given: outdoor educator, outdoor leader, and NOLS instructor. The outdoor-educator certificate is awarded to skills-program graduates who demonstrate an ability to teach "no trace" outdoor skills; the outdoor-leader certificate is awarded to graduates of longer courses who demonstrate the ability to lead groups in the outdoors; and the NOLS instructor certificate is given to outdoor leaders who pass the specialized instructor course, who apprentice for one season, and who effectively carry out the philosophy of the National Outdoor Leadership School.

The Wilderness Education Association (WEA) was founded in 1976 to promote professionalism in outdoor leadership, to improve the safety of outdoor trips, and to enhance the conservation of the wild outdoors. WEA offers the National Standard Program for Outdoor Leadership Certification (NSP), which emphasize experiential teaching and learning in a standard basic 18 topic curriculum under field conditions. The curriculum is taught by WEA certified instructors under the auspices of accredited universities or agencies. The NSP for outdoor leadership certification is an expedition-based program that addresses all components of the curriculum in one of three formats, each of which is part of the context of a longer course that must be completed within one year: at least three weeks of continuous wilderness travel; two wilderness field trips of two continuous weeks; or one two-week wilderness field experience with two additional continuous one-week wilderness field trips.

The Certification Issue in the United States

At first glance, it seems quite remarkable that there is no nationally recognized certification system for outdoor leaders in the United States, except for the narrowly-focused programs such as skiing, scuba diving, and small craft. While many excellent generalized leadership training programs have been developed, such as those of Wilderness Education Association (WEA), National Outdoor Leadership School (NOLS), and Outward Bound (OB), no one program reaches more than a tiny fraction of the nation's outdoor leaders.

Collectively, there are large numbers of people involved in hiking, camping, backpacking, mountaineering, rock climbing, nordic and alpine skiing, rafting, canoeing, kayaking, and a host of other activities, and participants in these activities often want and/or need guidance, instruction, and/or leadership. It is also apparent that these activities have much in common. All take place outdoors, generally in remote areas, often in wilderness or on wild rivers. Most of the knowledge and skills necessary for safe and responsible performance as a guide, instructor, or leader are common to all of these activities. Why not define a basic "tool kit" of skills and knowledge and provide standardized training? Such a program, perhaps modeled on some of the best examples in other countries, might ensure higher levels of competence, reduce risks (and thus potentially affect insurance rates), and enhance the quality of services provided.

A nationally accepted program sounds like a good idea, and every few years, someone initiates a new attempt to muster widespread support for such a program. Typically, a successful local training scheme is proposed as a model for a national program. Inevitably, the proposed national design is repeatedly trimmed and modified in response to input from prospective participants, until it loses form completely or is reduced to the prototypical local design on which it was originally based. The proponents of such plans sometimes seem bewildered, or even frustrated, by the success of national programs in other countries, particularly in Europe.

The reasons for relative success in the implementation of national programs in Europe are clear. Most European nations are small, with few exceeding the size of a typical state in the U.S. More importantly, European nations are social democracies in which collective interests are weighted more heavily in both public and personal decisions than is the case in the United States, where individualism is a cultural expectation. It is far easier to develop an acceptable set of national standards in a relatively small country, especially when the population is more inclined to consider the broader social consequences of a measure.

In the U.S., not only are potential participants less inclined to compromise—there are also greater real obstacles to the development of meaningful common standards. Geographically, the U.S. includes far more variety than exists in any single European country. Even when the issue is limited to "basic outdoor skills," geographical diversity results in intractable disagreements. Leaders in the cool, wet Northwest insist that thorough knowledge of hypothermia prevention and treatment are essential, and that no gear list, even for a day hike, is acceptable without rainwear as a required item. Experienced leaders from the desert Southwest may balk at the emphasis on wet, cold conditions but insist instead upon inclusion of skills and information related to acquisition and use of water, and skill and knowledge in the prevention and treatment of heat-related conditions. Those in the humid tropical climates from Florida to Louisiana have other perceptions.

The situation becomes more complicated when attempts are made to define common techniques for specific activities. All of this is not to imply that there are no common grounds. Certainly there are common principles and common needs. There are, however, enough differences to complicate attempts to develop broad national support for any one set of standards, and there is not enough incentive to motivate the sustained individual and collective effort necessary to overcome the obstacles.

Seeking Employment as an Outdoor Leader

Many would-be outdoor leaders gain their first experience in informal circumstances. Typically, some leadership responsibilities are accepted in the context of an outing with a group of friends. Once the fledgling leader gains confidence, he/she might organize and lead a group of other friends to a favorite site, or volunteer to teach them some basic outdoor skills. If the leader does a good job, it may not be long before his/her services are sought by others. With luck and patience, this progression may lead to significant professional opportunities.

More often, however, the leader must actively seek positions in which to develop leadership skills and/or generate income for his/her services. The first step is to identify existing employment opportunities. A survey of local park and recreation departments or districts, public or private schools, youth camps, ski schools, guide services, and outfitters will help identify what services are being provided in the area and may reveal job opportunities. A good source of information about available positions nationwide is the *Jobs Clearinghouse,* a monthly publication of the Association for Experiential Education, University of Colorado, Box 249, Boulder, CO 80309. Information about youth camp positions may be procured from the American Camping Association, 5000 State Rd 67, North, Martinsville, IN 46151.

It is a good idea to look into each of the existing programs that might offer employment to ascertain the quality and reputation of the program as a whole and of the current leaders of each activity. This knowledge can be invaluable and is worth a substantial investment of time. The beginning leader may well do himself/herself a disservice by becoming associated with an organization that does not have a good reputation for quality and for adherence to high standards for safety and environmental ethics. On the other hand, especially for experienced leaders with excellent reputations, an institution or company with a poor reputation may represent an opportunity for involvement either internally or as an outside consultant, to help develop a more positive image.

Getting a job takes real effort which requires a great deal of time, patience, self-assurance, and sometimes a considerable amount of expense. Before selling yourself to a prospective employer, it is necessary to verify your credibility as an outdoor leader. Suggestions for enhancing this credibility include:

1. Know as much as possible about the particular activities that you would like to lead. If you want to "get ahead of the pack," read every major book on the activity and keep up-to-date on current activity-specific periodicals. Read carefully. Don't just skim over the technical details. Study every available shred of material on safety issues, concerns, and skills related to the activity. Attend clinics and conferences to stay abreast of what's happening.

2. Whatever the activity, do it well and often. Participate and practice as often as necessary to become expert and to develop a reputation as a competent, safe and responsible practitioner. Serve as a volunteer with youth agencies to get more practice.

3. Obtain any applicable certification in the activity itself and in any relevant safety skills. For virtually any outdoor leader, this also includes first aid and CPR certification. Advanced Red Cross certification may or may not suffice. Outdoor-oriented courses emphasizing improvisation and long-term care are better and, in many cases employers prefer or require First Responder or EMT certification. Wilderness EMT courses are becoming more readily available and are usually the preferred option.

4. Teach safety related courses. Employers need to be assured that leaders are capable of conducting activities safely. It helps to have taken safety courses (first aid, rescue techniques, avalanche safety, or whatever is applicable), but it means a great deal more to have *taught* the topic or skill. Teaching requires (or at least

implies) a level of understanding of the topic that is considerably greater than that of the average participant or student.

5. Understand why you want to lead outdoor activities. Think about it. Talk to others as a means of clarifying your own thoughts. There are many legitimate reasons. Most employers will ask you why you want the job, and most will see right through an answer that doesn't come from the heart. Incidentally, "Because I like to do the activity" is not a sufficient reason for leading others! Employers will not hire those whose goals are entirely self-serving.

6. Try to expand your horizons beyond the local area. Whatever the activity, there is much to be learned from participation outside the immediate area. In virtually every activity, there are local customs and practices. Often, local practices do not reflect broader trends. By participating outside of the area or region, you can gain new insights, and others can gain from you. Travel to other areas produces real benefits for you as a leader, makes you more valuable as a resource, and, sometimes out of proportion to any real gains, can add to your credibility. Climbing in the Alps of Europe or in several of the states in the U.S. may enhance one's perspectives and will probably result in the development of new skills or ideas. Almost certainly it will add substantially to the credibility of the climbing instructor whose previous credentials covered only two western states.

7. Keep a logbook. It helps to organize your experiences so that you can obtain the greatest benefit from all that you have done. The logbook is invaluable when constructing a professional resume. One way to log in experiences is to have a page reserved for each activity that you are involved in, such as hiking, skiing, and rafting. Reserve the front side of each page for a chronological listing of each experience in the activity (for example, a hike up Old Baldy with dates and description). Reserve the top half of the other side for classes, clinics, or other training you have had in the activity and reserve the bottom half for any leadership or instructional

experience. Too often, potentially impressive arrays of experience are simply compressed into "lots of hiking experience" as time passes and memories fade. Particularly for the leader who has not yet established a substantial employment record, a well-organized presentation is impressive because of the data itself and because it demonstrates an ability to keep organized records.

8. Learn to write well. With a good investment of time and energy, many skilled participants are capable of becoming excellent outdoor leaders. It may be hard to see beyond the initial goal of becoming a field leader or instructor, and, at this level, it is often not necessary to have excellent writing skills. However, at some point, the leader will probably aspire to positions "up the ladder." Many supervisory field positions require an ability to write professional quality reports, and most administrative positions and virtually all academic positions require an ability to construct and edit copy-ready professional documents. The leader who has not invested sufficient time and effort in the development of writing skills is not likely to be among the few field leaders who eventually become directors and administrators.

Applications and Resumes

Once a potential employer is identified, the exact details of the application process can usually be determined in a simple phone call. Then the work begins. Usually, a written application is submitted first, and an interview is scheduled later. The written application may or may not include a resume. Sometimes, a written statement is required, wherein the candidate discusses his/her reasons for wanting the position, and why he/she is qualified. In any case, the application represents an opportunity to demonstrate one's ability. An application that is completed in exact compliance with the requests and is carefully typed or (if permitted) very neatly filled out in printing or longhand reflects well upon the applicant. The employer will assume that the application represents the very best work that the applicant can produce. An application that contains typos, misspelled words, poor

grammar, or is sloppy or incomplete will not inspire confidence. It is a good idea to make at least one copy of the application prior to filling it out. Then a practice copy can be completed and checked carefully before the final copy is made. Remember that generic application forms may not be well-suited to expressing your particular talents and abilities. Supplementary written material is usually welcome and should be included when it will help the reader to understand better your qualifications for the job. One's signature should be legible. Prospective employers are not impressed by the ego-scrawl affected by some who think it is a sign of sophistication to write illegibly.

The resume is a very valuable tool. Like the application, it will be taken by the employer as an example of the best work that the candidate can produce. Before beginning the task, it is helpful to look at many examples of possible formats. Schools, colleges, and universities usually have offices that provide employment counseling, and there one can find examples of resumes. Many public libraries and most public employment agencies have examples to review. In spite of the fact that some people have been advised to submit one-page resumes (generally to companies that screen hundreds of applicants), resumes can be several pages in length as long as the material is germane to the experience.

Typically, your name and address appear at the top of the first page. If you plan to move soon, insert a permanent address at which you can always be reached. Many jobs are lost by college students who leave school with no forwarding address. If you know exactly what job you want, it might be listed under the heading of *Job Objective*. The next headings are usually *Education* and *Experience*, in each case listed in reverse chronological order. If you have kept a good logbook or can recall many details, this information can be incorporated here. Training in outdoor skills or leadership and any related certifications can be included under education while personal and leadership experience may be organized under *Experience*. Be consistent throughout each section; use the same pattern and provide the same type and extent of information for each entry. *Military Service*, if any, could be listed, followed by *Personal Data*.

This can include anything that might be relevant such as foreign language, hobbies, travel, related activities in youth agencies, and awards. Avoid diluting the effect of the resume by tossing in facts not relevant to your qualifications for the position.

Address the letter and resume in accordance with the established application process, or, if no formal processes exist, to the person responsible for hiring employees. Avoid the generic "Dear Ms.", or "Dear Sir" and expressions such as "Hello" or "Gentle People." Identify the person in charge, and be sure to spell the name and title correctly.

References

References are especially important in outdoor pursuits, as many aspects of leadership are subjective and not easily assessed in writing. Maturity and good judgement, for example, are often best evaluated by direct observation in the field and through referees who have such firsthand knowledge. When possible, solicit letters of reference from people who have direct knowledge of your performance in the field. It is always best to use referees who are known to be credible, and, ideally, who are known by the prospective employer. Remember that letters reviewed by the applicant carry far less weight than letters sent directly to the employer. It is better to have a few select references sent to the employer than to send or carry in a great stack of letters that you have had a chance to survey. The employer will assume that the applicant will have withheld any letters containing negative comments, and might assume that those writing the letters may have been swayed toward kinder evaluations knowing that they would be read by the applicant. Select reference parties carefully, ask their permission to list them as references or ask them if they are willing to write a letter of recommendation to the agency, then trust them.

Interviews

Sometimes, interviews are scheduled for every applicant, though, in most cases, interviews are scheduled only for the top few candidates. Whenever possible, interviews are done in person, though, in some cases, they can be conducted over the phone. In the realm of outdoor pursuits, it is not unusual for conventional interview processes to be supplemented by field experiences in which the applicant has an opportunity to demonstrate activity skills and leadership ability.

Anxiety is normal and to be expected. You can keep anxiety to a minimum by being prepared well in advance and by keeping a healthy perspective on the process. Remember that the purpose of the interview is to determine whether or not you are the right person for the job, and whether this is the right position for you. The following suggestions may help:

1. Dress up. Look your best. The employer will assume that what is seen is just about the best you will look on the job. In both public and private sectors, image is an issue. Your appearance may or may not be a major factor, depending upon the position. When it is important to convey an impression of professional competence, personal appearance is often important. Ski schools want staff to look sharp; city park departments want employees who will be acceptable to the taxpayers; and summer camp operators want staff who look wholesome and credible so that parents will be comfortable leaving their children with them. What is functional, in style, and acceptable as a devotee of an activity may not be acceptable to employers whose success and/or public image depends upon the appearance and behavior of staff members. (Refer to Chapter Thirteen, "Marketing the Outdoor Program").

2. Be enthusiastic. This is the time to bring forth your best attributes. The interviewer is looking for facts and clues to your personality and approach to life and work.

3. Answer all questions completely. If it is a simple "yes" or "no" question, try to give some additional information. Show that you know what you are talking about, without being overbearing. Be truthful! Ethics aside, there is no advantage, in the long run, to distortions. Be sure to include the "yes" or the "no," then go on and elaborate.

4. Don't be swayed or made anxious if the interviewer pauses for a while or asks very difficult questions. This may be a direct attempt to see how you handle stress, or it may be inadvertent. If you need a moment to think, just say so. "That's a tough question! May I have a moment to think about it or would you like my immediate response?" would be a reasonable reply to an exceptionally complex or challenging question.

5. Come prepared with a list of any questions you may have about the position. If you have done your homework, you will be well-acquainted with the company or agency and the position before you arrive at the interview. Asking the right questions about the job can indicate your interest in a successful matching of your abilities and the needs of the organization.

Summary

Outdoor leadership requires the understanding of participants and the role and function of leadership. Outdoor pursuit participants possess all the properties of other groups of people. They have reasons for being followers and needs for having leaders, and are affected by many external and internal forces. Every individual in a group has specific responsibilities for himself/herself, and all groups have responsibilities to individuals and to society.

Leaders may be selected in several ways, and all leaders exert several types of power on the followers. Outdoor leaders may have certain recognizable traits, but no list guarantees that the possessor will be an effective or adequate leader. Outdoor leaders can agree on the relative importance of some competencies; however, regional and activity differences make it necessary to develop additional competencies that

may be mandatory in one situation and inappropriate in others. Several models of leadership tell us that leadership style depends upon the level of maturity of the group as it relates to the demands of the task to be performed and as it is affected by a series of conditions.

The outdoor pursuit leader needs to understand the interrelationships of participant and group characteristics, leadership theory, and leader competencies before embarking with a group.

While there are several outdoor leader training programs in the United States, there is no single nationally recognized program of certification of outdoor leaders. Other English-speaking countries have a wide variety of leadership training programs that are based upon experience and may lead to a form of certification.

References

Buell, L. (1978). *Leader's guide to the 24-hour experience.* Greenfield, MA: Environmental Awareness Publications.

Cousineau, C. (1977). *A Delphi consensus on a set of principles for the development of a certification system for education in the outdoor adventure programs.* Unpublished doctoral dissertation, University of Northern Colorado.

Edginton, C., & Ford, P. (1985). *Leadership of recreation and leisure service organizations.* New York, NY: John Wiley and Sons.

French, J. R. P. Jr., & Raven, B. (1959). The basis of social power. In Cartwright, D. (Ed.), *Studies in social power.* Ann Arbor, MI: Institute for Social Research, University of Michigan.

Hersey, P., & Blanchard, K. H. (1977). *Management of organizational behavior: Utilizing human resources, (3rd ed.).* Englewood Cliffs, NJ: Prentice-Hall, Inc.

Miles, J., & Priest, S. (Eds.). (1990). *Adventure education.* State College, PA: Venture Publishing Inc.

Phipps, M. (1991). Educating the leader in the use of leadership styles to enable greater motivation of followers. *Proceedings.* National Conference for Outdoor Leaders: Public, Commercial and Non-profit Partnerships in Outdoor Recreation. Crested Butte, CO: Colorado State College.

Priest, S., & Chase R. (1989). The conditional theory of outdoor leadership: An exercise in flexibility. *Leisure Studies, 10*(2).

Sessoms, H. D., & Stevenson, J. L. (1981). *Leadership and group dynamics in recreation services.* Boston, MA: Allyn and Bacon, Inc.

Shivers, J. S. (1980). *Recreational leadership.* Princeton, NJ: Princeton Book Company.

Swiderski, M. J. (1981). *Outdoor leadership competencies identified by outdoor leaders in five western regions.* Unpublished doctoral dissertation, University of Oregon.

BASIC ADMINISTRATIVE PLANNING

Regardless of the type of enterprise, the organizational pattern or the size of the staff, there are certain generic administrative tasks that must be undertaken prior to leading a group into the outdoors. Primary administrative functions are programming, staffing, scheduling, budgeting, and evaluation. They may be the responsibility of the leader, the supervisor, the organization's directors, or a combination of all three. Ideally, each person keeps in close communication with the others so that there is no misunderstanding about policies, planning, or implementation. Each of the functions is related to the others, and the administrator must develop and modify all of them concurrently.

Programming

Programming is a widely studied and documented topic among professionals in the recreation services field. It is discussed in several books that offer the reader both theoretical and practical points. The material presented here is based upon current practices and recommendations for programming in all recreational activities. Program is defined as the practical implementation of the sponsoring agency's goals and objectives. In other words, the program is the vehicle through which an organization meets its goals. In reality, the program is everything—planned and unplanned—that affects the participants. Unexpected storms, poor tasting meals, transportation that breaks down, beautiful

sunsets, and the joy of making new friends are all part of what the participants perceive to be portions of the program. Basically, programming entails planning for everything that should occur as well as the things that might occur.

Programming, the planning of programs, must begin with a well-defined set of goals and objectives. "Well-defined" means well-thought out and well-understood, but not fixed or immutable. Planning is a dynamic, interactive process. Initial targets and directions are essential in any enterprise, but almost always must be modified as one develops a clearer picture of the actual program. Before a program is planned, the programmer should understand the objectives of the organization. If these objectives are in conflict with those of the program planner, the plans should be aborted immediately. If the goals of the organization are related to teaching minimum camping skills to beginners and the leader wishes to take the group up a 10,000 foot peak to teach ice climbing techniques, the goals of the leader are in conflict with those of the organization. For ethical and legal reasons, no program should be implemented unless it is consistent with the purposes of the sponsoring organization.

The goals and objectives of sponsoring organizations and, consequently, the outdoor recreation programs themselves vary widely. Some may focus on environmental awareness or education; others will emphasize some aspect of personal growth, recreation, or skill development.

Certainly, the objectives of outdoor programs planned for such diverse groups as a college recreation program, a college academic program, a youth agency, a community center, a private enterprise offering vacation trips, or a group of learning disabled adults will all differ. While any outing affords many benefits, program goals determine the area or areas to be emphasized, and program objectives determine the activities and methods to be employed. Goals are statements of general direction or purpose. For example, a goal of a college outdoor leadership class might be expressed as "to provide opportunities for outdoor leadership development," or "to develop skilled, ethical, and responsible outdoor leaders."

Program objectives should be attainable and measurable, and it should be possible to verify that they were met. The following guidelines may help in writing objectives.

In form, each objective should:

1. Start with the word "to" followed by an action verb (e.g., to carry a 35-pound pack 8 miles a day for 5 days).
2. Specify a single result to be accomplished.
3. Specify a target date for the accomplishment (e.g., upon completion of the course).
4. Be as specific and quantitative (hence, measurable and verifiable) as possible.
5. Specify only the "what" and "when." Avoid the "why" and "how."

In content, each objective should:

1. Relate directly to the goals of the organization.
2. Be readily understandable by those who will be contributing to its attainment.
3. Be realistic and attainable, but represent a significant challenge.
4. Be consistent with the resources available or anticipated.
5. Be consistent with the basic policies and practices of the organization.
6. Be willingly agreed to by all parties without undue pressure or coercion.

Examples of objectives for an outdoor leadership course could be:

Upon completion of the program participants will be able:

a. To teach basic canoeing skills to beginning paddlers.
b. To teach group cooperation through a two-day and one-night canoe trip on a flatwater lake.
c. To organize and implement an eight-week canoeing class for sixteen participants which develops their ability to travel safely and responsibly by canoe on flat water for two days.

Program Contents

Recreational programs are often categorized according to activity types such as arts and crafts, music, drama, literature, dance, sports and games, and outdoor activities. In actuality, it is possible to incorporate all the other types of activities into the outdoors.

Another way of categorizing programs is by activity format which refers to the form or organization of the activity. The number of program activities with land- and water-based outdoor foci is surprising if one considers the possibilities within each of the formats. The following list describes the formats and includes some examples of programs that may be developed around each of them. The list reflects the terminology used currently by several authors. While the major part of this book centers on land- and water-based activities carried out in the natural environment away from the comforts and security of the urban environment, other activities may be included as integral parts of such programs. Such activities may be carried out during pre-trip training, on the trip, or at post-trip review sessions. Or they may be used as programs offered to complement and/or supplement the outdoor-pursuit offering.

Activity Formats

Competitive events: (These are games and contests between individuals and groups.)

Orienteering contests
Tent pitching races
Softball on snowshoes
Identification contests
Outdoor cooking contests
Cross-country ski races

Self-directed activities: (This includes drop-in, open facility, and special interest activities. No organization or program structure is needed for these activities. They are self-interest activities usually taking place in a reference room, library, or multipurpose room. The participants "drop-in" and stay only as long as they wish. Supervision is mainly for the purposes of safety; however, there may be some incidental instruction.)

Map reading practice
Knot-tying boards
Reading reference books
Working on personal equipment

Social activities:

(1) Interest Groups: (These are groups of people with no common bond other than an interest in the topic. Interest groups have no organizational structure and are made up of individuals who attend as they wish. A great many outdoor trips, climbs, and other activities come under this format.)

Lectures, slide shows, and films
Nature walks
Municipal outings
Commercial trips and tours

(2) Clubs: (Clubs are membership groups with organized operating codes or policies, officers, and usually a dues structure.)

Hiking clubs
Youth agency troops
Natural history associations

Special events, including performance and spectator activities: (These are activities that occur only occasionally, require careful planning, and usually have no prerequisites or follow-up programs. They occur on specified dates and times.)

Winter carnivals
Pot lucks
Progressive cook outs
Award programs
Recognition nights
Litter clean up trips
Trail building trips
Fund raisers (e.g., sponsoring hikers or boaters for $ 0.50 or $1.00 per mile.)

Self-improvement or educational activities: (These instructional programs offer specific knowledge or skills. They meet at specific times with planned progressions. Participants usually attend from the first session to the end and usually pay for the block of lessons. In a recreational situation, educational activities are voluntary; nevertheless, the same program formats and ideas can be incorporated into school and college classes.)

First aid
Weather
Map and compass
Plant identification
Geology
Outdoor cooking
Swimming
Photography
Astronomy
Animal tracks
Bird watching
Care and repair of equipment
Making and remodeling equipment
Mountaineering

In addition to different formats, programs can be developed for different age and skill levels, and can be organized by season, month, and sometimes week. All outdoor-pursuit leadership does not occur on a trail or river; some may happen indoors, in town, and in structured lectures. Working one or more of the activity formats into the program may help one meet the interests and needs of many participants.

Recreation Programming Principles

Recreation programs are based upon certain principles generally agreed upon by professionals in the recreation field. One may think of a principle as a "guiding rule to action" (e.g., a rule of conduct). By incorporating these principles into program planning, the programmer can provide the participant with the same quality program that he/she expects from other similar programs. This is tantamount to quality control used in the manufacturing of market goods, as it controls the quality of the program. The length, type, and content of every program should be based upon the consideration of both the group itself and individuals within the group.

Group-Centered Principles

The extent to which each principle will be followed varies according to the type of group. Groups consisting of single categories of individuals (i.e., Boy Scouts) will be less affected by some guidelines than groups made up of a wider range of individuals (i.e., participants from a community center). Accordingly, the following ten principles do not apply equally to all groups; however, each should be considered.

1. Planners must consider the needs and interests of the group, and the available leadership, equipment, finances, and resources (land or water).

2. The program should be planned for many age ranges and abilities within the group. For example, a youth group may range from ages ten to sixteen, include beginners and experts, and consist of both able-bodied and disabled members. A college class may consist of people who range in age from seventeen to over sixty and who portray a wide range of abilities, conditions, and interests. A community center group usually consists of a wide range of ages, abilities, socio-economic levels, and interests. Obviously, the municipal outdoor programmer has a much more diversified clientele than does the planner of a program for a narrowly-defined group.

3. The program should offer a majority of activities within the financial budgets of all potential participants. If some members of the target group cannot afford the program, either the program should be altered or expenses should be somehow defrayed (through scholarships, donations, borrowing, renting, improvising). (This recreation programming principle applies largely to tax-supported programs.)

4. The program must be operated in a manner that serves as a model for participants. Program standards for safety and environmental responsibility will be reflected in the behavior of participants when they conduct personal ventures. (It is better to turn back in an emergency and refund some money than to endanger the lives of the participants.)

5. When possible, programs should offer the continuity of year-round operation. Courses about care and repair of equipment, first aid, meteorology, geology, map and compass, etc., all contribute to the overall outdoor program and can be offered during what is often called the "off-season."

6. The program should provide activities that are varied and progressive (new places, new activities, new levels).

7. The program should be a supplement, or complement, to what is already offered and available within the community.

8. Planning should be long-range, to ensure future leadership, finances, facilities, and equipment.

9. The program should be based upon the standards developed by national agencies or research studies. (Ratios of leaders to participants, leader competencies, progressions, equipment, etc.)

10. The program should follow the best current practices in the field.

Individual-Centered Principles

Planners also need to consider each individual by keeping the following principles in mind:

1. The program should provide the individual with an outlet for expressing skills and interests.

2. The individual should be provided with the widest possible range of individual choices in a variety of activities. This will vary with different groups. A prescribed outdoor course or a college class will have fewer choices than one sponsored by a municipal recreation department or one offered to private individuals seeking leisure experiences outdoors.

3. Individual differences should be recognized and accommodated when possible.

4. Every program should provide the opportunity for social interaction and fellowship.

5. Every program should create and develop an interest in self-leadership, self-sufficiency, and self-reliance. The program that makes groups and individuals reliant on the leader may be missing a primary potential purpose of outdoor pursuits—that of developing self-reliance. "Full-service" guiding may or may not move clients toward self-sufficiency. In order to avoid overconfidence, clients in "full-service" programs must be made to understand their own capabilities and limitations. They must understand that they are not investing in a program that automatically gives them the ability to duplicate the same trip without the service of the guide.

6. The program should involve the participant in the planning process and, insofar as possible, in the decision-making process.

7. The program should provide the opportunity for creative expression. Singing, storytelling, menu-making, cooking, and joking are all forms of self-expression.

8. The program should provide the opportunity for adventure and new experience. Even though the leader has been there and done something a hundred times, it must be treated as a new and wondrous adventure to the beginner. Instead of belittling a climb with "Oh, I've done that route lots of times," a leader could say, "Isn't the view from the ridge spectacular?" or "What did you think of the steep pitch just before the summit?"

When trying to follow the principles, one might consider inserting some of the program formats mentioned above into the program. Some of the formats can help the programmer meet specific principles better than others, and by using several formats, there is a better chance of implementing all the principles.

Staffing

Staffing is perhaps the greatest single challenge for administrators of outdoor programs. Safe, high-quality experiences for clientele, and, ultimately, the success of the program depend upon the abilities of field staff working in potentially hazardous remote field locations. The administrator faces the formidable task of determining the size and qualifications of staff members, locating and assessing potential employees, and hiring, training, and supervising the staff. The easiest way to attack this complex problem may be to divide it into manageable parts, as in the following material.

Many of the decisions that must be made with regard to staffing require a sound, current, working knowledge of the realities of field leadership of the activity in question. More often than not, the administrator faced with the responsibility for staffing decisions is not a participant in the activity, much less an experienced, active leader or instructor in the activity. Given the importance of making good decisions in terms of both program quality and personal and program liability, and given the large amounts of time and expense involved in the staffing process, the administrator is strongly advised to seek assistance from those who have the necessary background and up-to-date expertise.

Identification of Needs

While identification of staffing needs is clearly prerequisite to initiation of a search for staff, one should be prepared to rethink the proposed program in light of the qualifications of the potential personnel identified in the search process. Often, some modifications in the proposed programs are needed to accommodate limitations in the abilities of the available staff or to take advantage of greater than anticipated staff capabilities. Nevertheless, probable needs must be identified to provide a starting point. The number of personnel required to operate a program is, to a large extent, dependent upon the abilities and workloads of each staff member. It is often easier to begin by listing the particular activities and/or outings that must be staffed, grouping similar elements together. For example, one might group hiking- and backpacking-related aspects of the program together, since these activities require similar skills. Activities, such as rock climbing and mountaineering, might be grouped together as they require expertise in rope handling and climbing skills.

While it may be possible to locate individuals capable of leading a wide-range of activities, it is most likely that a search will yield individuals with relatively narrow fields of expertise. It is relatively easy, for example, to locate individuals who have extensive backpacking expertise and adequate leadership potential. It is considerably more difficult to find experienced mountaineers, much less mountaineers who have the additional safety and rescue training necessary to conduct activities safely. Too often, ardent outdoor enthusiasts focus almost exclusively on one aspect of land or water activity, and have, at most, a passing familiarity with activities outside of their special area of interest.

As a result, it is often necessary to define staffing needs on the assumption that several specialists must be hired. While cumbersome, this often results in superior initial program quality, and may provide flexibility and improved continuity if, through in-house apprenticeships and training, staff can be encouraged to broaden their horizons.

Assume that you are faced with the relatively simple task of staffing a weekend backpacking program. Where do you begin? First, it is important to know as much as possible about the proposed program. How many outings are planned? What is the expected group size? Who will participate, and what is the nature of the group? Where and during what season will the outings take place? Many factors must be considered before determining the number of leaders needed. In a few cases, it may be sufficient to provide a single leader. More often, and certainly in the case of most multi-day backcountry outings, at least two leaders will be needed. (For suggestions on leadership ratios and qualifications for various activities, refer to Chapters Sixteen and Seventeen.) Typically, such outings are staffed by a fully-qualified leader and a competent but less experienced assistant.

The specific minimum qualifications of each depend upon the nature and purpose of the outing. The staff must be capable of safely facilitating achievement of the program objectives. While basic safety and group management skills are needed by leaders of any backpacking outing, program objectives often define additional leadership requirements. Basic leadership skills may suffice for the leaders of beginning level summer day hikes; however, considerable additional experience and skill may be required for off-season travel, longer outings, or programs designed to accomplish specific objectives such as enhancement of self-confidence, development of advanced skills, or learning about the environment.

Each situation is unique, and the program administrator may lack the experience necessary to define the number and qualifications of staff needed for a particular outing. Advice and assistance can often be obtained from administrators or leaders of highly regarded programs with similar content. Contacts with providers of such programs can provide valuable insights and advice, and an awareness of what comparable institutions regard as minimal staff qualifications and participant/staff ratios. In this critical realm, the administrator cannot afford, from a legal perspective, to set standards less stringent than those of other institutions or organizations offering similar programs. As a caveat, one must be sure that the persons from whom advice is sought are highly regarded as leaders in the field. Requesting advice from someone just because his/her program has been in business for several years is risky, as the enterprise may be operating below the standard recognized as acceptable.

Job Announcements, Descriptions, and Analyses

Job announcements are brief notices of position openings with broadly stated duties and general as well as specific qualifications. *Job descriptions* are lists of the general and specific duties expected of the employee. *Job analyses* are descriptions of what the employee actually does, often accompanied with notations on the length of time needed to accomplish each task.

Once needs are identified, general and specific duties and responsibilities can be described for each proposed position—the job description. These "in-house" descriptions may then be summarized to create announcements of openings suitable for posting or publication. The final job analysis often cannot be developed until the staff member is identified and actually performs the assigned duties. Employees have the right to expect their duties to be spelled out on their job descriptions. When the job analysis is not consistent with the job description, one or both should be modified.

Created prior to the search for a new staff member, the initial job description is relatively easy to generate. While the modification of this tentative description into a form suitable for use in a job announcement appears to be a simple process, it in fact deserves careful consideration and often requires the involvement of personnel managers or institutional committees. Hiring processes are often subject to special protocols, conventions, and rules. A small private guide service may be free to describe a position and define criteria and qualifications for employment in whatever manner deemed most likely to achieve results in the particular

advertising medium. At the opposite extreme, a publicly-funded educational institution may have to comply with a complex and frequently changing array of local, state, and federal regulations as well as established institutional policies. Fortunately for the program administrator, most institutions have one or more individuals on staff to assist in this process. The operator of a small private business can often obtain advice or assistance from local government agencies. Contact with an established reputable service-oriented business in the area may be useful as a means of identifying which governmental agencies need to be contacted.

Regardless of the extent of regulation and constraint, it is often best to avoid being overly specific when advertising the position. Minimum requirements should be stated clearly; however, care must be taken not to turn away qualified individuals. Before stating minimum requirements as a fixed number of years of a specified kind of employment, or as a requirement for a specific academic degree or certificate, consider whether a person might be acceptable given some alternative combination of experience. The most common way of accomplishing this is to append "or equivalent" to the specific, preferred conditions. When stating salaries or wages, it is often best to state the range and to append with the words "commensurate with experience" (or equivalent wording) if flexibility is possible.

Figure 11.1 (page 222) illustrates an outline for a basic job description. Figure 11.2 (page 223) shows an example of a job description modified from one used by the Northwest Youth Corporation.

In most cases, the final working job description cannot be written until the new employee has been identified. Even in the case of a new "single-purpose" part-time employee, it is often necessary to make some adjustment in the initial job description to reflect the individual's strengths, limitations, interests and time constraints. Failure to adjust is unfair to both the new employee and the enterprise, and it could be a contributing factor to legal action in an ensuing case of negligence.

> **FIGURE 11.1   A Generic Outline for a Job Description**
>
> 1. Position Title
> 2. Dates of Employment
> 3. Program Description
> 4. General Description of Job
> 5. Specific Job Responsibilities
> 6. Work Conditions and Hours
> 7. Pay
> 8. Qualifications
> 9. How to Apply

Locating Potential Staff

Most positions require highly skilled individuals who can work effectively in unsupervised field settings. The work schedules are often irregular, the hours are long, and the pay is often marginal. Even in a large metropolitan area, there may be only a few potential employees. Fortunately, however, there are reasonably efficient ways of gaining the attention of these individuals. One of the easiest and most productive approaches is to spread the word within the community of participants in the activity in question. For example, a search for a backpacking instructor might be initiated by a few phone calls to one or more backpacking instructors or hiking club leaders in the area. They may offer suggestions and help spread the word throughout the regions. Inform as many dedicated participants as possible. Some may be potential leaders or know of possible candidates. Try posting notices in the clubhouses and newsletters of local hiking or climbing clubs, and in stores that sell hiking equipment. Colleges and universities sometimes have outing clubs or outdoor pursuits courses, and a few offer outdoor leadership training. All are potential sources of staff.

Assessment of Candidates

How can the best candidate be selected from a pool of applicants? The goal is to select the candidate who will be the greatest asset to the program. The person or persons charged with selecting the new employee thus need to be thoroughly familiar with the program as a whole as well as with the specific job description.

Initial screening of applicants is usually accomplished through a review of written applications and references. The efficiency of the screening process depends in large part upon the quality and quantity of information provided by each candidate. The application form and other materials sent to applicants need to be carefully constructed to ensure that the reviewers will have adequate information upon which to base their decisions. If a standard institutional application form must be used, it may be necessary to request specific kinds of additional information in a cover letter or supplemental application form.

Most application forms include spaces for:

Date
Applicant's name
Street address
City
State
Zip code
Work and home telephone numbers
Social Security number (This may not be required until after the hiring process is finished, or it may be required in order to reimburse travel expenses. It depends upon the agency.)
Position applied for
Education (date, institutions, and degrees)
Employment history (dates, employer, position, brief job description, wage or salary may be optional)
Other relevant experience and training (special skills, training or certification, familiarity with outdoor resources in the area; hobbies and interests, etc.)

In some cases, it may also be useful to know the applicant's age, gender, marital status, number of dependents, medical history and physical limitations, driving record, military service and discharge record, and police record. Before requesting any of the above information, it's best to review institutional policies and governmental regulations applicable to the search. There are situations, especially in the United States,

FIGURE 11.2   An Example of a Job Description

NORTHWEST YOUTH CORPS

POSITION: Crew leader
DATES: Summer: June-September   **Fall:** September-October

PROGRAM BACKGROUND

Northwest Youth Corps (NYC) is a summer education and job training program for high school youth, aged 16-19. Youth crews work on projects for government and industry in a format stressing job skills and environmental education. During the week, crews camp near the job sites, live in tents, and cook their own meals over a campfire or Coleman stove. Weekends are devoted to recreational outings and educational activities.

JOB DESCRIPTION

Crewleaders live and work with their crew in a full-time capacity. They supervise work projects, implement a daily environmental education program, coordinate meal preparation, and transport their crew in a 15-passenger van. They are also required to learn the skills necessary to operate a chainsaw in a safe, efficient manner.

DUTIES AND RESPONSIBILITIES

Corpsmember Supervision:
Crewleaders are responsible for coordinating all the daily operations of a ten (10) member teenage work crew. They delegate responsibilities to crewmembers, maintain crew discipline, and establish crew morale.
Work Project Supervision:
Crewleaders are responsible for the safe completion of assigned work projects and direct corpsmembers with specific attention to safe work practices, proper use of tools, work quality, and efficiency of production.
Recordkeeping:
Crewleaders are responsible for maintaining daily work reports, corpsmember time sheets, written corpsmember evaluations, and a variety of other paperwork.
Education:
Crewmembers are responsible for integrating NYC's environmental education program into each day's work schedule and for assisting in the coordination of an ongoing recreation program.

DESIRED QUALIFICATIONS

Education:
Minimum one year college education in outdoor recreation, forestry, environmental education, resource management, landscape architecture, or a related field.
Experience:
Applications will be reviewed considering all revelant experience relating to youth leadership, outdoor recreation, environmental education, or forestry background. Previous experience operating chainsaws is desirable.
Certification:
A current first aid card and CPR certification is required. Life-saving certification is desirable. Applicants must be able to demonstrate an acceptable driving record during the last three years.

HOURS

NYC is a residential program requiring long days, high energy, and love of challenge. There will be a five-day break between sessions; additional unpaid days off will also be scheduled.

PAY SCALE

In 1991 first-year Crewleaders earned a minimum of $50/day plus meals and potential bonuses. Staff Performance Bonuses ranged from $98 to $165, and Productivity Bonuses ranged from zero to $232.

TO APPLY

Application requirements include a completed application, resume, and references. Interviews will be scheduled as applications are received.

wherein employers are prohibited from requesting certain kinds of information about prospective employees. Where it can be shown that the position demands a specific age, gender, or marital status and is not discriminatory against any individual, it may be possible to require such information. Driving and police records are standard requests in cases where the prospective employee will work with youth, and/or funds, and will be involved in vehicular transportation. Requesting information that does not, or should not, affect the carrying out of the job responsibilities serves no purpose.

The nature and specificity of additional information needed to make a hiring decision varies widely from case to case. In a relatively simple case, when selecting a "single-purpose" part-time employee, all that may be needed is information specific to the particular job. For example, when selecting a backpacking leader who will have no other function in the program, it is often sufficient to have the candidate detail (1) personal experience in backpacking, (2) any courses or training in related skills, and (3) any leadership or teaching experience in backpacking or related activities.

Remember that the written application is only a screening process. Final decisions will be made only after the interview process is completed. When the new employee may be expected to perform a variety of functions, more information is needed about the breadth of a candidate's experience. Figure 11.3 might be used as an aid in screening candidates for a position in a program that includes hiking, backpacking, rock climbing, mountaineering, and rafting. Using such a form can facilitate comparisons and is especially useful when there are many applicants for a position.

At some point in the selection process, it will be necessary to conduct a more thorough assessment of a candidate's knowledge of, and ability to teach each activity. Usually, this more detailed assessment will apply only to those candidates who have met initial criteria and have survived an initial screening of applications and references. There are several possible ways of determining specific abilities. The best method or methods will vary depending upon the nature of the position, the expertise of those conducting

the search process, the extent to which it is possible to communicate with the candidates, and the nature and reliability of references. Assessment of a prospective outdoor leader is not an easy task, even for experienced professionals well-versed in the specific activities in question. One of the first things most experienced administrators do is call for help!

Given the importance of making a good decision, and the difficulty of assessing a candidate, references can be extremely important. Nothing is more useful than being able to discuss the prospective employee with an experienced and reputable colleague who has had an opportunity to gain firsthand knowledge of the candidate. A few minutes on the telephone can sometimes eliminate the need for hours of interviews. If the applicant lists an organization as a former employer, it is wise to inquire exactly why the person left the organization. Sometimes it was because of poor job performance!

If references cannot provide enough information, the importance of the interview and alternative assessment techniques is increased. It is often worthwhile to use a written exam and/or a preestablished series of questions in an oral exam or interview format. A written or oral examination is useful if, and only if, the questions are appropriate and if, and only if, the responses can be evaluated by people experienced in activity leadership to which the candidate may be assigned.

It is often best to utilize various types of questions, to assess both objective skill and the candidate's judgement. For example, a candidate for a position as a mountaineering instructor might be asked to draw or construct a 3:1 pulley system suitable for use on a glacier, using standard mountaineering devices and knots. The candidate might then be asked to describe what actions he/she might take in response to a specified set of circumstances. A set of a dozen questions could include one or more dealing with first aid, environmental hazards, clothing and equipment needs, climbing and rescue skills, environmental ethics, group control, and teaching methods, as well as various open-ended questions to shed light on the candidate's ability to use good judgment in resolving complex dilemmas.

FIGURE 11.3   Outdoor Skills and Teaching Experience Summary

Applicant's Name: _____

Position Applied For: _____

For each of the activities listed below please indicate the extent of your **experience and skills**. Use the following codes:

0. No experience
1. Beginning or novice level
2. Intermediate level
3. Advanced or expert level

Also indicate your **ability to teach** each activity at the beginning, intermediate and advanced levels. Use the following codes:

0. Not qualified to teach at this level
1. Could teach, but no teaching experience at this level
2. Have some teaching experience at this level
3. Have extensive teaching experience at this level

Activities	Personal Experience and Skill in Activity	Ability to Teach levels:		
		Beginning	Intermediate	Advanced
Hiking				
Backpacking				
Rock climbing				
Rafting				

In some cases, it is necessary to observe the candidate in the field. For example, in the absence of reputable certification or references, a potential ski instructor should be observed while skiing and while teaching this activity. Although the candidate's talents might be conveyed in a videotape, direct observation is generally more revealing. While there is always much to be gained from direct observation in the field, circumstances and budgetary constraints may make it difficult or impossible to arrange. For example, it may be possible to arrange a two-hour session in which to assess a candidate's ability to teach skiing, but it may be difficult to assess the ability of a mountaineering instructor unless several full days can be scheduled.

In practice, decisions are usually based upon information derived from the written application, letters of recommendation and telephone conversations with references, interviews with the candidate, and written or verbal examination, supplemented, where possible, with direct field observations.

It is common to identify more than one individual who meets all the performance criteria of the job in question. Unless one person seems clearly more qualified than the others, vis-à-vis the specific job description, the decisions may be based in part upon the possibility of ancillary contributions to the program. For example, in the case of the search for a backpacking instructor, an individual who can also teach kayaking might be selected from a set of otherwise equally qualified individuals if the program happens to need additional help in kayaking.

Staff Orientation and Training

For most administrators, a new or reassigned employee is both a blessing and a burden. The relief felt at finally identifying and hiring the new staff member is followed immediately by a new set of challenges. Even when a long-time employee is reassigned, it is necessary to commit time and energy to orient the person to a new role in the organization. Inevitably, there is a period of inefficiency during which the new staff member is learning how to accomplish the necessary tasks. A new employee must be made familiar with the general structure, policies, and procedures of the organization or institution in addition to the job orientation itself. In some large operations there may be established indoctrination processes and materials. More often, the entire task falls on the shoulder of the individual's immediate supervisor.

Consideration of orientation and training should be part of the initial decision to fill the position. Funding and allocations of supervisory time need to be considered as part of the essential costs associated with the position. When several staff members are hired simultaneously, time and energy can be saved by conducting general orientation sessions for all new employees and volunteers, so that the time required for individual sessions is minimized.

Orientation sessions for new staff generally include detailed surveys of relevant policies and procedures, including payroll issues, employee work rules and benefits, and safety policies and procedures. All of these areas should also be explained clearly in up-to-date documents. Very often, such documents are not kept up-to-date. The need to orient new employees often provides the incentive to review and update written policy statements. Involving the new employee in this process can be worthwhile for everyone. The organization gains from having fresh insight, and the new employee gains a sense of involvement and respect, as well as a better understanding of the rationales supporting policies and regulations.

The amount of specific training that is necessary depends upon the circumstances. If there are other employees doing similar work, it may be sufficient to have the new staff member work with an experienced employee as an assistant or co-leader. When there is no possibility of an "apprenticeship," it is usually best to assign the new leader to tasks that are relatively easy. A new backpacking leader might be assigned to a few small, beginning level weekend group outings before being assigned to a more challenging experience. Even if the new employee has considerable experience as a leader, it takes time to adjust to a new job and to become familiar with new terrain.

Specific skill deficits may be dealt with by providing in-house training sessions if expertise is available. However, it is often more efficient to "farm out" the training, especially if the skills are reasonably standardized. Using outside sources may not cost much more than using in-house personnel, unless the in-house experts have nothing else to do with their time. When employees attend "outside" clinics or when outside experts are brought in to conduct training sessions, new ideas and techniques are made available. In the case of first-aid and CPR training and other safety-related skills, it is often best to defer to the American Red Cross or to other sources of nationally recognized standardized training and certification. In some larger communities, especially in the western states, there are specially designed first-aid courses available for outdoor leaders, ski patrol and mountain rescue personnel. These courses include material relevant to the special needs of people who work in backcountry areas, and may offer Emergency Medical Technician, First Responder, Red Cross Advanced First Aid, or other nationally recognized certificates.

Staff training is an on-going process, and must be considered as an inherent cost of operation of the program. In some cases, all of the costs of staff training, including the costs of maintaining first aid, CPR and other certification are born by the employer. More often, the employer supports a portion of the expense. Typically, training that is specific to the job and not of general value outside of the organization is fully funded by the employer, while the costs of maintaining first aid, CPR and other required certificates are shared or considered to be the employee's responsibility.

Compensation

There is always a need to compensate leaders for the time they spend working with programs. While money is the most widespread form of compensation, it is by no means the only option. The following summary includes some of the most common forms of employee compensation.

Money. It sounds simple enough, doesn't it? In many if not most cases, it's the most efficient and effective form of compensation, and it's the primary form of compensation for most workers. However, as any experienced administrator knows, the actual process of providing monetary compensation is anything but simple. To begin with, how much should the person receive? Should the pay be hourly, daily, weekly, monthly, by salary, or by the job? What is the actual cost of a given rate of pay, given the various taxes, payments to local, state, and federal programs, employee insurance and other benefit costs?

Establishment of a pay scale is a complex process. It's important to consider the pay rates for similar work as comparable organizations in the region, the cost of employee benefits, and the costs of the various governmental taxes and fees that must be paid in proportion to employee wages. The scale needs to allow for reasonable raises over time, as well as for overtime compensation and raises for outstanding performance. Establishing a fair pay scale is difficult, even in the case of an office worker assigned to regular working hours. The process is far more complex in the case of most outdoor leaders, due to the irregular work patterns and long hours. The nature, intensity, and risk levels of the work also vary markedly within the course of a typical assignment.

In some cases, pay is determined in part on the basis of the difficulty and risk level which adds yet another dimension to the puzzle. The following table shows the major tasks associated with operation of a typical basic weekend backpacking course. In the example, it is assumed that the leader is responsible for each of the listed responsibilities. Note that programming, budgeting, scheduling, marketing, registration of participants, and other critical tasks are not included here as they are normally considered to be the responsibility of the program administrators. While some planning and scouting time may be saved by operating multiple similar trips in the same location, the total amount of staff time required is still remarkably large. See Table 11.1 (page 228).

Given the amount of time required to staff even a simple weekend backpacking course, it isn't surprising that many organizations rely heavily on volunteers, at least as assistant leaders. It is also not surprising that in the private sector such courses are expensive for participants. Even at only $10.00 per hour, the costs of direct leadership for a two-day field outing may approach $1,000.00. Administrative costs, insurance, general overhead, transportation costs, and other expenses may well add another $800.00 or more so that each participant must pay $50.00-$70.00 per day just to cover expenses. It is no wonder, then, that many private outfitters, guide services, and schools must charge $100 per day or more (in 1993 dollars) to make a reasonable profit.

Fortunately for the general public, many tax-supported institutions can offer outdoor activities at more affordable rates because of lower overhead and insurance costs. Unfortunately for leaders, many private and public operators keep their costs down by paying very low wages or by paying for only part of the time invested by the leader. Sometimes it is possible to hire capable leaders for evening or weekend outings on a part-time per day or per outing basis for as little as $50.00 per day or $100.00 per weekend (in 1993 dollars). This may be a satisfactory arrangement when the individual is a full-time student or otherwise fully employed. Teachers, for example, may make good reliable part-time employees. If the individual is totally reliant upon income from leadership, however, it is unlikely that he/she can afford to accept the position. Full-time, well-paid employees

TABLE 11.1   **Hours to be Considered for Compensation for a Typical Weekend Backpacking Outing**

	LEADER HOURS	ASSISTANT LEADER HOURS
Pre-trip planning [1]	4	0
Pre-trip scouting [2]	12	12
Pre- and post-trip meetings [3]	6	4
Group gear preparation [4]	1.5	0
Personal gear packing	2	2
Conduct of outing [5]	24	24
Group gear cleaning, repair and storage	1	1
Follow up evaluations and reports	1	0.5
Personal gear cleaning, repair and storage	2	2
TOTAL	**53.5**	**45.5**

[1] Includes planning, vehicle reservations, generation of course descriptions, agendas and other handouts, etc. Repeated trips on the same basic plan require less time.

[2] Assumes ability to scout a two-day beginning trip in a single day by a fast, fit pair of leaders. Repeated trips to the same site usually do not require scouting.

[3] Assuming two pre-trip meetings at 1.5 hours each, one post-trip meeting at 1 hour, and set-up and follow-up time.

[4] Assumes a need to organize a moderate amount of group gear. It is assumed here that personal gear is provided by individual participants.

[5] Leaders are responsible for the group from time of assembly until return to town. In addition, leaders must usually arrive at least 30 minutes early to prepare vehicles and gear, and after the outing they must return vehicles and, in some cases, transport participants home. Therefore, the 12 hours per day assumed here are minimal. Some organizations pay for an additional 12 hours of evening and night duty at a reduced or "on-call" rate.

are generally the most committed and reliable personnel. The next best alternative is a part-time employee who has a secure full-time paid position in the community. When students or other members of transient populations are hired on a part-time basis, frequent changes of staff can be expected, with the resultant costs of training and lack of continuity.

Obviously, all of the above issues must be viewed with one eye on the budget. In most cases, all costs of operation must be borne by the participants, at least in the private sector. Unless some other source of income is available,

market forces often lead to an uneasy compromise wherein participant fees are uncomfortably high, and staff wages are uncomfortably low.

Sometimes there is an advantage to contracting or subcontracting for the needed services. As a contractor, the leader receives no direct benefits other than a fee, which is often greater than the wage that would have been received as an employee, and the fee seems larger still since no taxes are withheld. The employer enjoys lower costs and may be afforded some degree of protection from liability for the actions of the contractor, especially if the contractor is insured. While such an arrangement may not be in the best long-term interests of the contractor, it may provide considerable short-term advantage. The primary stumbling block may be liability insurance. Unless the program's liability coverage automatically extends to contractors, the contractor may have to obtain his/her own insurance. In many cases, the costs of obtaining adequate coverage exceed any monetary advantage gained by contracting.

Health Insurance and Retirement Benefits

Health insurance and retirement programs are valuable benefits, especially in the United States. Even in the majority of developed nations, which have national health-care plans, there are usually a variety of supplemental health and retirement programs that can be provided for full-time, and in some cases for part-time employees. The typical full coverage group health plan in the U.S. is very costly; however, it is a benefit needed and appreciated by employees. In many cases, employers are required by law to offer certain health insurance and/or retirement benefits. Employers should consult with the appropriate local and state agencies to determine what rules apply given the size and nature of the organization.

Training Opportunities

As discussed earlier, some or all of the staff training sessions may be paid for by the employer. Whether or not training is viewed as a benefit depends upon the employee's attitude, company policy, and the quality and scheduling of the sessions. Well-run, valuable sessions may be appreciated by employees even if they have to pay part or all of the costs. They may consider being allowed to participate as a benefit of employment. On the other hand, less exciting sessions may be viewed as unpleasant additional burdens.

The activities themselves are ongoing "training sessions" for the leaders. For many, the opportunity to improve activity and leadership skills is a prime motivator and benefit of employment. By providing an occasional training

session, clinic or seminar, the employer can help maintain enthusiasm for learning. It is a good idea to encourage post-trip meetings of groups and leaders, wherein the leaders can solicit feedback from the participants. It is especially useful to follow the full group post-trip meetings with a leaders-only meeting, to allow uninhibited exchange of ideas and constructive criticism. Such meetings can be of great value in upgrading program quality, leadership ability, esprit de corp and job satisfaction.

Equipment, Food, and Transportation

Most outdoor pursuits are highly gear intensive, and most take place at some distance from town. Gear, food, and transportation are all potential employee benefits. There is great variation in the way these items are dealt with in different programs. Transportation to and from the outing site is almost always provided at no cost to the leader. When carpools are used, the leader is compensated fully for use of his/her vehicle, or rides in someone else's vehicle at no cost, with expenses picked up by the program or by the pool of participants. Gear is sometimes provided. For example, ropes, carabiners, helmets, and other specialized gear are almost always provided for rock climbing and mountaineering participants and leaders. Backpacking leaders may be offered a backpack, tent, sleeping bag, and stove. Equipment is usually provided when it is clearly needed by the leader in order to conduct the course, or when the leader will be working enough to incur significant wear and tear on personal equipment. Such equipment usually is not considered employee property, and remains with the company on termination of the employee. Sometimes, when it is not needed by the program, gear belonging to the organization may be borrowed by employees. While appreciated by employees, this can be a costly "can of worms" for the employers. The practice is not recommended unless strict guidelines are applied.

Clothing is rarely provided. Even when uniforms are required, as is common in ski schools, for example, special group or even wholesale prices may be arranged, but the costs are paid by the employee. The clothing is maintained by the employee and is retained as personal property once employment has ended. There are exceptions to the rule, especially when a uniform is distinctly marked and cannot be modified for "civilian" use. Such clothing may be paid fully or in part by the employer and is kept by the employer for reuse by new employees.

Some programs provide the leaders' food. As a general rule, if the program provides the food for the participants, the leaders are provided with food as well. In such cases, leader food is a benefit paid for out of the program budget. When food is not provided for participants, it is not usually provided for leaders. Compensation may be provided in the form of a "per diem" allotment to cover food costs, or no compensation may be provided based upon the rationale that the leader would have to provide his/her own food in town anyway.

Recognition and Praise

Everyone appreciates a pat on the back. Recognition of work well-done can take many forms, from informal comments to formal presentation of awards. Exceptional or newsworthy accomplishments by staff may be showcased on bulletin boards, in newsletters, in local newspapers, or, in some cases, on television. Many outdoor pursuits activities have exciting visual potential. Often a local TV station can be enticed into doing a human interest or sport story featuring an outstanding employee or program.

Other Compensation

Some of the most obvious employee benefits are often forgotten. It might be worthwhile to review the section on the values of outdoor pursuits, in Chapter One. The physical, philosophical and aesthetic benefits that attract participants to outdoor pursuits are no less attractive to leaders. At least when the weather is good and all is going well, many an outdoor leader has secretly chuckled at the thought that he/she is being paid to do what others must pay to do!

Volunteer Benefits

Essentially all of the benefits available to paid employees are available to volunteers, except, of course, money. In many cases, volunteers can claim a "benefit" not available to paid personnel. Many extremely valuable programs and services simply could not exist without volunteers. In such cases, volunteers can rightfully feel proud, as they are unselfishly helping others by providing services and skills that would otherwise be unavailable.

It is important to appreciate volunteers as individuals, and to understand their particular needs and motives for wanting to serve. It is also important to maintain a clear focus on the needs of the program, in particular vis-à-vis program safety and quality. It may be tempting to try to accommodate an enthusiastic volunteer when in fact there is no real need for that individual's particular set of talents. In the long run, it is always best to maintain high standards and expectations for performance. Whether paid or not, staff morale is very much determined by the extent to which there is a real basis for pride in the quality of the program. Like paid personnel, volunteers appreciate clear definitions of responsibility, ongoing feedback, and recognition for their accomplishments.

Supervision of Staff

Leadership is probably the single most important factor in the success of an outdoor recreation program. For this reason, an outdoor-recreation administrator should spend the majority of his/her time working with, and for, the leaders of the program.

Leaders are a resource, and what a program receives from this resource may depend entirely, on the administration and the supervisor.

The key is good supervision. Many times, it seems that a supervisor in actuality becomes a "snoopervisor," which in general fouls communications and inadvertently has a bad effect on the program. Among all personnel, rapport should be such that there is little change in the program (or the leader's feelings) when supervisory/administrative persons are at the site. Too often, supervisors are looking only for what is wrong rather than what is right.

In an age when there is the perception of "administration pollution," there are always persons who appear (in an effort to show their importance) to question each small facet of a program. This action, commonly called "nitpicking," is one of the best ways of robbing leadership of the enthusiasm and resourcefulness which are so necessary to outdoor programming.

By nature, outdoor leaders are individualists. This is good. In the outdoors, these leaders have learned to be self-reliant; they have tasted the freedom and naturalness of the nonsynthetic world. When a leader is confronted by an administrator who appears to speak only from books, the leader may lose his/her drive and enthusiasm about the program very quickly. When people are hired to do jobs, they should be allowed to perform them. They need administrative support and supervision but, assuming that qualified leaders were hired in the first place, they should need little or no administrative interference.

Scheduling

Scheduling refers here to the process of setting dates and times for activities and events. Agendas, as specific plans for the content and timing of meetings, outings and events, are discussed in the section on tactical planning in Chapter Fifteen. Scheduling is critically important to the success of any program. Outdoor pursuits are, in general, very time intensive. Participants must find room in their personal schedules for pre-trip meetings, acquisition and preparation of clothing and equipment, outings, post-outing repairs, cleaning, and storage. Planners must be highly sensitive to the lifestyle and preferences of potential participants. Vacation patterns, school calendars, work schedules, and potentially competitive, or conflicting, events have to be assessed and considered. The situation is compounded by resource access. River levels, snow levels, road conditions, weather conditions, usage levels, management controls, and permit stipulations are only some of the considerations surrounding access to resource

lands and waters. As if this isn't enough confusion, there must be enough qualified staff available, and facilities, transportation, and lodging must be available. The scheduler must often juggle half a dozen variables when seeking the best possible time for a given event or activity.

Most outdoor pursuits, as leisure activities, must be scheduled at times that do not conflict with, or interfere least with, those activities and responsibilities that a given participant sees as obligations. For this reason, unless the prospective clients are retired, longer events or activities must be scheduled during vacation periods. Short excursions may be scheduled on weekends, or during the summer, for students and many teachers and faculty. Meetings or other in-town events are generally held on week nights, as staff are often busy leading field excursions on weekends. There is no one best evening. Monday through Thursday evenings are the most frequently used for classes and meetings, with Friday and Saturday evenings customarily committed to social events. Thus, a purely social, recreational event usually has a better chance of success on a Friday or Saturday evening than on an earlier night, while a clinic, course or business meeting is not likely to go over well on either Friday or Saturday evening. For various reasons (such as religious observances, family activities, school work, and relaxation), Sunday evening is rarely used for any kind of meeting. There is a general reluctance to commit the last evening of the weekend to any structured event.

If participants may have a need for, or interest in, more than one activity, this must be considered when setting the order in which events will occur. Failure to do so inhibits the participant's ability to enroll in multiple events, and so reduces enrollment potentials for the sponsor. For example, in a large program with multiple offerings, a beginning backpacking outing should be scheduled before an intermediate backpacking meeting, and ideally before any other outings for which the beginning backpacking outing is a prerequisite. The timing is important, as well as the sequence. It is best, for example, to leave at least one or two weekends between two outings in a sequence, since few people can schedule two weekends "back-to-back." Especially when the activity is physically or psychologically demanding, it is important to give the participant a chance to rest, recover, reorganize gear, get caught up on chores, and become mentally ready for a new adventure.

Evening preparatory sessions should be scheduled far enough in advance of an event so that everyone has an opportunity to do whatever is necessary prior to the event, be it studying, exercising, skill practice, gear acquisition, or breaking in a new pair of boots. Meeting times set too early interfere with evening meals, but meetings set too late may be unproductive, because retention diminishes as people tire. Most evening meetings are scheduled to start between 6:30 and 7:30 p.m., and usually last no longer than two hours. It is often best to limit the total number of sessions by extending them as much as possible. For example, it is usually easier and more efficient for both the instructor and the participants to schedule two long evenings than four short evenings. Beginning instructors are invariably amazed by how long it takes to cover what may seem like a short list of topics. Even experienced and efficient instructors usually prefer having several hours with a group before heading for the field. Nevertheless, keep the attention spans and personal time constraints of participants in mind. If a meeting is scheduled for two hours or more, it is likely that some people will avoid it altogether, and it takes a particularly adept instructor to maintain the interest and attention of any audience for that long.

Registration

Registration, the enrollment or "signing up" of clients, is an integral part of any program. It is important from a business and clerical perspective; it influences client attitudes towards the program; and it can represent a major cost in both time and money. From a business perspective, registration is generally the point at which fees are paid or at least committed to by the clients. It is at this point, if not before, that clients need to be made aware of any and all terms and conditions related to payment. In essence, this is the point at which a contractual agreement is being struck between the sponsor and client. As in any contract, it is wise to have the particulars reduced to writing. Figure 11.4 illustrates a typical registration form.

Registration is usually accomplished, by telephone, by mail, or in person. Each has its advantages, and, in some cases, it may be best to use a combination of approaches. Normally, the choice is based upon a desire to maximize the number of clients given the resources available. Many small businesses utilize all three methods, allowing clients to enter the program by whatever means is most convenient for them. Usually at least some exchange of paperwork is necessary, by mail or personal contact. Large institutions, such as colleges and community recreation departments that provide multiple offerings to people living in a limited geographic area, may conduct a well-advertised "arena" registration at a centrally located facility.

The following suggestions may help. Remember that whichever techniques are used, a friendly and professional approach, well-designed forms, and carefully written documents pay dividends in efficient and, most importantly, in client perceptions of the program.

Telephone registration is becoming increasingly popular, due to improved technology. Incoming WATS, "800" service, FAX machines, and a host of computerized telephone enhancements and services have increased the efficiency and, at least for clients, made telephone use more attractive. Many large institutions employ sophisticated interactive systems that allow the caller to "punch in" codes on a touch-tone telephone, and even to pay using various credit cards. Such systems can often keep track of group sizes, limit enrollments, and convey prerecorded messages in response to preestablished caller input. While highly efficient for some applications, these "high tech" systems lack the important element of real-human intervention. In normal telephone registration, the caller can speak to someone who can, ideally, answer questions and perhaps allay some anxiety. A good "fit" between clients and programs is essential, and there is no good substitute for conversation with a knowledgeable person. Usually,

---

FIGURE 11.4   An Example of a Registration Form

Name: _____ Age: _____ Gender: _____

Address: _____
      #   street   city   state   zip code

Phone (home): _____ Phone (work): _____

Class Name	Dates	Times	Place	Instructor	Class Fee

Total Due: _____ Amount Paid: _____ (cash, check, or charge): _____

Balance Due: _____

SIGNATURE: _____ DATE: _____

SIGNATURE: _____
               (parent or guardian if under 18)

---

a phone call only serves to reserve a place in an activity, and it must be followed by an exchange of paperwork in the mail unless the person can come to the office within a day or two. Even when the call taker is highly knowledgeable and able to answer the caller's questions fully, it is important to provide the vital information in written form.

Registration by mail may be initiated by the client, for example, by sending registration forms clipped from a local newspaper, along with payment. More often than not, it is initiated by the sponsor in response to the client's telephone call or letter of inquiry. Mail-in registrations can be costly if not arranged carefully, in part because of the delay inherent in mailings. Hopefully, bulk mailing rates can help keep costs down in large programs.

Registration in person, whether one at a time or in an arena with several hundred people, offers the best chance to ensure that the client knows exactly for what he/she is signing up. It also gives the staff a chance to assess the client more effectively, and saves postage and telephone costs. One-to-one contracts are ideal from a communication standpoint, if the sponsor's representative is thoroughly knowledgeable. On the other hand, such contacts are very inefficient for other than very small programs, as similar messages and processes must be repeated at considerable expense in time. At the opposite extreme, mass registration is very efficient in terms of time spent per client, at the expense of disallowing relaxed and thorough discussion of issues. If the large group registration session is for closely related activities, it may be possible to begin the session with program descriptions and a question and answer period. In a diverse program, any discussion would have to be limited to common issues and registration procedures. The components of a successful arena registration are (1) adequate numbers of registrars, (2) availability of information (it must be possible to answer all important questions quickly), and (3) simplicity.

One tempting way to avoid long lines is to provide a form for each potential client, on which they can record their name, address, phone number, and any other necessary information, and list the courses, activities, or events in which they wish to register. The problem with this system involves the inadequacy to monitor enrollments; some people would leave thinking they are enrolled, when in fact the offering was full. Having people sign up for specific activities takes somewhat more time, but it allows those who are unable to enroll in a given activity the chance to select an alternative activity in which space is still available.

In this process, time can be saved by using the form mentioned above so that the client doesn't need to record the data repeatedly should he/she enroll in more than one activity. Registrars for each activity can initial the form and note the activity and fee, for assessment and payment or billing at a separate desk. Statements of terms and conditions, activity descriptions, schedules of events, agendas, health forms, releases and acknowledgements of risks, parent/guardian release forms, and a clear statement of refund policies should be provided to each participant at this point.

Whatever technique is used for registration, it is important to gather enough information to serve the needs of the client and of the program. In addition to the obvious information (name, address, and home and work telephone numbers), it may also be useful to record the client's date of birth, social security and driver's license numbers. Parent or guardian and/or emergency contact information is handy to have in the registration files, even if it is also included on the health form.

For most organizations, the greatest challenge is that of drawing in enough clientele. For this reason, it is very helpful to know how the client initially learned of the program and to know as much as possible about what inspired participation. Such information is invaluable in planning future marketing schemes. Knowing the person's age and specific interests can help when planning programs and in targeting mailings or other marketing schemes.

Registration does not guarantee that the enrollee will participate. As anyone who has ever arranged group events is all too aware, it is common for people to sign up and then not participate. The range of reasons runs from illness or accident to unpredictable time conflicts to loss of interest, excess anxiety, or forgetfulness, to name just a few possibilities. The result can be unnecessarily costly and frustrating unless care is taken to establish fair policies and convey them in writing to clients in advance of registration. There are two principal areas of concern. The issue of most immediate interest to the nonparticipant, and to the organization as well, is the fee. There are many possible schemes for determining what portion of the fee, if any, will be refunded. Most organizations establish a schedule of refunds based upon the time of leaving the program and the reasons for leaving. Whatever schedule is applied, it is far easier and more comfortable for the organization to hold a deposit or part of a fee if the client was warned, in writing, at registration.

The second area of concern is the possibility of potential client loss in the program, activity, or event. Although little can be done about this at the last moment before an outing or once well into a progression, it may be possible to enroll someone else to fill the vacant place if the absence occurs very early in the program. Care must be taken, however, to avoid adding someone who will be handicapped or less safe due to having missed one or more meetings, lessons, or training sessions. One way to avoid wasting a space is to maintain a "waiting list" of potential alternative participants. When the first meeting of a program is mandatory or very important, those on the waiting list may be required to attend. Absentees may then be replaced immediately from among the alternates in attendance. This is an especially useful tactic in the realm of outdoor pursuits, wherein the material addressed in pre-outing sessions is important to safety, and being part of the program from the beginning helps the participant develop a sense of full membership in the group enterprise. This, of course, is not feasible in the program where clients come from many widely separated geographical areas.

Budgeting

Needless to say, every agency, organization, or business is different in regards to the structure and dimensions of its budget. Furthermore, while the owner/operator of a small guide service must, of necessity, be in complete control of his/her budget, a leader (or even administrator) of programs imbedded in large institutional structures may have little knowledge, much less control, of the budget. The small business operator would probably like to spend less energy dealing with finances and more time doing other more appealing tasks, while those at the other extreme may be frustrated by the lack of understanding and control. At least a partial solution for both sets of people may be to conduct a careful review of the existing budget, using as many sources of information as possible, while being as objective as possible.

Budget planning is usually too complex to do strictly in one's head. It is not unusual to see budgets for modest programs that occupy several pages. Having a written budget is very useful from a planning perspective, and a post-event budget summary is an invaluable aid in accounting for expenses, tax form preparation, and in planning similar future events. When constructing a budget form, consider the various end uses of the information, including the requirements of accountants, the IRS and other taxing entities, and utility for future planning. Especially for the small business, a well-constructed form can save precious time. Many computer software manufacturers make programs that are specially designed for these purposes, and most good spreadsheet programs can be used to create budget plans that are easy to use. Such programs are especially handy for planning, as predictions can be entered easily, with almost instantaneous display of "bottom lines." All such programs also allow quick and easy generation of hard copies, and many have interactive word processing capability so that the budget may be modified and included directly in reports.

Data base programs are particularly useful for keeping track of purchases and expenses, especially when there are many expenditures over the fiscal or tax year. Data bases allow each entry to be described, dated, and coded so that each category of expense can be separated, totalled, and printed out in a few minutes.

There are many expenses that might be incurred in operating an outdoor recreation business. The following list is not all inclusive, and, for any given business, some items may not apply. Small business operators especially may find it convenient to list or group the various items in a way that is compatible with the requirements and forms of the IRS or other taxing entities. Note that in some cases (such as for a facility), the expense listed for a particular program may represent only a portion of the actual facility's expenses, or none at all, depending upon the extent to which the program is expected to share the burden of those expenses.

A Sample of Possible Business Expenses

1. Salaries
   Administrative
   Staff
       Full-time
       Part-time
   Secretarial
   Contracted
   Other (lawyers, CPAs)
2. Taxes
3. Withholding
   Federal
   State
   Local
   FICA (social security)
4. Insurance
   Workman's Compensation
   State Accident
   Business liability, property
   Employee liability, accident
   Volunteer liability, accident
   Participant, accident
5. Facilities
   Buildings and offices
   Pools and recreational facilities
   Maintenance and supplies
6. Utilities

7. Office Expenses
   Telephone
   Postage
   Printing
   Supplies
   Equipment
8. Marketing and Promotion
   Advertisements
   Materials
9. Equipment
   Purchase
   Rental
   Maintenance and repair
   Replacement
10. Publications
    Trade journals and magazines
    Books and reference materials
    Maps
11. Transportation
    Licenses
    Purchase of vehicles
    Rental of vehicles
    Tickets and fares
    Safety equipment
    Maintenance and repairs
    Vehicle replacement
    Gas and oil, etc.
    Tolls and fares
12. Accommodations or Resources
    Lodging and campsite
    User and access fees
13. Food
    Staff
    Participant
14. Miscellaneous expenses
    Incidental costs
    First aid materials
    Refunds

Other possible expense categories include livestock, capital improvement, and investments.

Income may come from a number of sources. In a small business, the situation is often very simple in that income may come only from client fees. In larger private organizations and in public institutions, income may also be derived from several sources. The income side of the ledger may be quite simple or may be set up as follows:

1. Investment
2. Fees
3. Sales
4. Refunds or rebates from manufacturers
5. Gifts
6. Grants
7. Donations

In the most simplistic sense, the "bottom line" can be calculated by subtracting the sum of all expenses from the total revenue, taking care to account for any refunds or other hidden variances. In practice, however, it is not always easy to interpret the "bottom line" in a budget, especially when its scope includes overhead costs and other expenses not directly incurred in carrying out the event or program. In setting up the initial budget, it is recommended that both small and large organizations seek the aid of qualified tax consultants. Even if the taxes are subsequently calculated by the program administrator, advice is usually necessary to determine deductions, expenses, "costs of doing business," overhead, and other items that may vary from case to case. Then the real situation can be grasped, and the true effects of changes in fees, income, or expenses can be comprehended. As a final thought, remember that a budget is a plan that may need to be modified. Anyone who has ever planned as simple a venture as a weekend at the beach (or even a trip to the market!) knows that it is wise to plan for contingencies.

Evaluation

Every program has goals or objectives, whether or not they are formally documented. Evaluation is the process of assessing the extent to which objectives were achieved and goals were approached. Evaluation may be formal or informal. Informal evaluation occurs throughout the program, as leaders and staff interact with the participants and observe their responses to each activity, event, or experience. Discussions of these observations at staff meetings can generate ideas for program improvement and reinforce effective elements of the program. Formal evaluation processes include the use of evaluation forms and structured discussions. See Figures 11.5, 11.6 (page 238), and 11.7 (page 239). In every case, it is important to solicit the views of the leaders, staff, administrators as well as the views of the participants.

Few programs are driven solely by participant interests. While participant satisfaction is almost always an important consideration, in many cases there are program goals, objectives, policies, and philosophical directives that must also be weighed heavily even though they may be at odds with attainment of maximal immediate enjoyment by participants. This is common in programs that have educational or therapeutic objectives, wherein the success of a program

may be measured in terms of institutional perceptions of what best serves the long-term interests of the participants. If the participant is unaware of or unable to recognize and appreciate the long-term benefits of an experience, he/she may be less satisfied with the program. Thus, an administrator or leader might evaluate a program as having been highly successful, while a participant might express serious reservations. For example, an overnight camping trip with a high school biology class might be judged wildly successful by the faculty if all of the teaching objectives seemed to have been met, and the students learned basic camping skills. Some of the students, however, might regard the outing

---

FIGURE 11.5   Outdoor Recreation Program Evaluation Form

ACTIVITY: _____

DATE: _____

We appreciate your comments. With your help and input, we can make improvements in our program.

1. Did you enjoy the program? yes ____ no ____
   Comments: _____

2. Did the program fulfill your expectations? yes ____ no ____
   Comments: _____

3. Please indicate your response below:

	EXCELLENT	GOOD	FAIR
Leader's knowledge of the material			
Leader's skill in activity			
Leader's teaching ability			
Location of activity			
Pace or speed of activity			
Length of program			

   Comments: _____

4. How did you hear about this program? _____

5. Would you recommend this program to a friend? yes ____ no ____
   Because: _____

6. Other comments: _____

7. Ideas for future trips? _____

FIGURE 11.6   Outing/Clinic Evaluation Form

OUTING/CLINIC TITLE: _____

DATE: _____   SEX: M ___ F ___

Please help to improve the quality of our program by filling out the evaluation form and turning it in to a staff member. Thank you.

Please rate the Outing/Clinic from EXCELLENT (5) to POOR (1)

Instructors:

	5	4	3	2	1
Knowledge and skill level _____					
Teaching ability_____					
Organization and efficiency _____					
Attitude towards participants _____					
Overall rating_____					

Comments:_____

_____

Overall Program:

	5	4	3	2	1
Pre-trip information _____					
Travel arrangements _____					
Accommodations (if applicable)_____					
Overall rating _____					

Comments:_____

_____

as a total failure, having had no chance to swim, little free time, and not enough bug repellant. Both viewpoints are important and should be taken seriously. This situation is not unusual, and it points to a need for better communication between, in this case, the faculty and students.

Poor evaluations by participants result when the experience did not meet their expectations. Poor evaluations by representatives of the organization result when objectives, which represent the expectation of the organization, are not achieved. When the perceptions of participants vary markedly from the perceptions of administrators, leaders, and staff, the usual cause is poor communication in the initial phases of the program. Good, early exchange of ideas can create realistic expectations by either changing participant preconceptions or by inspiring more realistic goals and objectives. Careful analysis

of input from all sources may identify ways in which the objectives may be modified without diminishing their value, or ways of achieving exciting objectives, so that participant satisfaction is increased without reducing the overall value of the program.

Open evaluation processes lead to better programs, and, perhaps even more important, to a sense of involvement, personal respect, power, and control by all who contribute. Too often, administrators, leaders, and staff all dread the evaluation process. Having invested time and energy in designing and carrying out a program, it is only natural for the planners to wish for total success and, at the same time, to fear failure. Negative evaluations imply failure— and that hurts. Most people thrive on praise and dislike criticism in any form. Administrators don't like to hear that the goals and objectives

FIGURE 11.7   Class Evaluation Form

NAME OF CLASS _____

INSTRUCTOR _____ DATE_____

Put a circle around the word that represents your objective judgment of the course or the instructor. Your response is confidential. A summary of all student evaluations in this class will be provided to the instructor.

1. Instructor's interest and enthusiasm for teaching the course

poor	fair	good	very good	excellent

seems personally uninterested; does not inspire learning	*moderately interested and enthusiastic; not especially stimulating*	*has sustained interest & enthusiasm for the course*

2. Preparation for class periods

poor	fair	good	very good	excellent

preparation usually haphazard	*usually well prepared*	*always well prepared*

3. Organization of the course

poor	fair	good	very good	excellent

little or no evident organization	*well organized but room for improvement*	*very well organized from start to finish*

4. Presentation of subject matter

poor	fair	good	very good	excellent

students bored; haphazard use of class time; voice and expression are inadequate	*keeps students interested; voice clear and expression distinct; class time well used*

5. Attitude toward students

poor	fair	good	very good	excellent

shows no personal interest in students; indifferent	*friendly, courteous and considerate*

6. Course objective: What to learn was clear

poor	fair	good	very good	excellent

no attempt was made to define course objectives	*objectives were clear from the beginning*

7. General ratings of the course

poor	fair	good	very good	excellent

learned very little	*good solid course; I learned much*

8. General rating of the instructor

poor	fair	good	very good	excellent

not bad, but could be better	*an exceptionally good teacher*

9. Facilities

poor	fair	good	very good	excellent

facilities were not appropriate	*adequate*	*facilities were suited for this particular class*

Comments: (On the back please comment on significant strengths and weaknesses of the course. How can this course be improved?)

they established were not appropriate, or that their planning was inadequate. Leaders and staff don't like to learn that certain activities were not successful, or that their leadership was flawed. It is well to remember, however, that (1) it is simply not possible to please everyone equally in any group situation, and (2) criticism is free advice. The advice may or may not be good advice, but the price is right!

Whether or not a program is successful in the long run is usually dependant upon the quality and value of the services that are delivered. Definitions and perceptions of quality and worth change constantly, so the successful program must be continually assessed and adjusted. A team approach can help administrators, leaders, and staff maximize program potential and minimize unnecessary anxiety. The keys to success are mutual respect and understanding and a sense of common purpose. Mutual respect and understanding are grounded in good communications, and one of the best ways to facilitate communication is for a key member of the team to take the lead.

For example, an administrator might begin a post-trip evaluation session by saying, "Let's see what we can do to improve next month's program. It seems from the evaluations that some of the objectives I set need to be changed or tossed out altogether. Can you help me?" This sets a tone that is conducive to constructive action. In such an atmosphere, the leader whose teaching style has been criticized may feel comfortable asking for advice. In a post-trip session with participants, informal group evaluation can be instigated by the leader, who might say to the group, "Let's talk about how the trip went for you. We want to do a better job for the next group, so you can do us, and the next participants, a big favor by giving us your honest appraisal of your experience."

It is often useful to focus discussions first on general issues, such as the location and agenda, then on the leadership. It is particularly valuable, if time allows, to focus one by one on the leaders in order to extract as much feedback as possible. By making it clear that every staff member, including the leader, is still learning, more direct and honest feedback is encouraged. To facilitate free exchange of ideas, the listeners

should take care to avoid defensive responses, but rather to express appreciation for the advice or idea. Later, after all of the group members have had a chance to speak freely, the staff may wish to explain why a particular action was taken, but this should be done only when necessary to correct serious misunderstandings on the part of the group. The post activity evaluation process is invaluable to the leader as well as to the organization, which benefits from the development of leader competence. Written evaluations can be used and are especially valuable when employed in conjunction with the verbal evaluations of the post-trip meeting process.

Ideally, the evaluation process should include post-trip verbal discussion by the group, written evaluations by group members, verbal discussion in a leaders-only post-trip meeting, and written evaluations of each leader. By "leader" we refer here to anyone who participated in a leadership capacity, including leaders, assistant leaders, drivers, and any other involved staff. For example, leaders and assistant leaders in a program may participate in group post-trip evaluations, meet in a leaders-only session to provide intensive feedback for every leader, and then receive a written evaluation from each head leader. Figure 11.8 is an example of a form for leader "peer evaluation" that includes both structured and open-ended elements.

The leaders are asked to arrive at the leader meeting with written evaluations of every leader with whom they worked. Distributing these evaluations after, rather than before or during, the meeting, facilitates communication by avoiding the tendency of leaders to become fixated on topics and issues in the written evaluation.

Post-trip leader meetings are discussed in greater detail under the section on bringing closure in Chapter Sixteen, "Leadership in the Field."

Program and leader evaluation requires a significant commitment of time and energy at a point when it is tempting to put the past behind and to focus upon immediate and future needs. Experienced administrators and leaders know, however, that the rewards of regular, thorough evaluation far outweigh the costs.

FIGURE 11.8   Post-Activity Leadership Evaluation Form

Activity:_____ Date of Activity:_____
Date of Evaluation: _____
Evaluator: _____ Evaluator's Position:_____
Subject: _____ Subject's Position:_____

OBJECTIVE   EVALUATION:

POINTS

Subject's:	1	2	3	4	5
1. Skill level in the activity					
2. Experience/general knowledge of activity					
3. Physical condition/ fitness					
4. Appropriateness of, and use of clothing and equipment					
5. Performance of assigned tasks					
6. Teaching and communication skills					
7. Apparent judgment and maturity					
8. Initiative and energy level					
9. Performance under stress					
10. Quality of summary write-up					

Rating System:
1 = Inadequate for leadership of this activity
2 = Adequate for leadership of this activity at assistant leader level
3 = Adequate for leadership of this activity at leader level
4 = Excellent and consistent with highest professional standards
NA = Insufficient basis for estimating competence or performance

SUBJECTIVE   EVALUATION: _____
_____
_____
_____
_____

Note:
The purpose of this evaluation is to provide any and all insights that could be of value to the leader. Please be as direct and honest as you would appreciate in an evaluation of yourself!

Summary

Basic administrative functions include programming, staffing, scheduling, registration, budgeting, and evaluation. Those considering administrative aspects of the outdoor pursuits field will be called upon to be familiar with the details of each of these topics and to be able to plan and modify them concurrently. Programming functions include developing various goals and objectives, incorporating various program formats, and following both individual-centered and group-centered principles. Staffing includes developing job descriptions and announcements, and locating, assessing, training, supervising, and compensating staff. The processes of scheduling and registration include many activities designed for the convenience of potential participants as they make arrangements to enroll in the outdoor pursuits program. Budgeting is a plan for income and expenses designed to result in an even financial balance or

a net gain for the organization. Evaluation of
the program from the point of view of both the
participant and the organization is a process of
documenting the extent to which the objectives
were achieved and the goals approached. These
administrative functions are basic to the operation of any outdoor enterprise.

References

Culkin, D. F., & Kirsch, S. L. (1986). *Managing human resources in recreation, parks
and leisure services.* New York, NY:
Macmillan Publishing Co.

Curtis, J. E., & Kraus, R. G. (1986). *Creative
management in recreation, parks, and leisure services.* St. Louis, MO: Times, Mir-
ror/Mosby College Publishing Co.

Deppe, T. (1983). *Management strategies in
financing parks and recreation.* New York,
NY: John Wiley & Sons.

Edginton, C. R., Hanson, C. J., & Edginton, S.
R. (1992). *Leisure programming: Concepts, trends and professional practice.*
Dubuque, IA: William C. Brown Communications, Inc.

Farrell, P., & Lundegren, H. M. (1991). *The
process of recreation programming:
Theory and technique (3rd ed.).* State College, PA: Venture Publishing, Inc.

Rossman, R. J. (1980). *Recreation programming: Designing leisure experiences.*
Champaign, IL: Sagamore Publishing Co.

LIABILITY, RISK MANAGEMENT AND INSURANCE

Liability, risk management, and insurance are of central importance to both administrators and leaders of outdoor pursuits. Both share the responsibility for the well-being of their clientele and thus should understand the legal context of their responsibility. Insurance acquisition is primarily an administrative function; however, liability and risk management are the concerns of both administrators and leaders. The risk management plan must be developed jointly and subsequently followed by the leaders. The topics of liability, risk management, and insurance are complex, and all three items have been combined into this chapter.

One of the reasons recreation administrators and some outdoor leaders choose not to offer activities such as canoeing, rafting, climbing, cross-country skiing, snowcamping, desert trips, ropes courses, and other events viewed as "risky" is a concern about accidents that may cause injury or death and subsequent litigation. In the United States, the practice of suing to recover money for actual damages is of concern to those offering activities that may appear to encompass an element of risk. At the onset of this chapter, it must be emphasized that, as providers of outdoor pursuit programs, our philosophical concern should be the welfare of the human beings entrusted to our care. We must recognize, however, that, in addition to our concern for the individual, there is another reason why we should be very careful to offer programs that encompass appropriate care. The possibility

of a lawsuit is a worrisome idea, in the least, and one that brings to mind the loss of hundreds of thousands of dollars, not to mention any anguish created by the possibility of being proven guilty of negligence.

It is a generally accepted tenet in most legal jurisdictions that no outdoor recreation program can be 100 percent safe, no matter how well it is run. Under certain circumstances the participants in an outdoor recreation activity may be expected to assume responsibility for some of the risks associated with their participation in the activity. In many parts of the world, including essentially all of Europe, all participants (except children and the mentally impaired) expect, and are expected, to assume much if not all of the risk except in extraordinary cases. In the United States, participants are far less likely to accept personal responsibility for their decisions and actions. In the United States, as in most countries, children under seven years of age rarely if ever assume any responsibility for the risks of participation. Seven- to fourteen-year-old youth in the U.S. may assume some risk, though rarely more than 20 percent. Fourteen- to twenty-one-year-old people are more likely to assume some part of the risk, and older persons are usually expected to assume part or, in very rare cases, all of the risk. In the United States, it is not unusual for adult participants to assume less than 50 percent of the risk, even when they were well-informed and/or acted irresponsibly.

Contributory negligence is a term that refers to the percentage by which awards may be reduced, based partly or solely upon the risk assumed by the participant. The courts might, for example, reduce a $100,000 award to $75,000, if the plaintiff was determined to have been 25 percent responsible; or in other words, to have assumed 25 percent of the risk. Even with such a reduced award for damages, no administrator wants to be involved in the anguish of a lawsuit with its accompanying publicity, time involved, loss of money, and damage to the organization's reputation.

If accidents can be lessened in both frequency and severity, it follows that there will be fewer lawsuits. With fewer lawsuits being fought, fewer suits will be lost, and less money will be due in damages. If the way to lessen accidents is through a well-developed and implemented risk management plan then every outdoor administrator and leader should consider it mandatory to develop risk management plans for every aspect of the program.

Defining risk management as wise fiscal management is, understandably, a valid approach. From a *philosophical* point of view, however, it may be stated that the *primary* purpose in risk management is the concern for the well-being of the participants and staff, while the *secondary* purpose is a concern for fiscal matters. Be that as it may, the elements of legal liability should be understood by all who undertake to lead others in any type of program.

While outdoor programmers should be concerned with all forms of legal liability, the type of liability related most to outdoor programs and the management of associated risks is "tort." A tort is a wrong doing against a person who suffers damages. While there are intentional torts (assault, fraud, slander, misrepresentation, etc.), the concern here is the *unintentional* tort. Unintentional torts are wrong doings based upon *negligence*. The actual damages may be paid by the wrongdoer to the one who was wronged.

In a court of law, in order to show that negligence occurred, the plaintiff must prove four elements:

1. A duty was owed. It must be shown first that the person(s) in charge (in this case, the administrator and the staff who directed the program) had the duty or responsibility to provide the participant with a safe environment and competent leadership. In any outdoor program with a designated leader, there is the responsibility to provide a safely operated program. This means a safe environment under normal conditions. One can never guarantee that there will not be unforeseen conditions such as July blizzards in areas normally above freezing or earthquakes in Michigan, but it does assume that the environment or situation will be as safe as is predictable. It can usually be assumed that *any* organization providing a recreational program owes the participants the duty of providing a safe environment and competent leadership.

2. The duty was breached. (There was a failure to perform this duty.) The plaintiff must show that the duty to provide the safe environment was breached by the leader (or administrator) who did not follow what the courts call a "standard of care."

3. There was resultant real injury or damage. If it can be shown that there was, in fact, a duty to provide a safe environment and that the duty was breached by the leader or administrator not following a standard of care, the plaintiff must then show that the failure to follow the standard of care was the proximate cause of the injury.

4. The injury actually resulted in damage of a nature serious enough to warrant the recovery of funds.

If these four elements can be proven, a defendant may be found guilty of negligence. In many cases, a jury decides the verdict. In the course of the defense, a risk management plan can be used to show how well the defendant followed the standard of care that is at issue in the second phase of the plaintiff's case.

Before discussing the standard of care and the development of the plan to manage the risks, it is advantageous to consider certain positive elements of risk and adventure activities. There is currently little information on the frequency of accidents in outdoor activities. All available sources tell us that the incidence of these accidents is minimal. In relation to accidents, injuries, and fatalities, three facts are known:

1. There is no evidence that outdoor recreational activities are inherently dangerous. The activity does not cause accidents; people cause the accidents. People in the wrong place, at the wrong time, with the wrong equipment, and/or making wrong decisions cause accidents.

2. People are risk takers. Individuals desire to test their skills, try new challenges, and have new adventures. Risk taking is found in all sorts of situations. There is probably less risk in terms of mental health in a whitewater trip than in accepting a new job. There is probably less physical risk in a canoeing trip than in driving a car. Outdoor participants are like everyone else; they will take risks.

Hans Selye, the Canadian psychiatrist, has written much on the aspects of positive stress (eustress). Stress that is self-imposed has a positive effect as it relieves boredom and increases the joy of living. Just participating in an outdoor activity in the first place may be an example of positive stress. With more opportunity for outdoor activities, more people will expose themselves to risk for the pure joy of it. The thrill of exploration by canoe, the exhilaration of paddling down a new river, and the feeling of accomplishment that follows the completion of a difficult climb are all the results of a natural inclination for risk and the accompanying eustress (positive stress). Unfortunately, there are times when some participants find that this positive stress turns into negative stress with resulting misadventure, accident, and even death. All leaders need to recognize the value of *perceived risk* while doing everything in their power to minimize *actual risk.*

Since it is recognized that people are risk takers who will try things without being aware of the risks, it becomes the responsibility of outdoor pursuit administrators and leaders to conduct activities wherein the risks are minimized and where self-imposed stress remains positive and beneficial. Responsible leaders teach the participants how to manage risks so

they can continue to participate in these outdoor recreation activities safely. They need skills to keep them from being in the wrong place at the wrong time with the wrong equipment and/or making wrong decisions long after they leave the sponsored programs.

3. In an outdoor pursuit program, as in any situation, the leaders are never guarantors or ensurers of safety. Unforeseen conditions, improper decisions, and/or improper behaviors on the part of the participants preclude guaranteed safety.

With the preceding three facts in mind, the tasks of the outdoor pursuit staff are managing risks and minimizing the possibility of accidents. By definition, a risk is a chance of encountering harm, injury, loss, hazard, or danger. Management refers to the act of controlling something. Thus, risk management is a control of injury, hazard, loss or danger. *A risk management plan is a set of regulations, policies, and procedures for conducting an activity that contains an inherent risk.*

Risk management is the responsibility of the leader of every program. While some activities have more potential for accidents than others and must be planned with extreme caution, there are potential hazards in nearly every program. The injury of a participant in the collapse of a broken chair or bench during a training session is of no less importance that the injury of a hiker who breaks a leg in a fall. As a matter of fact, in the former case, the responsibility was probably entirely that of the agency that permitted the use of faulty equipment (a weak chair). In the case of the hiker, it might be claimed that the participant contributed partly to the accident through improper behavior. It *may* be shown that the hiker was running down a steep hill contrary to instructions that warned against such behavior.

The management of risks is based upon the premise that people should be able to pursue their natural inclinations toward activities involving risk; however, the possibility of accidents resulting from such activities should be minimized through plans to control them. We might also agree that it is philosophically wrong to deny people the right to participate in activities of potential, yet controlled, risk. People want to test themselves, to move faster, to climb higher, to explore the unknown, to attempt the unattempted. No program should deny the participant the chance to succeed at what was not previously attempted or performed, as long as the activity is one that the program can offer competently. Every participant has the right to fail without serious physical, mental, or emotional consequences. Also inherent in that right is the right to try again. One goal of the participant is to have a positive experience. If the participant returns home unscathed and able to try again, it is relatively unimportant that the goals of achieving or mastering the skill were not reached.

"Comprehensive risk management planning" takes into account all aspects or elements of the activity, and results in clear, concise policies and directions for dealing with all foreseeable risks. These risks may result from individual elements or from the interaction of these elements. Of concern in a typical outdoor-pursuit activity are resource lands and facilities, the weather, access routes, transportation modes, group and individual equipment, and several categories of people who are directly or indirectly affected by the activity. These people include the public at-large (via taxes, insurance rates, associations with individuals directly involved in the activity, or an obligation to respond to an emergency, i.e., search and rescue teams), the public directly involved (co-users of the area or facility), land or facility managers, administrators and officials of the sponsoring agency, the staff and leaders of the activity, and, of course, the participants.

When people and resources interact, potential problems are created. The list of these problems is virtually endless; however, most can be contained in three categories: (1) injuries or health problems, (2) damage or loss to property or resources, or (3) failure to meet participant expectations. Accurate identification of potential problems and assessment of risks requires a thorough understanding of the site(s), the facilities and possible weather conditions, the activity to be pursued, and (too often minimized) the

goals, objectives, and limitations of the program, the leaders, and the participants. Developing effective policies and procedures for containing and minimizing these risks demands an awareness of applicable management regulations and laws and a sensitivity to social and legal conventions. In order to assure concern for the welfare of the participant, the risk management plan should be developed so that it gives evidence of an attempt to follow a "standard of care."

Standard of Care

When an individual accepts responsibility for leading a group, he/she is, in effect, declaring competence. Defining the term "competent" may appear to be difficult; however, in the courts of law in the United States, this competency is equated with that of a *reasonable and prudent professional who utilizes the best and most current professional practices.* A reasonable and prudent (or careful) professional, establishes what is known as a *standard of care.* In cases where litigation occurs and the leader(s) or administrator(s) are sued, the defense is made that the best standard of care was followed. In other words, in order to be judged as competent, the leader must show that a standard of care comparable with that of the best professional practices was followed.

For example, a mountaineering leader deciding between two routes may have good reason to regard both route "A" and route "B" as acceptably safe alternatives for the ascent of a peak. He/she may feel that route "A" is a slightly better route on that particular day. However, if the majority of local guides consider route "B" to be the safer route, the leader must weigh this fact very heavily before committing the group to route "A." If an accident should occur on route "A," the leader could face the additional burden of having to justify his/her decision. If the case should go to court, expert witnesses (professional guides and experienced climbers familiar with both routes) may be called in, and they would probably cite route "B" as the safer route. This would cast doubt on the performance of the leader and, thus, on the "standard of care" provided to the participants.

Careful and conservative leaders and administrators always consider, at *every* decision point, both the real risks *and* the implications of having to justify the decision before a panel of peers.

There are three major aspects of the standard of care: supervision, conducting the activity, and environmental understanding. A standard of care may be met by following the points made on the outline listed and explained below:

I. Supervision
   A. General Supervision
      1. Supervisory plan and number and location of supervisors
      2. Awareness of dangerous conditions
      3. Knowledge of first aid
   B. Specific Supervision
      1. Communication at level of participant
      2. Participant understands and adheres to safety practices
      3. Alert to changing conditions

II. Conducting the Activity
   A. Adequate Instructions and Progressions
   B. Understanding the Participants
      1. Age and size
      2. Skill and maturity
      3. Special conditions (mental, physical, etc.)
   C. Warning of Dangers and Mandating Use of Protective Devices

III. Understanding the Environment
   A. Equipment Checks
   B. Conditions Checks
      1. Man-made structures
      2. Natural hazards
   C. Layout and Design

If it can be shown that each of the above points was addressed and followed carefully, the leader has a better chance of proving competence than if there is no evidence that an attempt was made to adhere to them. Many times, there is no activity instruction involved; yet, the activities must be supervised. Supervision refers to monitoring the situation, regardless of instruction, while conducting the activity refers to the actual instruction and how the activities will be conducted. These components may be explained as follows:

Supervision

Supervision is divided into *A. General* and *B. Specific.* General Supervision requires three considerations:

1. Supervisory plan. The leader should have a written supervisory plan that includes an adequate number, placement, and qualifications of all the staff in each program or else a standard of care cannot be proven for the activity. Regardless of the activity, the administrator and leader have the responsibility to ascertain in advance the number and qualifications of all needed staff and to make it known to all in the group of where staff members will be located. It should be so clear that all the group members have equal opportunity to understand it.

On youth overnight trips, there should be one leader plus one extra for every eight campers (American Camping Association Standard) which calculates into two leaders for eight hikers and three for sixteen. Furthermore, there should be one person (perhaps a participant) designated as head of the line and another designated as tail of the line with all the others in between the head and tail. It means following Red Cross standards for the number of lifeguards and their positions near the swimming area. Leader/participant ratios for other activities are discussed in Chapter Seventeen, "Leadership of Selected Activities."

2. Awareness of dangerous conditions. The leader or program director must show that, for whatever would be considered "normal" dangerous conditions, there was thought and planning put into the activity. Is there an area of fast running water in the river? Is it tornado season? Are forest fires a possibility? Is there a drop-off in the water or a hidden stump? Avalanche possibility? Lack of water? All staff must be able to recognize dangerous conditions or signs of trouble and to report them correctly.

3. Knowledge of first aid. All leaders have the responsibility to know how to administer immediate first aid. There can be no time for looking things up in the book or guessing or hoping to remember. A standard of care assumes that the leader will have immediate recall of first aid needed for situations unique to the activity. The leader who does nothing may be as negligent as the one who acts rapidly but incorrectly. Swimming staff are expected to know CPR; trip leaders should also know about cuts, bruises, sprains, burns, insect bites, and most other injuries as well as emergency care in wilderness situations.

Under *Specific Supervision*, there are also three components of care:

1. Communicating at the level, and in the language of, the participant. This means that the leader must be able to relate to the age, intelligence, and language of the participant. Younger participants, beginners, and those who may be frightened or apprehensive need different explanations than those given to advanced groups. They may need to hear things several times; they may need a simpler vocabulary. It is the responsibility of the leaders to be sure that everyone in the group understands what is said. It should be so clear that afterward most of the participants in the group will agree consistently to what was said.

2. Participant understands and adheres to safety practices. The participant must understand what the safety practices are and why they are practiced that way. Clearly, the instructor must not ask the participant to do anything unreasonable and imprudent, nor to undertake any unreasonable risk or exposure to foreseeable harm. If the participant is told not to swim at night, the reason for not swimming at night (unless in a lighted pool) must be given. (People can understand that it is difficult to see a swimmer in trouble in the dark, but they may not realize that depth perception is lost in the darkness, and things are further away than they seem to be.) If participants are to adhere to the safety practices, it should be with the understanding

of the reasons behind them. If they don't understand while under the supervision of a sponsored program, they may never understand when out on their own!

3. Be alert to changing conditions. This refers to changing conditions in the participant. Fear, fatigue, the onset of hypothermia, unsafe practices, and skills which are too advanced for the participants are but some of the conditions all staff must be able to recognize. Plans should be made in advance for frequent rest, early stops, and for changes in the route if the condition of any participant indicates the necessity of such decisions. Psychological, physical, and mental conditions often change without warning. The leader should be aware of all possibilities and make plans accordingly and then implement the plans when necessary. On a trip, what does one do when a participant becomes ill? Or when a leaking canoe soaks all paddlers to the bone? Leaders must anticipate the possibilities and plan for them.

Conducting the Activity

Conducting the activity covers three areas:

A. *Adequate instructions and progressions.* This means that the leader/instructor must know not only how to perform the skill to be taught but how to analyze the skill in terms of its component parts in order to help the participant move from the simple to the complex, from the basic to the advanced, along logical progressions that are within his/her ability. For example, a cross-country skiing instructor should teach the participant how to put on the equipment and how to do some "in place" movements such as getting up from a simple fall, before teaching the skills that result in falls. Instructors should be familiar with the current literature of their field to keep current with the latest thinking on the teaching of special activity skills. The agency or leader without ready access to reference books on their specific outdoor activity may have trouble validating that the staff had adequate information on instructing that activity.

Not only must the leader be able to teach the skills in logical progression, he/she must be able to modify the plans to meet the age, skill, experience, and maturity of the participant. Here, maturity refers to both chronological maturity and maturity in terms of knowledge of the activity. The 12-year-old who has gone on a series of well-led backpack trips is likely to be more mature in backpacking than a 50-year-old who has never been on a hiking trail.

B. *Understanding the participants* is broken into understanding the age, size, skill, maturity, and the special conditions of every participant. The tall leader needs to realize that the short climber or trail user cannot place his/her feet on the same spots that the leader uses. The very young hiker or paddler may have much more initial energy than the older one who may, in turn, have more endurance than the younger one. The words of encouragement used for the seven-year-old will differ from those used for the 17-year-old or the adult of 67. The obese participant may not have the energy to move as rapidly as those who have less body weight to carry. Beginners must be made to feel that they are able to learn new skills regardless of age. There is a different plan of instruction to be undertaken with the novice and with the expert. The inexperienced do not perform in the same manner as the experienced. The leader who forgets that the task is to teach people—not activities—is not acting as a reasonable and prudent professional. Furthermore, the group may include several individuals with either physical or mental disabilities that require modification of the activity and of the instruction.

C. *Warning of dangers and mandating use of protective devices and practices.* The participant may not understand the dangers and potential consequences of incorrect performance regardless of the earlier mentioned instruction concerning safety practices. It is the leader's responsibility to explain all potential risks and consequences in a clear manner and insist on proper behavior from the participants.

Certain clothing or protective devices, such as helmets, personal flotation devices, or rain gear, may be required. If the gear is needed for safety, the leader has little choice but to be autocratic, to make no exceptions, and to refuse to permit those without proper gear to participate. In the adherence to a standard of care, there is no room for group decisions related to protective devices and practices. In the interest of performing at an acceptable standard of care, the leader is justified in excluding those without proper equipment from participating in the activity. It is not enough for the leader to suggest the use of equipment that is considered essential for safety; such items must be required, and all participants must be checked to be sure that all such items are present, in good condition, and used properly.

Understanding the Environment

Understanding the environment refers to both the natural and the man-made environment.

A. *Equipment checks* must be made on vehicles used for transportation and on all "man-made" equipment. In essence, every piece of equipment used should be checked for good condition before it is used. Equipment must be appropriate for the size and experience of the camper. The right size paddle and flotation device, the tent that doesn't leak, the stove that must be clean and in excellent operating condition are but four examples.

An assessment of gear would probably begin with a review of the program's written gear requirements list and policies. Every program should have, *on hand*, clear and specific lists of the clothing and equipment required of participants in each activity, as well as supplemental lists of gear required for leaders of each activity. While an essential starting point is a well-thought out list, such lists are of little or no value if, in practice, they are not adhered to. In a postaccident review, one of the first things an investigator may do is try to learn exactly what gear was actually on-site.

All too often the leader fails to enforce gear requirements effectively, leaving the participant less protected and the leader and program in a highly vulnerable position. Gear lists should be carefully designed, thoughtfully amended in writing on the basis of needs particular to each outing, and then enforced to the letter. When designing the lists of minimum requirements (items without which an individual will not be allowed to participate), it is wise to seek the advice of administrators and leaders of similar programs. In a case of litigation, one's gear list might be reviewed by other professionals and compared to gear lists used by other providers of similar service. It is only prudent when creating minimal gear lists and gear check policies to develop lists that are as complete and specific as those of comparative agencies or institutions.

B. *Condition checks.* This refers to the conditions on both man-made facilities, such as buildings and roads, and on any natural hazards usually expected on such a trip. Hidden rocks, deep drop offs in the lake, time of sunset, poisonous plants, high tide, low rivers, etc., are all things that might be expected and checked out before the trip. The leader who finds broken, loose, or weakened equipment should not permit its use.

The suitability of the natural environment depends upon the geography of the site, the nature and condition of travel routes, the weather, the proximity of support services such as rescue teams, and the intended activity. An area of gentle rolling hills at moderate elevations, with good trails may seem implicitly well-suited for a beginning hiking course. On one hand, if the area is known for its severe storms and rapid weather changes or if the area is exceptionally remote, risk levels may be unacceptable for other than highly-experienced participants. On the other hand, a rugged and spectacular high alpine region may be reasonable for beginners if the weather is moderate and reasonably predictable, and if the area is not too remote and there are good escape routes.

C. *Checking the layout or design* means more than checking the stairs, emergency exits, lights, and windows. It also means checking the source of emergency help on a trip away

from home, locating telephones and sources of aid, and planning emergency routes that may be taken to leave the area. In short, it means checking not only the condition of the area to be used, but checking all surrounding areas for possible use and for exit in case of emergency. On trips, this means alternate routes in the event or fire, flood, storm, or injury. It also may mean finding safe shelter.

Special care must be taken whenever a site is modified or a structure is built by the participants and leaders. For example, if a bridge is built to cross a stream or if a shelter is built, those responsible for creating the bridge or shelter assume virtually all of the responsibility for its safety. If, on the other hand, a decision is made to cross a natural log bridge or to use a natural cave for shelter, the leader would simply be required to use due caution in making the decisions to use the bridge or cave. Leaders and (if the leaders have been doing an effective communication job) participants alike know that long bridges and caves sometimes collapse. The point here is not to argue against the use of structures built by the group, but to remind leaders to be extra cautious when considering the creation and/or the use of such structures.

The material just covered is an explanation of the components of a "standard of care," the legal term on which the defendant makes the case for innocence of negligence. If the defendant in a negligence suit can show that the duty to provide a safe environment and competent leadership was not breached, the plaintiff may have a difficult time proving negligence. If each outdoor-pursuit program has a risk management plan based upon these components, there will be some evidence that the leader was acting as a reasonable and prudent professional. Although there are many different outdoor-pursuit programs, it seems reasonable that each leader follow a similar *outline* to develop a plan to manage risks. The following recommendation for a risk management plan outline addresses each of the components for the standard of care yet encompasses only ten sections.

The Risk Management Plan

Up to this point, it may be perceived that risk management is a complex and time consuming task. It is little wonder that many outdoor leaders or administrators learn of the foregoing material, and deciding that programs which entail risk are "not worth the effort," and they do not offer them (or, worse, offer them without planning to "manage" the risks). While the topic may be complex, there are ways to manage risks efficiently and practically. The following material is devoted to the management of risks in all outdoor-pursuit programs. Note that there is no mention of *eliminating* risks. The intention is to *manage* them.

How is the risk management plan developed? Assume that, at the moment, you have decided to explore the possibility of providing an outdoor experience. At this point, the situation is quite simple; no responsibility has been assumed and no activity-related risks exist. Now is the time to begin the risk management planning process. From the very beginning, the administrator/ leader of the potential program should be attentive to all potential hazards. Again, there is no need for anything approaching paranoia since the elimination of risk is not intended. What is required is a conscientious and consistent review of each aspect or element of the proposed event.

The first order of business is to "rough out" the idea, to investigate the availability of the essential ingredients—land or water resources, suitable participants, capable leaders, those "connections" between resources and people, dollars, transportation, clothing, and equipment. As this initial survey is conducted, potential problems should be identified, and all identifiable risks should be found either: (1) inherently low enough to be acceptable, or (2) capable of being rendered acceptably low by some reasonable modification of the activity. Finally, assuming that all of the "ingredients" are accessible and that no unacceptable and unavoidable risks exist, it is time to plan the details of the activity itself.

At this point, written expression of the full and detailed risk management plan should begin. Keep in mind that the people responsible for implementing the activity will need easy access to the information, policies, and directions in the plan. One method of presenting the material is to follow a topical order so that staff or leaders can locate needed information quickly by following a logical sequence.

For the purposes of this text, we have followed the outline in Figure 12.1 (page 252) in our discussion of risk management planning. Such an outline is very useful as a reminder to consider every aspect of risk management, and our figure could serve as an outline for a comprehensive risk management plan incorporated in a single document. In actual practice, the written risk management plan usually consists of a set of documents which, taken collectively, cover or include all of the relevant facts, policies, and procedures. For example, the "risk management plan" for a college mountaineering course may consist of: a copy of the institution's goals and objectives for the program; a copy of the standard safety policies and procedures document for the program (which should specify student-to-leader ratios and leader qualifications as well as all applicable transportation policies, emergency procedures, and safety policies); a copy of the course description (which should include a detailed list of course goals and objectives); gear requirement lists (if not included in the safety policies document); pre-trip meeting agendas; an outing agenda specifying the location, access points, escape routes, times, dates, leaders and participants on the outing; and, copies of all waivers, and releases, and health forms. The outline in Figure 12.1 could serve as a checklist to ensure that each item is covered in the appropriate document.

Immediately following an activity, the leaders should file a detailed account of the outing. In the event of a mishap, the above listed documents (if well-constructed and up-to-date), the leader's post-trip report, and a complete set of waivers and health forms would be invaluable resources.

Considering all of the items in Figure 12.1 (page 252) and compiling a written risk management plan may seem to encompass a ponderous amount of work. For the institution or organization just beginning to offer outdoor activities,

---

FIGURE 12.1

Outline for Risk Management Plan

1. GENERAL DESCRIPTION
   a. Name of Program
   b. Type of Activity
   c. Level
2. DATES AND TIMES
   a. Dates
   b. Times
3. GOALS AND OBJECTIVES
   a. Organizational
   b. Activity
4. LOCATION
   a. Site/Area
   b. Weather
   c. Routes/Campsites
   d. Facilities
5. TRANSPORTATION
   a. Mode
   b. Routes/Destinations
6. PARTICIPANTS
   a. Number
   b. Skill Level
   c. Characteristics
7. LEADERS
   a. Number/Roles
   b. Qualifications
8. EQUIPMENT
   a. Type and Amount
   b. Control
9. CONDUCTING THE ACTIVITY
   a. Preactivity Preparation
   b. Group Control
   c. Teaching Strategy
   d. Time Management
10. EMERGENCY PREPAREDNESS
    a. Policies
    b. Health Forms
    c. Telephone Numbers

---

this may prove to be a valid perception. Given the magnitude of the task, it is often worthwhile to hire a consultant who can create the necessary documents more efficiently, and usually at a net savings when considering the value of in-house employee time. Many, if not most, organizations will have many aspects of the risk management plan already committed to writing. The process may then involve collecting materials, updating, and editing, with little need for development of new documents. When constructing the risk management plan, remember that, while the primary objective is to provide direction for managing risks, the written plan may also be used to document or reveal the standards of care employed by the institution in the conduct of the program or activity for which the plan was developed.

The first step is to look at every program separately and ascertain if the sponsor can provide the necessary basic ingredients to manage risks. Each program must be analyzed to see if there will be suitable participants, capable leaders, adequate facilities, and appropriate equipment. There is no sense in going any further if it is found that the prospective participants are not mature enough, qualified instructors cannot be hired, or if there is not enough, or adequate equipment. For every possible program, all identified risks should be either low enough to be acceptable (i.e., stubbed toes, skinned knees) or capable of being made low by some type of modification (i.e., gloves, helmets, climbing protection, and proper clothing).

Assuming that there will be participants of the right age and ability, capable instructors, adequate facilities, and appropriate equipment, and that no unacceptable or avoidable risks exist, one can start to plan the details of a risk management plan for each activity.

1. *General Description*
   a. Name of Program, Course, or Event
      What is the advertised title of the course or event, and who is the sponsor (if not implicit under the circumstances)? By designating the program, the leader starts to form a picture of the types of risks to be managed. Probably a good way to start is to have each program staff list the potential risks perceived in each program. Swimming conjures up notions of drowning, choking, fear, underwater rocks, hypothermia, and others. A hiking program includes the possibility of being lost, caught in a storm or a fire, hypothermia, thirst, fatigue, sunburn or sunstroke, being caught out after dark, the need to stay out all night, and other problems.

b. Type of Activity

What activity or activities are planned? A general answer is sufficient here, such as "kayaking" for a recreational outing, or "kayak roll clinic" for a class.

c. Level of Activity

Terms, such as beginning, intermediate, advanced, expert, or instructor level, may suffice. The activity may have its own set of terms; use whatever terms best describe the activity. In some cases, an outing or course is designed to provide different levels of instruction, or the outing may have alternative routes at higher or lower skill levels. Be sure to note the presence of alternatives or options if they are available. Activity levels are discussed in Chapter Seventeen, "Leading Specific Activities."

Each program must be examined on its own merit in terms of the characteristics of the participants, the site, and the level of skill. Some people may classify activities as high, medium, or low risk; however, these labels may not accurately reflect the risk involved. The risk can change depending upon the situation and participants. For example, one may want to classify climbing as a dangerous or high-risk activity, when in actuality an advanced climber demonstrating a skill on the climbing wall of an indoor facility is probably involved in a low-risk activity as compared to an inexperienced senior citizen climbing a vertical cliff of crumbling basalt located ten miles from the road. Each is a "climbing" activity, but the risk in each activity wouldn't be classified as the same, and the risk management plans for each should be quite different.

2. Date(s) and Time(s)

Dates and times must be identified so that one can plan carefully for various contingencies. The program that operates in the winter will have to make allowances for short hours of daylight compared to programs offered in July. The time of sunrise, twilight, sunset and darkness are important considerations.

Time is important because we need to consider the working time of the leaders and the possible set-in of fatigue, especially in away-from-home trips. A leader who is the driver, guide, lunch hour supervisor, and song leader for a 12-hour trip, without a break, may not be thinking as clearly as the leader who has shared duties and responsibilities with another leader. An outdoor activity of several hours is certainly more demanding on the staff than an activity that lasts only one hour. An overnight trip brings to mind a different type of risk management than a two-mile nature hike on level ground. The agenda or time-management plans, covered under "Field Leadership" (Chapter Sixteen) might well be attached here.

3. Goals and Objectives

The objectives of the activity are stressed here because they are often left out of risk management plans. Goals are vital to program coherence and thus to effectiveness; they give purpose and direction to the activities, and they allow estimation of acceptable and justifiable risks. Clearly, program goals and objectives must be understood by both leader and follower right from the start. If the objective is only to reach the top of the mountain or end of the river, there is a problem. The written objective defining a destination must be followed by the objective to return to camp safe and sound. If the objective is only to reach the top or end, what are we teaching about group interaction, leisure activities, and safety for lifelong leisure enjoyment? And how are the risks for the return trip addressed? (The reader might want to review Chapter Eleven for material on writing objectives.)

a. Goals and Objectives of the Organization.

Both for the institution or organization as a whole and for the program in question, the sponsor's goals and objectives are of considerable importance. Risks are always present; but, to be acceptable, they must be justified in terms of the goals and objectives of the institution and program as well as those of the specific activity.

b. Activity Goals and Objectives

The goals and objectives of the activity need to be understood not just by the initiator of the event, but also by leaders and participants. Written concise goals and objectives allow valuable scrutiny which help insure that they are reasonable. Too often, disaster, or at least disappointment, is built into an event right from the start!

In Chapter Eleven, the section on evaluation addresses the need to evaluate from the viewpoints of both the participants and the organization. Listing the objectives on the risk management plan will help this process.

4. *Location*

Where the program is held necessitates control of different types of potential accidents. The conditions that exist at the location will also affect the potential for risks.

a. Activity Site or Area

It may be generally sufficient to describe the area by name, giving enough detail to allow the reader to locate the site on a map—for example, "near Green Lakes, in the Three Sisters Wilderness Area west of Bend, Oregon." While the physical characteristic of the area (geography, plant and animal life, etc.) must be considered in order to assess potential hazards, it is usually not practical to attempt a comprehensive written description. One can state the overall character of the area and cite any special hazards. It is assumed that the risk management plan is based upon a good, current knowledge of the area and its potential hazards. Such knowledge is critical to the development of specific plans for the outing and for such documents as the Statement of Risks. Usually, the best way to assess the site is by direct observation by the leader, supplemented by study of maps and guidebooks, and discussion with others familiar with the site.

b. Weather and Climate

When considering the location of the proposed activity, the leader needs to consider such things as the weather forecast and to prepare for possible thunderstorms, tornadoes, or excessive heat. Trips to the ocean require knowledge of the times and heights of the tides. Unusually high or low water in rivers, dry conditions in forests, avalanche conditions on glaciated peaks, times of sunrise and sunset, heavy traffic, and dust storms are all examples of things to be considered.

It is sometimes hard to know where to draw the line in terms of probability of severe weather occurrence. When in doubt, it is always better to hedge on the conservative side, and to discuss all of the possibilities. For example, the conditions for a trek high in the mountains of Honshu, Japan, in July, might be described as: "Mostly warm days and cool nights, with highs seldom above 75°F and lows rarely below 35°F. Frequent heavy afternoon thunderstorms with occasional snow showers at higher elevations. Moderate to severe hurricanes have hit the area on an average of once every three years during the period of our trek."

c. Routes and Campsites

These should be specified precisely in the written plan, and the written description should be supplemented by a clearly marked map. "Escape routes"—to be used in the event of emergencies or in a need to avoid the primary route—should also be described and shown on the map, along with campsites, alternative campsites, key water sources, and special hazards.

d. Facilities

In the written document, facilities should be described and when appropriate located on a map. All facilities, from playing fields to ropes courses, gyms, and swimming pools, must be carefully inspected for safety hazards. The leaders must know how to use the facility safely and how to deal with emergencies. Though it may seem too obvious to mention, leaders should know the location of fire extinguishers, fire alarms, telephones, emergency exits, electrical circuit breakers, light switches, and any other safety-related features. Sometimes, it is necessary to move an outdoor course indoors, and, of course, most pre- and post-trip meetings are indoors. Like most people, leaders are sometimes lax when it comes to safety in buildings; yet, in an emergency, the leader would be expected to give immediate, correct instructions to the group.

When ropes courses, bridges, or manufactured contrivances are used, special care must be taken to assess structural safety and hazards related to any use of the structure. As mentioned earlier, the use of man-made structures adds a new dimension of responsibilities to those assumed in the conduct of activities in a natural setting.

5. *Transportation*
   a. Mode of Transportation
   The type and number of vehicles should be specified, together with any rules, policies, or conditions not set forth in the safety policies below. It is also important to know the general transportation plan, e.g.,"Participants will be transported to and from the site in a chartered 45 passenger bus driven by an ICC approved driver;" "Students will be transported in State Motor Pool vans driven by approved leaders and staff;" or "Transportation will be by private vehicles; any car pool arrangements are the sole responsibility of the participants." If transportation is not provided, this should be clearly stated, e.g., "The program begins and ends at (the activity site). We do not provide transportation to or from the site."

   b. Routes and Distances
   Routes and distances should be specified when the institution is directly involved in transportation or if there is only one possible route. In the case of carpools, it is better, from a liability perspective, to simply provide advice on how to find the site and warnings about routes known to be hazardous; but, otherwise, let each driver decide the best route.

   The transportation of staff and participants to and from the site is often the most dangerous portion of the entire program. The responsibility for reaching the field may rest with the program, the participants, a contracting agency, or it may be shared by everyone. Whatever the case, the responsibilities of the program should be clearly delineated in the risk management plan. In the case of transportation, if the program bears responsibility, policies and directions must clearly provide for reliable safety-checked vehicles and for competent drivers.

   A thorough plan will include specific reference to common-sense (but too often ignored) issues such as the use of seat belts, drinking and drugs, speeding, and compliance with traffic laws. The plan must also anticipate accidents, injuries, breakdowns, and getting lost, and the plan must provide clear directions for resolving these situations. Vehicle security while parked is an increasingly important issue. The plan should include any policies or procedures designed to ensure that vehicles are safe and useable upon return, and that keys are safe and accessible. Another concern usually addressed in this section of the plan is the return of participants to town and/or their homes. The plan should address the exceptional potential for accidents caused by tired drivers at the end of the outing, especially when long days, long drives, or multiple-day outings are involved.

   Since transportation issues are common to many kinds of programs and activities, transportation safety policies are often included in comprehensive safety policies and procedures documents. When constructing or assembling a risk management plan in a specific program or activity, it is a good idea to review the organization's established transportation policies carefully. This can be a good opportunity to update this important document.

6. Participants

a. Number

How many clients or participants are expected, and what are the maximum and minimum numbers that will be allowed? Enrollment limits (maximums and minimums) are often affected by economics and by concerns about program quality, environmental impact, or group size restrictions by land managers. These are all valid concerns; however, for the purposes of risk management (and liability) it is important to give priority to safety considerations. In many activities, risks may increase if party sizes are either too small or too large. Very small parties may be less able to resolve emergencies in remote areas; however, large parties may increase risk by slowing movement or complicating group control. The maximum and minimum number of participants must be consistent with the budget and other concerns mentioned above, but in every case must be within limits that can be justified on the basis of participant safety.

b. Skill level

The skill level of participants must be considered and activities must be planned and conducted accordingly. In most cases, beginning, novice, intermediate, advanced, and expert level experiences in a given activity are conducted differently and require different risk management strategies and policies.

c. Characteristics

In some cases, it is sufficient to be nonspecific here, while, in other cases, it is important to know many things about the participants. How much needs to be known depends upon the activity, the level of the activity, the site, and many other factors. When planning the activity, care must obviously be taken to consider the needs of the prospective participants, and needs may be affected by such factors as age, gender, physical and mental ability, experience, and skill level. While it may be adequate to identify participants in a Parks Department beginning backpacking class as "adults in good physical condition," such broad terminology provides marginal guidance to leaders. Especially when higher risk activities are involved, it is also important to define any prerequisite such as prior successful completion of a certain course, or an ability to pass a specified fitness test. The words "or equivalent" may be added to give the leader greater leeway. In any case, it is important to clarify who may participate, and under what conditions participation is allowed. Doing so in writing can assist in the safe operation of the program and can document attempts to ensure a safe "fit" between the participants and the activity.

The sex of the group members should be noted, even for programs that are not coed. It may be appropriate or deemed necessary for male staff to accompany certain female away-from-home activities in the role of drivers, guides, etc. In situations involving minors, tents should not be shared by members of the opposite sex even if it means carrying extra weight. The policy on this topic may be set by the sponsoring agency and should be followed carefully.

The methods of leading will differ for different groups. Third graders, sixth graders, high schoolers, the mentally and physically disabled, and sometimes different socio-economic groups require different sets of guidelines for managing risks. Even within these categories, there may be great differences. Some sixth graders may be physically limited, some high schoolers may have asthma. Developmentally disabled individuals may be institutionalized or mainstreamed. Every possible variable must be considered. Every participant (and their family members) expects that the program will be conducted with thoughtfulness and care. In short, every different participant must be recognized and considered in the management of risks. Unusual or atypical characteristics, therefore, must be listed.

7. Leaders

a. Number and Roles

The leaders should be listed, along with their roles or job titles. It is good to incorporate copies of appropriate job descriptions in the written plan. The number of leaders (and/or assistants) required for an outing depends upon the activity, the site, participant characteristics, and leadership capabilities, among other factors. (Typical minimum ratios are given for a variety of activities in Chapter Seventeen "Leadership of Selected Activities.") Since staff usually account for the largest single expense in the budget of an outdoor program, there is great temptation to keep expenses in line by reducing the number of staff. Before dropping below the minimums suggested in Chapter Seventeen, one should consider the risks with great care, be prepared to justify the decision in terms of risk management and provision of an adequate standard of care, and remember that adequate staffing may be the first item to be assessed should a mishap occur.

b. Qualifications

In a written report, it is generally adequate to list the current certifications and years of experience of staff members; however, in the event of an investigation, detailed resumes and copies of current cards and certificates may be requested. In any case, care must be taken to define standards that are "consistent with the norms in the trade," which, in practical terms, means that hiring standards and assessment should be at least as stringent as those of comparable organizations in the region. Suggestions for staff qualifications for various activities are provided in Chapter Seventeen.

8. Equipment

a. Type and Amount

The type of equipment used should be identified to show the quality of the effort to control accidents. Coast Guard approved floatation devices are mandatory for boating and should be listed on the risk management plan. It is important to know the type of camping stove to be used since the risks vary with different fuels and the risk management plan must address these differences. The leader who indicates what type of equipment is to be used shows an attempt to manage the risks involved in the activity.

It is necessary to note the amount of equipment to be used in order to indicate if proper safety practices were followed. The leader who uses two three-person tents for a group of eight on a trip obviously assumes that two people won't need a tent or that a three-person tent is adequate for four persons. Each of these decisions indicates less than prudent and careful consideration (unless the tenters are very small). On a backpacking trip, the list might read: one tent per two people, one stove per four people, one complete first-aid kit for the group, and one backpack per person.

The risk management plan must include lists of the clothing and equipment required of participants, leader gear requirements (if they vary from those for participants), and group gear requirements for the outing. Clothing and equipment requirements are discussed in detail in Chapter Six, "Preparation for Survival" and Chapter Seventeen, "Leadership of Selected Activities."

b. Control of Equipment

Sometimes, equipment is put away when it is not clean nor dry nor in good repair. It is essential to check all gear before use. Equipment that is damaged, frayed, or in poor condition should not be used. If a staff member finds a problem with either a facility or piece of equipment, that item should not be used by anyone until it is repaired. The staff member who says, "It will probably be safe for this one time," or "Let's hope it lasts," is not acting as a reasonable and prudent professional. All gear should be checked carefully, cleaned, and repaired immediately upon return from outings. Any unfit gear that must be kept should be clearly marked and removed from use.

The plan should include policies and procedures for assuring compliance with the gear requirements (i.e., who will check the gear prior to the outing; how will the check be done, and what will the consequences of failure to arrive without proper gear), check and maintaining the condition of safety-related gear, and the use of safety gear (for example, who is to carry the first-aid kit assigned to each independent field group). In most cases, the above information will be included in the program safety policies and procedures document.

Although not central to the risk management plan, it is convenient to also include policies for assignment of responsibility for gear items, including check-out and check-in of gear, post-trip cleanup, storage and inspection.

9. Conduct of the Program, Course or Event

a. Preactivity Preparations

The plan should include the dates, times, and agendas of pre-trip meetings, which are discussed at length in the section on tactical planning found in Chapter Fifteen.

b. Group Control

The risk management plan should address all aspects of group control, including roll and attendance keeping (who is there, and how will the leaders keep track during the outing?), issuance of warnings and safety instructions (when, where, and what topics are to be covered?), informing participants of plans (what is going to happen, and who is responsible for what, for whom, and to whom?), and checking on the participant welfare throughout the outing. These issues are discussed in Chapter Sixteen, "Leadership in the Field."

c. Teaching Strategy

Progressions and teaching methods affect risk levels, so they should be documented carefully. It is important to be prepared to justify the use of any nonstandard progressions or methods. Teaching methods and progressions are discus-sed in Chapter Ten, "Outdoor Pursuits Leadership," Chapter Sixteen, "Leadership in the Field," and Chapter Seventeen, "Leadership of Specific Activities."

d. Time Management Plan

A time management plan is a time-ordered agenda that gives the predicted starting and ending times of every major activity or event. It provides a clear picture of what happens when, and of how much time is to be devoted to each element of the program, course, or outing. A carefully constructed time management plan is an essential component of a good risk management plan. It is an invaluable planning tool and aid to field staff, and it allows the reader to assess sequencing, time allotments, and the overall format of the course or outing. Time management plans are discussed in Chapter Fifteen, "Strategic and Tactical Planning."

10. Emergency Preparedness

Here, we are concerned with policies and procedures designed to facilitate effective response to emergency situations. There should be standard policies for specific emergencies such as fire, storm, flood, lost or missing persons, first aid, group or individual survival, and/or other emergencies.

Policies should specify that group leaders carry copies of health forms, which should contain emergency telephone contact numbers for each participant. Each independent group needs to be self-sufficient in these regards so that, in the event of an accident or illness, the group leader can immediately access health information and emergency contact numbers. A typical "health form" is illustrated in Figure 12.2.

The leader should carry adequate change to use a public telephone and a list of emergency telephone numbers such as ambulance and police services and key administrators of the outdoor program. It cannot be assumed that all areas of the country (or world) use the 911 system or that they all require the same amount of change for a pay phone. Only advance planning can assure access to emergency help.

FIGURE 12.2   Health Information Form

NAME _____

OUTING _____

TERM _____ YEAR _____

Please describe any illness or injury, current or past, that might affect your ability to participate fully and safely in this course, **including but not limited to** back and knee problems, cardiac or respiratory ailments, diabetes, allergies, migraines, fear of heights, or sensitivity to cold. _____

_____

List any drugs or medications you are currently taking: _____

_____

List any allergies or other adverse reactions to medications: _____

_____

CONTACT INFORMATION

Yourself: _____
       (address)   (city)   (state)   (phone)

Social security #: _____   Driver's license # and state: _____

Local contact: _____
      (address)   (city)   (state)   (phone)

Parent or relative: _____
      (address)   (city)   (state)   (phone)

Physician: _____
      (address)   (city)   (state)   (phone)

GENERAL INFORMATION

Briefly describe your experience level in this activity: _____

_____

Do you have first aid or medical training? Describe: _____

_____

Now that all the components of the program have been addressed, any additional policies can be developed. The event, participants, instructors, and equipment available are used to develop the plan for managing the risks. The same list of policies and practices may be developed for several similar programs, or parts of several programs. In these cases, there may be some standard operating procedures for the activities. The use of standard operating procedures is common among outdoor programmers. Such documents are easily inserted in risk management plans at this point.

Waivers, Releases, and Statements of Risk

Many people feel that a liability waiver signed by a participant of legal age will preclude that participant suing for negligence. This is, with rare exceptions, not true. The majority of U.S. courts have held that public agencies providing services to the public cannot contract to absolve themselves of liability to the public to whom the services are rendered. Private enterprises are usually considered similarly. In other words, in most cases, waivers do not provide real protection from suits. Nevertheless, most public and private providers of outdoor recreation services require all participants to sign one or more documents—commonly known as waivers—prior to participation in any activity where the risk of injury or damage to personal property is, or is perceived as, elevated.

To understand why waivers are so often used, it is important to know what a waiver is, and what it does. The typical waiver has three distinct elements: the *release*, wherein the participant, the institution or organization, and its administrators, staff, and agents form part or all liability; the *statement of risks* in which the participant acknowledges awareness of certain general and specific risks inherent in participation in the activity; and the *assumption of risk*, wherein the participant agrees to personally assume responsibility for some or all of the risks associated with participation in the activity.

The *release* usually has no real substance in court, but it does tend to reduce the likelihood of being sued. A person who has signed a release may believe that it is no longer possible to bring suit, may be too embarrassed to do so having signed a release, or may feel ethically bound to fulfill the contractual agreement not to sue. The *statement of risk* and related *assumption of risk* may discourage some individuals from suing ("after all, they did tell me this could happen, and did so in writing"); but, more importantly, these elements help the provider show that the risks were made clear to the participant prior to the outing or event which may affect the extent to which the plaintiff in a suit may be expected to assume responsibility for whatever has taken place. On a positive note, waivers remind participants of risk and of the need to remain alert; thus, waivers reduce the real risk levels. Carefully written waivers, when used correctly, are well worth the effort.

Often a liability waiver for a minor is signed by one or both parents (or legal guardians) who state they will not sue for negligence. Administrators and leaders should be aware of the fact that, while the parent/guardian may indeed not sue, no parent/guardian has the right to sign away a child's right to sue upon reaching the age of majority up to a legally determined statutory limitation. The statute of limitations varies from state to state. An administrator should always seek information from a legal advisor on the use and development of liability waivers. Not to do so would normally be an instance of failure to act as a reasonable and prudent professional, because the administrator is rarely an attorney.

Some providers include all three elements (release, statement of risks, and assumption of risks) in a single document. Others provide separate documents for all three, or combine the elements in various ways. Examples of various formats are provided below. The first example, Figures 12.3a and 12.3b (page 262), from Best of the Alps Trekking, illustrates the use of separate documents, printed for convenience on two sides of a single sheet of paper. The "Statement of Risks" and the "Release and Assumption of Risks" are signed and dated

FIGURE 12.3a   Statement of Risks Form

STATEMENT OF RISKS

This trek involves travel by rail, motor vehicle, cable car, tramway, chair lift and other mechanical means. Motor vehicle accidents or accidents while traveling by any other conveyance could result in serious injury or death. This trek also involves travel by foot or by animal or other conveyance in rugged, mountainous terrain, sometimes at great distances from rescue or other forms of assistance, including medical aid. The weather in the mountains is unpredictable and can change rapidly. Severe weather conditions can occur in the mountains even during the summer months. Slips, falls, rockfall, avalanches, floods, lightning strikes and other traumatic events are possible as are serious medical conditions such as hyperthermia or hypothermia, any of which could lead to permanent injury or death.

I understand that the leaders of the trek are well-trained but may make mistakes and/or may be unable to solve problems or to prevent accidents. Therefore, I understand that my personal safety depends largely upon my alertness, upon my care and attention to the environment and to my physical and emotional state, and upon my use of good judgement. I further understand that it is my responsibility to understand, to assess and to accept or reject any and all plans set forth by the trek leaders.

I, the undersigned, hereby acknowledge that I understand the risks inherent in the "BEST OF THE ALPS" trek.

SIGNED: _____

DATE: _____

separately. It may be a good idea to use two, or even three, signature lines when, as in this case, one or more elements are quite lengthy. Some institutions even require each paragraph to be initialed in an attempt to ensure that the entire document is read by the participant. The second example, Figure 12.4a (page 263), illustrates an incorporation of the statement of risks, the assumption of risk, and a release as worded into a single one-page document. Following the complete document are examples of replacement wording for use in conjunction with water-based or bicycling courses (Figure 12.4b, page 264).

The first example is from a small private company catering primarily to mature adults. The second example is from a major public institution catering primarily to college students of ages 18 and older. The third example is

from a high school in a state wherein age 19 is the age of majority. This document, therefore, includes a signature line for both the applicant and his/her guardian or parent.

The exact wording and form of the documents will vary between programs and may vary between activities within a program. In any case, the wording should be suited to the clientele, and it should be appropriate to the specific activity. The language and composition should be such that it is easily intelligible to the readers. The statement of risks must be as inclusive as possible and as specific as possible to the intended site and activity. Finally, the wording of the release must meet the legal requirements of the particular circumstance. Therefore, proposed statements of risks, assumptions of risk, and releases should be carefully reviewed by

---

FIGURE 12.3b   Release and Assumption of Risk Form

RELEASE AND ASSUMPTION OF RISK

Please read carefully:

In consideration of, and as part of the payment for, the right to participate in this trip arranged by "BEST OF THE ALPS TREKKING" and it's owners, agents and associates, I have and do hereby assume the risks explained in the Statement of Risks form and will hold the above mentioned company, owners, agents and associates harmless from and defend them from any and all actions, causes of actions, suits, debts, demands and claims of every kind and nature whatsoever which I now have or which may hereafter arise out of or in connection with this trip.

This agreement shall serve as a release and assumption of risk for myself and for my heirs, administrators, executors and for all members of my family, including any minors accompanying me.

By signing this form I acknowledge that I have read, understand and do agree to the terms and conditions set forth in the above statement and in the "General Information, Terms and Conditions" document.

Signed: _____

Date: _____

Signature of parent or legal guardian if applicant is under 21 years of age:

_____

---

the program administrators, by the field instructors knowledgeable of the actual site and activity, and by the institution's legal counsel or by an attorney experienced in such matters. Having a common interest in such matters, most providers of outdoor recreation services are happy to share their insights. A review of the document used by a similar program in your local area may provide a good starting point for development of an effective set of documents.

Insurance

Given the nature of outdoor pursuits and the tendency of modern day U.S. citizens to sue, it would seem that every provider of outdoor activities would be heavily insured. In fact, many providers carry no insurance at all; others are only marginally insured, and a large percentage of public agencies are "self-insured," having, presumably, sufficient financial reserves

to cover potential costs. Generally speaking, it is the smaller organizations and businesses that operate with little or no insurance, and the most frequently cited reason is cost. Insurance rates are soaring, businesses often face intense competition, and other providers may suffer from chronically tight budgets. While not unusual, the practice of operating in an underinsured capacity is not recommended and may be illegal in certain circumstances. For example, virtually all organized group use of federal lands must be conducted under what are generally known as "Special Use" or "Outfitter Guide" permits. With few exceptions, such users are required to have in effect specific forms of liability insurance, in amounts set by the land manager. The amount varies widely, even for identical types of activity in different National Parks. The typical range is from $250,000 to $1,000,000 which makes it extremely costly for the entrepreneur who operates only a few

FIGURE 12.4a   Statement of Risks, Assumption of Risks, and Release Form

UNIVERSITY OF OREGON
**OUTDOOR PURSUITS AND OUTDOOR LEADERSHIP
TRAINING PROGRAMS**
Land-based Courses and Outings

STATEMENT OF RISKS, ASSUMPTION OF RISKS, AND RELEASE

I, the undersigned, am aware that the _____ course or outing may be physically and emotionally demanding.

I understand that this course or outing involves activities in rugged terrain in all extremes of weather, far from any professional or medical services. I understand that rescues may take more than 24 hours and all medical and rescue costs are my responsibility. I understand the importance of obtaining sufficient medical and accident insurance before participation in the activity.

I understand that I may be exposed to real risks of injury, or even death, from such hazards or events as falls, rockfall, avalanches, lightning, river crossings, hypothermia, frostbite or cold injuries, bites and stings, and accidents traveling to and from the activity site. I understand that equipment may fail, and that such failure could cause or contribute to my injury or death.

I acknowledge that the leaders cannot foresee all of the risks and hazards associated with this course or outing.

I acknowledge that my safety is my personal responsibility, and that my safety depends upon my alertness and my use of good judgment. I understand that I can reduce risks by paying careful attention to the environment, my physical and emotional state, the condition of all safety related clothing and equipment, and by participating only in those activities that are well within my mental and physical capabilities.

I have been encouraged to develop a questioning attitude and to ask activity leaders to explain any decision with which I am uncomfortable, and I will not engage in any activity unless I have considered it carefully and accept responsibility for all related risks.

I understand that the State of Oregon, State System of Higher Education, and the University of Oregon, its agents officers and employees shall assume no responsibility or liability for me for accident, illness, or loss of or damage to personal property resulting from participation in this course or outing.

By my signature below, I hereby warrant that I:

    (1) have read the above statement and understand the risks associated with participation in this course or outing, and
    (2) am aware of and have met all of the prerequisites to participation in this course or outing. This includes having fulfilled all of the requirements of all prerequisite courses or outings and enrollment in good standing in all corequisite courses or outings, and
    (3) assume full responsibility for the consequences of my choosing to participate in this course or outing, and
    (4) hereby hold the State of Oregon, Oregon State System of Higher Education, and the University of Oregon, its agents, officers and employees harmless for any and all liability, action, claims and damage of any kind and nature whatsoever.

SIGNED: _____ DATE:_____

NAME (Please print neatly): _____

PARENT OR GUARDIAN SIGNATURE (If under 18 yrs.): _____

FIGURE 12.4b

STATEMENT OF RISKS, ASSUMPTION OF RISKS, AND RELEASE

NOTICE:

For water-based outings replace the first sentence of the third paragraph of the land-based document with:

I understand that I may be exposed to real risks of injury, or even death, from such hazards or events as falling or being thrown from watercraft, immersion in cold water, hypothermia, cold injuries, insect bites or stings, drowning, collisions with and/or being pinned against or under watercraft, logs or rocks, and accidents while traveling to and from the activity site.

For bicycling outings replace the first sentence of the third paragraph of the land-based document with:

I understand that I may be exposed to real risks of injury, or even death, from such hazards or events as hypothermia or hyperthermia, insect bites or stings, falling or being thrown from my bicycle, collisions with motor vehicles or other bicycles and accidents while traveling to and from the activity site.

---

trips per year. With very few exceptions, only large, established operators can absorb the high insurance premiums, can spread the costs over enough clients, and still can remain competitive. As a result, most small businesses that wish to operate on federal land, subcontract to, or join forces with, larger entities, in order to either avoid or share the insurance costs. Another practice is to operate only overseas which avoids not only insurance requirements but a host of additional costs and fees that are unique to operating on U.S. public lands.

A variety of types of insurance are available to meet the needs of the organization or business, its employees and volunteers, and its participants or clients. The principle areas of concern are liability of the organization or business, employee and volunteer liability and accidents, and participant accidents. The most common pattern seems to be one in which the company or organization pays for a broad liability policy and accident insurance for employees (which, in some areas, is mandated by law). The company recommends accident and liability insurance to its volunteers, liability insurance to its employees, and accident insurance to its participants or clients, but the company does not offer to pay for the additional insurance. An argument can be made, however, for the company to negotiate

a policy (or set of policies) to cover all of those areas. The total expense is likely to be less than the costs of individual policies; everyone is covered; and the costs may be considered, in part, as a benefit of employment.

Unfortunately, insurance is very costly, and may be especially so when purchased specifically for outdoor-pursuits activities. While a large organization that is already insured at normal rates can often add a few outdoor activities without affecting rates, the small, specialized operator who seeks coverage for a climbing school may receive outlandish price quotes or no quote at all. It is important for the small, specialized operator to do a lot of shopping, and one of the best approaches is to ask the advice of similar operators from around the country. There are insurance companies who will offer policies at rates that reflect an understanding of the real, rather than the popularly perceived, risks in outdoor pursuits.

Summary

The management of risks in an outdoor program is based upon the premise that participants have natural inclinations to pursue activities involving the potential for accidents. While the sponsors cannot guarantee freedom from accident, risks can be managed so that the likelihood of an accident is lessened. Every outdoor leader should perform at the competency of a reasonable and prudent professional who follows the best and most current professional practices. Such performance is known as practicing "a standard of care." A standard of care adheres to specific points related to supervision, conducting the activity, and understanding the environment. One way to practice a standard of care is to develop and follow a risk management plan that identifies potential dangers and outlines how the activity may be managed to lessen the risk.

Waivers and insurance policies are administrative concerns that require legal advice. It is the responsibility of administrators and leaders to carry adequate insurance and to utilize appropriate documents (statements of risk, assumption of risk, and releases) that have been approved by legal counsel.

References

Christiansen, M. L. (1986). How to avoid negligence suits: Reducing hazards to prevent injuries. *Journal of Physical Education, Recreation and Dance 57*(2), 46-52.

Cockrell, D. (Ed.). (1991). *The wilderness educator: The Wilderness Education Association curriculum guide.* Merrillville, IN: ICS Books, Inc.

Kaufman, J. E., & Lazarus, B. I. (May-June 1987). Programming Options. *Employee services management.* pp. 10-14.

Raines, T. J. (January 1991). Adventure programs, can the risk be taken? *Journal of Physical Education and Recreation 62*(1), 64-67.

Rankin, J. (April 1990). The risk of risk: Program liability in high adventure activities. *Journal of Physical Education, Recreation, and Dance 61*(4), 39-42.

van der Smissen, B. (1980). *Legal liability—adventure activities.* Las Cruces, NM: Educational Resources Information Center.

van der Smissen, B. (1982). Minimizing legal liability risks in adventure programs. *Journal of Experiential Education 4*, 10-17.

Wade, I. (1990). Safety Management. In J.C. Miles and S. Priest (Eds.) *Adventure education.* State College, PA: Venture Publishing, Inc.

MARKETING THE OUTDOOR PROGRAM

Many people, both in traditional business and in the service industry, hold a variety of misconceptions about what marketing entails and often confuse marketing with promotion, advertising, and public relations. Promotion is one aspect of marketing and is discussed in depth later in this chapter. Advertising is one of several forms of promotion. Public relations is a process inherent in every marketing plan. Basically, public relations relates to the people-oriented aspects of the marketing plan, the relationship between the organization and its various publics. It is the planned effort to influence public attitudes towards a program or organization. It implies a concerted effort in the direction of developing positive opinion. Marketing involves much more, including product/service development, location decisions, pricing, and promotion.

Marketing is the process of planning and executing the conception, pricing, promotion, and distribution of ideas, goods, and services to create exchanges that satisfy the objectives of both the customer and the organization. Implementing the marketing concept entails that businesses and organizations: (1) design their products/services to meet customer needs and wants, (2) focus on specific market segments rather than the entire (mass) market, and (3) develop integrated marketing mix strategies.

Effective and continuous marketing is necessary for all products, but it is especially important for the service businesses which include the sponsorship of outdoor programs. Recreation marketing is still very much in its infancy for a number of reasons. First, there still remains a great deal of confusion with respect to what marketing entails. A second reason is that many outdoor program administrators believe they don't have enough money, time, information, or expertise to develop and implement a marketing strategy. Finally, we continue to rely on theories, concepts, and methods that have been used to market manufactured goods. We continue to market recreational experiences much the same way that we market refrigerators and television sets. Little attention has been directed at the important differences between marketing tangible manufactured products and recreational/educational experiences. A canoe trip or a tour of high mountain lakes cannot be marketed the same way as a product sold in a retail store.

Differences Between Recreational Experiences and Physical Goods

Outdoor program marketing is different from marketing manufactured goods in a number of important respects. First, the outdoor experience must be consumed (i.e. experienced) on-site. The product cannot be produced, stockpiled, and then transported to a distribution point more convenient to clients. Nor can the service be delivered fully to the participant. Instead, the participants must travel to the production point.

Directors of outdoor programs need to understand that they are not marketing a facility, program, or even a combination of facilities and programs, but rather, an outdoor experience. Outdoor recreational experiences involve five distinct phases, which were identified by Clawson and Knetsch as: (1) Anticipation and planning, (2) Travel to the site, (3) On-site experiences and activities, (4) Travel back home, and (5) Recollection. Too many directors have failed to recognize the important role marketing can play in improving the off-site elements of the experience as well as the outdoor activities themselves. The total experience should be marketed—not just the outdoor experiences and activities.

Outdoor program marketing also differs from the marketing of manufactured goods in that outdoor experiences share many of the same characteristics as *services*. Outdoor experiences, like services, are special kinds of "goods" that are intangible. A service is an *activity* that has value to the buyer. Outdoor services are ephemeral and experiential in nature. They can be experienced, but not possessed; there is no transfer of ownership. They cannot be felt, tasted, or touched in the same way as physical goods. Nor can they usually be examined, demonstrated, and tested prior to the purchase/participation.

Outdoor experiences are first purchased, and then produced and consumed at the same time. Manufactured goods, on the other hand, are produced, then sold and then consumed. A product may be recalled, but an experience is permanent. Once it has occurred, it cannot be cancelled, changed, nor returned. The customer/ participant is actively involved in the production of the experience, and the quality of the experience is, in part, dependent upon the participant's performance.

The participant serves the dual role of consumer and producer; thus, the experience cannot be standardized but is different for each individual. Even if it were possible to standardize for individuals, complete standardization would not be possible because of the intervening

conditions of weather, actions, attitudes, and behaviors of the staff and other participants. The outdoor experience also differs from most physical goods in that it is an instantaneously perishable commodity. It is also difficult to determine exactly the cost of producing one unit of the experience (e.g., what it costs to produce one day or one week of an outdoor experience for one person).

A Marketing Plan for Outdoor Programs

In spite of the differences between traditionally manufactured goods and the outdoor program experience, it is possible to develop a simple marketing plan that will generate satisfied clients. The marketing plan as shown in Figure 13.1, has been modified from plans recommended for all businesses (service as well as industry) and will be explained point by point. This outline is the basic framework for a marketing plan, regardless of whether it is for a traditional business or a service (e.g., outdoor program) business. The remainder of this chapter will describe the different components of this plan as they relate to the outdoor program.

First, it must be realized that many of the steps in the marketing plan include actions already undertaken by the administrator/director of any outdoor program. Many times, they appear to be logical actions and are not considered as part of an overall plan. If the administrator/ leader analyzes the following steps, it may be seen that many of them are already in place, that some may need modification, and that others can be added easily. The important thing is to see the actions in their entirety and to realize that, *in toto*, they are a well-developed marketing plan— not merely a list of things "to be done" because it seems appropriate. The well-organized administrator/leader acts purposefully at all stages of the outdoor-pursuit program. When logical activities appear as part of a well-developed marketing plan, more credence is given to their existence, and it can be seen where they fit into the overall organization of the administration.

Taken step-by-step, the marketing plan sections can be explained as follows:

FIGURE 13.1   Marketing Plan

I. OVERALL OBJECTIVES
II. MARKET ANALYSIS
   A. *Demographics and Lifestyles*
   B. *Economic Conditions*
   C. *Laws and Government Regulations*
   D. *Technology*
   E. *Competition*
III. BUSINESS PROFILE
IV. TARGET MARKET IDENTIFICATION
V. TARGET MARKET OBJECTIVES
VI. MARKETING MIXES
   A. *Traditional*
      1. Product/Service/Location
      2. Place/Distribution
      3. Price
      4. Promotion
         a. Personal Selling
         b. Advertising
         c. Sales Promotions
         d. Publicity
         e. Word-of-Mouth
   B. *Interactive*
      1. Client-Employee
      2. Client-Community
      3. Client-Client
      4. Client-Environment
   C. *Internal*
      1. Orientation to Client
      2. Customer Management
      3. Personnel Training
      4. Personnel Policies and Incentives
      5. Organizational Communication
VII. BUDGET
VIII. IMPLEMENTATION
 IX. EVALUATION

Overall Objectives

Program objectives have been discussed earlier in Chapter Eleven, "Basic Administrative Planning," and might well be reviewed at this point. Objectives for the marketing plan itself might be stated in terms of numbers of clients, developing new images, or adding new programs, and usually will relate to the financial growth of the organization. Examples of three different fiscally-related objectives for a marketing plan might be:

- To increase the number of one-week trips by five percent in three years.
- To offer three new locations for adult tours (Scotland, The Everglades, and New Zealand) in the next three years.
- To increase the number of clients by 20 percent in the next five years.

Market Analysis

When developing the market plan, one must assess the impact of changes in demographics and lifestyles, economic conditions, laws and government actions, technology, and competition on the present and future markets. In other words, one must analyze the current market for the business.

Demographics and Lifestyles

Program providers need to understand the changing demographics and lifestyles of potential clients. Included today are the increase in single parent families, the decreasing size of the middle-class and above family, the rise (or decline) in family income, the number of two wage households with two different vacation times, the great increase in healthy retirees with the financial ability to travel, and the increase in minorities, mainstreamed, disabled, and "latch key" youth (those whose parents are not home when school is over). Knowing current facts about people will help one to identify feasible categories of potential clients.

Economic Conditions

Businesses and agencies need to monitor and assess the likely impact of changes in economic factors such as unemployment rates, real family income, rate of inflation, credit availability, terms and interest rates, and prices of complementary and competitive services (e.g., travel costs, equipment, and other program providers).

Laws and Government Regulations

The regulations concerning use permits, fire permits and policies, insurance, credentials, transportation of groups, etc., must all be understood and adhered to. Understanding these regulations will help determine the potential market for certain types of programs.

Technology

Just like all other segments of society, the outdoor program field has been impacted by technological changes. All-terrain vehicles, wind surfing, hang gliding, ski boarding, recreational vehicles, and motor homes have all provided new ways for people to be involved in the outdoors and have fragmented the recreation market. Radios, cellular phones, and sensing devices have changed the communication patterns of outdoor users. The effect of technology can impact the outdoor pursuit program and must be considered before developing a marketing plan.

Competition

It is important to analyze the competition's marketing strategies. What are their features and the quality of the program? Where are their outdoor program locations in relationship to their clients' homes? What are their promotional messages and themes? How are their prices comparable? What types of clients are they attracting? How can your program differ from the competition so that potential clients will find your program attractive?

Some examples of items to consider when doing an analysis of the marketing environment include the following: The best weather for a trip to Scotland is probably the end of the summer, while the best weather for a trip to New Zealand is probably from the end of fall to the middle of spring. The Everglades might be best before the summer heat and humidity is too high. Even at home, one might need to make alternate plans because of drought, fires, floods, or any number of natural conditions that will deter the clients from attending or give them an experience that forebodes repeating.

Transportation is a changing element. The prices of air fare, bus fare, or gasoline will play a part in the marketing of all programs. The political situation in various countries is a vital facet, and, even at home, important elections may impact on the interest of participants being away from home. The dollar fluctuation in other countries may mean the difference between a full tour and a limited one—as well as play a big part in the generation of gross income for the business.

Activities that are "in" may increase participation and may also increase the competition. Trips to the rain forest in South America or to any wildlife area are influenced by current issues, interests of clients, and the numbers of other tours and/or trips to the same areas. Certainly, the location of the Olympic competitions may influence certain potential clients to add an outdoor tour to their sport-viewing vacation. Terrorism, political activity, nuclear disaster, volcanic activity, past forest fire, or insect devastation, and many other factors can influence the potential of certain locales as prospects for outdoor programs—both new and long established. Analysis of the business environment creates the opportunity to make, strengthen, change, or delete plans for certain programs. Information on the above can be gathered by reviewing brochures, ads, and advertising produced by the competition.

Business Profile

The business profile is, in reality, an inventory of exactly what the business has to offer. In this case it means the types of services (backpacking, climbing, rafting, birding tours, etc.) that are offered, number and quality of staff, the equipment available (tents, cabins, huts, packs, ice axes, rafts, floatation devices, etc.), the image people have of the business now (unknown, dangerous, exclusive to the young, fit and adventuresome, for the affluent only, etc.), the satisfaction level, and the opinion of past clients. One needs to make a detailed list of exactly what is being offered to the client. Only then can the business be marketed completely and accurately.

Target Market Identification

After the first three steps are taken, the director can decide upon what part of the market to serve. One outdoor program cannot be all things to all people. The same program will not appeal to those who want a guided tour with all services provided and no responsibilities included, and to those who aspire to become leaders or avid participants in similar activities. The same program will probably not appeal equally to the novice canoeist and the advanced river runner.

Target marketing (or market segmentation) is the process of grouping potential or existing clients with similar preferences into groups known as market segments. The most promising segments are selected as target markets, and marketing mixes are designed which satisfy the special needs, desires, and behaviors of the targeted populations. Families with children aged ten or above, a mixture of disabled and their caring siblings, retirees interested in learning about natural resources while experiencing their first backpacking trip, and advanced climbers interested in glacier travel on high peaks are all different marketing segments. Potential clients can be grouped by location of residence, age, income, family status, interest in long- or short-term trips, settings of certain activities, and preferences for certain activities. At least one segment should consist of a group large enough to justify specialized marketing strategies. Other segments may be included by employing additional marketing strategies if the cost benefit analysis is favorable toward them.

After the potential market segments (or targets) have been identified, an assessment should be conducted to include: the existing and future potential of each target, the amount and strength of competition within each segment, the pro-gram's ability to offer a mix that will be successful in attracting different segments, the cost of servicing different segments, and whether and how much serving different segments will contribute to the overall objectives of the program. It is often wiser to target smaller segments that are presently not being served, or are being served inadequately, than to go after larger segments for which there is a great deal of competition. Programs might target families, senior citizens, single parents on vacation and their children, those with beginning, intermediate or advanced skills, or other segments.

Target Market Objectives

For each segment, different market objectives should be identified. Again, these objectives should be expressed in quantitative terms; they should be measurable; they should specify the target market, and indicate the time period in which the objective is to be accomplished.

These objectives are different from those developed for the marketing plan and should address the target markets specifically. For example:
- Increase the number of programs for retired persons by ten percent over the next five years.
- Increase the number of family programs focusing on natural history by five percent over the next five years.
- Add two one-week programs specifically for the physically disabled in the next two years.

Marketing Mixes

In the past, business directors thought of marketing as consisting of the traditional "four P's" approach—product, place, price, and promotion. Today, marketing is thought of in three types of mixes: traditional, interactive, and internal.

Traditional Marketing Mixes

Traditionally, marketing has consisted of emphasizing product, place, price, and promotion. Today, these four items are only a small segment of the entire marketing plan and is only one of three segments of what is known as the "marketing mix."

Product. Relative to the product, the outdoor program administrator must consider all aspects of the experience. It is not just a backpacking trip; it is meals, transportation, sleeping arrangements, rest stops and all other components combined to meet the clients' expectations.

Place. While place usually means one location, in outdoor pursuits, it is an analysis of a means of travel, transportation routes, stops for meals, sites for the program, accessibility, alternate sites, distances, and attractions en route.

Price. The price of the experience must be determined accurately, based upon the cost of producing the experience. The price for each segment of the program must be based on the business and target market objectives, full cost of producing, delivering, and promoting the experience, the willingness of the target market to pay for the product provided, prices charged by competitors, availability of substitutes or alternative programs, and the economic climate of the time. Different pricing strategies may encourage different dates, longer stays, group enrollments, special rates for families, and special packages such as weekends, holidays, etc. People often equate price with "quality" and may select a service that charges above the competition because they assume it to be of higher "quality." There is, however, both an upper and a lower threshold of recreation demand curves, above and below which the target segments will not purchase the service. With this fact in mind, the business should promote and provide evidence of the value of the offerings—not just the price.

Promotion. Promotion should be both useful to the potential client and accurate. Misrepresentation may lead to dissatisfied clients and is illegal. Promotion seems like a simple idea; however, it consists of five different methods: personal selling, advertising, sales, publicity and word-of-mouth. Because most entrepreneurs spend much time and money on promotion, this topic is treated in greater depth at the end of the major section on marketing.

Interactive Marketing

Interactive marketing refers to the relations between the people in the outdoor group (the clients) and others (such as representatives or the organization and members of the community). Interactive marketing is the process of developing the best possible relations among all the publics that might be influenced by the enterprise in question. It involves the principles of public relations, and it is involved with several types of client relations.

Client-Organization/Employee. Clients and potential clients often make no distinction between the experience and the staff that produce it. Unpleasant experiences with staff make for totally unpleasant experiences with the program—regardless of beautiful sunsets and breathtaking views.

Client-Community. Being a people-oriented business, the outdoor-pursuit program can make optimal use of the human element in public relations. Probably the best tool is the group itself. The relations between the clients and the greater community may determine the public

image of the organization. Part of participant-created public opinion is generated while the group is en route to or from the outing site. How they look and talk in restaurants and gas stations directs public opinion. While they are on the trail, lake, or river, they can also influence the opinion of those who see and/or hear them. It comes from what is seen on the news media, reading the messages printed on the T-shirts, watching the group eat hamburgers at a rest stop, and witnessing staff behavior on days off. It includes the opinions formed by persons they meet on the trail or river, government agency personnel, and the local businesses that serve the organization.

Leaders are included in all the preceding situations, as they can exert a great influence on public perception of the program. Whenever the leader discusses his/her experiences, and/or appears among those who are aware of the programs, opinions are formed. He/she represents the sponsoring organization, and the reputation of the various programs offered by that organization may rise or fall because of the effect of the leader's behavior even in situations unrelated to the site or the activity. The effects continue after the outing, when participants are at home relating the positive and negative aspects of their experiences to family and friends.

Client-Client. It goes without saying that all clients will not like each other equally; however, all clients must get along well enough to work, eat, travel, and recreate together. Interpersonal conflict resolution is an important part of staff training, and how it is implemented is crucial to the opinion clients form as they react together.

Client-Environment. The relationship of the customer and the environment (i.e., total surroundings) is important. A good relationship does not necessarily depend upon an easy trail and warm sunshine. A client may have had a hard day in the rain on a rough trail but can become comfortable with warm food, a dry tent, and the vision of a good breakfast the next day. The opinion formed of the entire organization and its leaders might well hinge on perceptions of experiences created by environmental conditions. "Perception" is the key word here. If the leader establishes an appropriate set of expectations in the minds of participants and conducts the program well, the clients will derive maximum rewards from the total experience, and end with an appreciation of, if not fondness for, the environments of the activity.

Internal Marketing

Internal marketing is directed at the staff rather than at the client.

Orientation to the client. The administrator must first market the job to the staff, then market the program to the potential participants. Employees must have high motivation and favorable attitudes toward the program. This means that the main objective of internal marketing is to employ and retain the best possible staff within an organizational system and philosophy that allows them to do their best. A second objective is to develop satisfied staff who will see the logic and payoff of courteous and empathetic behavior toward the participants.

Customer-Oriented Management. The administrator/leader must educate the rest of the staff to the similarities and differences among the characteristics, needs, and abilities of the participants through a process of client orientation. The leaders and staff must be "participant oriented." It starts from the top down—from the administrators and chief instructors down to the apprentices. It means a positive interaction with the participants.

Personnel Training. Too often the training of staff focuses on technical aspects of the job. It is just as important to focus on aspects of dealing with the client. Training in participant relation skills (e.g., dealing constructively with complainers) is even more essential if the staff consists of people who have not worked previously in human contact positions. Training should also consist of verbal and nonverbal communication skills. Listening skills are equally important, as are sales techniques that consist of how to interpret the outdoor program to others.

Personnel Policies and Incentives. The material presented in Chapter Eleven related to the value of good personnel policies and incentives. These are inherent functions of internal marketing. One might consider that higher wages could be offset by increased participant

satisfaction and lower employee turnover costs. The recommendations of satisfied staff may play a crucial role in recruiting new clients.

Organizational Communication. A final aspect of internal marketing is organizational communication which, in essence, means letting the staff know what is going on. Staff who know the marketing objectives can help to recruit new clients. Staff who know about current and future programs can provide clients with information that may result in more enrollments. Communication is also a two-way street. Staff must be able to relate both positive and negative participant comments to the administration. They can facilitate client feedback by encouraging input from clients and communicating it to the administration.

Marketing Budget

The marketing budget should be based upon the marketing objectives. If one of the objectives of the marketing plan is "to offer three new locations for adult tours in the next three years," the fiscal plan for marketing the program should reflect the costs anticipated to meet this objective. The marketing budget should also be based upon estimated income generated by meeting the marketing objectives. The budget should be flexible but modified only after careful consideration of the impact of the change on the marketing mix and accomplishment of objectives. The adage, "It takes money to make money," can be recalled here.

Implementation

Implementing the market plan for the outdoor pursuit program can be accomplished through: (1) informing the employees about the marketing plan (e.g., rationale, objectives, and strategies); (2) identifying specific tasks to be accomplished; (3) assigning specific responsibilities for different tasks; (4) developing time lines and deadlines; and (5) adhering to the budget and monitoring progress. It should be obvious by now that many of the points in the marketing plans will be covered, at least in part, by other administrative functions. No administrative functions are independent of any other!

Evaluation

Evaluation is an essential, but often overlooked, element of a marketing plan. The purpose of evaluation is to improve the effectiveness of marketing strategies by identifying differences between actual results and expected performance, and determining likely reasons for the success or failure to realize objectives. Marketing mix strategies must be continually evaluated rather than waiting for a crisis.

Developing the Market Plan

To develop the marketing plan, one can take the outline presented here and write down how each topic and subtopic is already being addressed. It will probably come as a surprise that many portions of the marketing plan are already in place or at least under consideration. Then complete the plan by adding modifications, by adding plans to topics left blank, and by reviewing the entire nine major topics for completeness.

Like planning a budget, a marketing plan is intended to be flexible and can be modified to fit the situation. It is not difficult to complete if the leader/administrator has already considered the generic functions of administration discussed in Chapter Eleven.

Promotion—A Major Marketing Function

Promotion is the second of the traditional marketing mixes described above. In the back of any outdoor magazine, the flyers of many city or county recreation departments, school and college papers and catalogs, club bulletins, and on the walls of outdoor-equipment stores are ads for all sorts of outings and courses. Unfortunately, many of these activities don't take place due to insufficient participation, which in turn is often due to inadequate or inefficient promotion.

Effective promotion of an outdoor pursuit activity requires an understanding of what prompts people to participate as well as an understanding of what stands in the way of participation. Motivation may be positive (driven by personal desires), or it may be negative (compelled by internal or external forces). Examples of positive motivation are interests in fitness enhancement or skill development, scientific or aesthetic interest in the environment, or the improvement of mental health via relaxation and recreation. Other possible advantages of taking part in outdoor pursuits are discussed in Chapter One, and any of these may prove to be positive motivators. Equally powerful motivation can come about through pressure to conform, as when spouses, close friends, or others in a peer group urge participation in an activity. Sometimes, the participant really has little choice, as is often the case with children, students, and military personnel assigned to the activity. When promoting an outing, keep the goals and objectives clearly in mind and be willing to consider modification of the approach as you become more familiar with the potential group and what may be motivating them.

Typically, the organizer of an outdoor program is a devotee of the activity who finds great satisfaction in it. It is easy to forget that the great majority of people have no comparable interest in the activity, no matter how exciting it may seem to the organizer. Before formulating the promotional scheme, look carefully at the people you hope to attract. Try to understand *their* view of the activity. People absorb new ideas slowly, so unless lots of time and money are available for massive educational promotion, it is often best to present the activity in a way that is consistent with the expectations of potential participants. Most people see what they *expect* to see. If your organization typically offers a certain kind of program and usually promotes programs in a certain way, an argument can be made for following this pattern if it has been successful in the past. If successful promotion channels already exist, it is best to continue the old format as much as possible since it usually saves money to plug into well-tested and successful systems. It is certainly possible to create completely new types of programs and to use new and eye-catching promotional techniques; however, this usually involves a high start-up cost, and outdoor-pursuit activities are often low-budget operations.

When designing the promotional scheme, and in fact the program itself, it is a good idea to bear in mind the reasons why people *don't* sign up for outdoor pursuits. For example, one common reason is the perception that great physical prowess and/or youth is a prerequisite to participation. When real barriers don't exist, the promotional scheme should include elements designed to break down these misconceptions. Good photographs can be invaluable in getting this sort of message across. Another, and all-too-often valid concern is the cost. What may seem a worthwhile expenditure to a devotee of outdoor pursuits may not seem worthwhile to one not yet involved. This points up the importance of emphasizing personal benefits in promotional materials.

Time is another major concern. Most people don't see themselves as having enough discretionary time. Weekends are spent mowing the lawn, cleaning house, washing the car, or other chores, and by voluntary or obligatory visits with friends or relatives.

Promoting an outdoor program is not just a matter of attracting people from some vacuous limbo. The program has to be seen as sufficiently rewarding to overcome the real or perceived constraints of everyday life. A good promotional campaign should simultaneously extol the virtues of the activity and attempt to reduce the effects of these constraints. This is especially important when dealing with true beginners, and when it argues for short duration, easy access, low cost, and low-obligation experiences. A person who might never commit to a weekend of high Alpine backpacking, no matter how easy and no matter how fabulous the scenery, may well sign up for a half- or full-day hike, especially if it is inexpensive and the children can be included.

Some suggestions for overcoming concerns about time commitment are:

1. Check the calendar carefully to avoid any obvious conflicts (athletic events, etc.).
2. Promote well in advance (a month or more) since people are much more likely to commit themselves to a distant date. A day or a month in the future seems much less significant than next weekend when the lawn needs mowing, the car needs washing, and other commitments have already been made.
3. Try to combine a *perception* of low commitment with a real commitment of money. A fee schedule that gives a substantial break for early payment but that disallows refund of part or all of the fee is usually perceived as fair, especially if the amount is small. Such a schedule helps minimize budget worries and tends to reduce the number of dropouts.
4. Counter the concern *directly* by pointing out the advantages of commitment to a program. Many people *appreciate* being obligated to go on an outing, since they recognize the mental and physical advantages of participation but have difficulty justifying involvement when faced with short-term pressures.

There are five principal methods of promotion, each of which involves a different strategy and each of which has a different purpose.

Personal Selling

Personal selling involves communicating information through personal, usually face-to-face, contact between the potential client and the employees or representatives of the program. Past participants themselves should be viewed as potential sales people. Staff who have participated in some hospitality training will serve as better sales persons than those who have no familiarity with how to influence people. One example of personal selling appropriate for outdoor-pursuit programs include everyday conversations wherein interested people ask questions or wherein the leaders, administrator, or staff member can initiate conversations relative to the program in question. Many times, there are "job fairs" or "vacation fairs" at universities and colleges for the purpose of helping people find summer jobs or vacations. Usually, personal selling is occasional and not scheduled. It should, however, be planned, accurate, and appealing; thus, a practice session on answering anticipated questions is invaluable.

The presentation of lecture, slide show, or movies is time consuming, and, in the case of slides and movies may call for significant investments in camera equipment, film, editing and processing, and projection equipment. It is also one of the most productive forms of personal selling, dollar for dollar, if good bookings can be arranged. The effectiveness of this method depends upon the topic matter, the quality of the material presented, how well it is presented, and to whom. An excellent slide presentation to a local club, school, or other gathering place for prospective clients or participants is likely to yield substantial interest, enhanced credibility for the organization, and opportunities for presentations to other groups.

Direct solicitation through door-to-door contacts and telephone messages should be avoided because they offend many people; they are time-consuming; and they seldom yield enough customers to warrant the effort. In many places, such solicitation is against local ordinances without the acquisition of special permits.

Advertising

The process of advertising involves the dissemination of promotional messages through "paid for" media such as newspapers, magazines, radio, television, and advertising through brochures and other printed means. These media are well-suited for quick delivery of information to widespread audiences. Effective advertising requires more than just well-designed or well-worded copy. The media and methods must be selected carefully in order for the process to yield the needed responses at a cost that is within budgetary limits (and, ideally, is minimal). There are many potential avenues, most of which exist even in smaller communities. These include various printed media, electronic media, and several more directed approaches. Suggestions for several types of advertising means are as follows:

Flyers

Flyers are small, typically letter- or legal-sized, advertisements printed on one or both sides. They are inexpensive, and, therefore, they may be printed or photocopied in large quantities at nominal cost. Because they are designed to be carried away and read at leisure, flyers can

contain a lot of information in addition to whatever illustrations, designs or words are used to attract attention. A well-designed flyer can serve as a mini-poster and also be folded for mailing. When distributed wisely, they can be very effective and yield prospective clients or participants at a very low cost per response. The key is finding places to leave stacks of flyers so that they will be seen and picked up by likely clientele. For example, a flyer for an advanced rock climbing course might be placed in an outdoor specialty store catering to experienced climbers, while it may be best to place flyers for entry level skiing or hiking courses in a general sporting goods store or in a fitness center. Schools and businesses often have bulletin boards available, but one should always check before posting to be sure of the organization's rules.

Posters

Posters are usually larger than flyers, are designed to attract attention, and are usually printed on one side only. Unlike flyers, which can be taken away and read later, posters remain on the wall or bulletin board. The message must be clear at a glance, leaving the viewer interested and aware of who to call or where to go for more information. Sometimes posters, which are costly, can pay for themselves if they are attractive enough to be sold at a nominal cost to those who collect such items to decorate their dormitory or bedroom walls.

A technique often used by large companies to help viewers remember important data is to provide a folder tray of cards, or even postage-paid postcards, attached to or near the poster. Tear-off tabs used by small companies may be effective but may be unsightly unless designed carefully. As with flyers, location is all important. Often, space is limited in stores and on bulletin boards, so the temptation to produce larger eye-catching sizes must be weighed against the greater likelihood of finding display positions for smaller sizes.

Pamphlets

Pamphlets are booklets produced on pages in multiples of four (4, 8, 12, 16). Frequently, pamphlets are folded to fit into a standard business envelope. A pamphlets may fit well in display racks commonly found in outdoor equipment stores, but usually it will not serve well unless the cover makes people want to pick it up and read it. The name of the sponsoring organization in large print is usually less effective than a curiosity whetting line like, "Get Away From It All."

When considering a pamphlets design, it is important to work with a knowledgeable printer. The costs of paper and printing vary over a remarkably wide range depending upon size, paper quality, whether the paper to be used is recyclable, if the final copy and ink are recyclable, the number of colors, whether or not photographs are used, and the printing processes involved. As with any type of printing, there are usually significant start up costs for each run, so it is important to predict needs accurately to take advantage of quantity discounts and avoid multiple orders.

Newsletters

Many organizations use newsletters, and their editors are chronically short of copy. Schools, clubs, churches, youth organizations, and fitness centers often print newsletters on a regular basis. A ski club, for example, might print an ad for a program for free or for a modest fee. Sometimes, an "ad" can be included either overtly or subtly, in a feature story or article. Most editors will jump at the opportunity to include material of interest to the newsletter's subscribers.

Some sponsors may find it worthwhile to circulate their own "newsletter," which might provide a mix of interesting articles and self-promotional material.

Flyers, pamphlets, or newsletters can be mailed to targeted individuals and agencies using mailing lists of previous participants and likely prospects. Lists of likely prospects can be compiled from referrals and responses to ads, or they may be obtained, in some cases, by

purchasing mailing lists from organizations who target similar populations. A ski school may not want to sell its list to another local ski school, but it may well agree to sell the list to a provider of summer rafting excursions. Special bulk mail rates are available for those who plan to mail at least several hundred items; check with the U.S. Postal Service for the latest quote on the ever changing rate structure to compare various options.

Newspaper Ads

Advertising through newspapers can be an excellent choice, especially when the activity has broad appeal. A series of rafting clinics or ski lessons might be effectively advertised in the paper, while an advanced level, technical clinic might be more effectively marketed in an appropriate specialty outfitter. There are several possible ways of publicizing a program in a newspaper. Display ads are usually quite effective, but good placement and adequate size are costly. Tabloid sections have the advantage of being designed to be removed and saved, but, like display ads they are costly. (See Mass Media below.)

Printed Materials

Every program uses the printed word for one or more purposes. Promotion flyers, sign-up sheets, equipment lists, report forms, instruction sheets, and numerous other printed materials are used to convey information. Needless to say, the quality of the material can be judged by both appearance and content. Gone is the day of smudgy mimeographed flyers or faint, illegible spirit-duplicator copies. New types of office machines capable of producing clear, crisp copies have left inferior ones far behind. No one can afford sloppy-looking material anymore.

The content of the printed material must likewise be precise. Incorrect language use and spelling reflect on the intelligence of the sponsor and thus create negative opinions of the entire program. Even the signature on written letters should be legible; an illegible scrawl may be interpreted as a sign of one who is pompous about his/her importance and who doesn't care for the reader enough to take the time to sign a name legibly.

Visual Media

Many times the sponsor of a program will use a slide show for promotion purposes. Sometimes, the sponsor or leader is so enthusiastic about the merits of the topic discussed that poor, fuzzy, or out-of-date pictures are shown as if the audience will imagine what good shots would look like. Until there are enough good slides to cover 100 percent of the program, no slide show should be given. Furthermore, no slides should be shown unless they are authentically related to the actual program. To be effective, the slides must be selected carefully. Older adults are not usually convinced of the ease of a trip if all they see are young, fit devotees of the activity. Nor would youth be convinced of the necessity for being in top shape if all they saw were older people at rest. The presentation must clearly depict the realities, and yet be understandable and appealing to the audience.

Mass Media

Mass media includes newspapers, radio, and television which are available to the majority of the general public. Ordinarily, one does not think of mass media as a prime method for generating public opinion about an outdoor-pursuit program. Paid radio and newspaper ads, however, can produce excellent results; however, the costs are very high, especially for "prime" times in the case of radio.

Suggestions. When designing the layout of advertisements, several points should be kept in mind:

1. Keep it simple. In most cases, people will not read very much printed information in an advertisement. Simply include what, when, where, and how much it costs, with, at most, a sentence or two extolling the virtues of the activity. When seeking participants for an introductory or beginning-level experience, it is important to mention the key benefits of the program. People are usually much more interested

in skills, thrills, or relaxation than in details other than time, place, and cost. A contact name, address, and phone number should be included. Think about the ads you see. What do you look for and remember? A good ad leaves the viewer eager for more information and aware of the name of the contact agency, which can be located later using a telephone directory.

2. Use sketches or photos if possible. As with the written portion, keep illustrations clear and simple. Most printed messages are only glanced at for a few seconds at most. When selecting or designing the illustration, try to find or create one that inspires curiosity. Photographs tend to do this, as the viewer may at least be curious as to when and where the picture was taken. You want the person to be drawn to the advertisement and stay fixed for a few seconds. Skiers tend to spot and fix attention on skiers, climbers on climbers, kayakers on kayakers, and so on. Be sure that body position, equipment, safety practices, and technique in the illustration are appropriate and correct. Beginners may not notice errors, but devotees and experts do and often make fun of an illustration that shows poor form or outdated gear which damages the image of the program. When trying to attract beginners, it is a good idea to elaborate on some aspects of the activity that may be especially appealing to them, even if it is not an especially important part of the sport for avid participants. A rockclimbing course, for example, might use an illustration of a rappel, taking care, of course, not to illustrate anything too scary. Most people seek a bit of excitement in outdoor pursuits, but, also like to think of themselves as growing old with all limbs still attached. A beginning ski class ad should show some appealing aspects of learning how to ski, and not show someone on the lunatic fringe descending an icy 60 degree chute.

Sales

Sales promotions, while not carried on extensively for outdoor pursuit organizations, still have a potential in terms of recruiting clients. Included could be raffles, sales of T-shirts, sweat shirts, bandannas, mugs, and banners.

Publicity

Like advertising, publicity uses mass media to communicate information. The difference is that you do not pay for publicity. In order to gain publicity, the information must be newsworthy and of potential interest to the media's audience. Youth agencies and public educational institutions can benefit most from positive media publicity that are public service announcements. Particularly interesting courses or events, however, may be written up by newspaper staff and published as regular news, and, sometimes, as with newsletters, a newspaper will print contributed stories, or at least edit or coauthor articles. Many newspapers have weekly columns devoted to outdoor related topics. While the majority seem to focus on hunting and fishing, most will consider featuring other outdoor recreation activities, especially if they are of current interest. Often there are weekly columns written by outdoors people, schedules of trips, where to get more information, and occasional articles and photographs related to successful ventures. These rarely, if ever, rate front-page space and are more likely relegated to the family section or hidden inside the paper as fillers. But if an accident or tragedy occurs, it is front-page and prime-time news.

There is an ongoing need for mass media coverage that depicts outdoor recreation activities as exciting, potentially challenging, accessible to all, and quite safe if approached thoughtfully and responsibly.

Radio and Television. Most radio and television stations accept public interest announcements, for which they charge no fee. However, the announcement usually has to come from, and/or address, a public-oriented non-profit activity or, for example, a fund raising event for a charitable cause. Typically, the broadcast times aren't ideal, so the message may only reach those who are still sitting glued to the set as the station is about to sign off at 1:30 a.m. Stations target their audiences and invest heavily in surveys of their viewers and listeners. This information can be helpful in locating the best stations for a particular purpose, especially in the context of a comparative review of the survey data of each station. Many outdoor activities are intriguing topics for discussion, and most have exciting visual potential. Staff experts may be welcome on radio "ask an expert" shows, to speak about seasonally popular activities. Radio and TV talk shows need interesting guests who can speak on topics of timely interest. During and immediately following major news stories, television stations often bring in "talking heads," experts who can interpret or comment on some aspect of the situation. By letting local stations know of the expertise of its employees, an organization may be afforded opportunities to gain exposure and enhance credibility.

Word-of-mouth

Much of an organization's promotional marketing is generated by word-of-mouth from satisfied and dissatisfied participants and staff, persons who do business with the agency and persons who meet the participants on their treks, trips, and tours. Most enterprises rely heavily on word-of-mouth. It is sometimes surprising how rapidly the word spreads if a product or service is viewed as worthwhile.

Discussion

In a sense, every investment in quality and every effort to keep the cost to participants as low as possible is an investment in advertising. Do a great job, then be very patient. For most businesses and institutions, several years are required before enough clients or participants are engaged to claim real success. One reason may be that, while word travels rapidly, it must reach a very large audience before the volume of regular clientele reaches the level necessary to sustain a program economically. The first few years of any enterprise may be very tough, but those who find the will and the means to keep providing an excellent service almost always succeed. Programs built on a foundation of good public perception are somewhat less reliant upon conventional advertising techniques and so are better able to afford further investments and improvements in program quality.

The development of a planned promotional campaign should be based upon: (1) the *target market* you wish to aim at; (2) the *image* you wish to create; (3) the *objectives* of the promotional program; (4) the *budget* for the promotion; (5) the *timing* of the materials; (6) the *media* that will most effectively and efficiently communicate your message; and (7) how the effect of the promotional campaign can be *evaluated.* The outdoor program should be promoted according to credible representation of the intangibles such as fun, adventure, education, friendship, self-concept, and a leisure experience. The program that wishes to inspire the element of quality may discuss the staff qualifications, equipment, program progression, etc.

Dissatisfaction often results when there is a discrepancy between perceived expectations and actual experience. The program that was promoted as moderate daily jaunts in the sunshine may be, in actuality, filled with several days of arduous travel in a cold downpour through mud and melting snow. Promotional materials must convey realistic impressions, and a good promotional campaign will include a mix of difficulties as well as joys of the outdoor experience. If the mountain streams will be too cold for swimming, the promise or suggestion of swimming may result in disgruntled participants. Mention of trout-filled streams is of no purpose unless the group will be given time for fishing, instruction, and a list of equipment to bring.

Other promotional methods include Christmas cards, T-shirts, thank you letters, newsletters, and group photographs. Contact with merchants, gas station operators, and restaurants in towns through which the group will travel can establish positive images in advance.

Public Relations Principles

Public relations is a planned effort to steer public opinion in a favorable direction. The following principles can help leaders and administrators achieve maximum benefit from a marketing program.

1. The public relations program should be continuous. This means that planning and implementation should be part of every program and an everyday occurrence. Every time the program and its sponsor are mentioned, by word-of-mouth or in print, opinions may be formed or altered. A program designed to influence public opinion *after* the fact is too late.

2. All aspects of the marketing program should be honest. In spite of the fact that one purpose of such a program is to arouse favorable opinion, the truth should never be stretched or altered to achieve this goal. An administrator who promotes a program through brochures that show photographs of areas not utilized in the program is dishonest. A brochure that identifies leader qualifications that do not exist is dishonest. Written *intentions* do not suffice for honest facts.

3. Public relations should be all-encompassing and comprehensive. The public needs to know the entire story. An organization that offers a "memorable canoe trip" interprets the outing incompletely unless the public is led to understand it occurs on a slow-moving river past spectacular scenery or on whitewater pouring through immense canyons.

Public Relations in Emergencies

When an accident occurs or when a search or rescue is called for, the public image of the organization may be seriously damaged. The potential damage depends partly upon the actual events and partly upon what the public *perceives* as the actual events. Much of the public perception of the event is dependent upon the statements of the organization's representatives, be they leaders and staff in the field or administrators. The special case of public relations at the scene of an emergency is discussed in Chapter Eight, "Search and Rescue."

The organization should have a plan for handling public relations in emergencies, wherein the roles and responsibilities of administrators and staff are well-defined. An administrator should be designated to serve as a spokesperson for the organization, and this person or another administrator should be assigned responsibility for overseeing the effort. There are several important responsibilities that must be attended to immediately. These include:

1. Notification of parents, guardians, relatives, or friends.

This should be done immediately, out of courtesy, and to reduce the chance of concerned individuals learning of the incident first via the media. Sometimes, public agencies can assist in emergency notifications. At least initially, the family does not need to know any graphic or shocking details, or any rumors unless the purpose is to deflate in advance a rumor that they might hear anyway.

2. Communications with involved staff.

Administrators must remain accessible to staff throughout the incident. When possible, the spokesperson should conduct the communications, and he/she should prompt the involved field personnel to record all necessary data at the scene.

3. Communications with the media and other agencies.

The spokesperson must remain accessible to the media throughout the incident and the period of media interest following the incident. The effectiveness of the "spokesperson" approach is greatly enhanced if all organization personnel know how to channel questions quickly and graciously to the spokesperson. The spokesperson should be direct, honest, positive in tone, and compassionate, but should avoid giving out unnecessary details, stating judgments or predictions, providing names until parents, guardians, or relatives have been notified, or releasing any information that could adversely affect the well-being of the injured or lost person. On the other hand, the spokesperson must not withhold any information if doing so would be detrimental to the victim's interests.

4. Develop a complete accident report.

This will usually include all of the information gathered at the accident scene, notes from debriefing sessions with involved staff, logs of administrative actions during the incident, copies of the logs of search and rescue, police, ambulance, or other agencies when available (these may provide accurate times for key events), and notes from later interviews with the injured or lost person.

5. Contact the victim and/or the family after the incident.

Phone calls and/or visits to a hospital or home indicate goodwill and facilitate friendly relationships. On the positive side, contacts can help the administrator understand what happened so that the chance of recurrences can be reduced, and increase the chance of the person resuming participation in the program. From a more pessimistic perspective, such contact may reduce the likelihood of lawsuits being filed, or at least demonstrate a caring attitude by administrators.

Summary

The marketing of recreation programs is based upon the understanding that the outdoor product is an experience—not a tangible product. Nevertheless, marketing plans for "service" businesses should follow the steps of marketing plans for "product" businesses. In this chapter, an nine-point marketing plan is recommended. Using this plan, the administrator of an outdoor program can develop marketing strategies which incorporate traditional, interactive, and internal strategies. The marketing plan should be directed as much toward satisfying and retaining old customers as it is toward attracting new ones. The program must also be marketed to the employees and the communities where they do business. Principles of public relations are incorporated into the recommended marketing plan, but additional specific public relations plans must be implemented for emergency situations.

References

Clawson, M., & Knetsch, J. L. (1966). *Economics of outdoor recreation.* Baltimore, MD: The Johns Hopkins Press.

Czepiel, J. A., Solomon, M., & Surprenant, C. (Eds.). (1985). *The service encounter.* Toronto, Canada: Lexington Books.

Donnelly, J. H., & George, W. (Eds.). (1981). *Marketing of services.* Chicago, IL: American Marketing Association.

George, W. R., & Barksdale, H. (October 1974). Marketing activities in the service industries." *Journal of Marketing,* 38, pp. 65-70.

Kotler, P. (1975). *Marketing for non-profit institutions.* Engelwood Cliffs, NJ: Prentice-Hall.

Lovelock, C.H. (1983). *Service marketing.* Englewood Cliffs, NJ: Prentice-Hall.

Mahoney, E. (1989). Lecture. U.S. Forest Service Marketing Symposium. East Lansing, MI: Department of Park and Recreation Resources, Michigan State University.

Rathmell, J. M. (July 1966). What is meant by services. *Journal of Marketing,* 27, pp. 32-36.

TRANSPORTATION

At first glimpse, the topic of transportation may not appear to be a component of an outdoor-pursuit program. It is, however, one of the most important components of outdoor recreation and one that must be understood by administrators and leaders alike. Because most outdoor pursuits are not held within walking distance of participants' homes or the facilities of the sponsoring agency, transportation becomes a major factor in planning and implementing a successful outdoor venture. Some administrators may be reluctant to offer programs away from their own facilities because of concerns about injuries, accidents, subsequent litigation, and potential liability. Certainly all the best planning for a successful experience in the field is of no value unless participants arrive at the site and return home safely. Just as certainly, there are real risks associated with transportation. Yet, with careful planning and effective management control, these risks can be reduced to acceptable levels.

Resources for Transportation

It goes without saying that modern transportation necessitates motorized travel (i.e., train, plane, bus, or automobile). Using trains and planes to transport participants to appropriate sites for outdoor pursuits will, in all likelihood, also entail cars and/or buses to move people from the depot or airport to the location of the activity. With this scenario in mind, much of this chapter will concentrate on automotive transportation.

Vehicle Types

The selection of vehicles may seem simple until one considers the pros and cons of the many alternatives: cars, station wagons, vans, and buses for passengers, and racks, trailers, and various vehicles for hauling equipment. It is also important to consider whether the vehicles are privately-owned, rented, or leased, or owned by the institution, and whether the drivers are professionals or volunteers, participants or nonparticipants, staff or nonstaff. These variables interact in innumerable ways. While there are some common patterns, virtually every permutation is employed in some program. In the interest of clarity, vehicle type, transportation of gear, ownership, and drivers will be addressed as separate issues. Later in the section, combinations that have worked well for many programs will be addressed along with safety issues and some practical tips.

There are usually several transportation options available to program planners and leaders. In most cases, automobiles are necessary for at least part of the journey. In general, safety is enhanced and costs are reduced by keeping the number of vehicles to a minimum. In other words, each vehicle should be filled to capacity. In many cases vehicle passenger capacity determines the limit for enrollment, as transportation costs may rise sharply with each additional vehicle (unless those vehicles are filled). When the group size is not limited by vehicle capacity, it is easiest to achieve the lowest possible cost per trip per participant when vehicles of various sizes are available. For example, a group of 20 dayhikers might be transported most efficiently in a 15-passenger van and a five passenger sedan, with day packs stowed in the sedan trunk and under or behind van seats. Twenty backpackers would probably require an additional cargo van or large (preferably covered) pickup truck. In either case, the cost per trip per person would probably be less than if four or five sedans were used.

There are other issues, however, that must be considered when deciding what vehicles to use. Smaller vehicles are generally easier to drive and may (especially in the case of four-wheel drive and other specialty vehicles) be better able to negotiate rough roads. Smaller vehicles, however, may mean more vehicles, which adds risk, requires more drivers, adds to the difficulty of keeping track of the group, and reduces opportunities for group socializing or discussions. Station wagons (and most of the new "minivans") may have more room for bulky gear such as backpacks; however, the space advantage may be slight compared to sedans with large trunks. In most cases, station wagons present a significant hazard unless a protective barrier is installed to restrain gear from flying forward in the event of a sudden stop or accident.

Vans are often the vehicle of choice, since their capacity is often close to the size of organized hiking or other outdoor groups. It is important to check with local authorities to determine whether or not a special license, such as a chauffeur's license, is required in order to drive the vehicle in question. In any case, it's important to recognize that driving a large van, especially when full of people, can be either more difficult or more intimidating than driving a passenger car. Drivers of vans should be experienced drivers, preferably with van driving

experience. Buses may be cost effective for large groups. While there are obvious advantages to having a large group all in one vehicle, the size of a bus presents some potential problems. Some backcountry roads, trailheads, and access points cannot accommodate large buses. In addition, most states require special licenses in order to operate buses; thus, it may be necessary to hire professional drivers.

Ownership

Vehicles may be private (that is owned by staff, participants, or others), rented, or leased, or owned by the institution. Each has advantages and disadvantages in terms of costs, liability, and convenience. Private vehicles are often used in situations wherein the frequency of need is low, and/or there is an abundance of available private vehicles. While the institution is spared a major capital investment and ongoing maintenance expenses, it always loses some control over the quality and maintenance of the vehicles and usually loses control of the driving of the vehicle. If, as is usually the case, the transportation of passengers and gear is considered to be part of the program, then any increase in the risks of transportation increases the exposure of the institution. If any mishap should occur, whether or not individual vehicle owners have insurance, the institution may be at risk financially.

Any institution or organization planning to use private vehicles should review their insurance situations carefully with an agent or attorney. Often, it is the owners and drivers of private vehicles who are most adversely affected. Cars are expensive to operate, and yet compensation schemes seldom are adequate to cover the full costs of use. If compensation is provided, then the drivers and/or owners might be considered commercial carriers, in which case their insurance may not apply. A nonowner policy may be procured for each vehicle not owned by the sponsoring organization, or participants whose cars are used may be insured at the expense of the sponsor. This is not an unusual practice among youth camps that use staff-owned cars in the summer. The use of private vehicles is commonplace but risky for the vehicle owners and the institutions. Given proper insurance and careful management, however, private vehicle use can be a reasonable and highly cost effective alternative. (See "Carpools.")

For many programs, even ones sponsoring large numbers of outings, rental is an attractive option. The number and type of vehicles can be set according to the specific needs of a program; there is no need to invest large amounts of capital in a fleet of vehicles; and, maintenance and storage costs are eliminated. There may also be some advantages regarding liability, in that some responsibility for certain aspects of safety maintenance may be borne by the rental agency. In addition, rental agency vehicles are usually no more than a few years old, so mechanical failure rates are relatively low. Government agencies are often able to rent vehicles from a motor pool. In this case, rates may be slightly less than from private rental agencies, though considerable advance notice may be required to obtain the desired vehicles.

Direct ownership of vehicles is ideal in terms of access and control. It is very convenient to have the program vehicles on-site and ready to go at all times; however, as any vehicle owner knows, there are many costs and potential frustrations associated with vehicle ownership. Purchase and maintenance costs (and all too frequently, replacement costs) are major barriers, especially for small organizations. Even after considering tax advantages, it is usually hard to justify vehicle purchase on a purely economic basis. Parking space, insurance, and licensing need to be considered. Liability insurance rates may reflect the greater level of responsibility inherent in vehicle ownership. An organization that owns a vehicle and maintains it can't defer some of the blame for inadequate maintenance to a rental agency.

Drivers

Few components of outdoor-pursuit activities are more hazardous, hour for hour, than driving. In many programs, there is more risk of serious injury or death on the highway than on the trail or river. While attention may be focused upon the skills of the leader and instructor, it is the

driver who may hurtle down the freeway at a mile a minute with a dozen people dozing in the back seats. All too often drivers are asked to drive large, unfamiliar vehicles full of passengers on unfamiliar roads, either early in the morning en route to an outing, or late in the afternoon, tired from a day or more of adventure, on the homeward drive. While it is obvious that no one should be allowed to drive unless qualified, alert, and willing, too often the list of criteria is shortened to simply *willing*. Sometimes, this is due to difficulty in finding enough drivers, and sometimes to a reluctance to question a driver's qualifications or even to act on concerns about a prospective driver's record.

There is no excuse, ethically or legally, for not making sure that all drivers are qualified and capable of safe driving. It is frustrating to have to cancel an outing for lack of drivers, and that shouldn't happen if the initial planning for the outing was done well. Nevertheless, such cancellation does happen now and then, and it must be accepted with no temptation to compromise on safety. Such compromise could lead to disaster, and certainly would send a clear signal that the organization puts convenience or economics before safety.

There are various ways of assessing potential drivers. The first criteria is generally that of appropriate licensing, which may include special notations, or a chauffeur's license in some areas, often depending upon the size of vehicle to be driven. Next, it is important to know if the person has had experience with the kind of vehicle in question. Even an experienced driver who hasn't driven vans should not be allowed to practice with a van full of people; however, the same person might be allowed to drive a cargo van. The road conditions are important as well. Many drivers are either uncomfortable with or inexperienced in night driving or driving on snow and ice. Again, vehicles carrying passengers must not be used for practice!

Most public institutions have driver clearance procedures whereby the driver's record is checked by computer through a police department. Typically, a scheme is devised wherein various traffic offenses are assigned points, which are gradually reduced over time. The driver's "score" must be below a certain level before the person may be allowed to drive public vehicles. The rules for access to driving records vary from state to state, especially with regard to access by private organizations. Many organizations, sometimes inspired (or urged on) by their insurance carriers, insist upon completion of a driver training or driver safety course before service as a driver. All drivers transporting youth must be screened for their records related to child abuse and similar conduct.

Smaller organizations may choose to send employees through a local driving program, while larger organizations may opt to develop their own training programs. While the needs of each organization vary, there are some objectives common to most driver training programs. At the end of this chapter, there is a list of objectives suggested for a basic driving safety refresher course for drivers of cars, pickups, vans, and other light vehicles. These objectives could be amended and revised to serve as a checklist or test for assessing potential drivers.

When selecting, assessing, and clearing drivers, it is important to provide alternative or backup people. Long drives usually require driver rotation, and there is always a chance that a driver may be unable to attend the outing or become ill, tired, or, for some other reason, may not be up to par when needed. Most organizations have found it worthwhile to plan for a minimum of one backup driver per vehicle. It is also common to have drivers follow an amended and easier agenda on the last day of an outing, to ensure that they will be well-rested. In other cases, fresh drivers may be transported to the exit point to drive the worn-out crew home safely.

Carpools

When private vehicles are used, they are usually driven by their owners in what is commonly known as a carpool. The owner/driver may be staff, participants, or nonparticipants in the outing. As discussed in the section on private vehicles, liability is a serious concern. The sponsor of the outing retains, under most circumstances, responsibility for the well-being of participants throughout the program; however, the sponsor loses direct control during the carpool

phase. The owner/drivers take on substantial risk and may not be protected by their normal insurance policies. Sponsors, owners, and drivers of vehicles should seek good counsel with regard to their particular circumstances. If insurance issues can be resolved, carpools can reduce costs for organizations and for participants. The owners of vehicles, though, typically end up donating substantial value. When one adds the cost of tire wear, tune-ups, and other maintenance, even a standard-size sedan costs a great deal to operate on a per mile basis. Gasoline and oil are only a fraction of the actual out of pocket costs associated with driving a car. All too often, "compensation" amounts only to sharing the cost of gas. Even if all of the gas is paid for by the passengers, the driver is stuck with real expenses that, in most cases, exceed the cost of gas.

There are various ways of computing a fair amount of compensation for the use of a car. The simplest schemes give each driver a fixed per mile sum paid by assessing each passenger the same amount regardless of the number of passengers in any one vehicle. This is fair to all drivers and passengers alike, especially when one car is full and another has only one or two passengers. The rate per mile should be between two and three times the average cost per mile of gasoline, so the amount the driver receives is roughly equal to the actual cost per mile of using the car. This results in per passenger costs that are much higher than simply "sharing the gas." The only people likely to express surprise are those who have not owned a car. Most car owners would rather pay a fair transportation fee than put miles on their own vehicles. Using a system that is fair to the car owner has advantages to the participants and organizers as well. Participants will probably feel good about having adequately offset the owner's costs, and the organization will find it easier to attract volunteer vehicles.

There are at least two important warnings that should be issued here. *The exchange of money for transportation may define the recipient as a commercial carrier, and most individual car insurance policies specifically exclude such activities.* Even the *promise* of payment may be enough evidence of intent, so it may not be sufficient to use the often recommended ploy of not paying the driver until the journey is safely completed. From the point of view of the sponsor, one alternative may be to program only from "trailhead to trailhead;" that is, the outing or event begins and ends at the activity site. The participants are then totally responsible for getting to and from the site. The participants, should they decide to use a carpool, may have one or more options as well. It is sometimes possible for the sponsor to obtain insurance for nonowned vehicles and liability insurance for volunteer drivers. The costs of such insurance are then added to the outing fee.

Sponsoring organizations need to be very cautious in their attempts to control carpools. Most simply suggest the idea, inject a warning about insurance, perhaps remind participants of the need to be fair to owners/drivers, and then back away. In fact, since very little control can be exercised over the actual behavior of drivers in a volunteer carpool, it may be best to stand back. If, for example, the sponsor facilitates the pool process, participants may expect the sponsor to be responsible for the safety of the resultant transportation options. Leaders, for example, are generally cautioned not to assign participants to particular vehicles. Such decisions should remain the responsibility of passengers.

Agency Owned or Rented Vehicles

Most organizations use their own and/or rented vehicles to transport participants and staff. Attention to the following suggestions can help avoid some of the most common headaches associated with the transportation phase of the outing.

1. Arrange for drivers. Reserve all vehicles many weeks in advance of the outing. Check regularly to reduce the chance of last minute "surprises." Be sure that adequate seat belts and safety equipment will be on hand.

2. Do safety checks (lights, chains, safety equipment, etc.) early enough so that if something is missing or broken, it can be replaced or repaired without unduly disrupting the agenda.

3. Make sure that each driver knows the rules (*no compromise* on seat belts, traffic laws, speed limits, drinking, etc.), and that each has a set of written instructions for accidents and emergencies.

4. Give each driver clear directions to the site, and preferably provide them with a map. On longer trips, determine meeting points at intervals of 1-2 hours, to meet and rotate drivers if necessary. The meeting points should be identified as locations with telephones, so that it is possible to call ahead (or back) should a vehicle be delayed. Be sure that all drivers have a contact telephone number in town as a backup for communication in an emergency.

5. It is often best for the leader to go last, so that he/she will be aware of any vehicle that is delayed along the way. Drivers should devote their attention to *driving*, and should not be distracted by watching the rear view mirror, or tempted to make heroic moves to catch the forward vehicles. Of course, when a leader goes first he/she can control the speed of all other vehicles, an action that may be wise in bad weather or other poor driving conditions. Each driver should adhere to the speed limits without concern for the locations of other vehicles.

6. If shuttles are necessary, consider leaving at least one vehicle at the entry point for a possible emergency retreat, unless it will be impossible to retreat from the outing (as on some river trips). When nonparticipant drivers are used, it is tempting to move all of the vehicles to the exit point; however, this may preclude retreat to the entry point if an emergency occurs less than halfway to the exit point.

7. Always park vehicles considerately, taking as little space as possible and leave vehicles in an apparently "stripped" condition (i. e., with absolutely no possessions visible from the outside). Carry the keys in a secure place, as it is

difficult to hide keys effectively. It is a good idea to have two sets of keys for each vehicle, especially at remote sites or when complex shuttles are necessary. The chance of losing or breaking a key may be small, but the consequences could be frustrating, time-consuming, or worse.

8. Be prepared for adversity. Have a back-up plan in mind for reasonably foreseeable contingencies. What if a vehicle is unavailable at the time of departure? What if a vehicle breaks down en route to, or from, the site? Where can replacement vehicles be obtained. How long would it take to get the participants and gear taken care of. What extra costs would be incurred?

9. If participants are allowed to use private transportation in lieu of that provided by the program, be prepared with the necessary paperwork. It is usually easier to keep on hand a supply of forms that contains the necessary language and blank spaces for details, name and date. When properly filled out, the form should document the intent of the participant not to take part in a specified part of the transportation phase of the program. The relinquished transportation should be defined clearly. This statement may be followed by a statement that for him/her the program begins and/or ends at specific points and times.

Transportation of Gear

Gear transportation is an important concern that is too often inadequately addressed and that results in unacceptable risk. Gear must be carried in a way that does not endanger passengers. Any item not secured can fly forward in a collision, and nothing should interfere with the ability of passengers to escape from the vehicle. The most common, and serious, mistake includes piling unsecured gear in the back seats of vehicles and piling gear (such as skis) along the inside of vans. Packs, or other gear, need to be either on the floor, wedged securely between the seat and the back of the next forward seat, or seat-belted to the seat itself, using clips

to secure the belt to override the ability of the belt to loosen. Better yet, the gear should be carried on an external rack on the roof or on the back of the vehicle. In any case, it is possible to exceed the manufacturer's weight limitations for the vehicle. When a vehicle is loaded near its capacity, it usually becomes less maneuverable and always requires a greater stopping distance, and thus greater caution when driving!

Trailers are sometimes very useful, and they may be essential when large items, such as canoes, must be carried in quantity. Anyone who has used a trailer can testify to some of the potential problems associated with trailers. The hitch must be properly installed on a vehicle capable of handling a trailer safely. Built-in hitches are generally the easiest and safest to use; however, add-on units are available for purchase or rent. Some are quite effective, but they must be selected carefully and installed properly to maximize safety and minimize damage to the rear bumper of the vehicle. Loading must be done carefully, especially with respect to tongue weight. Driving with a trailer can be both hazardous and frustrating. Anyone charged with the responsibility of driving a vehicle that is pulling a trailer should be well-aware of procedures for safe towing, and should have practice in backing up and maneuvering.

For many groups, the ideal solution is to use a pickup or cargo van. Such vehicles are designed specifically for this purpose and are well-worth some additional expense. When loading gear in such rigs, be attentive to the weight distribution, and keep in mind the effects of even a few minutes of vibration and swaying. An amazing amount of damage can be done in a very short time to packs, skis, boats, or any object allowed to rub back and forth on vehicle walls, floor, or sharp or abrasive objects. Fragile items should be well-secured, boxed, or padded—especially when considering the costs of modern "high-tech" gear.

The following material consists of several lengthy lists of suggestions for safe driving. When the risk management planning document is developed, many of the policies may be drawn from this material. Not all will apply equally to any one program; nevertheless, what follows can be used or modified to fit your own unique situation.

Suggestions for Safe Driving

A Basic Safety Refresher Course

Even though drivers possess valid licenses, a test developed and administrated by the agency can often identify sloppy or unacceptable driving habits. The agency can then prescribe driving refresher safety courses administered by private organizations or by the agency itself. Upon completion of the course, the driver should be able to demonstrate:

General Skills

1. An ability to conduct a thorough vehicle check prior to departure, including the items listed below in the section on *Safety Policies*.
2. A knowledge of the functions and shifting procedures for automatic and manual transmissions.
3. Smooth starts and stops.
4. Proper use of feet (i.e., right foot only) in vehicles with automatic transmissions.
5. Use of sufficient signals in advance of all turns.
6. A procedure of looking over either the left or right shoulder prior to making a turn in order to check for vehicles that may be in the "blind spot." (This procedure is mandatory in some states.)
7. Proper use of mirrors, including automatic check in rear-view mirror prior to every braking maneuver.
8. Proper stops (at sidewalk *and* curb) when entering roadway.
9. Smooth and controlled panic stops from 35 mph, first using brake pedal only, and then using emergency brake only.

10. An ability to maintain vehicle in a safe lane position, without crossing lines or corners.
11. An ability to maintain attention to driving, in particular to keep the eyes on the road while conversing with passengers.
12. An awareness of hazards seen during the driving period.
13. A considerate and courteous attitude toward other drivers, bicyclists, pedestrians, and animals.
14. An ability to back up safely and efficiently, including proper use of the horn and mirrors.
15. An ability to turn around safely on a narrow road with an unguarded drop-off on one side. (A test site may be simulated.)
16. Competence in mountain road driving skills, including the use of the horn on blind corners, turnarounds in tight spaces, and techniques for preventing overheating of brakes on long descents. (If such a site is unavailable, response may be verbal.)
17. Safe parking skills, including the proper use of gears and proper positioning of tires when parking on steep hills.
18. A high level of caution, awareness, and safety habits while driving.

Winter Driving

19. An awareness of how to start a cold or flooded engine.
20. How to perform a safe battery jump start.
21. An ability to install and dismount tire chains quickly and safely.
22. An ability to maintain control of each type of vehicle on icy and snow-covered roads.
23. An ability to recover smoothly and safely from a skid.
24. An ability to stop both chained and unchained vehicles smoothly and safely in panic stops from 20 mph using the brake pedal and using the emergency brake (on rear-wheel drive vehicles).

Passenger and Gear Loading Skills

25. Awareness of vehicle load limits and the effects of added weight.
26. Knowledge of safe gear storage procedures, and of the dangers of unsecured gear and of gear blocking exits.
27. A willingness to enforce seat belt use by all passengers at all times.
28. Awareness of the dangers of slumping or slouching in seats, and of the importance of reminding passengers to keep seat belts snugly over their laps.

Emergency Response

29. Knowledge of how to attempt to remedy common types of mechanical failure, including flat tires, flooded engine, and safe jump starting.
30. Awareness of basic procedures in the event of an imminent accident, including instructions to passengers.
31. Awareness of basic procedures and priorities following an accident to maximize safety of passengers.
32. Knowledge of the organization's policies with regard to injuries, property damage, towing, repairs, contacts with supervisors, and information releases following an accident.

Winter Driving Skills

Driving under winter conditions presents many hazards that are unfamiliar to the summer driver. Packed snow, "black ice," white-outs, blizzards, and blocked traffic are only a few of the problems with which drivers should be prepared to cope. In any winter outdoor activity, driving to and from the recreation-site is probably the most dangerous aspect of the outing. Proper preparation of the vehicle and knowledge of winter driving techniques can help ensure safe and enjoyable excursions. Knowing how to drive a car on ice and snow requires judgment, good instruction, and experience.

1. Make sure your vehicle is in good operating condition: wipers, lights, brakes, steering, tires, etc.

2. Slow down, but remember large vehicles, such as trucks, must maintain their momentum to retain traction. It is unlawful in most states, to hold up traffic by traveling below the speed limit; however, the number of vehicles and the time or distance over which they may be held back varies widely from state to state. Recommended maximum speed when using chains is 30 mph.
3. Drive with lights and seat belts ON!
4. Driving when tired and sleepy is doubly dangerous on slippery roads. Let someone else drive or pull off and refresh with fresh air, sleep, or coffee.
5. Allow plenty of time to make the trip. Don't try to make up time on the road. "Better late than never."
6. If conditions are slippery, use your gears to slow down. Use brakes with extreme caution. Pump lightly to slow down.
7. Start with an easy foot on the accelerator and slip the clutch. Don't spin the wheels. Traction is greatest just before the wheels spin.
8. If the wheels spin, try rocking the car forward and backward. Also try sand, gravel, or traction mats to get out of a pocket.
9. Once underway, try to keep up your momentum. When approaching a hill, keep far enough behind the next vehicle so you will not have to slow down or stop.
10. Icy surfaces make steering difficult. Slow down *before* reaching curves. It is very difficult to judge the exact speed at which to make a corner. If the corner is perfectly flat (unbanked), the concern is only that the car may go too fast and slide toward the outside. If the road is banked, then going too *slowly* may cause the vehicle to slide into the inside of the corner. Either mistake can send the car off the road or into oncoming traffic.
11. On a winter day when the road surface is clear, watch for icy patches in shaded areas beneath overpasses and on bridges. These can easily cause a skid if you are

going too fast. (For advice on recovering from skids, see "Driving Emergencies," page 292.)

Chains

Although snow tires and studded tires offer somewhat better traction than regular tires, they do not replace the need for tire chains. Cars without tire chains may be cited by police when chains are required, even if they have studded tires. In many states, studded snow tires are prohibited.

1. Carry tire chains that fit the car's tires. Try them on at home to make sure they fit and are in good condition. "Cables," "strap," and other recent innovations are almost never as good as old-fashioned steel-link chains. Be a cautious consumer.
2. Carry a few repair links (and pliers to put them on).
3. If rubber chain tighteners are used, most normal operations require only that they be hooked at three points, forming a triangle. Putting them on too tight can cause excessive wear on the sidewalls of the tires. Carry a spare, as they are easily broken or lost.
4. If possible, avoid jacking up the car to put chains on. Do not crawl under a jacked-up car.
5. An inexpensive rainsuit and gloves make chaining up somewhat comfortable.
6. Park in a plowed turnout; never block traffic nor park on a blind turn nor steep grade.
7. Chain up *before* you have to. Getting pulled out of a snow bank is more costly and time consuming than chaining up early.
8. Check chains after a few miles of driving or sooner if you hear signs of looseness.
9. Chains offer better traction but not necessarily better control (steering). *Slow down!*
10. It should take a total time of *less than ten minutes* to chain up a car or van using this system:

a. Park safely off the road! Warn participants to watch for uncontrolled vehicles sliding into chain up areas!
b. Lay the chains out behind the rear wheels (or behind front wheels on front-wheel drive vehicles) with ice bar down, the inside hook on the inside next to the tire, and the outside latch on the outside next to the tire.
c. Back onto the chains until the hook and latch ends are accessible, just in front of the tire. (About a foot of chain should be loose).
d. Flop the chain up and over the tire and hook the inside hook.
e. Vigorously pull the chain tight on the outside and latch it.
f. Add the tighteners (rubber loops with hooks).
g. Drive forward and back a few times, then retighten the chains again.

Parking

1. Park only in plowed turnouts, as far from the roadway as possible.
2. Park in the direction you wish to leave from (or downhill); and, if it is snowing or a storm is pending, put your chains on before you leave on your excursion (especially overnights).
3. Do not block other cars from getting out.
4. If engaged, your emergency break can freeze *on*. Park in gear.
5. If parking overnight, mark your car with a flag on the antenna to avoid being crunched by a snowplow when your car becomes covered by snow.

Remember it's better to be late or to cancel an outing, than to risk an accident. If the driving conditions are not reasonable, stay home! Almost every experienced leader has had to delay or cancel outings. Too often, however, the inexperienced leader may be caught up in the excitement and take on a hazardous drive as a challenge. Winter driving may be the most hazardous aspect of a leader's duties. Bravado cannot be allowed to interfere with good judgment.

Jump Starting

Jump start only between same voltage and same type (alternator or generator) systems. If different, remove battery cable from good battery to protect donor's system. Connect one jumper cable (red) from positive side of donor's battery to positive (+) side of ineffective battery. Connect the other (black) cable from the negative (-) side of the donor's battery to *suitable ground* on the non-starting engine. Start engine and remove cables—in reverse order (negative first). *Do not make the final connection at the battery!* Hydrogen gas is present and may explode if ignited by the spark, blowing the battery apart and possibly covering you with acid. Connect the final negative (ground) terminal to some part of the engine or frame away from the battery!

Driving Emergencies

The quality of driver reactions usually determines the difference between a close call and a collision. The many variations and complications of emergency situations make it difficult to prepare for every one. The following emergencies have been selected to stimulate thought and assist in preparing for decisions.

1. Recovering From a Skid
   a. Avoid braking on icy pavement;
   b. When in a vehicle with rear-wheel drive, steer in the direction in which the rear end of the vehicle is skidding. When in a vehicle with front-wheel drive, and there is no one in front of you, keep the front wheels pointed straight ahead, and rear wheels will follow. If on a curve or close behind someone, steer car in the direction you want it to go. Rear wheels should follow.
2. Running Off Pavement
   a. Release accelerator pedal;
   b. Keep firm grip on steering wheel;
   c. *Resist the urge* to return to pavement immediately;
   d. Straddle pavement edge until vehicle is *moving slowly*;

2. Running Off Pavement (continued)
   e. When pavement level is nearly even with shoulder, turn sharply back onto pavement.
3. Deep Ruts and/or Holes in Road
   a. Reduce speed;
   b. Try to avoid ruts and holes if such action can be done safely;
   c. Before wheel drops in rut or hole, let up on brakes so wheel will turn;
   d. Maintain firm grip on steering wheel.
4. Animals on the Road
   a. Avoid hitting an animal only if you can do so safely by braking and steering. Do not swerve so drastically that you lose control. It may be better to strike the animal.
5. Bee in Vehicle
   a. Ignore while driving;
   b. Stop on shoulder and *then* remove bee.
6. Dropped Articles
   a. Do not try to retrieve anything from the floor of vehicle while the vehicle is moving—stop, then recover, or dispose of dropped items.
7. Blinding Lights
   a. Dim lights even if other driver does not;
   b. Look at the right edge of the road;
   c. Slow down.
8. Tire Blowouts
   a. Keep firm grip on steering wheel;
   b. Keep wheels as straight as possible;
   c. Gradually release accelerator pedal;
   d. Pump brakes lightly;
   e. Reduce speed to 15 mph or less before pulling off onto shoulder;
   f. Have vehicle well off the road to change tire.
9. Brake Failure
   a. Take foot off accelerator pedal;
   b. Pump brake pedal repeatedly;
   c. Shift to lower gear;
   d. Engage parking brake;
   e. Turn off ignition;
   f. Rub tire against curbing if on a steep city hill;
   g. Rub fender against cliff or run into bushes before picking up speed if on a mountain road.

10. Steering Failure
    a. If hard steering develops, pull off road and check for low tire or broken power-steering belt;
    b. Complete failure: apply brakes moderately to prevent skidding.
11. Lights Fail
    a. Try other lights, such as high or low beam, turning signal, parking lights, fog lights, or brake lights, since the problem may be in one of the switches or fuses.
12. Accelerator Sticks
    a. Pump accelerator pedal with several sharp jabs to release;
    b. Turn off ignition;
    c. Apply brakes and pull off highway.
13. Flooding of Carburetor
    a. Do not pump pedal. Hold accelerator pedal against the floor or, on newer models, do not touch accelerator;
    b. Engage starter for 5 to 10 seconds, let starter motor cool, and repeat if necessary.
14. Hood Flies Up
    a. Look ahead out of left window;
    b. Decelerate as rapidly as can safely be done;
    c. Do not cross center line;
    d. Pull off road as soon as possible.
15. Stalling on Railroad Tracks
    a. If train is coming, leave vehicle immediately. Leave area of impact and move away from the train;
    b. If in a vehicle with a manual transmission, and train is not coming, place gear shift lever in low or reverse, engage clutch, and engage starter, and push. For automatic transmission, place in neutral and push or pull with another vehicle.
16. Submerged Vehicle
    a. Escape through open window, before water reaches window level, if possible.
    b. Most vehicles will float for several minutes;

16. Submerged Vehicle (continued)
    c. If vehicle sinks too rapidly, move to the rear of passenger compartment to breath trapped air while planning to escape;
    d. Open side window or knock out back window;
    e. Open door when water pressure is equalized.
17. Vehicle Catches on Fire or Gasoline Leak
    a. Evacuate passengers immediately;
    b. Cut off electrical power if possible;
    c. Throw mud, dirt, or snow on blaze.
18. Rear-end Collision Imminent
    a. Use your arm to support the back of your head and neck, or slump down so your head hits the back of the seat, and encourage riders to do the same.
19. When an Accident is Imminent (Head-on or front-corner impact)
    a. Warn passengers;
    b. Steer until accident is unavoidable;
    c. Immediately before impact, driver should cross arms over face, and press head and arms against steering wheel.
20. After an accident, if there is the danger of spilled gasoline, or if the vehicle severely damaged, turn off ignition. Do not allow anyone to smoke anywhere in the vicinity of the vehicle! Vapors travel a long way.
21. Render first aid and *send for professional help.*
22. *Warn other drivers*—place flares to warn traffic in both directions. Place at least two flares about 150 ft. (50 yds.) and 250 ft. (85 yds.) behind accident. Place at least one flare 150 ft. ahead of accident. These are bare minimums! Remember, it takes 125 ft. for a car to stop on *good, dry pavement* when going 40 mph. Protect yourself and others: *warn other drivers far enough away that they will be able to stop safely if they have to.* Snow and/or ice can easily *triple* stopped distances!

23. Protect yourself and others from the environment; stay warm and dry.
24. Be cautious about accepting *towing* help from nonprofessional passersby. They may do more harm than good and cost you more than a professional.

If you are not involved but decide to stop at an accident scene:

25. Have a reason for stopping. No sightseers, please!
26. Drive past the accident and stop/park in a safe place.
27. *Warn other drivers*—place flares, add additional ones, or replace dying ones.
28. Do not attempt to pull out a snowbound vehicle without realizing the extreme dangers in which you place yourself and others. *Towing is best left to the professionals.* You must not cause other accidents. *You may be held liable for any problems that arise.*

If you are unable to stop, you can often help by tossing out a few flares (unlighted) as you drive slowly by.

Transportation Safety Policies

In almost every circumstance, transporting staff and participants to and from the activity site involves greater risk, especially relative to major injury, than any other aspect of an outing. Administrators, leaders, and drivers must be vigilant and uncompromising with regards to safety.

Every organization that is responsible for transporting participants needs to develop a set of clearly defined transportation policies and procedures as part of the risk management planning process. The following transportation safety policies, when supplemented by a description of maximum driver qualifications are suggested as starting points for administrators or leaders charged with the task of risk management planning.

1. All participants are to meet at the facility and must be transported to and from the activity site in agency vehicles only. Exceptions may be granted at the discretion of the program supervisor if the request and signed documentation are submitted in advance of the outing.
2. Only approved drivers are to drive agency vehicles. Approved drivers may not delegate or authorize nonapproved drivers to drive agency vehicles.
3. No vehicle is to be driven by a person who is, in the opinion of the outing leader or instructor, unable for any reason to perform in a normal, alert, and safe manner.
4. No alcoholic beverages or intoxicating substances of any kind are to be used by drivers, leaders, staff, or participants during the outing. This includes the period from group assembly before departure to formal dismissal of the group following return. No drivers, leaders, staff, or participants are to arrive at the group assembly before departure while under the influence of alcohol or any intoxicating substance. No exceptions can be made for the transportation phase of the outing, including stops en route.
5. It is the driver's responsibility to check all of the following safety-related functions and to check for the presence of all of the following safety equipment prior to departure. Any deficits or malfunctions must be corrected prior to leaving town.

Under the Hood:
- Radiator water level (antifreeze)
- Battery water level
- Battery connection
- Oil level
- Automatic-transmission fluid level (if applicable)
- Windshield-washer fluid level

In the Car:
- Windshield-washer operation
- Windshield-wiper operation and effectiveness

- Horn
- Emergency brake
- Seat belts for everyone (in place and ready to use)
- Indicator lights for oil, amps, high beam, etc.
- Fuel gauge (and know what kind of gas the vehicle uses!)
- How to unlock hood, trunk, gas cap and how to remove ignition key
- First-aid kit (fully stocked, clean, and dry!)
- Jumper cables
- Ice scraper (in season)
- Snow shovel (in season)
- Flashlight (with fresh batteries!)
- Emergency flares (6 minimum)
- Fire extinguisher
- Emergency calls list
- Health and contact forms for all passengers
- Vehicle accident forms
- Credit cards
- Maps (if needed)
- Jack/handle/lug wrench
- Tire chains (that you *know* fit) and tighteners

Out of the Car:
- Headlights (high/low beams all working)
- Taillights
- Turn signals (front and rear)
- Brake lights
- Emergency flashes
- Tire-tread depth (should be excellent) and wear
- Spare tire (inflated)
- Mirror position

6. No vehicle shall contain more passengers than the manufacturer's intended maximum, nor more passengers than the number of functional and accessible seat belts.

7. No vehicle shall be loaded in excess of manufacturer's specifications, and load limits should be reduced if necessitated by vehicle or road conditions.

8. Gear in passenger vehicles must be loaded below seat level unless fully restricted from forward motion. Doors must not be blocked by gear. Gear on racks must be firmly secured.

9. All occupants of vehicles are to use seat belts at all times when the vehicle is in motion. No passenger is to be transported unless a seat belt is available. It is the driver's responsibility to inform participants of this rule and to enforce this policy. No exceptions are allowed.

10. The driver must warn passengers not to slump or slouch in their seats, nor for any other reason, to allow the lap belt to ride above their hips. (Note: Improper use of lap belts can result in spinal damage even in low speed impacts.)

11. All applicable motor vehicle laws, including all speed limits, must be obeyed explicitly.

12. Conversation, games, songs, or activities are allowed if, and only if, they do not interfere with the driver's concentration. It is the driver's responsibility to inform passengers or to stop the vehicle, as needed.

13. Drivers are to take into consideration the public image of the agency when conducting business, parking, or engaged in activities near the vehicle.

14. Key and spare key locations are to be known by all drivers, leaders, and staff.

15. In the event of an accident, the driver's first responsibility is the safety of participants. (See Chapter Seven, "Backcountry First Aid," for a detailed description of actions one should take at the scene of an accident.) Briefly stated, the driver should:

  a. Stabilize the scene, administer first aid, and call for assistance if needed.

  b. Refer questions about the accident to the program supervisors, unless participant safety requires an immediate response.

  c. Contact the program supervisor or appropriate agency representative as soon as possible.

  d. File the required reports immediately or as instructed by the supervisor.

Summary

Transporting participants for outdoor pursuit activities requires planning on the part of both the administrator and principle leader. Decisions on vehicles, drivers, transporting gear, and driving policies must be made and implemented early in the planning process for any outdoor venture. Drivers should be tested for acceptable driving habits and required to demonstrate a wide-variety of driving-related skills. Winter driving and reaction in emergencies require special and different considerations. Lists of suggestions for safe driving and for transportation policies can be used to develop the risk management plan of individual outdoor pursuit programs.

References

The material for this chapter had been taken from driving safety manuals of many states, driver training course manuals and programs used by public and private organizations involved in transporting participants. Both authors have written similar material for municipal and educational programs.

part four

PLANNING
&
FIELD LEADERSHIP

chapter
fifteen

STRATEGIC AND TACTICAL PLANNING

This section covers the implementation of material in the previous sections. It is assumed that the reader is familiar with that material and can move forward to actual planning and leading participants into backcountry settings. The components of the process include the strategy of planning the event followed by the tactics of leading the participants in the field. This chapter addresses both types of planning, and where and how each relates to the previous chapters.

The materials for Chapters Fifteen, Sixteen, and Seventeen come from many years of experience in teaching, administration and field leadership. Thus, there are no references given in these chapters. The material has been compiled, modified and verified after many sucessful repetitions. It is the integration of all the material given in the preceding sectons of the book into steps for leading outdoor pursuits safely and reasonably, employing the most current professional practices.

The Process of Strategic Planning

Strategic planning consists of all the background planning that must take place prior to the actual departure for a trip. It usually entails quite a bit of "paperwork" and it takes place at a desk and on a telephone and in conference with other people. The planning process begins at the moment one is inspired to accomplish something. "Let's see if we can arrange a backpack outing during the peak wildflower season" is a typical beginning. Soon the ideas begin to flow. Excitement builds as the planners begin to visualize themselves engaged in an idealized backpacking adventure. The initial plans are usually characterized by lack of specificity and by wholehearted optimism. Such enthusiasm is normal, healthy, and probably essential to the ongoing development of a dynamic program.

Inevitably, however, reality begins to intrude. "Wouldn't it be great if" is replaced by "Can we do it?" Inspiration moves to analysis. The primary question is, of course, whether or not the likelihood of success is sufficient to warrant commitment of resources to continued planning. Planning is costly, at least in terms of time, so it is best to take a look at feasibility first. What is needed to carry out the plan, and what could interfere? A list of the elements of strategic planning is shown in Figure 15.1 (page 300).

It can be seen that there are ten items to consider when planning an outdoor activity. Several have been discussed in depth in previous chapters and are mentioned here only briefly in order to indicate the total process of planning. Participant issues must be considered first; however, beyond that, there is no specific order of the considerations. The fact is, all ten elements must be planned carefully or the program should not be offered.

```
┌─────────────────────────────────────────┐
│                                           │
│  FIGURE 15.1                              │
│  Ten Elements of Strategic Planning       │
│                                           │
│                                           │
│   1. Participant Issues                   │
│   2. Clothing and Equipment               │
│   3. Food and Water                       │
│   4. Lodging and Facilities               │
│   5. Leadership                           │
│   6. Access to Land and Water Resources   │
│   7. Funding                              │
│   8. Administrative Approval              │
│   9. Transportation                       │
│  10. Evaluation                           │
│                                           │
└─────────────────────────────────────────┘
```

Participant Issues

The best-planned outing can fail due to lack of participation. All too often, time and energy is put into developing what seems to be an outstanding outing or course, only to have too few people sign up. There is no sense in continuing to plan a program unless there will be enough clients to justify its existence. The actual number of participants is often substantially less than the number of initial registrants. A decrease in the rate of attrition can sometimes be obtained if the organizer has some leverage (like grades or nonrefundable deposits), and yet, even then, some people inevitably drop out. Since outdoor activities are often pursued with friends or relatives, the loss of one person may result in the loss of several others as well. It is best to be very conservative in estimating the actual participant tally. One way to address the fluctuating number of enrollees is to *plan for a range of participants;* for example, anticipate a minimum of 12 and a maximum of 16.

Limits and Prerequisites

Outdoor programs begin with an idea, an image of one or more people engaged in some form of outdoor activity. These people are at the center of the entire planning process. How the planner defines the people who will participate in the program affects every aspect of the plan, so the ultimate success of the program is determined,

in large measure, by the clarity and accuracy of the planner's vision. Ideally, the program will produce the greatest possible good (measured in terms of movement toward the sponsor's goals), given the available resources.

Does maximizing benefits mean maximizing enrollment? Not necessarily. Perhaps, more collective good is afforded by a program that provides an extremely valuable service to a select group than by committing the same resources to a modestly rewarding program of broad appeal. In fact, it is rarely possible to maximize the efficiency with which resources (staff, facilities, lands and waters, etc.) are employed without narrowing the focus to a select subset of the general population. The target population must be defined with great care. A definition that is too narrow may result in too few participants to sustain an entrepreneurial venture or to justify the expense in a public sector institution; however, in many cases, the very fact of exclusivity or focus may inspire participation. In any case, an overly narrow definition may needlessly disallow participation which wastes valuable resources.

On the other hand, too broad a definition (i.e., inadequate limitations) may degrade program quality, increase risks, or preclude attainment of objectives. For example, general interest programs designed exclusively for men or for women are sometimes highly successful even though they each exclude half of the population. However, when the programs are further limited, say to experienced mountaineers, the pool of potential clients may be too small to achieve a viable response. The extent to which it is possible to specialize is largely determined by the number of potential clientele in the target group and within range of the program. Target marketing was discussed in Chapter Thirteen, "Marketing the Outdoor Program." Even when there are abundant potential clientele, it is usually best to draw the limits or to define the prerequisites as broadly as possible. This requires an intimate familiarity with the activity, the site, the specific plans, and the program goals and objectives, which argues for the field leaders involvement in establishing criteria and prerequisites for enrollment.

Limits and prerequisites should be based upon considerations of program safety and quality. Absolutes should be stated only in those rare cases where absolute and exclusive criteria are intended. Examples would be programs for women only, park district residents only, or persons who must be of a certain age due to insurance regulations. Otherwise, it is generally best to state the nature of the program clearly, perhaps along with a recommendation. For example: "This is an intermediate rock climbing course, recommended for adults who have completed the beginning rock climbing course." A more rigid expression of these criteria might be: "This is an intermediate rock climbing course for adults 18 years and over. Prerequisites: Successful completion of the beginning course, or consent of instructor." Leaving some flexibility is important. Unless it is legally or otherwise necessary to enforce a certain criteria firmly, care should be taken to avoid unnecessary exclusions based upon false preconceptions.

Assessment

Whatever the criteria, limits, or prerequisites may be, they must be expressed clearly and unambiguously. Remember that people interpret everything in terms of their own past experience. For example, a prerequisite of experience on "steep, rough terrain" may be interpreted in good faith by someone for whom steep means "a ball might roll," and "rough" means "the paths are not paved." Potential participants must understand the criteria but not be unnecessarily deferred, and leaders must be able to apply them effectively. When the criteria are specific and an application form is used, it is helpful to include spaces for the applicant to indicate compliance with the prerequisite or state the case for exceptions. This helps the leader determine eligibility and provides a small measure of advantages from a liability perspective, in that the applicant has indicated, in writing, that he/she has met the prerequisites.

It is easiest to define prerequisite skills or knowledge in terms of something concrete, such as "passing the Beginning Backpacking Course with a grade of C or better." Usually, however, it isn't possible or desirable to be so specific.

Therefore, the leader has to be able to establish usable criteria for assessing whether or not the individual is prepared for the program. *Safety* is the key issue in all cases. Enjoyment for the individual and for all of the group is important but secondary to safety concerns. The criteria should be as objective as possible and should be applied uniformly to all applicants. A written list of criteria is useful, as a means of maintaining consistency and as future verification of intent, should an accident occur. For example, as guidelines, a leader of an intermediate backpacking class might list all of the possible experiences that would constitute adequate preparation, such as "recent participation in a substantive backpacking course involving at least two nights of camping, or at least one week (or longer) backpacking outing, or a total of ten nights of personal backpacking in the last two years."

Sometimes, specific skills may be used as criteria. It may suffice to simply ask a prospective ski student, "Can you do a parallel turn?" when the program consists of only two or three levels of instruction. If more levels are offered, it is usually necessary to see the individuals actually perform to assess subtle differences in skill level. In mountaineering courses, skills, such as belaying and knot tying, may be demonstrated without having to go to a field site. Participants in water-based programs may be asked to demonstrate their abilities in a swimming pool. When asked if they can do something, some people may answer, "Yes," in order to avoid embarrassment. Those who say they *can* do things that they are incapable of doing can endanger their own lives as well as the lives of others. By demonstrating the skill, they remove all doubt!

Fitness

All that has been previously said applies to the establishment of fitness criteria and the assessment of fitness levels. While most outdoor activities require some degree of physical fitness, the amount and specific nature of necessary physical prowess varies widely between and within activities. For example, hiking short distances on level ground requires little physical fitness, while long distance hiking in rugged mountain terrain at a fast pace can be extraordinarily demanding. Also, anyone who has engaged in strenuous activities can appreciate the fact that an ability to participate successfully may depend as much upon psychological factors as upon physical strength. Furthermore, each activity requires a specialized type of fitness and the development of certain muscles. Runners, hikers, climbers, skiers, and bikers, for example, each have special needs and define "fitness" as a particular set of mental and physical capabilities.

While wanting to ensure adequate fitness among participants to allow safe attainment of program objectives, the leader must be aware of what constitutes adequate fitness for the specific activity. When the program is designed for people who are already somewhat involved in the activity, it may be possible to express fitness in terms of an ability to do something they may have done, such as "ski ten kilometers in one hour" on a specified course, or "gain 1,000 vertical feet on a specified steep trail in an hour or less." It is more often necessary, however, to rely upon more common indices of fitness, especially when the prospective clients are beginners. The usual solution, when actual activity measures aren't practical, is running or jogging. While proficiency in running is not a perfect indicator of a person's ability to hike, climb, or ski, it is an excellent and easily applied measure, and it is reliable enough to meet the needs of most programs. With care, running can be used quite successfully as a measure of an individual's chances of success. For example, in one university program, running has been used for many years as a measure of fitness prior to participation in backcountry outings. Participants must be able to run two miles in 20 minutes or less to be eligible to participate in beginning backpacking or snowcamping outings, and they must complete the run in 18 minutes or less to participate in advanced backpacking or mountaineering outings.

The standards have been developed experientially over a period of years. It became clear that those who came in from the test runs ahead of the standard times very rarely had great difficulty with the pace of the course and seldom slowed the group, while those who were even slightly slower than this pace very often were overtaxed and/or could not maintain a reasonable pace. These running tests have proven effective where they have been carefully calibrated to serve a particular need. An important side benefit of this form of assessment is the opportunity for leaders to observe the participants engaged in strenuous and challenging activity. It is very helpful to see how each person responds to the situation. It is especially helpful to observe relative speeds of various group members, as this knowledge can facilitate planning effective field management strategies.

Not uncommonly, someone will be unable to run but will be able to hike or climb. In some cases, the reason is chronic; however, in most cases, it is temporary minor trauma to the knee or ankle which would be aggravated by running. Typically, the individual believes that he/she will be able to perform adequately by the time of the outing. This puts the instructor in the position of having to disallow participation, to find an alternative testing method, or to simply accept the individual's self-assessment. In many cases, the first alternative may be mandated by circumstances. If the outing is especially demanding or risky, it may be best to take the "hard line" and deny access to the trip. It certainly never hurts to establish a precedent of being firm relative to safety issues. It may, on the other hand, be reasonable to accept the individual's judgement, if the outing is such that the consequences of poor fitness or difficulty in performing would not be serious. In this case, however, it would be wise to have the individual sign a written statement of understanding. The statement should acknowledge the participant's awareness of the standard fitness test, the reason for not taking part in the standard test, and his/her self-assessment of fitness equal to, or greater than, that required to pass the standard test.

One alternative, that has been used successfully by several organizations, is a modified form of the Harvard Step Test. Less jarring than running, it provides a reasonable measure of fitness. To conduct one version of the test, find or build a step about 16 inches high for people 5' 9" tall, adding or subtracting a few inches for substantially taller or shorter people.

Have the respective client step up and down, alternating feet, for 4 minutes. At the 4 minute point, he/she should rest quietly for 60 seconds, then count his/her pulse for 30 seconds. Have the client wait 30 more seconds (to the 2 minute post-activity point), and again count his/her pulse for 30 seconds. He/she should wait 30 more seconds (to the 3 minute post-activity point), and count the pulse for again 30 seconds. For the sake of example, assume that the three 30-second pulse counts are: 65, 45, and 35. The Recovery Index (RI) may be calculated as follows:

$$RI = \frac{Duration\ of\ exercise\ in\ seconds\ x\ 100}{Sum\ of\ 3\ pulse\ counts\ x\ 2}$$

Using the listed examples, this calculation translates to:

$$RI = \frac{Duration\ x\ 100}{Sum\ x\ 2}\ or\ \frac{D\ x\ 50}{Sum}$$

Therefore: $RI = \frac{240\ x\ 50}{150}$ or $\frac{12,000}{150} = 80$

The resultant score may be interpreted as follows:

60 or less = poor,
61-70 = fair,
71-80 = good,
81-90 = very good,
91-100 = excellent.

In the example, the participant's score of 80 may be interpreted as "good," and that person may be advised to run, jog, or exercise more in order to move into the very good or excellent category. Because improper exercise regimens can be dangerous, it is best to suggest that individuals consult a professional athletic trainer and/or their physician before engaging in activities that are significantly more strenuous than normal. Certainly, there is a need to consider the particular fitness requirements of the event or outing, and to use good judgement when applying *any* fitness test, to avoid any activity or stress level that may be harmful or dangerous to the individual.

Clothing and Equipment

The practical requirements of minimum gear were discussed in depth in Chapters Five "Understanding Human Needs" and Chapter Six, "Preparation for Survival." A different aspect of clothing and gear is the great amount of gear some participants feel obliged to carry wherever they are.

Philosophical Implications

Leaders can expect to have to explain, discuss, debate, and justify the requirements set for participants. For every individual concerned about the consequence of taking too much equipment on an outing, there is another individual who can't wait to try out the latest technological advance, or at least his/her latest acquisition. Gear acquisition has become an avocation in its own right. Many people enjoy the process of putting together assemblages of equipment, as much (or more) for the sake of the equipment as for the activity itself. This may be primarily for the sake of showing off the superb kit and/or for keeping up with the latest innovations.

Outdoor leaders must be prepared to address these issues. The negative factors of cost, weight, size, maintenance, and isolation from the very environment the participant has worked so hard to get to must be recognized. And the penalties for excessive gear use go beyond these obvious elements. Excessive amounts of gear, especially certain high-technology items, put unneeded strain on an already overtaxed ecosystem. Over-consumption of material goods—a chronic problem in most of the Western world—seems especially out of place in a wilderness or backcountry setting.

The foregoing concerns are important and should be considered carefully, but must be balanced against the consequences of inadequate clothing and equipment. While requiring too much gear may eliminate potential participants (due to cost barriers), may perpetuate the dependence upon material goods, and otherwise may degrade the experience, requiring too little gear may have far more serious consequences.

Somewhere in the planning, perhaps in the pre-trip meeting, the leader must be prepared to stress the minimum clothing and equipment required and to share concern and to give advice relative to the over-amount of gear that might be better left behind. The first aspect requires leader assertion, while the second requires leader sensitivity. Prospective leaders might refer to Chapters Five and Six for a review of the minimum gear required for safety.

Acquisition, Storage, Maintenance and Control

Most organizations or agencies must acquire, store, maintain, and control some gear. There are several reasons for needing to have some equipment and clothing on hand. Most often, it is because the type, number, and condition of specialized items, such as rafts, large group tarps, or group first-aid kits, are the responsibility of the sponsor. Individuals should not supply what is considered to be required safety equipment for the group. Tents, sleeping bags, foam pads, backpacks, stoves, and other gear may be needed when the typical client doesn't own such equipment, and rentals are unavailable or not affordable by the client. Skis, snowshoes, ice axes, crampons, and helmets may have to be obtained for similar reasons. Ropes, slings, carabiners, and specialized safety gear generally cannot (and should not) be rented because of the vulnerability to damage and the need for strict quality control. Clothing may need to be provided, especially for beginners and for young participants, who may not own enough insulation or wind and rain layers. By supplying gear, a program may become more accessible and thus will increase the number of potential participants.

Before investing in equipment or clothing, there are a few factors to consider:

1. Gear is *very* costly, and it is rarely possible to cut corners on cost. Loaner or rental gear tends to take an inordinate amount of abuse and may not be as safe as gear owned and controlled by the agency.

2. Gear may be tax-deductible, which may offset up to 25 percent or more of the initial investment; however, state and local personal property taxes may consume any initial savings within a few years.

3. Insurance on gear and equipment is usually essential. It is usually quite expensive, and rates seem to increase annually.

4. Relative to replacement costs, some items, like ice axes, may last for many years. Most items, like skis, rafts, and tents, last for several years only by virtue of continual maintenance. Ropes and slings must be frequently replaced as they age even if not used, and clothing and footwear may survive only two or three years in a loaner or rental program.

5. Maintenance is on-going and costly in materials and time. *Something* is *always* returned damaged or broken from an outing. Someone, usually the leader, must take the time (and find the money) to repair the item. Hole patching, zipper replacement, and ridding gear of mud, clay, and pitch are common and surprisingly time-consuming chores.

6. Storage requires space and not just *any* space. The space must be large enough, have good ventilation (gear often comes back soaking wet), have adequate shelves and hooks, and must be located conveniently.

7. Security is a major concern. Keys and locks may be sufficient, although alarm systems are becoming more important, especially in some urban areas.

8. Control of equipment is time consuming and never perfect. Policies and procedures must be devised so that each item is assigned to an individual. Typically, personal items are signed for by each individual, using a standardized "gear checkout" form. Leaders or assistant leaders sign out group gear, but losses may still occur. Even when the policy (which should be clearly stated on the checkout form) places financial responsibility squarely on the shoulders of the borrower, it is sometimes impossible to recoup the value of the missing item. Often, this is due to confusing circumstances. For example, a carabiner, originally issued to a student, was used by the assistant leader in a group exercise, and is now missing. Who pays? Unfortunately, it is very difficult to prevent theft

altogether. Strict policies for issuance of gear, daily counts of group items, and personal inventories can help, but it's hard to prevent someone from walking away with valuable items if they are intent upon thievery.

9. Liability may be increased substantially, since the institution has accepted responsibility for selecting and maintaining the gear. This implies a need to be extraordinarily cautious in selecting equipment, extremely conscientious about maintenance, and quick to dispose of any questionable items. No gear on which safety depends (i.e., carabiners, ropes, pitons, etc.) should be purchased except for items that meet the safety standards of the industry and are stated in writing to withstand use up to specified limits.

All things considered, for the organization to have some gear on hand is usually essential, but having more on hand than is truly necessary is wasteful of time and money. Participants can usually borrow acceptable items if given adequate advice and lead time. Rentals may be available in the community, and most rental houses and specialty shops are amenable to group discounts. Low budget options are usually available in any sport. Leaders should be aware of local sources of used or inexpensive options that will serve the necessary function just as well as the high style new item on the rack in the specialty shop. A careful analysis of the budget may reveal that it is actually less expensive to cut participant fees and to provide some additional financial support for paid employees to cover their gear expenses than to invest in and maintain a large program gear cache.

In addition to considering the needs of individual participants and the group as a whole, it is usually worthwhile to develop a list of instructor gear. While the minimal requirements for a participant should, in theory, be more than adequate for a leader, in fact, leaders are often called upon to assist participants or to supplement their gear, and they may have to respond to an emergency. For these reasons, leaders are generally expected to be somewhat better prepared than participants. Typically, items required of leaders beyond those required of participants include extra clothing, tools, and safety gear.

There are many possible configurations for gear lists, and these are discussed both in Chapter Six, "Preparation for Survival" and in Chapter Seventeen under "Leadership of Selected Activities."

Food and Water

Planning must include sources of an adequate food and water supply for the participants and staff. In some cases, this may mean handing out a list of food to be provided by the participants and staff (i.e., three breakfasts, four lunches, and three dinners) and planning a trip to a back-country site that has an abundant safe water supply. On the other hand, the provision of food and water can be a major challenge on longer trips, in most areas where water must be purified before consumption, on trips where the organization is responsible for providing the meals, or for trips to other parts of the world where food is different in both ingredients and in quality. One cannot plan to eat the same foods in developing nations as are consumed in most of North America, Europe, Australia, and New Zealand. In some cases, special diets must be accommodated, and climate conditions complicate food storage.

Providing a safe water supply is essential as was discussed in depth in Chapter Six, "Preparation for Survival." Plans for the provision of water generally include equipment and/or chemicals for boiling, filtering, or chemically treating natural sources of water. It is also necessary to assess the potential water sources within the proposed site to assure that water will be available at the time of the outing.

Lodging and Facilities

Once the travel route and the activity are established, lodging needs can be determined so that costs and availability may be ascertained quite easily. It is also wise to consider alternative lodgings and/or deposits to ensure that needed facilities will be available. Care must be taken to ascertain the numbers of other individuals or groups already scheduled to use the facilities. In parts of the United States, one must either make reservations to use shelters and campsites or wait for dates to be assigned. This is necessary because of the preponderance of people requesting space. On trips requiring extensive travel, lodging en route to the outdoor site must be planned, budgeted, and reserved.

Planning for the activity sites and routes is covered in depth under "Tactical Planning" in this chapter.

Leadership

As has been pointed out throughout this book, the number and qualifications of leaders is of prime importance. Material on leaders can be found in Chapters Ten, Eleven, and Twelve and in Chapters Sixteen and Seventeen. Recommendations for appropriate numbers of qualified leaders should be followed. If, in the planning process, it is determined that adequate leadership is not available, the activity must be modified accordingly.

Access to Land and Water Resources

Is the resource suitable for the activity in mind? Is it accessible? Access to an area usually depends upon at least four factors: (1) distance to the site, (2) condition of access roads, (3) condition of trails or routes, and (4) permission of the land manager or owner. It is not at all uncommon to find that the site isn't accessible due to snow, blocked roads, or problems in obtaining permission to use the site. The best and easiest way to clarify these issues is simply to call the managing agency or the landowner and to discuss the possibilities directly. If this contact provides reasonable assurance of clear access and site suitability, the next step should be to locate good maps (topographic and current, and with a scale of at least 1:50,000 if possible) and a person thoroughly familiar with the area.

While the managing agency or owner can usually be located easily, finding a person who knows a particular site can be more of a challenge. It may well be that the instigator of the idea knows the area well. Managing agencies, land owners, local sporting goods shops, outing clubs, or parks and recreation districts may also be able to help. Colleges and universities usually have outdoor programs or classes, and they can often provide access to information, maps, and expertise. Ideally, find someone who knows the site well, who knows the condition of the area at the time of year you want to use it, and who also understands what it is you want to do. A person who has never led a group similar to yours may not be very useful in assessing the appropriateness of the site. In case the person you find knows the site but isn't familiar with either the participants or the activity, then it will be essential to find someone who is.

At this point, sit down at a table with the maps and experts on hand and rough out a plan. Sketch out some possible routes and work through some time sequences in sufficient detail to convince yourself that the great idea is feasible.

Funding

While the budget of a total outdoor-pursuits related business was discussed in Chapter Eleven, "Basic Administrative Planning," the leader should understand what is often referred to as activity or functional budgeting. This refers to the financial planning for one function or one activity. Typically, the activity budget does not incorporate such costs as utilities, salaries of full-time employees, costs of equipment used by other programs (unless prorated) or basic administrative costs of insurance, clerical help, marketing, etc. Included in the expenditures anticipated for one function could be:

- Transportation (including gasoline, oil, tolls, parking)
- Permits and user fees
- Salaries of part-time leaders and drivers (including insurance and taxes)
- Food
- Equipment purchased specifically for this program
- Supplies incidental to this program (including special promotional material)

Income could consist of the fees generated by participants. In most cases, the minimum number of participants needed to justify a program is a compromise between program ideals and economic realities. Vehicle capacities, shelter or lodging space, and instructor ratios usually result in a step sequence, where actual expenses move up in increments as additional vehicles, shelters, or instructors are added. The result is fluctuation in the real cost of the outing per participant. As each participant is added, for example, costs per person drop with each additional person seated in a van until the van is full, then rise dramatically as the next person is added, which requires a second vehicle. The budget of the activity is predicated on a maximum and minimum number of participants and often by numbers in between. The budget of the activity is developed with several scenarios in mind.

One of the purposes of the activity budget is to compare the cost of the function to the cost of other programs offered by the organization. Certainly, there are wide variances in program costs. A bus tour for 60 retirees to view fall foliage is far less costly than a river running trip of ten days for a group of 12. A look at the budgets of several activities can show an organization if a balance in income generating programs exists and of those programs, which ones barely break even or operate at a slight loss. A budgeting principle in recreational enterprises assumes that the income from some programs will help defray the expenses in others. Still, the administration must be cognizant of the balance. Too many programs that operate at a loss cannot be justified by excessive charges for programs that are truly very cost effective.

A stronger reason for requiring a budget for a single activity is to compare the expenses to similar activities. Each weekend backpacking trip should cost relatively the same. Transportation distances may increase the expenses of some trips and, therefore, justify additional costs. Participants will appreciated knowing why Trip A costs more or less than Trip B. Planners may find it necessary to change a trip site to one closer to home if the extra cost for transportation prevents potential participants from enrolling and thus makes the activity a financial liability.

Administrative Approval

Unlike the activities of organizations such as the National Outdoor Leadership School and the Wilderness Education Association, in many organizations, the outdoor-pursuit program is one of many other offerings. College courses in a department of physical education, trips offered to certain youth agency groups, special trips in youth camps and churches, special programs of natural history societies and others may need special administrative approval. This approval is often requested by a group of leaders or by a single individual within the larger organization. Generally speaking, authorization from the administration is much more likely to be forthcoming if the basic feasibility of the outing is determined in advance, and if a clear rationale can be given for it. Thus, whatever the purpose of the outing, it should be clearly thought out, with supporting arguments in mind.

The decision to approve the venture will probably be based upon some form of cost/benefit analysis. The greater the apparent benefits, the greater the chance of approval of the program, as long as costs remain within the norms and potentials of the institution. Often, outdoor-pursuits programs are disallowed due to insufficient awareness of the value of outdoor activities. Managers may not be, or even know, active participants in outdoor pursuits, and they may see such activities as unreasonably costly and hazardous. The request for the program should be accompanied with a strong rationale for the attributes of the program. Ideally, not with the passive nod, but the support and encouragement are needed of the institution.

In addition to the key elements discussed above, it is important to be aware of how the program will interact with existing programs in the area. Take a good look around the community to see if similar programs are being offered. There are several reasons for this. First, it may save a lot of time and expense if your efforts can be combined with another program, or if your participants simply enroll in the other program. At the very least, there may be much to learn from those who have already developed a similar program. If two programs are to be developed, this is the time to check out potential conflicts over the use of land or water resources, transportation, lodging, and potential staff. Viewed positively, it is common courtesy to locate and contact those who have already invested time and energy in developing similar programs, and, viewed selfishly, it is simply good politics to do so. Private and public sector organizations struggling to fill their rosters do not appreciate more competition. A friendly contact can usually minimize the problem.

Transportation

The topic of transportation and many suggestions for developing safe travel policies was the focus of Chapter Fourteen. It is an element in the strategic planning process and relates very closely to the development of a risk management plan.

Evaluation

While evaluation was discussed in Chapter Eleven, "Basic Administrative Planning," plans for implementing the evaluation must be made at the same time as the plans for implementing the activity. Evaluation of both the staff and the program itself are necessary, and the timing of these evaluations is important. Right after the program may be too soon as the participants may be too tired and want nothing more than a quick return to home, a hot shower, a home-cooked meal, and a night's sleep on a comfortable mattress. On the other hand, waiting until after the participants return home usually results in increased postage and a large percentage of no responses.

Ideally, the evaluation process should include post-trip verbal discussion by the group, written evaluations by group members, verbal discussion in a leaders-only post-trip meeting, and written evaluations of each leader. How these are to be collected is a topic for early planning.

The entire initial phase of planning may seem quite ponderous, and yet it can usually be completed in a few hours. The length of time needed depends a lot upon the experience of the planners and also upon luck in making contact with resource managers and others with needed information.

A common mistake that people make in planning is to underestimate the time required to accomplish a task. In the strategic planning phase, a work plan can facilitate planning by serving as a reminder of the overall timeline, key dates, and times. It is not unusual to have to reserve lodging and vehicles many months in advance. In large organizations, arrangements for scheduled activities and for staff may have to be made six months or more in advance, and budgets may be set as much as a year in advance! A work plan or calendar notations can help avoid embarrassing and potentially costly oversights. Lead time (the amount of time needed in advance of an event for arrangements to be made) is also frequently underestimated. The planner can note all the dates by which arrangements must be made and the dates to start working on those arrangements. Time management planning for the actual outing is addressed next under the heading of "The Process of Tactical Planning."

Documentation is an integral and essential part of the planning process. Some documents, such as the work plan, are created solely for immediate administrative purposes. Others, including most of the documents in the risk management plan, also facilitate smooth operation of the program itself. Good documentation is especially appreciated by those who must plan future programs.

The Process of Tactical Planning

The topic of tactical planning includes the face-to-face contact with the participants. It is planning for a meeting with the participants and leading them in their selected activities.

Route and Site Planning

For some outdoor pursuits, the selection of sites and routes may be the most critical element of the tactical planning process. While it is true that one may be able to hike, ski, or climb in a wide variety of areas, it is also true that the nature and quality of the experience will invariably be affected by the site or route. In most cases, the planner does not have a broad range of alternative sites from which to choose, so the basic design of the program is determined largely by the limitations and possibilities of the available sites or routes. One of the earliest planning tasks is to determine what suitable sites and routes, if any, are accessible to, and appropriate for, the program. Preliminary concerns include:

Proximity: Is the area within a reasonable travel distance?

Access: Can permission be obtained to use the area?

Rules and regulations: Can the program operate successfully given the rules and regulations governing use of the area?

Usage levels: Is the area overused or overcrowded, and will the program contribute to problems or be adversely affected by the presence of other users?

Timing: Is the area in suitable condition for the program at the time of the scheduled activities? What is the chance of unexpected changes in conditions?

Suitability: Does the area contain sites, routes, features, and terrain suitable for conduct of the program? Are better sites available elsewhere?

Safety: What are the on-site hazards? Are there acceptable escape routes? Is effective search and rescue assistance available, and how distant are the closest telephones, of rescue teams, and emergency services?

Environmental issues: Is the area able to withstand the type of activities that are planned? Are more durable sites available?

All of the above topics must be addressed before the planning process may continue. Unless the planner has access to detailed firsthand knowledge of the area, it will probably be necessary to conduct an on-site visit. The proliferation of guidebooks in recent years, coupled with advances in map making, and aerial and satellite photography has resulted in an abundance of descriptive information being available to the planner. As a consequence, it is now sometimes possible to conduct initial planning without ever having been on the site. This is especially true when popular sites are chosen, as these tend to be described in more guidebooks, and there are often better and more detailed maps available.

Once an area has been selected, the detailed plan may be developed. At this point, there may be no reasonable alternative to firsthand knowledge of the site, especially if the activity is risky or if there are specific teaching objectives for the program. The success of any program designed to teach skills or to teach about the environment is largely determined by how well the site or route is utilized, which in turn depends upon how well it is known and understood by the leaders. Experienced ski instructors, for example, know that terrain selection affects the "learning curve" greatly. The route taken by a mountaineering party is also critical. On mountains and glaciers, safe terrain conducive to learning, and hazardous or even life threatening conditions may be as little as a few feet apart. Knowledge of a site enhances safety by lessening the chance of becoming lost, improves the chances of success in conducting searches or rescues of lost or injured subjects, and may greatly improve the quality of decisions made in emergencies. Many programs intentionally subject participants to challenges wherein the perceived risks are greater than the real risks. The effectiveness and safety of such programs depend upon the ability of the leader to assess the real risks of a given combination of site, route, and activity. Thorough knowledge of the area is critical under these circumstances.

Sufficient resources should be built into the budget to allow the leader and key staff members to obtain the necessary maps and guidebooks and to conduct on-site assessments. If a program is repeated, using the same site and routes, and if there is significant carryover in staff so that at least one person with on-site experience can accompany each outing to the area, then many of these expenses are incurred only once. Normally, the institution should assign the leader, and at least one assistant leader, to the task, employing them on a standard basis for the necessary period. Administrators should be careful to assign no less than the minimum number of people, with appropriate skills, to accomplish the task safely. Sometimes, the leader and/or assistant leaders will volunteer to scout the site. While this may be ideal from the perspective of immediate costs to the program, care must be taken to clearly define who is responsible for any unforeseen injuries, damages, or costs that might arise from the scouting mission. When the task is clearly necessary and being done primarily for the benefit of the institution, a leader injured while scouting might well expect to be covered by institutional insurance. In these cases, it may be advisable to "employ" the scouting group as official volunteers, who would be covered by whatever agreements and benefits are normally afforded by the institution. Certainly, there are times when leaders will explore prospective sites "on their own" as part of their own personal avocational interest.

The on-site inspectors, or "scouts," can usually travel far faster than a full party. Even the vehicular transportation portion is likely to be more efficient due to fewer and shorter stops along the way. Care must be taken to estimate how long it will take the group for each portion of the route. In most cases, the scouts are fit and experienced, and they can cover in one day what a group of a dozen people would cover in two or three days. It is common, for example, to scout a three day backpack outing in a day, carrying only a day pack. A three-day mountaineering outing may require additional time to scout, depending upon the route to be climbed. These estimates are based upon the assumption that the scouts find everything on the initial planned route to be satisfactory! Therefore, it is important to allow a day or more of extra time, in case it is necessary to develop a new plan and scout alternative sites and routes. Note taking may be inconvenient in the field, but often pays dividends after the trip. One of the easiest methods is to carry a small note pad and one or two photocopies of the map on which to make notes and locate sites and routes.

It is usually easy to identify the experienced scout—it is the individual who is noting the location and travel time to every possible campsite, water source, activity site, practice area, alternative route, and escape route, rather than simply noting the intended sites and routes. The experienced scout is a pessimist, knowing

full well how often plans must be modified in mid-outing. River routes should also be scouted very carefully, noting all possible take-out points, campsites, and places that could be hazardous should stream flows vary. On land or water, a group's potential for environmental damage must be carefully considered. Terrain that shows little sign of the passage of a small scouting party may be ravaged by even the most considerate group of a dozen campers. Often one of the greatest challenges facing the leader is that of finding sites and routes that can accommodate groups without suffering significant environmental damage. Scouting parties may need to make major adjustments in the initial plans after on-site inspection of proposed sites.

There is more to the task of scouting than just identifying the possibilities. They should also be attentive to the aesthetic values of the area. When is the sun on the meadows? Can we see the peak from this side of the lake? At what time of day will it be most pleasant to hike this trail? The psychological effects of the sequence of sites and events must also be considered. Assume that an area is identified for a three day on-trail beginners backpacking outing. There is only one trail, which runs from a trailhead at a large lake up a steep four miles to a spectacular summit, then down two miles to a good campsite by a small lake. The trail then winds through a series of small lakes and ponds, all in big timber, to another campsite eight miles from the first campsite. Then the trail follows a creek downstream six miles to another trailhead. If you were planning this route, which way would you prefer to go? While it might be tempting to go in the direction described above, ascending the peak immediately and descending to camp, it might be hard on beginners to start with a steep ascent. More importantly, think of the overall dynamic of the outing. The peak (and the grand view of the lake below) is likely to be the high point of the trip, both literally and psychologically. Perhaps it would be better to ascend the stream side trail while spirits and energy levels are naturally high, move through the lake area on the second day with excitement maintained by the prospect of the peak ascent, and finish the trip with the climb, lunch on top, and a steep descent to the lake. This direction is not ideal from the perspective of wear and tear on the feet and knees, but it is probably the best in terms of the attitudes and enjoyment levels of the group members.

It may be easy for administrators and leaders to become caught up in the details of timing, logistics, and the accomplishment of objectives, and forget why they themselves were attracted to the out of doors in the first place. Safety and environmental responsibility are essential, and efficiency is ideal, but all of these qualities combined don't guarantee an outing that will fulfill its potential. Through sensitive but deliberate planning, sites and sensations are beautifully orchestrated and the outing conducted by the leader feels right and complete.

Activity Planning

Activity planning and route planning (discussed in the previous section) are interactive processes. The success of any activity is, to a large extent, predetermined by the activity site and extant conditions, and by the timing of the activity with the context of the program as a whole. This is true regardless of the nature of the activity, from games to experiential activities to structured teaching sessions. Thus, it is important to consider the site and the entire programmatic context as well as the actual structure and content of the activity.

Sites affect activities in several ways. The physical characteristics of the site directly affect any physical activity. Any given site lends itself to and may even facilitate certain types of activity while rendering other activities difficult is impossible. It is also important to be sensitive to the psychological effects of the site! Towering cliffs, raging rivers, or deep, dark forests may excite the experienced outdoor person, but intimidate the beginner. At the least, dramatic scenery can be distracting in situations where careful attention to the instructor is needed. To cite a simple example, a groomed, gentle, wide slope may facilitate learning of certain beginning ski maneuvers, but be useless for teaching beginning off-site technique. In the context of a multi-day beginning backcountry ski tour, this site may be very useful if it is the first site encountered on the tour, but may be of little value

when encountered near the end of the tour. A gentle ungroomed slope in open timber, ideal for first lessons in off-site touring, may be useless at the start of the tour, but ideal if encountered at an appropriate time late in the tour. Thus, it's necessary to have a clear understanding of the objectives of the program and of what kind of sites are needed before beginning the process of defining a route. On the other hand, without knowing the area and the potential routes and sites, it may be difficult or impossible to determine exactly what can be accomplished on the outing.

Time Management Plans

Time management planning refers to the development of time ordered work plans, schedules, and agendas on which are specified the intended starting points and durations of events. The focus of this section is the development of an agenda which, if well constructed, can serve simultaneously as a planning tool, as an aid to conducting an activity, and as a reference for participants. The key to success in implementing plans lies in the ability to predict correctly how long it will take to accomplish each of the many actions or activities that collectively form an event. As skill is developed, predictions become more accurate.

The best way to develop the art of estimating time needs is to practice throughout every program and outing, and apply conscientious effort to improving accuracy. Make a game of it! Challenge other leaders. "How long will it take the group to make it to the top of the ridge?" An experienced leader, given basic information about the group, the route, and the ground cover, and using only a topographic map, should be able to estimate travel time with an error of 20 percent or less, and should be able to reduce possible error to less than 10 percent once in the field. Learning to estimate accurately is not easy. Predict, compare, and evaluate continually, and before long it will be possible to estimate time to within 5 percent for durations of an hour or less.

There are several reasons for placing so much emphasis on accuracy. First, most activities and events take far longer to complete than most people expect, so attention is necessary to correct this misconception. Second, most sponsors, leaders, and participants have wholeheartedly embraced the concept of efficiency, and, therefore, believe that time should be used as productively as possible. Third, it is a matter of good business to end an activity at the time the participants were informed the activity would end. Last, but not least, skill in time management is of great potential value in emergencies. The success or failure of emergency response often depends upon the leader's ability to use resources and personnel in ways that are maximally effective.

Using a one-day hike to a lookout tower on top of a mountain as an example, the following material explains how to develop a time management plan. For the sake of brevity, the distances here are not expressed in the metric system. Assume that you intend to take a dozen people on a day hike to a lookout tower on top of a mountain. The trailhead is 70 miles from town, partly by paved highway and partly by unpaved back roads, and the trail is five miles long, gaining a total of 2,500 feet between the trailhead and the summit.

Where do you start your plan? It is often best to start where you want to end up, which is at home, at the end of the trip. This may seem awkward, but it can save a good deal of erasing and reworking the day's plans, since there is a tendency to overfill the day unless turnaround or departure times from the field are established early. For example, if the participants need to be at their homes by 7:00 p.m., then arrival in town cannot be later than 6:15 p.m. (if you assume 20 minutes of unloading, checking in gear and last minute discussion, followed by 25 minutes of commuting). Staff may be delayed further, with vehicles to clean and return, gear to clean and store, and reports to file. If the group is to return to town by 6:15 p.m., it must leave the trailhead no later than 4:30 p.m., assuming 30 minutes on 15 miles of gravel road, 60 minutes for 55 miles of highway, and 15 minutes for fast food milk shakes "to go" along the way. Loading vehicles usually takes close to 30 minutes, so the group should plan to be at the trailhead no later than 4:00 p.m. Note that arrival at this time would allow plenty of extra daylight

for emergencies except in late fall or early winter, when the planned arrival time would need to be moved up to at least 3:00 p.m. to allow a safe margin of daylight.

Arrival at the trailhead by 4:00 p.m. would require leaving the summit lookout by at least 1:30, assuming a consistent 2 1/2 mile per hour downhill pace and a 30 minute "pad." A moderate downhill grade coupled with the "horse returning to the barn" syndrome usually results in a snappy pace on the exit leg of a hike, but even a minor knee or ankle injury or pulled muscle can make even downhill travel extremely slow, so don't be too optimistic! Having established the latest time of departure from the summit, you can now plan either as you have been going ("backwards" in time) or begin in the early morning hours and work your way toward the summit. The latter process seems to be a more natural direction in which to plan; however, in doing so, you run a somewhat higher risk of having to rework the morning plan if you don't start early enough to reach the summit before it's time to leave. Of course, whichever way you develop the plan, it is possible that the outing can't be done in a day, or at least not by the hoped for return time. Continue to plan "backwards" in time. If you must leave the summit at 1:30 p.m. and want at least an hour on top for lunch and sightseeing, add a bit of pad and put the arrival time at the summit at noon.

If you assume a dry, reasonably good trail with a grade that slowly increases to a moderate gradient as the summit is approached, it should take about 3 1/2 hours to reach the summit. This is based upon a 2 mile per hour pace, with an additional 60 minutes of stops for water, rest, and pictures along the way. The overall percentage grade is about 9 percent (2,500 feet of gain in 5 x 5,280 or 26,400 feet of horizontal travel) so the pace will be moderate, and most people will need occasional breaks. Therefore, in order to reach the summit by noon, hiking has to begin no later than 8:30 a.m.

That means that you must be at the trailhead at 8:00 a.m., as it will take at *least* 30 minutes to let everyone use the outhouse, get boots and clothing on, organize and orient the group, and address basic safety issues. Arrival at the trailhead at 8:00 a.m. means that departure from town must be by or before 6:30 a.m., assuming no stops along the way. Since this is a day hike, gear checking will only take about 15 minutes. If health forms and waivers were dealt with at a pre-trip meeting, departure at 6:30 may be possible if everyone is at the departure point by or before 6:00 a.m. (which for many participants will mean awakening at 4:30 or 5:00 a.m.). The leaders may have to be up even earlier, as they will need to arrive at least 15 minutes earlier than the participants, to meet, arrange gear, and get the vehicles ready.

Is this *too* early? It may be for some groups, although experienced groups will appreciate the value of an early start. Depending upon the available daylight, it might be possible to push the entire agenda back an hour. Failing that, the only alternative may be to select a closer or shorter hike. This is a common dilemma, as leaders often choose a destination that they personally favor, and think of it in terms of the time it took them to hike, perhaps with another experienced friend. A party of one or two speedy, experienced people, intent upon reaching the summit at a good clip, could probably leave at 8:00 a.m. and be home by 5:30 p.m. or sooner! Remember, groups are inherently slow.

Every aspect of the trip will consume significantly more time than would be the case for one or two individuals. In addition, more people mean more chances for sprained ankles and for other unforeseeable causes of slow pace or delay. Therefore, it is important to set times for return to the trailhead (or pull out point on a river trip) that leave a comfortable margin of available daylight for resolving problems. Besides, the return trip by vehicle may well be the most dangerous part of the journey, so it is far better to make a daylight trip with wide-awake drivers than to risk having to drive at night with tired drivers.

Factors Affecting Travel Speeds

The above agenda is based upon assumptions of prompt departures and ideal driving, hiking, and climbing conditions. While most people are familiar with the effect of weather and traffic conditions on driving time, estimating trail travel rates is an art that requires the consideration of many factors. There are many factors that affect travel speed. Each must be understood and considered before one can make a reasonable time management plan for any outing. Throughout the following discussion, the speeds suggested are based upon a fit adult backpacker carrying a pack weighing approximately 20 percent of the body weight.

Terrain. Flat or gently rolling terrain allows maximal speeds. Rugged, convoluted, or brushy terrain can greatly reduce efficiency by making it impossible to achieve a steady pace, whether on-trail or off-trail.

Trail Condition. Trails vary widely in tread quality, width, and grade, but almost always allow faster travel than is possible off-trail. Hiking speeds are very vulnerable to maintenance status. Windstorms in wooded areas can reduce passability greatly in a matter of hours. Many trails are not maintained each year, and older maps may show abandoned trails. Trail hiking speeds vary from nearly 4 mph (6.4 kph) to about 1 1/2 mph (2.4 kph) for poorly maintained trails.

Off-Trail Travel. Speeds vary widely, from about 3 1/2 mph in open meadows, dry lake beds, or on some shores and beaches, to several hours per mile in rugged, steep, or brushy terrain. Off-trail walking is seldom as efficient as trail walking since the route rarely is straight for more than a few feet at a time, and the overall route may be inefficient as well. Boulder fields, talus slopes, and loose sand may be particularly time consuming, especially if group members have difficulty with balance and footing. More time is spent on navigation.

Snow Cover. Hiking speeds are affected very little by up to an inch or so of new dry snow. Wet new snow may ball up under footwear and cause loss of traction. More than an inch of snow begins to slow the pace. Six inches of new snow reduces travel speeds by about 25 percent if it is heavy and pasty. Hiking is usually possible in up to about 18 inches of new dry and light snow. This much snow will slow one or two walkers by about 50 percent; however, the pace can be maintained by rotation of trail breakers in a group. Those not breaking trail will have an easier, more restful pace.

The situation is different when hiking takes place on a surface of old frozen consolidated snow in the mornings, and in deep slush in the afternoon. Tree wells and other surface irregularities result in optimal paces of about 70 percent of dry trail rates when the surface is frozen or hard enough to keep penetration to about an inch or less. Warm conditions can rapidly convert snowpacks to a slushy condition wherein travel speeds may be reduced to no more than 30 percent of dry trail rates; which is a common cause of delay for parties traveling in spring and early summer.

One can snowshoe in snow of almost any texture and depth, but it is a relatively slow process. Very loose, steep snow, and slippery side slopes are particularly tedious on snowshoes. Speeds under ideal circumstances vary widely, from as high as perhaps 70 percent of dry trail hiking speed to under a mile per hour. Nordic skiing also tends to be rather slow except under special conditions. Runners using nordic ski tracks during the dry season consistently travel faster than skiers do during the winter. On slightly downhill runs well within the capabilities of the skier, travel speeds on skis can be very high; however, the skier is vulnerable to snow conditions and variations in terrain. On level, groomed tracks, an excellent skier may double normal dry land hiking rates for short distances, but the average backcountry skier will do well to attain 50-70 percent of the speed one would predict for dry land hiking on the same route. Skiing *feels* fast, but seldom is faster than walking, except under ideal circumstances.

Distance. Hiking speeds vary with route distance because most hikers will tire slowly throughout the route. Once people have warmed up, early morning paces are generally faster than paces later in the day. Most people can sustain a regular pace for two miles on moderate terrain, but, as route length increases, allowances must be made for a slackening of pace. There may be considerable reduction in speed due to blisters and sore muscles if a route exceeds the distance for which the group is prepared by recent training.

Timing. People tend to be eager in the morning, a bit lazy after lunch, and eager to return to the trailhead at the end of a trip. No matter how wonderful the trip is, the "horses returning to the barn" effect often results in faster travel speeds on the final leg of the journey. As a result, many people become injured or lost at this point in a trip, necessitating careful supervision by the leader(s).

Elevation. Absolute elevation affects one's ability to produce energy. While speed on a level route may be little affected below 10,000 feet in elevation, the ability to walk up an incline may be noticeably reduced at elevations as low as 4,500 feet. For example, a person who can carry a 50 pound backpack from sea level to 1,000 feet in an hour may need 90 minutes to carry the same pack from 10,000 to 11,000 feet. Elevation differences are very important and may, in many cases, be more important than distance in determining travel times. A common rule of thumb is to allow about one hour for every thousand feet of ascent. This is a reasonable estimate for the fit adult who carries a pack weighing 20 percent of body weight (the example used throughout this discussion) for ascents of three or four thousand feet at moderate elevations on steep but well-groomed trails.

A single thousand foot climb could be done in as little as 30 minutes, while ascents of more than about 4,000 feet would require more rests and a slower pace. On a trail with a 10 percent grade (1,000 feet per 2 x 5,280 = 10,560 feet of horizontal travel) the hiker can also cover approximately 2 miles *and* ascend 1,000 feet in an hour, due in part to being able to take advantage of the efficiency of a fluid trail stride. When planning time allotments for descents, allow plenty of time for elevation *losses*. Figure 15.2 is typical of graphs that are printed on many European hiking maps. From the chart it is possible to estimate hiking times given the elevation gain or loss and the trail distance.

Gradients. Trail gradients were explained in Chapter Nine, "Land Navigation," and that material should be understood here. Hiking efficiency and speed is little affected by gradients of up to about 5 percent. Some loss of efficiency occurs beyond 5 percent, and, as uphill gradients increase beyond about 20 percent, walking efficiency begins to diminish noticeably. The leg must be lifted more than swung, and traction begins to become a concern. Downhill gradients

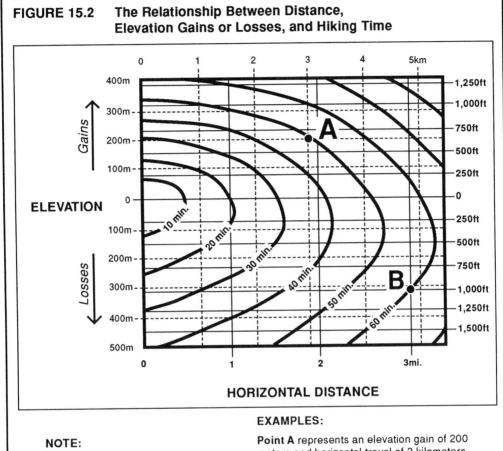

FIGURE 15.2   The Relationship Between Distance, Elevation Gains or Losses, and Hiking Time

HORIZONTAL DISTANCE

NOTE:

The hiking times are estimates for fit, adult hikers carrying moderate loads on smooth trail surfaces, at elevations below 6,000 feet (1,800 meters).

EXAMPLES:

Point A represents an elevation gain of 200 meters and horizontal travel of 3 kilometers. Estimated hiking time is 50 minutes.

Point B represents an elevation loss of 1,000 feet and horizontal travel of 3 miles. Estimated hiking time is 60 minutes.

are especially important but too often inadequately considered. While very gentle downhill gradients (2-4 percent) typically allow optimal hiking speeds, greater gradients usually force a reduced pace. On downhill gradients of as little as 10 percent, slipping is far more likely than on equivalent uphill slopes. Most knee and ankle injuries are aggravated more by downhill than by uphill travel. Very steep gradients may actually take longer to descend than to ascend.

Weather. While it is true that extreme weather can slow a party, and some routes become slippery or even treacherous when wet, foul weather usually *increases* travel rates. This

seems contrary to one's first image of soggy hikers in full rain gear, slogging slowly up the trail. In fact, the group slogging along in cool weather is likely to be in camp far earlier than would be the case on a sunny, warm day. On a drippy day, there is little or no temptation to stop and gaze at the scenery, and, when a break is announced, the participants quickly become chilled and thus anxious to hit the trail again. It is important to be aware of this tendency, so that plans can be made to either utilize or minimize the extra time in camp. Some of the extra time may be needed to deal with wet gear, less efficient meal cooking, etc.

Daylight. Travel speeds off-trail and in rugged terrain are strongly affected by available light. Navigation is impaired, group control requires greater attention, and the actual process of hiking, skiing, or snowshoeing may be rendered more difficult due to difficulty sensing the details of ground cover and lack of depth perception. In brushy or hazardous terrain, safety may make it unwise to travel at all in less than excellent lighting. Nevertheless, travel is usually possible at night, albeit at a much reduced pace. Depending upon the number and condition of flashlights, the extent of moonlight, and the terrain, hiking speed at night may range from 50 percent of normal daylight speed to as much as 80 percent. Greater caution must be exercised in group control, but by using "buddy" systems, etc., it is usually possible to move along smoothly.

Group Size. The total group size is important, but somewhat less so than the manner in which the group is organized. A large group of 20 people will travel slowly if it is kept tightly together. On the other hand, if the group travels as four independent squads of five people each, travel speed may be considerably increased. In a large group, everyone must stop every time one individual stops. While it is true that the overall pace of the 20 people (however they may be structured) cannot exceed that of the slowest person, in a massive group the slowest person is slowed even more by having to wait at stops requested by other members. In the smaller groups described above, there should be only one-fourth as many incidental stops. Typically, groups of 4 or 5 people can travel at about 90 percent of normal travel speed, groups of 10 to 12 people will travel at 70 percent of normal speed, and groups of 20 people will travel at about 50 percent of normal speed.

Ability. A person's ability to move at a given speed depends upon fitness, endurance, attitude, health, and skill, all of which are interrelated. There are many incidents of very fit individuals who were unable to maintain a reasonable pace due to a lack of one of the other necessary components. There are lots individuals who have accomplished amazing feats despite weaknesses in one or more areas. When estimating travel times, it is extremely useful to know as much as possible about the *individuals* who will make up the group. It is easy to be fooled by appearance and preconceptions! An enthusiastic three-year-old may complete a seven mile hike carrying a five-pound pack at a 1 1/2 mile per hour pace, and be ready for a game of hide and seek upon return to the trailhead, while a healthy adult may be footsore and ready for a nap after the same walk. Seventy-five-year-old hikers who know how to use the rest-stop and how to walk efficiency on soft sand or snow may set a pace that exhausts even highly "fit" young adults. Attitude and skill must not be underestimated.

The time plan must be so constructed as to allow options in the event that the ability of one or more individuals changes during the course of an outing. Illness, injury, or changes in attitude can profoundly and rapidly alter a person's ability to maintain a normal pace.

Pack Weights. Basically, the heavier the pack, the slower the pace. In practice, it is more complex because individuals vary in their physical ability to carry a pack and their psychological response to being burdened. The type and fit of the pack are also critical. The following suggestions assume an excellent pack design, well-fitted to an individual used to carrying a pack. A pack of up to 10 percent of body weight will usually slow people by not more than 5 percent from their speed with no pack. At 15 percent of body weight, slowing may be about 10 percent. At 20 percent of body weight (the standard used here for "normal hiking rates"), expect about a 30 percent reduction in speed, and expect packs weighing 30 percent of body weight to reduce speed by as much as 50 percent over moderate distances. This means that while small loads have little effect, additional weight increments of the same size have markedly greater effect on travel speeds.

Personal Interests. How fast a person travels is largely dependent upon what kind of an experience he/she is seeking. The individual intent upon relaxing and photographing wild flowers may not have an interest, intent, or willingness to march at a pace close to that of the "standard hiker." On the other hand, the fitness buff doing calisthenics at the trailhead may be bored, frustrated, or simply angry if he/she has to plod along at a "normal" pace.

Program Goals and Objectives. The interests of the sponsor may well determine how fast or how slow the group must travel. Before beginning to calculate travel times, it is essential to know why the group is traveling, and what activities or processes might affect the pace of the group. Teaching sessions, counseling sessions, group dynamics, exercises, or other activities may delay a group, while a group organized with the intent of developing fitness or conquering summits may well exceed the norms.

Trip Planning Work Sheets

After examining all the facets of time management and the factors that affect travel time, the leader can develop a reasonable trip planning work sheet, such as the one shown in Figure 15.3 (page 318). This document should be viewed as a mandatory and final aspect of the trip planning process since it covers the material presented in the section of "The Process of Tactical Planning" up to this point. It is this planning work sheet that verifies the rationale for leading a group into a specific area for a given amount of time. True, it is *an estimate* of times; however, the estimates are based upon logical planning, not just guess work. From a liability point of view, this sheet may be used as evidence of a leader acting as a reasonable and prudent professional using the best current information.

Pre-Trip and Post-Trip Meetings

Pre-trip contacts can reduce risks and enhance the quality of the experience for participants, while rewarding leaders with a great reduction in the number and severity of delays, equipment failures, and problems caused by misunderstood expectations. When a good deal of information critical to safety or to the efficient operation of the program will be conveyed, such meetings are often required and considered a prerequisite to the outing. In cases where participants come from many locations and distances, written communication can explain much of the information participants must have prior to the trip.

In other cases, it may be up to the instructor to see to it that everyone who misses the meetings is thoroughly informed before the outing.

Pre-trip meetings must be scheduled (or correspondence received) far enough in advance of the outing so that necessary preparations can be made. This may include training, fitness development, or acquisition of food, and almost always obtaining equipment. When the outing is a simple short day hike, for which all of the requirements for which can be explained on a printed handout, no pre-trip meeting may be required. For longer or potentially hazardous day trips and for virtually all multi-day excursions, at least one pre-trip meeting is necessary. With the possible exception of beginning level recreational trips, two or more pre-trip meetings are needed to cover all of the necessary material in a timely manner.

For those within commuting distance, the pre-trip meeting might consist of a series of evening two-hour sessions, preferably early in the week. Equipment requirements and options for borrowing, purchasing, or renting, as well as fitness requirements and conditioning suggestions, can be covered at the first session. If the first session is at least two weeks prior to the outing, participants may have adequate time for preparation. The last session should be scheduled during the week preceding the outing. It should be close enough to the outing to ensure good recall but at least a full day prior to the outing so that there is enough time in which to conduct last minute business. In general, a session length of 1 1/2 to 2 hours works best. Shorter periods are usually insufficient unless conducted with exceptional efficiency, and longer sessions overtax even the seasoned student who is used to sitting still for long periods.

For those coming from greater distances, correspondence can serve as initial instructional material and contain much of the information given in a face-to-face training session. Once the participants have assembled at the base of the operations, intensive training can occur over two to four or more days. Some programs consist of classroom sessions over a period of several weeks, and others cover several concentrated sessions over the period of two to four

FIGURE 15.3   Trip Planning Worksheet

This worksheet is to be used in conjunction with the route description for your outing. The completed worksheet is due at the last pre-trip session prior to your outing.

The purpose of this worksheet is to ensure that every participant has carefully studied the route prior to departure. We want no lemmings on our trips! Careful study of the maps and plans prior to the outing will add to your enjoyment and comprehension, and is good preparation for planning your own trips. Warning: Allow at least 2 hours to complete this exercise!

Please provide all of the following information.

YOUR NAME:_____   DATE: _____

INSTRUCTOR: _____   OUTING OR PROGRAM: _____

General location of outing: _____
Driving distance to the site: _____ Driving time to site: _____
If vehicle shuttle is planned – Total distance:_____ Time: _____
Names and scales of map(s) of the area: _____

DAY ONE

Time of departure from campus: _____
Time of arrival at the site: _____
Time of departure on trail: _____
Time of arrival at campsite: _____
Elevation of the trailhead: _____
Total of elevation gains today: _____
Total of elevation losses today: _____
Elevation of the campsite: _____
Overall (net) change in elevation: _____
Trail miles traveled today: _____
Off-trail miles traveled today: _____

DAY TWO

Time of departure from camp: _____
Time of arrival at campsite: _____
Total of elevation gains today: _____
Total of elevation losses today: _____
Elevation of the campsite: _____
Overall (net) change in elevation: _____
Trail miles traveled today: _____
Off-trail miles traveled today: _____

DAY THREE

Time of departure from camp: _____
Time of arrival at trailhead: _____
Time of departure in vehicles: _____
Time of arrival at campus: _____
Time of departure from campus: _____
Total of elevation gains today: _____
Total of elevation losses today: _____
Elevation of the end trailhead: _____
Overall (net) change in elevation: _____
Trail miles traveled today: _____
Off-trail miles traveled today: _____

DAILY SUMMARIES:

All times are your best estimates based on the outing description, the outing agenda, and your study of the maps. Elevation changes refer to the hiking, climbing or skiing portions of the outing.

ROUTE:

Attach copies of topographic maps on a scale of 1:100,000 or less that cover the entire hiking, climbing or skiing area. Use colored pens or pencils to clearly identify the following:
1. The starting and ending points
2. The route
3. The intended campsites
4. True north

days. There is a wide variety of scheduling formats for pre-trip sessions but the contents can be relatively similar.

A general outline for an orientation program might look like the following:

I.   Introduction
     A. Leader(s)
     B. Assistants
     C. The organization
     D. Purpose of the program or event
     E. Participants (including clarification of pronunciation, addresses, telephone numbers, and other relevant information)

II. Orientation to program
     A. Explanation of format of the training session
     B. Hand out copies of the schedule and explain it

III. Orientation to the outing
     A. Explanation of the events
     B. Hand out copies of the agenda and explain it (See Figure 15.4, page 320)
     C. Discuss hazards and risks

IV. Activity Requirements
     A. Participant fitness and skills
     B. Participant responsibilities
     C. Health forms
     D. Costs beyond initial (if any)

V.   Equipment requirements
     A. Required (with rationale)
     B. Optional (with rationale)
     C. Group
     D. Food and meal preparation

VI. Expectations for Participant Behavior
     A. Interpersonal
     B. Environmental, sanitation, minimum impact

VII. Travel arrangements, accommodations, tenting arrangements, etc.

VIII. Skills
     A. Map reading
     B. Navigation
     C. Trail or river travel
     D. Others

IX. Risk management and liability waivers

X.   Review and finalize plans for the outing

A copy of a tentative agenda for a three day backpacking outing is presented here in order to illustrate the type of handout that is helpful to participants and to show the type of careful planning that went into the outing.

While it can be modified for use by any leader, Figure 15.4 is an actual agenda used in a university program in which every student in every outing is required to complete with a grade of 80 percent before being permitted to participate in the outing.

Somewhere the instructor(s) should help the participants feel calm and dispel imagined or real fears. The following ideas may help:

a. Try to reduce excessive anxieties by reminding the group that everyone will have an opportunity to participate in decision making, and that no one will be required to do anything against his/her will. If skills or techniques are to be taught, remind people that you will progress one step at a time, with personal improvement and enjoyment, not competition, as a goal.

b. A lot of sleep is lost over fears of not getting enough sleep. Thus, two points seem worth making to outing groups; first, most people can miss an occasional complete night of sleep and yet function quite well all day, and, second, just being perfectly still and relaxed results in about half of the rest of actual sleep. Even a whole night of sleeplessness, then, can still provide the equivalent of several hours of sleep. While such a night may not be very restful psychologically, the body will usually feel fine. Furthermore, just keeping these thoughts in mind is often enough to reduce tensions and allow sleep.

FIGURE 15.4   A Tentative Agenda for a Three Day Backpacking Outing

	FRIDAY		SATURDAY		SUNDAY
AM		**AM**		**AM**	
5:45	Leaders assemble	5:30	Leaders up	5:15	Leaders up
6:00	Participants assemble	6:00	Students up	5:45	Students up
6:15	Gear check	6:30	Staff meeting	6:00	Staff meeting
6:30	Group meeting	7:00	*Tour of homes*	7:00	Hiking
6:45	Dispense group gear	8:00	Packing up	8:00	*Small group*
7:00	Depart	9:00	Hiking		*navigation practice*
9:00	Arrive at trailhead	9:15	*Navigation practice*	9:15	*Environmental*
9:45	Hiking	11:30	Lunch break?		*awareness*
10:15	*Techniques for safe,*			11:30	Lunch break?
	low impact, efficient				
	travel on trails				
PM		**PM**		**PM**	
1:00	Lunch break	12:30	Hiking	12:30	Hiking
2:00	Hiking	1:30	Arrive at	2:00	Arrive at vehicles
2:30	*Environmental*		mountain top	2:30	Depart
	awareness	2:00	*Navigation and*	4:30	Back in town
3:30	Arrive at campsite		*map reading*	5:00	Students free
4:00	*Campsite issues*	3:00	Hiking	5:30	Staff return gear
4:30	*Site selection*	4:00	Arrive at camp site		and vehicles
	and cooking skills	5:00	Dinner	6:00	Staff free
5:00	Dinner	6:00	Evening hikes		
6:30	Evening meeting	6:30	*Survival exercise*		
7:00	Staff meeting	8:00	Group meeting		
8:00	Night hike?	8:30	Staff meeting		
9:00	*Star talk?*	9:00	*Star Talk?*		

NOTE:

1. Instructional topics are shown in italics.
2. The above agenda is based on assumptions of prompt departures and ideal driving and hiking conditions. Changes in the agenda or in the topics of instructional sessions may be necessary during the outing.
3. In addition to achieving the skills objectives of the class, we hope that you gain an understanding and appreciation of the area in which we are traveling. Please share your observations and knowledge with the group and ask the instructors and other group members if you have any questions about the area's history, geology, plants or animals.

---

c. When the alarm is set for an earlier hour than usual, it is easy to sleep right through it. Suggest that participants either set two alarms or, better yet, that they exchange phone numbers and arrange to call one another at a certain hour, usually ten or fifteen minutes after the alarms are supposed to go off. This system has at least two advantages: first, there is no worry about not hearing the alarm, and second, if one of the two individuals is ill or will be late in arriving at the meeting point, the leaders can be given this message by the other person.

Discussion

Regardless of what is being done or being taught, the participants at the beginning of the outing are not identical to the participants at or near the end of the outing! Each experience changes people. Skills improve, fitness may improve, and/or the body may begin to tire, health and attitude may improve or may, with sore muscles and fatigue, decline. Fears are conquered, and limits expanded, while new anxieties and unknown limits are discovered. Social relationships within the group are dynamic and powerful. Simultaneously, there is a psychological rhythm to every outing; anticipation and anxiety, fresh enjoyment and commitment and exhilaration flow into concerns about the return to the real world at the same time as fatigue, growing discomfort, and "homesickness" begin to edge into consciousness. Planners must be aware of the likely patterns of changes in order to plan effective activities, and leaders need to be continually sensitive to each individual and to the overall attitudinal state of the group.

As if this isn't enough of a challenge, there is yet another, and potentially even greater concern facing the leader. As any experienced leader knows, no matter how good the plans are, environmental conditions may make it difficult or impossible to carry out the activity. Returning to the example of a ski tour, what happens when, despite a good long-term forecast, it rains and snows so hard throughout the first day that it is virtually impossible to teach skiing on the groomed slope, and there are no other comparable slopes along the intended route? It may be necessary to restructure the entire outing on the spot. It is in such circumstances that experience in leadership really counts.

Be optimistic and put the blinders on for awhile, focusing upon a specific activity. Assume the broadest definition of activity here, which might include anything—a game of hide and seek, a group dynamics exercise, a philosophical discussion in a group format, a hike to a lake, a nature talk, an ice climbing seminar, ski lesson, or any other definable use of time. Regardless of the activity, several basic principles apply to the planning process. These are:

1. Know why the activity is being conducted. Each activity should be clearly related to, and consistent with, the goals and objectives of the outing program, and sponsoring institution.

2. Know the site well enough to assess its suitability under expected conditions and to predict the effects of reasonably foreseeable changes in the weather, surface conditions, or stream flows. By "suitable" we mean that the desired activity can be conducted safely, legally, and with no adverse social or environmental impacts.

3. Consider the physical and mental conditions of the participants. What are their abilities and weaknesses? What skills do they have and what is the range of skill levels within the group? Are they fit and rested? When does the activity occur in the outing, and will attitudes and interests be compatible with the activity?

4. Structure the overall sequence of activities so that participants will be prepared for, and able to, safely accomplish the next activity. For example, it might be inappropriate to conduct a night hike late in the evening if a climb is planned to leave early the next morning.

5. Structure the sequence of events within the activity so that the participants will be prepared for, and receptive to, each successive experience or element of the activity. This is the underlying concept of the progression. For some activities, standard or at least customary progressions exist. For example, there are a number of well-documented "standard" progressions used by instructors of skiing, mountaineering, sailing, canoeing, kayaking, hang gliding, scuba diving, and other popular activities. In most cases, there are many "standard" progressions in use within each activity area, each promoted by local or regional organizations, and each constantly evolving as technology, methodology, and the sports themselves advance. Using locally accepted progressions is usually a good idea. By using sequences and terminology that are common to the region, it is easier to communicate with and advance the skills of experienced participants, and all participants will find it easier to obtain further instruction within the region. From a legal perspective, the use of accepted progression may also help establish consistency with local or

regional "standards in the trade." In any case, whether or not standard progressions exist, the sequence of events or of topics may profoundly affect the efficiency and safety of the activity. Especially when there are risks inherent in the activity, the progressions to be used should be documented in the risk management plan, and instructors should be advised of the need to carefully consider any deviations from the accepted sequences.

6. Be prepared for contingencies. What if the activity must start late, or takes longer than expected? What if it takes much less time than expected? What if conditions make it unsafe or unproductive to conduct the activity, or interfere with key elements of the intended plans?

Many outdoor leaders and administrators are educators, often highly experienced in planning and conducting classroom activities. They have learned how to prepare for and compensate for the differences between various classes, and the difference between, for example, a morning class and a late afternoon class. Nevertheless, many a schoolteacher has been caught unprepared as a leader of a backwoods outing. The range and intensity of forces acting upon the group is far greater than in the relatively controlled and repetitive school setting, and there is no thermostat, not to mention walls nor roof.

LEADERSHIP IN THE FIELD

It is assumed at this point that you, the reader, have assimilated all the material in Chapters One through Fifteen and are now ready to cover the primary issues and concerns likely to be encountered in each phase of an outing, beginning with the assembly of the group immediately prior to departure and ending with the return to home after the completion of the outing.

Assembly to Time of Departure

When selecting a meeting point from which to depart for the outing, parking space may be the only essential. However, checking and loading equipment in the rain is hardly pleasant, and there is frequently a need for toilets and access to telephones so the best meeting point is a building that offers shelter, rest rooms, and a telephone. There will need to be a spot to leave the "trip plan" as well as any waivers that haven't been given to someone in advance.

Leaders should arrive early to get things organized and underway. If several staff members are available, then it may be possible to complete several chores simultaneously and save a good deal of time, especially if responsibilities are delegated. The following tasks are common to the assembly phase of most outdoor-pursuits activities.

1. Be sure that vehicles or transportation arrangements are in order, and that someone takes responsibility for checking the safety conditions of each vehicle thoroughly. See Chapter Fourteen, "Transportation," for a check list.

2. Check on road conditions and get the latest weather forecast. This should be done by the principle leader before he/she leaves home!

3. Take roll. If necessary, also collect fees and check registration.

4. Call and check on missing participants, unless, by virtue of the "phone-buddy" system, absences are already explained.

5. If it wasn't done the previous evening and left at the site of the agency, check all gear. Be sure that *everybody* has *all* required items. One staff member can check the gear of ten participants in about twenty minutes if the process is carried out efficiently. Rather than "Did you bring item X?", say either "Let me see your _____" or at least "What sort of _____ did you bring?" The latter approach is usually adequate for an experienced adult group; however, the only foolproof system is direct visual inspection. Beginners may have packed items that are totally inadequate. In any case, it is good to see what each person has along so that a mental note can be made of any marginal items.

It is best to think about what do in the case of missing items well in advance since it is bound to occur. Letting people participate without required items is not a viable option. If the list is what the leader considers a reasonable minimum, then he/she should insist on compliance. If a person is allowed to participate without a complete set of gear, the results may include increased risk, degradation of program quality due to substitutions for the missing items, increased environmental impact, and serious legal jeopardy for the leaders and program administrators.

Another concern is that the participant may view required items as not really important. If someone gets by once without raingear on a mountain hike, he/she may well fail to carry it on the next outing. Leaders should expect to encounter people who feel very strongly that strict gear requirements infringe upon their individual rights.

What if a person does not have the required gear? Having discovered that a small investment in some used but adequate gear saves lots of problems, some leaders surreptitiously bring a sackful of the more frequently forgotten items to the meeting place. (If people *know* that gaps in the list will be filled by the instructor, they might get sloppy in fulfilling their equipment responsibilities.)

The only other alternative, short of denying participation in the outing, is to let the person return home or to go to a nearby store to obtain the item. If the gear requirements and the possibility of being denied access to the trip were made clear prior to the trip then the leader should not feel obligated to delay the group. If anyone feels the delay would be unreasonable, simply send the person home. When young people are involved, though, it is important to make sure that parents or others are aware of this change in plans.

In the case of some groups, packs can be organized the night before and left with the leader or at the site of the agency office. This prevents any items from being removed or added. (This is an often-used technique in youth agency groups, where even the group gear is distributed and all packs weighed to be sure

none are over the limited weight. In case of a "no-show," the group gear can be redistributed the next day.)

6. Sign out any items for which the participants will be personally responsible. It is common for programs to provide such things as compasses or life jackets. Experience has shown that the only way to recover everything at the end of the activity is to sign out each item. Each item should have been numbered and labeled so that they cannot be interchanged. When a set or kit of gear is to be checked out, it also saves time if the staff makes up the appropriate number of full sets in advance and uses a standard checkout form. In this way, simply note the identification number of each item as it is handed to a participant, then have the participant sign the form.

7. Sort out the group gear. Every activity has its own requirements, but, in most cases, there will be substantial amounts of group equipment. If more than one group is being outfitted, each should have a separate array of gear. This is needed, for instance, when there are two or more rafting, hiking, or climbing units which will travel independently perhaps even on the same route. Separate equipment simplifies and speeds the process. Each set of gear, first-aid kits, ropes, rafts, or whatever, can then be easily checked for completeness and turned over to each group leader.

8. Distribute the group gear. It is often necessary for participants to help carry communal equipment. In fact, a good case can be made for requiring this whenever possible since it makes participants more aware of the equipment requirements of the activity and promotes a feeling of full participation.

Probably the fairest and fastest system is for the staff to make an appropriate number of nearly equal piles, letting participants then choose whatever items they prefer or those that will fit in their packs. This system works well, if supervised thoughtfully, to see to it that no one ends up with an unreasonable load. Children, for instance, should be given little or nothing to carry, except perhaps token items, until they are big enough for adult loads.

Weigh the packs to make sure no one is carrying more than a fair share. This is particularly necessary for beginners or youth, but also useful for adults. The leader should be aware of pack weights relative to participant strengths and body weights.

Strength, skill, experience, and the quality of backpacks are appropriate criteria for distributing loads—age and gender are not. Remember that excessively heavy loads are dangerous, and a big athletic person is not immune to a sprained back or ankle. Also, a person carrying too much of the group gear disallows others from accepting their responsibility which can be a valuable part of the experience and provide a sense of contribution. Overweight men may to want to carry great loads as though the fat were muscle, only to risk exhaustion if not cardiac problems. Some men may insist upon carrying far more weight than others in the group. Some women may insist upon carrying loads fully equal to those of the men, thinking this is in fact a fair and equal sharing of the responsibility. Weight should be distributed according to ability, not by equal shares.

A larger, stronger, and more fit person can carry a given load more easily, with greater speed and fewer risks than someone smaller or less fit. "Fit" means not only in the cardiovascular sense but in conditioning to the activity as well. A light but strong and fit woman can sometimes carry a bigger load than a larger unconditioned male. Usually, men can carry more due to greater strength and body mass, and so the weight should be divided accordingly. The other concern is that some women expect the men to carry the majority of the weight, and resist carrying a fair share based upon their ability. The leader should, in any case, weigh or lift all of the packs and keep a mental note of how much group gear each person is carrying.

It is also important, when backpacking, to check the fit and design of packs. A poorly designed, fitted, or sized pack can necessitate a much lighter load. Also take note of each person's health and degree of fatigue. Those who were up half of the night won't be as able to carry a load as those who are well-rested. Remember, too, that beginners are much less efficient than experienced participants and may have a far harder time just keeping up, much less lugging gear loads. This is especially true in skiing and climbing. Usually, small shifts can be made without objection, and arrangements can often be made to shift at least group, if not personal, gear at rest breaks, lunch stops, or with each day's travel.

Note who has what group items. A written list can be a real time-saver later in the trip when searching for things. Many programs formally sign out group gear to students at this point.

9. Collect and review all health forms. These should be taken along on the outing, and carried by the appropriate group leaders.

10. Have participants sign and return waiver forms and statements of risks of the outing. (See Chapter Twelve.) The waiver form should be signed as closely as possible to the start of the outing itself, while health forms and risk statements may be signed earlier. All of these should be stored in town, not taken on the outing.

11. Assemble the group, and check to be sure that everyone is ready to go, feels well, and knows the overall plan.

12. Meet with the driver, review the destination and route, the plans for handling delays or emergencies, and the basic "rules of the road." Be sure to follow the suggestions given in Chapter Fourteen, "Transportation."

13. Load the gear according to the material presented in Chapter Fourteen.

14. Load the people. Given the reluctance of some to buckle up, check carefully to be sure that seat belts are in use, and remind people that they must wear their seatbelts whenever the vehicle is moving. (Virtually every major outdoor program in the U.S., Europe, and Japan requires that all participants and staff be buckled up at all times when the vehicle is moving.) Again, follow the principles in Chapter Fourteen.

FIGURE 16.1   Outing Plan

Class: _____
Departure (day, date and time): _____
Return (day, date and time): _____
Vehicles Used (type, owner and license plate): _____

General Destination: _____
County(ies): _____
Ranger District(s): _____
Maps (be specific): _____
Number and Type of Watercraft/Bikes etc.: _____
Entry Trailhead(s) or Take-out Point(s): _____
_____

Agenda (describe fully or attach detailed agenda): _____
_____
_____
_____
_____

Route (describe in detail or attach clearly marked map): _____
_____
_____
_____
_____

Instructors: Participants:
_____   _____
_____   _____
_____   _____

Assistant Instructors: _____
_____   _____
_____   _____
_____   _____
_____   _____
_____   _____
_____   _____
                                        _____
                                        _____
                                        _____
                                        _____

15. Finalize the Outing Plan by adding any missing information. A sample outing plan is shown in Figure 16.1. Typically, this includes the final list of participants and any details that could not be recorded in advance. Be sure that a map is attached, on which the route, all campsites, and key activity sites are clearly shown. This information serves as an aid to anyone who may be called upon to render search and rescue assistance, serves as a

resource for administrators in the event he/she needs to know where the group is, and serves as a good starting point from which to construct a final report following the outing.

16. Be sure that the group understands the need to meet upon arrival at the parking area. This means that if more than one vehicle is used, instructions for when and where to meet must be made clear before the last leg of the journey. Otherwise, the leader may arrive to find participants scattered and waste a lot of time just getting everybody together. It is always easier to exercise control from the start than to try to gain it later.

Transportation To and From the Site

Transportation is an item to be considered under field leadership because it involves face-to-face contact with participants. It has been covered in Chapter Fourteen, and the leader is advised to cover every facet of the suggested policies. Applying them as firm policy can benefit the leader and the institution in a legal sense by showing good intent and good planning on the part of staff. Anything less might be considered dereliction of duty in the eyes of many professional outdoor leaders and administrators. There should also be a good first-aid kit in each vehicle and, preferably, a first-aider.

Be sure the navigator knows the stopping places along the way. Usually, the safest and most convenient plan when using several vehicles is to designate meeting points at one- to two-hour intervals at specific points with telephones. No one should leave these areas until all vehicles are accounted for, and the leader should go *last* so that any problems along the way—flat tires, breakdowns, or accidents—will be seen and dealt with. This can save a great deal of anxiety and time in resolving such situations since the leader can simply phone ahead to the assembly point and notify the rest of the party. When going to a backcountry trailhead or put-in point, the group should be sure to assemble at the last telephone en route.

Backcountry roads can be very confusing, so it is best to explain them carefully then have vehicles follow a lead car containing someone familiar with the correct route.

Trailhead and Launch Site Issues

Once at the trailhead or launch site, there is usually collective relief at being able to get out of the vehicles, a heightened sense of anticipation, and sometimes anxiety about the adventure that is about to begin. The last thing anybody wants is to have to sit or stand around while the instructor gives instructions, and yet there is much that must be said and done before the group can actually set off for the backcountry, or push off from shore. The following suggestions may help speed the process, or at least make life easier for the staff:

1. Assemble the group and set a time and place for reassembly. Ten minutes is plenty of time. Have participants use the time to use the rest rooms or outhouses. If no facilities are available, give advice as to where to go with the reminder to follow instructions given at the pre-trip meetings.

2. Assemble the group again and supervise the unloading of the vehicles. Have the participants don their boots if they did not wear them in the vehicle, and pack away their "in camp" shoes. They may be at higher elevations than when they started out and may need to put on warmer clothing right away. If group gear has not already been assigned, now is the time to do it (but there may be no way to weigh the packs!). Reassembly should be possible in a maximum of 20 minutes.

3. At this point, the staff should be moving quickly to change their clothes if needed, and circulate among the participants to provide assistance.

4. Make sure that the group leader or a qualified first aider carries the first-aid kit.

5. Check every participant's pack to be sure everything is adequately (i.e., very securely) fastened and that rain protection is adequate if this seems necessary.

6. Recheck vehicles to be sure that absolutely no gear or clothing is visible from the outside. Vehicles are often broken into for very small items. The simple precaution of hiding everything left in the vehicle can greatly reduce the chance of break in. The rules are simple— if *you* can see it, so can anyone looking for things to take.

7. Remember the advice in Chapter Fourteen to carry two sets of keys; inform the participants who will be carrying each set. Do not plan to "hide" keys and retrieve them at the end of the trip. A thief won't take long to check all of the common hiding places!

8. Meet briefly with the staff to finalize plans for the day.

9. Meet with the participants and get ready to head up the trail or out to the water. There are several important points to be covered in a brief talk before starting. It is usually easiest to do this as a large group.

a. Review the plans for the day. Every adult should have a map, except on short river or lake journeys where a sketch might be sufficient. Go over the route and encourage the frequent use of the maps during the day. If, as in most programs, independence is a goal, then this is essential. Map reading is a basic and necessary skill in most outdoor activities, and it is learned only by repeated prediction, observation, and subsequent review. Participants should also be made aware of the timing of rest breaks, lunch, and alternatives in the event of unexpected changes in the weather, etc.

b. Explain the method to be employed for keeping track of everybody. Whether you're on a trail or on a river, this usually involves staying between a lead and a tail person and being responsible for those following. This is often the hardest point

to get across. The specifics of these plans are important and will be discussed in detail later in this chapter.

c. Review what to do if anyone loses contact with the group for more than a specified period of time. (Follow the material in Chapter Six, "Preparation for Survival.")

d. Review how to deal with sanitation issues. (Follow the material in Chapter Four, "Care of the Environment," and the material you covered in the pre-trip meetings.)

e. Suggest the appropriate clothing in which to begin the activity, and then break into travel or task groups. If this hasn't already been done, it is usually easiest to have individual group leaders stand as far apart as possible to completely separate the units.

10. Repark the vehicles to occupy the least possible space, as a matter of courtesy to other users.

11. As a last chore, it is a good idea to spend just a few minutes cleaning up the area. Whether it is a trailhead or a landing, inconsiderate people have probably left at least some litter. Picking it up as a group is very easy, takes very little time, does a valuable community service, temporarily reduces the amount of litter that will be dropped (clean sites tend to stay clean), and perhaps most important of all, may have a lasting positive effect on participant behavior. People are much less likely to litter if they have actually had to pick up after others.

12. Head up the trail.

Decision Making

Decision making is an ongoing process wherein the leader must integrate all aspects of his/her knowledge. While the process must be based upon reason and logic, it is inevitably colored by the leader's attitudes and feelings, and limited by factors beyond the leader's control. Lack of knowledge or skill, lack of sensitivity to changes in the participants or in the environment, unrealistic emotional biases, and lack of foresight all detract from the quality of decisions.

Most leadership decisions are highly complex, requiring consideration of many factors. Even a "simple" choice between two routes may require information about such issues as the alternative routes, the weather, the time of day, and the status of staff and participants. While it might be ideal to devote large measures of time to each decision, in practice this would be impractical. Therefore, the first and perhaps most critical decision to be made is an assessment of the *importance* of the issue. This requires a quick but accurate survey of the total situation, and a quick and, if anything, pessimistic assessment of the worst case results should a bad decision be made. The worse the potential outcome, the more critical the decision.

In *Leading to Share; Sharing to Lead*, (Council of Outdoor Educators of Sudbury, Ontario, Canada, 1979), R.J. Rogers outlines the essential components of the decision making process to be:

1. Physiological Forces (micro and macro climates, first aid, hypothermia and hyperthermia, physical fitness);
2. Social-psychological Forces (human behavior, personal interaction, small-group dynamics, valuing);
3. Environmental Forces (weather, ecology, environmental land ethic);
4. Safety Forces (accident and emergency procedures, group security, special hazards, search and rescue); and
5. Technical Forces (navigation, program planning, route planning and expedition planning, group travel, personal and group equipment, wilderness skills, legal liabilities, outdoor clubs, and community opportunities).

Making a decision should be an act based upon a step-by-step process of rational action, not precipitous action. These logical steps are as follows:

1. Consider the task. What is the situation and what must be done?
2. Consider the resources. These are the five external factors listed above.

3. Consider a range of alternative actions, then evaluate each in respect to the five external factors. For example, you could go on, but how does each external factor affect this decision? What are the effects of each if you stay? If you go back?
4. Write down all possible ideas and pick the best one. This is your decision. If you can't write them down, discuss them and then pick one, remembering that the responsibility rests with the leader. You can't pass the buck and say, "*They* told me to do it that way."
5. Put the decision into action positively and emphatically. Don't waste time discussing or thinking about, "What if?" "What if" is out of the picture. Stick to your decision.
6. In the end, evaluate the results of your decision. It might influence future ones.

Most decisions made by the leader affect staff or participants. The circumstances will determine when and to what extent the decision should be expressed to those involved. If the decision was arrived at democratically among the participants and staff, this may be a moot point. Often, however, the decision needs to be conveyed to the staff or participants, and, in a field setting, this normally involves face-to-face verbal communication.

When other leaders are involved, whether a single assistant leader or a complex hierarchy of team leaders and assistants, the decision maker is advised to meet with and inform the entire leadership team or at least those at the top of the subordinate hierarchy before informing the participants. This is more than just a courtesy. The other members of the staff may have information unavailable to the leader at the time he/she made the decision, and subgroup or team leaders may be better able to communicate messages within their smaller units. This also tends to foster respect for the message bearers, or at least may be less disruptive than having the prime leader step into the unit to enact decisions. On the other hand, it may be best to communicate decisions that are complex, controversial, or exceptionally important in full group settings, after a full briefing of staff.

Group Control

The term "group control" may seem to imply rigid, autocratic discipline. The term, as used here, may in fact refer to any level or manner of control that is sufficient to maintain acceptable safety of the group, minimal impact on the natural resource, minimal impact on other users of the area, and accomplishment of the objectives of the outing. As any experienced leader knows, the appropriate level of control varies widely depending upon the participants, the objectives of the program, and the immediate circumstances.

Levels of Control

In general, it is usually desirable to use the least coercive, "lowest profile" approach that will meet the needs of the moment. This may mean a softer voice, less strict rules for behavior, or a greater physical distance between the leaders and the participants. There are several advantages to a lower key or "gentler" style. Such approaches are more restful for both staff and participants and are generally preferred by participants seeking relaxation with no particularly strong destination, knowledge, or skill objectives for the outing.

Often, leaders and staff intentionally create a sense of lessened control or of greater distance from participants, in order to *generate* anxiety. In circumstances wherein the participants need inspiration to think for themselves, this is an effective strategy. By backing off and transferring responsibility to the group members, learning is usually accelerated, which in turn fosters the development of self-confidence. While such techniques are widely-employed, extreme care must be taken to maintain sufficient control to avoid unacceptable risks. Under most circumstances, increasing *perceived* risks for participants increases many of the potential benefits of the experience. However, doing so often means

accepting increased *real* risk. If the leader attempts to create anxiety by loosening perceived control, it must be done in such a way as to protect participants from risks that are unjustified by the goals of the program. Another important hidden danger is the possibility of giving participants a false sense of the level of control necessary in a given set of circumstances.

While it is usually best to be no more assertive than necessary, there are times and places wherein greater control is called for. Whenever there are specific objectives for an outing, it is more important to exert control over the actions of the group. In emergencies, very strict and efficient control may have to be instigated immediately. The experienced leader is able to adjust the level of control to the needs of the moment and apply effective control techniques. Doing so implies an ability to make good decisions, communicate well, and establish effective procedures. The material in Chapter Ten, "Outdoor Pursuits Leadership," discusses this topic in the section on leadership models.

Control On and Off the Trail

Three general principles for group control that are useful regardless of the level of control or the process by which decisions are made are listed as follows:

1. Gain the understanding and support of the group prior to the need for control. If the group understands the need for control and the way in which control is to be maintained, the process is likely to operate reasonably well with minimal need for intervention by staff. Additional efficiency can often be gained by assigning clearly defined roles and responsibilities to each group member prior to situations where optimal control is needed. For example, individuals might be assigned specific positions in line and specific duties.

2. Begin with control levels that are as strict as the most stringent levels that will be required on the outing. This is especially important with

younger groups, wherein it is easy to move to less firm control methods, but relatively difficult to increase the level of control unless a precedent has been established.

3. The control strategy must be monitored at all times and must be adjusted to fit the circumstances. No control system is perfect, and participants and staff, regardless of age or experience, may fail to perform their roles in the process. A control system that is appropriate in the morning in fine weather may be inadequate later in the day due to fatigue, changes in terrain or weather, or other change in the circumstances.

Whether on land or water, the leader must ensure that the group members are directly supervised so that each participant can be immediately reached by a capable staff member in the event of an emergency or a need to intervene to prevent unsafe behavior. The control system must also allow gathering of the entire group, should it become necessary to issue directions or pool resources in an emergency.

When traveling on land or water, the usual procedure is to confine the group between a lead person or "scout" and a tail person, often referred to as a "sweep" or "caboose." This system works well if:

a. The slowest person travels just behind the leader.
b. No passing is allowed.
c. The group stops at all junctions, decision points, and points of possible confusion.
d. Every person is responsible for, and keeps track of, the following person.
e. If one person stops, the whole group stops.

This system works well on-trails, streams, and other linear features, once the group members learn to keep track of the person *behind* them. With large groups, it is helpful to give the tail person something visible to wear or carry. In this way, the lead person can easily keep track of the tail person. In very large groups or at night, it may be helpful to add a mid-person who will keep track of the tail, so the lead person doesn't have to wait as often for a view of

the caboose. Having the lead person keep track of the sweep may seem somewhat excessive, since in theory the whole line will stop if any one person stops. As experienced leaders know, however, this is a case wherein redundancy is very worthwhile and often necessary.

Especially in off-trail travel, it is helpful to assign the task of keeping track of the sweep to the *second* person in line, so the lead person is free to focus on route finding. There are many configurations possible, in which certain people in the line are given responsibility for tasks such as timekeeper, recordkeeper, or navigator.

The leader and/or assistant leaders may or may not assume the roles of lead person or sweep. Unless the participants are young or the risk level is high, it is often best to have group members assume the roles, if not all of the responsibility, for group control. There is no better way to learn, and when group members assist, the staff is free to move within the group. Nevertheless, the leader or assistant may need to stay near the front to control the pace, to determine rest stops, to make route decisions, and to ensure that the tail person is in sight at regular intervals. "Leading from the rear" is appropriate only in low risk situations with experienced participants, as it is very difficult to exert the necessary leadership from a position at the end of the line.

Finally, there may be times when it is reasonable to loosen control, and let people walk at their own paces, out of sight of one another; however, this low level of control is seldom appropriate except in fine weather and safe terrain with experienced people. Even then it is best to have a good sweep person, and a rule that people are to leave a pack on the trail if they leave the trail momentarily, and wait at every junction to be sure the next person goes the right way.

Off-trail travel or open water travel can be far more difficult to control, since the group is not confined to a linear feature. Many leaders can relate tales of having lost track, at least momentarily, of individuals in brushy or rough terrain, in foul weather on land, in rough seas or in fog on open water. Under such circumstances, extraordinary care must be taken. The most obvious and useful technique is to maintain continual close visual contact with all members. Pairing up can also help. The "buddy system" is reassuring to group members and staff, and it offers real security by reducing the chance of a single person being lost alone and by increasing the likelihood of an absence being noticed quickly. As discussed earlier, each participant should carry certain basic safety items, including a whistle. During off-trail travel, it is a good idea to have individuals carry their whistles in accessible pockets or on neck cords tucked into their shirts.

In truly foul weather, especially at night or in hazardous terrain, one of the most effective systems is to simply tie everyone together! While this is usually done in a mountaineering context using a climbing rope, any strong cord would suffice unless it might be needed to arrest a fall. The leader normally ties onto the front end of the line, then the slowest person ties in, or ideally attaches with a sliding carabiner, followed by the rest of the group with the sweep tied to the rear end of the line. If nothing else, this system provides great peace of mind for the leader, who can concentrate fully on route finding, with the knowledge that no member of his/her flock can stray.

There is, by the way, another interesting way of using a cord to control a group. In Tokyo and in several other large cities around the world, groups of school kids are surrounded by a circular elastic cord before entering large, crowded areas such as amusement parks or central subway stations. It's quite a sight to see fifty youngsters flow amoeba-like through the crowded halls and corridors of Tokyo Station, and it helps to put other control problems in perspective.

In areas over rock, where the way is marked by rockpiles (cairns, ducks, birds), it is a common practice in dense fog for the leader to tie the end of a ball of twine around one wrist and to set out in the fog, trying to locate the next cairn. The rest of the group stays together on the last located cairn with an assistant playing out the twine. When the leader locates the next marker, he/she gives a previously agreed upon number of firm tugs on the line and "reels" in the group to that next cairn. The group *never*

leaves one cairn until the next one is found. If the next one is not located, the leader is "reeled" back to the group, and a bivouac is made until the fog lifts, or until the cairn can be located.

Control in the Campsite

Often, problems arise while in camp or while spending a prolonged period at an activity site. In such settings, there is a tendency for everyone, participants and leaders alike, to relax. Many searches have been conducted for people who "wandered off" from camp. Clearly, the need for control measures depends upon the group and the setting. Nevertheless, it is best to err on the side of security. Even with competent adults, some control is normal and, once explained is generally appreciated. In hazardous, brushy, or confusing areas, strict controls may be required with any group, including the staff.

The most common problems stem from single individuals or small groups of inexperienced people who venture away from the group to explore, seek water, firewood, or photographic opportunities, or privacy with friends. Young people may also be inclined to move away from the group just to see if they can get to exciting, but prohibited nearby sites to play games or to engage in some form of proscribed activity.

The leader can reduce the risks in several ways. One very useful action is to ensure that everyone on-site is aware of where they are, the shape and orientation of the land, and the exact location and nature of hazards. A "buddy system" may suffice; however, in hazardous or very bushy terrain, or with young people, it may be necessary to insist that no one leave camp without a leader. If the group members are capable and responsible, notification of a leader may suffice, or, in the case of mature and experienced adults, one might ask that no one leave camp alone, though, even in this case, it is helpful to ask that a leader be notified, a precaution that any truly experienced participant will understand and respect.

One of the most common and frustrating problems arises at night, particularly in brushy terrain. Campers slip out to relieve themselves, only to grope around for hours, or all night, unable to find the tent when returning in the dark.

It happens all too often, but it can be avoided if tent mates stay awake during the absence and, ideally, have a candle or flashlight on as a homing beacon. In addition to whatever real safety these measures may add, there are real psychological benefits. The participants feel more secure, and the leader and staff will sleep more soundly.

Group Travel in Hazardous Terrain

Hazardous terrain can be defined loosely as terrain wherein extra caution is required to maintain a risk level equivalent to that encountered in normal hiking situations. Assume that the leader is well-versed in the particular hazards associated with individual travel in each of the circumstances described, and has or is aware of the skills and knowledge necessary for safe individual travel in these areas. In this section we will discuss travel in hazardous terrain as it relates to *groups and group leadership*.

Even though the solo traveler may not be likely to have an accident or become ill or lost, there may be no one available to provide assistance. A small group of two or three people may be two or three times more likely to encounter difficulty. The chance of a sprained ankle, for example, is roughly proportional to the number of ankles in the group. The small group, however, can at least provide basic assistance on scene, and can go for more help if necessary.

In a large group, something odd happens. For example, in a group of 15 people, the risk of a sprained ankle may be *more* than 15 times the risk for one person. While we know of no credible academic study of this phenomena, it appears to be the case in personal observations of hundreds of large group outings under a wide range of conditions. It seems that, in a large group, several factors may interact to increase the risk level above what might be estimated by simply multiplying the risk for one person times the number of people in the group. Perhaps the most obvious factors are skill level and experience. Participants in large group outings tend to be less experienced than those who go out solo or in small groups. Perhaps, more importantly,

people in groups are often distracted by socializing, and, in such situations, may become either relaxed and inattentive or excessively playful which increases the risk of injury. Another common cause of increased risk, related largely to experience level, is anxiety, often compounded by fatigue.

In a large group, there is pressure to conform to a schedule, pace, and route that may be overly stressful for some individuals. For example, think of a group of off-trail hikers or skiers traversing a fairly steep sidehill. Anyone who is anxious will tend to lean toward the hill which, of course, leads to a slip, greater anxiety, and rapid depletion of energy reserves. In addition, there is a tendency to push one's limit to appear more capable to others in the group. One of the key responsibilities of the leader is to monitor all participants continually so that individual needs are not overlooked. While there may be certain safety advantages to large groups with proper skills, ability, and equipment to carry out injured persons or conduct limited searches, leaders need to assess the risks of large groups very carefully. When the effects of large groups and hazardous terrain are combined, the interaction can stack the odds against success.

There are many areas wherein large group travel is not appropriate, even when it might be conducted safely. Large groups have a great potential for causing damage to backcountry areas, as well as to impact seriously the experiences of other users. Often, the areas that we think of as hazardous—deserts, steep slopes, and high mountains—are most vulnerable to damage. While it may be possible, by following the suggestions given below and in the section on minimizing environmental impacts (see Chapter Four), to maintain an acceptably "low profile" in some areas, there are many areas where large groups should not be taken. As the managers of outdoor resources are the first to admit, their rules and regulations cannot possibly identify every area in which large group travel is or is not likely to cause unacceptable impact.

Streams and Rivers

Stream and river crossing can be a highlight of an outing or an opportunity for disaster. The leader needs first to assess the group, as it can only succeed if *every* member is capable of whatever type of crossing is intended. It is also essential to consider how slowly a large group moves. It's one thing for one or two people to be in a draw when flash floods are possible, and quite another thing to have a large group in such a setting, as the large group may take far longer to scramble out of the way of rising water. Even a simple log crossing can take an unbearably long time with a large group, so it is often necessary to modify the plan accordingly. It may be easier and faster to march a group across a creek than to spend excessive time keeping the feet dry.

Leaders should be well-versed in the dangers of cold water, swift currents, and silt, the various systems for crossing streams, and safe use of ropes in river crossings. With a group, there is sometimes reluctance to look very long for the best place to cross. Sometimes, it's best to let the group relax while leaders scout upstream and downstream, as most streams and rivers offer a considerable variety of features. Meanwhile, the group can get ready for the crossing. It's best to be pessimistic and conservative here, and to be sure that everyone is prepared for a plunge. Rain pants and jackets with tight cuffs can be dangerous as they fill with water. Hip suspension belts on packs should be released to allow easy escape.

It is good to get in the habit of always using spotters downstream, each equipped with a pole, throw bag, or rope, and not wearing packs so they are as agile as possible. The first person across should be the appointed spotter for the far side, and the last person to cross should be the spotter on the approach side. In this way, the two spotters, usually leaders, are each protected by one spotter when they cross, and each group member has the benefit of two spotters, one on each side.

There are many possible ways to cross, from wading or swimming (floating packs on sleeping pads), to log bridges, constructed bridges, or Tyrolean traverses. Each has certain advantages and certain disadvantages and risks. When deciding on the best method, leaders need to consider the abilities and anxieties of the group members, the size of the group, and the length of time available. Whatever method is chosen, it's important to set a good example. The leader who boldly walks across the log over the stream, with no protection or spotters, will be emulated by participants. Even if the group is asked to use more cautious methods at the time, it will be more difficult to obtain full compliance if a more exciting or challenging option has been demonstrated.

Leaders also need to be sensitive to the lowest level of competence, and should normally establish and demonstrate a standard crossing method that everyone can accomplish safely. If a faster but more difficult method is appropriate for all but one or two group members, it may be worthwhile using it if time is short. However care must be taken to help the less experienced people across in an appropriate manner, and leaders need to be sensitive to the psychological and social effects of such a plan. The less competent members may feel uncomfortable if singled out for special treatment. The experienced leader can usually turn these situations into positive experiences, as opportunities for demonstrating other techniques and for discussing group leadership processes.

Steep Terrain

Steep slopes present another set of challenges. The dangers are usually related to slips or falls, and the risk of natural or group-caused rockfall. Groups can also do extensive damage to almost any slope if tight control is not exercised. There are several things that a leader can do before heading up or down steep terrain. The group members need to be informed of the risks that are not obvious. For example, many people may not understand the potential seriousness of even a short slip or slide when carrying a large pack, how much damage even a small rock can do, or the importance of *never* turning one's back on a steep rocky slope. Groups tend to flush game, and any animals spooked by the group may send rocks down from far above.

The group also needs to understand *how* to reduce risks, or the plan for the ascent or descent needs to be clearly explained before approaching the slope. It is important to keep the pace well within the comfort zone of *all* participants, as tired people are far more prone to kick loose rocks, let brush snap back, or not pay attention to the possibility of encountering poison oak, rattlesnakes, or other hazards. If the rest step has not been demonstrated earlier, it should be practiced before ascents, to help maintain a relaxed, slow pace. Many people, especially nonskiers, need to be reminded of the need to stay away from the hill, as "leaning in," a natural tendency, promotes slips, increased rock displacement, and soil damage.

There are any number of possible surfaces that can present a hazard if sufficiently inclined. While we tend to be naturally leery of steep rocky slopes, relatively gentle slopes may allow rocks to accelerate to lethal velocity. Snow surfaces are obviously dangerous when the surface is frozen or wind crusted or when the conditions result in the possibility of avalanches. One of the least obvious but most hazardous surfaces is wet grass. The classic example is a frosty, steep meadow, or, worse yet, a dew covered, freshly cut alpine pasture. Many a climber in the Alps has safely negotiated an airy climbing route, only to take a hair-raising ride down a rain slicked, freshly mowed farmer's field.

The best plan is usually to use existing trails if they exist. Even a game trail usually offers considerable advantage over off-trail travel, as traction is enhanced, rockfall is reduced, and environmental damage is minimized. While a small group might safely traverse, ascend, or descend a given steep slope with no problem, large groups have so much potential for dislodging rocks and disturbing soil and plant life as to warrant extreme care by using every possible means of reducing risk and impact. Ridge routes are preferable to gullies, at least in terms of rockfall, since it tends to flow away from people on a ridge.

When the group moves in a line, switch backing up or down a hill; tight control is needed if loose rock is present to ensure that the group stops or clusters up at the end of each traverse. In this way, no one is ever below anyone else.

Without good control, the front of the line will be on the next switchback before the rear of the line gets off of the first switchback. When the terrain doesn't allow clustering the group at the end of a traverse, consider ending the ascending or descending traverse with a horizontal traverse long enough to accommodate the whole group. Then the next traverse can be done by reversing the marching order, without having to cluster up or to put anyone above or below anyone else.

When the large group is broken into smaller groups or when individuals are each asked to zigzag independently (two good ways of reducing impact on some types of ground), it is important to prevent any person or group from getting above any other individual or group. This is not easy to do! The group needs to clearly understand the plan, and they should have tight visual contact with a leader or individual who sets the pace and, by his/her position, establishes the elevation for all parties. By having everyone at the same elevation at all times, no one is in the target zone for rockfall. Speaking of target zones, it is amazing to see a group cautiously ascend steep terrain by taking care to avoid rockfall, only to stop and rest on a scree slope with their backs to the cliff source of the rocks on which they are sitting. At the *very least* a pair of reliable spotters need to be assigned to watch for rockfall, and, better yet, the whole group should "face the danger" or find a better place to rest.

Rope Use

Sometimes, on very steep terrain, ropes may be used for security. Of course, the leader who contemplates the use of ropes should be very thoroughly versed in the technical aspects of ropes and rope use. Fixed lines can be a real asset, and they can be used with reasonable efficiency if each person is equipped with slings, carabiners, or other necessary gear. Whenever ropes are considered, it is probably also time to consider requiring helmets on all staff and participants.

Rappels should be avoided with any large group, unless conditions allow plenty of time, since it's necessary to allow 5-10 minutes per person, plus setup and take-down time. Also, it is virtually impossible to avoid scarring the surface when many people rappel from the same point.

Snow and Ice

Any leader who plans to lead groups on snowfields and glaciers should be completely familiar with current and standard practices in the fields of mountaineering and crevasse rescue. Most of the abundant written material on these topics focuses, as it should, on small group travel. Larger groups present some special problems. Aside from the obvious potential for major environmental and social effects, large groups in technically challenging situations are slow.

Climbing routes often have "bottlenecks," and a large group may simply be unable to pass through some parts of the route quickly enough. In cold weather, the time required for roping up and putting on crampons can be painfully long for a large group. These effects, along with the inherently slow pace of a large group, can greatly increase risks on some routes. In many cases, safe travel on snowfields and glaciers requires an ability to pass over certain areas during critical periods of relative stability. A large, slow party may still be high on a mountain, fighting peak late afternoon rockfall, soft snow bridges, fading light, afternoon lightning storms, and growing fatigue, while leaner, faster teams are long since safely down in camp.

Leaders must be careful to consider routes in terms of group paces and needs. The route or climb, rated easy or moderate in the guidebook and done by the leader and two friends in a total of seven hours, may well deserve a moderate to difficult rating for a large group and require eleven or twelve hours to complete.

When using ropes, consider some in-town or low elevation practice to establish standard procedures, even if the group members are all highly experienced. Each rope team should have at least one leader or fully rescue-competent member, and weaker members of the group should be allocated to center positions or rope. While, for teaching purposes, one can make a good case for using conventional small party roping systems, there are alternatives that may be of use under some circumstances. In Europe,

for example, vast herds of tourists are taken onto glaciers in groups of up to twenty on a single long rope, and one of the authors has counted seventy-two Austrian mountain troops marching up the Dachstein, all on one long interconnected set of ropes. We aren't suggesting that such systems are safe or appropriate in all circumstances, but there are times when effective group management requires creative extensions of more conventional techniques designed for small groups.

Be careful when designing or employing any nonstandard technique. Be sure that the system will work before using it in a situation wherein participants might be endangered. You don't want to inadvertently increase risk, and you don't want to be the "Lone Ranger" in a courtroom defense of your actions.

Be especially careful on ice. One tends to develop a sense of the thickness of ice needed to support a person or a small group, but a much greater thickness may be required for a large group, especially if they even momentarily assemble in a small area. In some parts of the country, an interesting and dangerous phenomena occurs on alpine lakes. In the Pacific Northwest and in parts of the Sierra Nevada, hard ice seldom forms due to the relatively warm conditions. In these areas, a thin and soft ice layer forms early in the season and is then buried in deep snows. It may then partially melt away, leaving little except a floating pad of snow. One skier or snowshoer, or a small group, may be able to cross safely or even sit in the middle of a lake and enjoy a long lunch with no problem; however, the weight of a large group may be enough to sink the pad. The result, which may be immediate or may take as much as an hour to occur, is water permeation of the upper layers of the snow cover, and then often rapid and very dangerous breakdown of the pad into a slurry of snow and water. Ice crossings are best avoided with large groups unless the surface is known to be sufficiently strong, and even then the party should be prepared with throw lines or other means of speedy rescue.

Terrain may be hazardous for group travel for many other reasons, including, but not limited to, extreme heat, lack of water, dangerous plants or animals, climate and weather phenomena, or attitude. Responsible leadership of any size of group requires awareness of the hazards that might be encountered on the route and the skill and knowledge normally expected of an expert practitioner of the activity. Leaders of large groups (the definition of "large" will vary with the activity) need to be sensitive to the possibility of increased risks, slower travel speeds, and greater environmental impacts, and they must be prepared to modify routes, plans, and control techniques accordingly.

Campsite Issues
Campsite Selection

Whether campsites are selected in advance or at the time of need, the key issues to be considered are safety, the potential for environmental and social impacts, the adequacy of water supplies, the suitability of the site considering the objectives of the program, the policies of the resource management agency, and any costs associated with use of the site. Comfort and aesthetics are usually secondary in importance, though these issues certainly need to be considered. Given a choice of sites that are fully acceptable in terms of the primary criteria, the choice of site is usually based upon such factors as exposure to wind or weather, the abundance of biting insects, the availability of shade, the likelihood of morning sun, and the view.

In addition, the distance to other occupied camps may be a very important issue for groups. Organized groups need to be especially sensitive to the social and aesthetic effects of camping near other groups. Small parties in the area, who may be seeking solitude or at least the illusion of solitude, generally do not appreciate the presence of large groups, organized or not. It is a simple matter of courtesy to make every effort to avoid disrupting the experience of other users of the resource. Sometimes, a choice must be made between sites near small parties or sites near other organized groups. Generally speaking, to minimize the effects on the small groups, it is better to move in near the large groups even though this may mean foregoing some privacy.

Safety Issues

There is no such thing as a perfectly safe site. It is the leader's responsibility to assess the risks associated with camping at the site, and to decide whether or not the risks are acceptable. Once a site is selected, the leader is obligated to inform participants of any significant risks associated with use of the site. Common hazards might include steep or otherwise hazardous terrain, hazardous bodies of water or waterfalls, unsafe water supplies, unsafe bridges or log crossings, poisonous insects or plants, dangerous animals, confusing trails, or brush cover that could contribute to someone becoming lost, to hazards related to people, to human activities or traffic, and to weakened or dead trees or branches that could fall on tents. The latter is a particular concern in old growth forests of the west, where a dead tree located 200 feet from a tent may pose a threat, and falling limbs may be lethal.

Tentsite Selection

Once a campsite has been reached, the next task is usually the selection of tent sites for each staff and participant tent group. The experienced leader will explain the rules for site selection, impact reductions, and sanitation, then set a time and place for reassembly before letting groups seek sites, unless everyone will camp close together. When beginners are involved, it is usually best to move about with the entire group so that the advantages and disadvantages of each site can be discussed as a part of the education of the group. Once enough sites have been found, a toilet area can be designated, then the tent sites can be assigned to tent groups. If time is short or foul weather exists, it may be best to have participants scout out sites, then seek the approval of staff members before erecting tents and tarps. Depending upon the skill level of the participants, it may be important to have a leader or experienced participant assist with tent setting. Direct leader supervision should always be provided when beginners are learning to use gasoline or pressurized gas stoves, or at any time when the weather or the condition of the participants warrants extra care.

In most group situations, there are one or more shelters occupied by leaders and staff and a larger number of shelters occupied by participants. Sometimes, the layout of the campsite is such that all of the shelters must be placed in close proximity. The advantages of a tight configuration are real, or at least psychological, security, sometimes appreciated by beginners, and ease of communications between tent groups and staff. During unusually cold or foul weather or when the group needs or wants an extra measure of security, it's a good idea to confine all of the shelters to a small area. Under such conditions, it may be worthwhile to "make the rounds" one or more times during the night. When camping with beginners or youngsters in foul weather, the staff should rotate duty and check each tent at appropriate intervals.

On the other hand, camping close together may preclude privacy, strain the carrying capacity of the site, and result in the campers losing an opportunity to experience the special feelings that come from camping out of sight of any other tent, where one can at least fantasize about true wilderness. Under stable, fair weather conditions in a relatively safe location, it may be reasonable and even advantageous to spread out a group, even if the participants are beginners. If adequate control measures are taken, every camper will have safe and sure access to a staff member.

When the group is spread over a wide area, the locations of staff shelters are important. Usually, the primary concern is accessibility. In general, the staff tent or tents should be positioned to ensure easy, safe, and sure access to staff by members of any of the tent groups, even in the dark. Sometimes, especially when there is only one staff tent, access can be facilitated by placing the tent at one end of the array of participant tents, or a line of cord or flagging may be used to orient and direct people to the tent at night.

Meals

In most camping situations, there are advantages to having a group meal experience. This may involve preparation of a common meal, or may simply be a matter of having a common cooking and eating area. There are several advantages to coming together for meals, including opportunities to share food and ideas for outdoor cooking, opportunities for socialization, and facilitation of communication between staff and participants. Especially when the participants are relatively new to camping, there is always much to be learned about fire site selection and fire building, stove selection, starting and using stoves, and basic outdoor cooking. Having everyone in a central location can allow the staff to provide better supervision and can allow participants to learn from the experiences of others. There are times, of course, when it's best to cook at individual tent sites. When the weather, temperature, or condition of participants requires maximal shelter, it may be best to have people at their own tent sites, so that all but one of the tentmates can be warm and dry in the tent during the cooking process. In this case, the staff usually needs to roam from site to site to be sure that fires or stoves are used safely and successfully, and that everyone is well-fed. With luck and a bit of experience at this routine, the instructor can usually manage to arrive on his/her second visit to a site just as the meal is ready to sample! While we're on the topic of meals, leaders and staff may need to plan somewhat different menus than their students, since they may be very busy during mealtime helping others to start fires or stoves or to cook meals, and may be busy conducting meetings or activities before and after dinner. It is often easier for staff to rely on foods that require little or no preparation, and to snack opportunistically throughout the meal period.

Meetings and Activities

Typically, the travel portion of the day ends late in the afternoon. By this time, people are usually anxious to set up camp and prepare a meal, so meetings need to be brief and limited to conveying the information necessary to establish camp, to organize the mealtime, and to set a time and place for after dinner activities. After dinner, people generally feel energetic for a short while, but soon they begin to slow down and retreat into their tents, especially after a strenuous or long day. If meetings or activities are planned, it's best to catch the group just after dinner and before they lose their enthusiasm for group activity.

Once they have settled in for the night, it can be difficult to get them up and out of their tents. An evening meeting is always a good idea. The day's events can be reviewed, and, depending upon the nature of the outing and group, there are usually many worthwhile issues and topics that can be discussed. With beginners, or with any group in exceptionally foul weather, it's a good idea to assess everyone's attitudes and health and to review ways of staying warm at night. (See Figure 16.2). Be sure to specify the rules pertaining to sanitation (where and how) and safety (limits, policies, and procedures when leaving the tent or camp).

Evening activities might include star talks, identifying the sounds of the area at night, or night hikes. With reasonable care, trail hiking at night can be safe. By having each person walk with one hand on the pack or shoulder of the person ahead, a large group can travel with only one flashlight on the darkest night. Night travel is exciting, interesting, sometimes challenging, and always fun, and can teach the skills and provide the confidence necessary for night travel in emergencies.

An activity that is especially valuable is the "Tour of Homes." This is usually best done in the morning, and consists of making the rounds from tentsite to tentsite with the entire group, and, at each site, carefully assessing the site for risks, environmental sensitivity, and comfort potential, and assessing the gear of the residents for functionality and suitability. One way to conduct the "Tour" is to have someone from each tentsite act as a tour guide or promoter of the property, while participants ask questions about the site and the equipment. The "Tour of Homes" provides a valuable opportunity for participants to learn from the experiences of others and to learn more about equipment. The "Tour" isn't just for beginners. Experienced participants are, if anything, even more enthusiastic about its benefits.

FIGURE 16.2   Suggestions for Staying Warm at Night

1. Use plenty of insulation between the bag and the ground.
2. Fluff the bag up well at least 30 minutes before bedtime.
3. Go to bed warm, i.e., exercise before turning in.
4. Go to bed dry. Never wear any damp clothing in the sleeping bag.
5. Wear extra clothing inside the bag, or put it over you.
6. Wear a hat!
7. Put a rolled sweater around your neck or create a barrier to prevent heat loss.
8. Keep your face out of the bag. Moisture defeats insulation value.
9. Zip two bags together. Two people together need less top loft. Three people fit into two bags, and require even less top loft.
10. Keep the fluffier side of the bag on top. Don't compress it by rolling onto it.
11. Huddle side to side with other people.
12. Use hot water bottles! One or two liter bottles of boiling water can keep a bag warm for hours, and drive excess moisture from the foot of the bag.
13. Eat and drink as needed during the night. Keep food and water nearby.
14. Do isometrics as needed to warm up.
15. Use a vapor barrier liner, or wear waterproof clothing inside the sleeping bag. Nonbreathable fabric works best to keep body moisture out of the bag.
16. Never use a tarp or other waterproof layer in contact with the outside of the bag. Without good ventilation water from perspiration will accumulate on and in the bag.

Teaching in the Outdoors

No matter what one does, or does not do, every participant in an outdoor program learns something, if only because people are *always* learning, no matter what they are doing. The leader who conducts an outing with no specific objectives may have no particular desire to teach, and yet by his/her actions *is* teaching, simply by virtue of acting out the role of a leader. It's unavoidable. We're all teachers, leaders, and participants alike, and we're all learners. Nevertheless, we use the term "teaching" to imply an overt attempt to convey ideas, information, or skills, and the term "teacher" to an individual who purposefully attempts to teach.

It is probably fair to say that every participant in every outing gains some awareness and knowledge of the environment, enjoys some measure of personal growth, and gains some useful skills, regardless of the nature of the program or the performance of the leaders. It is also true that, in virtually every case, leaders are expected to move the participants towards the goals of the program, and, when possible, to see that each participant achieves certain specified knowledge, skill, or behavioral objectives. In other words, the leader is expected to teach.

It is beyond the scope of this book to attempt even a summary of the wealth of information and advice in the many excellent texts available on the topic of teaching. Rather, the intent here is to address the subject in terms of the immediate practical needs of the outdoor leader. For efficient teaching to take place, the learner must be receptive, and the teacher must be able to communicate effectively. The listener must be comfortable, rested, and undistracted before information can be absorbed, and the setting must allow each person to hear and see the speaker easily. These conditions are fundamental to any learning situation but must be supplemented by other conditions.

Before one can plan an effective teaching method, the program goals and audience must be understood. To understand the goals of the program, it may be necessary to refer back to the written description of the program and to discuss the issue in detail with program administrators. It is also essential to understand the audience, or, to be more precise, the individuals who comprise the body of prospective learners. Why are they there? What do they want? What do they think they need? What do you, or what does the program, think they need? What are they capable of learning? *How* do they learn best? These are not easy questions to answer; however, they all bear on the task at hand. Once again, the more we know, the better we can accomplish our mission. (See Chapter Ten for more information about participants.)

Needless to say, there is no perfect method or venue for teaching any topic or any type of person. In fact, there are usually many ways in which a given topic may be taught to any specified audience. It is up to the teacher—in this case, the outdoor leader—to determine the best methods given the opportunities and constraints of the particular situation. Given the complexity of the outdoor experience, it is often necessary for the leader/teacher to change techniques on the spur of the moment due to changes in the weather, an inability to reach preferred sites, or other unexpected events. The uncertainty inherent in outdoor teaching shouldn't be used as an excuse for not planning, but as a reminder of the need to plan for more than one approach to the task.

Communication Skills

Everyone knows that verbal communication is often a less than perfect way of conveying ideas even between two people in the quiet and comfortable setting of a living room. Consider the leader who must convey an important message to a group of twelve tired and hungry hikers descending a narrow trail in cold wind and rain. It is impossible to get everyone close together, the wind obscures all but the loudest voices, and no one is in the mood to stop and risk getting colder.

The only reasonable solution in the above example would probably be to move to the head of the group, slow the pace enough to ensure that the group is walking in close order, then stop at the next wide and sheltered spot. The message should be delivered only after *every* person is huddled together and attentive. It should be given quickly and clearly so that the group is moving again within three or four minutes.

For communication to be effective, the audience must be receptive, which in an outdoor setting usually means undistracted by personal discomfort, tiredness, anxiety, social interactions, or scenery. Their desire to hear the message has to override all other interests. For example, it may be very difficult to address a group just about to begin a long anticipated activity, or a group that is about to leave for home. They also need to be able to hear, and preferably see, the speaker. In general, this requires that the leader be sensitive to the needs of the group. Sometimes, it may be necessary to allow time for rest, eating, or trips for toileting before trying to communicate more than the simplest messages. At other times, the leader must act quickly before the listeners become chilled or anxious to move on.

The setting is also important. Ideally, the site should be quiet, away from streams, waterfalls, or wind sounds, and the listeners should be positioned with their backs to the sun, and wind, and to distracting scenery. On inclined ground, it is usually best to have the leader downhill of the group so he/she can be seen easily. If the leader is uphill, the group members have to look uphill. This can be hard on neck muscles, and, from such a position, the speaker may be silhouetted against the horizon.

It isn't often that one finds a perfect "amphitheater" just when it's needed, and rarer still to have the sun in the right place and the wind from the right direction. More often, the leader must make the best of a less than ideal set of circumstances. Recognizing the importance of good communication, the experienced leader is sensitive to the listener's needs and adjusts the content and length of messages, and even the program agenda, according to the circumstances.

One of the best ways to learn about teaching is to observe experienced teachers in a variety of settings. Most of us can also recall useful observations from our own histories as students. What we are likely to discover is that the best and most experienced teachers are highly sensitive to their audiences, very excited about their topics, and adept at suiting their teaching style to the needs of the moment, seldom dwelling on one approach for very long. Lectures alternate with discussion sessions. The teacher may begin by expressing some key ideas or by providing some background information, and then facilitate involvement by the students. When individuals in the group are guided to personal discovery, the information or concepts are intrinsically connected to the learner's world and are more likely to be retained and effectively utilized.

While classroom settings are relatively standardized and generally provide a high level of comfort and freedom from distraction, outdoor settings come in essentially limitless variety, may or may not be comfortable, and often abound in distracting elements. For these reasons, it is often desirable to teach some skills and basic information in a classroom setting. For example, a few hours of pre-trip meeting time spent teaching basic safety issues, environmental ethics and map and compass use can greatly reduce the risks, lower the impact, and increase the efficiency of a beginner backpacking outing. By covering some topics in a lecture/discussion format in town, less time needs to be spent in the field on topics that require relatively formal and necessarily sedentary approaches. Instead, more time can be spent in more active, hands-on experiences that cannot be easily conducted in the conventional classroom setting.

Given the variability and frequently less than ideal conditions encountered in outdoor sites, it is a good idea to divide the material to be covered into relatively small parcels. This also makes it easier to fit needed teaching into small intervals of time. One of the best ways to take advantage of the inherent variability of circumstances and to accommodate the need to keep people active is to be prepared for opportunistic teaching; that is, be prepared to use "teachable moments." Thus, the wildflower patch by the trail provides an opportunity for discussion of plant adoption, the rockslide across the trail elicits a lecture on geology, or the sprained ankle becomes a training session in first aid and an important lesson in group dynamics.

Speaking and Learning

Speaking to groups is a basic leadership skill. Most leaders soon develop enough self-confidence to address small groups and to convey the information necessary for control of the program. The ability to speak at length on a topic is not so easily learned. Most of us recall, with some embarrassment, our first attempt to present a lecture. It can be intimidating to stand before an expectant audience. One's anxiety is usually proportional to the size of the group and inversely proportional to one's understanding of the topic. It's easiest to practice group speaking before small groups of friends, on a familiar topic. Remember that any group, no matter how large, is composed of individuals. Think of speaking to these individuals, rather than to the whole group. Each lecture on a given topic is easier, as one discovers effective ways of expressing ideas.

There are several relatively simple points that one can do to improve the effectiveness of lectures.

1. The topic and the session length should be determined by what the speaker is fully prepared to address.

2. Use notes or materials as needed to provide the needed reminders and data, but do not expect to use or read full sentences. Prepared speeches are difficult to deliver under ideal circumstances and seldom have value in field teaching sessions.

3. Tell the audience what to expect. In fact, it's a good idea to follow the time-tested adage, "Tell them what you are going to tell them. Tell them, and then tell them what you told them." It's also a good idea to tell the group when the lecture session is scheduled to end, so individuals can prepare themselves.

4. Be positive whenever possible, and avoid negative examples. This is especially important in skills instruction, but applies to lecturing as well. For example, if someone says, "Don't think *blue*, think *red*," what do you think of first? Red may follow blue, but some of the blue image remains. When conveying complex ideas, residual memories of negative examples may interfere with later attempts to recall the positive example.

5. Try to make the presentation interesting. Attention can be improved by using visual examples, by moving around (within reason!), and by varying the cadence, pitch, tone, intensity, and volume of speech patterns. Humor can, if used carefully, help maintain interest and attention. Try engaging individuals in discussion, so that everyone feels involved. This is both an effective teaching technique and a means of determining the effectiveness of the presentation. Soliciting input from the group also helps keep everything in perspective. No one person knows everything about any topic, and, on any topic, there are often as many individual viewpoints as there are members of the audience. If group discussion seems to blur the distinction between teacher and learner, enjoy, and listen carefully.

Teaching a Lesson

Teaching is really a method of facilitating change. Through the lesson, knowledge, attitudes, or skills are changed (hopefully for the better). The following three general components for teaching a lesson can be used to help prepare for teaching any kind of lesson. The leader needs to make plans for each item.

1. The contents or "what" to be taught.
2. The method of delivery (teaching style), or "how" the material will be taught.
3. Effecting the change or the "why" the material will be taught.

The three steps to teaching include preparation, teaching, and implementation of the lesson.

Step I. Lesson Preparation (either in the outdoors or indoors)
  A. Plan the activity mentally (what to do, equipment needed).
  B. Write up the plan including contents, risk management, goals, organization of groups, and equipment.

Step II. Teach the Lesson
  A. Meet the participants. Be there in advance, check roll and condition of participants, introduce the contents and expectations, and end the lesson on time.
  B. Be a leader (guide, teacher, instructor or facilitator). Practice the most appropriate style: laissez-faire, dominant assertive, or effective facilitator.
  C. Supervise the group.
  D. Manage the group behavior.
  E. Use your voice effectively.
  F. Use your hands effectively; do not wave them around.
  G. Use your eyes to see unsafe practices. Include everyone, express interest, notice inattention or bewilderment, and focus on the learner.
  H. Use your ears to hear when participants ask questions.

Step III. Lesson implementation (Effect the change you are trying to make)
  A. Be a professional model with your own style, opinions, and methods.
  B. Use your brain to think, criticize, analyze, talk, and try new things.
  C. Evaluate all situations objectively.
  D. Be enthusiastic.
  E. Be creative and skillful.

Through these three steps, you may affect change in the participants and yourself.

The Homeward Journey

The last few hours before arrival at the vehicles may test the skills of any leader. No matter how much fun the group is having, and even if it has only been a one-day trip, the "horses returning to the barn" syndrome takes over. People lead with their minds, and, by the time they are heading toward the trailhead or take-out point, they are already mentally engrossed in whatever awaits in town. It is essential that the leader anticipate this and gain firm control before there is a mad dash for the vehicles. Usually, this requires that one of the leaders move to the front of the group, holding the lead to a reasonable pace whether walking, skiing, boating, or biking. Innumerable search-and-rescue operations have resulted from inadequate control during this period. A little extra speed and lack of attention greatly increase the risk of missing a trail or making a technical error. Usually, people are at least a little bit tired, which makes a slow pace and caution even more important. Without emphatic reemphasis, most people tend to forget all about whoever is following, even when the habit seemed well-engrained after a long trip. A good plan is to stop perhaps three hours before the end of the day and explain the need to "run a tight ship" all the way to the vehicles.

Procedures and Concerns Upon Return to the Vehicles

People are almost always happy to get back to their cars. Even the most ardent mountaineer, canoeist, or nature lover usually savors this transition to "civilization." If time is short, and there is a concern for efficiency in returning to town, the leader needs to maintain control from the moment of arrival at the trailhead. Once relieved of packs or watercraft, people who are not tired will have a tendency to scatter, and anyone who is tired is likely to be found snoring in a back seat of a van if he/she is not put to use getting gear quickly stowed away.

Take roll carefully to be sure that everyone is accounted for. When group gear has been issued, it is best to collect it at the trailhead, especially when darkness, rain, or other inconveniences are expected back in town. This can be a fast and efficient process if it is well-organized. The leader should assemble the group and have each person extract all group gear from his/her pack or gear bag. The process is made even easier if participants are reminded of the need to keep these items accessible when packing on the last morning. If forms were used to sign out equipment, it is a simple matter to check items back in. These items can then be secured and loaded separately from personal gear. The entire process takes just a few minutes and saves time and energy. Once back in town, people will be even more tired and eager to get home, resistant to having to empty a pack or gear bag to find some missing items, and more likely to make errors in the check-in process.

As per the initial leg of the journey, the policies for stowing gear and transportation listed in Chapter Fourteen must be followed with great care. Again, the drivers might benefit from a check list to remind them of their responsibilities.

Once the gear is completely loaded, take a careful look around the parking area for items left behind. This is a very common occurrence and worth a special effort. As a last chore, it is a good idea to spend just a few minutes cleaning up the area, just as was done before the group started up the trail.

For several reasons, the return trip may be far more hazardous than the outbound one. Drivers are usually not as well-rested; return trips often involve night-time driving; drivers may be anxious to return home; and the group is likely to be either asleep and not supportive or awake and excited, laughing, joking, and distracting him/her. On trips to the site, the group is usually awake but not yet cohesive and not so likely to be rambunctious.

The most important points to consider when getting ready for the trip home are:

1. Be sure that the driver(s) are fit to drive.

2. Check the vehicle safety features again.

3. Be firm about the use of seat belts and restate warnings about the dangers of slumping down in the belts. They *must* remain over the hips.

4. Once everyone is belted down, it is easier to count, so now is the time to confirm that the correct number of people are on board, and that no one is left behind.

5. Use a series of meeting points on the return. Usually, drivers should have a break or be replaced every hour on the return trip, instead of every two hours as when traveling *to* the site.

6. Again, it is usually best for the leader to be the last vehicle on the road so that any problems can be known and handled efficiently. There is a potential problem, however, in that, just as in the field, the party may try to go too far in their eagerness to get home. It may be best to put another staff person, or at least the most trustworthy driver, in the lead to keep speeds down. Remember that many return trips are downhill, and that downhill driving can be much more dangerous than uphill. A stretch of road that is safe at 55 miles per hour uphill may have to be driven downhill at 40 miles per hour or less to maintain the same braking distance and control.

"Back to the Barn"

Remember that, by the time people arrive back in town, they don't want to stand around and listen to lengthy discussions. Before the vehicle stops, be sure to explain any final procedures. Usually, this is a matter of checking in gear (if not done at the trailhead or landing), helping clean and return group gear to storage, and reminding participants of the time and place for the post-trip meeting.

Remember that the journey is not yet over for participants. The leader has to be sure that everyone has a way to get home. Anyone without a ride or too tired to drive will need assistance.

The staff usually have a number of chores facing them after the participants have gone home. Gear needs to be cleaned, dried, counted, and stored; vehicles need to be cleaned and parked or returned to the supplier.

The need for staff to stay on duty after the participants have left is too often forgotten in the planning of the outing. It is important to consider the post-return chores when establishing the agenda for the final day, so that staff interests and needs are reflected in the final plan. By the end of an outing, the staff are often at least as tired as the participants. The time of return (and, thus, perhaps the entire day's agenda) needs to be set to allow the staff to complete their chores and be able to return home safely and at a reasonable hour. In situations wherein staff and participants share rides, or when public transportation schedules must be considered, it may be important to inform participants of the staff post-outing schedule. This is most easily accomplished if estimated times are included in the published agenda for the outing.

Post-Trip Meetings and Procedures

What happens after an outing activity can be extremely important in terms of the value of the experience for both participants and staff. This is especially important in programs wherein the major purpose was classroom oriented. Post-trip contacts with participants provide an opportunity to review the experience, reinforcing the positive aspects of the trip, and minimizing the effects of any negative aspects. If the outing was skill-oriented, this meeting provides an opportunity to clarify techniques, answer questions, and provide guidance for continued development. Personal and social benefits are included in the objectives of many programs and are, in fact, inevitable on virtually any outing. These areas can be explored as well, often to great advantage if the leader is skillful in guiding the discussion.

Staff invariably benefit from a thorough critique of the experience by participants. A technique of special value is to have participants direct comments and suggestions to each staff member. The discussion can be initiated by first eliciting general ideas about what the participants expected of the staff prior to the outing and then thoughts about what actually happened. Staff find this extremely useful with regard to future outings, and participants learn something about the demands of leadership.

Scheduling the meeting well in advance is a good idea, so it can be announced along with the pre-trip meetings. After a weekend outing, the following Monday or Tuesday evenings are usually best in terms of attendance. A meeting held a week later will likely attract fewer people, but it has the advantage of allowing enough time for them to relax and think things over. A delayed post-trip meeting also allows time for photos to be developed; however, this can be a disadvantage in that the viewing of picture can,

and too often does, dominate the meeting at the expense of discussion of more valuable topics. If photos are shared, it's usually best to schedule a time for this at the end of the meeting.

Evaluation forms can also help the leader and the institution responsible for the program. These give the institution at least a limited form of feedback as to the qualities of the program and the staff, and to provide helpful information for the leader. It is almost always best to have participants fill them out at the post-trip meeting. Unless some sort of control over the participants is available, the return rate is likely to be low for any take-home form. (Examples of evaluation forms are included in Chapter Eleven.)

Staff post-trip meetings should always be conducted. Refer to Chapter Eleven for a review of the evaluation process. Finally, the leader should review the program in writing. As suggested earlier in this chapter, one should leave a copy of the outing plans, an agenda, and a map showing the route in an accessible, prearranged place before departure. If this was done, the post-outing report can be easily done by marking the *actual* route on the map, along with any key sites or locations of incidents. The agenda can be annotated to show the actual times of events, and a review of the program can be written on the back of the initial outing plan. If these steps are taken conscientiously, the result is a valuable resource for future leaders and staff.

In addition to the program review or summary, there is often additional paperwork that must be completed. Accident reports are particularly important. While some organizations may require that accident forms be completed only in the event of serious injury, it is advisable to document every injury or serious illness involving participants or staff. Failure to document such incidents in a timely manner may compromise future claims for medical care by staff, and may make it more difficult for the organization to defend itself in the event of litigation.

Some organizations require "near-misses" to be reported. This is certainly a good idea. If a separate report isn't required, "near-miss" incidents should be noted in the outing review document and should be adequately discussed in staff meetings. A close call is an important learning opportunity that should not be dismissed without analysis and, if necessary, corrective action to reduce or eliminate possible recurrences.

When the organization provides equipment, control of the inventory is an ongoing concern, and is often a headache, for those responsible for maintaining the gear. Many organizations require leaders to complete inventory control forms upon return of equipment to the storage area.

Finally, it is often necessary to produce written evaluations of staff and/or participants. The evaluation process is, if done well, quite time consuming. It may also be one of the most difficult tasks facing the leader. Nevertheless, evaluation is often extremely valuable for the recipient, and well worth mustering the needed extra energy.

LEADERSHIP OF SELECTED ACTIVITIES

This chapter is designated to assist administrators and field leaders to implement specific activities. For each activity, a brief description is followed by a discussion of impacts and resource requirements. Easy, moderate and difficult levels of the activity are defined and objectives are suggested for beginning, intermediate and advanced courses or outings. The objectives are written in a form appropriate for formal classes. The reader planning a less structured program will find the objectives useful reminders of program potentials. Clothing and equipment requirements are discussed and listed whenever possible with reference to the basic lists for hiking to avoid unnecessary duplication. In application, it will be necessary for the reader to adjust the lists to meet the specific needs of his/her program. Minimum leadership qualifications and leadership ratios are suggested and common formats discussed.

Hiking

Description

Hiking is one of the most popular of all land-based outdoor pursuits. By definition, a hike is a walk taken for pleasure, over a significant distance, in a natural setting, and lasting, at the most, for a day. The range of hiking possibilities includes anything from relatively short and easy strolls to rugged, limit-testing adventures. Multi-day travel is regarded here as trekking or backpacking, and will be considered separately.

Hazards and Risks

Hiking is probably one of the safest of all recreational pursuits as long as participants exercise good common sense. (As has been mentioned in Chapter Twelve, no activity is hazardous by itself.) If the planning process includes a thorough assessment of potential environmental hazards and if the information developed is conscientiously applied to route and equipment selection, then serious mishaps are unlikely. Because hiking in itself is a simple activity, it is here that a great many beginning leaders and participants make serious mistakes that are magnified when they attempt more advanced outdoor pursuits.

In a country as diverse as the United States, there can be no single way of examining the hazards of hiking, except to advise careful planning that relates to the specific area of the country. The climate and life zones of the U.S. include Tropical, Lower Sonoran, Upper Sonoran, Dry Temperate, Wet Temperate, Canadian, Hudsonian, Arctic-Alpine, and all the intermediate climates such as the Wet Temperate Coastal and many more. Within a 100-mile distance, one may encounter as many as five of these climate zones.

Furthermore, because of latitude and elevation, the seasonal weather is different in various parts of the country. When the official day of spring occurs on March 20 or 21, some parts of the country may seem like the middle of summer while other locations seem like the middle of the winter. On a day in June, summer flowers blooming might be blooming on the south side of a small mountain while 10 feet of packed snow might lie on the north side of the same peak, both at the elevation of 5,000 feet. The summit of Mt. Washington in New Hampshire, at barely one mile in elevation, reputedly has the worst weather in the country—even in the midst of summer! And hiking weather, at any given latitude, varies not only as one goes up in elevation, but as one travels across the country from the Atlantic to the Pacific Ocean.

A person who has hiked safely along the Appalachians in Maryland and Virginia may be surprised by the conditions encountered on a hike in Arizona, Florida, or any of the mountainous states west of the Mississippi River. The fact is, assumptions that are valid in one area can get one into life-threatening trouble in other areas. Thus, while hiking in itself is safe, the hiker needs to know the hazards of the area in which the hike takes place.

Environmental and Social Impacts

Hiking is a relatively low impact activity, especially since it does not include overnight camping. Nevertheless, there is significant potential for damage to the environment and for interference with the experiences of other users. The most obvious effects stem from the cumulative wear and tear of foot traffic, especially on fragile soils. There are examples worldwide of damage resulting from excessive use of trails. (See Chapter Four.) Generally speaking, the more vulnerable an area is, the more essential it becomes to keep group sizes (and total usage) low and to restrict travel to developed trails or, in off-trail travel, to game trails and rocky or more durable surfaces. Extra caution is also warranted in any area that has become popular and thus heavily used. Some impacts are inevitable, but

conscientious leaders will choose routes that can withstand use, and will control impacts by education, example, and enforcement of behavioral standards, and facilitate participant awareness, sensitivity, and caring relative to environmental issues.

Resource Requirements

All that is needed for a hike is the freedom to walk. Good hikes are possible in any terrain and in almost every conceivable setting. Many cities have urban or suburban parks large enough to allow long, all-day hikes. A surprising number of major metropolitan areas adjoin relatively natural lands. Hong Kong is one such city. There, you can begin a hike from a downtown hotel, walk all day in monkey-inhabited semi-tropical forests, and wander back into town in the evening.

Most hiking utilizes trails, paths, and back roads. There are very few barriers to participation, as most paths and trails are free, and no special skill, fitness, or equipment are required to begin. Hiking is an option for able-bodied people of all ages and fitness levels, and, in recent years, many routes have been rendered accessible to the blind, and/or have been graded or leveled to allow wheelchair access. Cross-country or "off-trail" travel is growing in popularity where it is allowed.

The popularity of hiking has resulted in an abundance of guidebooks covering most parts of the world. Guidebooks can provide a survey of local options; however, caution is advised because many guidebooks are inaccurate, incomplete, poorly translated, or out-of-date. Other sources include land-management agencies, local park and recreation districts and departments, and local suppliers of hiking gear. It is always important to check with the resource manager as soon as possible to find out about policies, regulations, and hiking permits since some areas require advance application.

Levels and Objectives

Levels. Hikes can be categorized by overall physical difficulty, as is usually the case with purely recreational hikes, or with regard to the level of challenge determined by the objectives for the outing. The terms "easy," "moderate," and "difficult" are used for levels based upon difficulty. Sometimes, when the activity involves specific skills and advanced knowledge, the terms "beginning," "intermediate," and "advanced" may be used. It is important to keep in mind that, while beginners usually need or seek easy ventures while advanced-level participants usually seek general challenges, any combination is possible.

The label "easy" implies hikes that stick mostly to trails and involve limited distances and elevation gains. Ventures labeled "easy" shouldn't exceed distances of six or seven miles (about ten kilometers) or elevation gains of more than 1,000 feet (about 300 meters), even on a full-day outing. Rough trails, steep terrain, or snow cover might reduce these figures considerably. A "moderate" hike may include up to twice the distance and elevation gains, including segments of off-trail travel. Any hike covering more than twelve miles (19 kilometers) or more than 2,500 feet (800 meters) of elevation gain is probably best labeled "difficult" unless the route is exceptionally forgiving.

Objectives "A" through "I" below are appropriate for any hike and should be the central focus of "beginning" level outings. Objectives "J" through "P" may be reasonable targets for "intermediate" level experiences. The remainder, while very much worthwhile, are probably attainable only after repeated experiences at the "intermediate" and/or "advanced" levels.

Objective "T" transcends all others in that it is the only objective that is not centered on the individual. It could be attained at any point in the progression, or never attained at all. Perhaps, more than for any other objective listed here, leadership by example is critical.

Suggested Objectives. The objectives of hiking are often limited to simple relaxation and exercise, but may cover a wide range of topic areas. In fact, it probably isn't possible to go on a hike without gaining at least fitness, relaxation, a sense of perspective, enhanced social awareness and communication skills, and greater awareness of the natural world. The following objectives are common to most hiking programs

and are, in fact, common to most outdoor-pursuit activities. Typically, the participant should be able to:

A. Enjoy the experience and anticipate pursuing the activity further;

B. Gain physical fitness and awareness of the fitness requirements of hiking;

C. Develop an awareness of, and sensitivity to, the environment;

D. Gain in walking skills, which include pacing, and other skills appropriate to the terrain and route;

E. Develop safety skills such as techniques for maintaining contact with group members;

F. Be aware of the major hazards inherent in the activity and ways of reducing or eliminating risks;

G. Understand the clothing and equipment requirements of hiking;

H. Understand the major types of environmental damage that can result from human usage, and ways in which such impacts can be reduced or eliminated;

I. Understand the basic principles of survival and the specific techniques needed to assume a reasonable chance of survival in the local environment;

J. Be aware of the principle landholders and/or agencies responsible for managing local recreation resource lands, and of the policies and regulations that apply to hiking on these lands;

K. Understand basic first aid for injuries and conditions likely to occur in a backcountry setting, including improvisation, long-term care, and a thorough understanding of hypothermia and hyperthermia;

L. Be aware of the capabilities and limitations of local search and rescue services, and of how to obtain and facilitate such assistance;

M. Be able to interpret planimetric and topographic maps, including an ability to measure distances, and to interpret contour lines to determine elevations, elevation differences, and land forms;

N. Be able to identify and assess potential hiking areas, trails, and routes using maps, guides, and other resources, including probable travel times, potential hazards, camping or bivouac sites, water sources, and alternate or "escape" routes;

O. Be able to follow marked routes in the field using maps, guides, and other resources;

P. Be able to measure bearings on a map and follow bearings in the field;

Q. Understand and be able to use resection and triangulation to determine field locations;

R. Develop the skills necessary for safe and environmentally sound off-trail travel;

S. Acquire the knowledge, skills, and experience necessary to independently plan and carry out a successful hiking outing;

T. Develop a level of understanding and concern for the environment that results in responsible actions on behalf of the environment.

Clothing and Equipment Requirements

While an all-day summer hike in a large suburban park might require nothing but comfortable loose clothing and enough cash to buy lunch and bus fare home, this book focuses upon outdoor pursuits in areas "remote from modern conveniences." A hike into a backcountry area only fifty miles away from town might require a substantial set of gear. Misfortunes are not likely to occur, but there are always possibilities. Such possibilities have led to many fatalities over the years when overconfident hikers have treated backcountry travel as casually as strolls in the park. Throughout this book, attention has been paid to minimum required equipment. The items that should be required on a hike depend upon the area's climate, season, terrain, and skills of the participants. Weather forecasts must be interpreted with great caution. When in doubt, it is best to be somewhat pessimistic with regard to the weather!

Participants on hiking outings are often naive, trusting, and used to being protected from natural hazards. Leaders have to be aware of this, and set and enforce standards based on their best judgment.

As has been mentioned, the leader should be familiar with the weather patterns of the part of the country in which the group is hiking, and

should plan equipment and clothing accordingly. Minimum requirements are the items listed in Chapter Six, "Preparation for Survival." Beyond that, lists generated for one part of the country may be ludicrous for other areas. The best advice leaders can give participants preparing for a simple hike is to prepare for the worst probable scenario for the part of the country in which the hike is to occur. Depending upon the site, that could mean blizzards in July, tornadoes in February, or flash floods in August or in March. Daily variance of 60°F or more in temperature are not uncommon in summer or winter in parts of the United States. We could go on and on. *The leader must help the participant prepare for at least one night out in the worst conditions probable!*

The following lists were designed for an environment with the potential for cool wet days and cold nights even in midsummer. These areas include the mountainous regions of North America as well as the coastal areas of both the Atlantic and Pacific Oceans, generally north of the 45th parallel. The gear shown here should be adequate for at least April through October in these areas. Few environments require more clothing and equipment, except during the winter months.

The group list includes items carried by each independent group in the field, and the individual list includes items that every individual (including instructors) needs to carry. Required items mean just that—*required*. Note that the optional lists contain some items which may, under certain circumstances, be necessary. For example, one might insist that sun hats be brought along in certain environments. (See Figure 17.1a-c, pages 351-353).

Leadership Qualifications

The minimum qualifications for a hiking leader depend largely upon the environment in which the hike is to be conducted. A short summer walk in a large suburban park might demand no more than reasonable maturity, common sense and responsibility, and an ability to find the route through signs or maps. On the other hand, even a modest backcountry adventure may require a leader with highly specialized

FIGURE 17.1a   Suggested Minimum Gear Requirements for Hiking in Mountainous and North Coastal Areas

INDIVIDUAL GEAR

Required Items (*Certain synthetics may be substituted at the discretion of the instructor.):

1. **Boots** (Weight and type specified for each outing)
2. **Wool* socks** (1 or 2 pair to wear)
3. **Wool* socks** (1 or 2 pair for complete change)
4. **Wool* layer for the legs** (Non-restricting pants, knickers and sox, or long johns)
5. **Long pants** (If long-johns option is chosen above, with belt if needed)
6. **Wool* layer for top** (Shirts and/or sweaters)
7. **Warm parka or vest** (Down or synthetic)
8. **Raingear** (Substantial fabric, hood-to-ankles; may be jacket or poncho plus pants or chaps, or may be cagoule and high gaiters)
9. **Wool* hat** (Must cover ears)
10. **Gloves or mittens** (Wool*)
11. **Sunglasses** (Good UV protection and side shields necessary in snow or at higher elevations)
12. **Sunscreen** (15 SPF or higher rating preferred)
13. **Water bottle** (1 liter or more, plastic; bring full)
14. **Matches** (12 or more, waterproof or in watertight container)
15. **Pocket knife** (A multi-tool "Swiss Army" type is nice but not essential)
16. **First-aid kit** (Small, including adhesive bandages and moleskin)
17. **Whistle**
18. **Flashlight** (Alkaline or lithium batteries preferred)
19. **Map(s)** (Protected in plastic bag)
20. **Compass**
21. **Candles** (1 or 2 votive type work well)
22. **Cup** (Metal, to melt snow or boil water)
23. **Food** (The appropriate edibles for the hike plus the equivalent of at least one full extra lunch as emergency food)
24. **Emergency shelter and ample cord to set it up** (Small tarp, "space blanket," or large poncho, with 15 meters of parachute cord)
25. **Day pack** (Large enough for all carried gear plus some group gear)

Optional Items (Some of these items may be required at the discretion of instructor.):

1. **Light shoes** (Sneakers)
2. **Liner socks**
3. **Gaiters**
4. **Shorts**
5. **Swimsuit**
6. **Underwear**

FIGURE 17.1b   Suggested Minimum Gear Requirements for Hiking in Mountainous and North Coastal Areas (continued)

Individual Optional Items (continued)
(All are recommended and may be required at the discretion of instructor.):

7. **Light cotton shirt(s)**
8. **Windshell** (Top and pants, especially if rainwear is urethane coated or other non-breathable fabric)
9. **Sun hat**
10. **Handkerchief**
11. **Umbrella**
12. **Pack cover** (Very valuable and may be required in rainy areas)
13. **Watch**
14. **Nylon cord** (15 feet or 5 meters, 1/8" or 3-4 mm multipurpose)
15. **Insect repellent**
16. **Personal medications and toiletries**
17. **Toilet paper**
18. **Binoculars**
19. **Camera and film**
20. **Notebook and pencil**
21. **Sit pad** (Of ensolite or equivalent closed cell foam; 15 inches by 24 inches is a convenient size)
22. **Extra food and water** (To be left in vehicle for the return trip)

GROUP GEAR

Required Items (For each independent field group):

1. **Insulated pad(s)** (Approximately 1, 2/3 length pad for every 4 participants on dry ground, and 1 for every 2 participants on snow or wet ground)
2. **Sleeping bag(s) or equivalent insulation** (Approximately 1 for every 12 participants in warm weather and 1 for every 8 participants in cold weather)
3. **Tarp(s)** (Adequate to provide rain, snow and wind protection for the entire group. One 15 x 15 foot (5 x 5 meter) or 2, 9 x 9 foot (3 x 3 meter) tarps will suffice for at least twelve people if used effectively)
4. **Container for heating water** (At least two quart (two liter) volume, to process drinking water and to make hot-water bottles for hypothermia treatment)
5. **First-aid kit** (See suggested contents in the first-aid section)

Optional Items:

1. **Portable stove and fuel** (Required in areas where natural fires would be impractical)
2. **Extra food** (Such as a bag of candy, soup mixes and bouillon)
3. **Extra clothing** (A complete change of clothes can be valuable, especially in wet weather or where falls into water are possible.)
4. **Wire saw** (To facilitate use of small trees or limbs for splints, litters, or emergency fires)
5. **Nylon cord** (50 feet **or** 20 meters of 1/8" or 3-4 mm)

**FIGURE 17.1c   Suggested Minimum Gear Requirements for Hiking
in Mountainous and North Coastal Areas (continued)**

Group Optional Items (continued):

6. **Nylon tubular webbing** (20 feet or 6 meters; many uses including security tie-in to assist participants on steep, slippery, or intimidating terrain)
7. **Climbing rope** (May be useful in steep, hazardous, or intimidating terrain and can be used to construct a litter. Eight mm climbers' static cord is adequate for most purposes; 120 feet is adequate to construct a rope liter; 9mm or larger dynamic rope is needed for belays.)
8. **Plastic flagging** (Very helpful in the event of a search for a missing person)
9. **Watch** (If not required of individuals)
10. **Insect repellent** (If not required of individuals)
11. **Sunscreen** (If not required of individuals)
12. **Toilet paper** (If not required of individuals)

LEADER GEAR

Required Items (In addition to individual gear list):

1. **Watch**
2. **Headlamp or flashlight, spare fresh batteries and bulb**
3. **One additional warm clothing layer for the torso**
4. **List of all participants and staff, health forms of all participants and staff, and list of emergency phone numbers**
5. **Notebook and pencil**

NOTE:

1.   *The leader may or may not choose to carry most of the group gear. While carrying the gear may reduce the chances of it becoming lost or being damaged, there is always a chance of the leader being lost with most of the group's survival gear. It is generally best to allocate the gear, for the foregoing reason, to share the burden, and most importantly to allow the participants an opportunity to see and appreciate the safety related gear carried.*

2.   *The above list is recommended for the parts of the USA where the weather conditions may be the worst. Leaders can start with the suggested survival items listed in Chapter six and add to them from items in the above list to reach a sensible kit. Beginning leaders should check with the most experienced leaders of an areas with which they are not familiar before recommending equipment to any group.*

skills and extensive experience, and who is able to inspire group attitude and action while remaining constantly alert to conditions in the environment. The bottom line is the same in either case; either outing must be conducted in a manner consistent with participant expectations and accepted leadership practices. Meeting participant expectations results in satisfied "customers," while compliance with accepted standards and practices provides substantial support in the event of a mishap resulting in a lawsuit against the leader or his/her employer. Any hiking leader should have at least the following attributes:

A. Maturity consistent with the responsibility of the job;

B. Evident intelligence and common sense;

C. An ability to relate to the employer and the participants in a friendly and personable manner;

D. An ability to assess the psychological and physical needs and limits of the participants with reasonable accuracy;

E. An ability to communicate ideas and instructions effectively and appropriately (This includes an awareness of the significance of the setting in which the communication is being attempted, appropriate physical appearance, timing, and the effective use of gestures and eye contact.);

F. An understanding of teaching methodology as required by program objectives (This includes an effective balance of verbal instructions, demonstration, and practice.);

G. A willingness and ability to exercise control over the actions of the group in conformance with the standards and policies of the employer;

H. Driving ability, if needed, and, if so, a satisfactory driving record, plus ample experience in similar vehicles and road and weather conditions as required by the program;

I. First-aid skills appropriate to the situation (This must include experience and training in improvisation and long-term care if any backcountry or wilderness travel is planned.);

J. Search and rescue training appropriate to the program (At a minimum this should at least include an awareness of the capabilities and limits of local search and rescue services and an understanding of how to control and use these services effectively.);

K. Knowledge of the area in sufficient detail to allow effective planning of the field portions of the program (This almost invariably requires a high level of competence in map reading, good maps, and at least some firsthand knowledge of the area.);

L. Specific outdoor skills and knowledge sufficient to conduct the program safely (This includes an ability to deal effectively with any foreseeable natural hazards such as steep terrain, rockfall, stream or ice crossings, insects or animals, or adverse weather, and may include advanced navigational skills.);

M. Leadership and organizational skills sufficient to conduct a safe program (This includes an ability to maintain control of the group at all times under any reasonably foreseeable condition and to maintain an awareness of, and concern for, the well-being of all participants at all times.);

N. Special skills and knowledge as necessary to meet the specific objectives of the program (This could include, for example, skills or knowledge in counseling, local history, natural science, or any other topic relevant to program objectives.);

O. An awareness of local environmental concerns and a willingness and ability to set an example for participants and to conduct an environmentally sound program;

P. An awareness of and willingness to conform to the rules and regulations of holders or managers of the resource lands on which the activity is to take place;

Q. Substantial experience in an environment similar to that of the intended program.

An individual with all of the above attributes should be able to do an adequate job of leading a hike. The attributes listed above are common to virtually every outdoor pursuit, and they will be referred to as basic leadership requirements when discussing leadership qualifications for other activities. Leadership qualifications are intentionally generalized in this section because hiking is such a varied activity.

Leadership Ratios

Because of its inherently low risk, hiking requires fewer leaders for a given group than most other outdoor pursuits. With the exception of backcountry travel or experience with special objectives, one leader can usually handle a dozen adult participants. Common sense dictates the bottom line. It is generally easier to maintain supervision over adults than children, and control on trails is simpler than in unconfined or rugged off-trail travel. Special program objectives may necessitate higher leadership ratios (meaning fewer participants per leader). In an urban or suburban setting, for example, a single leader may be sufficient if the participants are mature and can cope temporarily with his/her absence or incapacitation. In a backcountry or wilderness setting, one leader is almost never sufficient since group control is more difficult and one has to consider the possible incapacitation of a leader, which could result in participants having to fend for themselves. Youth camps recommend one leader for every eight hikers plus one extra in all situations.

There are few situations wherein a single leader can provide reasonable service to more than twelve participants. In any significant backcountry travel, this ratio should not exceed one instructor for every eight participants, with at least two leaders on-site. This puts an upper limit on a group size of eighteen people, which is very large and unwieldy, likely to provide less than a satisfactory experience for participants, and may well infringe on the enjoyment of other users of the area. Such a large group may also exceed the group-size limits of resource-management agencies. Many organizations set an upper limit of twelve-to-fifteen people, including at least two leaders, for any backcountry hiking.

Suggested Formats

Easy hikes in the summer may require only a pre-trip information sheet specifying the nature of the outing, fitness and equipment standards, and the time and place of start and return. This can be distributed at the time of registration. More rigorous outings or outings with special objectives may require more pre-trip meetings to allow time to convey the necessary information and, most importantly, to enable leaders to assess the participants and adjust the program (or participant expectations) accordingly. If only one pre-trip meeting is planned, it should occur several days prior to the outing, especially if gear acquisition may be a problem.

Weekends are the most popular times for hikes, for obvious reasons. Saturdays or Sundays may be the only free days common to a group of people. A surprising number of people can get away on weekdays, however, including some students, shift workers, and homemakers, as well as many retirees, self-employed and professional people. Weekdays offer great advantages in areas where trails are congested on weekends. A rewarding three- or four-hour hike can be scheduled after school hours or even after normal working hours in late spring and early summer.

Recommended Reading

Hart, J. (1984). *Walking softly in the wilderness.* San Francisco, CA: Sierra Club Books.

Backpacking

Description

Backpacking is a popular activity in most economically advanced countries, especially in those which have relatively large expanses of roadless land and relatively few huts. Backpacking is different from hiking or trekking in that all provisions necessary for overnight travel are carried in the pack. The result is larger loads and a slower pace but a greater sense of independence. Backpackers can set up camp on almost any flat piece of ground rather than having to return at night to the roadhead or to a hut. Under most weather conditions, modern gear provides a high level of comfort plus a good deal more privacy than that attainable in most huts.

Backpacking has advocates and committed participants of all ages. While many are young adults, and the typical backpacker has an above-average income and education, no demographic category is unrepresented.

Hazards and Risks

The hazards encountered in backpacking are similar to those in hiking. Greater loads slightly increase the possibility of strains and sprains. Backpackers also travel farther into the backcountry than hikers, especially on multi-day outings, increasing the significance of any given mishap by lengthening the distance to outside services. On the other hand, backpackers are relatively independent in terms of shelter and provisions, so the dangers inherent in getting lost or becoming stranded are reduced. Overall, backpacking ranks as one of the safest outdoor pursuits, if the participants prepare for the conditions of the part of the country in which they are backpacking.

Environmental and Social Impacts

Backpacking combines hiking and camping, and so has considerable potential for causing environmental and social impacts. Most of the impacts in most wilderness and backcountry areas are directly related to backpacking, and in particular to camping. A review of Chapter Four, "Care of the Environment," might be useful here. Camping can result in damage to campsite areas, through compaction or abrasion of soils, various forms of pollution, and, if fires are used, through overuse of natural fuels. Leaders have a special responsibility when leading backpacking outings to select appropriate sites, to teach and enforce behaviors that minimize impacts and leave meticulous no-trace camps, and to guide the participants toward responsible independently determined actions when they backpack on their own.

Resource Requirements

All backpackers need is access to walkable routes and places to camp. Some areas have an abundance of freely accessible resources, while, in others, these may be limited by road or trail conditions, steep or densely vegetated terrain, adverse climate or weather, insect pests, animal hazards, or limits on travel or camping. Limits on access or camping privileges are usually based upon safety or environmental concerns. Local resource managers are a good source of information about potential backpacking sites, as are local providers of goods and services related to backpacking, guidebooks, and hiking or backpacking clubs. In any case, it is important to check with the resource manager to find out about regulations, policies, and any permit requirements. Resource managers can also provide current information about the condition of access roads, trails, and campsites, and they can usually provide accurate maps.

Levels and Objectives

Levels. A successful outing depends upon meeting participants' needs and expectations. As in hiking, beginners don't necessarily want easy outings, and advanced practitioners don't necessarily want the challenge of a difficult trip. Dividing outings into levels based upon difficulty or objective content can assist participants in selecting appropriate experiences. The following suggestions for categorizing outings are consistent with common practice, although there is considerable local and regional variation. Outings are often described in terms of both difficulty and objective content; though, the latter system is primarily associated with classes or outings within educational settings.

Many factors affect the difficulty of an outing. A backpacking experience is a complex event affected by terrain, ground cover, trail conditions, length and specifications of the route, nature and condition of campsites and water supplies, the type and amount of gear carried, the weather, and the fitness, experience, and attitudes of the participants. An "easy" weekend backpacking trip seldom involves trail distances of more than five to six miles (8 to 10 km) and total elevation increases of more than 1,000 feet (300 m) per day. On easy trips, it is best not to assume travel rates in excess of two miles (3 km or so) per hour of walking, which will result in only about 1 1/2 miles (about 2 1/2 km) per hour of travel when rest stops are included. An additional hour is usually required for every 1,000 feet (300 km) of elevation gain.

On longer trips, the distances might be somewhat increased on days other than the first and last, because several hours of the first and last days are usually committed to vehicular travel. For example, an easy three-day backpacking trip might involve up to five miles (8 km) of moderate uphill travel on day one, up to ten miles (16 km) of relatively level travel on day two, and six miles (10 km) of gentle downhill travel on day three. These suggestions assume reasonably fit and well-equipped adult participants in good weather and walking conditions. When planning an easy trip, it is usually best to be conservative and opt for the shorter, gentler alternatives since any number of factors can increase travel times and difficulties.

A "moderate" trip might involve longer distances [perhaps six to eight miles (10-13 km) on first and last days, and ten to twelve miles on middle days], greater elevation gains (up to 2,500 feet or so) or portions of rugged, snow-covered, or off-trail travel of up to 20 percent of the total distance. Trips longer than three or four days are often labeled "moderate" even when

they conform to "easy" standards of distance and elevation due to the inevitable extra stresses and pack weights.

Any backpacking trip covering more than eight to ten miles (13 to 16 km) on first and last days, and twelve miles (19 km) on middle days is usually considered "difficult" even if the route follows trails. This label is probably appropriate for any backpack route involving elevation gains in excess of 2,500 feet (800 m), or major sections of snow-covered or rugged off-trail travel.

Objectives "A" through "C" and all of the objectives suggested for hiking are appropriate for a beginning-level backpacking outing, and can often be attained on a two-day trip, assuming good planning, experienced leaders, and a bit of luck. A pair of two-day outings or one three-day outing is usually ample to meet these objectives under most conditions. Objectives "D" and "E" and all previous objectives are appropriate for intermediate outings and usually require at least 2 weekends or an additional three-day outing beyond the beginning level. Intermediate backpacking courses are often designed to give participants the ability to backpack on their own with no outside assistance. Much of the basic information necessary to attainment of these objectives can be taught very effectively in a classroom setting, thus accelerates the progress on outings. This is especially true of first aid and some aspects of map and compass use. Objective "F" is typical for advanced outings.

Objectives. The following list of objectives includes those appropriate for beginning, intermediate, and advanced level outings. Those common to all backpacking outings are listed first. More advanced objectives are grouped toward the end of the list.

No two leaders are likely to agree on the exact order, or wording of, objectives, and every leader will want to make additions, subtractions, or modifications to the list. It is valuable, however, to review the list carefully and to establish an appropriate set of objectives before leading any outing. If the activity is part of a class, especially in an educational institution, it may be necessary to construct a formal written list. In any case, it is often useful to carry notes into the field to help ensure that key topics are addressed.

Typical objectives for backpacking include all of the objectives suggested for hiking. In addition, it is expected that the participant will be able to:

A. Understand the clothing and equipment requirements of backpacking (This includes selection, acquisition, maintenance, and packing.);

B. Be able to identify potential campsites and to assess the site for natural hazards and potential for environmental damage;

C. Be able to set up a safe, comfortable and environmentally sound campsite, to use the site effectively, and to leave the site clean and un-damaged (This implies an understanding of how to set up tents and/or tarps, how to use tents, pads, sleeping bags, stoves or fires, how to cook, and other skills as appropriate.);

D. Be able to identify and to assess potential backpacking areas, trails, and routes using maps, guides, and other resources (This includes probable travel times and potential hazards, camping or bivouac sites, water sources, and alternate or "escape" routes.);

E. Acquire the knowledge, skills, and experience necessary to independently plan and carry out a successful backpacking outing;

F. Develop the skills necessary for safe and environmentally sound off-trail travel.

Clothing and Equipment

The basic essentials for backpacking include little more than the essentials for hiking, plus shelter, a sleeping bag, and more food and water. It is important to include all items necessary for safety for the area of the country while resisting the temptation to pack excessive gear. For information on pack weights, see Chapter Fifteen, "Strategic and Tactical Planning."

Degradation of the experience can also result from the use of gear that is not necessary. For example, a good mountain tent, which may be a necessity on a high Alpine climb, may actually be a liability on a summer low-elevation outing. When a simple tarp provides more than ample protection, why isolate participants from the wilderness, blocking the breezes, the moon, and the stars with an expensive, heavy and portable high-tech mobile home?

The following suggested equipment list is based, like the hiker's lists (pages 351-353), upon travel between April and October in mountainous regions west of the Mississippi River where the weather may be cold and wet, even during the summer months. Note that the individual list is identical to that for hiking except for items 24 and 25 on the individual required list and item 19 on the individual optional list. Group requirements vary from the hiking list in that only item 5, the first-aid kit, is listed as required since individuals each carry sleeping bags and some form of shelter. Groups that backpack in other parts of the country where the situations are less severe should consult with the experts in those areas to determine what items, if any, could be safely omitted. In some areas, there may be additional requirements (e.g., in desert areas, additional water containers may be essential).

Participants should understand that function is more important than form, and they should be made aware of low-budget sources of gear, including homemade, borrowed, or rented items. (See Figure 17.2.)

Leadership Ratios

Leadership ratios in backpacking, at least in theory, can be the lowest of any outdoor pursuit if safety alone is considered. The closest comparable activity is backcountry hiking, wherein two leaders might be able to handle up to sixteen experienced adult participants in ideal conditions. In theory, experienced backpacking leaders might be able to handle this many back-packers, since each individual is self-contained and in relatively less danger should he/she become separated from the group.

In practice, however, such group sizes and leadership ratios are rarely seen because of several problems with such large parties. First, many land managers will not allow parties of twenty or more due to concern about environmental impact and degradation of the experiences of other users. Limits as low as twelve people per group, including leaders, are widely

FIGURE 17.2   Suggested Minimum Gear Requirements for Backpacking

INDIVIDUAL GEAR

Required Items   (Items 1 through 23 on the required list for hiking, plus):
1. **Large pack** (To carry all of the above plus some group gear)
2. **Shelter** (May be shared, however, each individual should carry a part, such as a tent body, tent fly or groundsheet, as an emergency shelter)
3. **Stove, fuel, and cooking utensils** (May be shared and listed as required only because this is often the case due to environmental concerns)

Optional Items   (Items 1 through 23 on the required list for hiking, plus):
1. **Repair kit** (Sewing supplies, extra buttons, wire, clevis pins, split rings, ripstop nylon-cloth repair tape, duct tape, and glass fiber tape are especially useful components, along with miniature scissors and pliers and a small screwdriver and awl.)
2. **Personal shelter** (If side trips are planned)
3. **Day pack** (If side trips are planned)

GROUP GEAR

Required Items   (For each independent field group):
1. **First-aid kit** (See suggested contents in the first-aid section.)
2. **Water purification system** (Unless required of individuals. Including provision of appropriate chemicals and filtration devices.)

Optional Items   (Items 2 through 12 on the optional group list for hiking, plus):
1. **Snow shovels** (Can be invaluable at high-elevation trailheads in early and late season to dig out cars)
2. **Snowshoes** (A small pair can be a great help in breaking trail in the event of unexpected snowstorms in early or late season.)

LEADER GEAR

Required Items   (In addition to individual gear plus items 1-5 on the list of required leader gear for hikers):
1. **Cord** (50 feet or 15 meters of 1/8 inch or 3-4 mm nylon)
2. **Alarm** (Watch or clock)
3. **Stove repair items** (Tools and cleaning wires for field repair of all stove types on the outing, or for personal stove if each stove owner is required to provide tools for his/her stove)
4. **General repair kit** (Needles, strong thread or dental floss, knife with awl and tools, clevis pins, wire, strong tape)
5. **One additional warm layer for the legs** (i.e., with hiking requirements means both extra torso and extra leg layers, for emergencies or to share with needy participants)

recommended and occasionally mandated by managers. (See Chapter Four, "Care of the Environment.")

Most organizations limit groups to twelve to fifteen people, including two leaders. Youth camps limit their groups to a maximum of sixteen campers, plus three leaders. These ratios are typically increased to one leader per three or four participants, again with a minimum of two leaders per group, for "outer-limits" activities such as rugged off-trail adventures. The reasons for having two leaders are the same as those for hiking. Any number of situations can result in the incapacitation of one leader, or in the need for leaders to be in two places at one time. Beyond the safety advantages, teaching objectives and the general comfort and satisfaction of the group are enhanced by having two leaders. Another distinct benefit not mentioned earlier is the potential for training leaders by employing those with less experience in assistant or apprenticeship roles.

Suggested Formats

The most common backpacking format is an overnight, two-day excursion, primarily because most participants have difficulty obtaining more free time. Certainly a two-day outing can be a pleasant and rewarding experience, and yet the advantages of longer trips are so great as to warrant an effort to extend trips when possible. Even one additional half-day provides a disproportionate increase in the potential value of the outing. The extra part or full day allows two nights' stay rather than one, opportunities for travel much farther into the backcountry, and/or much more time for attainment of other objectives. Participants on three-day or longer outings appreciate having a full day untainted by the need to travel to or from the trailhead. Many people feel that three-day to five-day outings are optimal since they allow attainment of the principle objectives of backpacking and yet don't require extremely heavy packs. Even in summer conditions, the food requirements of ventures longer than five days can result in uncomfortably heavy loads.

Whatever the trip length, backpacking outings usually warrant at least one pre-trip meeting. Two meetings are better, with one about ten days prior to the outing and one about three days prior to the outing. The first meeting can be used to introduce participants to backpacking and to the specific nature of the outing and to establish correspondence between participant and leader expectations. Gear requirements can also be detailed, allowing plenty of time to locate appropriate items. The second meeting provides an opportunity for last-minute adjustments and final directions to participants, facilitating a smooth departure on the outing day.

Recommended Reading

Fletcher, C. (1974). *The complete walker.* New York, NY: Alfred A. Knopf.

Manning, H. (1986). *Backpacking: One step at a time.* Seattle, WA: Recreation Equipment, Inc.

Simer, P., & Sullivan, J. (1985). *The National Outdoor Leadership School's wilderness guide.* New York, NY: Simon & Schuster.

Snowcamping

Description

By its broadest definition, snowcamping includes any camping in the snow, even though, to some, the term connotes only the use of igloos, snow caves, and other shelters made of snow. While acknowledging the importance of snow-shelter construction and use, we'll use the broader definition here. Camping in the snow, especially in show shelters, seems to many nonparticipants to be an intrinsically miserable activity to be avoided at all costs. In fact, with proper equipment and a few skills beyond those of ordinary backpacking, it can be amazingly comfortable. As advocates quickly point out, there are even a few advantages over summer camping, including little or no competition for campsites (due to far fewer users and far more potential sites), a guaranteed soft or at least adjustable surface, no distance to water (just melt the snow), no dust, no mud, and no insects! Many snowcampers use some form of shelter excavated or constructed from snow blocks; however, almost all carry fabric shelters as insurance against poor construction conditions or insufficient time for construction. Snowcampers use skis or snowshoes, transporting their somewhat heavier than bare-ground loads in backpacks or on sleds (pulks). Distances are usually fairly short due to the inherent slow pace of winter travel, short days, and the extra time needed to construct snow shelters. Because snow muffles sounds and conceals so well, and because there are so few other users of the backcountry in winter, it is often possible to find a sense of wilderness less than a mile from a road. Camping in the snow extends the backpacking and mountaineering seasons, allows backcountry skiers access to remote sites, and is an exciting and thoroughly enjoyable activity in and of itself.

Snowcamping isn't nearly as popular as backpacking or ski touring, and yet a surprising number of people do camp in the snow, at least occasionally. Most participants are experienced backpackers or mountaineers who do it to extend the hiking or climbing season, gain access to the peaks (which may require camping on

snow well into summer in some areas), or simply to experiment with the intriguing notion of sleeping in snow shelters. Because of the need for, or at least desirability of, previous backpacking experience and the need for extra gear, there are relatively fewer potential candidates for snowcamping than for backpacking programs. Children and adults alike are usually fascinated by the concept of the igloo, so single-day or carefully controlled near-the-road overnight experiences may appeal to relative camping newcomers as well as to backpackers.

Hazards and Risks

Aside from the risks normally associated with backpacking, the greatest concerns are medical problems related to prolonged exposure to cold, frostbite, and trench foot, and the dangers of avalanches, snow bridge collapses, and weak ice or snow surfaces on bodies of water. Travel itself isn't necessarily hazardous if conducted on snowshoes; however, ski travel with a large pack or a sled in tow can be risky. A nicely initiated maneuver on skis can end in disaster if the skier doesn't compensate for the momentum of the pack precisely or if the sled decides to pass on the wrong side of the tree. There is also a special kind of "double whammie" face plant peculiar to ski travel with loose-heel bindings and a large backpack, wherein the skier unfortunate enough to make a conventional face plant is, milliseconds later, smashed another several inches into the snow by the backpack. A more common occurrence, potentially dangerous on hard or crusty surfaces, is the sudden planting of rear and elbows. Finally, the infamous knee-in-the-snow forward fall on skis is far more dangerous with a large pack since the momentum of the extra mass can easily lead to a posterior dislocation of the femur.

There are also a few hazards associated with the camping process itself. Especially when using tents, avoid camping beneath snow-laden branches or trees likely to be overloaded during the night. In relatively warm maritime climates, snow accumulation in the trees can be extremely heavy and capable of developing devastating energy in a long fall. The best of tents can be crushed by such "tree dumps," which may contain branches as well. Snow caves, igloos, quinzees, and other shelters may also collapse; however, this is a rare event, and the dangers are usually more from unplanned lack of shelter than from burial. The greatest danger in caves and igloos, and tents for that matter, have poor air quality and excess humidity due to inadequate ventilation. The buildup of toxic fumes due to stove use within shelters has caused fatalities.

Despite the potential hazards, snowcamping can be conducted safely. Virtually all risks can be avoided by careful planning and by utilizing common sense.

Environmental and Social Impacts

Snowcamping is potentially a very low impact activity. The ground is protected by snow; most wildlife has usually left the area or is safely in hibernation; and, in most cases there are very few other users with whom to conflict. Unfortunately, snowcampers sometimes cause considerable damage. Too often, campers don't think about the aftereffects of leaving caves and igloos intact or leaving deposits of toilet paper and fecal matter. Shelters eventually weaken and become traps for unwary deer and elk. People may also fall in, though they are better equipped to monkey their way out than the hapless elk who plunges in head first. Shelters should be collapsed and filled nearly level. Besides, the destruction process is instructive; it is the best way to assess construction results. Shelter destruction is typically easy to initiate; however, people tend to lose energy for the harder and less exciting task of filling the exposed pits.

Winter campers are usually less cautious than summer campers about where they go to defecate or urinate, when, in fact, they should be more cautious. Contrary to the popular self-serving myth, toilet paper, fecal matter and urine do not cease to exist simply because they are buried in snow. Preserved by the cold, they are deposited in the spring. Many summer parks and campgrounds are used for winter camping as they are easy to reach via snow-covered roads.

Too often, picnic tables, buried by snow in midwinter, catch the thawing debris in the spring. Leaders need to place campsites carefully, knowing that under winter conditions participants will not want to travel far for toileting purposes. The recommended procedure is to place the frozen fecal material into plastic baggies for removal to proper disposal facilities.

Resource Requirements

All that is really needed for snowcamping is a little snow and a safe and attractive site. The earlier suggestions for backpacking sites apply here; however, in general, smaller areas are needed due to the shorter distances that must be traveled under winter conditions. Parking can sometimes be a problem, too, since some trailheads limited to day use aren't plowed or require permits.

Little snow is needed since many types of shelters can be constructed from snow gathered and piled or processed into blocks. Depending upon the ground surface, six inches (about 15 cm) of snow may be enough to make good pile shelters, while three feet or so (about one meter) on level ground is sometimes enough for snow caves if wind action has created deep drifts.

Levels and Objectives

Levels. An "easy" snowcamping outing rarely involves travel distances of more than a few miles (up to five km) with little elevation gain per day. When shelter construction is a primary goal and the group is made up of beginners, a mile of travel may be the limit since so much time will be needed to build the shelters. A "moderate" trip might involve considerably more distance; however, even with experienced participants, a lot of time has to be allocated for shelter construction. In most cases, it is necessary to allow at least two hours for experienced individuals and three hours for beginners to build snow shelters. Setting up tents, by comparison, takes about thirty minutes at most, and fifteen minutes is usually sufficient for experienced backpackers if the snow surface needs little packing. A moderate trip might, therefore, cover up to 5 or 6 miles (8 or 10 km) on tenting days but only 3 or 4 miles (5 to 6 1/2 km) on shelter-building days. Shorter distances may be required if significant elevation gains are included.

Snow travel is so variable in speed and efficiency that it's very difficult to give specific guidelines here, and, on the best planned outing, variances from predicted paces can be anticipated. Snow conditions in some areas can vary quickly from a firm boot-walkable surface to deep snow that forces a snail's pace on skis or snowshoes. Any trip covering more than about seven miles (11 km or so), or elevation increases greater than 2,000 ft (600 m) probably ought to be labeled "difficult" unless the travel conditions are exceptionally good.

A "beginning" snowcamping outing can be "easy," "moderate," or "difficult" in terms of the effort needed, though most beginning trips are "easy" since "beginners" need to devote most of their attention to developing skills and techniques. If participants have limited backpacking experience prior to the outing, it may be necessary to limit the objectives of the outing to "A" through "E" suggested below, plus an appropriate selection from those suggested for backpacking. With substantial prior backpacking experience, objective "F" can usually be attained partially on a two-day trip and wholly on a two-night, three-day trip. "Intermediate" experiences may focus on construction techniques, adding new shelter types, and improving efficiency. Some intermediate groups use the available time to travel greater distances, utilizing tents or very basic snow shelters. "Advanced" outings might also focus on shelters, stressing speed of construction or construction in shallow snow, ice, or other difficult conditions. They might instead take the form of long-distance adventures, perhaps following popular summer hiking or backpacking routes. Attainment of objective "G" may require many outings in a range of conditions.

Objectives. The objectives suggested for backpacking also apply to snowcamping and should be reviewed carefully. The objectives listed below are specific to travel and camping in the snow and typically require that the participant will, in addition to meeting the appropriate goals of backpacking, be able to:

A. Understand the special equipment and clothing requirements of snowcamping;

B. Understand the special hazards of travel in snow-covered terrain (This includes avalanches and hazards related to cornices, snow bridges, and other snow formations.);

C. Recognize, treat, and minimize the risks of hypothermia, frostbite, trench foot, and other cold-related conditions and injuries;

D. Locate safe and environmentally sound campsites, and find safe tent or shelter sites within the campsite;

E. Set up a safe and comfortable camp using tents or tarps, and use sleeping bags, stoves, and other gear effectively;

F. Construct safe and reasonably comfortable snow shelters (This should include at least two types of shelters selected from mound types, snow caves, and blockhouses or igloos, and at least one survival-type shelter such as kick-holes or tree-well caves.);

G. Develop the skills, knowledge, and experience necessary to independently plan and carry out a successful snowcamping outing.

Clothing and Equipment

It is important for the leader to understand that snowcamping conditions are different from summer camping conditions. The gear and equipment lists must be generated from the lists used in cold and wet parts of the country—not from the lists generated from the areas the participants may have backpacked in the spring and summer months. See Figures 17.3 a-c (pages 364-366).

Leadership Qualifications

A snowcamping outing leader should possess all of the attributes and qualifications of a backpacking leader and, in addition, possess:

A. Understanding and experience vis-à-vis cold injuries, including the prevention and treatment of frostbite and trench foot;

B. Experience in the construction of quinzees, igloos, snow caves, block shelters, and emergency shelters, including the safe use of all related tools;

FIGURE 17.3a   Suggested Minimium Gear Requirements
for Snowcamping

INDIVIDUAL GEAR

Required Items   (In addition to the requirements for backpacking):

1. **Extra insulation** (This usually includes two layers of wool or better fabric for the legs and torso, instead of the one layer needed for three-season backpacking.)
2. **Turtleneck or other neck covering** (A wool scarf will suffice, but zippered turtlenecks are especially versatile.)
3. **Extra hand coverings** (At least two layers, including substantial wool or artificial fiber mittens. Wool or polypropylene glove liners and ski gloves are useful.)
4. **Warm footwear** (There are many possibilities, including mountaineering boots or insulated hiking boots, snowmobile boots, Sorel type insulated boots, some types of ski boots, and various insulated gaiters and overboots. Snowcampers often bring two pairs of footwear—one to travel in and one to wear around camp.)
5. **Gaiters** (The high type are usually best.)
6. **Warm sleeping bag** (Depending on the area, 3 inches or more of top layer loft may be needed.)
7. **Warm sleeping pad** (Closed-cell pads of three-eighths inch [9 mm] or greater thickness are usually needed on snow. Air mattresses are not recommended.)
8. **Substantial shelter** (Tarps work very well, as do many types of tents; however, fabric types, construction quality, and design are more critical in snow and winter weather.)
9. **Skis, boots, and poles, or snowshoes** (Most modern light touring skis are strong enough for winter backpacking. Seventy-five millimeter three-pin bindings and substantial boots with torsionally stiff soles are desirable unless the route follows prepared tracks or gentle roads. There are some "backcountry" versions of track skiing boot and binding combinations that are almost as stable as a good 75 mm three-pin combination.)

Optional Items   (In addition to the optional items suggested for backpacking):

1. **Avalanche cord, probes, or beacon** (May be required)
2. **Extra water bottle** (Hot-water bottles in sleeping bags are especially nice in cold weather, help to drive excess moisture out of the bags and greatly increase comfort. When water must be provided by melting snow, the increased storage volume is also very useful.)
3. **Insulation for stove bottom** (A small square of asbestos or foil-covered ensolite is needed for some hot-bottomed stoves, while for others an unprotected square of ensolite is adequate.)
4. **Sleeping-bag covers or bivouac sacks** (Note that these may inhibit the escape of vapor from sleeping bags, causing loss of insulation value, and should be unnecessary in well-constructed shelters kept at temperatures below freezing.)
5. **Additional candles** (Winter nights are long, and a single candle can light a large cave or igloo.)

FIGURE 17.3b   Suggested Minimium Gear Requirements for Snowcamping (continued)

Individual Optional Items (continued):

6. **Sieve or screen for water** (Melting snow for water often results in a thin soup of leaves or tree needles, mosses, and other vegetable matter. Coffee strainers, tea strainers, a piece of cotton cloth or a small square of plastic window screen can quickly remove most of this.)
7. **Ski poles** (If snowshoes are elected on required list)
8. **Shovel** (Essential for excavation of snow caves or construction of pile or mound shelters, and useful in building igloos. Large grain-scoop types are useful, however, small portables are far superior for work inside caves and in hardened snow such as in avalanche rescue work.)
9. **Snow saw or snow knife** (The snow saw is usually considered the more valuable tool.)
10. **Sled or pulk** (This is a great way to transport gear over snow on certain types of terrain. Like skiing, the basic idea is simple, but proper gear and a certain amount of technique are essential for enjoyment and safety!)

GROUP GEAR

Required Items   (In addition to the requirements for backpacking):

1. **Snow shovels** (If not carried by each individual, at least one for every four party members for avalanche-rescue purposes, and at least one for every shelter to be constructed.)
2. **Snow saws or snow knives** (At a ratio of one for each snow-block shelter to be constructed)
3. **Repair kit** (In addition to the contents suggested for backpacking, the kit should contain any pieces, parts, or tools needed for maintenance and repair of snowshoes, snowshoe bindings, skis, ski bindings, or ski poles, and extra waxes, if needed.)

Optional Items:

1. **Snow-removal tarps** (Old tarps or sheets of plastic, nylon, or other strong, slippery material are useful for dragging snow out of insides and entrances during construction of caves and mound structures. Good tents, tarps, or ground sheets can be used but are likely to be damaged.)
2. **Sled or pulk** (There can be a great safety advantage to having a substantial sled along, especially if it is long enough to use as an emergency transport device for injured group members. On trips that will push more than a few miles into the backcountry, this can greatly shorten rescue times. Such a sled can also be used to haul group gear, thus reducing pack weights and the risk of ski injuries caused by traveling with extra-heavy loads. It's also useful to have a way of transporting all of a participant's load in the event of a minor sprain or strain that would otherwise slow or stop the group.)

FIGURE 17.3c   Suggested Minimium Gear Requirements for Snowcamping (continued)

LEADER GEAR

Required Items (In addition to individual gear, plus required items for backpacking leaders):

1. **Spare sunglasses** (High UV-rating with sideshields. It is common to need sunglasses on snow, and common for participants to lose or break them.)
2. **A second flashlight and/or additional spare batteries, and spare bulbs** (Winter nights are long, cold weather saps battery efficiency, and a small spare flashlight can save the large light when it's bright light isn't needed, and having a second light facilitates battery changing.)
3. **Ski maintenance items** (If skis are used by participants) These include:
   a. Glide waxes (For the possible temperature range, even when "no-wax" skis are used)
   b. One or more "sticky" waxes (Enough to provide traction for "problem" skis)
   c. Scraper
   d. Oversized screws (At least several each in different sizes, for binding repair)
   e. Posi-drive and standard blade screwdrivers (Short, with good grips)
   f. An extra basket or two (No one basket type fits all poles)
   g. Fiber tape (At least 8 feet or 2.5 meters)

NOTE:

Once again, the above list only covers suggestions beyond those given earlier for backpacking, so those lists must be reviewed carefully. Everything on the backpacking list is appropriate for snowcamping with the exception, of course, of insect repellent.

C. Training and competence in estimating avalanche and other snow structure or ice-related hazards, including route selection and avalanche rescue;

D. Competence in ski touring and/or snowshoeing sufficient to demonstrate and provide basic instruction in these skills.

Leadership Ratios

Snowcamping outings planned as clinics in shelter building gain from having at least one instructor or experienced shelter builder for every two construction-sites. Groups traveling on skis or snowshoes need at least two leaders (a leader and an assistant) per group, and a ratio of not more than five skiers per leader or six snowshoers per leader. Compared to backpacking, travel paces and distances are usually reduced, and, under most conditions, tracking is possible, making it easier to find missing persons. On the other hand, visibility and sound travel are often restricted; the senses are muffled by hats and hoods; and the cold and the excitement of skiing or snowshoeing are distracting. These factors combine to impair communication and sometimes to reduce participant focus on basic safety issues.

Suggested Formats

Snowcamping outings, like backpacking outings, are usually conducted as two-day overnight excursions. While there are many advantages to longer trips, the average outing length on snow tends to be less than for similar dry-land excursions. Snow travel is potentially more tiring, the cold weather adds a certain amount of stress, and pack loads are usually fairly heavy even without additional food. It's often useful or even necessary to have several pre-trip meetings instead of the one or two recommended for backpacking. Even though participants in snowcamping are presumably experienced in backpacking, all of the gear requirements for this activity need to be reviewed in addition to the special needs related to snow travel and camping. Time spent in chalkboard discussions of shelter construction can reduce frustrations and speed construction in the field. A comprehensive avalanche-safety lecture is always a worthwhile addition to snowcamping courses and an essential component of any program that will involve the use of avalanche-prone areas.

Recommended Reading

Cary, B. (1979). *Winter camping.* Brattleboro, VT: Stephen Greene Press.

Gorman, S. (1990). *AMC guide to winter camping.* Boston, MA: Appalachian Mountain Club.

Mountaineering

Description

Mountaineering encompasses all of the elements of hiking, backpacking, and often snowcamping, as well as the climbing activities central to the popular image. High-angle rock and ice climbing and summit attempts are often part of the experience but aren't an essential part of this activity. The typical trip begins with travel via trails and off-trail routes to the point where climbing skills become necessary, then centers on some combination of snow, ice, or rock climbing until the return trip back down to the realm of hikers and backpackers.

Like all outdoor pursuits, mountaineering attracts avid participants of all ages and demographic backgrounds. Enthusiasts tend, however, to be older and to have even higher incomes and educational levels than those of backpackers. Also, the need for backpacking experience and the higher risks, fitness requirements, and equipment needs in mountaineering combine to reduce the number of potential participants to well below that for other outdoor pursuits. Some programs reduce entrance barriers by providing some of the needed equipment opportunities for fitness training, and review of backpacking skills. "Mini-lessons" in climbing skills while backpacking can encourage participants to move on to mountaineering.

Hazards and Risks

Mountaineering is no doubt more dangerous than backpacking; however, the exact level of risk is hard to estimate accurately. There are natural hazards in mountainous terrain, including steep slopes of snow, ice, and rock, crevasses, avalanches, rockfall, and raging streams. These, however, present little danger to people who follow accepted mountaineering practices and good common sense. Just as on the highway, virtually all accidents are the result of poor planning and/or poor judgment. The frightening numbers of mountain fatalities in Japan (about 550 annually) are attributable to the very large numbers of inexperienced people who have access to very steep terrain in these areas. In the United States, where only about sixty people die each year in the mountains, getting to such terrain usually requires considerable time and effort, which greatly reduces the total number of inexperienced people involved in this activity. U.S. attitudes toward safety are also much more conservative than in Europe or Japan and may contribute to the relatively low fatality rate. In any case, serious accidents are rare in organized mountaineering outings employing qualified leaders and instructors who adhere to modern teaching standards and practices.

Environmental and Social Impacts

Mountaineering has great potential for causing serious damage to the environment, which has, unfortunately, been demonstrated on countless peaks worldwide. Climbers, who by virtue of their above average education should be among the most aware of environmental concerns, are a major problem for many land managers. Too often, climbers know what is best for the environment but justify exceptions in order to achieve their goals of conquering peaks or routes. The fragile high alpine campsite is selected over the more durable site a half-mile below timberline because the higher camp saves an hour on the next day's climb. Running down a scree slope is faster and more fun than walking down a solid ridge nearby, so the scree runs are usually selected despite the effects. Routes on heather or flower covered meadows are selected for ease rather than potential for impact. Most of the world's famous and popular peaks are strewn with litter, including great heaps of debris left by major expeditions, much of it dumped into crevasses for convenience, ensuring a nearly permanent supply of ground up materials to pollute stream systems fed by the glacier.

It is possible to climb with little impact. Whether this happens or not depends upon the competence and values of the mountaineer.

Resource Requirements

Almost any mountainous area has some interesting routes to offer, and specific resource needs will depend upon the nature of the outing. If the trip is purely recreational and the participants are experienced, then the possibilities are nearly unlimited for anyone living near the mountains. Outings with specific objectives may require special types of terrain such as steep slopes of rock, snow, or ice, crevassed glaciers, or accessible summits. When skills teaching is intended, site specifications can be critical, further limiting the options. While the ideal mountaineering course should include a range of techniques for rock, snow, and ice climbing, the realities of terrain, season, and weather often require either additional outings or a compromise of objectives. Maps, guidebooks, and local expertise often provide all the information necessary for planning a modest recreational venture with experienced participants. However, when teaching is intended, secondhand knowledge of the resource is rarely adequate. Leaders of such outings should make every effort to personally scout the area to determine the series of sites best suited for learning various skills. Snow slopes for self-arrest practice, beginning belay practice, or any activity where an uncontrolled slide could occur should have safe, gentle runouts. Rock-climbing practice sites should be free of rockfall and allow upper belays and easy, safe access to the top.

Levels and Objectives

Levels. Like other outdoor pursuits, mountaineering trips can be described according to level of difficulty, objectives, or both, and several standard systems describe the difficulty of climbs and climbing routes. Detailed comparisons of these systems can be found in some mountaineering texts, though some refer only to the technical difficulty of individual pitches while others attempt to include consideration of distance, time, and necessary effort. One serious drawback to any such system lies in the fact that even minor changes in the weather or the ground or snow surface can profoundly

affect the difficulty of the route. Leaders must be prepared to adjust routes and activities as necessitated by unexpected conditions.

An "easy" mountaineering trip almost always requires more expertise, skill, and fitness than an easy backpacking trip. Most "easy" trips involve two- or three-day outings unless the high country can be reached in just a few hours. Even when access is not difficult, the benefits of acclimatization may make two- or three-day trips more enjoyable. Outings that take longer than three days can be wearing on people not used to the stresses of higher elevations.

"Easy" mountaineering trips usually involve no more than about 3,000 feet (1,000 m) of gain on the climb, assuming good conditions, fit participants, and few delays caused by roping up or belaying. Typically, an easy trip includes some sections of scrambling or climbing where ropes may be needed for psychological, if not real, security, and very limited sections requiring belays, rappels, or other techniques.

A "moderate" outing might involve more difficult access to the mountain, slightly greater elevation gains on the climbing route, and more sections requiring technical climbing skills and techniques. Routes that might be easy under good conditions may well be called moderate or even difficult in different seasons or bad weather, or when attempted within a shorter time frame. A route that requires very high levels of fitness, mastery of basic climbing skills, total elevation gains of more than 6,000 feet (1,800 m), or maximum elevation of over 14,000 feet (4,300 m) should be listed as "difficult."

Planners of mountaineering outings may find it difficult to keep program objectives within realistic limits. Outings and classes for beginners usually need to cover, or at least review, many of the basic skills associated with hiking, trekking, backpacking, snowcamping, and rock climbing before addressing specific mountaineering topics. As a result, little time may remain in beginning-level outings for more than cursory review of a limited number of topics and skills. This is an argument for extensive use of pre-trip meetings or multiple outings at the beginning level in any mountaineering program. When planning beginning programs, it is often

necessary to decide between nontechnical ascents and the inclusion of more skills training.
Even basic lessons in knots, ice axe use, crampon use, glacier travel, and the many related
skills and topics can gobble up days on the
mountainside, leaving little time for summit
attempts unless planners compromise on content or depth of instruction, or add additional
outing time.

Intermediate-level experiences typically assume that participants already have basic backcountry and mountaineering experience and that
they have at least a limited ability to utilize the
tools and techniques of the sport. Some programs devote all of the attention in beginning
classes to skill development and reserve the label
"intermediate" for easy to moderately difficult
teaching outings wherein the participants integrate their knowledge and skills in a summit attempt. In other cases, the intermediate level may
involve skills training in any number of specialized activities for participants with basic experience or training. Popular topics include snow or
ice climbing, rock climbing in alpine settings, or
rescue techniques. Some review of basic concepts is invariably required in these courses.

Advanced-level outings probably vary more
in content than those of any other level due, in
part, to widely varying conceptions of what
constitutes advanced skills; it also takes many
years of experience and practice to attain anything approaching mastery of any of the several
activities that constitute mountaineering. Most
mountaineering programs are designed to introduce participants to the sport, and these tend to
label as "advanced" any outings for which a
few basic or intermediate ones are prerequisites. Such "advanced" trips are similar to
those at the intermediate level in that a review
of basics is usually necessary, from in-depth
training in specific topics to routes requiring
the use of intermediate or higher skills. A few
programs offer truly advanced experiences involving participants in lead climbing, outing
planning, group leadership, and other areas
necessary for full mastery of all the suggested
objectives, including independent participation
in the sport.

Objectives. No two mountaineering outings
are identical, no matter how hard leaders may
try to conform to standard plans. Nevertheless,
it is always worthwhile to set forth principal
objectives. Without a clear understanding of
these, it is difficult to plan effectively and impossible to present potential participants with a
clear picture of what goals to attain. At the same
time, it is probably more important in mountaineering than in any other outdoor pursuit to
emphasize the uncertainties inherent in the activity. The alpine environment changes constantly,
and the conditions necessary for safe travel and
for conduct of many of the component activities
of mountaineering may or may not exist on a
given outing.

Some outings have very few objectives. This
is especially true of casual recreational events
with experienced participants. Others have
many, as is usually the case in mountaineering
classes and schools.

The following list includes only those objectives not suggested elsewhere in the text for
hiking, trekking, backpacking, snowcamping,
and rock climbing. These activities are included
in the broad definition of mountaineering, and
skill in these areas is usually considered a prerequisite to participation in mountaineering. In
those cases where prior skill development is
not required, the mountaineering course has to
be extended to cover these topics before moving
on to more advanced topics. All of the objectives of the prerequisite areas are therefore potentially valid for mountaineering outings
and should be reviewed carefully. The reader
should review objectives for hiking, backpacking, snowcamping, and rock climbing.

When selecting goals for a specific outing
or program, it is important not to overestimate
participants' abilities and to choose objectives
that are reasonably attainable. As implied above,
it is also important to have alternatives in mind
for any alpine adventure. Common objectives
specific to mountaineering are that participants
will be able to:

1. Identify potential sites for mountaineering, using maps, guides, and other resources;

2. Understand the fitness requirements of mountaineering and appropriate conditioning exercises;

3. Understand the gear requirements for mountaineering and be able to construct an appropriate list of equipment and specifications given a description of the location, route, and season;

4. Be aware of the physiological effects of altitude and extreme cold, including the recognition, treatment, and prevention of resulting medical problems;

5. Understand avalanches and snow-structure hazards, including avalanche hazard prediction, route finding, and avalanche rescue in backcountry settings;

6. Understand the special hazards of mountain weather, and be able to predict changes and respond appropriately;

7. Understand the environmental concerns characteristic of alpine and subalpine regions, and the ways of minimizing or eliminating impacts in those zones;

8. Be able to select and assess climbing routes based upon direct observation, maps, photographs, and guidebooks, including estimation of hazards, gear needs, best approaches, safest conditions, timing for ascent and descent, total time required, and suitability for various party sizes and experience levels;

9. Be able to tie the most important knots used in mountaineering, including, but not limited to, the figure eight on a bight, figure eight follow-through, single bowline, bowline on a coil and double fisherman (grapevine) knots, and prusik, clove and Muenter hitches;

10. Be able to use the ice axe effectively and safely to cut steps, to provide balance and security using the French technique positions, and to engage in self-arrest up to and including arrest from a head-first, on-the-back position;

11. Understand the strengths and limits of ropes and the other fabrics used in slings, harnesses, and carabiners, and be able to tie in ways appropriate for climbing on snow and glaciers;

12. Understand the strengths, weaknesses, and proper use of bollards, flukes, pickets, ice axes, ice screws, pitons, nuts, bolts, and other anchors used in mountaineering;

13. Demonstrate competence in setting up, securing, and carrying out sitting hip, foot-axe, and friction-device-assisted belays;

14. Be able to select, adjust, fit, and attach crampons securely and to use them effectively on a variety of snow and ice surfaces using appropriate French and Austrian techniques;

15. Understand the techniques for crossing glaciers, including route selection, roping up, and ways of reducing the chance of falling into a crevasse;

16. Be able to respond effectively if another party member falls on a cliff or into a crevasse. This includes an ability to set up appropriate systems for accessing and extricating the victim;

17. Be able to respond effectively after falling while roped. This includes an ability to utilize slings, prusik knots, and mechanical ascenders;

18. Acquire the skills and knowledge necessary to independently plan and carry out a safe, environmentally responsible, and enjoyable mountaineering outing that integrates all aspects of the sport.

Clothing and Equipment

Gear requirements for mountaineering vary widely. Most outings involve some backcountry hiking, and overnight trips require backpacking gear unless huts or accommodations are available. In some cases, the climbing portions of the outing may require no special equipment or clothing, while, in others, these may be extensive. Items commonly needed for climbing include helmets, ice axes, crampons, ropes, slings, harnesses, various kinds of anchors, and specialized footwear. Highly specialized clothing and a vast array of technical hardware and devices may also be essential for some types of climbing.

The following gear lists assume that the outing involves hiking, backpacking, or snow-camping, and that the appropriate equipment will be carried for these activities. The array of required items assumes that the climbing portions of the outing include glacier travel and basic rock climbing at middle latitudes from early spring to late fall. (See Figures 17.4 a-c, pages 373-375.)

Leadership Qualifications

A mountaineering leader should possess all of the attributes of a backpacking leader, as well as the ability to conduct the climbing portion of the outing.

Specific additional attributes include:

A. Substantial general mountaineering experience in terrain and climate conditions similar to those in the area of the intended outing. Mountain conditions are complex and variable, and many outings are necessary to build an adequate depth of experience;

B. An ability to select and assess climbing routes based upon direct observation, maps, photographs, and guidebooks, including estimation of hazards, gear needs, best approaches, safest conditions, timing for ascents and descents, total time required, and suitability for various party sizes and ability levels;

C. Training and competence in estimating avalanche and other snow structure hazards, in selecting safe routes, and in avalanche rescue under backcountry, as opposed to ski-area, conditions;

D. An understanding of rope, sling, and climbing hardware strengths and characteristics;

E. An ability to tie all of the basic mountaineering knots, including at least the figure eight on a bight, the figure eight follow-through, the single bowline, the bowline on a coil and the double fisherman's (grapevine) knots, and the prusik, Muenter, and clove hitches;

F. An ability to use ropes, slings, and hardware effectively in establishing both natural and artificial anchors in snow, ice, and rock, using pickets, flukes, screws, pitons, nuts, bolts, bollards, and other means;

G. Competence in belaying, using both manual and device-assisted techniques in snow and on rock. This should include the use of

standard signals, sitting hip and boot-axe belays, and belays using Sticht plates, Muenter hitches, and "figure eight" descenders;

H. Competence in the use of the ice axe, including the various positions of the French technique, step cutting, and self-arrest on a variety of snow surfaces;

I. Experience in glacier travel, including route selection and the use of accepted techniques for roping up and roped travel on glaciers;

J. Competence in crevasse-rescue techniques, including hands-on practice with Bilgeri, 2:1 and 3:1 "Z" systems, prusik and mechanically assisted rope-climbing techniques, and the construction of rope litters;

K. Competence in rappeling using at least the Dulfersitz, carabiner brake and figure eight systems, and the lowering of others using the figure eight and Muenter hitch;

L. An understanding of mountain weather and the weather patterns peculiar to the site of the intended outing;

M. An understanding of altitude-related stresses and physiologic responses, including hypoxia, AMS, HAPE, CE, and recognition, treatment, and prevention of these conditions;

N. An understanding of the effects of cold, wind, exhaustion, and anxiety on the mental and physical conditions of climbers. This includes an awareness of how these stresses affect the learning process, and of techniques for maximizing receptivity and communication;

O. Fitness and climbing ability exceeding the demands of the route to be led or of the class to be taught;

P. Snowcamping skills and snowshoeing or ski touring ability appropriate for the terrain, climate, and season of the intended outing.

Leadership Ratios

Mountaineering outings generally require high leadership ratios. Recreational ventures following standard routes well within the abilities of the participants are sometimes led by one fully qualified leader and an assistant who has similar skills but less experience. In this case, the pair of leaders may be able to handle as

**FIGURE 17.4a   Suggested Minimum Gear
Requirements for Mountaineering**

INDIVIDUAL GEAR

Required items   (In addition to the items required for backpacking or hiking):

1. **Suitable boots** (Stiff lug soles, plus stiff leather or plastic uppers if crampons are to be used. Fit, durability, waterproofness and insulation are also critical.)
2. **Gaiters** (High type is necessary if deep snow is expected or if pants are used rather than knickers when using crampons.)
3. **Additional insulation** (Two layers rather than one layer of wool or better fabric, and neck covering such as a turtleneck)
4. **Dark, full coverage sunglasses** (With good UV protection; side shields are very useful.)
5. **Carabiners** (Often required. Two locking types and one non-locking type meet most needs. Many may be required for some technical routes.)
6. **Ice axe** (Axe specifications should be set by the instructor and all axes carefully inspected prior to the outing.)
7. **Crampons and straps or attachment system** (Specifications should be set by the instructor. Crampon fit and attachment security must be carefully checked before the outing.)
8. **Helmet** (To instructor's specifications)
9. **Harnesses** (Often required. Many types of seat, chest and combination harnesses are available commercially. Inexpensive versions suitable for basic glacier travel and climbing can be made from tubular webbing.)
10. **Prusik loops** (To instructor's specifications)
11. **Climbing slings** (Often required. Careful inspection of sling fabric and construction is essential.)

Optional Items   (In addition to requirements for hiking or backpacking; may be required at option of instructor):

1. **Skis, ski boots, ski poles, or snowshoes** (If needed)
2. **Avalanche probes** (At 2-4 meters per person, and snow shovels at one for every four people)
3. **Avalanche beacons** (Rarely essential though always an advantage in avalanche terrain, beacons serve no purpose unless participants are trained in their use, and neither device should be allowed to induce a false sense of security.)
4. **Headlamps** (Extremely useful for the night travel common in mountaineering, almost essential for night climbing or skiing, and often required. Alkaline or other cold-resistant batteries are needed as normal cells are useless in temperatures below freezing.)
5. **Wind protection** (Wind-resistant parkas and pants that don't trap moisture are valuable for hard work in cool, windy environments.)

FIGURE 17.4b   Suggested Minimum Gear
Requirements for Mountaineering (continued)

GROUP GEAR

Required Items   (In addition to the requirements for backpacking):

1. **Tarp or bivouac shelter** (Any group traveling above timberline needs to be able to shelter an injured party member and one or two companions for extended periods until outside help can be obtained. Failure to carry such shelter has resulted in many fatalities.)
2. **Sleeping bag or equivalent extra insulation** (A half bag or "elephant's foot" plus a vest and parka might suffice. This is an essential adjunct to the above shelter.)
3. **Foam pads** (At least enough for an injured party and companions. In snow above timberline one three-quarter length sleeping pad for every two party members meets the basic needs and also provides comfortable seating during breaks.)
4. **Stove, pot, and fuel** (These are considered basic requirements for climbing groups because they provide access to water if ice is available and can provide essential warmth in the form of hot drinks and hot-water bottles.)
5. **Avalanche probes** (These should be considered required items at any time that avalanches are possible, which is most of the time in the mid-latitude mountains assumed in this list. Ideally, each person should have a 6 to 12 foot (7 to 8 m) good-quality probe or a pair of avalanche probe ski poles.)
6. **Shovels** (Portable folding shovels are invaluable should an avalanche bury a person or gear, and should, like the probes, be considered required items in any situation where avalanches might occur. One shovel for every four climbers is probably adequate.)
7. **Climbing ropes** (The type, quality, and condition of the ropes is critical and must be reviewed carefully by the instructor. Kernmantle ropes are the easiest to handle and provide safety advantages in certain technical climbing applications, but are costly and hard to assess for damage. Laid ropes provide adequate security for most purposes and are less costly and easier to inspect for damage; thus, they are generally more suitable for use with classes and large groups. *Static* lines may be useful for fixed lines and special purposes but must not be confused with *dynamic* ropes. In most cases it's sufficient to provide one rope for every three climbers. Larger parties often carry a spare rope as well, and still others may be required by climbing schools or classes.)
8. **Hardware** (The exact needs depend upon the route and conditions during the climb. Often-needed items include pickets, flukes, and other snow anchors, screws and other ice anchors, and pitons, nuts or other rock anchors, as well as belay devices, rappel devices, pulleys, rope-ascending devices, specialized tools for steep ice work.)
9. **Software** (Various-sized loops made from different diameters of rope and widths of webbing are used to secure anchors such as tie-ins and for a multitude of other purposes. As with hardware, group needs must be carefully assessed to avoid over as well as undersupply, and communal needs may be partly met by gear carried by individuals.)

**FIGURE 17.4c   Suggested Minimum Gear
Requirements for Mountaineering (continued)**

Group Optional Items:

1. **Wands** (Especially useful when changing conditions or poor visibility might make route-finding difficult. They are used most often on glaciers and snowfields)
2. **Altimeter** (Sometimes useful for route finding, especially for poor visibility or night travel. Rarely essential.)
3. **Aerial photographs and guidebooks** (Especially useful if the outing has specific objectives that require efficient use of the terrain and the exact locations of certain routes and areas.)

LEADER GEAR

Required Items (In addition to individual gear and the required items for backpacking leaders, plus the items required for leaders of snowcamping and/or rock climbing if these skills are included):

1. **Carabiners** (A personal supply of locking and non-locking carabiners sufficient to lead the route and execute basic rescue procedures)
2. **Slings** (A personal supply of 1 inch (2.5 cm) tubular or equivalent slings and 6-7 mm kernmantle prusiks sufficient to lead the route and execute basic rescues procedures)
3. **Hardware** (Belay devices, pulleys, and anchors for personal use in leading, sufficient to execute basic rescue procedures)
4. **Tools and replacement screws** (For adjusting crampons)

NOTE:

Remember that the above suggestions are based on mixed glacier and rock climbing at mid-latitudes in situations requiring access to the mountains by foot. Review the gear suggestions for hiking, trekking, backpacking, snowcamping, and rock climbing as well as the items suggested here before specifying the gear requirements for a mountaineering venture. Consider both the dangers of being caught with inadequate gear and the penalties that accrue from carrying too much. Comfort, safety, and liability considerations must also be addressed. Unneeded extra gear can overburden the back, drain the wallet, and degrade the experience by clouding the relationship between the participant and the environment. However, cost and inconvenience is no excuse for not carrying basic mountaineering safety gear.

---

many as 12 participants if there are no technical "bottlenecks" on the route. There are several possible objections to this size party. First, it may be disallowed by resource managers. Such parties have the potential to overtax campsites in fragile areas near timberlines, and they can seriously interfere with other parties attempting the same route. Safety is also a concern, because a large party kicks loose a lot of rock, inevitably bombing itself, and may be so slow as to greatly extend the time spent on the mountains. This in turn increases dangers.

The only substantive counter-argument is that large groups can, in theory, carry out their own wounded. Large parties can be reasonable, but only if travel, especially camping, is largely on ground protected by snow, and if the season, timing, and route preclude conflict with other climbing parties. The route itself needs to be relatively nontechnical, since belays, rappels, and even the use of fixed lines can cause long delays and require incredible patience. Consider that a group of five people can usually rappel off a cliff in about twenty-five minutes while a group of twenty would require at least an additional full hour!

Any outing that attempts a challenging route or wherein teaching is intended should be limited to about eight participants and two leaders. Many organizations provide a leader or an assistant leader for every three or four participants for all levels of outings.

Suggested Formats

There are many possible formats for mountaineering trips and classes. Two-day or longer outings are the norm since considerable time is usually required just to access mountainous terrain. When difficult routes or summit attempts are intended, mountaineers usually try to begin climbing very early in the morning, often well before sunrise. This almost always requires travel to a high base camp or hut on the preceding day, and makes for a very long second day if a return to town is necessary by that evening.

Some mountaineering programs that emphasize teaching break up the activity into component parts, offering single-day or evening courses in knot-tying, rock climbing, and other skills that can be taught in or near town, followed by one or more extended outings to teach snow climbing and glacier travel and to integrate various activities. Such a series might include courses covering the mountain environment, a review of backpacking skills, knot-tying and rope use, map-and-compass use on-trail and off-trail, basic rock climbing, mountain-rescue skills, and first aid for mountaineers, followed by a two-day or three-day glacier school and a two-day or three-day summit attempt combining glacier travel, snow climbing, and rock climbing.

Pre-trip meetings are essential. When the outing has specific educational objectives, at least two meetings are usually required to allow time to describe the outing, assess the participants, review basic skills (knots, rope handling, and belaying), and explain the gear requirements. The first meeting should be held at least ten days prior to the outing to allow time for the participants to acquire the necessary gear. The second should be held just a few days before the outing, close enough in time so that directions will be remembered and commitments upheld while still allowing time for last-minute adjustments. Because so much gear is involved in mountaineering, a lot of time can be saved by checking participant gear at the last pre-trip meeting or perhaps at a special meeting on the evening prior to the outing. Missing items or misfitted crampons are far easier to deal with prior to the time of departure, after which the only option is often to leave the person behind.

Recommended Reading

Blackshaw, A. (1968). *Mountaineering.* Baltimore, MD: Penguin Books.

Chouinard, Y. (1977). *Climbing ice.* San Francisco, CA: Sierra Club Books.

Cliff, P. (1987). *Ski-mountaineering.* Seattle, WA: Pacific Search Press.

Fyffe, A., & Peter, I. (1990). *The handbook of climbing.* London, England: Stephen Greene Press.

Graydon, D. (Ed.). (1992). *Mountaineering: The freedom of the hills.* Seattle, WA: The Mountaineers.

Rock Climbing

Description

Rock climbing was once viewed only as an element of the broader sport of mountaineering. In recent years, it has become a specialized activity in its own right. Devotees of "sport climbing" usually climb with top belays on small cliffs, boulders, or artificial walls. Some move on to lead climbing and the realm of conventional mountaineering. In recent years, sport climbing has become increasingly popular, leading to the establishment of routes of ever-increasing difficulty.

Hazards and Risks

There are several potential hazards in rock climbing. These include falls, injury from falling rock, and a range of general environmental perils. Minor injuries, such as bashed knuckles and scraped elbows, are fairly common, especially on certain types of rock and in more advanced climbing. The chance of major injury can be reduced to a low level if participants and leaders use common sense, standard safety procedures, and top-quality equipment.

Environmental and Social Impacts

There are two principle types of impact associated with rock climbing. The most obvious is damage to the rock itself. Many clean, sharp fissures and cracks, even in solid granite, have been beaten into rounded grooves, mostly by climbers of earlier decades who used pitons as anchors. Most, though not all, climbers have switched to less abusive anchor systems (nuts, chocks, and their high-tech offspring). However, sport climbers now drill permanent holes for expansion bolts, and decorate routes with a mixture of chalk and skin oils.

While most climbers are aware of the effects of heavy traffic on access paths and slopes, nevertheless the most popular rock climbing areas suffer considerable damage. Leaders can help

reduce impacts by making sure that participants are aware of the potential for damage, by adjusting plans and routes to avoid sensitive or overused sites, and by demonstrating behaviors and techniques that are consistent with sound environmental practices.

Resource Requirements

Even when there are no good natural rock climbing sites nearby, indoor or outdoor artificial climbing walls can meet a wide range of needs. Belaying and rappeling practice require only small cliffs or a moderately high wall and appropriate anchor points, and basic skills can be taught even on low artificial walls. Climbing techniques are best taught on rock inclines and cliffs, though primary moves, balance, and conditioning can be replicated on manmade surfaces using wood, metal, concrete, and plastic to simulate natural handholds, footholds, cracks, and corners. There are many publications devoted to the designs and suggestions for artificial climbing-practice structures.

Natural sites range from large boulders to great cliffs or mountain peaks. Accessibility is a key concern, including distance, time, and permission to use the site. Land managers in both public and private sectors may have legitimate concerns about safety and liability, environmental damage to the site, and access routes or campsites. Private owners may be concerned about privacy and security compromises caused by the presence of strangers on their property. Most practice areas have a limited number of good sites for teaching certain skills, so coordination can be essential.

Rock types are important as well. Granite, limestone, dolomite, basalt, and certain sandstones and welded tuffs are among the better known and most popular climbing surfaces; however, many of these outcrops are unfit due to local peculiarities in composition, structure, or weathering. The rock must be tough and hang together well and not be subject to excessive rockfall. Quarries, road cuts, sea cliffs, and fault zones can offer superb climbing but need to be carefully checked for instability caused by blasting, earth movement, or rapid erosion.

Except in the case of very advanced programs, it is also vital to have easy access to the top of the climbing face and some means of placing anchors. Common anchors include substantial, healthy, well-rooted trees or solid rock suitable for bolting, but the best of cliffs may be useless if topped by sloping soil or loose rock. Some marginal sites can be improved by removing loose material, though this process should be avoided until the environmental implications have been carefully considered.

Except for advanced classes focusing on multi-pitch climbs, there is no need for great height. Routes of 30 to 60 feet (10 to 20 m) allow easy communication from top to bottom, bottom belays using standard climbing rope lengths, and enough height to provide excitement and challenge. Local equipment stores, guidebooks, and climbers can usually provide an inventory of local options.

Levels and Objectives

Levels. Rock climbing outings and programs can be described by reference to the technical difficulty of the climbs or the objectives of the program. The technical difficulty of a climb is usually expressed in terms of numbers or letters in a rating scheme, but there are several problems inherent in such systems, including lack of uniformity among the dozen or more "standard" ones. These schemes have evolved over the years in several countries, and are based upon various criteria such as individual move difficulty, overall technical difficulty of the route, strenuousness of the route, or the equipment needed. For our purposes here, it will suffice to describe outings according to course objectives and to separate group outings into beginning, intermediate, and advanced levels.

Beginning outings start with no assumptions about climbing or rope handling ability, and they focus on orientation to the sport, knot typing, belaying, and basic climbing skills. Climbing activities at this level are always top-roped if more than a few feet off the ground. Objectives A through H are reasonable for beginning programs. Rappeling, the subject of Objective I, is often included in beginning programs because

it's flashy and fun; however, due to time constraints, the session might better be spent practicing down climbing. After careful review of basic skills, intermediate programs might attempt to achieve Objectives I through L. Much of the intermediate class time is usually spent on skill development with top ropes. Advanced programs are usually designed to meet Objectives M and N, with at least initial experience in "leading" while belayed from above.

Objectives. The following suggested objectives are listed here in the order in which the subject matter is usually addressed. On completion of the program, participants should be able to:

A. Identify potential sites for rock climbing using maps, guides, and other resources;

B. Understand the fitness requirements of rock climbing and appropriate conditioning exercises;

C. Understand the basic gear requirements of the activity and construct an appropriate list of gear needs given a description of the site and routes;

D. Tie the more important knots used in rock climbing, including the figure eight on a bight, figure eight follow-through, single bowline, bowline on a coil, and double fisherman's knots, and the prusik, Muenter, and Clove hitches. Ideally, participants should be able to tie these knots quickly behind the back. This requires a greater comprehension of the knot but ensures long-term retention of the skills;

E. Understand the strengths and weaknesses of ropes, slings, carabiners, and any other hardware used in the program;

F. Be able to locate, assess, set, and utilize natural anchors and preset artificial anchors safely and without causing environmental damage;

G. Demonstrate competence in setting, securing, and carrying out sitting-hip and friction-device-assisted belays using standard signals. This includes proper tie-in to the belay using both rope only and rope-and-harness systems in upper belay climbing;

H. Demonstrate an understanding of the three-point rule and of basic climbing techniques including friction, slab, and face climbing, mantling, and jamming, stemming, bridging, lay-backs, and other counter-force moves, as well as traverse and down climbing;

I. Set up and safely use at least the Dulfersitz, carabiner brake, and figure eight and/or other friction-device-assisted rappel techniques;

J. Respond effectively after falling while roped. This includes the use of slings and prusik knots or mechanical ascenders;

K. Respond effectively to assist a fallen climber on belay. This includes tying off sitting hip, figure eight, Sticht Plate, and Muenter hitch belays;

L. Select, place, and safely utilize artificial anchors such as nuts and pitons. This includes an awareness of safety concerns and potentials for environmental impact;

M. Set up and employ appropriate anchors, belays, and other techniques in lead climbing;

N. Acquire the skills and knowledge necessary to independently plan and carry out a safe, environmentally sound, and enjoyable rock climbing outing.

Clothing and Equipment

See Figures 17.5 a-c (pages 380-382).

Leadership Qualifications

The keys to safety in a rock climbing program are awareness, preventive actions, and constant alertness. Rock climbing instructors have to be able to assess potential hazards and design, implement, and reinforce safety procedures and policies. They must also instill a sense of personal responsibility in participants. The nature of the risks in rock climbing is such that there are seldom second chances; if rocks or people fall, there are no extended periods during which to ponder alternatives or seek advice. Prevention of accidents and preparation for emergency action are essential and depend upon the technical skills and group leadership ability of an experienced leader.

The minimum attributes of a rock climbing leader include:

A. All of the attributes recommended for hiking leaders;

B. Applicable items from the trekking, backpacking, or mountaineering lists if rock climbing will take place in the context of these activities;

C. Rock climbing experience and skill at a level well beyond that to be taught in the program;

D. A thorough understanding of rope slings, climbing hardware strengths and characteristics, and maintenance procedures;

E. An ability to tie all of the basic rock climbing and mountaineering knots, including at least the figure eight on a bight, figure eight follow-through, single bowline, bowline on a coil and double fisherman's (grapevine) knots, and the prusik, Muenter and clove hitches. The leader should be able to tie any of these quickly and perfectly beyond the back and be able to teach them effectively;

F. An ability to use ropes, slings, and hardware to establish anchors in rock and other natural features. This includes a thorough understanding of the effects on system strength of loading angles, bending angles around objects, and the positioning of knots and anchors;

G. Competence in belaying, using both manual and device-assisted techniques. This should include the sitting-hip belay and the use of figure eights, Sticht Plates, and Muenter hitches, as well as standard signals for belaying;

H. Competence in rappeling using Dulfersitz, carabiner brake and figure eight systems;

I. Competence in rescue techniques, including hands-on practice in self-rescue, prusik and mechanically assisted rope-climbing techniques, lowering systems, construction and use of piggy-back carries, and rope-basket litters and stretchers;

J. Familiarity with the proposed site, including the characteristics of the rock, the routes, the potential for rockfall, and potential and existing anchor locations.

Leaders of rock climbing programs need to be exceptionally alert and conscientious about detail, and willing and able to maintain close,

FIGURE 17.5a   Suggested Minimum Gear Requirements for Rock Climbing

INDIVIDUAL GEAR

Required Items:

1. **Suitable footwear** (There are many possibilities. Beginners may find that sneakers are adequate so long as the soles don't protrude further than the uppers. It is important that the weight be placed directly above the edge of the sole, and many running shoes, designed with broad soles to increase stability, make it almost impossible to stand on narrow ledges. Lug-sole hiking or climbing boots may also be used, although Norwegian welts should be avoided. A host of highly specialized rock climbing shoes are available. They are rarely needed by beginners but can offer superb grip and edging capabilities.)

2. **Helmet** (Specifically designed for climbing. Most bicycle and motorcycle helmets are not appropriate. Helmets are essential whenever rockfall or falls by the climber are possible. They are routinely used by lead climbers and by those who are rock climbing in the context of mountaineering. They are also required in virtually all U.S. climbing schools and by many European and Japanese rock climbing schools, since rockfall or head-knocking "inversion" type falls can never be ruled out, even in "sport climbing." However, most recreational sport climbers do not wear helmets. Most sport climbers are young, tend therefore to feel immortal, and are more concerned with current style and images. Unfortunately, the current style mandates Lycra tights and a bare head.)

Optional items:

1. **Harnesses** (Many types of seat, chest, and combination harnesses are available commercially, and acceptable alternatives can be made from tubular nylon webbing. Designs and specifications must be very carefully assessed–a well-designed and well-made harness can provide a considerable margin of safety if used properly, yet some commercial and many popular "homemade" types have serious flaws.)

2. **Carabiners** (For beginners one or two locking types and one or two non-locking types are usually plenty, if not included as group gear.)

3. **Slings** (A variety of sizes and types are sometimes used as personal gear, though again these may in many cases be considered group gear.)

4. **Hardware** (More advanced climbers sometimes carry a rappel device, a chalk bag, a variety of anchors and other tools as personal gear, though in some class or program settings these items are considered group gear.)

**FIGURE 17.5b   Suggested Minimum Gear Requirements
for Rock Climbing (continued)**

GROUP GEAR

Required Items:

1. **Climbing rope** (For most instructional purposes relatively short ropes of 120 feet (35 meters) in length are adequate. Dynamic kernmantle ropes are the easiest to handle and provide several safety advantages in lead climbing, yet are expensive and hard to assess for damages. Dynamic laid or braided types offer more than ample strength for upper belays, are cheaper, and are much easier to inspect for damage. Static lines serve well if they are used appropriately, i.e., for upper belays only and in no situation (such as lead climbing) where heavy peak loading could occur. The number of ropes needed for a rock climbing session depends upon the skills to be taught, the number of available anchors and routes, the number of students, the number of routes or positions that can be supervised at one time, and the need for additional ropes to establish anchor points. Typically, one instructor can only supervise one or two routes (each with a belayer and climber) at one time. Therefore it's usually sufficient to allow one rope per two students up to the total that can be supervised, plus any extras that may be needed. Ropes have a limited safe life span, must be carefully checked before each use for any signs of damage, and should not be expected to last more than a few years even with the best of care.)

2. **First-aid kit** (Sufficient for conditions. Size and contents will depend on distance from medical assistance.)

3. **Anchors, hangers, slings, etc.** (As needed to establish anchors and edge protection at site)

Optional Items:

1. **Software** (There seems always to be a need for nylon webbing slings and cord loops of various sizes. Exact needs depend on the site, route, and techniques employed. It's important to date all slings and to inspect them carefully before, during, and after use. Webbing fabric is especially vulnerable to weathering and abrasion, and knots in such fabric tend to loosen easily. Webbing should be cut up and discarded if any doubt exists as to strength. It should not be expected to last as long as rope.)

2. **Hardware** (This may include carabiners, rappel devices, ascenders, pulleys, bolts and bolting tools, pitons, nuts and high-tech anchor devices, hammers and extraction tools, and a host of other specialized items.)

NOTE:
Remember that the above suggestions assume a site in town or at least close to the road. Review hiking, trekking, backpacking, or mountaineering lists for suggestions about trips away from the road, overnight, or in mountainous terrain. When teaching knot-tying, it is a big help to have a supply of 12 to 15 foot (4 to 5 m) ropes. These can be anything from old cotton clothesline to sections of old climbing rope.

**FIGURE 17.5c   Suggested Minimum Gear Requirements
for Rock Climbing (continued)**

LEADER GEAR

*Required Items (In addition to individual gear, above, and leader gear for
hiking, backpacking or mountaineering, as needed):*

1. **Set of hardware for demonstrations** (Various items depending upon level
   of outing or class)
2. **Set of gear adequate to conduct rescue** (Harness, descending device, slings,
   and prusik sufficient to go to the aid of a fallen climber, harness to be worn
   at all times, other items to be carried or close at hand at all times)

---

ongoing supervision of myriad details. Every knot, every anchor, every tie-in, and every move is significant in this activity. There is no room for "Space Cadets" among the ranks of rock climbing instructors.

Leadership Ratios. Safe and efficient rock climbing instruction usually demands a high ratio of staff to participants. It is hard for one instructor to adequately supervise more than two climbing routes at one time, and this is possible only if the routes are short, close together, and relatively uncomplicated. This means that one instructor can rarely handle more than four active participants (two belayers and two climbers) at one time. The overall ratio can be expanded by including other participants who might watch, practice knots, or participate in some safe, unsupervised alternative activity, although this is generally not a good idea since it can lead to distractions for the instructor and the belayers.

A counterargument is that one onlooker per route can gain from observation and provide assistance should some mishap require the instructor to focus on one climber or belayer; thus, some programs allow up to six participants per leader or qualified assistant. There are exceptions, of course, as in knot-tying and belaying practice where no one is actually exposed to danger and can be supervised at a ratio of perhaps a dozen participants per leader.

In any case, the rock climbing leader should always be assisted by at least one other qualified person so that fast and safe rescue of an injured individual is possible. Minimum qualifications of assistant leaders varies according to the nature of the site and routes, and may range from a competent program graduate to no less than a fully qualified leader.

Suggested Formats

If adequate artificial or natural practice sites are available nearby, rock climbing can be one of the easiest activities to schedule. Many of the basic skills can be taught in a classroom setting; knot-tying, for example, is probably better taught indoors than outdoors since participants can focus on learning the complex movements and patterns undistracted by weather and terrain. Once in the field, it's harder to focus participant attention on details.

Most rock climbing programs begin with one or more indoor sessions that serve as pre-trip meetings and an opportunity to discuss ropes, slings, hardware, and basic climbing techniques and to practice knot-tying and belaying. The length of time necessary for actual climbing practice depends upon access, set-up and take-down times. Some indoor facilities require only a few minutes to set up and take down, so that significant progress can be achieved in an hour or less.

Most field sites, however, require substantial time to get ready even when top anchors are in place. It is usually necessary to allow about a half-hour to get a few top anchors in place for belay stances or change of direction pulleys, and as much time at the end of the session to remove the slings and hardware and to coil ropes. Add to this the time needed to sign out and distribute equipment (if, as is usually the case, helmets and other items are provided by the program) and the time needed to collect, sign in, and return the equipment to storage.

In some cases, leaders or assistants may be able to set up and take down equipment before and after the scheduled program; however, this isn't always possible and may not be desirable. The placement of anchors and other systems and the proper dispatching and care of equipment are important components of any instructional program. As a result, sessions of less than two hours may allow little actual climbing time. If the routes are relatively short (half a rope length or so), an hour of actual climbing time is usually sufficient to allow two or three climb cycles. If two or three participants are assigned to a route and rotate the roles of climber, belayer, or observer, all should be able to climb once in an hour.

Whatever the length of individual sessions, it is important to develop skills and techniques in a logical progression. Each session should somewhat overlap the contents of the prior session, and leaders should make sure that every participant has prerequisite skills and knowledge before proceeding to the next level of skill.

Recommended Reading

Long, J. (1989). *How to rock climb.* Evergreen, CO: Chockstone Press.

Long, J. (1991). *Face climbing.* Evergreen, CO: Chockstone Press.

Robbins, R. (1970). *Basic rockcraft.* Glendale, CA: La Siesta Press.

Robbins, R. (1973). *Advanced rockcraft.* Glendale, CA: La Siesta Press.

Snowshoeing

Description

Snowshoeing is fun, practical, and relatively easier and safer than skiing. Where skiing evokes images of thrills and spills, snowshoeing offers peaceful, if sometimes strenuous, enjoyment of the winter backcountry, free of anxiety about high-speed collisions with the scenery. Snowshoes have distinct advantages over skis on steep slopes with abundant trees or other obstacles. The snowshoer can usually plod straight uphill or downhill, while the skier may have to traverse back and forth on the way up, and choose between very long traverses or linked face plants on the way down. In such terrain, the snowshoer, much to the frustration of the skier, usually covers the ground faster and with less expenditure of energy. Little skill or balance is necessary to snowshoe on gentle slopes, and nothing beats snowshoes for carrying large, heavy, or awkward loads or pulling sleds uphill. Skis do have an advantage over snowshoes on steep side hills, especially on hard or slick surfaces, and in good ski conditions on slopes well within the ability of the skier.

Here, snowshoeing is defined as the winter equivalent of hiking, as opposed to snowcamping, which is the winter equivalent of backpacking. Travel over snow on snowshoes is rarely as fast as travel over the same terrain by foot on bare ground. Routes therefore tend to be relatively short, especially in midwinter when daylight is limited.

Snowshoeing has advocates throughout the snowy parts of the world. There is good evidence that this activity was pursued as far back as 4,000 BC, and all manner of foot-surface-expanding contraptions have been used ever since. Because snowshoeing requires little balance, almost anyone can do it, at least on gentle terrain. Before the advent of modern ski equipment, snowshoeing was enjoyed by a larger proportion of winter recreationists; however, the absolute number of snowshoers is probably higher now than at any time in the past. Attracted to winter sports by skiing, many people turn occasionally to snowshoeing for relaxation or for the several practical advantages of this activity for special purposes. Rescue groups often find snowshoes superior to skis since "shoes" assure steady travel relatively unaffected by snow conditions, terrain, loads carried, or the ski skills of participants, and because they are uninterrupted by waxing stops. Snowmobilers and pilots often carry snowshoes for emergency use.

Hazards and Risks

Snowshoeing isn't inherently hazardous; the dangers in this sport are related to the weather and snow cover. Hypothermia, frostbite, and avalanches can cause grief for the unaware traveler. Ice- or snow-covered water can often be crossed more safely on snowshoes than on foot; however, real danger still exists and great care is essential. Safety in such environments depends upon a combination of knowledge, alertness, a willingness to modify plans to maximize safety margins, proper equipment, and the skills necessary to respond to mishaps. Becoming lost or injured in a winter environment is generally more serious than similar events in the summer. Communications are impaired, and travel and transport times are all lengthened dramatically in the cold season. Both search efficiency and survival times are reduced. Nevertheless, snowshoeing is probably the safest of all winter outdoor pursuits if the activity is conducted well.

Environmental Impacts

Snowshoeing can be a very low impact activity if conducted carefully, even when travel is off-trail, since the snow provides a measure of protection for the vegetation. Snowshoeing therefore has somewhat less potential for impact than hiking. Some potential impacts of snowshoeing are perhaps not well known. Leaders should avoid conducting groups into areas that are used as retreats, shelter zones, or critical feeding areas for wildlife during the winter months. While some animals migrate or hibernate, others do not or cannot leave the snow-covered areas, and they can be very vulnerable to disturbance. The primary social impact of snowshoeing has to do with skiers! While skiers may appreciate and use a well-packed snowshoe route in extremely deep snow, they do not appreciate carefully set ski tracks being destroyed by snowshoers. Conscientious snowshoers avoid walking on ski trails for this reason and for their own safety because not all skiers are able to avoid unexpected slow moving obstacles in their tracks.

Resource Requirements

The resource requirements for good snowshoeing are minimal, and, in most cases, they are similar to those for hiking with, of course, the addition of enough snow to justify their use. Walking on foot is usually the best option in soft snow depths of up to about 1 foot (0.3 m) on the level and 2 feet (0.6 m) on hillsides. Beyond these depths, snowshoes usually provide an advantage unless the snow surface is very firm. It is not unusual in the winter for conditions to change rapidly. Late spring snow packs usually don't require snowshoes early in the day, though they may be required in the afternoon. Routes should avoid lengthy sidehills if possible and need not be long since travel is generally slower than on bare ground. Great care must be used in selecting routes to allow options in the event of avalanche conditions or unsafe snow bridges. Parking can also be a problem since trailheads are not always plowed in the winter, and, even if they are, may require permits.

Levels and Objectives

Levels. Snowshoe trips, like hikes, can be described by level of physical difficulty (easy, moderate, or difficult) or by objectives and prerequisites (beginning, intermediate, and advanced). Since winter travel is by nature either slower or more strenuous than walking on bare ground, snowshoe trips need to be considerably shorter than summer equivalents. For example, where an easy summer hike might cover 6 or 7 miles, an easy snowshoe hike might be limited to 3 or 4 miles (4.8 to 6.4 km) with elevation gains of 1,000 feet (about 300 m) or less even on a full-day outing in good snow conditions and good weather. If a "full day" is defined by

daylight, then the number of hours available for travel during winter months may be extremely limited. On shorter days and/or in difficult snow or adverse weather, a trip of even half this distance may not be easy. It is difficult to be precise since so much depends upon conditions and the efficiency with which the group is able to break and pack their trail. "Moderate" day trips might double these figures. Any snowshoe trip covering more than 8 miles (12.9 km) or 3,000 vertical feet (914 m) probably ought to be called "difficult."

"Beginning" trips are designed to meet the needs of those who haven't snowshoed before. Objectives "A" and "B," and at least the essence of Objectives "C" and "D" are appropriate for beginning trips, in addition to the objectives for beginning hiking. "Intermediate" outing participants may be expected to meet Objectives "C," "D," and "E," while Objective "F" may not be attained until the participant has substantial experience at the intermediate or "advanced" level. Most of the objectives for hiking are also appropriate at the intermediate or advanced level of snowshoeing.

Objectives. Any of the objectives suggested earlier for hiking may be appropriate for outings on snowshoes. Other objectives specific to snowshoeing are that the participant will be able to:

A. Learn how to put on and use at least one type of snowshoe and binding combination. This includes maintenance, adjustment, and repair in the field;

B. Understand clothing and equipment requirements specific to snowshoeing and winter travel;

C. Understand the recognition, treatment, and prevention of hypothermia, frostbite, and other cold-related conditions;

D. Understand basic avalanche theory, avalanche-hazard estimation, route selection in snow-covered terrain, and avalanche rescue in backcountry settings;

E. Understand the various types of snowshoes and bindings that are available, and be able to select the appropriate types for any specified combination of terrain, snow conditions, and intended use;

F. Be able to travel efficiently on snowshoes (smoothly and with minimal energy) and be able to kick steps, traverse, stem turn, kick turn, and descend using good technique in a wide range of snow conditions.

Clothing and Equipment

See Figure 17.6.

Leadership Qualifications

The leader should possess at least the qualifications suggested for hiking, plus specific snowshoeing and winter-travel skills and experience.

Specifically, the leader should have:

A. Substantial experience on snowshoes, preferably on snow conditions and in terrain similar to that of the intended site;

B. Training and competence in estimating avalanche and other snow-structure hazards, selecting safe routes, and avalanche rescue under backcountry conditions;

C. Familiarity with the intended site and route sufficient to allow safe and effective utilization of the resource under winter conditions. Knowledge of an area under summer conditions may not be adequate;

D. An understanding of snowshoe and binding types sufficient to assist participants in using, maintaining, and repairing their equipment;

E. An understanding of the recognition, treatment, and prevention of hypothermia, frostbite, and other cold-related injuries.

Leadership Ratios

The risks of travel in winter are somewhat higher than in summer. Travel is more difficult, slips and falls more likely, and a variety of snow-related hazards may exist. Visibility is impaired by bad weather, and snow muffles sounds which impairs verbal communication and the range of audible signals. In addition, participants may be distracted or less attentive than when basking in summer warmth. Also, any mishap that occurs may have far more serious consequences than in the summer due to decreased survival times and protracted search and rescue times.

These considerations must be kept in mind when establishing minimum leader ratios. While one leader might conduct a dozen people on a short tour near a lodge or ski area, backcountry travel requires at least two leaders per group, with a normal limit of six participants per leader.

Suggested Formats

By our definition, snowshoeing is a single-day activity. Most of what has been said about hiking, applies to snowshoeing, but pre-trip meetings should be extended in length or number to allow thorough pre-outing discussions of snow and cold-related safety topics.

Recommended Reading

Prater, G. (1988). *Snowshoeing (3rd ed.)*. Seattle, WA: The Mountaineers.

FIGURE 17.6   Suggested Minimum Gear Requirements for Snowshoeing

INDIVIDUAL GEAR

Required Items (In addition to requirements for hiking):

1. **Snowshoes and bindings** (Type and fit specified by the instructor)
2. **Warm boots** (There are advocates of everything from high-top moccasins to mountaineering boots. Ski boots, snowmobile boots, and shoe-pacs are also popular.)
3. **Extra insulation** (Two layers of wool or better for the legs and the top, two pairs of gloves or mittens, and a total top insulation of at least 1 inch (2.5 cm) should be adequate in most climates, though local adjustments will be necessary.)
4. **Gaiters** (High type is preferable)

Optional Items (None beyond those for hiking)

GROUP GEAR

Required Items (In addition to the requirements for hiking):

1. **Shovels** (Always useful for making emergency shelters and invaluable in avalanche rescue. A ratio of one portable snow shovel per four participants is probably sufficient for most purposes.)
2. **Avalanche probes, cords or beacons** (As needed)
3. **Repair items for snowshoes** (Cord and whatever pieces, parts, and tools may be necessary in the event of breakage)
4. **Snowshoe repair kit** (Tools, tape, screws or bolts, cord, etc., sufficient to adjust, maintain and repair the types of snowshoes and poles to be used on the outing.)

Optional Items (None beyond those of hiking, although attention should be paid to the greater importance of insulating pads, insulation, and strong, weatherpoof shelter.)

LEADER GEAR

Required Items:

1. Items 1-5 on the list for hiking leaders
2. Items 1 and 5 on the list for backpacking leaders
3. Items 1-2 on the list for snowcamping leaders

Optional Items:

1. Items 2-4 on the list for backpacking leaders are appropriate for overnight trips.

NOTE:
The above suggestions are for day trips only, and do not include gear for overnight travel. For overnight trips, see the gear lists for snowcamping.

Backcountry Skiing

Description

Skiing probably began when early users of snowshoes discovered that a narrow and relatively smooth "snowshoe" would slide, allowing faster travel at least on downward sloping surfaces. The first illustrated descriptions, from the 1600s, show the use of two skis, one long "glider" and one short "pusher" used in conjunction with a single staff or pole for propulsion and balance. Today, there are many specialized forms of skiing, usually grouped into two major categories, alpine and nordic. Sometimes called "downhill" skiing, alpine skiing employs techniques and equipment for negotiating steep slopes, while nordic skiing employs techniques and equipment for travel across rolling or gentle terrain, thus coining the popular term "cross-country" (or "XC") skiing.

There are many highly specialized activities within each major category. Within the realm of alpine skiing are such specialties as recreational lift skiing, helicopter skiing, slalom, giant slalom, and downhill racing. Some of the popular nordic specialties are cross-country skiing in groomed tracks, cross-country skiing on roads and trails, cross-country racing, ski-jumping, cross-country downhill skiing, ski-touring, and ski-mountaineering. If cross-country trail skiing is the winter equivalent of hiking, then ski-touring is the winter equivalent of backpacking. Some of the specialties clearly contain elements of both alpine and nordic skiing. Examples of this are cross-country downhill, a sport of rapidly increasing popularity wherein skiers use nordic equipment on steep slopes, often sharing the slopes and lifts with alpine skiers, and ski-mountaineering, wherein modified alpine gear and technique are used by mountaineers on winter and spring climbs.

We have used the term "backcountry" skiing due to the fact that our focus is on the realm outside of developed ski areas. We acknowledge, however, that "backcountry" conditions may prevail in parts of some ski areas, and that skiers sometimes traverse "developed" and "backcountry" realms in a single outing, and sometimes in a single run. Backcountry skiers may employ any combination of alpine and nordic gear and technique. During the last two decades, as developed ski areas have become increasingly crowded and costly, the number of participants in backcountry skiing has increased disproportionately. The trend appears to be continuing, as disgruntled lift skiers seek a less crowded and costly alternative to developed sites and as hikers and backpackers seek exercise, an escape from urban pressures, and closeness to the natural world during the snowy months.

Hazards and Risks

It is difficult to make a general statement about the safety of backpacking skiing because of the wide range of activities encompassed by this term. Cross-country skiing on moderate-to-flat terrain is inherently quite safe. Speeds tend to be low, and the lightweight, flexible gear make fall-related injuries unlikely. Certainly, track skiing in and around ski areas is far safer by the hour than lift serviced alpine skiing. On the other hand, ski-tourers and ski-mountaineers may be subject to significant danger from avalanches and other snow- and ice-related hazards, from the perils of getting lost, and from injury due to the greater dangers of skiing with packs on ungroomed surfaces. Nordic downhillers face risks similar to those of alpine skiers, making this a relatively high-risk activity in terms of fractures, sprains, and strains. The consequences of such injuries are substantially controlled, however, when the activity takes place within alpine ski areas and resorts due to the availability of ski-patrol services. While the risks of mishap in backcountry skiing are relatively low, the consequences can be serious due to the effect of cold weather, less daylight and greater difficulty for searchers which results in slower and more difficult rescue.

Environmental and Social Impacts

While developed ski areas have wreaked havoc on countless hillsides worldwide, backcountry skiing causes relatively little serious environmental impact. Since the terrain is somewhat protected by snow, direct damage to vegetation and soils is minimal. There are some potential impacts, however, which have been discussed earlier in the context of hiking and snowshoeing. Ski-tourers and ski-mountaineers may wish to reread the "Environmental and Social Impacts" section of the earlier discussions of backpacking, snowcamping, and mountaineering.

Resource Requirements

If there's snow, nordic skiing is at least a possibility. Some basic rules of thumb are that it takes about 2 inches (5 cm) of snow to "ski" a lawn or golf course, a foot (30 cm) of snow to ski roads (especially unpaved roads), 2 feet (60 cm or so) of snow to ski most hiking trails, and 3 feet (90 cm or so) of snow to ski off-trail in most terrain. Clearly, it is necessary to assess each site on its own; these figures assume fairly dense snow—not fluff.

Cross-country skiers often enjoy skiing in the prepared tracks found in or near many alpine ski areas and winter resorts. Fees are usually charged to use these tracks, which are often scoffed at by skiers until they try them once. In fact, a well set track is a delight to ski on and can greatly improve technique for even the most hardened backcountry skier. Nordic downhillers also tend to favor alpine ski areas since groomed slopes, like prepared tracks, speed the learning process. Ski lifts are a real asset once basic skills have been mastered; with marked roads, tracks, or routes on mixed terrain, one can ski many miles without having to walk uphill.

The popularity of nordic skiing has resulted in an abundance of maps, guides, and other information on facilities and resources in most areas. Ski shops, and public and private land-management offices can usually provide these materials, and local advice and expertise is often available from clubs, the outdoor programs of recreation departments and schools, and private-sector ski schools.

Levels and Objectives

Levels. The terms "easy," "moderate," and "difficult" apply to backcountry ski-touring or ski-mountaineering outings but have little application to activities within developed areas, where physical stress can usually be adjusted to meet the needs of individuals, and where technique rather than strength or endurance are required. An "easy" ski tour rarely involves more than three or four miles (4.8 or 6.4 km) of skiing, with elevation gains of less than 1,000 feet (about 300 m). Ski ability and ski conditions, however, can vary this considerably. "Moderate" outings may double these limits, and any outing covering more than eight miles (13 km) or 2,000 vertical feet (about 600 m), is usually best described as "difficult" unless the route and conditions are exceptionally favorable or the participants are exceptionally fit and skilled.

The terms "beginning," "intermediate," and "advanced" are usually applied to technique-oriented classes. "Beginning" outings typically address the needs of those, who haven't skied before, haven't skied on nordic gear even though experience has been gained on alpine gear, or who have limited nordic experience. The following topics, maneuvers, or techniques are generally considered appropriate for beginning courses. All might be included in a two-day format, while only selected portions of the progression should be attempted in more limited blocks of time:

> Equipment review
> Safety discussion
> Tip paddle turn
> Tail paddle turn
> Sidestep
> Kick turn
> Tip crossover turn
> Tail crossover turn
> Falling
> Getting up
> Walking
> Basic diagonal stride
> One-Step
> Uphill stride
> Herringbone

Straight running
Step turn
Single plow
Snowplow
Snowplow turn
Traverse
Stem turn
Basic telemark turn
Double poling

"Intermediate" outings typically involve a review of beginning maneuvers, followed by instruction in part or all of the following maneuvers:

Advanced diagonal stride
Skating
Pole use
Traverse sidestep
Sideslip
Forward sideslip
Unweighting
Uphill christie
Stem christie
Parallel turns
Telemark turns

"Advanced" outings also typically begin with review of the basics, then focus on parallel and/or advanced telemark turns, or on some selected interest such as specialized turns, deep snow, ice, crust and crud skiing, skiing with packs, or skiing steep terrain and/or refinement of skating and track techniques.

While the terms "easy" and "beginner" are useful and fairly well-understood by most skiers and potential skiers, there is often confusion over what constitutes an "intermediate" or "advanced" level of competence. It is usually best to combine the term with a statement or two about the skills people need before participation. For example, the statement—"An intermediate level outing for those who can do basic snowplow turns"—helps clarify what is required and offered.

Backcountry outings are sometimes described by a combination of difficulty level and prerequisite skiing ability. This provides a range from "easy" trips for "beginners" to "difficult" trips for skiers with "advanced" skills.

Objectives. Some skiing outings have very specific objectives. An example is a nordic downhill class which might focus on one specific aspect of the sport, such as deep snow skiing or a particular turn. Ski-touring and ski-mountaineering outings may have very broad objectives similar to those of hiking, backpacking, snowcamping, or mountaineering. Thus, the suggested objectives for these activities should be reviewed carefully.

Typical objectives for skills-oriented cross-country and nordic-downhill classes are that the participant will be able to:

A. Enjoy the experience and want to pursue the activity further;

B. Gain a fitness and an awareness of the fitness requirements of the activity;

C. Develop an awareness of the hazards inherent in the activity and of ways of reducing these risks. This includes hazards related to cold and to avalanches;

D. Understand the clothing and equipment requirements of the sport, including selection, maintenance, and repair;

E. Be able to identify potential resources and facilities for the activity. This includes an awareness of managing agencies or landholder policies and regulations;

F. Improve in skiing ability. This objective is often expressed in terms of specific skills or maneuvers. Specification is useful in certain educational settings wherein grading is based upon attainment of objectives, and, in most cases, can help clarify leader and participant expectations with regard to course direction and content;

G. Develop an awareness of and sensitivity to the environment. (This objective is too often forgotten in skills-oriented classes!)

Typical objectives of ski-touring and ski-mountaineering outings include, in addition to those suggested above, that the participant will be able to:

A. Be able to navigate under winter conditions, which includes an ability to use maps and compasses effectively;

B. Be able to identify potential sites for emergency bivouacs, and construct adequate shelters using the minimal equipment carried;

C. Be aware of the capabilities and limitations of local SAR units under winter conditions;

D. Acquire the skills and knowledge necessary to independently plan and carry out a successful ski-touring or ski-mountaineering day outing.

Clothing and Equipment

Specific gear requirements for nordic skiing depend upon the activity and setting. When the activity will take place entirely within the confines of a ski area or resort and on well-marked trails that form a closed and limited system, it is sometimes reasonable to ski without survival equipment, just as alpine skiers do. In this case, gear requirements depend solely on the type of skiing to be done. Those who travel outside of developed areas need additional gear for the same reasons that hikers do, and have some special needs as well. First, it is easy to get lost while ski touring, despite the popular myth that one can always turn around and follow the tracks back. Whoever invented that idea apparently never tried to follow tracks on an icy or wind-packed surface, through a maze left by others, or after a half-hour of windblown new snow! It is not only easy to get lost; the consequences are far more serious when it does occur. Winter days are short; temperatures are low; and SAR response times are lengthened. Still another concern is the increased likelihood of being forced to spend an unplanned night out due to injury or gear failure. A relatively minor injury can also make skiing difficult or impossible. Breaking a ski or binding or even a ski pole can slow progress to a snail's pace—a cold snail's pace. Still another possibility is reduced speed due to such delights as ice, breakable crusts, and deep, wet "mashed potato" snow.

Skis, boots, and poles are constantly evolving, with new models on the market every year. Participants are often confused by the vast array of options and combinations, and all too often buy before they understand their needs. Encourage participants to borrow and use rental gear, and to make consumer education a part of every course. Enjoyment of the sport can be enhanced by carefully matching gear to the particular needs of each participant. Factors to consider include the type(s) of activity, current and projected skill level, aggressiveness, physical strength, and weight, as well as the amount of money the individual can afford to spend.

From a top view, skis vary from slightly "boat"-shaped to slightly "hourglass"-shaped. This shape is called "sidecut," and it is one of the factors that determines how easily the ski turns. Boat-shaped skis and skis with parallel side walls tend to stay in tracks and run straight, while skis with a lot of sidecut (hourglass shapes) tend to turn more easily. Good skiers can make any type of ski go straight or turn, but shape does make a difference, especially for beginners trying to learn and for experts pushing the limits.

Ski length is also an important and often misunderstood dimension, and instructors would do well to pay careful attention to the length of participants' skis—especially in advance of outings when adjustments can be made. While it is true, in a limited sense, that short skis are easier to turn than long ones, much more is involved. Ease of turning is also affected by the shape of the ski, its flex pattern, torsional rigidity, bottom-surface qualities, and other factors.

Ski length is too often determined solely by the height of the skier. While most ski shops have charts relating height to ski length, the skier's total weight is in fact the issue. A slender or overweight person or anyone who will be carrying a large pack, and fitted by using standard charts, may be given skis too short or long. Either error can seriously impair progress and enjoyment. Skis function best when they are loaded or pressed onto the snow with the correct amount of force, and that force is determined by the weight of the skis, the pack, and the skier's strength and technique. Some shops have weight charts, but even these must be used carefully.

A good test that has become popular in recent years is to have the skier stand squarely on both skis on a smooth, perfectly flat surface. In this condition, cross-country or touring skis should not touch the floor for at least 2 feet (60 cm) in the region just ahead of and behind the foot when both skis are weighted equally. Test this by slipping a small card or piece of paper back and forth between the ski and the floor. As a rule, the better, stronger skiers will want more clearance to insure they'll glide on tip and tail surfaces, not the surface underfoot. No-wax skis, in general, should be fitted with more clearance. No-wax skis that are too short or not stiff enough drag which produces friction and noise. There is also a second part to the test: Have the person put all his/her weight on one ski to see if it can be depressed enough to grab the piece of paper. Beginners should be able to do this just by standing still, while experts may want to find a ski requiring a slight downward push, especially if a pack will be carried. The "paper test," as it's commonly known, doesn't apply to skis designed strictly for downhill skiing since there is no need to maintain a "wax pocket" on such skis.

To wax or not to wax? This is an area of rapidly evolving technology wherein any specific recommendations would be quickly out of date. Without a doubt, waxed skis are still delightful to use in temperatures below about 25°F (approximately -4°C). On the other hand, the patterns of no-wax ski bottoms ensure pleasant skiing at almost any temperature with wax required only on the tip and tail to enhance glide. Nevertheless, there are plenty of "purists" who decry the no-wax bases as being too "high-tech" while they fumble through tubes and sticks of complex compounds developed by the chemical industry to deal with the myriad texture and temperature conditions of the snow surface. Instructors should discuss and if possible, demonstrate the virtues of both systems, but they should consider using no-wax skis for beginning classes and for any other class or outing where temperatures will hover near the freezing mark. Under these conditions, waxing may consume a substantial amount of time. It is a valuable skill, but having to devote a lot of time to the process can be frustrating for those who would prefer to be skiing.

The value of metal edges is often debated among nordic skiers. Metal edges grip better on very hard surfaces and may be essential on truly icy slopes, and most nordic downhillers and ski-mountaineers prefer them since such conditions

are common in alpine ski areas and on the high peaks. Even in these areas, however, skis without metal edges work perfectly well most of the time, and ski-tourers and cross-country skiers rarely need them. When conditions are so icy that metal edges are really essential, it's probably best to pop the skis off and walk! Metal edges are expensive, add to maintenance problems, add weight, modify flex patterns, mutilate the opposite ski, chop-up ski poles, and can be dangerous in a fall. Any instructor can recall having students ski over his/her skis and if the student's skis had metal edges can still point out the grooves. It's also worth noting that even the most skilled instructor will eventually hit a participant's ski or pole, and the damage (and potential obligation) will be far greater if the instructor uses metal edges.

Bindings are important as well, and should be suited to the activity. As with skis, almost any type can be used, but maximal enjoyment depends upon a good match of equipment. Narrow racing or track-type binding systems are ideal for use with light boots and shoes in tracks and for gentle turns in good conditions. There are several very stable, heavy duty types designed for use with substantial boots on backcountry trails and in untracked off-trail areas, as well as for turning on downhill runs. Either type of binding can be used for either set of activities, though with less ease and efficiency. Beginners usually prefer the relatively stable options until enough confidence has been developed to move to the narrower binding/boot combinations. Advanced skiers prefer light gear for track skiing, and wider bindings and torsionally stiff boots for backcountry use. Boots are extremely important. Participants who will be renting should be given clear directions for fitting them, how to check for torsional rigidity and proper fit in the bindings, and how to contact the heel plate or "pop-up."

Ski poles vary in length, basket design, and grip style. Racers and cross-country track skiers favor relatively long poles (at least a tight fit in the armpit is a common measure), and small, sometimes wedge or "half-moon" baskets. Ski-tourers usually prefer slightly shorter poles with full, round baskets, while nordic downhillers often use the shorter alpine style. Grip and strap design is also very important and often overlooked. Efficient technique depends, in part, upon an ability to relax the hand without losing control of the pole, and this requires adjustable straps and at least an inch or so (two to three cm) of pole top to protrude above the point where the strap enters it. Beginning participants often come to an outing with poles that don't have this "top knob," in which case adhesive tape can be used to bind down the top part of the strap.

Waxes are another essential common to all types of skiing. Even when "no-wax" skis are used, "running," "glide," or "speed" waxes are needed to provide fast tip and tail gliding surfaces. Also useful for reducing snow build-up on the kicker surfaces of no-wax skis, wax kits can be complex sets of waxes and klisters or simplified systems using only two or three, waxes or waxes and klisters.

There is much more to be said about skis, boots, and poles, and every season brings advances in technology and technique. It's difficult to stay abreast of every new advance while maintaining a sense of perspective on the relationship between skiing and ski equipment. On one hand, matching individuals with the best possible types of ski gear for a given activity can make a big difference in terms of ease of learning and avoidance of frustration. On the other hand, it's very easy to become overly concerned about gear. Almost any type of skiing can be done on almost any type of gear. The importance of having the equipment well-matched to the activity increases when skill development is the central focus of an outing. (See Figures 17.7 a-b, pages 394-395.)

Leadership Qualifications

Backcountry skiing is an immensely varied realm. The reader should review the suggested qualifications of hiking leaders, as all are appropriate for leaders or instructors in backcountry skiing.

The reader should also review the suggested qualifications for snowcamping and/or mountaineering leaders if these activities may be part of the program. Additional attributes include:

A. Familiarity with the techniques to be taught, including an ability to perform the maneuvers or skills with a high degree of expertise, since modeling is the key to instruction, and a thorough understanding of the physical and biomechanical aspects of the maneuvers;

B. A knowledge of both modeling and analytical approaches to instruction. This includes a thorough understanding of effective progressions, an ability to identify errors, and an ability to formulate constructive positive comments and strategies leading to improvements in participant skill levels. Leaders should also know how to recognize and to minimize the effects of cold weather and anxiety on the teaching process;

C. An understanding of ski clothing and equipment, including waxing, skis, bindings, boot and pole design, function, maintenance, and repair;

D. An understanding of cold-related trauma, including the recognition, treatment, and prevention of hypothermia and frostbite;

E. An understanding of avalanche and other snow and ice hazards, including rescue techniques and methods of reducing risks.

Leadership Ratios

Cross-country and nordic-downhill instruction within or very near developed areas often requires only one leader for each group. In such closed and relatively protected areas, the leader is "seconded" by the ski patrol. Additional leaders or assistants can be useful, however, as ski instruction is best performed in small groups. A group of three or four students is probably ideal, allowing plenty of individual attention while moderating the stress on each person. On the other hand, group control becomes difficult and individual attention inadequate if group size exceeds about ten participants. Modeling is extremely important and requires frequent reinforcement of images, so the instructor usually needs to demonstrate frequently. If demonstrations follow every third student's attempt at a maneuver, the instructor will be performing at a pace near the limits of his/her endurance in a class of nine.

**FIGURE 17.7a   Suggested Minimum Gear Requirements
for Backcountry Skiing**

INDIVIDUAL GEAR

Required Items (In addition to requirements for hiking):

1. **Ski boots and poles**
2. **Additional insulation** (Extra clothing beyond the requirements for hiking
   sufficient to allow the skier to survive an unplanned night out even if one layer
   is soaked by rain or sweat; this usually requires two layers of light-to-moderate
   thickness for both torso and legs, plus a combination of torso-insulating layers
   such as vests or parkas totalling more than an inch (2.5 cm) in thickness and
   two pairs of gloves or mittens.)
3. **Basic tool kit for skis** (Screwdriver, etc., plus basic wax kit and scraper)

Optional Items:

1. **Avalanche cords or beacons** (May be required; useless without training)
2. **Extra gloves and mittens**
3. **Insulating pad** (Small pad, or better, a 2/3 length pad; far superior to bough
   beds in survival situations, required if boughs unavailable, and easier on
   ecosystem)
4. **Extra batteries** (Alkaline, lithium, or other cold-resistant types)
5. **Climbing skins** (Many ski-mountaineers and some ski-tourers prefer
   "climbers" to waxes when using waxing skis in certain types of snow and terrain.)
6. **Pack cover** (Almost essential for keeping gear dry in rain or very wet snow,
   and always handy. Large plastic bags can be used, though fitted covers of
   coated nylon are preferable.)
7. **Sun hat** (Preferably with visor or brim)

GROUP GEAR

Required Items:

1. **Tool kit** (Screwdrivers, extra screws, binding and pole parts including at least
   one basket, tape, scrapers, files, and other maintenance-and-repair items)
2. **Insulating pads** (At least one 2/3 length pad for every two or three people
   unless carried by individuals)
3. **Sleeping bags or half bag** (Essential in the event an injured person must be
   stabilized until SAR assistance can be obtained)
4. **Tarp or small tent** (Adequate to provide shelter for an injured person and one
   to two attendants; tarps are usually more versatile. Don't forget sufficient cord
   to set up the tarp!)
5. **Stove, fuel, and pot** (In a survival situation, a portable backpacking-type or
   mountaineering-type stove with plenty of fuel and at least a two-liter container
   can provide drinking water and water for hot-water bottles.)
6. **Shovels** (One for every four people, for avalanche rescue and to aid in shelter
   construction in unplanned bivouacs.)

**FIGURE 17.7b   Suggested Minimum Gear Requirements
for Backcountry Skiing (continued)**

Group Required Items (continued):

7. **Plastic flagging** (To mark routes in the event of emergencies; ski tracks cannot be relied upon)
8. **First-aid kit** (Substantial kit; see first-aid section)

Optional Items:

1. **Avalanche probes** (May be required; should be carried if avalanche danger exists, at a ratio of at least one 6-foot (2 m) or longer probe per participant. In situations where substantial avalanche danger exists, beacons or at least cords should be carried and used by all participants. Training in avalanche rescue is essential for this equipment to be of value.)
2. **Extra food** (A supply of high-energy foods can be very helpful, at least in terms of maintaining positive attitudes in emergency bivouacs and unexpectedly extended outings.)
3. **Sled or pulk** (This can be useful for hauling group gear and, if large enough for use as a rescue sled can be a great asset in the event of an injury.)

LEADER GEAR

Required Items:

1. Items 1-5 on the list for hiking leaders
2. Items 1 and 5 on the list for backpacking leaders
3. Items 1-3 on the list for snowcamping leaders

Optional Items:

1. Items 2-4 on the list for backpacking leaders are appropriate for overnight trips.

NOTE:
The above suggestions are for day trips only, and do not include gear for overnight travel. For extended ski tours or ski-mountaineering outings, consult the backpacking, snowcamping, and mountaineering lists.

On backcountry cross-country routes or on ski-touring or ski-mountaineering outings, a second leader or assistant is necessary for the safety reasons expressed in earlier discussions of hiking and backpacking. Groups of more than a dozen can be awkward since safety and the inherent variability of skiing paces extends the distance between skiers on a trail. Group control is often more difficult than in backpacking, while the consequences of inadequate control are often more severe. Two leaders can supervise no more than ten to twelve skiers under most circumstances. Minimum requirements for these activities should thus be two leaders for up to twelve participants, plus an additional leader or qualified assistant for each additional unit of up to six participants.

Suggested Formats

Cross-country and nordic-downhill classes are often taught as a series of short lessons. A one-and-a-half-hour format seems to be ideal for periods of direct instruction since attention spans, limits of endurance, and the stresses of winter weather make longer sessions relatively unproductive. A full-day format involving two one-and-a-half-hour segments separated by breaks for practice and lunch fills most of the available daylight in midwinter and pushes the patience and interest limits of the most earnest student. The use of one-hour teaching segments is not recommended unless utilized in sequence form during a day. Such short sessions actually provide only about fifty minutes of instructional time, and the initial session may be largely consumed by attempts to assess the skills of participants. Whenever the total time is limited, session objectives should be narrowed appropriately; it's far better to make substantial progress on a small point than to overwhelm and frustrate participants with unrealistic and unattainable expectations.

Cross-country outings typically involve fewer hours of travel than equivalent summer activities because of shorter days. Except for ideal gentle downhill runs well within the ability of all participants, travel rates will also be much less than for hiking. While it often feels as though skiing is faster than walking, this is rarely the case.

Overnight ski tours usually involve extra distances and elevation gains so such outings often require pre-dawn starts and late-night returns.

Pre-trip meetings are valuable for any ski outing. Beyond the values of these meetings discussed for hiking, backpacking, and other activities, they can provide opportunities to discuss and explain gear requirements and teach technique. Very substantial improvement in skills can result from studying films and videotapes of skiers demonstrating techniques. Pre-trip meetings should occur far enough in advance of the outing to allow participants to arrange for rentals or to borrow ski gear. One session two weeks prior to the outing and one session just a few days prior to the outing works well.

Recommended Reading

Abraham, H. (1980). *Teaching concepts ATM.* Boulder, CO: Professional Ski Instructors of America.

Bein, V. (1982). *Mountain skiing.* Seattle, WA: The Mountaineers.

Brady, M. (1979). *Cross-country skiing.* Seattle, WA: The Mountaineers.

Gillette, N. (1979). *Cross-country ski gear.* Seattle, WA: The Mountaineers.

PSIA Board of Directors. (1966). *The official American ski technique.* Boulder, CO: Professional Ski Instructors of America.

PSIA Steering Committee. (1989). *Teaching nordic.* Boulder, CO: Professional Ski Instructors of America.

Tejada-Flores, L. (1981). *Backcountry skiing.* San Francisco, CA: Sierra Club Books.

Watters, R. (1979). *Ski camping.* Moscow, ID: Solstice Press.

Bike Touring

Description

Bike touring is a popular activity encompassing everything from short day trips to extended world tours. Tourists pack their gear, from basic tools and a picnic lunch to a complete repair-and-maintenance kit and camping equipment, in panniers (special bags suspended from racks over handlebars and wheels). Some tourists venture off paved roads, often using bikes with reinforced frames and wider tires, or specifically designed "mountain bikes."

Bike touring offers many of the benefits of wilderness and backcountry activities, and yet with the exception of some mountain trail biking, most activity takes place in relatively close proximity to civilization. As a result, the bike tourist is seldom deprived of the amenities of civilization for more than a few hours at a time.

By the broadest definition, just about everyone has at one time or another gone on a bike tour—that is, if packing up a picnic lunch and riding across town to the park is accepted as "touring." On the other hand, full-blown modern bike touring, with panniers stuffed and cycle shoes in toe clips, has a relatively limited appeal. Even more than nordic skiing, bike touring has an image of strenuousness. This is unfortunate and generally inaccurate since, as in any outdoor pursuit, the pace is usually self-determined and can be as leisurely as desired. Most devotees of bike touring are fit and relatively young, and, like participants in wilderness and backcountry pursuits, tend to be well-educated and/or well-off financially. One clue to the number of potential clients for a bike-touring program, aside from the above demographic considerations, is the abundance of bicycle shops in the community. Many of the bicycles sold for general commuting and recreation are adequate for at least beginning touring, so people with such bikes are at least over the primary hurdle of initial purchase.

Bicycling is currently experiencing a wave of popularity, probably sustained in part by recent high levels of interest in general fitness. This should result in an expansion of interest in touring as some bike owners begin to push the limits of the sport.

Hazards and Risks

If asked to list "high risk" outdoor activities, most people wouldn't think of bike touring, at least not before a long list of such activities as skiing or climbing. In fact, bike touring probably ought to be included at or near the top. Even at modest speeds, equipment failure, an unexpected chuckhole, grating, rock, slippery spot, or an error in jugdement can send the pedaler over the handlebars or into a ditch. Worse yet, most tourists share the road with motor vehicles, and collisions, even grazing sideswipes, can be devastating.

Careful attention to safety rules and procedures, the use of high-visibility clothing, gear, and/or flags, and helmets can all help reduce the risk of accident and injury. At best, however, an element of risk remains since falls cannot be completely eliminated, and the most cautious biker is subject to danger caused by careless drivers. On the positive side, such incidents don't occur often, and professional care and equipment is often accessible within minutes (in cities) or within an hour or so on most country roads. Nevertheless, the overall chance of serious injury or death is probably higher for bike touring than for any other outdoor pursuit unless the activity is very carefully controlled and all applicable safety measures employed.

Environmental and Social Impacts

Bike touring is one of the only land-based outdoor pursuit activities that does not necessarily take place in wilderness or backcountry areas. Since bicyclists usually stay on roads and camp in developed campsites or at other relatively durable sites, there is little potential for damage to backcountry areas. In fact, since bike tourers are often also hikers and backpackers, a decision to go biking is likely to be made at the expense of taking a hike or an overnight trip into the backcountry, and thus reduces the impact on more fragile resources.

Nevertheless, there are instances of rather serious impact due to the increasing popularity of "mountain biking." Despite the efforts of land managers, many hiking trails and some off-trail areas have been extensively damaged by excessive use by mountain bikers. Some soil and vegetation types are highly vulnerable to rutting and other effects of wheeled vehicles. The result is not unlike the damage caused by excessive horse use, in particular, deep mires of mud caused by use during periods when the soil is excessively dry or damp. The loosening of soil speeds erosion and loss of vegetation unless the managers can afford the usually costly process of graveling, or otherwise hardening, the route.

There are social consequences of bicycle use as well. Hikers and other users of trails damaged by bikers do not appreciate either the sights or the inconvenience of mudholes and ruts. Cyclists on pavement also cause unnecessary annoyance and sometimes risk to motorists, when they fail to adhere to safe and customary traffic regulations. Whether through ignorance or lack of consideration, many bikers ignore basic rules of the road, including stop signs. Both adverse social effects are particularly unfortunate as they could be avoided entirely by the exercise of common sense and consideration. Leaders of biking courses or outings have an excellent opportunity to shed light on these issues, demonstrate considerate biking, and guide participants in the development of constructive behaviors.

Resource Requirements

Most bike tourists need access to reasonably smooth paths or roads. It's most convenient to begin from town or wherever the program would normally meet, though this isn't necessary if vans, pickups, or other transportation can be used to carry tourists and bikes to the starting point. Traffic safety and local regulations may preclude the use of certain roads and highways. On the other hand, many communities have developed extensive pathways primarily for bicyclists, and, in some areas special bike lanes have been designated. For many areas, guidebooks are also available which show recommended touring routes. These can be especially valuable when initially investigating areas with extensive urban and rural road systems since checking out all of the possibilities can be a formidable task.

In many areas, land managers can provide detailed maps of logging roads and other secondary roadways that can provide excellent opportunities for mountain biking.

Levels and Objectives

Levels. Like hiking or backpacking, bike touring can proceed at almost any pace, so virtually any distance or type of terrain can be negotiated with ease, given enough time. It is, however, convenient when describing outings to assign adjectives such as "easy," "moderate," or "difficult." If a full-day tour is planned, it may well be possible to include six to eight hours or more of riding. Beginners, however, will find so much time "in the saddle" tiring and likely to result in sore limbs and seat. Since most programs deal with beginners, three hours or so of actual riding should be considered maximal for an "easy" tour, and distances on flat roads should rarely exceed 30 miles (about 50 km). Hills, rough pavement, head winds, foul weather, or substantial gear loads may substantially reduce these limits. A "moderate" tour may involve twice as much distance and four to six hours of riding, while any tour covering more than 60 miles (about 100 km) should be called "difficult"—especially if the loads are heavy and/or the route is anything less than ideal.

Objectives "A" through "D" or "E" are usually appropriate for "beginning" classes, while "intermediate" classes typically reinforce objectives "D" and "E" and move participants toward Objectives "F," "G,", and "H." "Advanced" classes often focus on Objective "I." At every level, considerable review is usually necessary, and integration of all basic skills should accompany attempts to attain more objectives.

Objectives. As in any other outdoor pursuit, there are many inherent benefits which may or may not be specifically addressed in a list of objectives. Typical objectives specific to bike touring are that the participant will be able to:

A. Enjoy the experience and want to pursue the activity further;

B. Gain an awareness of the fitness requirements of bike touring;

C. Understand the hazards inherent in bike touring and basic safety procedures to reduce the chance of accidents or injuries;

D. Understand the equipment and clothing requirements of bike touring. This includes the selection, maintenance, and repair of bicycles and related gear;

E. Develop skills in bike riding and touring, allowing more efficient, comfortable, and safe travel by bicycle;

F. Understand sufficient first aid and emergency care to stabilize injuries until professional assistance can be obtained;

G. Be aware of the resources available for bike touring in the area;

H. Acquire the knowledge and skills necessary to independently plan and carry out a successful bike-touring day outing;

I. Acquire the knowledge and skills necessary to independently plan and carry out a successful bike tour involving overnight camping.

Clothing and Equipment

The gear requirements for bike touring depend upon the length (in time and in miles) of the trip, where it will take place, the season and likely weather, and the tourists' willingness to face being stranded by equipment failure. For the purposes of this list, assume that the outing consists of a long full day, covering perhaps 50 miles (80 km) on fairly remote rural roads. Gear requirements might be less in urban areas, but will be greatly increased if overnight camping is planned, in which case the backpacking list should be reviewed for appropriate items. (See Figures 17.8 a -b, pages 400-401.)

Leader Qualifications

Most bike-touring programs either include overnight camping or focus on the skills necessary to begin this type of touring. Therefore, leaders and instructors usually need skills and experience in camping, especially bike tour camping, as well as substantial skill and experience in riding, bicycle maintenance, and repair. Any bike-touring leader should have at least Attributes A through F suggested for hiking leaders and:

A. A willingness and ability to exercise control over the actions of the group in conformance with the standards and policies of the employer, highway and traffic safety rules, and any other applicable policies, rules, or laws. This includes an ability to organize the group, employing leader-caboose or other appropriate control situations effectively in any reasonably foreseeable weather and traffic conditions while maintaining an awareness of the well-being of all participants at all times;

B. If driving is required by the program, appropriate licenses and a satisfactory driving record;

C. Appropriate first-aid skills. This must include training and experience in long-term care and improvisation if the route includes areas where professional care and emergency equipment are not readily accessible. Leaders should be especially well-versed in hypothermia and hyperthermic conditions and on the importance of hydration and nutritional considerations if the tours will be long or strenuous;

D. An awareness of emergency services available throughout the program area, including procedures for obtaining such assistance in emergencies;

E. Expertise in the skills and techniques of bike riding, including pacing and rhythm;

F. Expertise in touring-bike evaluation, maintenance, and repair;

G. Special skills and experience as needed for the program. This usually includes overnight camping, which requires experience in gear selection, packing, riding with full camping gear, side selection, and camping;

H. Substantial bike-touring experience in the area to be used by the program, or basic familiarity with the area backed by substantial experience under very similar conditions.

Leadership Ratios

The number of leaders required on a tour depends upon the nature of the tour, its setting, and the age and number of the participants. Since most tours operate on or near roads and not distant from "civilization," at least in the form of telephones, the incapacitation of a leader is unlikely to be a serious threat to the security of

**FIGURE 17.8a   Suggested Minimum Gear Requirements
for Bike Touring**

INDIVIDUAL GEAR

Required Items:

1. **Bicycle** (In good repair. There are many aspects of frame, wheel, and component design and construction that affect both comfort and safety. Expensive specialized bicycles are not essential to enjoyable beginning touring. Care should be taken to assess all safety-related aspects of any bicycle prior to a tour.)
2. **Rack(s)** (Racks for the front and/or rear are essential since it's dangerous to carry anything on one's back while riding. Both front and rear racks may be essential for overnight trips involving camping.)
3. **Panniers** (Panniers or other containers that can be carried on the rack are essential for most types of gear. A full set of panniers, including a handlebar bag, may be needed for overnight tours involving camping.)
4. **Helmet** (Investigate each model carefully. Not all available types provide adequate protection.)
5. **A pint (500cc) water bottle** (Or larger plastic bottle is usually adequate)
6. **Small tool kit** (Patch kit, pump, knife, and screwdriver, if not part of group gear)
7. **First-aid kit** (Adequate personal kit to stabilize broken bones, bleeding, and other possible injuries if it isn't carried as group gear)
8. **Protective clothing** (This will vary with locale and season, but may include rain protection, wind protection, and insulation appropriate for the possible weather and temperatures.)
9. **Driver's license and/or other identification** (Required in some areas for operating a bicycle on roadways)
10. **Maps of the area**

Optional Items:

1. **Light and batteries or generator** (Essential if any night riding may be done)
2. **Rear and side reflectors** (Also essential if night riding is possible)
3. **Warning flag** (A bright flag or pennant on a pole is always a good idea and may be especially valuable in rolling terrain.)
4. **Lock and chain** (Unfortunately essential if the bike is to be left unguarded in some parts of the world)
5. **Toe clips and straps** (Very useful and considered essential by some)
6. **Cycling gloves** (A good pair can increase comfort and reduce damage to the hands.)
7. **Cycling shoes** (Proper shoes can increase comfort and efficiency.)
8. **Sunglasses**
9. **Watch**
10. **A trailer** (Some trailers can safely haul enough camping gear for two people!)

FIGURE 17.8b   Suggested Minimum Gear Requirements for Bike Touring (continued)

GROUP GEAR

Required Items:

1. **Small tool kit** (Unless carried by individuals)
2. **First-aid kit** (Unless carried by individuals)

Optional Items:

1. **Full tool kit** (In addition to small tool-kit contents, possible contents include two tire irons, Allen wrenches, adjustable wrench, universal wrench, spoke wrench, spokes, "third hand" free-wheel extractor, chain breaker, assorted nuts and bolts, and a spare tube.)
2. **Warning flag or sign** (In traffic it is sometimes worthwhile to use a bright flag or pennant on a pole and/or a sign warning of bikers ahead to be worn by the last biker in line.)

NOTE:

Overnight camping is often an important part of the touring experience. If camping is planned each tourist will need to carry a sleeping bag, an insulating pad to sleep on, and cup and spoon, and arrange for shared access to shelter (a tarp and ground sheet, or a tent) and cooking gear (a stove, pot, and fuel). Review the backpacking list for other useful items, but bear in mind that unnecessary gear adds complexity, a lot of extra work when climbing hills, and risk, since extra weight reduces stability and control.

LEADER GEAR

Required Items (In addition to individual gear):

1. **Watch**
2. **List of participants and staff, health forms for all participants, list of emergency phone numbers**

---

adult participants. One leader can usually supervise about ten adults, though this can be difficult in certain traffic situations and results in very long spreads when riding single file with safe spacings between riders. Five to seven riders per leader are usually easily manageable and should be considered the maximum if the participants are young or require closer attention or supervision.

Recommended Reading

Bridge, R. (1979). *Bike touring: The Sierra Club guide to outings on wheels.* San Francisco, CA: Sierra Club Books.

Rafting

Description

Rafting has been with us since the first person wobbled out across the water on a drifting log. It probably wasn't long before several logs were lashed together, and designs and materials have continued to evolve to this day. The simplicity and inherent stability of rafts is appealing enough to offset their characteristic lack of maneuverability relative to canoes, kayaks, and other solid-hull watercraft. Rafts are either paddled or rowed. Outings vary from short, leisurely drifting to ambitious multi-day whitewater runs on rivers with fast currents and obstacles that ensure an exciting ride.

Rafting is an extremely popular activity, in part because it can be enjoyed by almost anyone regardless of physical capability. A large raft fitted with a frame and oarlocks can usually be controlled by one person, so passengers have nothing to do but enjoy the ride. On the other hand, paddle rafting usually involves the entire crew who, guided by the "raft captain," propel and steer the raft. While rafts are costly, there are often rentals available.

Hazards and Risks

As a watercraft activity, rafting has certain inherent hazards caused by proximity to water. The precise level of risk is dependent upon the nature of the body of water, the kind of activity, the type and condition of the craft, and the extent to which the participants employ common sense and adhere to safety rules and procedures. Rafts are relatively stable; however, swamping and rollovers are common. The same physical characteristics that lend stability to the craft also, unfortunately, increase resistance to turning and movement, so to a certain extent, rafts are at the mercy of the currents—at least much more so than canoes or kayaks. Getting tossed overboard is a common event in all but the mildest whitewater, and it is often impossible to maneuver the craft to facilitate a quick retrieval.

Perhaps the greatest danger specifically attributable to rafts is their apparent stability; they lull users into believing that it would be almost impossible to fall overboard, or for the raft to flip. Another danger that is sometimes greater in rafting than in other watercraft activities is entanglement in lines and gear. Rafts have great load-bearing capacity, and it's common for lots of equipment to be lashed and stowed on board for multi-day trips. Rafters have to be careful to avoid entrapment in this cargo or its securing ties if the craft should capsize.

A hazard common to all watercraft activities is hypothermia. Rafters may be particularly vulnerable to both chronic and immersion hypothermia. Paddling a raft is often an intermittent process; an exciting fast water section of river is likely to result in wet clothing from paddling and/or sweat, while the period of relative inactivity between rapids may result in insufficient metabolic heat production to sustain a healthy core temperature. If someone falls in, immersion hypothermia is a possibility whenever water temperature is much below body temperature, and very likely if the water temperature is below about 60°F (15°C). A rafter experiencing mild chronic hypothermia from prolonged chilling prior to going overboard may be especially vulnerable to the high rate of heat loss characteristic of water immersion.

Rafters and others exposed to such conditions should always wear wet suits if the combined air and water temperatures total less than 120°F (49°C). Some programs require wetsuits whenever the water temperature is below 50°F (10°C) regardless of the air temperature. Many programs require participants to pass a swim or survival swim test, or to possess current certification in basic swim skills from an organization such as the Red Cross. A very high percentage of watercraft accidents, drownings, and cases of immersion hypothermia are alcohol related. Leaders should establish policies with regard to alcohol use and convey such policies verbally and in writing at the first pre-trip meeting.

Environmental and Social Impacts

Rivers are linear features, so that all use is concentrated in a narrow zone. In many areas, the zone adjacent to rivers and streams (called the riparian zone) is highly sensitive and easily damaged. Fortunately, most river activity is in the form of day trips. Nevertheless, there is potential for damage when groups overuse takeout points. Typically, any given section of river or streams will have a limited number of good places to stop for breaks or lunch. Leaders should seek local advice from land managers prior to planning trips, so that stops can be scheduled on less used and/or more sites. Littering is also a problem on raft trips. This seems to stem from a combination of factors including the great capacity of rafts for carrying extra weight. Whereas a hiker might take an efficient, modest lunch, the rafter can usually take whatever he/she pleases, wrappers, cans, and all. Because rafting is accessible to all, many rafters are not indoctrinated in the ways of low impact use of natural resource areas. The leader can help determine the future behaviors of his/her participants by making them aware of the need for care and consideration of the environment, by setting a good example, and by establishing and enforcing biocentric policies and procedures.

Overnight river excursions are common, and they have to be controlled very carefully to minimize damage. Good campsites are not abundant on most rivers, and usually there are very few conveniently located sites. These may see excessive use on popular rivers. Most organized groups now routinely use "porta-potties," sometimes made from military surplus rocket boxes or ammo cans, to contain and remove all fecal matter. Fires are built on metal plates (old garbage can lids work well) to reduce blackening of rocks and sand. Leaders should check with the landholder or land management agency to determine what sites can best withstand the impact of the intended outing, and what impact reducing practices are encouraged or required.

Resource Requirements

Beginners may enjoy practice in pools, ponds, lakes, and gentle streams. Soon, however, even novice rafters seek rivers with sufficient current to provide exciting action. The popularity of rafting has led to the proliferation of guides and guidebooks for most regions. Many rivers are very heavily used during the warmer months.

Fortunately, some of the finest rivers have been wholly or partially protected from development by designation as Wild, Scenic, or Recreational Rivers. Both private landholders and public land managers have often had to resort to some form of regulation of use in order to maintain the long-term quality of these limited resources. Users should always check well in advance to find out about rules, regulations, and permit requirements. Some rivers are so popular that permits must be obtained a year or more in advance! Beleaguered managers usually set aside some permits for private parties and a larger number for commercial operators, since experienced guides can usually take more people down a river with less environmental impact per person. However, the balance of commercial vs. private permits never seems to please either group. There are many fine rafting rivers for which no permits are required or for which they are easy to obtain.

Levels and Objectives

Levels. As in land-based pursuits, it's useful to categorize rafting outings by both level of difficulty (easy, moderate, or difficult) and by objective content (beginning, intermediate, and advanced). Rating the difficulty of a river isn't easy since it is based upon the opinions of the observers, and water-level fluctuation can dramatically alter the size and energy of rapids and other features. As in land-based activities, myriad factors, such as the weather, the water temperature, the equipment used, and the overall length of the trip, can profoundly influence the overall experience. Still, there are several "standard" rating systems. The most universal of these was derived from the I-VI climbing classification system of Europe, and uses six levels to cover the spectrum from easy, minor riffles barely noticeable in a raft (Class I) to next-to-impossible cataracts rarely challenged even by the lunatic fringe. Runs are often described by overall difficulty, with any tougher exceptions pointed out (for example "a Class II run with two short Class III rapids"). For rafters, Class I and II rapids are usually considered "easy," Class III "moderate," and Class IV "difficult." Class V rapids are so tough that "difficult" is probably an inadequate term. These are for experienced experts only. Class VI waters are usually considered negotiable only with supernatural aid!

Another important consideration when describing the difficulty of a run is its length, measured not so much in terms of distance as in time. It's also important to consider whether the raft can be rowed or paddled since paddling usually involves all of the passengers in frequent rotation, while rowing may involve only the leader or perhaps a succession of rowers. River currents and the number and frequency of stops determine the route of travel.

Beginners usually appreciate easy water at first but quickly develop a taste for Class III rapids. Thus, Objectives "A" through "C" or "D" are usually appropriate for beginning-level courses. Intermediate-level participants will appreciate Class III rapids and perhaps one or more carefully chosen and scouted Class IV thrills. At this level, Objectives "D" through "G" can be added, along with emphasis on greater development of paddling or rowing skills. Advanced classes further refine skills in pursuit of Objectives "H" and "I."

Objectives. Many rafting excursions are designed only to provide relaxation or thrills, while others are designed to teach rafting skills or for specific educational purposes such as study of the riparian environment. The following objectives are suggested for day trips designed to teach rafting skills. Leaders planning overnight rafting outings should also review the objectives suggested for backpacking.

Typical objectives of a rafting outing are that the participants will be able to:

A. Enjoy the experience and want to pursue the activity further;

B. Develop an awareness of, and sensitivity to the environment;

C. Learn how to travel safely by raft, which includes competency in basic paddling and/or rowing techniques, self-rescue techniques, techniques for assisting in the rescue of others, and techniques for avoiding and treating hypothermia;

D. Understand how to minimize social and physical impacts on the river and riverbank environment;

E. Understand river dynamics and develop an ability to read the river by direct observation;

F. Develop an ability to interpret river charts, maps, and guides;

G. Become aware of the capabilities and limitations of local water search and rescue resources, and of the most effective means of accessing these resources;

H. Acquire the skills and knowledge necessary to independently plan and carry out a successful rafting outing;

I. Develop a level of understanding and concern for the environment that leads to responsible actions on behalf of the environment.

Clothing and Equipment

As in any outdoor pursuit, gear and clothing requirements vary depending upon the demands of the particular activity, its duration, the site, and the qualifications and abilities of the participants. Clearly, a raft is required, and here the possibilities are almost endless, from one-person general-purpose models to immense craft with highly specialized designs. Most are inflatables made of neoprene-coated nylon or other abrasion resistant fabric. All have several air compartments that provide security should one section lose air. Rafts can be purchased; however, quality rafts can be costly. Rental has some distinct advantages for those who don't raft often, who want to learn more about the sport or certain raft types before purchasing, or who want to eliminate overhead and maintenance costs.

Life jackets (personal flotation devices or "PFD's") are also an essential item common to all water activities. The American Whitewater Affiliation recommends a minimum flotation weight of 15 pounds (6.8 k) for adults and 12 pounds (5.4 k) for children under 100 pounds (45.4 k). PFD's are rated in the United States by style and function as Type I, II, III, IV, and V. Types I and II are efficient and usually large types that all but guarantee a face-up floating position; however, they are somewhat restrictive for rafters or others needing to paddle or work while wearing the devices. Type III's are less effective in that they don't, in their simplest form, automatically bring the face out of the water. However, because of their slim, vest-like fit, they do allow easy paddling and so are very popular with rafters, canoeists, and kayakers. Type IV's don't really count in activities like rafting; they are only intended to be tossed, like life rings. Type V refers to all sorts of highly specialized devices, and some new versions are essentially Type III's with flotation collars, a distinct advantage for anyone whose swimming ability is low, or for any very rough water. Most organizations that offer rafting excursions or classes require that all participants wear a Type III or better PFD at all times. Common sense dictates that the only way to reap the benefits of a PFD is to wear it and to wear it properly fitted and secured. Planning to put it on if you have an accident is as inane as planning to buckle a seat belt before a car crash. Just as in driving, the statistics verify a tremendous reduction in mortality rates when these simple measures are taken in advance.

What else needs to be taken? This depends upon the river and the weather, and, of course, on the length of the trip. (See Figures 17.9 a-c, pages 406-408.)

Leader Qualifications

A rafting leader should possess all of the qualifications listed earlier for hiking leaders since these attributes are no less vital here. In addition, the leader should have:

A. Substantial general experience on and about water and watercraft;

B. Substantial experience in the type of water environment likely to be encountered on the outing in question;

C. Familiarity with the type of craft to be employed, including an understanding of its proper and effective use, limits and weaknesses, field maintenance, and proper handling during transportation to and from the site;

D. Familiarity with the proper use of all safety equipment to be taken on the outing in question (PFD's, throw-lines, ropes and pulleys, helmets, etc.);

E. A willingness to enforce the use of personal safety equipment at all appropriate times;

F. Swimming and water-safety skills appropriate to the activity and site (Many employers require certification by the Red Cross or other agencies.);

G. Rescue and recovery skills appropriate to the craft and site. (This includes the salvage of overturned or swamped craft and the freeing of craft pinned against obstacles. Many employers require leaders to take specified water rescue courses.)

The above qualifications are appropriate for the "captain" of each raft. In addition, the leader of each group of up to three, or in rare cases four, rafts (the usual limits of effective control) should possess:

H. Familiarity with the stretch of river to be run. (This normally requires at least two recent runs on the section of river in question, including at least one in similar craft and at similar stream-flow rates.)

Leadership Ratios

Leadership ratios are largely dependent upon the ability of a leader to control the course of events. Rafts may hold several people in a rather confined space, making control within a craft relatively easy. On the other hand, rafts are to a certain extent at the mercy of the currents, and communication between them is extremely difficult. Travel upstream can be next to impossible; leaders of multi-raft parties have to choose between taking the usually favored position in the lead, which may be necessary for scouting purposes even though the route is well-known, and taking the rear position, which allows relatively easy supervision and access to any other raft should a mishap occur.

As a result, one fully qualified group leader is usually required for every three (or in rare cases four) rafts. This leader should possess all of the attributes listed above ("A" through "H"). Each raft needs a leader or "captain" with qualities "A" through "G" at least, since it's entirely possible that any one raft could have serious problems and be inaccessible to the others for

**FIGURE 17.9a   Suggested Minimum Gear Requirements
for Rafting**

The following lists are based on single-day outings in cool water during the warmer six months of the year.

INDIVIDUAL GEAR

Required Items   (*Certain synthetics may be substituted at the discretion of the instructor):

1. **Shoes** (Sneakers with wool* socks, or wet-suit boots, preferably with wool socks)
2. **Wool* layer(s) for the legs** (The instructor may require additional layers. A wet suit is required if the combined air and water temperatures are less than 120° F [49° C].)
3. **Rainwear for the legs** (If wet suit not worn. Rainwear leg bottoms must not be sealed.)
4. **Wool* layer for the torso** (Two or more if specified by the instructor. At least a "Farmer John" style wet suit top is required if the combined air and water temperatures are less than 120° F [49° C]. Short-sleeved wet suits don't replace wool layers; full wetsuits are required below 110° F [43° C] combined temperatures.)
5. **Rainwear for the torso** (Even if a short-sleeved wet suit is used, to protect wool layers and to reduce convective and evaporative heat loss. Garments must have either a tight neck or loose cuffs and bottom to avoid water build-up when swimming.)
6. **Personal floatation device ("PFD")** (Type III or better)
7. **Wool* hat** (Tight knit, to cover ears)
8. **Sunglasses** (With retaining strap! The glare from rivers can be intense.)
9. **Water bottle** (Plastic with "leash" attached, one liter or more capacity. Bring full!)
10. **Lunch** (Preferably durable items or in a sturdy plastic box to withstand the abuse of being mashed into a dry bag!)

Optional Items   (All are recommended and may be required at the discretion of the instructor.):

1. **Helmet** (Usually considered a device for kayakers, this item is valuable in wild water rafting in Class III or higher-rated streams.)
2. **Whistle** (Commonly required and useful for signaling)
3. **Knife** (A small, fixed-blade knife in a sturdy locking sheath can be useful in an emergency for cutting away tangled ropes or cords. Often required)
4. **Cap** (Light color with a bill for sun protection)
5. **Sunscreen** (Obviously something with water repellency is best.)
6. **Windshell** (Not in place of, but in addition to a rainsuit. A windsuit "breathes" and may be more comfortable in some conditions.)
7. **Dry clothes and a towel** (To leave at the car. It is common to return to the vehicle soaking wet, so a change from head to toe is a good idea.)
8. **Dry bag** (If not carried by the group or if extra room is needed)

FIGURE 17.9b   Suggested Minimum Gear Requirements for Rafting (continued)

RAFT GEAR

Required Items (To be carried in each raft. Combine with required group gear if group consists of only one raft.):

1. **Throwline** (A standard sack type using 50-100 feet [15-30 m] 3/8 inches [9 mm] polypropylene)
2. **Knife** (As above if not carried by individuals)
3. **Whistle** (As above if not carried by individuals)
4. **Dry bags** (As needed for gear)
5. **Bailing can** (One or two plastic "bleach bottle" types attached by cord are useful.)

Optional Items:

1. **First-aid kit** (Carefully sealed to avoid water damage. Often required, it should be carried in each raft unless the group is always moving together.)
2. **Emergency kit** (See group gear below.)
3. **Spare personal floatation device ("PFD")** (In case of lost or damaged PFD)

GROUP GEAR

Required Items (For groups of up to three rafts. Note that these items must travel in the last raft!):

1. **First-aid kit** (If not carried in each raft)
2. **Emergency kit** (If not carried by each raft, to contain 120 feet [about 36 m] of strong nylon or polypro rope [3/8 inch or 9 mm or larger diameter], two carabiners, two pulleys [or two additional carabiners], a repair kit for patching leaks, a pump with appropriate fittings, a backpackers' style stove, pot and fuel and/or fire-starting materials, a tarp or other shelter, an ensolite or other insulating pad, and a sleeping bag or half-bag.)

Optional Items:

1. **Come-along** (This can be a useful addition to the emergency kit for retrieving lodged rafts, especially in swift currents.)
2. **Thermos** (Full of hot chocolate, hot soup, or other hot drinks, it can be useful in assisting the warming of mildly hypothermic participants.)
3. **Maps and compass** (Unless the guides or leaders are intimately familiar with the river, these should be considered required items!)
4. **Flashlight(s)** (If there is a chance of getting back near or after dark)

FIGURE 17.9c   Suggested Minimum Gear Requirements for Rafting (continued)

NOTE:

1.   *When selecting gear, also consider a few prohibitions, i.e., no hard-soled shoes or boots, rubber boots with higher than six-inch tops, no cotton long pants or heavy cotton (chamois or flannel) shirts, and no rain ponchos. All can be dangerous to the craft or to the wearer.*

2.   *The previous suggestions are for single-day outings. Supplementary gear for overnight camping might include shelters, sleeping pads, sleeping bags, more food, fire pan and/or portable stove, cooking gear and porta-potty as well as additional clothing, personal toiletries and medications, and flashlights. Dry bags and great care in packing are essential for obvious reasons. Consult the clothing and equipment lists for backpacking or hiking for more suggestions.*

LEADER GEAR

Required Items (In addition to required Individual Gear):

1.   **List of participants and staff, health forms for all participants and staff, and emergency phone numbers**
2.   **Notebook and pencil**

---

significant periods of time. Good group management (such as having the craft with rescue gear last and always traveling so closely that no one is out of sight for more than a few minutes or a few hundred yards, whichever is least) can shorten emergency access times. Yet, at best, these access times are likely to exceed the survival time of a person pinned underwater.

The bottom line then depends upon raft size. If, for example, the rafts hold six people each, then a group leader and two qualified assistants are needed for a total of fifteen participants in three rafts.

Suggested Formats

Most rafting is done within the limits of a single day. Getting rafts to the put-in point, inflating them, making shuttle arrangements, and other logistical concerns make full-day trips more practical than short trips, at least in terms of the labor-to-fun ratio. Overnight trips are also popular, and they can extend as long as desired, even on rivers that aren't long enough to allow travel each day. One campsite can be used for several days while participants hike, swim, or perhaps use other types of paddlecraft to explore the adjacent stretch of river.

Pre-trip meetings are always valuable and are essential before multi-day outings. It's best to have at least one meeting well in advance of the outing so that people have time to assemble the requisite gear, especially if an overnight adventure is planned. Many programs require participants to pass swim or survival float tests, and this should be held or at least scheduled at an early date. A meeting just prior to the outing (perhaps on an evening two or three days ahead) can fine tune the program, increasing the likelihood of a smooth start on the morning of departure. As in all outdoor pursuits, a post-trip meeting can be immensely valuable in maximizing the value of the experience for both participants and staff.

Recommended Reading

Watters, R. (1982). *The whitewater river book.* Seattle, WA: Pacific Search Press.

Canoeing
Description

Canoeing is a popular activity with a long history beginning with utilitarian use in prehistoric times. The canoe is an elegant and inviting craft that is easy to handle in a wide range of conditions. Canoes can carry surprisingly large loads and still glide smoothly over flat-water lakes. With a little practice, Class II rapids are no problem, and skilled canoeists regularly run Class III rivers. Beyond this level, however, most people prefer the more stable raft or more maneuverable and watershedding kayak.

Canoe trips range from short paddles on flat water to adventurous multi-day outings that can include combinations of flat and wild water, sometimes linked by "portages" wherein canoes and gear are carried between bodies of water.

Canoeing is a standard activity at many youth camps and outdoor centers, and canoe lessons are often the first water-based additions to park and recreation or school-based programs. Rental opportunities increase the ease of entry into the sport, which appeals to people of all ages. Since the canoe lends itself to so many types of use, it is found in one form or another in most countries around the world.

Hazards and Risks

Most of what has been said about hazards in rafting applies to canoeing as well. Canoes tend to be a good deal less stable than rafts, and generally require more skill in paddling. However, these drawbacks are largely compensated for by greater control and maneuverability. In most cases, canoeists stay drier than rafters—a distinct safety (and comfort) advantage. Most canoes are fitted with flotation devices which, while not equalling the flotation of a raft, do provide enough lift to support two people in a swamped craft. Again, the comments in the rafting section should be reviewed.

Environmental and Social Impacts

Most of the comments made earlier relative to rafting apply to canoeing as well.

Resource Requirements

Canoes are equally enjoyable on flat water or modest whitewater, so it is almost always possible to find someplace to go. Beginners tend to favor ponds, lakes, or even swimming pools in which to practice beginning strokes. Many tend to stay on flat water, perhaps extending their adventures to include multi-day camping excursions. Large lakes or bays can provide this option, as can some very large rivers where there are no significant rapids. Others prefer the excitement of running rivers, and it doesn't take more than Class II rapids to provide thrills and occasional spills. For most people, Class III rapids are more than tough enough. Since canoes can be shouldered and carried easily by two people and tolerably well by one, it is often possible to canoe sections not accessible by rafts or heavier craft. In many cases, the canoe can even be paddled upstream through rapids, so a full day can be spent in a rather small area. These can be distinct advantages over rafting, depending upon the configuration of water resources.

Levels and Objectives

Levels. Canoes are somewhat less suited to rapids than either rafts or kayaks. As a result, while Class II rapids may not be too exciting in a raft or kayak, they offer plenty of thrills for beginning canoeists and are good practice grounds even at the intermediate level. Class III rapids, which might be considered "moderate" by rafters, would be "difficult" for most canoeists. Advanced canoe classes, however, might polish technique and play in some Class III rapids.

Objectives. The objectives suggested for rafting are appropriate for canoeing. Specific skill objectives may be determined by studying canoeing texts.

Clothing and Equipment

Canoes come in a wide range of sizes, shapes, and materials. The selection of a particular model depends upon the intended primary use, alternative uses, and, of course, on the amount of money available. Often, the best plan is to utilize local rental options until the possibilities are well-understood. Even then rentals may be the best way to go, considering storage, maintenance, and insurance costs, unless canoeing is a major part of the agency's program offerings.

Transporting canoes can be a problem. Rooftop carriers for cars or vans can be constructed at a low cost, but while appropriate for small numbers of canoes, the rooftop option is inadequate for large groups. Canoe trailers come in a variety of configurations, often homemade modifications of small flat-bed trailers designed to carry up to a dozen canoes. Some canoe-rental businesses also rent such trailers, and this option should be considered if annual usage will be limited.

The suggested gear requirements for rafting (Figures 17.9 a-c, pages 406-408) apply to canoeing outings, with a few exceptions. Since canoes are far more maneuverable, it is not usually considered necessary to have a throw line on each craft. One throw line for each group of up to four or five canoes is probably adequate if the canoes travel closely together, and the canoe with the throw line stays in a position allowing rapid access to the others. Where rafting groups usually must be limited to three or four craft, canoe groups can usually consist of up to eight or nine. For obvious reasons, the pump isn't necessary in the repair kit.

When portaging is anticipated, some sort of carrying device is needed. Any sort of pack will do, though the favorite for hauling gear is the Duluth pack or recent super-waterproof alternatives that resemble duffel bags with pack straps.

Leader Qualifications

The suggestions in the rafting section are appropriate here as well.

Leader Ratios

Canoes are far more maneuverable than rafts, which allows the leaders more opportunity to move about at will. This same mobility, however, is also available to participants, so while the leaders are more mobile the task of group control is compounded. Under most circumstances, a reasonable level of control can be maintained over a total of eight canoes by two leaders, one each in two of the eight canoes. That is, the group consists of six canoes, each carrying two participants, and two canoes, each carrying a leader with or without a participant. If the leaders are skilled and attentive and maintain themselves at lead and sweep positions, assistance and communication can usually be maintained. This results in a ratio of two leaders per fourteen participants, which is slightly less than for rafting. Certainly, this ratio should be increased (other leaders added) if outing risks are greater than normal due to more treacherous water, less experienced participants, or any situation that lessens control.

Suggested Formats

Canoeing is a somewhat more skills-oriented activity than rafting. Many paddle strokes can be practiced in swimming pools prior to open-water use. Upstream travel or even portaging allow short segments of river to be used for extended practice sessions, thereby eliminating shuttle problems. Otherwise, the possibilities are, as in rafting, nearly unlimited. Canoe camping is popular, and bodies of water can be linked by portages to allow extended voyages.

Recommended Reading

American Red Cross. (1974). *Canoeing.* Garden City, NY: Doubleday & Co.

Jabobson, C. (1984). *Canoeing wild rivers.* Merriville, IN: ICS Books.

Mason, B. (1984). *Path of the paddle.* Toronto, Canada: Van Nostrand Reinhold.

McNair, R.E., McNair, M. L., & Landry, P. A. (1990). *Basic river canoeing.* Martinsville, IN: American Camping Association.

Watters, R. (1982). *The whitewater river book.* Seattle, WA: Pacific Search Press.

Kayaking

Description

Kayaks evolved along the northern sea coasts, where rough water and foul weather demanded covered craft and resistance to swamping. These sleek, fast craft offer great maneuverability and a good deal more stability than commonly attributed to them. While most kayaks aren't as stable as the typical canoe, the low body position in a kayak (relative to the kneeling position of canoeing) is an advantage, and sitting also allows greater comfort on long trips. Some kayaks are designed to carry large loads, and some can even be fitted with sails. The light weight of modern designs makes transportation by vehicle at least as easy as for canoes, and the availability of rentals and instruction have rocketed this sport into widespread popularity. No other craft gives such an intimate sense of contact with the water. Kayaking is the most skill-oriented of the watercraft activities discussed in this text. Kayak outings range from practice sessions in pools to long-ranging voyages by sea, lake, or stream.

It is not easy to find a major stream or body of water not bearing at least a few kayaks during the warmer months. Even though the basic craft have been in use by Eskimos for centuries, kayaking as a sport is very young. Participants also tend to be young, although the average age is increasing as people continue to kayak into later years. Industry figures on kayak sales show continued and growing interest from an ever-broadening demographic segment.

Hazards and Risks

Kayaking isn't inherently more dangerous than canoeing or rafting if certain precautions are taken. Since the craft are somewhat more likely to capsize, it's important that the spray skirt that seals the kayaker to the craft is instantly removable should attempts at rolling be unsuccessful. Helmets are essential if the craft is used in rapids. Kayakers are in danger of sustaining shoulder and back injuries if poor technique is used. Common sense and good judgment are also critical since the sport typically involves the development of skills and the challenge of ever more energetic and difficult rapids. Just as in its closest land-based equivalent, alpine skiing, most kayaking accidents are related to overly ambitious activities. Serious mishaps are rare if limits of skill and craft design are respected. A review of the section on rafting hazards is advised especially vis-à-vis PFD's and hypothermia, since these concerns are no less valid here.

Environmental and Social Impacts

Most of the concerns addressed in the discussion of the potential impacts of rafting apply here as well.

Resource Requirements

Like canoeing, kayaking can be enjoyed on any water. Pool practice sessions are especially valuable for kayakers, who find the still, clear, warm water perfect for mastering one or more of the several types of rolls so crucial to successful mastery of Class III or higher rapids. Some people enjoy sea or lake kayaking, and multi-day outings can be made as easily in kayaks as canoes if proper craft are selected. Most kayakers, however, seem to prefer river running, and virtually any stretch is worth considering if it contains enough water flow and challenging rapids. There are shops in most major cities specializing in paddle craft, and these usually stock guidebooks identifying local resources. Clubs, schools, and parks and recreation departments can also usually provide information about suitable sites.

Levels and Objectives

Levels. Kayakers will find Class I and II rapids adequate at "beginning" levels, after initial skill-training sessions in swimming pools. "Intermediate" kayakers (those able to do rolls while in moving water) will enjoy most Class III rapids but should expect to spend many hours developing skills at this level. Few devotees push beyond this level even after years of kayaking. "Advanced" outings might expose participants to carefully selected Class IV rapids, though such groups usually focus on perfection of skills in upper Class III conditions.

Objectives. The general objectives suggested for rafting are appropriate for kayaking. Specific skill objectives can be extracted from kayaking texts.

Clothing and Equipment

Kayaks come in many specialized shapes, usually constructed of fiberglass or high-tech plastic. Equipment requirements are essentially the same as for rafting and canoeing, except that kayakers need a spray screen and a helmet. (See Figures 17.9 a-c, pages 406-408.)

Leader Qualifications

The suggestions in the rafting section are appropriate here as well.

Leadership Ratios

Kayaking leadership ratios tend to be greater than in canoeing since control of individual craft is as difficult with single occupation as when each craft contains two participants. Two leaders are needed to supervise six or seven people, but exceptions can be made in pools or perhaps other tightly controlled situations that are not in moving water. In such cases, one leader might be able to supervise eight or nine boats.

Suggested Formats

Kayaking classes are often conducted as a series of short sessions (one to three hours) wherein participants spend a short time in the classroom and most of the time on the water. Several initial sessions can be spent in a swimming pool, where basic strokes and the roll(s) can be taught more effectively. When possible, a small lake, bay, or other protected body of still water can be used to extend basic skills and practice rolls under more natural (and usually colder and less clear) conditions. Once skills are improved and confidence is up, streams of increasing difficulty can be attempted. These early lessons are usually short since attention spans and energy

reserves rarely extend beyond a few hours. Later outings can consist of river runs or take tours with skills sessions as brief interludes throughout the day.

Recommended Reading

Nealy, W. (1992). *Kayak.* Birmingham, AL: Menasha Ridge Press.

Tejada-Flores, L. (1978). *Wildwater: The Sierra Club guide to kayaking and whitewater boating.* San Francisco, CA: Sierra Club Books.

Trekking

Description

The term "trek" originally meant an Afrikaaner migration by ox cart. Its current meaning was popularized by Colonel Jimmy Roberts, who founded Mountain Travel Nepal. He first used it to describe organized commercial expeditions into the mountains with pack animals and porters carrying all of the client's gear. While several providers still adhere to this conventional definition, others take a broader view and use the term to encompass any adventure travel that is "off the beaten path." We'll focus here on trips that meet the latter definition and include an emphasis on self-propelled travel, be it hiking, backpacking, backcountry skiing, climbing, biking, rafting, canoeing, or kayaking. Treks may involve anything from easy hiking to expeditionary high alpine mountaineering. Travel may be entirely by foot, bike, or watercraft, or it may be partially by mechanized means or on horseback. Lodgings range from upscale hotels to primitive bivouacs.

There are now hundreds of companies offering adventure travel tours that meet our definition of trekking, and they offer, collectively, several thousand treks per year to every corner of the world. Clientele for treks are typically well-off professionals who are fit and accustomed to the kind of activity around which the trek is centered. About 30 percent of the clientele are couples over 50 years of age, while younger couples make up another 30 percent or so. The remaining 40 percent are single or married persons traveling singly with an average age of about 40 years. Fitness and skill requirements vary widely, from an ability to walk a few miles per day to superb fitness and advanced technical skills.

Hazards and Risks

Trekking may include virtually any outdoor pursuit, anywhere on the planet. General hazards include those normally associated with long distance travel, the medical and political risks associated with foreign travel, and the hazards and risks inherent in the type of activity to be engaged in. During conventional recreational participation in outdoor pursuits, risks are controlled by carrying a proper set of protective clothing and safety gear, maintaining a focus on safety, and using sound judgement. All too often, participants on treks, unless effectively guided, may tend to compromise on equipment and clothing due to the difficulty of transporting gear, may be distracted by new surroundings, and may suspend common sense when making critical decisions. Leaders need to set and enforce appropriate standards for gear and prerequisite skills, and be aware of the tendency to exceed reasonable limits. When one has invested large amounts of time and money in reaching a destination, it is tempting to take risks that one might not accept in another context.

Environmental and Social Impacts

The specific on-site potential effects of trekking are as varied as the activities and sites involved. While some may argue that "progress" is inevitable, it is also true that commercial trekking has "opened" many remote parts of the world, often sowing the seeds of profound environmental and social change. One or two trekking parties passing through a remote village each year may or may not be disruptive, depending upon the particular circumstances and culture. Typically, the extent of influence by outsiders is related to the size of the village or town and the party size, duration of stay, extent of contact, and amount of trade for goods or services. A large group using porters or buying provisions may have a substantial impact on a small village, whereas a small, self-contained party might enjoy a day of visiting with the local residents without major effect. Leaders of treks need to address the philosophical and practical implications of trekking before planning treks into sensitive regions. Through careful planning, it is sometimes possible to offer opportunities for cultural contact without unacceptable environmental and social risks.

Resource Requirements

Virtually any area that lends itself to access by foot or watercraft is a potential trekking destination. Access to most land and water resources worldwide is free of cost or permit requirements once visa and/or travel requirements have been met. There are significant exceptions, however. In many countries, permits must be obtained to run certain rivers or to climb certain peaks. Several countries require permits to enter wilderness areas, though these are generally without any associated fee. The primary exception is the United States where commercial users must obtain a special use permit and show proof of liability insurance (amounts range from $250,000 to $1,000,000 coverage), and they must pay a fee based upon the number of person-days of use. National parks are generally free, though in some countries commercial groups must obtain a permit. In the United States, commercial groups wishing to enter national parks must show proof of insurance and must pay an application fee, a substantial permit fee, entry fees and a fee per person per day, and, in most cases, they must pay a percentage of profits. In a few countries, governments exercise a monopoly on guided trips within certain parks or reserves, and, in the United States and Canada, the government has granted exclusive rights to certain private guides and outfitters in some national parks. Others wishing to lead a trip into the park may be denied permission to do so or be required to pay an "in lieu" fee to the designated guide service. Whether or not a permit is required, users of national parks, wilderness areas, game reserves, or any lands or waters are responsible for knowing and complying with all applicable rules and regulations.

In the realm of trekking, transportation and lodging resources cannot be assumed as readily as in conventional domestic outdoor activities. Airline or ship reservations may need to be made six months or more in advance, and local transportation can require extensive planning, research, and on-site review. Group discounts are commonly given but the rules and amounts vary widely. Advance application is almost always required for group discounts, or for group reservations on mass transit. Lodging may have to be reserved as much as a year in advance on popular routes in some areas.

It is important to check with each proposed lodging well in advance to be sure that the facility will be open, available to the group, and have enough room. Private operators sometimes limit usage to certain clubs or organizations, and reservations (with deposits) are often required. It's often possible to obtain substantial discounts on housing and/or meals by joining the appropriate organizations. Extensive public and private hut systems exist throughout the mountainous portions of Eastern and Western Europe and Japan, and in some mountain regions of Australia, New Zealand, Great Britain, Canada, the United States, the Soviet Union, and many other countries. Huts are usually staffed, and provide meals and sleeping accommodations at a reasonable cost for hikers and climbers. In many cases, especially in areas of extensive hut development, there is little choice but to use the system since virtually every place suitable for camping has become a hut site. Not uncommonly, camping is prohibited in such areas for economic or environmental reasons.

Levels and Objectives

Levels. Since treks are seldom skill-oriented, it is usually sufficient to categorize them in terms of overall levels of difficulty (such as "easy," "moderate," and "strenuous"). However, it may be useful or even necessary to define certain treks in terms of skill levels as well. Many providers of adventure tours employ a grading system consisting of five or six levels. In one system, the tours or treks are graded "A" through "E." "A" tours are nontrekking. Any hiking or camping is optional. "B" treks include easy hiking, biking, or water activity, and may or may not require camping. "C" treks include required moderate hiking, cycling, water activity, or easy climbing, and may include short sections of required strenuous activity. Difficult hiking and moderate climbing may be included but are optional. "D" treks include required strenuous hiking, biking, water activity, or moderate climbing, and may involve optional strenuous or technical climbs. "E" treks include required technical climbing or river running experience, sometimes under remote expeditionary conditions. For example, a three-week trek involving daily hiking of five to eight miles (8 to 13 km), average elevation gains of 2,000 feet (about 600 m) or less per day, and optional single day climbs of peaks in the area might be rated "C," while a two-week expedition to kayak a challenging river gorge may be rated "E."

Objectives. Most treks include one or more of the activities we have discussed earlier. Many of the objectives for these activities also apply when the activity is pursued in the context of trekking. Foreign treks are often characterized by an emphasis on enhancing cultural understandings, the study of geography, nature study, or skills such as photography. A clear set of objectives can facilitate the planning process and help the leader direct the field experience. Such a set may be developed by combining appropriate objectives for the component activities and objectives related to the particular trek.

Clothing and Equipment

The clothing and equipment requirements of trekking are determined by the nature of the activities involved. For example, if the trek consists entirely of hiking from hut to hut (see "Suggested Formats," for an explanation of huts), then the requirements for trekking may not vary significantly from those suggested earlier in this text for hiking. Even on long trips, little extra clothing is needed since most huts have a water supply ample enough to allow washing and a place to dry clothes in wet weather. Many huts outside the United States require the use of slippers when inside the hut, though they are usually provided.

The hiking list should serve the trekking party well if attention is paid to the social, if not real, survival value of some of the optional hikers' gear like toilet paper and a spare clean shirt.

Before discounting any of the required items for hiking, or for whatever activities are involved, consider the consequences of requiring insufficient gear, and having to replace it at the destination point. The following suggestions

are for a grade "B" or "C" trek involving only hiking, in mountainous terrain at mid-latitudes during the summer, as this is probably the most frequently offered type of trek. The requirements for other types of treks may vary substantially, and no single list can adequately suit all possibilities. (See Figure 17.10, page 418.)

Leader Qualifications

For domestic treks, the qualifications suggested for hiking may be adequate. Longer trips or foreign travel can be far more demanding; the process of scheduling transportation, lodging, and meals can become quite complex and difficult, and may require the handling of substantial amounts of money. The leader of a domestic trip can often rely on telephone communications and well-established credit systems, while the leader on a foreign trip may have to solve problems without recourse to the employer's advice, negotiate prices, and make payments using foreign currencies and credit systems, and often the leader does all of this in another language.

The leader of a trek, therefore, needs all of the attributes of a hiking leader, plus:

A. An awareness of available lodgings, accommodations, and procedures for securing access to needed facilities;

B. In the case of foreign travel, an ability to efficiently conduct the group through such bureaucratic and urban delights as passport controls, currency exchanges, and chaotic mass-transit systems en route to the trekking area. This may require competency in the local language;

C. An ability to conduct whatever financial affairs may be necessary. In some instances, this may require a willingness and ability to carry large sums of money, establish pricing agreements, pay bills, and keep acceptable records of transactions;

D. An ability to respond effectively to the psychological and physical stresses of extended travel. This includes personal stresses as well as those of participants.

FIGURE 17.10   Suggested Gear and Clothing Requirements for Trekking

INDIVIDUAL GEAR

Required items (In addition to the items required for hiking, with the exception of items 21 and 22):

1. **Passport** (With current visas, to be carried at all times)
2. **Money** (It is usually convenient to arrive with a small amount of the local currency.)
3. **Duffel bag** (Big and water repellent, as luggage to contain pack and gear on air flights, and for storing gear in hotels, vans, lockers, etc.)

Optional Items (In addition to items on the Optional List for hiking):

1. **Cotton shirts** (One or two spares as laundry may be infrequent.)
2. **City clothes** (Depends upon route. May include walking shoes and socks, shirt or blouse, slacks, tie, sport coat, or dress)
3. **Boot bag** (Coated nylon or sturdy plastic sack, for boots in huts and tents)
4. **Ice axe or walking stick** (Required on some routes)
5. **Lead bag for film** (Need depends on route. Most airports will, or must, hand check film on request.)
6. **Towel** (Small, thin types dry well, doubles as washcloth)

GROUP GEAR

The required and optional items suggested for hiking are appropriate here if the hiking will be in areas where the group may have to be self-sufficient for many hours prior to the arrival of outside help. In more remote areas, more gear may be required and more advanced first-aid or medical supplies may be called for. When hikes remain in proximity to aid, less group gear may be needed.

LEADER GEAR

The suggestions for hiking leaders may suffice. It is very helpful to carry a compact notebook containing all important details of the itinerary, daily agendas, lodging and other key addresses and phone numbers, contact persons, the budget, transportation schedules, and all client health and contact information. The same notebook can be used to record expenses and as a log and diary.

Leadership Ratios

As in hiking, acceptable ratios vary considerably. One leader may be able to supervise twelve to fifteen participants on a popular well-marked path in good weather; however, higher leadership ratios generally improve program quality and safety. Each case has to be assessed separately, and it is vital to consider the potential consequences should a leader become incapacitated or out of touch with the group. Just as in hiking, a strong case can be made for two leaders on any wilderness or backcountry trek, and many people feel that any foreign treks warrant this extra attention. In any case, the total party size has to be consistent with available space in lodgings since large groups may have considerable difficulty finding space, even with advance notice.

Suggested Formats

Domestic trips are usually run on a three-day to two-week basis, usually during the summer months when children are out of school and vacations are commonly taken. These trips are best planned with work schedules in mind, since vacations most often involve taking full work weeks off. Foreign treks are usually scheduled as two-, three-, or four-week adventures, largely because of the high cost of transportation. Longer trips are rare since few people can obtain or afford longer vacations.

Lodging on treks varies from hotels to campsites or bivouacs. Hotels are usually used only when needed at the beginning and end of a trek, and when the route includes cities where no other accommodations are available. Most trekking parties favor smaller facilities such as inns, guest houses, or huts. Hiking from hut to hut, sometimes called "hut-hopping," is more popular than backpacking in many parts of the world. The term "hut" is used loosely here to include any suitable lodging that provides bedding and, usually, meals. Many countries have extensive systems of mountain huts, which vary from unattended cabin-sized structures to huge storm-proof full-service mountain hotels housing 2,000 guests.

Hiking from hut to hut has distinct advantages over backpacking in terms of the loads that must be carried, allowing relatively small packs and commensurate comfort and freedom of motion. The disadvantages compared to backpacking include higher daily costs, less freedom of choice in choosing where to spend the night, and less privacy. Depending upon the circumstances, these advantages may be offset by reduced expenditure on equipment (shelter and cooking supplies, large packs, etc.), dense arrays of huts and opportunities to escape the crowd during the day, given the much lighter loads that need to be carried. One of the strongest arguments in favor of the use of huts is that while the impact on the hut site itself is usually heavy, the overall impact of human use is reduced since the vicinity is not subjected to the abuse of many small camps, each adding cumulative damage through fuel use, soil compaction, and pollution.

Camping is far less expensive than using huts or inns; however, it requires far more gear and can be unpleasant if the weather is uncooperative. A day or two of rain is tolerable, but several days can lead to damp gear and damper spirits. In some cases the costs of the extra gear or the costs of transporting the gear may outweigh the savings. Nevertheless, camping is a commonly employed method, and it can be a great success if rain is infrequent.

In any case, treks require substantial contact with participants, by mail and/or pre-trip meetings, well in advance of the excursion, to insure that passports, visas, tickets, inoculations, and all necessary gear is in order well in advance of the departure date

index

copyright credits

Copyrighted works, listed in the order of appearance, are printed by permission of the following: